Artificial Higher Order Neural Networks for Modeling and Simulation

Ming Zhang
Christopher Newport University, USA

Managing Director:	Lindsay Johnston
Editorial Director:	Joel Gamon
Book Production Manager:	Jennifer Romanchak
Publishing Systems Analyst:	Adrienne Freeland
Assistant Acquisitions Editor:	Kayla Wolfe
Typesetter:	Lisandro Gonzalez
Cover Design:	Nick Newcomer

Published in the United States of America by
Information Science Reference (an imprint of IGI Global)
701 E. Chocolate Avenue
Hershey PA 17033
Tel: 717-533-8845
Fax: 717-533-8661
E-mail: cust@igi-global.com
Web site: http://www.igi-global.com

Library of Congress Cataloging-in-Publication Data

Artificial higher order neural networks for modeling and simulation for computer science and engineering : trends for emerging applications / Ming Zhang, editor.
     p. cm.
  Includes bibliographical references and index.
  Summary: "This book introduces Higher Order Neural Networks (HONNs) to computer scientists and computer engineers as an open box neural networks tool when compared to traditional artificial neural networks"--Provided by publisher.
  ISBN 978-1-4666-2175-6 (hardcover) -- ISBN 978-1-4666-2176-3 (ebook) -- ISBN 978-1-4666-2177-0 (print & perpetual access) 1. Neural networks (Computer science) 2. Computer science--Data processing. 3. Computer engineering--Data processing. I. Zhang, Ming, 1949 July 29-
  QA76.87.A698 2012
  006.3'2--dc23
                                        2012019279

British Cataloguing in Publication Data
A Cataloguing in Publication record for this book is available from the British Library.

All work contributed to this book is new, previously-unpublished material. The views expressed in this book are those of the authors, but not necessarily of the publisher.

This book is dedicated to Professor Dingbo Kuang, Fellow of the Chinese Academy of Sciences, and Senior Scientist of the Shanghai Institute of Technical Physics, Shanghai, China.

This book is also dedicated to Professor Huixing Gong, Fellow of the Chinese Academy of Engineering, and Senior Scientist of the Shanghai Institute of Technical Physics, Shanghai, China.

Table of Contents

Preface.. xiv

Acknowledgment.. xxi

Section 1
Artificial Higher Order Neural Networks for Modeling

Chapter 1

Artificial Multi-Polynomial Higher Order Neural Network Models 1
Ming Zhang, Christopher Newport University, USA

Chapter 2

Artificial Higher Order Neural Networks for Modeling MIMO Discrete-Time Nonlinear System 30
Michel Lopez-Franco, Universidad de Guadalajara, Mexico
Alma Y. Alanis, Universidad de Guadalajara, Mexico
Nancy Arana-Daniel, Universidad de Guadalajara, Mexico
Carlos Lopez-Franco, Universidad de Guadalajara, Mexico

Chapter 3

Artificial Higher Order Neural Networks for Modeling Combinatorial Optimization Problems 44
Yuxin Ding, Harbin Institute of Technology, China

Chapter 4

Needle Insertion Force Modeling using Genetic Programming Polynomial Higher Order
Neural Network 58
Mehdi Fallahnezhad, Norwegian University of Science and Technology (NTNU), Norway
Hashem Yousefi, Amirkabir University of Technology (Tehran Polytechnic), Iran

Section 2
Artificial Higher Order Neural Networks for Simulation

Chapter 5
Artificial Polynomial and Trigonometric Higher Order Neural Network Group Models 78
Ming Zhang, Christopher Newport University, USA

Chapter 6
Fundamentals of Higher Order Neural Networks for Modeling and Simulation 103
Madan M. Gupta, University of Saskatchewan, Canada
Ivo Bukovsky, Czech Technical University in Prague, Czech Republic
Noriyasu Homma, Tohoku University, Japan
Ashu M. G. Solo, Maverick Technologies America Inc., USA
Zeng-Guang Hou, The Chinese Academy of Sciences, China

Chapter 7
High Order Neuro-Fuzzy Dynamic Regulation of General Nonlinear Multi-Variable Systems 134
Dimitris C. Theodoridis, Democritus University of Thrace, Greece
Yiannis S. Boutalis, Democritus University of Thrace, Greece
Manolis A. Christodoulou, Technical University of Crete, Greece

Chapter 8
Modeling and Simulation of Alternative Energy Generation Processes using HONN 162
Salvador Carlos Hernández, Cinvestav del IPN, Unidad Saltillo, México
Edgar Nelson Sanchez Camperos, Cinvestav del IPN, Unidad Guadalajara, México
Rocío Carrasco Navarro, Cinvestav del IPN, Unidad Guadalajara, México
Joel Kelly Gurubel Tun, Cinvestav del IPN, Unidad Guadalajara, México
José Andrés Bueno García, Cinvestav del IPN, Unidad Guadalajara, México

Section 3
Artificial Higher Order Neural Networks for Control and Predication

Chapter 9
Distributed Adaptive Control for Multi-Agent Systems with Pseudo Higher Order Neural Net 194
Abhijit Das, Automation and Robotics Research Institute, USA
Frank Lewis, Automation and Robotics Research Institute, USA

Chapter 10
Cooperative Control of Unknown Networked Lagrange Systems using Higher Order
Neural Networks 214
Gang Chen, Chongqing University, China
Frank L. Lewis, University of Texas at Arlington, USA

Chapter 11
Symbolic Function Network: Application to Telecommunication Networks Prediction 237
George S. Eskander, ETS, Quebec University, Canada
Amir Atiya, Cairo University, Egypt

Chapter 12
Time Series Forecasting via a Higher Order Neural Network trained with the Extended
Kalman Filter for Smart Grid Applications 254
Luis J. Ricalde, Universidad Autonoma de Yucatan, Mexico
Glendy A. Catzin, Universidad Autonoma de Yucatan, Mexico
Alma Y. Alanis, Universidad de Guadalajara, Mexico
Edgar N. Sanchez, Universidad de Guadalajara, Mexico

Section 4
Artificial Higher Order Neural Network Models and Applications

Chapter 13
HONNs with Extreme Learning Machine to Handle Incomplete Datasets 276
Shuxiang Xu, University of Tasmania, Australia

Chapter 14
Symbolic Function Network: Theory and Implementation 293
George S. Eskander, ETS, Quebec University, Canada
Amir Atiya, Cairo University, Egypt

Chapter 15
City Manager Compensation and Performance: An Artificial Intelligence Approach 325
Jean X. Zhang, Virginia Commonwealth University, USA

Chapter 16
On Some Dynamical Properties of Randomly Connected Higher Order Neural Networks 333
Hiromi Miyajima, Kagoshima University, Japan
Noritaka Shigei, Kagoshima University, Japan
Shuji Yatsuki, Kyoto Software Research, Inc., Japan

Chapter 17
A Hybrid Higher Order Neural Structure for Pattern Recognition 364
Mehdi Fallahnezhad, Norwegian University of Science and Technology (NTNU), Norway
Salman Zaferanlouei, Amirkabir University of Technology (Tehran Polytechnic), Iran

Compilation of References 388

About the Contributors 419

Index 428

Detailed Table of Contents

Preface xiv

Acknowledgment xxi

Section 1
Artificial Higher Order Neural Networks for Modeling

Chapter 1
Artificial Multi-Polynomial Higher Order Neural Network Models 1
    Ming Zhang, Christopher Newport University, USA

This chapter introduces Multi-Polynomial Higher Order Neural Network (MPHONN) models with higher accuracy. Using Sun workstation, C++, and Motif, a MPHONN Simulator has been built. Real world data cannot always be modeled simply and simulated with high accuracy by single polynomial functions. Thus, ordinary higher order neural networks could fail to simulate complicated real world data, but the MPHONN model can simulate multi-polynomial functions and produce results with improved accuracy through experiments.

Chapter 2
Artificial Higher Order Neural Networks for Modeling MIMO Discrete-Time Nonlinear System 30
    Michel Lopez-Franco, Universidad de Guadalajara, Mexico
    Alma Y. Alanis, Universidad de Guadalajara, Mexico
    Nancy Arana-Daniel, Universidad de Guadalajara, Mexico
    Carlos Lopez-Franco, Universidad de Guadalajara, Mexico

In this chapter, a Recurrent Higher Order Neural Network (RHONN) is used to identify the plant model of discrete time nonlinear systems, under the assumption that all the state is available for measurement. Then the Extended Kalman Filter (EKF) is used to train the RHONN. The applicability of this scheme is illustrated by identification for an electrically driven nonholonomic mobile robot.

Chapter 3
Artificial Higher Order Neural Networks for Modeling Combinatorial Optimization Problems 44
    Yuxin Ding, Harbin Institute of Technology, China

The traditional Hopfield network has been widely used to solve combinatorial optimization problems. However, the high order Hopfiled network, as an expansion of the traditional Hopfield network, is seldom used to solve combinatorial optimization problem. In theory, compared with low order networks, high order networks have better properties, such as stronger approximation properties and faster convergence rates.

Chapter 4

Needle Insertion Force Modeling using Genetic Programming Polynomial Higher Order
Neural Network 58

Mehdi Fallahnezhad, Norwegian University of Science and Technology (NTNU), Norway
Hashem Yousefi, Amirkabir University of Technology (Tehran Polytechnic), Iran

In this chapter, the authors use a 0.98 mm diameter needle with a real-time recording of force, displacement, and velocity of needle through biological tissue during in-vitro insertions. Using constant velocity experiments from 5 mm/min up to 300 mm/min, the data set for the force-displacement graph of insertion was gathered. Tissue deformation with a small puncture and a constant velocity penetration are the two first phases in the needle insertion process. Direct effects of different parameters and their correlations during the process are modeled using a polynomial higher order neural network.

Section 2
Artificial Higher Order Neural Networks for Simulation

Chapter 5

Artificial Polynomial and Trigonometric Higher Order Neural Network Group Models 78
Ming Zhang, Christopher Newport University, USA

Real world financial data is often discontinuous and non-smooth. Accuracy will be a problem if one attempts to use neural networks to simulate such functions. Neural network group models can perform this function with more accuracy. Both the Polynomial Higher Order Neural Network Group (PHONNG) and the Trigonometric polynomial Higher Order Neural Network Group (THONNG) models are studied in this chapter. These PHONNG and THONNG models are open box, convergent models capable of approximating any kind of piecewise continuous function to any degree of accuracy. Moreover, they are capable of handling higher frequency, higher order nonlinear, and discontinuous data.

Chapter 6

Fundamentals of Higher Order Neural Networks for Modeling and Simulation 103
Madan M. Gupta, University of Saskatchewan, Canada
Ivo Bukovsky, Czech Technical University in Prague, Czech Republic
Noriyasu Homma, Tohoku University, Japan
Ashu M. G. Solo, Maverick Technologies America Inc., USA
Zeng-Guang Hou, The Chinese Academy of Sciences, China

In this chapter, the authors provide fundamental principles of Higher Order Neural Units (HONUs) and Higher Order Neural Networks (HONNs) for modeling and simulation. An essential core of HONNs can be found in higher order weighted combinations or correlations between the input variables and HONU. Despite the high quality of nonlinear approximation of static HONUs, the capability of dynamic HONUs for the modeling of dynamic systems is shown and compared to conventional recurrent neural networks when a practical learning algorithm is used.

Chapter 7

High Order Neuro-Fuzzy Dynamic Regulation of General Nonlinear Multi-Variable Systems 134

Dimitris C. Theodoridis, Democritus University of Thrace, Greece

Yiannis S. Boutalis, Democritus University of Thrace, Greece

Manolis A. Christodoulou, Technical University of Crete, Greece

The direct adaptive dynamic regulation of unknown nonlinear multi-variable systems is investigated in this chapter in order to address the problem of controlling non-Brunovsky and non-square systems with control inputs less than the number of states. The proposed neuro-fuzzy model acts as a universal approximator, while with careful selection of the Lyapunov-like function, we prove the stability of the proposed control algorithm. Weight updating laws derived from the Lyapunov analysis assures the boundedness of the closed-loop signals incorporating the well-known modified parameter hopping.

Chapter 8

Modeling and Simulation of Alternative Energy Generation Processes using HONN 162

Salvador Carlos Hernández, Cinvestav del IPN, Unidad Saltillo, México

Edgar Nelson Sanchez Camperos, Cinvestav del IPN, Unidad Guadalajara, México

Rocío Carrasco Navarro, Cinvestav del IPN, Unidad Guadalajara, México

Joel Kelly Gurubel Tun, Cinvestav del IPN, Unidad Guadalajara, México

José Andrés Bueno García, Cinvestav del IPN, Unidad Guadalajara, México

This chapter deals with the application of Higher Order Neural Networks (HONN) to the modeling and simulation of two processes commonly used to produce gas with energy potential: anaerobic digestion and gasification. Two control strategies for anaerobic digestion are proposed in order to obtain a high biomethane flow rate from degradation of organic wastes, such as wastewater. A neurofuzzy scheme, which is composed of a neural observer, a fuzzy supervisor, and two control actions is presented first. After that, a speed-gradient inverse optimal neural control for trajectory tracking is designed and applied to an anaerobic digestion model.

Section 3
Artificial Higher Order Neural Networks for Control and Predication

Chapter 9

Distributed Adaptive Control for Multi-Agent Systems with Pseudo Higher Order Neural Net 194

Abhijit Das, Automation and Robotics Research Institute, USA

Frank Lewis, Automation and Robotics Research Institute, USA

In this chapter, a distributed control methodology has been presented, where nonidentical nonlinear agents communicate among themselves following directed graph topology. In addition, the nonlinear dynamics are considered unknown. While the pinning control strategy has been adopted to distribute the input command among the agents, a Pseudo Higher Order Neural Net (PHONN)-based identification strategy is introduced for identifying the unknown dynamics. These two strategies are combined beautifully, such that the stability of the system is assured even with minimum interaction among the agents. A detailed stability analysis is presented based on Lyapunov theory, and a simulation study is performed to verify the theoretical claims.

Chapter 10
Cooperative Control of Unknown Networked Lagrange Systems using Higher Order
Neural Networks 214
Gang Chen, Chongqing University, China
Frank L. Lewis, University of Texas at Arlington, USA

This chapter investigates the cooperative control problem for a group of Lagrange systems with a target system to be tracked. The development is suitable for the case that the desired trajectory of the target node is only available to a portion of the networked systems. All the networked systems can have different dynamics. The dynamics of the networked systems, as well as the target system, are all assumed unknown. A higher-order neural network is used at each node to approximate the distributed unknown dynamics. A distributed adaptive neural network control protocol is proposed so that the networked systems synchronize to the motion of the target node. The theoretical analysis shows that the synchronization error can be made arbitrarily small by appropriately tuning the design parameters.

Chapter 11
Symbolic Function Network: Application to Telecommunication Networks Prediction 237
George S. Eskander, ETS, Quebec University, Canada
Amir Atiya, Cairo University, Egypt

Quality of Service (QoS) of telecommunication networks could be enhanced by applying predictive control methods. Such controllers rely on utilizing good and fast (real-time) predictions of the network traffic and quality parameters. Accuracy and recall speed of the traditional Neural Network models are not satisfactory to support such critical real time applications. The Symbolic Function Network (SFN) is a HONN-like model that was originally motivated by the current needs of developing more enhanced and fast predictors for such applications. In this chapter, we use the SFN model to design fast and accurate predictors for the telecommunication network's quality control applications.

Chapter 12
Time Series Forecasting via a Higher Order Neural Network trained with the Extended
Kalman Filter for Smart Grid Applications 254
Luis J. Ricalde, Universidad Autonoma de Yucatan, Mexico
Glendy A. Catzin, Universidad Autonoma de Yucatan, Mexico
Alma Y. Alanis, Universidad de Guadalajara, Mexico
Edgar N. Sanchez, Universidad de Guadalajara, Mexico

This chapter presents the design of a neural network that combines higher order terms in its input layer and an Extended Kalman Filter (EKF)-based algorithm for its training. The neural network-based scheme is defined as a Higher Order Neural Network (HONN), and its applicability is illustrated by means of time series forecasting for three important variables present in smart grids: Electric Load Demand (ELD), Wind Speed (WS), and Wind Energy Generation (WEG). The proposed model is trained and tested using real data values taken from a microgrid system in the UADY School of Engineering. The length of the regression vector is determined via the Lipschitz quotient's methodology.

Section 4
Artificial Higher Order Neural Network Models and Applications

Chapter 13
HONNs with Extreme Learning Machine to Handle Incomplete Datasets 276
Shuxiang Xu, University of Tasmania, Australia

This chapter uses the Extreme Learning Machine (ELM) algorithm for HONN models and applies it in several significant business cases, which involve missing datasets. The experimental results demonstrate that Higher Order Neural Network (HONN) models with the ELM algorithm offer significant advantages over standard HONN models, such as faster training, as well as improved generalization abilities.

Chapter 14
Symbolic Function Network: Theory and Implementation 293
George S. Eskander, ETS, Quebec University, Canada
Amir Atiya, Cairo University, Egypt

This chapter reviews a recent HONN-like model called Symbolic Function Network (SFN). This model is designed with the goal to impart more flexibility than both traditional and HONNs neural networks. The main idea behind this scheme is the fact that different functional forms suit different applications and that no specific architecture is best for all. Accordingly, the model is designed as an evolving network that can discover the best functional basis, adapt its parameters, and select its structure simultaneously.

Chapter 15
City Manager Compensation and Performance: An Artificial Intelligence Approach 325
Jean X. Zhang, Virginia Commonwealth University, USA

This chapter proposes a nonlinear artificial Higher Order Neural Network (HONN) model to study the relation between manager compensation and performance in the governmental sector. Using a HONN simulator, this study analyzes city manager compensation as a function of local government performance and compares the results with those from a linear regression model. This chapter shows that the nonlinear model generated from HONN has a smaller Root Mean Squared Error (Root MSE) of 0.0020 as compared to 0.06598 from a linear regression model. This study shows that artificial HONN is an effective tool in modeling city manager compensation.

Chapter 16
On Some Dynamical Properties of Randomly Connected Higher Order Neural Networks 333
Hiromi Miyajima, Kagoshima University, Japan
Noritaka Shigei, Kagoshima University, Japan
Shuji Yatsuki, Kyoto Software Research, Inc., Japan

This chapter presents macroscopic properties of higher order neural networks. Randomly connected Neural Networks (RNNs) are known as a convenient model to investigate the macroscopic properties of neural networks. They are investigated by using the statistical method of neuro-dynamics. By applying the approach to higher order neural networks, macroscopic properties of them are made clear.

Chapter 17
A Hybrid Higher Order Neural Structure for Pattern Recognition 364
Mehdi Fallahnezhad, Norwegian University of Science and Technology (NTNU), Norway
Salman Zaferanlouei, Amirkabir University of Technology (Tehran Polytechnic), Iran

This chapter introduces a hybrid structure of higher order neural networks, which can be generally applied in various branches of pattern recognition. Structure, learning algorithm, and network configuration are introduced, and structure is applied either as a classifier (where it is called HHONC) to different benchmark statistical data sets or as a functional behavior approximation (where it is called HHONN) to a heat and mass transfer dilemma. In each structure, results are compared with previous studies, which show its superior performance along with its other mentioned advantages.

Compilation of References 388

About the Contributors 419

Index 428

Preface

Artificial Higher Order Neural Networks for Economics and Business was published by IGI Global in 2009. In 2010, *Artificial Higher Order Neural Networks for Computer Science and Engineering* was published by IGI. *Artificial Higher Order Neural Networks for Modeling and Simulation* is the third book published by IGI Global in the Higher Order Neural Network (HONN) area.

Artificial Higher Order Neural Networks for Modeling and Simulation is the first book that introduces artificial Higher Order Neural Networks (HONNs) to people working in the fields of modeling and simulation, and presents to them that HONN is an open-box artificial neural network tool as compared to traditional artificial neural networks. This is the first book that includes details of the most popular HONN models and provides opportunities for millions of people working in the modeling and simulation areas to know about HONNs, and how to use HONNs in modeling and simulation areas.

Artificial Neural Networks (ANNs) are known to excel in pattern recognition, pattern matching, and mathematical function approximation. However, they suffer from several well-known limitations—they can often become stuck in local, rather than global, minima, as well as taking unacceptably long time to converge in practice. Another limitation of ANN is the "black box" nature—meaning that explanations for their decisions are not immediately obvious, unlike techniques such as decision trees. This is then the motivation for developing artificial Higher Order Neural Networks, since HONNs are "open-box" models, and each neuron/weight is mapped to formula variable/coefficient.

In recent years, researchers have used HONNs for pattern recognition, nonlinear simulation, classification, and prediction in the modeling and simulation areas. The results show that HONNs are always faster, more accurate, and easier to explain. This is the second motivation for using HONNs in modeling and simulation areas, since HONNs can automatically select the initial coefficients, even automatically select the model for applications in the modeling and simulation area.

Objectives of this book are:

- This is the first book that introduces HONNs to people working in the fields of modeling and simulation.
- This is the first book that introduces to researchers in the modeling and simulation areas that HONNs are open-box neural network tools compared to traditional artificial neural networks.
- This is the first book that includes the most popular HONNs software packages and detailed information for researchers to successfully use these HONNs software packages.
- This is the first book that provides opportunities for millions of people working in the modeling and simulation areas to know about HONNs, and how to use HONNs in modeling and simulation areas.

- This book introduces the HONN group models and adaptive HONNs, and allows people working in the modeling and simulation areas to understand HONN group models, which can simulate not only nonlinear data, but also discontinuous and unsmooth nonlinear data.

The mission of this book is to let millions of people working in the modeling and simulation areas know that HONNs are much easier to use and can have better simulation results. In addition, this book allows people to understand how to successfully use HONNs software packages and hardware designs for nonlinear data modeling and simulation. HONNs will challenge traditional artificial neural network products and change the research methodology that people are currently using in modeling and simulation areas.

Artificial neural network research is one of the new directions for new generation computers. Current research suggests that open-box artificial HONNs play an important role in this new direction. Since HONNs are open-box models, they can be easily accepted and used by people working in the modeling and simulation studies.

Currently, no book has been published in the modeling and simulation areas using HONNs. This book will be the first book that collects chapters on HONNs for modeling and simulation. With this book, more people in modeling and simulation can use HONNs for modeling, pattern recognition, nonlinear simulation, and system control. More researchers in the modeling, simulation, economics, and business areas can use HONNs for time series analysis, data simulation, and market prediction.

This is the first book that will provide opportunities for millions of people working in the modeling and simulation areas to know what HONNs are and how to use HONNs in modeling and simulation areas. This book explains why HONNs can approximate any nonlinear data to any degree of accuracy, and make sure that people working in the modeling and simulation can understand why HONNs are much easier to use, and HONNs can have better nonlinear data simulation accuracy than SAS nonlinear (NLIN) procedures.

Chapter 1, "Artificial Multi-Polynomial Higher Order Neural Network Models," introduces Multi-Polynomial Higher Order Neural Network (MPHONN) models with higher accuracy. Using Sun workstation, C++, and Motif, a MPHONN Simulator has been built. Real-world data cannot always be modeled simply and simulated with high accuracy by a single polynomial function. Thus, ordinary higher order neural networks could fail to simulate complicated real-world data, but the MPHONN model can simulate multi-polynomial functions and produce results with improved accuracy through experiments. By using MPHONN for financial modeling and simulation, experimental results show that MPHONN can always have 0.5051% to 0.8661% more accuracy than ordinary higher order neural network models.

In chapter 2, "Artificial Higher Order Neural Networks for Modeling MIMO Discrete-Time Nonlinear System," a Recurrent Higher Order Neural Network (RHONN) is used to identify the plant model of discrete time nonlinear systems, under the assumption that all the state is available for measurement. Then the Extended Kalman Filter (EKF) is used to train the RHONN. The applicability of this scheme is illustrated by identification for an electrically driven nonholonomic mobile robot. Traditionally, modeling of mobile robots only considers its kinematics. It has been well known that the actuator dynamics are an important part of the design of the complete robot dynamics. However, most of the reported results in literature do not consider all parametric uncertainties for mobile robots at the actuator level. This is because the modeling problem would become extremely difficult as the complexity of the system dynamics increases, and when the mobile robot model includes the uncertainties of the actuator dynamics as well as the uncertainties of the robot kinematics and dynamics.

In chapter 3, "Artificial Higher Order Neural Networks for Modeling Combinatorial Optimization Problems," a high order Hopfiled network, as an expansion of the traditional Hopfield network, is used to solve combinatorial optimization problems. In theory, compared with low order network, high order network has better properties, such as stronger approximation property and faster convergence rate. In this chapter, the authors focus on how to use high order network to model combinatorial optimization problems. Firstly, the high order discrete Hopfield Network is introduced. Then the authors discuss how to find the high order inputs of a neuron. Finally, the construction method of energy function and the neural computing algorithm are presented. In this chapter, N queens problem and crossbar switch problem, which are NP-complete problems, are used as examples to illustrate how to model practical problems using high order neural networks. The authors also discuss the performance of high order network for modeling the two combinatorial optimization problems.

Chapter 4, "Needle Insertion Force Modeling using Genetic Programming Polynomial Higher Order Neural Network," suggested that precise insertion of medical needle as end-effecter of robotic or computer-aided system into the biological tissue is an important issue, which should be considered in different operations, such as brain biopsy, prostate brachytherapy, and percutaneous therapies. Proper understanding of the whole procedure leads to a better performance by operator or system. In this chapter, the authors use a 0.98 mm diameter needle with a real-time recording of force, displacement, and velocity of needle through biological tissue during in-vitro insertions. Using constant velocity experiments from 5 mm/min up to 300 mm/min, the data set for the force-displacement graph of insertion was gathered. Tissue deformation with a small puncture and a constant velocity penetration are the two first phases in the needle insertion process. Direct effects of different parameters and their correlations during the process are modeled using a polynomial neural network. The authors develop different networks in 2nd and 3rd orders to model the two first phases of insertion separately. Modeling accuracies were 98% and 86% in phase 1 and 2, respectively.

Chapter 5, "Artificial Polynomial and Trigonometric Higher Order Neural Network Group Models," introduces that real-world financial data is often discontinuous and non-smooth. Accuracy will be a problem, if one attempts to use neural networks to simulate such functions. Higher order neural network group models can perform this function with more accuracy. Both Polynomial Higher Order Neural Network Group (PHONNG) and Trigonometric polynomial Higher Order Neural Network Group (THONNG) models are studied in this chapter. These PHONNG and THONNG models are open box, convergent models capable of approximating any kind of piecewise continuous function to any degree of accuracy. Moreover, they are capable of handling higher frequency, higher order nonlinear, and discontinuous data. Results obtained using Polynomial Higher Order Neural Network Group and Trigonometric polynomial Higher Order Neural Network Group financial simulators are presented, which confirm that PHONNG and THONNG group models converge without difficulty and are considerably more accurate (0.7542% - 1.0715%) than neural network models, such as using Polynomial Higher Order Neural Network (PHONN) and Trigonometric polynomial Higher Order Neural Network (THONN) models.

In chapter 6, "Fundamentals of Higher Order Neural Networks for Modeling and Simulation," the authors provide fundamental principles of Higher Order Neural Units (HONUs) and Higher Order Neural Networks (HONNs) for modeling and simulation. An essential core of HONNs can be found in higher order weighted combinations or correlations between the input variables and HONU. Despite the high quality of nonlinear approximation of static HONUs, the capability of dynamic HONUs for modeling of dynamic systems is shown and compared to conventional recurrent neural networks when a practical learning algorithm is used. In addition, the potential of continuous dynamic HONUs to approximate high dynamic-order systems is discussed as adaptable time delays can be implemented. By using some typical examples, this chapter describes how and why higher order combinations or correlations can be effective for modeling of systems.

In chapter 7, "High Order Neuro-Fuzzy Dynamic Regulation of General Nonlinear Multi-Variable Systems," the direct adaptive dynamic regulation of unknown nonlinear multi-variable systems is investigated in order to address the problem of controlling non-Brunovsky and non-square systems with control inputs less than the number of states. The proposed neuron-fuzzy model acts as a universal approximator, while with careful selection of Lyapunov-like function, the authors prove the stability of the proposed control algorithm. Weight updating laws derived from the Lyapunov analysis assures the boundedness of the closed-loop signals incorporating the well-known modified parameter hopping. Also, the proposed algorithm shows robustness when we face modelling errors, and therefore, the state trajectories present uniform ultimate boundedness. The proposed dynamic controller proved to control those general nonlinear systems, which are difficult or even impossible to control with other algorithms. Simulation results on well-known benchmark problems demonstrate the applicability and effectiveness of the method.

Chapter 8, "Modeling and Simulation of Alternative Energy Generation Processes by using HONN," deals with the application of Higher Order Neural Networks (HONN) on modeling and simulation of two processes commonly used to produce gas with energy potential: anaerobic digestion and gasification. Two control strategies for anaerobic digestion are proposed in order to obtain a high biomethane flow rate from the degradation of organic wastes such as wastewater. A neurofuzzy scheme, which is composed by a neural observer, a fuzzy supervisor, and two control actions, is presented first. After that, a speed-gradient inverse optimal neural control for trajectory tracking is designed and applied to an anaerobic digestion model. The control law calculates dilution rate and bicarbonate in order to track a methane production reference trajectory under controlled conditions and avoid washout. A nonlinear discrete-time neural observer (RHONO) for unknown nonlinear systems in presence of external disturbances and parameter uncertainties is used to estimate the biomass concentration, substrate degradation, and inorganic carbon. On the other side, a high order neural network structure is developed for the process identification in a gasification reactor; the gas, composed mainly of hydrogen and carbon monoxide (synthesis gas or syngas), is produced from termochemical transformation of solid organic wastes. The identifier is developed in order to reproduce a kinetic model of a biomass gasifier. In both cases (biological and thermochemical processes), the Extended Kalman Filter (EKF) is used as the training algorithm. The proposed methodologies application is illustrated via numerical simulations.

Chapter 9, "Distributed Adaptive Control for Multi-Agent Systems with Pseudo Higher Order Neural Net," suggests that the idea of using multi-agent systems is growing more popular every day. It not only saves time and resources but also eliminates the requirement of large human coordination. These ideas are especially effective in combating zone where multiple unmanned aerial vehicles are required for achieving multiple simultaneous objectives or targets. The evolution of distributed control has started with simple integrator systems and then gradually different control methodologies have been adopted for more and more complex nonlinear systems. In addition, from a practical standpoint, the dynamics of the agents involved in networked control architecture might not be identical. Therefore, an ideal distributed control should accommodate multiple agents, which are nonlinear systems associated with unknown dynamics. In this chapter, a distributed control methodology has been presented, where nonidentical nonlinear agents communicate among themselves following directed graph topology. In addition, the nonlinear dynamics are considered unknown. While the pinning control strategy has been adopted to distribute the input command among the agents, a Pseudo Higher Order Neural Net (PHONN)-based identification strategy is introduced for identifying the unknown dynamics. These two strategies are combined beautifully so that the stability of the system is assured even with minimum interaction among the agents. A detailed stability analysis is presented based on the Lyapunov theory, and a simulation study is performed to verify the theoretical claims.

Chapter 10, "Cooperative Control of Unknown Networked Lagrange Systems using Higher Order Neural Networks," investigates the cooperative control problem for a group of Lagrange systems with a target system to be tracked. The development is suitable for the case that the desired trajectory of the target node is only available to a portion of the networked systems. All the networked systems can have different dynamics. The dynamics of the networked systems, as well as the target system, are all assumed unknown. A higher-order neural network is used at each node to approximate the distributed unknown dynamics. A distributed adaptive neural network control protocol is proposed so that the networked systems synchronize to the motion of the target node. The theoretical analysis shows that the synchronization error can be made arbitrarily small by appropriately tuning the design parameters.

Chapter 11, "Symbolic Function Network: Application to Telecommunication Networks Prediction," introduces that Quality of Service (QoS) of telecommunication networks could be enhanced by applying predictive control methods. Such controllers rely on utilizing good and fast (real-time) predictions of the network traffic and quality parameters. Accuracy and recall speed of the traditional Neural Network models are not satisfactory to support such critical real-time applications. The Symbolic Function Network (SFN) is a HONN-like model that was originally motivated by the current needs of developing more enhanced and fast predictors for such applications. In this chapter, authors use the SFN model to design fast and accurate predictors for the telecommunication networks quality control applications. Three predictors are designed and tested for the network traffic, packet loss, and round trip delay. This chapter aims to open a door for researchers to investigate the applicability of SFN in other prediction tasks and to develop more accurate and faster predictors.

Chapter 12, "Time Series Forecasting via Higher Order Neural Network trained with the Extended Kalman Filter for Smart Grid Applications," presents the design of a neural network that combines higher order terms in its input layer and an Extended Kalman Filter (EKF)-based algorithm for its training. The neural network-based scheme is defined as a Higher Order Neural Network (HONN), and its applicability is illustrated by means of time series forecasting for three important variables present in smart grids: Electric Load Demand (ELD), Wind Speed (WS), and Wind Energy Generation (WEG). The proposed model is trained and tested using real data values taken from a microgrid system in the UADY School of Engineering. The length of the regression vector is determined via the Lipschitz quotients methodology.

Chapter 13, "HONNs with Extreme Learning Machine to Handle Incomplete Datasets," introduces that Extreme Learning Machine (ELM) randomly chooses hidden neurons and analytically determines the output weights. With ELM algorithm, only the connection weights between hidden layer and output layer are adjusted. ELM algorithm tends to generalize better at a very fast learning speed: it can learn thousands of times faster than conventionally popular learning algorithms. Artificial Neural Networks (ANNs) have been widely used as powerful information processing models and adopted in applications such as bankruptcy prediction, predicting costs, forecasting revenue, forecasting share prices and exchange rates, processing documents, and many more. Higher Order Neural Networks (HONNs) are ANNs in which the net input to a computational neuron is a weighted sum of products of its inputs. Real-world data are not usually perfect. They may contain wrong data, incomplete, or vague data. Hence, it is usual to find missing data in many information sources used. Missing data is a common problem in statistical analysis. This chapter uses Extreme Learning Machine (ELM) algorithm for HONN models and applies it in several significant business cases involving missing datasets. The experimental results demonstrate that HONN models with ELM algorithms offer significant advantages over standard HONN models, such as faster training and improved generalization abilities.

Chapter 14, "Symbolic Function Network: Theory and Implementation," reviews a recent HONN-like model called Symbolic Function Network (SFN). This model is designed with the goal to impart more flexibility than both traditional and HONNs neural networks. The main idea behind this scheme is the fact that different functional forms suit different applications and that no specific architecture is best for all. Accordingly, the model is designed as an evolving network that can discover the best functional basis, adapt its parameters, and select its structure simultaneously. Despite the high modeling capability of SFN, it is considered a starting point for developing more powerful models. This chapter aims to open a door for researchers to propose new formulations and techniques that impart more flexibility and result in sparser and more accurate models. Through this chapter, the theoretical basis of SFN is discussed. The model optimization computations are deeply illustrated to enable researchers to easily implement and test the model.

The chapter 15, "City Manager Compensation and Performance: An Artificial Intelligence Approach," proposes a nonlinear artificial Higher Order Neural Network (HONN) model to study the relation between manager compensation and performance in the governmental sector. Using a HONN simulator, this study analyzes city manager compensation as a function of local government performance and compares the results with those from a linear regression model. This chapter shows that the nonlinear model generated from HONN has a smaller Root Mean Squared Error (Root MSE) of 0.0020 as compared to 0.06598 from a linear regression model. This study shows that artificial HONN is an effective tool in modeling city manager compensation.

The chapter 16, "On Some Dynamical Properties of Randomly Connected Higher Order Neural Networks," presents macroscopic properties of higher order neural networks. Randomly connected Neural Networks (RNNs) are known as a convenient model to investigate the macroscopic properties of neural networks. They are investigated by using the statistical method of neuro-dynamics. By applying the approach to higher order neural networks, macroscopic properties of them are made clear. The approach establishes: (a) there are differences between stability of RNNs and Randomly connected Higher Order Neural Networks (RHONNs) in the cases of the digital state $\{-1,1\}$-model and the analog state $[-1,1]$-model; (b) there is no difference between stability of RNNs and RHONNs in the cases of the digital state $\{0,1\}$-model and the analog state $[0,1]$-model; (c) with neural networks with oscillation, there are large difference between RNNs and RHONNs in the cases of the digital state $\{-1,1\}$-model and the analog state $[-1,1]$-model, that is, there exists complex dynamics in each model for $k=2$; (d) behavior of groups composed of RHONNs is represented as combination of behavior of each RHONN.

Chapter 17, "A Hybrid Higher Order Neural Structure for Pattern Recognition," considers that high order correlations of selected features next to the raw features of input can facilitate target pattern recognition. In artificial intelligence, this is usually addressed by Higher Order Neural Networks (HONNs). In general, HONN structures provide superior specifications (e.g. resolving dilemma of choosing number of neurons and layers of network, better fitting specs, quicker, and open-box specificity) to traditional neural networks. This chapter introduces a hybrid structure of higher order neural networks that can be generally applied in various branches of pattern recognition. Structure, learning algorithm, and network configuration are introduced, and structure is applied either as classifier (where it is called HHONC) to different benchmark statistical data sets or as a functional behavior approximation (where it is called HHONN) to a heat and mass transfer dilemma. In each structure, results are compared with previous studies, which show its superior performance next to other mentioned advantages.

Ming Zhang
Christopher Newport University, USA

Acknowledgment

The editor would like to acknowledge the help of all involved in the collation and the review process of the book, without whose support the project could not have been satisfactorily completed. Deep appreciation and gratitude are due to Prof. David Doughty, Dean of the College of Natural and Behavior Sciences, Prof. Douglas Gordon, former Dean of the College of Liberal Arts and Sciences, and Prof. George Webb, former Dean of the College of Sciences, Christopher Newport University, for giving me grants to support my research and to edit this book. Deep appreciation and gratitude are also due to Dr. Edward Brash, Chair of the Department of Physics, Computer Science, and Engineering, Professor. A. Martin Buoncristiani and Professor Randall Caton, former Chairs of the Department of Physics, Computer Science, and Engineering, Christopher Newport University, for providing research funding to support my research.

I would like to thank my supervisor, Dr. Rod Scofield, retired Senior Scientist of the National Oceanic and Atmospheric Administration (NOAA), Washington DC, USA, for supporting my artificial neural network research and awarding me USA National Research Council Postdoctoral Fellow (1991-1992) and Senior USA National Research Council Research Associate (1999-2000). I would like to thank Dr. John Fulcher, retired Professor of the University of Wollongong in Australia, for a long research collaboration in the artificial neural network area, since 1992.

I would like to thank Professor Dingbo Kuang, Fellow of the Chinese Academy of Sciences, and Senior Scientist of the Shanghai Institute of Technical Physics, Shanghai, China. Thank you for being my postdoctoral advisor from 1989 to 1991, when I was a postdoctoral researcher. I would like to thank Professor Huixing Gong, Fellow of the Chinese Academy of Engineering, and Senior Scientist of the Shanghai Institute of Technical Physics, Shanghai, China. Thank you for inspiring me in research from 1989 to 1991, when I was a postdoctoral researcher.

I want to thank all the Editorial Advisory Board members for their excellent advising and great help to this book. I also want to thank all of the authors for their insights and excellent contributions to this book. Most of the authors of chapters included in this book also served as referees for chapters written by other authors. Thanks go to all the reviewers who provided constructive and comprehensive reviews and suggestions.

Special thanks also go to the publishing team at IGI Global, whose contributions throughout the whole process from inception of the initial idea to final publication have been invaluable. In particular, to Joel Gamon, who continuously prodded via e-mail, for keeping the project on schedule, and to Erika Carter, Kristin M. Klinger, and Jan Travers, whose enthusiasm motivated me to initially accept this invitation for taking on this project.

Special thanks go to my family for their continuous support and encouragement, in particular to my wife, Zhao Qing Zhang, for her unfailing support and encouragement during the years it took to give birth to this book.

Ming Zhang
Christopher Newport University, USA
March 31st, 2012

Section 1
Artificial Higher Order Neural Networks for Modeling

Chapter 1
Artificial Multi-Polynomial Higher Order Neural Network Models

Ming Zhang
Christopher Newport University, USA

ABSTRACT

This chapter introduces Multi-Polynomial Higher Order Neural Network (MPHONN) models with higher accuracy. Using Sun workstation, C++, and Motif, a MPHONN Simulator has been built. Real world data cannot always be modeled simply and simulated with high accuracy by a single polynomial function. Thus, ordinary higher order neural networks could fail to simulate complicated real world data. However, the MPHONN model can simulate multi-polynomial functions, and can produce results with improved accuracy through experiments. By using MPHONN for financial modeling and simulation, experimental results show that MPHONN can always have 0.5051% to 0.8661% more accuracy than ordinary higher order neural network models.

INTRODUCTION

HONN Applications

Artificial Higher Order Neural Network (HONN) has a lot of applications in different areas. Barron, Gilstrap, and Shrier (1987) develop polynomial and neural networks for analogies and engineering applications. An, Mniszewski, Lee, Papcun, and Doolen (1988) test a learning procedure, based on a default hierarchy of high-order neural net-

works, which exhibited an enhanced capability of generalization and a good efficiency to learn to read English. Mao, Selviah, Tao, and Midwinter (1991) design a holographic high order associative memory system in holographic area. Mendel (1991) study higher-order statistics (spectra) system theory and use it in signal processing. Rovithakis, Kosmatopoulos, and Christodoulou (1993) research robust adaptive control of unknown plants using recurrent high order neural networks for the application of mechanical systems. Miyajima, Yatsuki, and Kubota (1995) build up higher order neural networks with product con-

DOI: 10.4018/978-1-4666-2175-6.ch001

nections that hold the weighted sum of products of input variables. It is shown that they are more superior in ability than traditional neural networks in applications. Xu, Liu, and Liao (2005) explore global asymptotic stability of high-order Hopfield type neural networks with time delays. There are two major ways of encoding a neural network into a chromosome, as required in design of a Genetic Algorithm (GA). These are explicit (direct) and implicit (indirect) encoding methods. Siddiqi (2005) genetically evolve higher order neural networks by direct encoding method. Ren and Cao (2006) provide LMI-based criteria for stability of high-order neural networks with time-varying delay for nonlinear analysis. Recently, Selviah (2009) describes the progress in using optical technology to construct high-speed artificial higher order neural network systems. The chapter reviews how optical technology can speed up searches within large databases in order to identify relationships and dependencies between individual data records, such as financial or business time-series, as well as trends and relationships within them. Epitropakis, Plagianakos, and Vrahatis (2010) intend evolutionary Algorithm Training of Higher Order Neural Networks, for the aims to further explore the capabilities of the Higher Order Neural Networks class and especially the Pi-Sigma Neural Networks. Selviah and Shawash (2010) celebrate 50 years of first and Higher Order Neural Network (HONN) implementations in terms of the physical layout and structure of electronic hardware, which offers high speed, low latency in compact, low cost, low power, mass produced systems. Low latency is essential for practical applications in real time control for which software implementations running on Center Process Units (CPUs) are too slow. Gupta, Homma, Hou, Solo, and Bukovsky (2010) give fundamental principles of Higher Order Neural Units (HONUs) and Higher Order Neural Networks (HONNs). An essential core of HONNs can be found in higher order weighted combinations or correlations between the input variables. By using some typical examples, this

chapter describes how and why higher order combinations or correlations can be effective. Das, Lewis, and Subbarao (2010) seek a dynamically tuned higher order like neural network approach; look into the control of quad-rotor. The dynamics of a quad-rotor is a simplified form of helicopter dynamics that exhibit the same basic problems of strong coupling, multi-input/multi-output design, and unknown nonlinearities. Yu (2010) offers a robust adaptive control using higher order neural networks and projection, and presents a novel robust adaptive approach for a class of unknown nonlinear systems. The structure is composed by two parts: the neuron-observer and the tracking controller. The simulations of a two-link robot show the effectiveness of the proposed algorithm.

Motivation

For modeling and simulation, there is no single neural network model that could handle the wide variety of complicated data and also perform with accuracy. Artificial Intelligent (AI) technique is one way to address this problem. Artificial Neural Network (ANN) computing is an area that is receiving increased research interest, since the classic artificial neural network model is a 'black box.' Artificial neuron network-based models are also not yet sufficiently powerful to characterize complex systems. Thus, a way of solving this problem is to develop new models with higher degree of accuracy for modeling and simulation. Multi-Polynomial Higher Order Neural Network Group (MPHONNG) models are "open box" models with improved accuracy are presented in this chapter.

Contributions

1. Multi-Polynomial Higher Order Neural Network models are studied.
2. Multi-Polynomial Higher Neural Network models learning algorithm has been provided.

3. MPHONN Simulator developed for data modeling has been developed.
4. MPHONN models have been tested by using data extracted from Reserve Bank.

BACKGROUND

HONN Modeling

Artificial higher order neural networks are used for modeling in a lot of areas. Zhang, Xu, and Fulcher (2002) find that real-world financial data is often nonlinear, comprises high-frequency multi-polynomial components, and is discontinuous (piecewise continuous). Not surprisingly, it is hard to model such data using classical neural networks. However, the neuron-adaptive higher order neural-network models can be used for automated financial data modeling. Seiffertt and Wunsch (2009) study the agent-based computational economics and finance grows, so do the need for appropriate techniques for the modeling of complex dynamic systems and the intelligence of the constructive agent. In particular, one area of computational intelligence, approximate dynamic programming, holds much promise for applications in this field and demonstrates the capacity for artificial higher order neural networks to add value in the social sciences and business. Chen, Wu, and Wu (2009) investigate higher order artificial neural networks for stock index modeling problems. New network architectures and their corresponding training algorithms are discussed. These structures demonstrate their processing capabilities over traditional artificial neural network architectures with a reduction in the number of processing elements. Dunis, Laws, and Evans (2009) analysis modeling and trading the soybean-oil crush spread with recurrent higher order networks. A traditional regression analysis is used as a benchmark against more sophisticated models such as a Multi-Layer Perceptron (MLP), Recurrent Neural Networks, and Higher Order Neural Networks. These are

then used to trade the spread. The implementation of a number of filtering techniques as used in the literature are utilized to further refine the trading statistics of the models. The results show that the best model before transactions costs both in- and out-of-sample is the Recurrent Higher Order Network generating a superior risk adjusted return to all other models investigated. Lu, Shieh, and Chen (2009) develop a systematic approach for optimizing the structure of artificial higher order neural networks for system modeling and function approximation. A new HONN topology, namely polynomial kernel networks, is proposed. Structurally, the polynomial kernel network can be viewed as a three-layer feed-forward neural network with a special polynomial activation function for the nodes in the hidden layer. Both quadratic programming and linear programming based training of the polynomial kernel network are investigated. Zhang (2010) finds that classical neural network models are unable to automatically determine the optimum model and appropriate order for data approximation. In order to solve this problem, Neuron-Adaptive Higher Order Neural Network (NAHONN) Models have been introduced. NAHONN models are shown to be "open box." These models are further shown to be capable of automatically finding not only the optimum model but also the appropriate order for high frequency, multi-polynomial, discontinuous data. Rainfall estimation experimental results confirm model convergence. When the artificial neuron-adaptive higher order neural network model was used for rainfall estimation, the average training error of rainfall estimation and the average test error of rainfall estimation are all better than classic artificial neural network techniques. Karnavas (2010) demonstrates a practical design of an intelligent type of controller using Higher Order Neural Network (HONN) concepts, for the excitation control of a practical power generating system. This type of controller is suitable for real time operation, and aims to improve the dynamic characteristics of the generating unit by acting properly on its original excitation system. The modeling of the power system under study consists of a synchronous generator connected via a transformer and a transmission line to an infinite bus. The computer simulation results obtained show clearly that the performance of the developed controllers offers competitive damping effects on the synchronous generator's oscillations.

HONN Models

For better application results, a lot of researchers focus on new HONN models development. Chen, Lee, Maxwell, Sun, Lee, and Giles (1986) build up high order correlation model for associative memory. Machado (1989) gives description of the combinatorial a neural model and a high-order neural network suitable for classification tasks. The model is based on fuzzy set theory, neural sciences studies, and expert knowledge analysis. Horan, Uecker, and Arimoto (1990) expand optical implementation of a second-order neural network discriminator model. Rovithakis, Gaganis, Perrakis, and Christodoulou (1996) learn a recurrent neural network model to describe manufacturing cell dynamics. A neural network approach to the manufacturing cell modeling problem is discussed. A Recurrent High-Order Neural Network structure (RHONN) is employed to identify cell dynamics, which is supposed to be unknown. Brucoli, Carnimeo, and Grassi (1997) provide a design method for associative memories using a new model of discrete-time high-order neural networks, which includes local interconnections among neurons. Burshtein (1998) examines long-term attraction in higher order neural networks for the memory storage capacity. Zhang, Xu, and Lu (1999) extend neuron-adaptive higher order neural network group models. Campos, Loukianov, and Sanchez (2003) deliver a nonlinear complete order model of a synchronous motor, which is identified using a dynamic neural network. Based on this model a sliding mode controller is derived. This neural network identifier and the proposed

control law allow rejecting external load. Kuroe (2004) supplies recurrent high-order neural network models for learning and identifying deterministic finite state automata. The proposed models are a class of high-order recurrent neural networks. Zhang (2006) widens linear and nonlinear HONN models for the power of chief elected officials and debt. Alanis, Sanchez, and Loukianov (2006) deal with the adaptive tracking problem for discrete time induction motor model in presence of bounded disturbances. A high order neural network structure is developed to identify the plant model. Butt and Shafiq (2006) present higher order neural network, based root-solving controller for adaptive tracking of stable nonlinear plants. Zhang, Simoff, and Zhang (2009) bring trigonometric polynomial higher order neural network group models and weighted kernel models for financial data simulation and prediction. Xu (2010) explores adaptive higher order neural network models for data mining. Zhang (2010) develops higher order neural network group-based adaptive tolerance trees for face recognition. Al-Rawi and Al-Rawi (2010) discuss the equivalence between ordinary neural networks and higher order neural networks. Ricalde, Sanchez, and Alanis (2010) test recurrent higher order neural network control for output trajectory tracking with neural observers and constrained inputs, and present the design of an adaptive recurrent neural observer-controller scheme for nonlinear systems whose model is assumed to be unknown and with constrained inputs. Sanchez, Urrego, Alanis, and Carlos-Hernandez (2010) study recurrent higher order neural observers for anaerobic processes, and propose the design of a discrete-time neural observer that requires no prior knowledge of the model of an anaerobic process. Najarian, Hosseini, and Fallahnezhad (2010) introduce a new medical instrument, namely, the Tactile Tumor Detector (TTD) able to simulate the sense of touch in clinical and surgical applications. The results show that by having an HONN model of nonlinear input-output mapping, there are many advantages compared with Artificial Neural Network (ANN) model, including faster running for new data, lesser Root Mean Square (RMS) error and better fitting properties.

HONN Theories

To build better HONN models, HONN theories have been studied. Jeffries (1989) presents a specific high-order neural network design that can store, using n neutrons, any number of any of the binomial n-strings. Baldi and Venkatesh (1993) study recurrent networks of polynomial threshold elements with random symmetric interactions. Precise asymptotic estimates are derived for the expected number of fixed points as a function of the margin of stability. Young and Downs (1993) discover that the theory of Pac-learning has provided statements about the generalization capability of linear threshold higher order neural networks. Tseng and Wu (1994) find that High-Order Neural Networks (HONN) are shown to decode some Bose Chaudhuri Hocquenghem (BCH) codes in constant-time with very low hardware complexity. HONN is a direct extension of the linear perceptron: it uses a polynomial consisting of a set of product terms Constant-time neural decoders for some BCH codes. Gupta, Homma, Hou, Solo, and Goto (2009) describe fundamental principles of Artificial Higher Order Neural Units (AHONUs) and Networks (AHONNs). An essential core of AHONNs can be found in higher order weighted combinations or correlations between the input variables.

Cao, Ren, and Liang (2009) concentrate on studying the dynamics of artificial Higher Order Neural Networks (HONNs) with delays. Both stability analysis and periodic oscillation are discussed for a class of delayed HONNs with (or without) impulses. Wang, Liu, and Liu (2009) deal with the analysis problem of the global exponential stability for a general class of stochastic artificial higher order neural networks with multiple mixed time delays and Markovian jumping parameters.

The mixed time delays under consideration comprise both the discrete time-varying delays and the distributed time-delays. Neto (2010) goes into discrete and recurrent artificial neural networks with a homogenous type of neuron. This chapter presents some uses of chaotic computations with the same neurons and synapses, and, thus, creating a hybrid system. Shawash and Selviah (2010) investigate the training of networks using Back Propagation and Levenberg-Marquardt algorithms in limited precision achieving high overall calculation accuracy, using on-line training, a new type of HONN known as the Correlation HONN (CHONN), discrete XOR and continuous optical waveguide sidewall roughness datasets by simulation to find the precision at which the training and operation is feasible. Boutalis, Christodoulou, and Theodoridis (2010) use a new neuron-fuzzy dynamical system definition based on high order neural network function approximators to study the nonlinear systems. Theodoridis, Christodoulou, and Boutalis (2010) deliver neuron–fuzzy control schemes based on high order neural network function approximators to study the control schemes. The indirect or direct adaptive regulation of unknown nonlinear dynamical systems is considered in this research. Dehuri and Chao (2010) present a theoretical and empirical study of Functional Link Neural Networks (FLNNs) for classification; focus on theoretical and empirical study of Functional Link Neural Networks (FLNNs) for classification. The computational results are then compared with other Higher Order Neural Networks (HONNs) like functional link neural network with a generic basis functions, Pi-Sigma Neural Network (PSNN), Radial Basis Function Neural Network (RBFNN), and Ridge Polynomial Neural Network (RPNN).

HIGHER ORDER NEURAL NETWORKS

Giles and Maxwell (1987) formulate the output from first-order neurons as follows in the equation:

$$y_i(x) = f[\sum_j^n W(i,j)x(j)]$$

where:

- $\{x(j)\}$ = an n-element input vector,
- $W(i,j)$=adaptable weights from all other neurons to neuron-i, and
- f = neuron threshold funciton (e.g. sigmoid).

Such units (neurons or nodes) are said to be linear, since they are only able to capture first-order correlations in the training data. Higher order correlations require more complex units, characterised by Giles and Maxwell (1987) in the following equation:

Units which include terms up to and including degree-k are referred to as kth-order nodes. An alternative (simpler) formulaition is equation of Lisboa and Perantonis (1991):

$$y_i = f[W_i^0$$
$$+\sum_i \sum_k \sum_l ....\sum_m W_{ikl....m,j}x_i.x_k.x_l....x_m]$$

where a single weight is applied to all n-tuples $xi .... xm$ in order to generate the output yi from that node. This formulation is reminiscent of the Sigma-Pi units of Rumelhart, Hinton, and Mc-Clelland (1986):

$$\sum Wij \prod ai1 ai2 ... aik$$

and for which they prove that the Generalised Delta Rule can be applied as readily as for simple additive units ($\sum$ Wijaij).

In summary, HONNs include multiplicative terms in their activation function. Now it is possible to perform these data multiplications within a preprocessing stage; the major computational load then becomes a function of the large number of weights. It should also be pointed out that the output of a *kth*-order single-layer HONN node is a nonlinear funciton of up to *kth*-order polynomials. Moreover, since no hidden layers are involved, both Hebbian and Perceptron learning rules can be used (Shin, 1991).

Polynomial Higher Order Neural Network (PHONN) model is that to use a combination of linear, power and multiplication neurons for simulation the data as follows:

$$Z_a = \sum_{k,j=0}^n (a_{kj}{}^o)\{a_{kj}{}^{hx}(a_k{}^x x)^k\}\{a_{kj}{}^{hy}(a_j{}^y y)^j\}$$

Trigonometric polynomial Higher Order Neural Network (THONN) model is an artificial neural network in which every element is a higher order trigonometric neural network. The domain of the neural network inputs is the n-dimensional real number R^n. Likewise; the outputs belong to the m-dimensional real number R^m. The neural network function f is a mapping from the inputs to its outputs as follows:

$$Z_c = \sum_{k,j=0}^n (c_{kj}{}^o)\{c_{kj}{}^{hx}\cos^k(c_k{}^x x)\}\{c_{kj}{}^{hy}\sin^j(c_j{}^y y)\}$$

Sigmoid polynomial Higher Order Neural Network (SPHONN) model is that to use a combination of sigmoid, linear, power and multiplication neurons for simulation the data as shown in Box 1.

Table 1. Canadian Dollar / US Dollar Exchange Rate. CAD$1.00 = UDS$0.9309 on November 3rd, 2009; USA Federal Reserve Bank Data January 6th, 2011.

USA Federal Reserve Bank Data				HONN Output				HONN Error Percentage			
Date	Rate and De- sired Output	Input 1 (2 month ago)	Input 2 (1 month ago)	PHONN	THONN	SPHONN	MPHONN	PHONN	THONN	SPHONN	MPHONN
11/2/2009	0.9309										
12/1/2009	0.9588										
1/4/2010	0.9637	0.9309	0.9588	0.9617	0.9243	0.9436	0.9336	0.2075	4.0884	2.0857	3.1234
2/1/2010	0.9389	0.9588	0.9637	0.9346	0.9456	0.9613	0.9524	0.4580	0.7136	2.3858	1.4379
3/1/2010	0.9596	0.9637	0.9389	0.9427	0.9216	0.9472	0.9397	1.7612	3.9600	1.2922	2.0738
4/1/2010	0.9928	0.9389	0.9596	0.9145	0.9337	0.9214	0.9812	7.8868	5.9529	7.1918	1.1684
5/3/2010	0.9869	0.9596	0.9928	0.9949	0.9196	0.9491	0.9631	0.8106	6.8193	3.8302	2.4116
6/1/2010	0.9546	0.9928	0.9869	0.9292	0.9708	0.9732	0.9673	2.6608	1.6970	1.9485	1.3304
7/1/2010	0.9414	0.9869	0.9546	0.9773	0.9069	0.9196	0.9172	3.8135	3.6648	2.3157	2.5706
8/2/2010	0.9778	0.9546	0.9414	0.9494	0.9476	0.9644	0.9585	2.9045	3.0886	1.3704	1.9738
9/1/2010	0.9527	0.9414	0.9778	0.9716	0.9882	0.9223	0.9286	1.9838	3.7263	3.1909	2.5297
10/1/2010	0.9790	0.9778	0.9527	0.9548	0.9644	0.9824	0.9548	2.4719	1.4913	0.3473	2.4719
11/1/2010	0.9869	0.9527	0.9790	0.9284	0.9192	0.9005	0.9349	5.9277	6.8599	8.7547	5.2690
12/1/2010	0.9843	0.9790	0.9869	0.9493	0.9212	0.9028	0.9344	3.5558	6.4106	8.2800	5.0696
Average Error (% Percentage)								2.8078	3.8238	3.1557	2.3964
Average Error pf PHONN, THONN, and SPHONN (% Percentage)								3.2625	MPHONN Better		0.8661

Box 1.

$$Z_r = \sum_{k,j=0}^{n} (r_{kj}{}^o)\{r_{kj}{}^{hx}[1 / (1 + \exp(-r_k{}^x x))]^k\}\{r_{kj}{}^{hy}[1 / (1 + \exp(-r_j{}^y y))]^j\}$$

MULTI-POLYNOMIAL HIGHER ORDER NEURAL NETWORK MODEL (MPHONN)

MPHONN is a multi-layer higher order neural network that consists of an input layer with input-units, and output layer with output-units, and two hidden layers consisting of intermediate processing units. Based on derivatives of MPONNG Model, a Back Propagation leaning algorithm has been developed. It is combined the characteristics of PHONN, THONN, and SPHONN (Box 2).

The derivatives of MPHONN model for polynomial, trigonometric polynomial neuron and sigmoid polynomial are:

Polynomial function:

$$\sum_{k,j=0}^{n} (a_{kj}{}^o)\{a_{kj}{}^{hx}(a_k{}^x x)^k\}\{a_{kj}{}^{hy}(a_j{}^y y)^j\}$$

Table 2. Canadian Dollar / US Dollar Exchange Rate. CAD$1.00 = UDS$0.9461 on November 30th, 2009; USA Federal Reserve Bank Data January 6th, 2011.

USA Federal Reserve Bank Data				HONN Output				HONN Error Percentage			
Date	Rate and Desired Output	Input 1 (2 month ago)	Input 2 (1 month ago)	PHONN	THONN	SPHONN	MPHONN	PHONN	THONN	SPHONN	MPHONN
11/30/2009	0.9461										
12/31/2009	0.9559										
1/29/2010	0.9388	0.8091	0.8170	0.9609	0.9366	0.9432	0.9446	2.3541	0.2343	0.4687	0.6178
2/26/2010	0.9506	0.8170	0.8087	0.9608	0.9257	0.9474	0.9055	1.0730	2.6194	0.3366	4.7444
3/31/2010	0.9846	0.8087	0.7868	0.9414	0.9129	0.9365	0.9503	4.3876	7.2821	4.8852	3.4836
4/30/2010	0.9889	0.7868	0.7933	0.9575	0.9484	0.9651	0.9672	3.1752	4.0955	2.4067	2.1944
5/28/2010	0.9527	0.7933	0.8376	0.9785	0.9723	0.9465	0.9544	2.7081	2.0573	0.6508	0.1784
6/30/2010	0.9429	0.8376	0.9127	0.9918	0.9712	0.9833	0.9095	5.1861	3.0014	4.2847	3.5423
7/30/2010	0.9715	0.9127	0.8601	0.9241	0.9782	0.9168	0.9421	4.8791	0.6897	5.6305	3.0262
8/31/2010	0.9398	0.8601	0.9267	0.9036	0.9715	0.9096	0.9275	3.8519	3.3731	3.2134	1.3088
9/30/2010	0.9715	0.9267	0.9118	0.9532	0.9381	0.9301	0.9683	1.8837	3.4380	4.2615	0.3294
10/30/2010	0.9816	0.9118	0.9329	0.9372	0.9279	0.9562	0.9356	4.5232	5.4707	2.5876	4.6862
11/30/2010	0.9741	0.9329	0.9288	0.9642	0.9604	0.9308	0.9598	1.0163	1.4064	4.4451	1.4680
12/30/2010	0.9991	0.9288	0.9461	0.9602	0.9567	0.9747	0.9407	3.8935	4.2438	2.4422	5.8453
Average Error (% Percentage)								3.2443	3.1593	2.9678	2.6187
Average Error of PHONN, THONN, and SPHONN (% Percentage)								3.1238	MPHONN Better		0.5051

Box 2.

$$Z = \sum_{k,j=0}^{n} (a_{kj}{}^{o})\{a_{kj}{}^{hx}(a_{k}{}^{x}x)^{k}\}\{a_{kj}{}^{hy}(a_{j}{}^{y}y)^{j}\}$$

$$+ \sum_{k,j=0}^{n} (c_{kj}{}^{o})\{c_{kj}{}^{hx}\cos^{k}(c_{k}{}^{x}x)\}\{c_{kj}{}^{hy}\sin^{j}(c_{j}{}^{y}y)\}$$

$$+ \sum_{k,j=0}^{n} (r_{kj}{}^{o})\{r_{kj}{}^{hx}[1/(1+\exp(-r_{k}{}^{x}x))]^{k}\}\{r_{kj}{}^{hy}[1/(1+\exp(-r_{j}{}^{y}y))]^{j}\}$$

Box 3.

$$\sum_{k,j=0}^{n} (r_{kj}{}^{o})\{r_{kj}{}^{hx}[1/(1+\exp(-r_{k}{}^{x}x))]^{k}\}\{r_{kj}{}^{hy}[1/(1+\exp(-r_{j}{}^{y}y))]^{j}\}$$

Box 4.

$$Z = a_{00}{}^0 + a_{01}{}^0 y + a_{02}{}^0 y^2 + a_{10}{}^0 x + a_{11}{}^0 xy + a_{12}{}^0 xy^2 + a_{20}{}^0 x^2 + a_{21}{}^0 x^2 y + a_{22}{}^0 x^2 y^2$$
$$+ c_{00}{}^0 + c_{01}{}^0 \cos(y) + c_{02}{}^0 \cos^2(y) + c_{10}{}^0 \sin(x) + c_{11}{}^0 \sin(x)\cos(y) + c_{12}{}^0 \sin(x)\cos^2(y)$$
$$+ b_{20}{}^0 \sin^2(x) + b_{21}{}^0 \sin^2(x)\cos(y) + b_{22}{}^0 \sin^2(x)\cos^2(y)$$
$$+ r_{00}{}^0 + \frac{r_{01}{}^0}{1+e^{-y}} + \frac{r_{02}{}^0}{(1+e^{-y})^2} + \frac{r_{10}{}^0}{1+e^{-x}} + \frac{r_{11}{}^0}{(1+e^{-x})(1+e^{-y})} + \frac{r_{12}{}^0}{(1+e^{-x})(1+e^{-y})^2}$$
$$+ \frac{r_{20}{}^0}{(1+e^{-x})^2} + \frac{r_{21}{}^0}{(1+e^{-x})^2(1+e^{-y})} + \frac{r_{22}{}^0}{(1+e^{-x})^2(1+e^{-y})^2}$$

Trigonometric polynomial function:

$$\sum_{k,j=0}^{n} (c_{kj}{}^o)\{c_{kj}{}^{hx} \cos^k (c_k{}^x x)\}\{c_{kj}{}^{hy} \sin^j (c_j{}^y y)\}$$

Sigmoid polynomial function (shown in Box 3).

Let $n = 2$,

$$a_{kj}{}^{hx} = a_k{}^x = a_{kj}{}^{hy} = a_j{}^y = 1$$
$$c_{kj}{}^{hx} = c_k{}^x = c_{kj}{}^{hy} = c_j{}^y = 1$$
$$r_{kj}{}^{hx} = r_k{}^x = r_{kj}{}^{hy} = r_j{}^y = 1$$

$$Z = \sum_{k,j=0}^{2} (a_{kj}{}^o)\{(x)^k\}\{(y)^j\}$$
$$+ \sum_{k,j=0}^{2} (c_{kj}{}^o)\{\cos^k (x)\}\{\sin^j (y)\}$$
$$+ \sum_{k,j=0}^{2} (r_{kj}{}^o)\{[1/(1+\exp(-x))]^k\}\{[1/(1+\exp(-y))]^j\}$$

The MPHONN Model can be described as shown in Box 4.

All the weights on the layer can be derived directly from the coefficients of the discrete analog form of the Polynomial, Trigonometric polynomial and sigmoid polynomial.

The structure of MPHONN and Learning algorithm are shown in the follows.

Output Neurons in HONN Model

MPHONN Structure is shown in Figure 1. Details of PHONN, THONN, and SPHONN structures are shown in Figure 2, Figure 3, and Figure 4.

The output layer weights are updated according to:

$$a_{kj}{}^o (t+1) = a_{kj}{}^o (t) - \eta(\partial E / \partial a_{kj}{}^o) \qquad \text{(A 1)}$$

where: η = learning rate (positive and usually < 1)

• *akj* = weight; index k an j = input index

(k, j=0, 1, 2,…,n means one of n*n input neurons from the second hidden layer)

• E = error
• t = training time
• = output layer

The output node equations are:

$$net^o = \sum_{k,j=1}^{n} a_{kj}{}^o i_{kj}{}^a + \sum_{k,j=1}^{n} c_{kj}{}^o i_{kj}{}^c + \sum_{k,j=1}^{n} r_{kj}{}^o i_{kj}{}^r$$
$$z = f^o(net^o) = \sum_{k,j=1}^{n} a_{kj}{}^o i_{kj}{}^a + \sum_{k,j=1}^{n} c_{kj}{}^o i_{kj}{}^c + \sum_{k,j=1}^{n} r_{kj}{}^o i_{kj}{}^r$$
$$\text{(A 2)}$$

Figure 1. MPHONN architecture

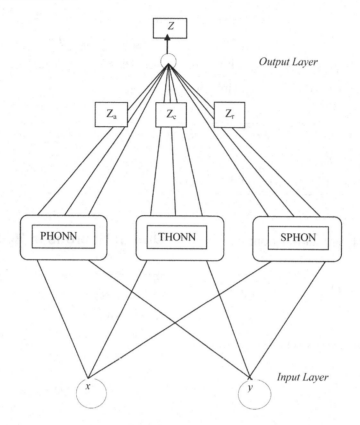

Here: $i_{kj}a$, $i_{kj}c$, $i_{kj}r$ input to the output neuron (= output from 2nd hidden layer)

- z = actual output from the output neuron
- f^o = output neuron activity function

The error at a particular output unit (neuron) will be:

$$\delta = (d - z) \qquad (A\,3)$$

where d = desired output value

The total error is the error of output unit, namely:

$$E = 0.5 * \delta^2 = 0.5 * (d - z)^2 \qquad (A\,4)$$

The derivatives $f^{o\prime}(net^o)$ are calculated as follows:

The output neuron function is linear function ($f^o(net^o) = net^o$):

$$f^{o\,\prime}(net^o)$$
$$= \partial f^o / \partial(net^o) = \partial(net^o) / \partial(net^o) = 1 \qquad (A\,5)$$

Gradients are calculated as follows:

$$\partial E / \partial a_{kj}^o$$
$$= (\partial E / \partial z)(\partial z / \partial(net^o))(\partial(net^o) / \partial a_{kj}^o) \qquad (A\,6)$$

$$\partial E / \partial z = \partial(0.5 * (d - z)^2) / \partial z$$
$$= 0.5 * (-2(d - z)) = -(d - z) \qquad (A\,7)$$

$$\partial z / \partial(net^o) = \partial f^o / \partial(net^o) = f^{o\,\prime}(net^o) \qquad (A\,8)$$

Figure 2. PHONN architecture

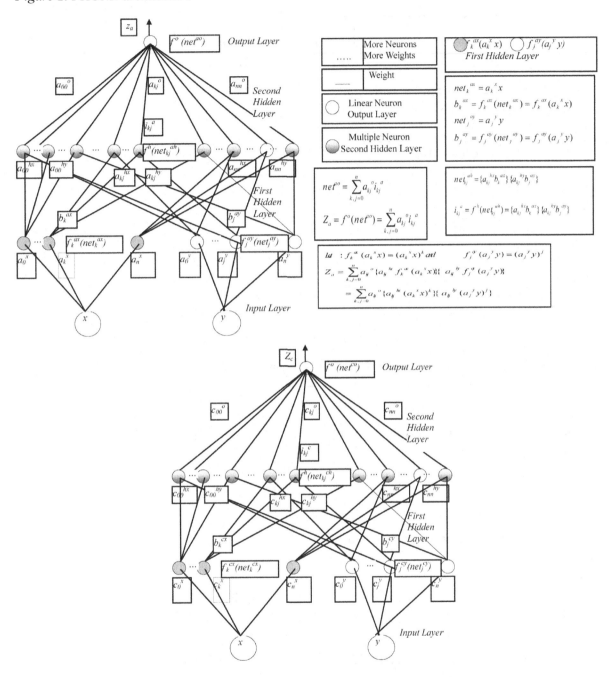

$$\partial(net^o)/\partial a_{kj}^{\;o}$$

$$= \partial(\sum_{k,j=0}^{n} a_{kj}^{\;o} i_{kj}^{\;a} + \sum_{k,j=0}^{n} c_{kj}^{\;o} i_{kj}^{\;c} + \sum_{k,j=0}^{n} r_{kj}^{\;o} i_{kj}^{\;r})/\partial a_{kj}^{\;o} = i_{kj}^{\;a}$$

$$(A 9)$$

Combining Equations A 6 through A 9, the negative gradient is:

$$-\partial E \;/\;\partial a_{kj}^{\;o} = (d - z)f^{o\;'}(net^o)i_{kj}^{\;a} \quad (A 10)$$

Figure 3. THONN architecture

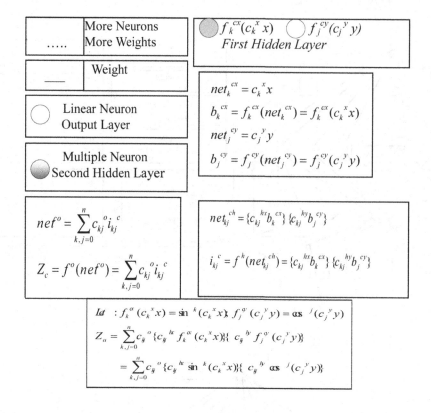

For a linear output neuron, this becomes, by combining Equations A 10 and A 5:

$$-\partial E \ / \ \partial a_{kj}^{\ o} = (d \ - z \ )f^{o\ '}(net^{\ o})i_{kj}^{\ a}$$
$$= (d \ - z \ )(1)i_{kj} = (d \ - z)i_{kj}^{\ a} \qquad (A\ 11)$$

The weight update equations are formulated as follows:

For linear output neurons, let:

$$\delta^{ol} = (d \ - z \ ) \qquad\qquad (A\ 12)$$

Combining Formulae A 1, A 11, and A 12:

$$a_{kj}^{\ o}(t+1) = a_{kj}^{\ o}(t) - \eta(\partial E \ / \ \partial a_{kj}^{\ o})$$
$$= a_{kj}^{\ o}(t) + \eta(d \ - z \ )f^{o\ '}(net^{\ o})i_{kj}^{\ a}$$
$$= a_{kj}^{\ o}(t) + \eta\delta^{\ ol}i_{kj}^{\ a}$$
$$where:$$
$$\delta^{ol} = (d - z)$$
$$f^{o'}(net^{\ o}) = 1 \qquad (linear \qquad neuron \qquad)$$
$$(A\ 13)$$

Based on Formulae A 13, we have:

$$c_{kj}^{\ o}(t+1) = c_{kj}^{\ o}(t) - \eta(\partial E \ / \ \partial c_{kj}^{\ o})$$
$$= c_{kj}^{\ o}(t) + \eta(d \ - z \ )f^{o\ '}(net^{\ o})i_{kj}^{\ c}$$
$$= c_{kj}^{\ o}(t) + \eta\delta^{\ ol}i_{kj}^{\ c}$$
$$where:$$
$$\delta^{ol} = (d - z)$$
$$f^{o'}(net^{\ o}) = 1 \qquad (linear \qquad neuron \qquad)$$
$$(A\ 14)$$

Figure 4. SPHONN architecture

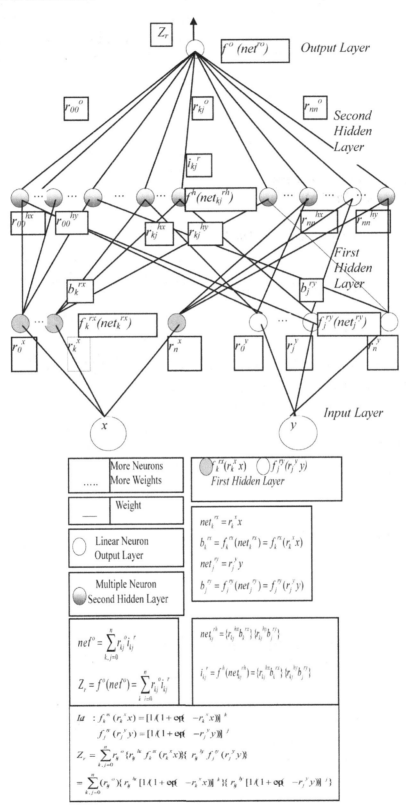

$$r_{kj}^{o}(t+1) = r_{kj}^{o}(t) - \eta(\partial E \,/\, \partial r_{kj}^{o})$$
$$= r_{kj}^{o}(t) + \eta(d - z)f^{o'}(net^{o})i_{kj}^{r}$$
$$= r_{kj}^{o}(t) + \eta\delta^{ol}i_{kj}^{r}$$
$$where :$$
$$\delta^{ol} = (d - z)$$
$$f^{o'}(net^{o}) = 1 \qquad (linear \qquad neuron \qquad)$$

$$(A\,15)$$

Second-Hidden Layer Neurons in HONN Model (Model 1b)

The second hidden layer weights are updated according to:

$$a_{kj}^{hx}(t+1) = a_{kj}^{hx}(t) - \eta(\partial E \,/\, \partial a_{kj}^{hx}) \qquad (B\,1)$$

where η = learning rate (positive & usually < 1)

* k,j = input index
* (k, j=0, 1, 2, …,n means one of 2*n*n input combinations from the first hidden layer)
* E = error
* t = training time
* hx = hidden layer, related to x input
* akj hx = hidden layer weight related to x input

The equations for the 2nd hidden layer node are:

$$net_{kj}^{h} = \{a_{kj}^{hx}b_{k}^{x}\}\{a_{kj}^{hy}b_{j}^{y}\}$$
$$i_{kj}^{a} = f^{h}(net_{kj}^{h}) \qquad\qquad (B\,2)$$

* where $i_{kj}a$ = output from 2nd hidden layer (= input to the output neuron)
* $_{bkx\ and\ by}y$ = input to 2nd hidden layer neuron
* (= output from the 1st hidden layer neuron)
* f^{h}= hidden neuron activation function
* hy = hidden layer, related to y input
* $akj\ hy$ = hidden layer weight related to y input

We call the neurons at the second layer are multiple neurons. Their activity function is linear and their inputs are the multiplication of two outputs of the first layer neuron output time their weights.

The error of a single output unit will be:

$$\delta = (d - z) \qquad\qquad (B\,3)$$

where d = desired output value of output layer neuron

* z = actual output value of output layer neuron

The total error is the sum of the squared errors across all output units, namely:

$$E_{p} = 0.5 * \delta^{2} = 0.5 * (d - z)^{2}$$
$$= 0.5 * (d - f^{o}(net^{o}))^{2}$$
$$= 0.5 * (d - f^{o}(\sum_{k,j=1}^{n} a_{kj}^{o}i_{kj}^{a} + \sum_{k,j=1}^{n} c_{kj}^{o}i_{kj}^{c} + \sum_{k,j=1}^{n} r_{kj}^{o}i_{kj}^{r}))^{2}$$

$$(B\,4)$$

The derivatives $f^{h'}(net^{h}_{kj})$ are calculated as follows, for a linear function of second layer neurons:

$$i_{kj}^{a} = f^{h}(net_{kj}^{h}) = net_{kj}^{h}$$
$$f^{h'}(net_{kj}^{h}) = 1 \qquad\qquad (B\,5)$$

The gradient (∂E/∂akjhx) is given by:

$$\partial E \,/\, \partial a_{kj}^{hx} = \partial(0.5 * (d - z)^{2}) \,/\, \partial a_{kj}^{hx}$$
$$= (\partial(0.5 * (d - z)^{2}) \,/\, \partial z)(\partial z \,/\, \partial(net^{o}))$$
$$(\partial(net^{o}) \,/\, \partial i_{kj}^{a})(\partial i_{kj}^{a} \,/\, \partial(net_{kj}^{ah}))(\partial(net_{kj}^{ah}) \,/\, \partial a_{kj}^{hx})$$

$$(B\,6)$$

$$\partial(0.5 * (d - z)^{2}) \,/\, \partial z = -(d - z) \qquad (B\,7)$$

$$\partial z \,/\, \partial(net^{o}) = (\partial f^{o} \,/\, \partial(net^{o}) = f_{k}^{o'}(net^{o})$$

$$(B\,8)$$

$$\partial(net^o) / \partial i_{kj}{}^a$$

$$= \partial(\sum_{k,j=0}^{n} a_{kj}{}^o i_{kj}{}^a + \sum_{k,j=0}^{n} c_{kj}{}^o i_{kj}{}^c + \sum_{k,j=0}^{n} r_{kj}{}^o i_{kj}{}^r) / \partial i_{kj}{}^a = a_{kj}{}^o$$

$$(B\ 9)$$

$$\partial i_{kj} / \partial(net_{kj}{}^{ah})$$

$$= \partial(f^h(net_{kj}{}^{ah})) / \partial(net_{kj}{}^{ah}) = f^h{}'(net_{kj}{}^{ah})$$

$$(B\ 10)$$

$$\partial(net_{kj}{}^{ah}) / \partial a_{kj}{}^{hx} = \partial(\{a_k{}^{hx}b_k{}^x\}\{a_{kj}{}^{hy}b_j{}^y\}) / \partial a_{kj}{}^{hx}$$

$$= b_k{}^{ax}a_{kj}{}^{hy}b_j{}^{ay} = \delta_{kj}{}^{hx}b_k{}^{ax}$$

$$where: \delta_{kj}{}^{hx} = a_{kj}{}^{hy}b_j{}^{ay}$$

$$(B\ 11)$$

Combining Equations B 6 through B 11, the negative gradient is:

$$-\partial E / \partial a_{kj}{}^{hx}$$

$$= (d-z)f^o{}'(net^o)a_{kj}{}^o f^h{}'(net_{kj}{}^{ah})\delta^{hx}b_k{}^{ax}$$

$$(B\ 12)$$

The weight update equations are formulated as follows:

let output neuron is a linear neuron:

$$\delta^{ol} = (d - z)f^o{}'_k(net^o) = (d - z) \qquad (B\ 13)$$

and also let the second layer neurons are linear neurons. Combining Formulae B 1, B 5, B 12, and B 13:

$$a_{kj}{}^{hx}(t+1) = a_{kj}{}^{hx}(t) - \eta(\partial E / \partial a_{kj}{}^{hx})$$

$$= a_{kj}{}^{hx}(t)$$

$$+\eta((d-z)f^o{}'(net^o)a_{kj}{}^o f^h{}'(net_{kj}{}^{ah})a_{kj}{}^{hy}b_j{}^{ay}b_k{}^{ax})$$

$$= a_{kj}{}^{hx}(t) + \eta(\delta^{ol}a_{kj}{}^o \delta_{kj}{}^{ahx}b_k{}^{ax})$$

$$where: \delta^{ol} = (d - z)$$

$$\delta_{kj}{}^{ahx} = a_{kj}{}^{hy}b_j{}^{ay}$$

$$f^o{}'(net^o) = 1(linear\ neuron)$$

$$f^h{}'(net_{kj}{}^{hx}) = 1(linear\ neuron)$$

$$(B\ 14)$$

Use the same rules, the weight update question for y input neurons is:

$$a_{kj}{}^{hy}(t+1) = a_{kj}{}^{hy}(t) - \eta(\partial E / \partial a_{kj}{}^{hy})$$

$$= a_{kj}{}^{hy}(t)$$

$$+\eta((d-z)f^o{}'(net^o)a_{kj}{}^o f^h{}'(net_{kj}{}^{ah})a_{kj}{}^{hx}b_k{}^{ax}b_j{}^{ay})$$

$$= a_{kj}{}^{hy}(t) + \eta(\delta^{ol}a_{kj}{}^o \delta_{kj}{}^{ahy}b_j{}^{ay})$$

$$where: \delta^{ol} = (d - z)$$

$$\delta_{kj}{}^{ahy} = a_{kj}{}^{hx}b_k{}^{ax}$$

$$f^o{}'(net^o) = 1\ (linear\ neuron)$$

$$f^h{}'(net_{kj}{}^{hy}) = 1\ (linear\ neuron)$$

$$(B\ 15)$$

Based on the Formulae (B 14) and (B 15) we have:

$$c_{kj}{}^{hx}(t+1) = c_{kj}{}^{hx}(t) - \eta(\partial E / \partial c_{kj}{}^{hx})$$

$$= c_{kj}{}^{hx}(t)$$

$$+\eta((d-z)f^o{}'(net^o)c_{kj}{}^o f^h{}'(net_{kj}{}^{ch})c_{kj}{}^{hy}b_j{}^{cy}b_k{}^{cx})$$

$$= c_{kj}{}^{hx}(t) + \eta(\delta^{ol}c_{kj}{}^o \delta_{kj}{}^{chx}b_k{}^{cx})$$

$$where: \delta^{ol} = (d - z)$$

$$\delta_{kj}{}^{chx} = c_{kj}{}^{hy}b_j{}^{cy}$$

$$f^o{}'(net^o) = 1\ (linear\ neuron)$$

$$f^h{}'(net_{kj}{}^{hx}) = 1\ (linear\ neuron)$$

$$(B\ 16)$$

$$c_{kj}{}^{hy}(t+1) = c_{kj}{}^{hy}(t) - \eta(\partial E / \partial c_{kj}{}^{hy})$$

$$= c_{kj}{}^{hy}(t)$$

$$+\eta((d-z)f^o{}'(net^o)c_{kj}{}^o f^h{}'(net_{kj}{}^{ch})c_{kj}{}^{hx}b_k{}^{cx}b_j{}^{cy})$$

$$= c_{kj}{}^{hy}(t) + \eta(\delta^{ol}a_{kj}{}^o \delta_{kj}{}^{chy}b_j{}^{cy})$$

$$where: \delta^{ol} = (d - z)$$

$$\delta_{kj}{}^{chy} = c_{kj}{}^{hx}b_k{}^{cx}$$

$$f^o{}'(net^o) = 1\ (linear\ neuron)$$

$$f^h{}'(net_{kj}{}^{hy}) = 1\ (linear\ neuron)$$

$$(B\ 17)$$

$$r_{kj}^{hx}(t+1) = r_{kj}^{hx}(t) - \eta(\partial E / \partial r_{kj}^{hx})$$
$$= r_{kj}^{hx}(t)$$
$$+\eta((d-z)f^{o}{}'(net^{o})r_{kj}^{o}f^{h}{}'(net_{kj}^{rh})r_{kj}^{hy}b_{j}^{ry}b_{k}^{rx})$$
$$= r_{kj}^{hx}(t) + \eta(\delta^{ol}r_{kj}^{o}\delta_{kj}^{rhx}b_{k}^{rx})$$

$$where: \delta^{ol} = (d-z)$$
$$\delta_{kj}^{rhx} = r_{kj}^{hy}b_{j}^{ry}$$
$$f^{o}{}'(net^{o}) = 1(linear\ neuron)$$
$$f^{h}{}'(net_{kj}^{hx}) = 1(linear\ neuron)$$

$$\text{(B 18)}$$

$$r_{kj}^{hy}(t+1) = r_{kj}^{hy}(t) - \eta(\partial E / \partial r_{kj}^{hy})$$
$$= r_{kj}^{hy}(t) + \eta((d-z)f^{o}{}'(net^{o})r_{kj}^{o}f^{h}{}'(net_{kj}^{rh})r_{kj}^{hx}b_{k}^{rx}b_{j}^{ry})$$
$$= r_{kj}^{hy}(t) + \eta(\delta^{ol}r_{kj}^{o}\delta_{kj}^{rhy}b_{j}^{ry})$$

$$where: \delta^{ol} = (d-z)$$
$$\delta_{kj}^{rhy} - r_{kj}^{hx}b_{k}^{rx}$$
$$f^{o}{}'(net^{o}) = 1\ (linear\ neuron)$$
$$f^{h}{}'(net_{kj}^{hy}) = 1\ (linear\ neuron)$$

$$\text{(B 19)}$$

First Hidden Layer Neurons in HONN

The 1st hidden layer weights are updated according to:

$$a_{k}^{x}(t+1) = a_{k}^{x}(t) - \eta(\partial E / \partial a_{k}^{x}) \qquad \text{(C 1)}$$

where η = learning rate (positive and usually < 1)

- k = kth neuron of first hidden layer
- E = error
- t = training time
- akx = 1st hidden layer weight for input x

The equations for the *k*th and *j*th node in the first hidden layer are:

$$net_{k}^{ax} = a_{k}^{x}x$$
$$b_{k}^{ax} = f_{k}^{ax}(net_{k}^{ax})$$
$$or \qquad \text{(C 2)}$$
$$net_{j}^{ay} = a_{j}^{y}y$$
$$b_{j}^{ay} = f_{j}^{ay}(net_{j}^{ay})$$

where $i_{kj}a$ = output from 2nd hidden layer (= input to the output neuron)

- $b_{k}ax$ and $bjay$ = output from the 1st hidden layer neuron (= input to 2nd hidden layer neuron)
- $fkax$ and $fjay$ are 1st hidden layer neuron activation functions.
- x and y = input to 1st hidden layer

The total error is the sum of the squared errors across all hidden units, namely:

$$E = 0.5 * \delta^{2} = 0.5 * (d-z)^{2}$$
$$= 0.5 * (d - f^{o}(net^{o}))^{2}$$
$$= 0.5 * (d - f^{o}(\sum_{k,j=1}^{n} a_{kj}^{o}i_{kj}^{a} + \sum_{k,j=1}^{n} c_{kj}^{o}i_{kj}^{c} + \sum_{k,j=1}^{n} r_{kj}^{o}i_{kj}^{r}))^{2}$$
$$\text{(C 3)}$$

The gradient ($\partial E / \partial a_{k}^{x}$) is given by:

$$\partial E / \partial a_{k}^{x} = \partial(0.5 * (d-z)^{2}) / \partial a_{k}^{x}$$
$$= (\partial(0.5 * (d-z)^{2}) / \partial z)(\partial z / \partial(net^{o}))$$
$$(\partial(net^{o}) / \partial i_{kj}^{a})(\partial i_{kj}^{a} / \partial(net_{kj}^{ah}))(\partial(net_{kj}^{ah}) / \partial b_{k}^{ax})$$
$$(\partial b_{k}^{ax} / \partial(net_{k}^{ax}))(\partial(net_{k}^{ax}) / \partial a_{k}^{x})$$
$$\text{(C 4)}$$

$$\partial(0.5 * (d-z)^{2} / \partial z = -(d-z) \qquad \text{(C 6)}$$

$$\partial z / \partial(net^{o}) = \partial f^{o} / \partial(net^{o}) = f^{o}{}'(net^{o})$$
$$\text{(C 7)}$$

$$\partial(net^{o}) / \partial i_{kj}^{a} = \partial(\sum_{k,j=1}^{n} (a_{kj}^{o}i_{kj}^{a}) / \partial i_{kj}^{a} = a_{kj}^{o}$$
$$\text{(C 8)}$$

$$\partial i_{kj}^{\ a} / \partial(net_{kj}^{\ ah}) = \partial(f^h(net_{kj}^{\ ah}))\partial(net_{kj}^{\ ah}) = f^{h\ \prime}(net_{kj}^{\ ah})$$

(C 9)

$$\partial net_{kj}^{\ ah} / \partial b_k^{\ ax}$$
$$= \partial((a_{kj}^{\ hx} * b_k^{\ ax}) * (a_{kj}^{\ hy} * b_j^{\ ay})) / \partial b_k^{\ ax}$$
$$= a_{kj}^{\ hx} * a_{kj}^{\ hy} * b_j^{\ ay}$$
$$= \delta_{kj}^{\ ahx} a_{kj}^{\ hx}$$
$$where : \delta_{kj}^{\ ahx} = a_{kj}^{\ hy} * b_j^{\ ay}$$

(C 10)

$$\partial b_k^{\ ax} / \partial(net_k^{\ ax}) = f_k^{\ ax\ \prime}(net_k^{\ ax})$$

(C 11)

$$\partial(net_k^{\ ax}) / \partial a_k^{\ x} = \partial(a_k^{\ x} * x) / \partial a_k^{\ x} = x$$

(C 12)

Combining Formulae C 5 through C 12, the negative gradient is:

$$-\partial E_p / \partial a_k^{\ x}$$
$$= (d - z)f^{o\ \prime}(net^{\ o})a_{kj}^{\ o} * f^{h\ \prime}(net_{kj}^{\ ah})\delta_{kj}^{\ ahx} a_{kj}^{\ hx} f_k^{\ x\ \prime}(net_k^{\ x})x$$

(C 13)

The weight update equations are calculated as follows:

Whereas for linear output neurons, this becomes:

$$\delta^{ol} = (d-z)$$

(C 14)

Whereas for linear neurons of second hidden layer, this becomes:

$$f^{h\ \prime}(net_{kj}^{\ hx}) = 1$$

(C 15)

The negative gradient is:

$$-\partial E_p / \partial a_k^{\ x} = (d - z)f^{o\ \prime}(net^{\ o})a_{kj}^{\ o}$$
$$* f^{h\ \prime}(net_{kj}^{\ ah})\delta_{kj}^{\ ahx} a_{kj}^{\ hx} f_k^{\ ax\ \prime}(net_k^{\ ax})x$$
$$= \delta^{\ ol} * a_{kj}^{\ o} * \delta_{kj}^{\ hx} * a_{kj}^{\ hx} * f_k^{\ ax\prime}(net_k^{\ ax}) * x$$

(C 16)

We have, for a linear 1st hidden layer neuron, as shown in Box 5.

Using the above procedure (Box 6).

For PHONN part, we have as shown in Box 7 and Box 8.

Box 5.

$$a_k^{\ x}(t+1) = a_k^{\ x}(t) - \eta(\partial E_p / \partial a_k^{\ x})$$
$$= a_x^{\ x}(t) + \eta(d - z)f^{o\ \prime}(net^{\ o})a_{kj}^{\ o} * f^{h\ \prime}(net_{kj}^{\ ah})a_{kj}^{\ hy} b_j^{\ ay} a_{kj}^{\ hx} f_k^{\ x\ \prime}(net_k^{\ ax})x$$
$$= a_x^{\ x}(t) + \eta * \delta^{\ ol} * a_{kj}^{\ o} * \delta_{kj}^{\ hx} * a_{kj}^{\ hx} * f_k^{\ ax\ \prime}(net_k^{\ ax}) * x$$
$$= a_x^{\ x}(t) + \eta * \delta^{\ ol} * a_{kj}^{\ o} * \delta_{kj}^{\ ahx} * a_{kj}^{\ hx} * \delta_k^{\ ax} * x$$

$$where :$$
$$\quad \delta^{\ ol} = (d - z)$$
$$\quad f^{o\ \prime}(net^{\ o}) = 1 \quad (linear \quad neuron)$$
$$\quad \delta_{kj}^{\ ahx} = a_{kj}^{\ hy} b_j^{\ ay}$$
$$\quad f^{h\ \prime}(net_{kj}^{\ h}) = 1 \quad (linear \quad neuron)$$
$$\quad \delta_k^{\ ax} = f_k^{\ ax\ \prime}(net_k^{\ ax})$$

(C 17)

Box 6.

$$a_j^{\,y}(t+1) = a_j^{\,y}(t) - \eta(\partial E_p \,/\, \partial a_j^{\,y})$$
$$= a_j^{\,y}(t) + \eta(d-z)f^{o\,\prime}(net^{\,o})a_{kj}^{\,o} * f^{h\,\prime}(net_{kj}^{\,ah})a_{kj}^{\,hx}b_k^{\,ax}a_{kj}^{\,hy}f_j^{\,y\,\prime}(net_j^{\,ay})y$$
$$= a_j^{\,y}(t) + \eta * \delta^{\,ol} * a_{kj}^{\,o} * \delta_{kj}^{\,ahy} * a_{kj}^{\,hy} * f_j^{\,ay\,\prime}(net_j^{\,ay}) * y$$
$$= a_j^{\,y}(t) + \eta * \delta^{\,ol} * a_{kj}^{\,o} * \delta_{kj}^{\,ahy} * a_{kj}^{\,hy} * \delta_j^{\,ay} * y$$

where :

$$\delta^{\,ol} = (d-z)$$
$$f^{o\,\prime}(net^{\,o}) = 1 \qquad (linear \qquad neuron)$$
$$\delta_{kj}^{\,ahy} = a_{kj}^{\,hx}b_k^{\,ax}$$
$$f^{h\,\prime}(net_{kj}^{\,hy}) = 1 \qquad (linear \qquad neuron)$$
$$\delta_j^{\,ay} = f_j^{\,ay\,\prime}(net_j^{\,ay})$$

(C 18)

Box 7.

$$a_k^{\,x}(t+1) = a_k^{\,x}(t) - \eta(\partial E_p \,/\, \partial a_k^{\,x})$$
$$= a_k^{\,x}(t) + \eta(d-z)f^{o\,\prime}(net^{\,o})a_{kj}^{\,o} * f^{h\,\prime}(net_{kj}^{\,ah})a_{kj}^{\,hy}b_j^{\,ay}a_{kj}^{\,hx}f_k^{\,ax\,\prime}(net_k^{\,ax})x$$
$$= a_k^{\,x}(t) + \eta * \delta^{\,ol} * a_{kj}^{\,o} * \delta_{kj}^{\,ahx} * a_{kj}^{\,hx} * f_k^{\,ax\,\prime}(net_k^{\,ax}) * x$$
$$= a_k^{\,x}(t) + \eta * \delta^{\,ol} * a_{kj}^{\,o} * \delta_{kj}^{\,ahx} * a_{kj}^{\,hx} * \delta_k^{\,ax} * x$$
$$= a_k^{\,x}(t) + \eta * \delta^{\,ol} * a_{kj}^{\,o} * \delta_{kj}^{\,ahx} * a_{kj}^{\,hx} * k * (a_k^{\,x} * x)^{k-1} * x$$

where :

$$\delta^{\,ol} = (d-z)$$
$$f^{o\,\prime}(net^{\,o}) = 1 \qquad (linear \qquad neuron)$$
$$\delta_{kj}^{\,ahx} = a_{kj}^{\,hy}b_j^{\,ay}$$
$$f^{h\,\prime}(net_{kj}^{\,h}) = 1 \qquad (linear \qquad neuron)$$
$$\delta_k^{\,ax} = f_k^{\,ax\,\prime}(net_k^{\,ax}) = \partial(net_k^{\,ax})^k \,/\, \partial(net_k^{\,ax}) = k * (net_k^{\,ax})^{k-1} = k * (a_k^{\,x} * x)^{k-1}$$

(C 19)

For TPHONN part and with c to replace a, we have as shown in Box 9 and Box 10.

For SPHONN part with r to replace a, we have as shown in Box 11 and Box 12.

APPLICATIONS OF MPHONN

This chapter uses the monthly Canadian dollar and USA dollar exchange rate from November 2009 to December 2010 (See Table 1 and Table 2) as the

Box 8.

$$a_j^{\ y}(t+1) = a_j^{\ y}(t) - \eta(\partial E_p \ / \ \partial a_j^{\ y})$$

$$= a_j^{\ y}(t) + \eta(d-z)f^{o\ \prime}(net^{\ o})a_{kj}^{\ o} * f^{h\ \prime}(net_{kj}^{\ ah})a_{kj}^{\ hx}b_k^{\ ax}a_{kj}^{\ hy}f_j^{\ ay\ \prime}(net_j^{\ ay})y$$

$$= a_j^{\ y}(t) + \eta * \delta^{\ ol} * a_{kj}^{\ o} * \delta_{kj}^{\ ahy} * a_{kj}^{\ hy} * f_j^{\ ay\ \prime}(net_j^{\ ay}) * y$$

$$= a_j^{\ y}(t) + \eta * \delta^{\ ol} * a_{kj}^{\ o} * \delta_{kj}^{\ ahy} * a_{kj}^{\ hy} * \delta_j^{\ ay} * y$$

$$= a_j^{\ y}(t) + \eta * \delta^{\ ol} * a_{kj}^{\ o} * \delta_{kj}^{\ ahy} * a_{kj}^{\ hy} * j * (a_j^{\ y} * y)^{j-1} * y$$

where : $\qquad\qquad$ (C.20)

$\qquad \delta^{\ ol} = (d-z)$

$\qquad f^{o\ \prime}(net^{\ o}) = 1 \qquad (linear \qquad neuron)$

$\qquad \delta_{kj}^{\ ahy} = a_{kj}^{\ hx}b_k^{\ ax}$

$\qquad f^{h\ \prime}(net_{kj}^{\ hy}) = 1 \qquad (linear \qquad neuron)$

$\qquad \delta_j^{\ ay} = f_j^{\ ay\ \prime}(net_j^{\ ay}) = \partial(net_j^{\ ay})^j \ / \ \partial(net_j^{\ ay}) = j * (net_j^{\ ay})^{j-1} = j * (a_j^{\ y} * y)^{j-1}$

Box 9.

$$c_k^{\ x}(t+1) = c_k^{\ x}(t) - \eta(\partial E_p \ / \ \partial c_k^{\ x})$$

$$= c_k^{\ x}(t) + \eta(d-z)f^{o\ \prime}(net^{\ o})c_{kj}^{\ o} * f^{h\ \prime}(net_{kj}^{\ ch})c_{kj}^{\ hy}b_j^{\ cy}c_{kj}^{\ hx}f_k^{\ cx\ \prime}(net_k^{\ cx})x$$

$$= c_k^{\ x}(t) + \eta * \delta^{\ ol} * c_{kj}^{\ o} * \delta_{kj}^{\ chx} * c_{kj}^{\ hx} * f_k^{\ cx\ \prime}(net_k^{\ cx}) * x$$

$$= c_k^{\ x}(t) + \eta * \delta^{\ ol} * c_{kj}^{\ o} * \delta_{kj}^{\ chx} * c_{kj}^{\ hx} * \delta_k^{\ cx} * x$$

$$= c_k^{\ x}(t) + \eta * \delta^{\ ol} * c_{kj}^{\ o} * \delta_{kj}^{\ chx} * c_{kj}^{\ hx} * k * (\sin^{k-1}(a_k^{\ x} * x)) * \cos(a_k^{\ x} * x) * x$$

where : $\qquad\qquad$ (C 21)

$\qquad \delta^{\ ol} = (d-z)$

$\qquad f^{o\ \prime}(net^{\ o}) = 1 \qquad (linear \qquad neuron)$

$\qquad \delta_{kj}^{\ chx} = c_{kj}^{\ hy}b_j^{\ cy}$

$\qquad f^{h\ \prime}(net_{kj}^{\ h}) = 1 \qquad (linear \qquad neuron)$

$\qquad \delta_k^{\ cx} = f_k^{\ cx\ \prime}(net_k^{\ cx}) = \partial(\sin^k(net_k^{\ cx})) \ / \ \partial(net_k^{\ cx})$

$\qquad = k * (\sin^{k-1}(net_k^{\ cx})) * \cos(net_k^{\ cx}) = k * (\sin^{k-1}(a_k^{\ x} * x)) * \cos(a_k^{\ x} * x)$

Box 10.

$$c_j^{\,y}(t+1) = c_j^{\,y}(t) - \eta(\partial E_p \,/\, \partial c_j^{\,y})$$

$$= c_j^{\,y}(t) + \eta(d-z)f^{o\,}{}'(net^{\,o})c_{kj}^{\,o} * f^{h\,}{}'(net_{kj}^{\,ch})c_{kj}^{\,hx}b_k^{\,cx}c_{kj}^{\,hy}f_j^{\,cy}{}'(net_j^{\,cy})y$$

$$= c_j^{\,y}(t) + \eta * \delta^{\,ol} * c_{kj}^{\,o} * \delta_{kj}^{\,chy} * c_{kj}^{\,hy} * f_j^{\,cy}{}'(net_j^{\,cy}) * y$$

$$= c_j^{\,y}(t) + \eta * \delta^{\,ol} * c_{kj}^{\,o} * \delta_{kj}^{\,chy} * c_{kj}^{\,hy} * \delta_j^{\,cy} * y$$

$$= c_j^{\,y}(t) + \eta * \delta^{\,ol} * c_{kj}^{\,o} * \delta_{kj}^{\,chy} * a_{kj}^{\,hy} * j * (a_j^{\,y} * y)^{j-1} * y$$

where : (C 22)

$$\delta^{\,ol} = (d-z)$$

$$f^{o\,}{}'(net^{\,o}) = 1 \qquad (linear \qquad neuron)$$

$$\delta_{kj}^{\,chy} = c_{kj}^{\,hx}b_k^{\,cx}$$

$$f^{h\,}{}'(net_{kj}^{\,hy}) = 1 \qquad (linear \qquad neuron)$$

$$\delta_j^{\,cy} = f_j^{\,cy}{}'(net_j^{\,cy}) = \partial(\cos^j(net_j^{\,cy})) \,/\, \partial(net_j^{\,cy})$$

$$= j * (\cos^{j-1}(net_j^{\,cy}))(-\sin(net_j^{\,cy})) = -j * (\cos^{j-1}(c_j^{\,y} * y)) * (\sin(c_j^{\,y} * y))$$

Box 11.

$$r_k^{\,x}(t+1) = r_k^{\,x}(t) - \eta(\partial E_p \,/\, \partial r_k^{\,x})$$

$$= r_k^{\,x}(t) + \eta(d-z)f^{o\,}{}'(net^{\,o})r_{kj}^{\,o} * f^{h\,}{}'(net_{kj}^{\,rh})r_{kj}^{\,hy}b_j^{\,ry}r_{kj}^{\,hx}f_k^{\,rx}{}'(net_k^{\,rx})x$$

$$= r_k^{\,x}(t) + \eta * \delta^{\,ol} * r_{kj}^{\,o} * \delta_{kj}^{\,rhx} * r_{kj}^{\,hx} * f_k^{\,rx}{}'(net_k^{\,rx}) * x$$

$$= r_k^{\,x}(t) + \eta * \delta^{\,ol} * r_{kj}^{\,o} * \delta_{kj}^{\,rhx} * r_{kj}^{\,hx} * \delta_k^{\,rx} * x$$

$$= r_k^{\,x}(t) + \eta * \delta^{\,ol} * r_{kj}^{\,o} * \delta_{kj}^{\,rhx} * r_{kj}^{\,hx} * k * [1\,/\,(1+\exp(-r_k^{\,x}x))]^{k-1} * (1+\exp(-r_k^{\,x}x))^{-2} * \exp(-r_k^{\,x} * x) * x$$

where :

$$\delta^{\,ol} = (d-z)$$

$$f^{o\,}{}'(net^{\,o}) = 1 \qquad (linear \qquad neuron)$$

$$\delta_{kj}^{\,rhx} = r_{kj}^{\,hy}b_j^{\,ry}$$

$$f^{h\,}{}'(net_{kj}^{\,h}) = 1 \qquad (linear \qquad neuron)$$

$$\delta_k^{\,rx} = f_k^{\,rx}{}'(net_k^{\,rx}) = \partial[1\,/\,(1+\exp(-net_k^{\,rx}))]^k \,/\, \partial(net_k^{\,rx})$$

$$= \partial[1\,/\,(1+\exp(-r_k^{\,x}x))]^k \,/\, \partial(r_k^{\,x}x)$$

$$= k * [1\,/\,(1+\exp(-r_k^{\,x}x))]^{k-1} * (1+\exp(-r_k^{\,x}x))^{-2} * \exp(-r_k^{\,x} * x)$$

(C 23)

Box 12.

$$r_j^{y}(t+1) = r_j^{y}(t) - \eta(\partial E_p / \partial r_j^{y})$$
$$= r_j^{y}(t) + \eta(d-z)f^{o}{}'(net^{o})r_{kj}^{o} * f^{h}{}'(net_{kj}^{rh})r_{kj}^{hx}b_k^{rx}r_{kj}^{hy}f_j^{ry}{}'(net_j^{ry})y$$
$$= r_j^{y}(t) + \eta * \delta^{ol} * r_{kj}^{o} * \delta_{kj}^{rhy} * r_{kj}^{hy} * f_j^{ry}{}'(net_j^{ry}) * y$$
$$= r_j^{y}(t) + \eta * \delta^{ol} * r_{kj}^{o} * \delta_{kj}^{rhy} * r_{kj}^{hy} * \delta_j^{ry} * y$$
$$= r_j^{y}(t) + \eta * \delta^{ol} * r_{kj}^{o} * \delta_{kj}^{rhy} * r_{kj}^{hy} * j * [1 / (1 + \exp(-r_j^{y} * y))]^{j-1} * (1 + \exp(-r_j^{y} * y))^{-2} * \exp(-r_j^{y} * y) * y$$

$where :$

$$\delta^{ol} = (d-z)$$
$$f^{o}{}'(net^{o}) = 1 \qquad (linear \qquad neuron)$$
$$\delta_{kj}^{rhy} = r_{kj}^{hx}b_k^{rx}$$
$$f^{h}{}'(net_{kj}^{hy}) = 1 \qquad (linear \qquad neuron)$$
$$\delta_j^{ry} = f_j^{ry}{}'(net_j^{ry}) = \partial[1 / (1 + \exp(-net_j^{ry}))]^{j} / \partial(net_j^{ry})$$
$$= \partial[1 / (1 + \exp(-r_j^{y}y))]^{j} / \partial(r_j^{y}y)$$
$$= j * [1 / (1 + \exp(-r_j^{y} * y))]^{j-1} * (1 + \exp(-r_j^{y} * y))^{-2} * \exp(-r_j^{y} * y)$$

(C 24)

test data for MPHONN models. Rate and desired output data, Rt, are from USA Federal Reserve Bank Data bank. Input1, Rt-2, are the data at time t-2. Input 2, Rt-1 is the data at time t-1. The values of Rt-2, Rt-1, and Rt are used as inputs and output in the MPHONN model. MPHONN model is used for Table 1 and Table 2. The test data of MPHONN orders 6 for using 10,000 epochs are shown on the tables.

In Table 1, CanadianDollar/USDollar Exchange Rate CAD$1.00 = USD$0.9309 on 2-Nov-2009, the average errors of PHONN, THONN, SPHONN, and MPHONN are 2.8037%, 3.8238%, 3.1557%, and 2.3964% respectively. The average error of PHONN, THONN, and SPHONN is 3.2625%. So MPHONN error is 0.8661% better than the average error of PHONN, THONN, and SPHONN models.

In Table 2, CanadianDollar/USDollar Exchange Rate CAD$1.00 = USD$0.9430 on 30-Nov-2009, the average errors of PHONN, THONN, SPHONN, and MPHONN are 3.2443%, 3.1593%, 2.9678%,

and 2.6187% respectively. The average error of PHONN, THONN, and SPHONN is 3.1238%. So MPHONN error is 0.5051% better than the average error of PHONN, THONN, and SPHONN models.

FUTURE RESEARCH DIRECTIONS

One of the topics for future research is to continue building models of higher order neural networks for different data series. The coefficients of the higher order models will be studied not only using artificial neural network techniques, but also statistical methods.

CONCLUSION

This chapter develops an open box and non-linear higher order neural network models of MPHONN. This chapter also provides the learning algorithm formulae for MPHONN, based on the structures of MPHONN. This chapter uses MPHONN simulator and tests the MPHONN models using high frequency data and the running results are compared with Polynomial Higher Order Neural Network (PHONN), Trigonometric Higher Order Neural Network (THONN), and Sigmoid Polynomial Higher Order Neural Network (SPHONN) models. Test results show that average error of MPHONN models are from 2.3964% to 2.6187%, and the average error of Polynomial Higher Order Neural Network (PHONN), Trigonometric Higher Order Neural Network (THONN), and Sigmoid Polynomial Higher Order Neural Network (SPHONN) models are from 2.8078% to 3.8238%. It means that MPHONN models are 0.5051% to 0.8661% better than the average of the PHONN, THONN, and SPHONN models.

ACKNOWLEDGMENT

The author would like to acknowledge the financial assistance of the following organizations in the development of Higher Order Neural Networks: Fujitsu Research Laboratories, Japan (1995-1996), Australian Research Council (1997-1998), the US National Research Council (1999-2000), and the Applied Research Centers and Dean's Office Grants of Christopher Newport University, USA (2000-2011).

REFERENCES

Al-Rawi, M. S., & Al-Rawi, K. R. (2010). On the equivalence between ordinary neural networks and higher order neural networks . In Zhang, M. (Ed.), *Artificial Higher Order Neural Networks for Computer Science and Engineering – Trends for Emerging Application* (pp. 138–158). Hershey, PA: IGI Global.

Alanis, A. Y., Sanchez, E. N., & Loukianov, A. G. (2006). Discrete-time recurrent neural induction motor control using Kalman learning. In *Proceedings of International Joint Conference on Neural Networks,* (pp. 1993 – 2000). IEEE.

An, Z. G., Mniszewski, S. M., Lee, Y. C., Papcun, G., & Doolen, G. D. (1988). HIERtalker: A default hierarchy of high order neural networks that learns to read English aloud. In *Proceedings of the Fourth Conference on Artificial Intelligence Applications,* (p. 388). IEEE.

Baldi, P., & Venkatesh, S. S. (1993). Random interactions in higher order neural networks. *IEEE Transactions on Information Theory, 39*(1), 274–283. doi:10.1109/18.179374

Barron, R., Gilstrap, L., & Shrier, S. (1987). Polynomial and neural networks: Analogies and engineering applications. In *Proceedings of International Conference of Neural Networks,* (Vol. 2), (pp. 431-439). New York, NY: IEEE.

Boutalis, Y. S., Christodoulou, M. A., & Theodoridis, D. C. (2010). Identification of nonlinear systems using a new neuro-fuzzy dynamical system definition based on high order neural network function approximators . In Zhang, M. (Ed.), *Artificial Higher Order Neural Networks for Computer Science and Engineering – Trends for Emerging Application* (pp. 423–449). Hershey, PA: IGI Global.

Brucoli, M., Carnimeo, L., & Grassi, G. (1997). Associative memory design using discrete-time second-order neural networks with local interconnections. *IEEE Transactions on Circuits and Systems. I, Fundamental Theory and Applications*, *44*(2), 153–158. doi:10.1109/81.554334

Burshtein, D. (1998). Long-term attraction in higher order neural networks. *IEEE Transactions on Neural Networks*, *9*(1), 42–50. doi:10.1109/72.655028

Butt, N. R., & Shafiq, M. (2006). Higher-order neural network based root-solving controller for adaptive tracking of stable nonlinear plants. In *Proceedings of IEEE International Conference on Engineering of Intelligent Systems*, (pp. 1–6). IEEE Press.

Campos, J., Loukianov, A. G., & Sanchez, E. N. (2003). Synchronous motor VSS control using recurrent high order neural networks. In *Proceedings of 42nd IEEE Conference on Decision and Control*, (vol. 4), (pp. 3894–3899). IEEE Press.

Cao, J., Ren, F., & Liang, J. (2009). Dynamics in artificial higher order neural networks with delays . In Zhang, M. (Ed.), *Artificial Higher Order Neural Networks for Economics and Business* (pp. 389–429). Hershey, PA: IGI Global. doi:10.4018/978-1-59904-897-0.ch018

Chen, H. H., Lee, Y. C., Maxwell, T., Sun, G. Z., Lee, H. Y., & Giles, C. L. (1986). High order correlation model for associative memory. *AIP Conference Proceedings*, *151*, 86. doi:10.1063/1.36224

Chen, Y., Wu, P., & Wu, Q. (2009b). Higher order neural networks for stock index modeling . In Zhang, M. (Ed.), *Artificial Higher Order Neural Networks for Economics and Business* (pp. 113–132). Hershey, PA: IGI Global. doi:10.4018/978-1-59904-897-0.ch006

Das, A., Lewis, F. L., & Subbarao, K. (2010). Back-stepping control of quadrotor: A dynamically tuned higher order like neural network approach . In Zhang, M. (Ed.), *Artificial Higher Order Neural Networks for Computer Science and Engineering – Trends for Emerging Application* (pp. 484–513). Hershey, PA: IGI Global.

Dehuri, S., & Chao, S. (2010). A theoretical and empirical study of functional link neural networks (FLANNs) for classification . In Zhang, M. (Ed.), *Artificial Higher Order Neural Networks for Computer Science and Engineering – Trends for Emerging Application* (pp. 545–573). Hershey, PA: IGI Global.

Dunis, C. L., Laws, J., & Evans, B. (2009). Modeling and trading the soybean-oil crush spread with recurrent and higher order networks: A comparative analysis . In Zhang, M. (Ed.), *Artificial Higher Order Neural Networks for Economics and Business* (pp. 348–367). Hershey, PA: IGI Global.

Epitropakis, M. G., Plagianakos, V. P., & Vrahatis, M. N. (2010). Evolutionary algorithm training of higher order neural networks . In Zhang, M. (Ed.), *Artificial Higher Order Neural Networks for Computer Science and Engineering – Trends for Emerging Application* (pp. 57–85). Hershey, PA: IGI Global. doi:10.1016/j.asoc.2009.08.010

Giles, L., & Maxwell, T. (1987). Learning, invariance and generalization in high-order neural networks. *Applied Optics*, *26*(23), 4972–4978. doi:10.1364/AO.26.004972

Gupta, M. M., Homma, N., Hou, Z., Solo, A. M. G., & Bukovsky, I. (2010). Higher order neural networks: Fundamental theory and applications . In Zhang, M. (Ed.), *Artificial Higher Order Neural Networks for Computer Science and Engineering – Trends for Emerging Application* (pp. 397–422). Hershey, PA: IGI Global.

Gupta, M. M., Homma, N., Hou, Z., Solo, A. M. G., & Goto, T. (2009). Fundamental theory of artificial higher order neural networks . In Zhang, M. (Ed.), *Artificial Higher Order Neural Networks for Economics and Business* (pp. 368–388). Hershey, PA: IGI Global. doi:10.4018/978-1-59904-897-0.ch017

Horan, P., Uecker, D., & Arimoto, A. (1990). Optical implementation of a second-order neural network discriminator model. *Japanese Journal of Applied Physics, 29*, 361–365. doi:10.1143/JJAP.29.L1328

Jeffries, C. (1989). Dense memory with high order neural networks. In *Proceedings of Twenty-First Southeastern Symposium on System Theory,* (pp. 436 – 439). Washington, DC: IEEE.

Karnavas, Y. L. (2010). Electrical machines excitation control via higher order neural networks . In Zhang, M. (Ed.), *Artificial Higher Order Neural Networks for Computer Science and Engineering – Trends for Emerging Application* (pp. 366–396). Hershey, PA: IGI Global.

Kuroe, Y. (2004). Learning and identifying finite state automata with recurrent high-order neural networks. In *Proceedings of SICE 2004 Annual Conference,* (vol. 3), (pp. 2241 – 2246). SICE.

Lisboa, P., & Perantonis, S. (1991). Invariant pattern recognition using third-order networks and zernlike moments. In *Proceedings of the IEEE International Joint Conference on Neural Networks,* (Vol. 2), (pp. 1421-1425). Singapore: IEEE Press.

Lu, Z., Shieh, L., & Chen, G. (2009). A new topology for artificial higher order neural networks - Polynomial kernel networks . In Zhang, M. (Ed.), *Artificial Higher Order Neural Networks for Economics and Business* (pp. 430–441). Hershey, PA: IGI Global.

Machado, R. J. (1989). Handling knowledge in high order neural networks: The combinatorial neural model. In *Proceedings of the International Joint Conference on Neural Networks,* (vol. 2), (pp. 582). IEEE.

Mao, Z. Q., Selviah, D. R., Tao, S., & Midwinter, J. E. (1991). Holographic high order associative memory system. In *Proceedings of the Third IEE International Conference on Holographic Systems, Components and Applications,* (vol 342), (pp. 132-136). Edinburgh, UK: IEE.

Mendel, J. M. (1991). Tutorial on higher-order statistics (spectra) in signal processing and system theory: Theoretical results and some applications. *Proceedings of the IEEE, 79*(3), 278–305. doi:10.1109/5.75086

Miyajima, H., Yatsuki, S., & Kubota, J. (1995). Dynamical properties of neural networks with product connections. In *Proceedings of the IEEE International Conference on Neural Networks,* (vol. 6), (pp. 3198 – 3203). IEEE Press.

Najarian, S., Hosseini, S. M., & Fallahnezhad, M. (2010). Artificial tactile sensing and robotic surgery using higher order neural networks . In Zhang, M. (Ed.), *Artificial Higher Order Neural Networks for Computer Science and Engineering – Trends for Emerging Application* (pp. 514–544). Hershey, PA: IGI Global.

Neto, J. P. (2010). Higher order neural networks for symbolic, sub-symbolic and chaotic computations . In Zhang, M. (Ed.), *Artificial Higher Order Neural Networks for Computer Science and Engineering – Trends for Emerging Application* (pp. 37–56). Hershey, PA: IGI Global.

Qi, H., Zhang, M., & Scofield, R. (2001). Rainfall estimation using M-PHONN model. In *Proceedings of the International Joint Conference on Neural Networks 2001,* (pp. 1620-1624). Washington, DC: IJCNN.

Ren, F., & Cao, J. (2006). LMI-based criteria for stability of high-order neural networks with time-varying delay. *Nonlinear Analysis Series B: Real World Applications, 7*(5), 967–979. doi:10.1016/j.nonrwa.2005.09.001

Ricalde, L., Sanchez, E., & Alanis, A. Y. (2010). Recurrent higher order neural network control for output trajectory tracking with neural observers and constrained inputs . In Zhang, M. (Ed.), *Artificial Higher Order Neural Networks for Computer Science and Engineering – Trends for Emerging Application* (pp. 286–311). Hershey, PA: IGI Global.

Rovithakis, G., Gaganis, V., Perrakis, S., & Christodoulou, M. (1996). A recurrent neural network model to describe manufacturing cell dynamics. In *Proceedings of the 35th IEEE Conference on Decision and Control,* (vol. 2), (pp. 1728 – 1733). IEEE Press.

Rovithakis, G. A., Kosmatopoulos, E. B., & Christodoulou, M. A. (1993). Robust adaptive control of unknown plants using recurrent high order neural networks-application to mechanical systems. In *Proceedings of International Conference on Systems, Man and Cybernetics,* (vol. 4), (pp. 57 – 62). IEEE.

Rumelhart, D., Hinton, G., & McClelland, J. (1986). Learning internal representations by error propagation. In D. Rumelhart & J. McClelland (Eds.), *Parallel Distributed Processing: Explorations in the Microstructure of Cognition, Volume 1: Foundations*. Cambridge, MA: MIT Press.

Sanchez, E., Urrego, D. A., Alanis, A. Y., & Carlos-Hernandez, S. (2010). Recurrent higher order neural observers for anaerobic processes . In Zhang, M. (Ed.), *Artificial Higher Order Neural Networks for Computer Science and Engineering – Trends for Emerging Application* (pp. 333–365). Hershey, PA: IGI Global.

Seiffertt, J., & Wunsch, D. C. II. (2009). Higher order neural network architectures for agent-based computational economics and finance . In Zhang, M. (Ed.), *Artificial Higher Order Neural Networks for Economics and Business* (pp. 79–93). Hershey, PA: IGI Global.

Selviah, D. (2009). High speed optical higher order neural network for discovering data trends and patterns in very large databases . In Zhang, M. (Ed.), *Artificial Higher Order Neural Networks for Economics and Business* (pp. 442–465). Hershey, PA: IGI Global.

Selviah, D., & Shawash, J. (2010). Fifty years of electronic hardware implementations of first and higher order neural networks . In Zhang, M. (Ed.), *Artificial Higher Order Neural Networks for Computer Science and Engineering – Trends for Emerging Application* (pp. 269–285). Hershey, PA: IGI Global.

Shawash, J., & Selviah, D. (2010). Artificial higher order neural network training on limited precision processors . In Zhang, M. (Ed.), *Artificial Higher Order Neural Networks for Computer Science and Engineering – Trends for Emerging Application* (pp. 312–332). Hershey, PA: IGI Global.

Shin, Y. (1991). The pi-sigma network: An efficient higher-order neural network for pattern classification and function approximation. In *Proceedings of the International Joint Conference on Neural Networks,* (Vol. 1), (pp. 13-18). Seattle, WA: IJCNN.

Siddiqi, A. A. (2005). Genetically evolving higher order neural networks by direct encoding method. In *Proceedings of Sixth International Conference on Computational Intelligence and Multimedia Applications,* (pp. 62 – 67). IEEE.

Theodoridis, D. C., Christodoulou, M. A., & Boutalis, Y. S. (2010). Neuro-fuzzy control schemes based on high order neural network function aproximators . In Zhang, M. (Ed.), *Artificial Higher Order Neural Networks for Computer Science and Engineering – Trends for Emerging Application* (pp. 450–483). Hershey, PA: IGI Global.

Tseng, Y.-H., & Wu, J.-L. (1994). Constant-time neural decoders for some BCH codes. In *Proceedings of IEEE International Symposium on Information Theory,* (p. 343). IEEE Press.

Wang, Z., Liu, Y., & Liu, X. (2009). On complex artificial higher order neural networks: Dealing with stochasticity, jumps and delays . In Zhang, M. (Ed.), *Artificial Higher Order Neural Networks for Economics and Business* (pp. 466–483). Hershey, PA: IGI Global.

Xu, B., Liu, X., & Liao, X. (2005). Global asymptotic stability of high-order Hopfield type neural networks with time delays. *Computers & Mathematics with Applications (Oxford, England)*, *45*(10-11), 1729–1737. doi:10.1016/S0898-1221(03)00151-2

Xu, S. (2010). Adaptive higher order neural network models for data mining . In Zhang, M. (Ed.), *Artificial Higher Order Neural Networks for Computer Science and Engineering – Trends for Emerging Application* (pp. 86–98). Hershey, PA: IGI Global.

Yatsuki, S., & Miyajima, H. (2000). Statistical dynamics of associative memory for higher order neural networks. In *Proceedings of The 2000 IEEE International Symposium on Circuits and Systems,* (Vol. 3), (pp. 670 – 673). Geneva, Switzerland: IEEE Press.

Young, S., & Downs, T. (1993). Generalisation in higher order neural networks. *Electronics Letters*, *29*(16), 1491–1493. doi:10.1049/el:19930996

Yu, W. (2010). Robust adaptive control using higher order neural networks and projection . In Zhang, M. (Ed.), *Artificial Higher Order Neural Networks for Computer Science and Engineering – Trends for Emerging Application* (pp. 99–137). Hershey, PA: IGI Global.

Zhang, J. (2006). *Linear and nonlinear models for the power of chief elected officials and debt*. Pittsburgh, PA: Mid-Atlantic Region American Accounting Association.

Zhang, L., Simoff, S. J., & Zhang, J. C. (2009). Trigonometric polynomial higher order neural network group models and weighted kernel models for financial data simulation and prediction . In Zhang, M. (Ed.), *Artificial Higher Order Neural Networks for Economics and Business* (pp. 484–503). Hershey, PA: IGI Global. doi:10.4018/978-1-59904-897-0.ch022

Zhang, M. (2010a). Higher order neural network group-based adaptive trees . In Zhang, M. (Ed.), *Artificial Higher Order Neural Networks for Computer Science and Engineering – Trends for Emerging Application* (pp. 1–36). Hershey, PA: IGI Global. doi:10.4018/978-1-61520-711-4.ch001

Zhang, M. (2010b). Rainfall estimation using neuron-adaptive artificial higher order neural networks . In Zhang, M. (Ed.), *Artificial Higher Order Neural Networks for Computer Science and Engineering – Trends for Emerging Application* (pp. 159–186). Hershey, PA: IGI Global. doi:10.4018/978-1-61520-711-4.ch007

Zhang, M., & Lu, B. (2001). Financial data simulation using M-PHONN model. In *Proceedings of the International Joint Conference on Neural Networks 2001*, (pp. 1828-1832). Washington, DC: IJCNN.

Zhang, M., Xu, S., & Fulcher, J. (2002). Neuron-adaptive higher order neural-network models for automated financial data modeling. *IEEE Transactions on Neural Networks, 13*(1), 188–204. doi:10.1109/72.977302

Zhang, M., Xu, S., & Lu, B. (1999). Neuron-adaptive higher order neural network group models. In *Proceedings of International Joint Conference on Neural Networks,* (Vol. 1), (pp. 333 - 336). IJCNN.

ADDITIONAL READING

Chen, Y., Wu, P., & Wu, Q. (2009a). Foreign exchange rate forecasting using higher order flexible neural tree . In Zhang, M. (Ed.), *Artificial Higher Order Neural Networks for Economics and Business* (pp. 94–112). Hershey, PA: IGI Global. doi:10.4018/978-1-59904-897-0.ch005

Draye, J. S., Pavisic, D. A., Cheron, G. A., & Libert, G. A. (1996). Dynamic recurrent neural networks: A dynamic analysis. *IEEE Transactions SMC- Part B, 26*(5), 692-706.

Dunis, C. L., Laws, J., & Evans, B. (2006b). Modelling and trading the soybean-oil crush spread with recurrent and higher order networks: A comparative analysis. *Neural Network World, 3*(6), 193–213.

Fulcher, G. E., & Brown, D. E. (1994). A polynomial neural network for predicting temperature distributions. *IEEE Transactions on Neural Networks, 5*(3), 372–379. doi:10.1109/72.286909

Ghazali, R., & Al-Jumeily, D. (2009). Application of pi-sigma neural networks and ridge polynomial neural networks to financial time series prediction . In Zhang, M. (Ed.), *Artificial Higher Order Neural Networks for Economics and Business* (pp. 271–294). Hershey, PA: IGI Global. doi:10.4018/978-1-59904-897-0.ch012

Ghazali, R., Hussain, A. J., & Nawi, N. M. (2010). Dynamic ridge polynomial higher order neural network . In Zhang, M. (Ed.), *Artificial Higher Order Neural Networks for Computer Science and Engineering – Trends for Emerging Application* (pp. 255–268). Hershey, PA: IGI Global.

Ghosh, J., & Shin, Y. (1992). Efficient higher-order neural networks for function approximation and classification. *International Journal of Neural Systems, 3*(4), 323–350. doi:10.1142/S0129065792000255

Hornik, K. (1991). Approximation capabilities of multilayer feedforward networks. *Neural Networks, 4*, 251–257. doi:10.1016/0893-6080(91)90009-T

Hu, Shengfa, & Yan, P. (1992). Level-by-level learning for artificial neural groups. *ACTA Electronica SINICA, 20*(10), 39-43.

Hussain, A., & Liatsis, P. (2009). A novel recurrent polynomial neural network for financial time series prediction . In Zhang, M. (Ed.), *Artificial Higher Order Neural Networks for Economics and Business* (pp. 190–211). Hershey, PA: IGI Global. doi:10.4018/978-1-59904-897-0.ch009

Inui, T., Tanabe, Y., & Onodera, Y. (1978). *Group theory and its application in physics*. Heidelberg, Germany: Springer-Verlag. doi:10.1007/978-3-642-80021-4

Jiang, M., Gielen, G., & Wang, L. (2010). Analysis of quantization effects on higher order function and multilayer feedforward neural networks . In Zhang, M. (Ed.), *Artificial Higher Order Neural Networks for Computer Science and Engineering – Trends for Emerging Application* (pp. 187–222). Hershey, PA: IGI Global.

Kariniotakis, G. N., Stavrakakis, G. S., & Nogaret, E. F. (1996). Wind power forecasting using advanced neural networks models. *IEEE Transactions on Energy Conversion, 11*(4), 762–767. doi:10.1109/60.556376

Knowles, A., Hussain, A., Deredy, W. E., Lisboa, P., & Dunis, C. L. (2009). Higher order neural networks with Bayesian confidence measure for the prediction of the EUR/USD exchange rate . In Zhang, M. (Ed.), *Artificial Higher Order Neural Networks for Economics and Business* (pp. 48–59). Hershey, PA: IGI Global. doi:10.4018/978-1-59904-897-0.ch002

Kosmatopoulos, E. B., Polycarpou, M. M., Christodoulou, M. A., & Ioannou, P. A. (1995). High-order neural network structures for identification of dynamical systems. *IEEE Transactions on Neural Networks*, *6*(2), 422–431. doi:10.1109/72.363477

Lee, M., Lee, S. Y., & Park, C. H. (1992). Neural controller of nonlinear dynamic systems using higher order neural networks. *Electronics Letters*, *28*(3), 276–277. doi:10.1049/el:19920170

Leshno, M., Lin, V., Ya, P. A., & Schocken, S. (1993). Multilayer feedforward networks with a nonpolynomial activation function can approximate any function. *Neural Networks*, *6*, 861–867. doi:10.1016/S0893-6080(05)80131-5

Liatsis, P., Hussain, A., & Milonidis, E. (2009). Artificial higher order pipeline recurrent neural networks for financial time series prediction . In Zhang, M. (Ed.), *Artificial Higher Order Neural Networks for Economics and Business* (pp. 164–189). Hershey, PA: IGI Global. doi:10.4018/978-1-59904-897-0.ch008

Lu, Z., Song, G., & Shieh, L. (2010). Improving sparsity in kernel principal component analysis by polynomial kernel higher order neural networks . In Zhang, M. (Ed.), *Artificial Higher Order Neural Networks for Computer Science and Engineering – Trends for Emerging Application* (pp. 223–238). Hershey, PA: IGI Global.

Lumer, E. D. (1992). Selective attention to perceptual groups: The phase tracking mechanism. *International Journal of Neural Systems*, *3*(1), 1–17. doi:10.1142/S0129065792000024

Murata, J. (2010). Analysis and improvement of function approximation capabilities of pi-sigma higher order neural networks . In Zhang, M. (Ed.), *Artificial Higher Order Neural Networks for Computer Science and Engineering – Trends for Emerging Application* (pp. 239–254). Hershey, PA: IGI Global.

Naimark, M. A., & Stern, A. I. (1982). *Theory of group representations*. Berlin, Germany: Springer-Verlag. doi:10.1007/978-1-4613-8142-6

Onwubolu, G. C. (2009). Artificial higher order neural networks in time series prediction . In Zhang, M. (Ed.), *Artificial Higher Order Neural Networks for Economics and Business* (pp. 250–270). Hershey, PA: IGI Global. doi:10.4018/978-1-59904-897-0.ch011

Rovithakis, G. A., Chalkiadakis, I., & Zervakis, M. E. (2004). High-order neural network structure selection for function approximation applications using genetic algorithms. *IEEE Transactions on Systems, Man and Cybernetics . Part B*, *34*(1), 150–158.

Saad, E. W., Prokhorov, D. V., & Wunsch, D. C. II. (1998). Comparative study of stock trend prediction using time delay recurrent and probabilistic neural networks. *IEEE Transactions on Neural Networks*, *9*(6), 1456–1470. doi:10.1109/72.728395

Sanchez, E. N., Alanis, A. Y., & Rico, J. (2009). Electric load demand and electricity prices forecasting using higher order neural networks trained by Kalman filtering . In Zhang, M. (Ed.), *Artificial Higher Order Neural Networks for Economics and Business* (pp. 295–313). Hershey, PA: IGI Global.

Selviah, D. R., & Shawash, J. (2009). Generalized correlation higher order neural networks for financial time series prediction. In Zhang, M. (Ed.), *Artificial Higher Order Neural Networks for Economics and Business* (pp. 212–249). Hershey, PA: IGI Global. doi:10.4018/978-1-59904-897-0.ch010

Shi, D., Tan, S., & Ge, S. S. (2009). Automatically identifying predictor variables for stock return prediction . In Zhang, M. (Ed.), *Artificial Higher Order Neural Networks for Economics and Business* (pp. 60–78). Hershey, PA: IGI Global. doi:10.4018/978-1-59904-897-0.ch003

Tenti, P. (1996). Forecasting foreign exchange rates using recurrent neural networks. *Applied Artificial Intelligence*, *10*, 567–581. doi:10.1080/088395196118434

Willcox, C. R. (1991). Understanding hierarchical neural network behavior: A renormalization group approach. *Journal of Physics. A. Mathematical Nuclear and General*, *24*, 2644–2655.

Xu, S. (2009). Adaptive higher order neural network models and their applications in business . In Zhang, M. (Ed.), *Artificial Higher Order Neural Networks for Economics and Business* (pp. 314–329). Hershey, PA: IGI Global. doi:10.4018/978-1-59904-897-0.ch014

Zhang, M. (2009a). Artificial higher order neural network nonlinear model - SAS NLIN or HONNs . In Zhang, M. (Ed.), *Artificial Higher Order Neural Networks for Economics and Business* (pp. 1–47). Hershey, PA: IGI Global.

Zhang, M. (2009b). Ultra high frequency trigonometric higher order neural networks for time series data analysis . In Zhang, M. (Ed.), *Artificial Higher Order Neural Networks for Economics and Business* (pp. 133–163). Hershey, PA: IGI Global. doi:10.4018/978-1-59904-897-0.ch007

Zhang, M., & Fulcher, J. (2004). Higher order neural networks for satellite weather prediction . In Fulcher, J., & Jain, L. C. (Eds.), *Applied Intelligent Systems* (*Vol. 153*, pp. 17–57). Berlin, Germany: Springer.

KEY TERMS AND DEFINITIONS

AHONUs: Artificial Higher Order Neural Units.

CHONN: Correlation HONN.

HONN: Artificial Higher Order Neural Network.

MPHONN: Multi-Polynomial Higher Order Neural Network models.

MPONNG: Multi-layer higher Order Neural Network Group model. It combines the characteristics of PHONN, THONN, and SPHONN.

NAHONN: Neuron-Adaptive Higher Order Neural Network.

PHONN: Polynomial Higher Order Neural Network.

RHONN: A Recurrent High-Order Neural Network structure.

SPHONN: Sigmoid Polynomial Higher Order Neural Network.

THONN: Trigonometric polynomial Higher Order Neural Network.

Chapter 2
Artificial Higher Order Neural Networks for Modeling MIMO Discrete-Time Nonlinear System

Michel Lopez-Franco
Universidad de Guadalajara, Mexico

Nancy Arana-Daniel
Universidad de Guadalajara, Mexico

Alma Y. Alanis
Universidad de Guadalajara, Mexico

Carlos Lopez-Franco
Universidad de Guadalajara, Mexico

ABSTRACT

In this chapter, a Recurrent Higher Order Neural Network (RHONN) is used to identify the plant model of discrete time nonlinear systems, under the assumption that all the state is available for measurement. Then the Extended Kalman Filter (EKF) is used to train the RHONN. The applicability of this scheme is illustrated by identification for an electrically driven nonholonomic mobile robot. Traditionally, modeling of mobile robots only considers its kinematics. It has been well known that the actuator dynamics is an important part of the design of the complete robot dynamics. However, most of the reported results in literature do not consider all parametric uncertainties for mobile robots at the actuator level. This is due to the modeling problem becoming extremely difficult as the complexity of the system dynamics increases, and the mobile robot model includes the uncertainties of the actuator dynamics as well as the uncertainties of the robot kinematics and dynamics.

INTRODUCTION

In control theory, it is widely known how to control linear systems, but it still has difficulties in controlling nonlinear systems. Extensive knowledge about the behavior of the dynamics control system is usually needed to control them. This knowledge is represented in terms of differential or difference equations, and this mathematical description of system dynamics modeling is called mathematical model or simply model (Khalil, 1996). The advantage of these models is that they have a physical interpretation of its parameters and

DOI: 10.4018/978-1-4666-2175-6.ch002

variables involved in the system's behavior. These models are complicated to build in many cases.

Operating conditions or climatic and other environmental factors can cause either system wear or degradation of its components. It is so extremely difficult to consider all the physical laws involved in the behavior of the system (Viuela & Galvn, 2004).

Additionally, current technological advances have generated an enormous variety of new problems and applications, and it is necessary to use new tools to model its dynamics with greater accuracy and robustness. A field of study that has held the attention of researchers for several years is system identification. This is to determine the mathematical model when some or all of the dynamics of the system are not known (Talebi, Abdollahi, Patel, & Khorasani, 2010).

Neural networks have grown to be a well-established methodology, which allows for solving very difficult problems in engineering, as exemplified by their applications to identification and control of general nonlinear and complex systems. In particular, the use of recurrent neural networks for modeling and learning has rapidly increased in recent years (Sanchez & Ricalde, 2003; and references therein).

There exist different training algorithms for neural networks, which normally encounter some technical problems such as local minima, slow learning, and high sensitivity to initial conditions, among others. As a viable alternative, new training algorithms, e.g., those based on Kalman filtering, have been proposed (Grover & Hwang, 1992; Haykin, 2001; Singhal & Wu, 1989). Due to the fact that training a neural network typically results in a nonlinear problem, the Extended Kalman Filter (EKF) is a common tool to use, instead of a linear Kalman filter (Haykin, 2001).

It is well known (Sanchez & Ricalde, 2003) that Recurrent Higher Order Neural Networks (RHONN) offer many advantages for the modeling of complex nonlinear systems. On the other hand,

EKF training for neural networks reduces the epoch size and the number of required neurons (Haykin, 2001). Considering these two facts, we propose the use of the EKF training for RHONN in order to model complex nonlinear systems.

The best-known training approach for Recurrent Neural Networks (RNN) is the back propagation through time learning (Singhal & Wu, 1989). However, it is a first order gradient descent method, and hence, its learning speed can be very slow (Singhal & Wu, 1989). Recently, the Extended Kalman Filter (EKF)-based algorithms have been introduced to train neural networks, in order to improve the learning convergence (Singhal & Wu, 1989). The EKF training of neural networks, both feed-forward and recurrent ones, has proven to be reliable and practical for many applications over the past ten years (Singhal & Wu, 1989).

In this chapter, a Recurrent High Order Neural Network (RHONN) is first used to identify the plant model, under the assumption that all the state is available for measurement. Then the RHONN is used to design an adaptive recurrent neural identifier for nonlinear systems, whose mathematical model is assumed to be unknown. The learning algorithm for the RHONN is implemented using an Extended Kalman Filter (EKF). The applicability of this scheme is illustrated by identification for an electrically driven nonholonomic mobile robot. Traditionally, modeling of mobile robots only considers its kinematics. It has been well known that the actuator dynamics are an important part of the design of the complete robot dynamics. However, most of the reported results in literature do not consider all parametric uncertainties for mobile robots at the actuator level. This is due to the modeling problem becoming extremely difficult as the complexity of the system dynamics increases, and the mobile robot model includes the uncertainties of the actuator dynamics as well as the uncertainties of the robot kinematics and dynamics.

BACKGROUND

Discrete-Time Higher Order Neural Networks

The use of multilayer neural networks is well known for pattern recognition and for modeling of static systems. The NN is trained to learn an input-output map. Theoretical works have proven that, even with just one hidden layer, a NN can uniformly approximate any continuous function over a compact domain, provided that the NN has a sufficient number of synaptic connections (Haykin, 2001).

Artificial neural network units (neurons) can be combined in different ways, and this fact is intimately linked with the learning algorithm used to train them. Commonly, neurons in a network are organized in layers. In the simplest form of a neural network, it is possible to find an input layer of source nodes, which projects onto an output layer of neurons (computation nodes), but not vice versa. In other words, this kind of neural network is strictly feedforward or acyclic. Basically, there are two kind of feedforward neural networks; the first one is called a single-layer network; such designation is referring to the output layer of neurons. The input layer is not taken into account due the fact that there are no neurons in it; therefore, no computation is performed there. Another class of feedforward neural network distinguishes itself by the presence of one or mode hidden layers, whose computation nodes are correspondingly called hidden neurons or hidden units. The function of hidden neurons is to intervene between the external input and the network output in some useful manner. By adding one or more hidden layers, the network is enable to extract important characteristics from input data, which is particularly valuable when the size of the input layer is large. The source nodes in the input layer of the network supply respective elements of the activation pattern (input vector), which constitute the input signals applied to the neurons in the second layer. The output signals of the second layer are used as inputs of the third layer, and so on for the rest of the network. The use of multilayer neural networks is well known for pattern recognition and for modeling of static systems. The NN is trained to learn an input-output map. Theoretical results establish that, even with just one hidden layer, a NN can uniformly approximate any continuous function over a compact domain, provided that the NN has a sufficient number of synaptic connections (Haykin, 2001).

The best well-known training approach for Recurrent Neural Networks (RNN) is the back propagation through time learning (Williams & Zipser, 1989). However, it is a first order gradient descent method, and hence, its learning speed can be very slow (Leunga & Chan, 2003). Recently, Extended Kalman Filter (EKF)-based algorithms have been introduced to train neural networks (Alanis, Sanchez, & Loukianov, 2010; Feldkamp, Prokhorov, & Feldkamp, 2003). With the EKF-based algorithm, the learning convergence is improved (Leunga & Chan, 2003). The EKF training of neural networks, both feedforward and recurrent ones, has proven to be reliable and practical for many applications over the past ten years (Feldkamp, Prokhorov, & Feldkamp, 2003).

It is known that Kalman Filtering (KF) estimates the state of a linear system with additive state and output white noises (Grover & Hwang, 1992; Song & Grizzle, 1995). For KF-based neural network training, the network weights become the states to be estimated. In this case, the error between the neural network output and the measured plant output can be considered as additive white noise. Due to the fact that the neural network mapping is nonlinear, an EKF-type is required (see Poznyak, Sanchez, & Yu, 2001; and references therein).

The training goal is to find the optimal weight values that minimize the prediction error. The EKF-based training algorithm is described by Grover and Hwang (1992):

$$M_i(k) = \left[R_i(k) + H_i^\top(k) P_i(k) H_i(k) \right]^{-1}$$

$$P_i(k+1) = P_i(k) - K_i(k) H_i^\top(k) P_i(k) + Q_i(k) \tag{1}$$

$$K_i(k) = P_i(k) H_i(k) M_i(k)$$

with

$$w_i(k+1) = w_i(k) + \eta_i K_i(k) e_i(k)$$

$$e_i(k) = x_i(k) - \hat{x}_i(k) \tag{2}$$

where $P_i \in \Re^{L_i \times L_i}$ is the prediction error associated covariance matrix, $w_i \in \Re^{L_i}$ is the weight (state) vector, L_i is the total number of neural network weights, $x_i \in \Re$ is the i-th plant state component, $\hat{x}_i \in \Re$ is the i-th neural state component, η_i is a design parameter, $K_i \in \Re^{L_i \times m}$ is the Kalman gain matrix, $Q_i \in \Re^{L_i \times L_i}$ is the state noise associated covariance matrix, $R_i \in \Re^{m \times m}$ is the measurement noise associated covariance matrix, $H_i \in \Re^{L_i \times m}$ is a matrix, for which each entry (H_{ij}) is the derivative of one of the neural network output, $(\hat{x}_i)$, with respect to one neural network weight (w_{ij}), as follows:

$$H_{ij}(k) = \left[\frac{\partial \hat{x}_i(k)}{\partial w_{ij}(k)} \right]$$

where $w_i(k) = \hat{w}_i(k+1)$, $i = 1, ..., n$, and $j = 1, ..., L_i$. Usually P_i, Q_i and R_i are initialized as diagonal matrices, with entries $P_i(0)$, $Q_i(0)$ and $R_i(0)$, respectively. It is important to note that $H_i(k)$, $K_i(k)$ and $P_i(k)$ for the EKF are bounded (Song & Grizzle, 1995).

For control tasks, extensions of the first order Hopfield model called Recurrent Higher Order Neural Networks (RHONN), which present more interactions among the neurons, are proposed (Narendra & Parthasarathy, 1990; Rovithakis & Chistodoulou, 2000). Additionally, the RHONN model is very flexible and allows incorporating to the neural model a priory information about the system structure.

A recurrent neural network distinguishes itself from a feedforward one in that it has at least one feedback loop. For example, a recurrent network may consist of a single layer of neurons with each neuron feeding its output signal back to the inputs of all other neurons.

The presence of feedback loops in a neural network has a profound impact on the learning capability of the network and on its performance. Moreover, feedback loops in a neural network result in a nonlinear dynamical behavior due to the use of nonlinear activation functions. This kind of neural network allows better understanding of biological structures. They can also offer great computational advantages. It is well known that feedforward (or static) neural networks are capable of approximating any continuous function (Haykin, 2001). However, the recurrent neural networks possess a rich repertoire of architectures, which qualifies them for various applications, which are not possible with feedforward neural networks; some of these applications are: Nonlinear prediction, modeling, control, and state space representation, among others.

The dynamic behavior of recurrent neural networks is due to the inclusion of recurrent connections, which facilitate the processing of temporal information or dynamic patterns, i.e. time-dependent patterns in the sense that the standard value at a given time depends on past values.

Consider the following discrete-time Recurrent Higher Order Neural Network (RHONN):

$$x_i(k+1) = w_i^\top \varphi_i(x(k), u(k)), \quad i = 1, \cdots, n \tag{3}$$

where $x_i (i = 1, 2, \cdots, n)$ is the state of the i - th neuron and L_i is the respective number of higher-order connections, $\{I_1, I_2, \cdots, I_{L_i}\}$ is a collection of non-ordered subsets of $\{1, 2, \cdots, n + m\}$, n is the state dimension, m is the number of external inputs, $w_i (i = 1, 2, \cdots, n)$ is the respective on-line adapted weight vector, and $\varphi_i(x(k), u(k))$ is given by

$$\varphi_i(x(k), u(k)) = \begin{bmatrix} \varphi_{i_1} \\ \varphi_{i_2} \\ \vdots \\ \varphi_{i_{L_i}} \end{bmatrix} = \begin{bmatrix} \prod_{j \in I_1} \Phi_{i_j}^{d_{i_j}(1)} \\ \prod_{j \in I_2} \Phi_{i_j}^{d_{ij}(2)} \\ \vdots \\ \prod_{j \in I_{L_i}} \Phi_{i_j}^{d_{i_j}(L_i)} \end{bmatrix} \quad (4)$$

with $d_{j_i}(k)$ being nonnegative integers, and Φ_i defined as follows:

$$\Phi_i = \begin{bmatrix} \Phi_{i_1} \\ \vdots \\ \Phi_{i_1} \\ \Phi_{i_{n+1}} \\ \vdots \\ \Phi_{i_{n+m}} \end{bmatrix} = \begin{bmatrix} S(x_1) \\ \vdots \\ S(x_n) \\ u_1 \\ \vdots \\ u_m \end{bmatrix} \quad (5)$$

In (5), $u = [u_1, u_2, \ldots, u_m]^\top$ is the input vector to the neural network, and $S(\bullet)$ is defined by

$$S(\varepsilon) = \frac{1}{1 + e^{-\beta \varepsilon}}, \quad \beta > 0$$

where ε is any real value variable.

Consider the problem to approximate the general discrete-time nonlinear system (6), by the following discrete-time RHONN series-parallel representation (Rovithakis & Chistodoulou, 2000):

$$\hat{x}_i (k + 1) = w_i^{*\top} \varphi_i \big(x(k), u(k)\big) + \epsilon_{z_i}, \quad i = 1, \cdots, n$$

where x_i is the i - th plant state, ϵ_{z_i} is a bounded approximation error, which can be reduced by increasing the number of the adjustable weights (Rovithakis & Chistodoulou, 2000). Assume that there exists an ideal weights vector w_i^* such that $\left\| \epsilon_{z_i} \right\|$ can be minimized on a compact set $\Omega_{z_i} \subset \Re^{L_i}$; the ideal weight vector w_i^* is an artificial quantity required for analytical purpose (Rovithakis & Chistodoulou, 2000). In general, it is assumed that this vector exists and is constant but unknown. Let us define its estimate as w_i and the estimation error as

$$\tilde{w}_i(k) = w_i(k) - w_i^*$$

The estimate w_i is used for stability analysis, which will be discussed later. Since w_i^* is constant, then

$$\tilde{w}_i(k + 1) - \tilde{w}_i(k) = w_i(k + 1) - w_i(k), \forall k \in 0 \cup \mathbf{Z}^+.$$

From (3) three possible models can be derived:

- Parallel model

$$\hat{x}_i(k + 1) = w_i^\top \varphi_i(\hat{x}(k), u(k)), \quad i = 1, \cdots, n$$

- Series-Parallel model

$$\hat{x}_i(k + 1) = w_i^\top \varphi_i(\chi(k), u(k)), \quad i = 1, \cdots, n$$

- Feedforward model (HONN)

$$\hat{x}_i(k) = w_i^\top \varphi_i(u(k)), \quad i = 1, \cdots, n$$

where $\hat{x}$ is the NN state vector, x is the plant state vector, and u is the input vector to the NN.

NEURAL IDENTIFICATION

Analysis of large-scale nonlinear system requires a lot of effort, since the real model parameters some times are so difficult to obtain (Gourdeau, 1997). Therefore, we derive a model based on Recurrent Higher Order Neural Network (RHONN) to identify the nonlinear system.

$$x(k+1) = F(x(k), u(k)) \qquad (6)$$

where $x \in \Re^n$, $u \in \Re^m$ and $F \in \Re^n \times \Re^m \to \Re^n$ is nonlinear function. To identify the system (6), we use a RHONN defined as:

$$\hat{x}_i(k+1) = w_i^\top \varphi_i(x(k), u(k)), \quad i = 1, \cdots, n \qquad (7)$$

where $\hat{x}_i (i = 1, 2, \cdots, n)$ is the state of the i-th neuron, L_i is the respective number of higher order connections, $\{I_1, I_2, \cdots, I_{L_i}\}$ is a collection of non-ordered subsets of $\{1, 2, \cdots, n+m\}$, n is the state dimension, m is the number of external inputs, $w_i (i = 1, 2, \cdots, n)$ is the respective on-line adapted weight vector, with $\varphi_i(x(k), u(k))$ as defined in (4). Consider the problem to approximate the general discrete-time nonlinear system (6), by the following discrete-time RHONN series-parallel representation (Rovithakis & Chistodoulou, 2000):

$$\hat{x}_i(k+1) = w_i^{*\top} \varphi_i(x(k), u(k)) + \epsilon_{z_i}, \quad i = 1, \cdots, n$$

where $\hat{x}_i$ is the i-th plant state, ϵ_{z_i} is a bounded approximation error, which can be reduced by increasing the number of the adjustable weights (Rovithakis & Chistodoulou, 2000). Assume that there exists an ideal weights vector w_i^* such that $\left\| \epsilon_{z_i} \right\|$ can be minimized on a compact set $\Omega_{z_i} \subset \Re^{L_i}$. The ideal weight vector w_i^* is an ar-

tificial quantity required for analytical purpose (Rovithakis & Chistodoulou, 2000). In general, it is assumed that this vector exists and is constant but unknown. Let us define its estimate as w_i and the estimation error as

$$w_i(k) = w_i(k) - w_i^* \qquad (8)$$

The RHONN is trained with an Extended Kalman Filter (EKF) algorithm (1). Then, the dynamics of the identification error (2) can be expressed as

$$e_i(k+1) = \tilde{w}_i(k) z_i(x(k), u(k)) + \epsilon_{z_i}$$

On the other hand the dynamics of (8) are

$$\tilde{w}_i(k+1) = \tilde{w}_i(k) - \eta_i K_i(k) e(k)$$

Now, we establish the first main result of this chapter in the following theorem.

Theorem 1 (Alanis, Sanchez, & Loukianov, 2010): The RHONN (7) trained with the EKF-based algorithm (1) to identify the nonlinear plant (6), ensures that the identification error (2) is Semi-Globally Uniformly Ultimately Bounded (SGUUB); moreover, the RHONN weights remain bounded.

APPLICATION

Applicability of the scheme is illustrated via simulation for an electrically driven nonholonomic mobile robot, whose model is considered to be unknown as well as all its parameters and disturbances.

In the past 20 years, the control of mobile robots has been regarded as the attractive problem due to the nature of nonholonomic constraints. Many efforts have been devoted to the tracking control of nonholonomic mobile robots (Park, Yoo, &

Park, 2010). Most of these schemes have ignored the dynamics coming from electric motors, which should be required to implement the mobile robots in the real environment, that is, the mobile robot model at the kinematics level or at the dynamics level has been only considered (Park, Yoo, & Park, 2010). It is important to note the controller design problem would become extremely difficult as the complexity of the system dynamics increases and when the mobile robot model includes the uncertainties of the actuator dynamics as well as the uncertainties of the robot kinematics and dynamics (Park, Yoo, & Park, 2010).

In this chapter a mobile robot with two actuated wheels as shown in Figure 1. The dynamic of an electrically driven nonholonomic mobile robot can be expressed in the following state-space model (Das & Kar, 2006; Do, Jiang, & Pan, 2004; Park, Yoo, & Park, 2010):

$$\dot{x}_1 = J\left(x_1\right)x_2$$
$$\dot{x}_2 = M^{-1}\left(-C(\dot{x}_1)x_2 - Dx_2 - \tau_d + NK_T x_3\right)$$
$$\dot{x}_3 = L_a^{-1}\left(u - R_a x_3 - NK_E x_2\right) \tag{9}$$

where each subsystem is defined as $x_1 = [x_{11}, x_{12}, x_{13}]^T$, $x_2 = [x_{21}, x_{22}]^T$, and $x_3 = [x_{31}, x_{32}]^T$, with:

$$J(x_1) = 0.5r \begin{bmatrix} \cos(x_{13}) & \cos(x_{13}) \\ \sin(x_{13}) & \sin(x_{13}) \\ R^{-1} & -R^{-1} \end{bmatrix}$$

$$M = \begin{bmatrix} m_{11} & m_{12} \\ m_{12} & m_{11} \end{bmatrix}$$

$$C(k) = 0.5R^{-1}r^2 m_c d \begin{bmatrix} 0 & \dot{x}_{13} \\ -\dot{x}_{13} & 0 \end{bmatrix}$$

$$D = \begin{bmatrix} d_{11} & 0 \\ 0 & d_{22} \end{bmatrix}$$

$$m_{11} = 0.25R^{-2}r^2(mR^2 + I) + I_w$$

$$m_{12} = 0.25R^{-2}r^2(mR^2 - I)$$

$$m = m_c + 2m_w$$

$$I = m_c d^2 + 2m_w R^2 + I_c + 2I_m$$

$$\tau = [\tau_1, \tau_2]^T$$

$$\tau_d = [\tau_{d1}, \tau_{d2}]^T$$

Figure 1. Mobile robot with two actuated wheels

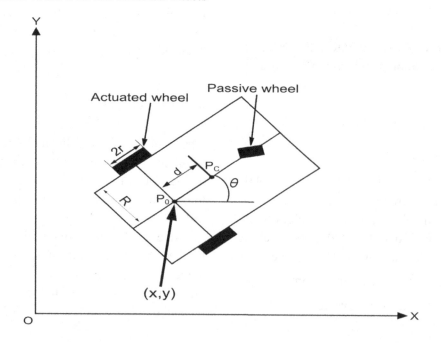

where $x_{11} = x$, $x_{12} = y$ are the coordinates of P_0, and $x_{13} = \theta$ is the heading angle of the mobile robot, $x_{21} = v_1$, $x_{22} = v_2$ represents the angular velocities of right and left wheels, respectively, and $x_{31} = i_{a1}$, $x_{32} = i_{a2}$ represents motor currents of the right and left wheels, respectively. R is half of the width of the mobile robot, and r is the radius of the wheel; d is the distance from the center of mass P_c of the mobile robot to the middle point P_0 between the right and left driving wheels. m_c and m_w are the mass of the body and the wheel with a motor, respectively. I_c, I_w, and I_m are the moment of inertia of the body about the vertical axis through P_c, the wheel with a motor about the wheel axis, and the wheel with a motor about the wheel diameter, respectively. The positive terms d_{ii}, $i = 1, 2$, are the damping coefficients. $\tau \in \Re^2$ is the control torque

applied to the wheels of the robot, $\tau_d \in \Re^2$ is a vector of disturbances including un-modeled dynamics. K_T is the motor torque constant, $i_a = [i_{a_1}, i_{a_2}]$ is the motor current vector, $u \in \Re^2$ is the input voltage, $R_a = diag[r_{a_1}, r_{a_2}]$ is the resistance, $L_a = diag[l_{a_1}, l_{a_2}]$ is the inductance, $K_E = diag[k_{e_1}, k_{e_2}]$ is the back electromotive force coefficient, and $N = diag[n_1, n_2]$ is the gear ratio. Here, $diag[\cdot]$ denotes the diagonal matrix. Model (9) is discretized using the Euler Methodology. The physical parameters for the mobile robot simulations are selected as shown in Box 1.

Simulation Results

We apply the neural identifier developed above to obtain a discrete-time neural model for the electrically driven nonholonomic mobile robot (9), with n = 7 trained with the EKF (1), as shown in Box 2.

Box 1.

$$d = 0.3m$$
$$d_{m1} = d_{m2} = 0.5N$$
$$I_c = 15.625 kgm^2$$
$$I_m = 0.0025 kgm^2$$
$$I_w = 0.005 kgm^2$$

$$K_E = diag[0.02, 0.02]V / (rad / s)$$
$$K_T = diag[0.2613, 0.2613]Nm / A$$
$$L_a = diag[0.048, 0.048]H$$
$$m_c = 30kg$$
$$m_w = 1kg$$

$$N = diag[62.55, 62.55]$$
$$R_a = diag[2.5, 2.5]\Omega$$
$$R = 0.75m$$
$$r = 0.15m$$

Box 2.

$$\hat{x}_1(k+1) = w_{11}(k)S(x_{11}(k)) + w_{12}(k)S(x_{12}(k))$$
$$\hat{x}_2(k+1) = w_{21}(k)S(x_{11}(k)) + w_{22}(k)S(x_{12}(k))$$
$$\hat{x}_3(k+1) = w_{31}(k)S(x_{11}(k)) + w_{32}(k)S(x_{12}(k))$$
$$\hat{x}_4(k+1) = w_{41}(k)S(x_{11}(k)) + w_{42}(k)S(x_{12}(k)) + w_{43}(k)S(x_{21}(k)) + w_{44}(k)S(x_{31}(k))$$
$$\hat{x}_5(k+1) = w_{51}(k)S(x_{11}(k)) + w_{52}(k)S(x_{12}(k)) + w_{53}(k)S(x_{22}(k)) + w_{54}(k)S(x_{32}(k))$$
$$\hat{x}_6(k+1) = w_{61}(k)S(x_{11}(k)) + w_{62}(k)S(x_{12}(k)) + w_{63}(k)S(x_{21}(k)) + w_{64}(k)S(x_{31}(k)) + G_1 u_{11}$$
$$\hat{x}_7(k+1) = w_{71}(k)S(x_{11}(k)) + w_{72}(k)S(x_{12}(k)) + w_{73}(k)S(x_{22}(k)) + w_{74}(k)S(x_{32}(k)) + G_2 u_{12} \qquad (10)$$

Box 3.

$$P_1(0) = 1 \times 10^8$$
$$P_2(0) = 1 \times 10^2$$
$$P_3(0) = 1 \times 10^8$$
$$P_4(0) = 1 \times 10^2$$
$$P_5(0) = 1 \times 10^2$$
$$P_6(0) = 1 \times 10^2$$
$$P_7(0) = 1 \times 10^2$$
$$G_1 = 0.00001$$

$$R_1(0) = 1 \times 10^4$$
$$R_2(0) = 5 \times 10^4$$
$$R_3(0) = 1 \times 10^4$$
$$R_4(0) = 1 \times 10^1$$
$$R_5(0) = 1 \times 10^1$$
$$R_6(0) = 1 \times 10^3$$
$$R_7(0) = 1 \times 10^3$$
$$G_2 = 0.00001$$

$$Q_1(0) = 5 \times 10^5$$
$$Q_2(0) = 5 \times 10^5$$
$$Q_3(0) = 5 \times 10^5$$
$$Q_4(0) = 1 \times 10^1$$
$$Q_5(0) = 1 \times 10^1$$
$$Q_6(0) = 1 \times 10^3$$
$$Q_7(0) = 1 \times 10^3$$

The inputs u_1 and u_2 are selected as chirp functions; Where $\hat{x}_7$ and $\hat{x}_6$ identify the motor currents of left and right wheels, respectively; $\hat{x}_5$ and $\hat{x}_4$ identify the angular velocities of left and right wheels, respectively; $\hat{x}_3$ identifies the robot angle; finally, $\hat{x}_2$ and $\hat{x}_1$ identify the y and x coordinates, respectively.

It is important to note that for conventional applications, it is unusual to use chirp signals (sine wave signal whose frequency increases at a linear rate with respect to time) as inputs. In this chapter, they are used for purposes of state estimation to excite most of the plant dynamics. For modeling of nonlinear system structures, it is important to represent a wide range of frequencies. Input signals attempting to meet this demand include Pseudo Random Binary Sequences (PRBS), random Gaussian noise, and chirp signals (swept sinusoid). All of these input signals have advantages which includes: independent noise estimation and reduction of data sets among others; however, chirp signals have been generally found to provide more consistent results and have been used successfully in the past for modeling the dynamics of complex nonlinear systems. For supplementary information, see also Haykin (2001). The NN training is performed on-line, and all of its states are initialized in a random

way. The RHONN parameters are heuristically selected as shown in Box 3.

It is important to consider that for the EKF-learning algorithm the covariances are used as design parameters (Feldkamp, Prokhorov, & Feldkamp, 2003; Haykin, 2001). The neural network structure (10) is determined heuristically in order to minimize the state estimation error. Simulation is performed with a sampling time of 0.01 s. The results are presented as follows: Figure 2 display the identification performance for x and y coordinates and the identification performance for the heading angle of the mobile robot; Figure 3 presents the identification performance for the angular velocities of right and left wheels, respectively; Figure 4 portrays the identification performance for motor currents of the right and left wheels. Finally, Figure 5 displays the control signals u_1 and u_2.

FUTURE RESEARCH DIRECTIONS

One forthcoming research is implementation of a control based on the proposed approaches in real-time mobile robots. The integrations of a visual servoing system will be considered in order to obtain measurements for position and speed for the robot. The selection of the design parameters

Figure 2. (Top) x-axis identification (plant signal in solid line and neural signal in dashed line); (middle) y-axis identification (plant signal in solid line and neural signal in dashed line); (bottom) angle identification (plant signal in solid line and neural signal in dashed line)

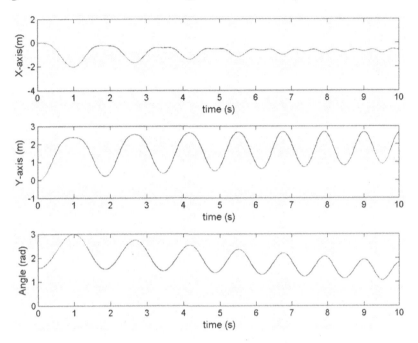

Figure 3. (Top) angular velocity v_1 identification (plant signal in solid line and neural signal in dashed line); (bottom) angular velocity v_2 identification (plant signal in solid line and neural signal in dashed line)

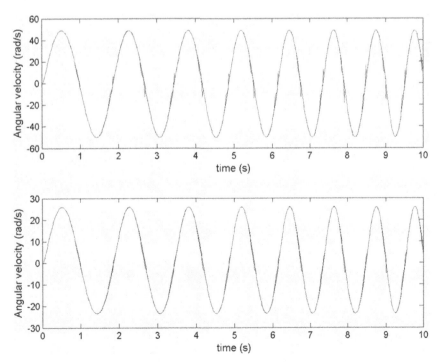

Figure 4. (Top) current i_{a_1} identification (plant signal in solid line and neural signal in dashed line); (bottom) current i_{a_1} identification (plant signal in solid line and neural signal in dashed line)

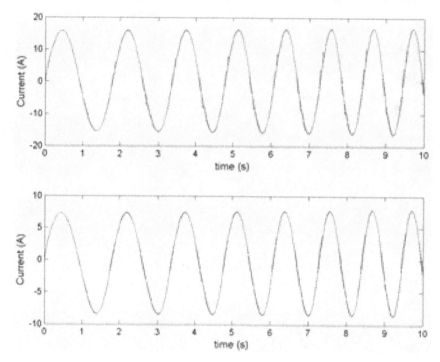

Figure 5. (Inputs.tif): (top) control signal u_1, (bottom) control signal u_2

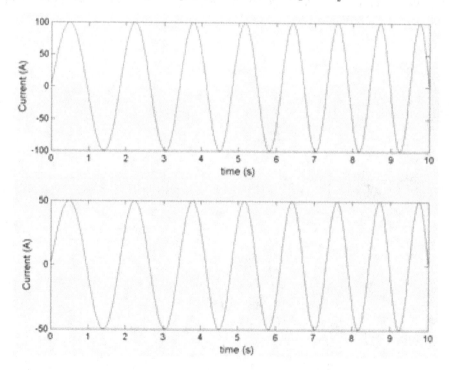

as covariances matrixes and learning rate are obtained heuristically; a future research direction is the development of an analytical methodology like particle swarm optimization. Finally, another future research direction is the development of the stability proof for the identifier proposed, based in the Lyapunov methodology.

CONCLUSION

A RHONN is used to identify the plant model of discrete time nonlinear systems, under the assumption that all the state is available for measurement. RHONN scheme is trained with an EKF-based algorithm, which is implemented on-line in a series parallel configuration. The RHONN training with the EKF-based algorithm presents good performance. This chapter deals only with identification for an electrically driven nonholonomic mobile robot. It presents a benefit when the dynamic of the system is unknown.

ACKNOWLEDGMENT

The authors thank the support of SEP Mexico, through Project PROMEP/103.5/07/2636, and CONACYT Mexico, through Project 103191Y.

REFERENCES

Alanis, A. Y., Sanchez, E. N., & Loukianov, A. G. (2010). Real-time discrete neural block control using sliding modes for electric induction motors. *IEEE Transactions on Control Systems Technology, 18,* 11–21. doi:10.1109/TCST.2008.2009466

Das, T., & Kar, I. N. (2006). Design and implementation of an adaptive fuzzy logic-based controller for wheeled mobile robots. *IEEE Transactions on Control Systems Technology, 14,* 501–510. doi:10.1109/TCST.2006.872536

Do, K. D., Jiang, Z. P., & Pan, J. (2004). Simultaneous tracking and stabilization of mobile robots: An adaptive approach. *IEEE Transactions on Automatic Control, 49,* 1147–1152. doi:10.1109/TAC.2004.831139

Feldkamp, L. A., Prokhorov, D. V., & Feldkamp, T. M. (2003). Simple and conditioned adaptive behavior from Kalman filter trained recurrent networks. *Neural Networks, 16,* 683–689. doi:10.1016/S0893-6080(03)00127-8

Ge, S. S., Zhang, J., & Lee, T. H. (2004). Adaptive neural network control for a class of MIMO nonlinear systems with disturbances in discrete-time. *IEEE Transactions on Systems, Man, and Cybernetics, 34,* 1–4.

Grover, R., & Hwang, P. Y. C. (1992). *Introduction to random signals and applied Kalman filtering* (2nd ed.). New York, NY: John Wiley and Sons.

Haykin, S. (Ed.). (2001). *Kalman filtering and neural networks.* New York, NY: John Wiley and Sons. doi:10.1002/0471221546

Khalil, H. (1996). *Nonlinear systems* (3rd ed.). Upper Saddle River, NJ: Pearson Education.

Leunga, C., & Chan, L. (2003). Dual extended Kalman filtering in recurrent neural networks. *Neural Networks, 16,* 223–239. doi:10.1016/S0893-6080(02)00230-7

Narendra, K. S., & Parthasarathy, K. (1990). Identification and control of dynamical systems using neural networks. *IEEE Transactions on Neural Networks, 1,* 4–27. doi:10.1109/72.80202

Park, B. S., Yoo, S. J., Park, J. B., & Choi, Y. H. (2010). A simple adaptive control approach for trajectory tracking of electrically driven nonholonomic mobile robots. *IEEE Transactions on Control Systems Technology, 18,* 1199–1206. doi:10.1109/TCST.2009.2034639

Poznyak, A. S., Sanchez, E. N., & Yu, W. (2001). *Differential neural networks for robust nonlinear control.* Singapore, Singapore: World Scientific.

Rovithakis, G. A., & Chistodoulou, M. A. (2000). *Adaptive control with recurrent high -order neural networks*. Berlin, Germany: Springer Verlag. doi:10.1007/978-1-4471-0785-9

Sanchez, E. N., & Ricalde, L. J. (2003). Trajectory tracking via adaptive recurrent neural control with input saturation. In *Proceedings of International Joint Conference on Neural Networks 2003*. Portland, OR: IJCNN.

Singhal, S., & Wu, L. (1989). In Touretzky, D. S. (Ed.), *Training multilayer perceptrons with the extended Kalman algorithm* (Vol. 1, pp. 133–140). Advances in Neural Information Processing Systems San Mateo, CA: Morgan Kaufmann.

Song, Y., & Grizzle, J. W. (1995). The extended Kalman filter as local asymptotic observer for discrete-time nonlinear systems. *Journal of Mathematical Systems . Estimation and Control, 5*, 59–78.

Talebi, H., Abdollahi, F., Patel, R., & Khorasani, K. (2010). *Neural network-based state estimation of nonlinear systems* (3rd ed.). New York, NY: Springer. doi:10.1007/978-1-4419-1438-5

Viuela, P. I., & Galvn, I. M. (2004). *Redes de neuronas artificiales un enfoque práctico* (3rd ed.). Madrid, Spain: Pearson, Prentice Hall.

Williams, R. J., & Zipser, D. (1989). A learning algorithm for continually running fully recurrent neural networks. *Neural Computation, 1*, 270–280. doi:10.1162/neco.1989.1.2.270

ADDITIONAL READING

Alanis, A. Y., Sanchez, E. N., & Loukianov, A. G. (2010). Real-time discrete neural block control using sliding modes for electric induction motors. *IEEE Transactions on Control Systems Technology, 18*, 11–21. doi:10.1109/TCST.2008.2009466

Chen, F., & Dunnigan, M. W. (2002). Comparative study of a sliding-mode observer and Kalman filters for full state estimation in an induction machine. *IEEE Proceedings on Electric Power Applications, 14*, 53-64.

Coutinho, D. F., & Pereira, L. P. (2005). A robust Luenberge-like observer for induction machines. In *Proceedings IEEE IECON 2005*. IEEE Press.

Das, T., & Kar, I. N. (2006). Design and implementation of an adaptive fuzzy logic-based controller for wheeled mobile robots. *IEEE Transactions on Control Systems Technology, 14*, 501–510. doi:10.1109/TCST.2006.872536

Do, K. D., Jiang, Z. P., & Pan, J. (2004). Simultaneous tracking and stabilization of mobile robots: An adaptive approach. *IEEE Transactions on Automatic Control, 49*, 1147–1152. doi:10.1109/TAC.2004.831139

Farrell, J. A., & Polycarpou, M. M. (2006). *Adaptive approximation based control: Unifying neural, fuzzy and traditional adaptive approximation approaches*. New York, NY: John Wiley and Sons. doi:10.1002/0471781819

Feldkamp, L. A., Prokhorov, D. V., & Feldkamp, T. M. (2003). Simple and conditioned adaptive behavior from Kalman filter trained recurrent networks. *Neural Networks, 16*, 683–689. doi:10.1016/S0893-6080(03)00127-8

Ge, S. S., Zhang, J., & Lee, T. H. (2004). Adaptive neural network control for a class of MIMO nonlinear systems with disturbances in discrete-time. *IEEE Transactions on Systems, Man, and Cybernetics, 34*, 1–4.

Grover, R., & Hwang, P. Y. C. (1992). *Introduction to random signals and applied Kalman filtering* (2nd ed.). New York, NY: John Wiley and Sons.

Haykin, S. (Ed.). (2001). *Kalman filtering and neural networks*. New York, NY: John Wiley and Sons. doi:10.1002/0471221546

Huang, H., Feng, G., & Cao, J. (2008). Robust state estimation for uncertain neural networks with time-varying delay. *IEEE Transactions on Neural Networks*, *19*, 1329–1339. doi:10.1109/TNN.2008.2000206

Jagannathan, S., & Lewis, F. L. (1996). Identification of nonlinear dynamical systems using multilayered neural networks. *Automatica*, *32*, 1707–1712. doi:10.1016/S0005-1098(96)80007-0

Khalil, H. (1996). *Nonlinear systems* (3rd ed.). Upper Saddle River, NJ: Pearson Education.

Kim, Y. H., & Lewis, F. L. (1998). *High-level feedback control with neural networks*. Singapore, Singapore: World Scientific.

Leunga, C., & Chan, L. (2003). Dual extended Kalman filtering in recurrent neural networks. *Neural Networks*, *16*, 223–239. doi:10.1016/S0893-6080(02)00230-7

Narendra, K. S., & Parthasarathy, K. (1990). Identification and control of dynamical systems using neural networks. *IEEE Transactions on Neural Networks*, *1*, 4–27. doi:10.1109/72.80202

Park, B. S., Yoo, S. J., Park, J. B., & Choi, Y. H. (2010). A simple adaptive control approach for trajectory tracking of electrically driven non-holonomic mobile robots. *IEEE Transactions on Control Systems Technology*, *18*, 1199–1206. doi:10.1109/TCST.2009.2034639

Poznyak, A. S., Sanchez, E. N., & Yu, W. (2001). *Differential neural networks for robust nonlinear control*. Singapore, Singapore: World Scientific.

Rovithakis, G. A., & Chistodoulou, M. A. (2000). *Adaptive control with recurrent high -order neural networks*. Berlin, Germany: Springer Verlag. doi:10.1007/978-1-4471-0785-9

Sanchez, E. N., & Ricalde, L. J. (2003). Trajectory tracking via adaptive recurrent neural control with input saturation. In *Proceedings of International Joint Conference on Neural Networks 2003*. Portland, OR: IJCNN.

Singhal, S., & Wu, L. (1989). In Touretzky, D. S. (Ed.), *Training multilayer perceptrons with the extended Kalman algorithm* (*Vol. 1*, pp. 133–140). Advances in Neural Information Processing Systems San Mateo, CA: Morgan Kaufmann.

Song, Y., & Grizzle, J. W. (1995). The extended Kalman filter as local asymptotic observer for discrete-time nonlinear systems. *Journal of Mathematical Systems . Estimation and Control*, *5*, 59–78.

Talebi, H., Abdollahi, F., Patel, R., & Khorasani, K. (2010). *Neural network-based state estimation of nonlinear systems* (3rd ed.). New York, NY: Springer. doi:10.1007/978-1-4419-1438-5

Utkin, V., Guldner, J., & Shi, J. (1999). *Sliding mode control in electromechanical systems*. Philadelphia, PA: Taylor and Francis.

Viuela, P. I., & Galvn, I. M. (2004). *Redes de neuronas artificiales un enfoque prctico* (3rd ed.). Madrid, Spain: Pearson, Prentice Hall.

Wang, Z., Ho, D. W. C., & Liu, X. (2005). State estimation for delayed neural networks. *IEEE Transactions on Neural Networks*, *16*, 279–284. doi:10.1109/TNN.2004.841813

Williams, R. J., & Zipser, D. (1989). A learning algorithm for continually running fully recurrent neural networks. *Neural Computation*, *1*, 270–280. doi:10.1162/neco.1989.1.2.270

Yu, W., & Li, X. (2004). Nonlinear system identification using discrete-time recurrent neural networks with stable learning algorithms. *Information Sciences*, *158*, 131–147. doi:10.1016/j.ins.2003.08.002

Chapter 3
Artificial Higher Order Neural Networks for Modeling Combinatorial Optimization Problems

Yuxin Ding
Harbin Institute of Technology, China

ABSTRACT

Traditional Hopfield networking has been widely used to solve combinatorial optimization problems. However, high order Hopfiled networks, as an expansion of traditional Hopfield networks, are seldom used to solve combinatorial optimization problems. In theory, compared with low order networks, high order networks have better properties, such as stronger approximations and faster convergence rates. In this chapter, the authors focus on how to use high order networks to model combinatorial optimization problems. Firstly, the high order discrete Hopfield Network is introduced, then the authors discuss how to find the high order inputs of a neuron. Finally, the construction method of energy function and the neural computing algorithm are presented. In this chapter, the N queens problem and the crossbar switch problem, which are NP-complete problems, are used as examples to illustrate how to model practical problems using high order neural networks. The authors also discuss the performance of high order networks for modeling the two combinatorial optimization problems.

1. INTRODUCTION

High-order neural networks have stronger approximation property, faster convergence rate, greater storage capacity, and higher fault tolerance than lower-order neural networks; therefore, they

DOI: 10.4018/978-1-4666-2175-6.ch003

have been intensively considered by researchers in recent years. At present, there have been extensive results on the problem of the existence and stability of equilibrium points and periodic solutions of high-order Hopfield Neural Networks (HHNNs), for example, the references Xu, Liu, and Teoc (2009), Yi, Shao, and Yu (2008), Ou (2008), and Gopalsamy (2007) all derive different sufficient conditions to guarantee the convergence of high-order neural network under different parameter settings. Due to the complexity of high-order networks, the above researches mainly focus on the second-order continuous high-order Hopfield network. The reference Cheung and Lee (1993) proves the stability of a special class of high-order discrete Hopfield neural network.

Although when compared with lower-order neural networks high-order networks have their own advantages, in practice they are seldom applied. For example, one interesting thing we found is that Hopfield Neural Network (HNN) has been widely used to solve the combinatorial optimization problem since it was proposed in the nineteen-eighties. For example, Hopfield firstly used it to solve the traveling salesman problem (Hopfield & Tank, 1985); since then, it has been used to solve different kinds of combinatorial optimization problems, such as map coloring (Galan-Marin, 2007), maximum cut problems (Wang, 2007), bipartite subgraph problems, (Wang & Tang, 2004), crossbar switch problems (Thangavel & Gladis, 2007), and the N queens problem. However, high order Hopfield networks as a variant of HNN have never been tried to solve combinatorial optimization problems. This is because constructing high order energy functions for optimization problems that satisfy the stability criteria of HHNNs is very difficult. In this chapter, we study how to use HHNN to solve combinatorial optimization problems. We mainly focus on two problems, one is how to construct high order energy functions and high order network topological structure for combinatorial optimization problems, and the other is using the high order network, instead of the first order HNN, to solve problems. They are the research motivations of this chapter.

The rest of the chapter includes the following parts. Section 2 introduces High-order Discrete Hopfield Neural Networks (HDHNN). In section 3, we propose the network construction method for the n queens problem and compare its performance with the first order HNN. In this section,

we also discuss the strategy to escape from local minimum. The last section offers the conclusion of this chapter.

2. HIGH-ORDER DISCRETE HOPFIELD NETWORK

In general, there are two types of Hopfield neural network, Continuous Hopfield Neural Network (CHNN) and Discrete Hopfield Neural Network (DHNN). In this chapter, we focus on DHNN. A DHNN with n neurons can be uniquely represented by an n × n real matrix $W = (w_{ij})_{n \times n}$ and an n-dimensional column vector $H = (h_1, h_2, ..., h_n)^T$. We denote a DHNN as $N = (W, H)$. DHNN working in serial mode can be described as follows:

Let $X(t) = (x_1, ..., x_n)^T$ be the network state vector at time t, of which $x_i \in \{-1, 1\}$. $X(t+1) = T(W, H, X(t))$, T is an operator as shown in the formula (1).

$$x_i(t+1) = \begin{cases} \text{sgn}(\sum_{j=1}^{n} w_{ij} x_j(t) - h_i), i \in \tau(t) \\ x_i(t), i \notin \tau(t) \end{cases}$$

$$(1)$$

where $\tau(t) \in \{1, 2, ..., n\}$. Equation (2) is the standard energy function of the network.

$$E(X) = -\frac{1}{2} X^T W X - X^T H \qquad (2)$$

If the connection weight matrix is symmetric and its diagonal elements are non-negative, DHNN working in a serial mode converges to a stable state corresponding to a local minimum of the Hopfield energy function. From (2) we can see that DHNN can only solve optimization problems whose energy functions can be expressed by a quadratic polynomial. If we want to use high order network to solve optimization problems, we need to construct high order energy functions for these problems. Equation (3) is the energy function of high-order discrete Hopfield network (Cheng, 1993). Equation (4) is the state-evolving function of neurons (Cheng, 1993).

$$E = -\frac{1}{n}\sum_{i_1}\sum_{i_2}\cdots\sum_{i_n} w_{i_1 i_2 \ldots i_n} x_{i_1} x_{i_2} \cdots x_{i_n}$$

$$-\frac{1}{n-1}\sum_{i_1}\sum_{i_2}\cdots\sum_{i_{n-1}} w_{i_1 i_2 \ldots i_{n-1}} x_{i_1} x_{i_2} \cdots x_{i_{n-1}}$$

$$-\ldots-\frac{1}{2}\sum_{i_1}\sum_{i_2} w_{i_1 i_2} x_{i_1} x_{i_2} - \sum_{i_1} I_{i_1} x_{i_1}$$

$$(3)$$

$$x_i(t+1) = f_h\left(-\frac{\partial E}{\partial x_i(t)}\right) \qquad (4)$$

The connection weight of high-order DHNN is also symmetrical, that is, the value of $w_{i_1 i_2 \ldots i_n}$ is independent of the ordering of the index, for example, $w_{123} = w_{132} = w_{213}\ldots$. As the energy function is a very complicated high-order polynomial, even if the weights are symmetrical, the convergence cannot be guaranteed. The reference Cheng (1993) proves the stability of a special class of high-order DHNN operating in a serial mode when $x_i^k = x_i$ is held. In general $f_h(y)$ is a binary function. If $y \leq 0$, $f_h(y) = 0$, otherwise $f_h(y) = 1$.

3. HIGH ORDER NETWORK MODELING COMBINATORIAL OPTIMIZATION PROBLEM

In this section, we discuss how to use high order network to solve combinatorial optimization problem. The content in this section is mainly based on our research work proposed in Ding (2010). Here we give a more deep analysis about the high order network modeling method.

3.1. First Order and High Order Networks

In the first order Hopfield network, the input of a neuron X_i is the weighted sum of the outputs from other neurons. Figure 1 shows the input of a neuron X_i in the first order Hopfield network. Let x_i denote the output of X_i. The input of a neuron can be described as Equation (5). In a high order network, the input of a neuron X_i is not a linear combination of the outputs of other neurons, and it is the product of the outputs of other neurons. Figure 2 gives a demonstration of the input of a high order neuron, and the input of the high order neuron X_i is defined as Equation (6). In Figure 2 denotes a multiplier. w_{ijk} and $w_{il\ldots k}$ are high order

Figure 1. Inputs of neuron for first order neural network

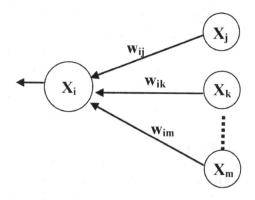

Figure 2. Inputs of neuron for high order network

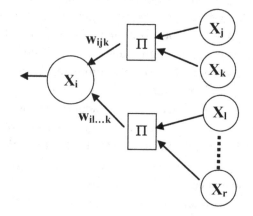

weighs. The first number in the subscript of the high order weight represents the index of a receiving neuron and other subscripts represent the indexes of outputting neurons. The input of each neuron is a high order multinomial of the output of other neurons; therefore, the energy function of the high order network is a high order multinomial shown as Equation (3). If we want to use high order network to model combinatorial optimization problem, the first thing we need to do is construct the high order energy functions for combinatorial optimization problems. In this chapter, we use a classical combinatorial optimization problem, n queens problem, as a sample to illustrate how to construct high order energy function and neural network topological structure.

$$input_{X_i} = w_{ij}x_j + w_{ik}x_k + ... + w_{im}x_m \qquad (5)$$

$$input_{X_i} = w_{ijk}x_jx_k + w_{il...r}x_l...x_r \qquad (6)$$

3.2. High Order Network Modeling N Queens Problem

3.2.1. N Queens Problem Description

N Queen's problem is that one has to place n chess queens on a square chessboard composed of n rows and n columns (n by n board) in such a way that they do not attack each other. In other words, any two different queens are not in the same line, not in the same row, and not in the same diagonal. Traditional Hopfield network and its major variants (Mafidziuk, 1995; Munehisa, Kobayashi, and Yamazakim, 2001; Noguchi & Pham, 2006) have been used to solve this problem, and they are the first order networks.

For the convenience of discussion, we make the following definitions. Let neuron $X_{i,j}$ corresponds the square of a board at i-th row and j-th column (0≤i,j<N). $x_{i,j}$ is the output of the neuron $X_{i,j}$, and $x_{i,j}$=1 represents a queen is placed at the square at i-th row and j-th column, otherwise $x_{i,j}$ = 0.

In the first order network (Mafidziuk, 1995; Munehisa, Kobayashi, & Yamazakim, 2001; Noguchi & Pham, 2006), different energy functions have been presented. Though these energy functions have different forms, there is no essential difference between them. In this chapter, we choose the energy function defined in (8). This energy function is shown as (7). In (7) the first term guarantees that only one queen is existed in each column. This means the first term have the minimum value, 0, if and only if one queen is placed in each column. In the same manner, the second term guarantees only one queen is placed in each row. The third and fourth terms guarantee at most one queen is placed in each diagonal line. The parameters A_1, A_2, B_1, and B_2 are constants. In this chapter we set them to one.

$$E = \frac{A_1}{2}\sum_{i=1}^{N}(\sum_{j=1}^{N}x_{ij}-1)^2 + \frac{A_2}{2}\sum_{j=1}^{N}(\sum_{i=1}^{N}x_{ij}-1)^2 +$$
$$\frac{B_1}{2}\sum_{i=1}^{N}\sum_{j=1}^{N}x_{ij}\sum_{k\neq0,1\leq i+k,j+k\leq N}x_{i+k,j+k} +$$
$$\frac{B_2}{2}\sum_{i=1}^{N}\sum_{j=1}^{N}x_{ij}\sum_{k\neq0,1\leq i+k,j-k\leq N}x_{i+k,j-k}$$
$$(7)$$

We take four queens problem as an example to illustrate Equation (7). Four queens problem is shown as Figure 3. According to Equation (7), the energy for the first line is $(x_{0,0} + x_{0,1} + x_{0,2} + x_{0,3} -1)^2$. We can see that if and only if one queen is placed in the first line, the energy for the first line is zero, and in any other cases, the energy for

Figure 3. Queens problem

$x_{0,0}$	$x_{0,1}$	$x_{0,2}$	$x_{0,3}$
$x_{1,0}$	$x_{1,1}$	$x_{1,2}$	$x_{1,3}$
$x_{2,0}$	$x_{2,1}$	$x_{2,2}$	$x_{2,3}$
$x_{3,0}$	$x_{3,1}$	$x_{3,2}$	$x_{3,3}$

the first line is greater than zero. The energy for the diagonal line (shown in gray color in Figure 3) is $x_{1,0}(x_{2,1}+x_{3,2})+x_{2,1}x_{3,2}$. We can see that if and only if no more than one queen is placed on the diagonal line, the energy for this diagonal line is zero, otherwise the energy is greater than zero. In the same way, we can construct the energy function for all the other rows, columns, and diagonal lines. Our target is to find all x_{ij} that satisfy the value of the energy function is zero.

3.2.2. Constructing the High Order Energy Function for n Queens Problem

The energy function for the first order Hopfield network is a quadratic polynomial. Only if we can find an energy function, which is a high order (at least cubic) polynomial, can we construct a high order network. Firstly, we construct the high order energy function for each row. We also take the four queens problem as an example. We construct the energy function for the first row. According the constrains of the problem, there should be a queen in each row. We construct the high order polynomial (8). We can see the polynomial (8) equals zero if and only if at least one queen is placed on the row. However, the polynomial (8) only satisfies one constrain of n queens problem for each row, it does not guarantee that only one queen is placed on the row. To address this problem, we construct another polynomial shown as (9). This polynomial consists of all products of any two variables in the first row. The polynomial (9) equals zero if and only if at most one queen is placed on the first row. Combining form (8) and form (9), we get the energy function for the first row. It guarantees that only one queen is placed on the first row when the energy function for the first row is zero.

In this same way, we can construct the energy function for other rows and columns. In high order network, the energy function for each diagonal line has the same form as the energy function in the first order network. For example, in the high order energy function the energy function for the diagonal line (shown in gray color in Figure 3) is $x_{1,0}(x_{2,1}+x_{3,2})+x_{2,1}x_{3,2}$ too, which consists of all products of any two variables in the same diagonal line.

Based on the above analysis, we construct the high order energy function for n queens problem as follows. The energy function for i-th row is represented as (10). In (5) the first item is zero if more than one queen are placed in i-th row; the second item is zero if at most one queen is placed in i-th row. Equation (10) is zero if and only if only one queen is placed in i-th row. In (10) the first item is a high order item. The energy function for all rows is represented as (11). Equation (11) equals zero if and only if only one queen is placed in each row.

We can construct the energy functions for columns and diagonals by the same way. Equation (12) defines the energy function for all columns; it is zero if and only if only one queen is placed in each column. Equation (13) defines the energy function for all diagonals from upper left to lower right; it is zero if and only if at most one queen is placed in each diagonal line from upper left to lower right. Equation (14) gives the energy function for all diagonals from upper right to lower left; it is zero if and only if at most one queen is placed in each diagonal from upper right to lower left. The Equation (15) gives the energy function for N- Queens problem, which is the sum of all above energy functions. Our target is to find all $x_{i,j}$ which make the Equation equal to zero.

$$(1-x_{0,0})(1-x_{0,1})(1-x_{0,2})(1-x_{0,3}) \qquad (8)$$

$$x_{0,0}(x_{0,1}+x_{0,2}+x_{0,3})+x_{0,1}(x_{0,2}+x_{0,3})+x_{0,2}x_{0,3} \qquad (9)$$

$$\prod_{j=0}^{N-1}(1-x_{i,j}) + \sum_{j=0}^{N-1}x_{i,j}\sum_{k=j+1}^{N-1}x_{i,k} \qquad (10)$$

$$E_1 = \sum_{i=0}^{N-1} (\prod_{j=0}^{N-1} (1 - x_{i,j})) + \sum_{i=0}^{N-1} \sum_{j=0}^{N-1} x_{i,j} \sum_{k=j+1}^{N-1} x_{i,k} \tag{11}$$

$$E_2 = \sum_{j=0}^{N-1} (\prod_{i=0}^{N-1} (1 - x_{i,j})) + \sum_{j=0}^{N-1} \sum_{i=0}^{N-1} x_{i,j} \sum_{k=i+1}^{N-1} x_{k,j} \tag{12}$$

$$E_3 = \sum_{j=0}^{N-2} \sum_{i=0}^{N-1-j} x_{i,i+j} \sum_{k=i+1}^{N-1-j} x_{k,k+j} + \\ \sum_{j=1}^{N-2} \sum_{i=j}^{N-1} x_{i,i-j} \sum_{k=i+1}^{N-1} x_{k,k-j} \tag{13}$$

$$E_4 = \sum_{j=1}^{N-1} \sum_{i=0}^{j} x_{i,j-i} \sum_{k=i+1}^{j} x_{k,j-k} + \\ \sum_{j=1}^{N-2} \sum_{i=j}^{N-1} x_{i,N-1+j-i} \sum_{k=i+1}^{N-1} x_{k,N-1+j-k} \tag{14}$$

$$E = E_1 + E_2 + E_3 + E_4 \tag{15}$$

Next, we need to prove that high order network defined by this high order energy function is convergent. We expand (15) and simplify it by combing like terms, notice in the simplified polynomial the exponent of each variable $x_{i,j}$ is 1. For any item $C x_{i_1 j_1} x_{i_2 j_2} \ldots x_{i_n j_n}$, we transform it into $\frac{-1}{n} (-n) C x_{i_1 j_1} x_{i_2 j_2} \ldots x_{i_n j_n}$, n is the number of variables in the term. Therefore, the energy function (15) has the same form as (3). $x_{i,j}$ satisfies $x_{i,j}^k = x_{i,j}$. This proves that (15) is a high order energy function of DHHNNs. $-nC$ is the value of one of high order weights among neurons X_{i_1,j_1}, ..., X_{i_n,j_n}. In this chapter a high order weight $w_{i_1 j_1, i_2 j_2, \ldots i_n j_n}$ represents the weight from neurons X_{i_2,j_2}, ..., X_{i_n,j_n} to X_{i_1,j_1}. The DHHNN constructed according to (15) and working in a serial mode converges to a stable point of the energy function. In fact, we need not expand (15)

to construct the high order network, and we can directly use (15) to construct the neural network. We will discuss it in the next section.

3.2.3. Constructing High Order Hopfield Neural Network

In order to construct the high order network we can expand the high order energy function and translate it into the form (3) to obtain connection weights. This is a very complex work when the number of neurons is large. In this section, we represent the topological structure of the network in another way.

In the high order energy function E each variable $x_{i,j}$ has two forms, one is $x_{i,j}$, the other is $1-x_{i,j}$. The neurons in DHHNN are binary neurons; their threshold function is a binary function. Therefore, we expand the structure of neurons as follows: each neuron has two outputs, one is $x_{i,j}$ named the positive output, and the other is $1-x_{i,j}$ named the negative output. The state-evolving function of the expanded neurons is still the same as (4). According to (4), the input of a neuron $X_{i,j}$ is the sum of the following six parts:

1. The product of the negative outputs of all neurons that are in the same row as $X_{i,j}$;
2. The negative of the sum of the positive outputs of all neurons that are in the same row as $X_{i,j}$;
3. The product of the negative outputs of all neurons that are in the same column as $X_{i,j}$;
4. The negative of the sum of the positive outputs of all neurons that are in the same column as $X_{i,j}$;
5. The negative of the sum of the positive outputs of all neurons that are in the same diagonal from upper left to lower right as $X_{i,j}$;
6. The negative of the sum of the positive outputs of all neurons that are in the same diagonal from upper right to lower left as $X_{i,j}$;

Figure 4. Neural network topology for n queen's problem

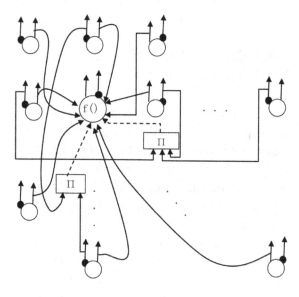

Among them, the first part and the third part represent high order weights.

The topological structure of n queens problem is shown in Figure 4. In Figure 4, the neural network is shown as a NxN neuron matrix corresponding to a NxN chessboard. Each neuron has two outputs, positive output and negative output (shown as black dot). Π is a multiplier. Figure 1 shows the inputs of neuron $X_{1,1}$;. $X_{1,1}$ has two high order weights represented by the dot line, and their

weight value is 1. From Figure 1, we can see that the high order network is not a fully connected network, the number of high-order connections is $2N^2$, the number of one order connections is smaller than $4(N-1)N^2$. The connection explosion problem that connections increase exponentially with the increase of neurons in a high order network does not exist. Each neuron has two kinds of output, 0 or 1; therefore, the output of the multiplier is 0 or 1. This shows the existence of high order weights do not affect the performance of the network.

The neural computing algorithm of the high order network working in serial mode is decried in Algorithm 1.

In Algorithm 1, the states of neurons are updated one by one. If all neurons' states are not changed, the network traps into local minimum. In some case, all neurons are assigned several states repeatedly, this also indicates the network traps into local minimum, the detection procedure is ignored in Algorithm 1.

3.2.4. Strategy for Escaping from Local Minim

High order Hopfield network is a gradient descent network. It is inevitably for the network to trap into local minimum. Usually we use two types of methods to help the network to escape from local

Algorithm 1. Neural computing algorithm

$t = 0$;
randomly initialize $x_{i,j}(0)$ to 1 or 0($i, j = 0, 1, ... N-1$)
For $i = 0$ to $N-1$
For $j = 0$ to $N-1$
{ $u_{ij}(t) = -\partial E / \partial x_{ij}(t)$
$x_{ij}(t+1) = f_h(u_{ij}(t))$
let all $x_{mn}(t+1) = x_{mn}(t)$, $(m \neq i$ or $n \neq j)$
$t = t + 1$;
}
if all $x_{ij}(t) = x_{ij}(t-1)$
return all $x_{ij}(t)$
else goto 3

Figure 5. The disturbance procedure of eight queens problem

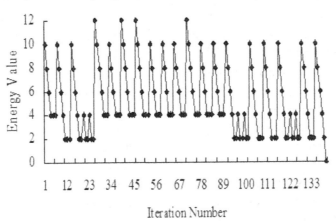

minima: deterministic approach and stochastic approach. The deterministic approaches include the "rock and roll" perturbation method (Lo, 1992), the "divide and conquer" method (Foo & Szu, 1989), and neurons' competitive learning method (Amartur, Piraino, & Takefuji, 1992). Stochastic approaches include genetic algorithm (Salcedo-Sanz & Yao, 2004), annealing theory (Wang, Li, Tian, & Fu, 2004), particle swarm optimization (Wang, 2007), ant colony algorithm (Li, 2008), and so on. In theory, stochastic approaches can reach the global optimum; however, in practice, it is very difficult to achieve. Stochastic approaches are time consuming and the most difficult is we cannot determine the termination conditions. Presently, the genetic algorithm is widely used. The high-order gradient descent network can use all the above-mentioned optimization strategies to escape from local minimum.

3.2.5. DHHNN for Eight Queens Problem

We use eight queens problem as an example to demonstrate the iteration procedure of the high order network. Firstly, we randomly initialize the state of each neuron to be 1 or 0. If the network traps into a local minimum, three neurons are randomly selected, and their states are randomly

modified. We call this operation a disturbance. The iteration procedure is shown in Figure 5. From Figure 5, we can see that at the beginning the value of energy function decreased quickly; after a few iterations, the energy value keeps at a small constant which indicates the network trapped into local minimum; under this situation, a disturbance was generated to modify the states of neurons, and the network escaped from local minimum and began a new iteration procedure. In this experiment, the network trapped in a local minimum 18 times, and it found a solution by iterating 130 times.

3.2.6. Performance Evaluation of High Order Network

In order to evaluate the performance of high order network, we compare it with a traditional binary Hopfield neural network (Hopfield, 1982). Both the networks use the same threshold functions, which is defined in Equation (1).

The energy function used in the first order network is defined in Equation (7). Our target is to compare the performances of the two networks caused by the difference of their topological structures (the high order network and the first order network); therefore, we do not use any global optimization strategies discussed in section

3.5. The binary HNN and the DHHNN use the simplest strategy to escape from local minimum. They use the following method to escape from local minimum: randomly select some variables x_{ij} and randomly change their states to be 1 or 0, and then repeat the iteration process. This procedure is called a disturbance. In order to keep the energy value not to be changed greatly, every time only several variables are selected and their states are changed.

We simulated different N-Queens problems, and N (number of queens) ranges from 8 to 100. For the convenience of comparison, each simulation was terminated until a solution was found, or the number of disturbance exceeded the maximum number of disturbance. The following conditions are set in each simulation for both networks: if N (number of queens) is smaller than 50, the maximum number of disturbances is 3500; if N is greater than 50, the maximum number of disturbances is 7000; a gradient descent search is terminated if the energy value equals zero, or keeps a constant. If the energy value equals zero, the simulation is stopped at once. We call the simulation a convergent simulation. If the energy is still greater than zero after the number of disturbances exceeds the maximum value, the simulation is stopped too, and we call this simulation not convergent.

Both networks operate in a serial mode. In an iteration, only one neuron is selected, and its state is updated. In the initializing procedure, variables are randomly set to be 0 or 1. To keep the energy at a low level in a disturbance, only a small percent of variables are randomly selected, and their values are changed. In our case, we set it to 2%. For each N we simulated 100 times. The hardware and software we used are: Windows XP, Intel CPU Pentium 4 3.0GHz.

The performance of the two networks is evaluated by the following 3 criteria:

- Convergence rate: the ratio of the number of convergent simulations to the total number of simulations

- Average iteration number: the ratio of the sum of number of iterations of all simulations to the total number of simulations
- Average time cost: the ratio of the sum of time cost of all simulations to the total number of simulations

As can be seen from Table 1 that, for the N Queens problems, the performance of the high order network is better than that of the first order network, especially for a larger N the improvement of performance is significant. The reason is that the high order network structure increases the convergence speed of the energy function. Figure 6 gives gradient descent procedures of energy functions for both networks to solve eight queens problem. We can see the energy value of the high order network decreased very quickly. The energy of the first order network declined slowly, especially at some stages its energy jumped back and from among certain values, we call such stages as oscillation stages. Compared with the first order network we found in most time the energy value of the high order network decreased monotonously, only when it trapped in local minimum its energy value maintained at a constant or jumped back and from among some values as shown in Figure 6. For the high order network, the oscillation stages seldom happed during the gradient descent procedure. Therefore, the first order network spent more time for each gradient descent search. Figure 6 only shows one gradient descent procedure for the high order network. In this procedure its energy did not become zero. That means it trapped into a local minimum. By adding disturbances, it can escape from local minimum.

3.3. High Order Network Modeling Crossbar Switch Problem

In the same way, we use high order network to solve crossbar switch problem which is a combinatorial optimization problem very similar with N Queen's problem.

Table 1. Performance comparison for n queens problem

N Queens	Converge Rate(%)		Avg. Iteration Num		Avg. Time(S)	
	High Order	First Order	High Order	First Order	High Order	First Order
8	100	100	130	166	0.01	0.01
10	100	100	280	479	0.02	0.03
16	100	100	500	1037	0.08	0.11
20	100	100	801	1724	0.19	0.23
30	100	100	1469	4041	0.81	1.44
32	100	100	1831	4547	1.16	1.68
40	100	100	2395	7961	2.43	5.1
48	100	100	3149	12604	5.48	12.97
50	100	100	3935	16395	5.68	18.97
60	100	100	6409	28177	14.52	58.43
64	100	100	6972	29431	23.47	75.31
70	100	100	9370	36665	40.51	122.71
80	100	100	12295	44911	67.68	220.64
90	100	100	14909	56317	87.88	389.68
100	100	100	16684	72995	119.21	661.69

Figure 6. Comparison of energy values

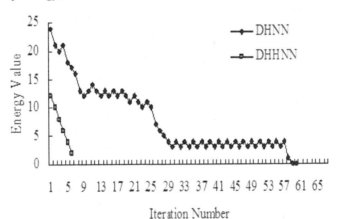

A crossbar switch is a switch connecting a set of N inputs and N outputs where each input can be connected to each output, as shown in Figure 7. When there is a request from the input to output to be satisfied, the Crosspoint switch will be closed. The constraints for the problem are as follows: in each input line only one output line can be connected; in each output line only one input line can be connected. That is to say, with two or more requests coming simultaneously for the same output line, only one request can be satisfied, and the other requests will be blocked.

A NxN crossbar switch can be represented by an NxN binary request matrix R. Rows and columns

Figure 7. NxN crossbar switch

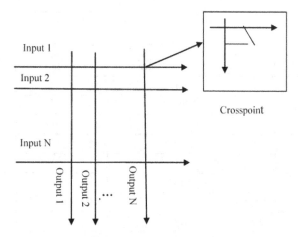

of the matrix R correspond to the inputs set and outputs set, respectively. Each element in the matrix R has exactly two values: 0 and 1. r_{ij}=1 means there is a request from the ith input line to the jth output line; r_{ij}=0 expresses there is no request. The state of the switch can be represent by an NxN binary configuration matrix C, where c_{ij}=1 indicates that the request from the ith input line to the jth output line is satisfied. c_{ij}=0 indicates that the request is discarded. For proper operations of the switch, there should be at most one request being satisfied in each row and each column. The throughput of the switch is optimal when the matrix C, which is a subset of the matrix R, contains at most a "1" in each row/column, and has a maximum overlap with R.

Traditional Hopfield network (DHNN) has been applied to solve this problem, usually the energy function for this problem is defined as Equation (16). It is a quadratic polynomial.

$$E = \frac{A}{2}\sum_{i=1}^{N}(\sum_{k=1}^{N}c_{ik}-1)^2 + \frac{B}{2}\sum_{j=1}^{N}(\sum_{k=1}^{N}c_{kj}-1)^2$$

(16)

In Equation (16) c_{ij} is the output of neuron ij. The first term is zero, if and only if there is no more than one request being satisfied in each row.

The second term is zero, if and only if there is no more than one request being satisfied in each column. The input u_{ij} of neuron ij is derived by the partial derivative of the energy function with respect to the output of neuron ij, u_{ij} is shown as Equation (17).

$$u_{ij} = -A(\sum_{k=1}^{N}c_{ik}-1) - B(\sum_{k=1}^{N}c_{kj}-1)$$

(17)

From (16) we can see that DHNN can only handle optimization problems whose energy functions can be expressed by a quadratic polynomial, if we want to deal with high-order problems, DHNN should be extend to high-order DHNN.

The state of a crossbar switch can be represented by a NxN binary configuration matrix C. c_{ij}=1 indicates that the request from ith input line to the jth output line is satisfied. c_{ij}=0 indicates that the request is discarded. Each c_{ij} is corresponding to r_{ij} in R. In crossbar problem we need to only consider the c_{ij} whose corresponding r_{ij} is 1 (all the other c_{ij} equals 0). For expression convenience, all of c_{ij} appear in the following equations; however, only c_{ij} whose corresponding r_{ij} is 1 is a variable, and all the other c_{ij} are constants whose value is 0. The constraint for the ith row is represented as form (18). Equation (18) equals zero, if and only if there is only one request be satisfied in ith row. In (18) the first term is a high order term. The constraint for all rows is represented as (19). Equation (19) equals zero, if and only if there is only one request be satisfied in each row. In the same way, the column constraints for crossbar switch problem can be constructed. Equation (20) is the energy function for all columns. It equals zero if and only if there is only one request satisfied in each column. The energy function for crossbar switch problem is the sum of (19) and (20), which is shown in Equation (21). When Equation (21) takes the minimum value 0, all c_{ij} are the solution of the problem.

Algorithm 2. Neural computing algorithm working in serial mode

Step 1: $t = 0$
Step 2: initialize all c_{ij} (0) to 1 for r_{ij} =1, and all c_{ij} (0) to 0 for r_{ij} =0 ($i, j = 0, 1, ... N - 1$)
Step 3: For $i = 0$ to $N - 1$
For $j = 0$ to $N - 1$ {
If r_{ij} =0 continue;
$d_{ij}(t) = -\partial E / \partial c_{ij}(t)$
$c_{ij}(t + 1) = f_h(d_{ij}(t))$
let all $c_{mn}(t + 1) = c_{mn}(t), \quad (m \neq i$ or $n \neq j)$
   $t = t + 1$ }
Step 4: if all $c_{ij}(t) = c_{ij}(t - 1)$ return all $c_{ij}(t)$ else goto step 3

$$\prod_{j=0}^{N-1}(1 - c_{ij}) + \sum_{j=0}^{N-2} c_{ij} \sum_{k=j+1}^{N-1} c_{ik} = 0 \qquad (18)$$

$$E_1 = \sum_{i=0}^{N-1} (\prod_{j=0}^{N-1}(1 - c_{ij})) + \sum_{i=0}^{N-1} \sum_{j=0}^{N-2} c_{ij} \sum_{k=j+1}^{N-1} c_{ik} \qquad (19)$$

$$E_2 = \sum_{j=0}^{N-1} (\prod_{i=0}^{N-1}(1 - c_{ij})) + \sum_{j=0}^{N-1} \sum_{i=0}^{N-2} c_{ij} \sum_{k=i+1}^{N-1} c_{kj} \qquad (20)$$

$$E = E_1 + E_2 \qquad (21)$$

The neural computing algorithm working in serial mode is shown in Algorithm 2.

In Algorithm 2, $f_h(y)$ is a hysteretic threshold function. If $y<0$, then $f_h(y)=0$; if $y>0$, then $f_h(y)=1$; when $y=0$, $f_h(y)$ remains unchanged (in fact, this function can be seen as a special case of the sig-moid function). E is the energy function defined in Equation (6). E is a polynomial function with respect to c_{ij}; therefore, it is easy to calculate the derivative term d_{ij}. The description of the high order energy function and the convergence of the high order network are discussed in detail in Xia, Tang, Li, and Wang (2005) and Cheung (1993).

In the experiments, the size N ranges from 20 to 100. For each crossbar switch problem, we simulated it 100 times, and in each simulation, the request matrix is randomly initialized. Each simulation is terminated if a solution is found or the iteration step exceeds the maximum iteration step 100. In this chapter, when all neurons are updated once, we call it an iteration step. In order to test the performance of high order network, we compare it with DHNN (Xia, Tang, Li, and Wang, 2005). The energy function of DHNN is defined as (16). The parameters A and B are set to 1.

Table 2. performance comparison for crossbar problem

N	Avg. Converge Rate (%)		Avg. Steps	
	High Order	**DHNN**	**High Order**	**DHNN**
20	100	100	4.02	13.54
30	100	100	3.99	17.42
50	100	100	3.72	29.29
80	100	100	3.49	45.43
100	100	100	3.72	57.89

From Table 2, we can see that all the three neural networks have 100% convergence rate. However, the performance of high order network is much better than DHNN. On average, high order network needs fewer steps than other networks to get a solution. For a larger N the improvement of the performance is significant. It is because the high order network structure accelerates the convergence speed of the energy function. Furthermore, we can see that the number of steps to get a solution for high order network is almost independent of the size of crossbar switches, while the iteration steps of DHNN increases greatly with the increase of the size of the problem.

4. SUMMARY

In this chapter, we discuss how to use high order networks to solve combinatorial optimization problems. We take N queens problem and crossbar switch problem as examples to illustrate the construction method for the high order energy function and the topological structure of the high order network. Although only two examples are analyzed in this chapter, we can extend this method to solve other combinatorial optimization problems. In the feature, we try to solve more classical combinatorial optimization problems, such as traveling salesman problem, map coloring. In theory if we can find a high order energy function for any combinational optimization problem, which has the same form as (3), we can solve this problem using high order network. The experimental results show higher order network has a quicker convergence speed than the first order network. It is valuable to construct high order network structures to solve practical problems.

REFERENCES

Amartur, S. C., Piraino, D., & Takefuji, Y. (1992). Optimization neural networks for the segmentation of magnetic resonance images. *IEEE Transactions on Medical Imaging, 11*(2), 215–220. doi:10.1109/42.141645

Cheung, K.-W., & Lee, T. (1993). On the convergence of neural network for higher order programming. In *Proceedings of IJCNN*, (vol 2), (pp. 1507—1511). IJCNN.

Ding, Y. (2010). A high order neural network to solve n-queens problem. In *Proceedings of IJCNN*, (pp. 1-6). IJCNN.

Foo, Y. P. S., & Szu, H. (1989). Solving large-scale optimization problems by divide-and-conquer neural networks. In *Proceedings of IJCNN*, (vol 1), (pp. 507—511). IJCNN.

Galán-Marín, G. (2007). A study into the improvement of binary hopfield networks for map coloring. *Lecture Notes in Computer Science, 4432*, 98–106. doi:10.1007/978-3-540-71629-7_12

Gopalsamy, K. (2007). Learning dynamics in second order networks. *Nonlinear Analysis Real World Applications, 8*(9), 688–698. doi:10.1016/j.nonrwa.2006.02.007

Hopfield, J. J. (1982). Neural networks and physical systems with emergent collective computational abilities. *Proceedings of the National Academy of Sciences of the United States of America, 79*(8), 2554–2558. doi:10.1073/pnas.79.8.2554

Hopfield, J. J., & Tank, D. W. (1985). Neural computation of decisions in optimization problems. *Biological Cybernetics, 52*(1), 141–152.

Li, Y. M. (2008). An improvement to ant colony optimization heuristic. *Lecture Notes in Computer Science, 5263*, 816–825. doi:10.1007/978-3-540-87732-5_90

Lo, J. T.-H. (1992). A new approach to global optimization and its applications to neural networks. *Neural Networks*, *2*(5), 367–373.

Mafidziuk, J. (1995). Solving the n-queens problem with a binary Hopfield-type network. *Biological Cybernetics*, *72*(1), 439–445. doi:10.1007/BF00201419

Munehisa, T., Kobayashi, M., & Yamazaki, H. (2001). Cooperative updating in the Hopfield model. *IEEE Transactions on Neural Networks*, *12*(5), 1243–1251. doi:10.1109/72.950153

Noguchi, W., & Pham, C.-K. (2006). A proposal to solve n-queens problems using maximum neuron model with a modified hill-climbing term. In *Proceedings of IJCNN*, (pp. 2679—2683). IJCNN.

Ou, C. (2008). Anti-periodic solutions for high-order Hopfield neural networks. *Computers & Mathematics with Applications (Oxford, England)*, *56*(3), 1838–1844. doi:10.1016/j.camwa.2008.04.029

Salcedo-Sanz, S., & Yao, X. (2004). A hybrid Hopfield network-genetic algorithm approach for the terminal assignment problem. *IEEE Transactions on Systems, Man, and Cybernetics*, *34*(6), 2343–2353. doi:10.1109/TSMCB.2004.836471

Thangavel, P., & Gladis, D. (2007). Hopfield hysteretic Hopfield network with dynamic tunneling for crossbar switch and N-queens problem. *Neurocomputing*, *70*, 2544–2551. doi:10.1016/j.neucom.2006.06.006

Wang, J. (2007). A memetic algorithm with genetic particle swarm optimization and neural network for maximum cut problems. *Lecture Notes in Computer Science*, *4688*, 297–306. doi:10.1007/978-3-540-74769-7_33

Wang, J., & Tang, Z. (2004). An improved optimal competitive Hopfield network for bipartite subgraph problems. *Neurocomputing*, *61*(5), 413–419. doi:10.1016/j.neucom.2004.03.012

Wang, L. P., Li, S., Tian, F. Y., & Fu, X. J. (2004). A noisy chaotic neural network for solving combinatorial optimization problems: Stochastic chaotic simulated annealing. *IEEE Transactions on Systems, Man, and Cybernetics. Part B, Cybernetics*, *34*(5), 2119–2125. doi:10.1109/TSMCB.2004.829778

Xia, G., Tang, Z., Li, Y., & Wang, J. (2005). A binary Hopfield neural network with hysteresis for large crossbar packet-switches. *Neurocomputing*, *67*, 417–425. doi:10.1016/j.neucom.2004.09.004

Xu, B., Liu, X., & Teoc, K. L. (2009). Global exponential stability of impulsive high-order Hopfield type neural networks with delays. *Computers & Mathematics with Applications (Oxford, England)*, *57*(3), 1959–1967. doi:10.1016/j.camwa.2008.10.001

Yi, X., Shao, J., & Yu, Y. (2008). Global exponential stability of impulsive high-order Hopfield type neural networks with delays. *Journal of Computational and Applied Mathematics*, *219*(3), 216–222. doi:10.1016/j.cam.2007.07.011

Chapter 4
Needle Insertion Force Modeling using Genetic Programming Polynomial Higher Order Neural Network

Mehdi Fallahnezhad
Norwegian University of Science and Technology (NTNU), Norway

Hashem Yousefi
Amirkabir University of Technology (Tehran Polytechnic), Iran

ABSTRACT

Precise insertion of a medical needle as an end-effecter of a robotic or computer-aided system into biological tissue is an important issue and should be considered in different operations, such as brain biopsy, prostate brachytherapy, and percutaneous therapies. Proper understanding of the whole procedure leads to a better performance by an operator or system. In this chapter, the authors use a 0.98 mm diameter needle with a real-time recording of force, displacement, and velocity of needle through biological tissue during in-vitro insertions. Using constant velocity experiments from 5 mm/min up to 300 mm/min, the data set for the force-displacement graph of insertion was gathered. Tissue deformation with a small puncture and a constant velocity penetration are the two first phases in the needle insertion process. Direct effects of different parameters and their correlations during the process is being modeled using a polynomial neural network. The authors develop different networks in 2nd and 3rd order to model the two first phases of insertion separately. Modeling accuracies were 98% and 86% in phase 1 and 2, respectively.

1. INTRODUCTION

Most of minimal invasive devices, computer-assisted or robotic surgery systems incorporate a needle insertion process (e.g. stereotactic brain biopsy, laparoscopy, radioactive seed-implanta-

tion, etc.). In such operations, accurate needle insertion process provides efficient access to the target area through biological tissues. In needle steering procedures, needle usually faces a soft and non-homogenous tissue, which causes more complexity of the process (Abolhassani, et al., 2007). In most applications, having a highly accurate process in both accessing the target and an

DOI: 10.4018/978-1-4666-2175-6.ch004

efficient insertion is essential. Some applications of percutaneous needle insertion can be observed in different works of prostate brachytherapy (Wei, 2004; Zivanovic & Davies, 2000), biopsy (Bishoff, 1998; Schwartz, 2005), and neurosurgery (Masamune, et al., 1995; Rizun, 2004). Some other applications such as deep needle insertion have been employed in the failure mechanism of ventricular tissue (Gasser, et al., 2009). In order to study tissue behavior, some researchers have used quasi-static needle insertion methods (see section 2 for detail). In addition, some other types of needle insertion such as rotational needle insertion, needle tapping, and fast needle insertions were also studied (Lagerburg, et al., 2006; Mahvash & Dupont, 2010).

Some phenomenological models were generated based on common needle insertion experiments, to describe the force-displacement graph of insertion as efficient set of terms including friction, inertia, viscous, deformation, and plasticity (Okamura, et al., 2004; Dimaio & Salcudean, 2003; TouficAzar & Hayward, 2008). In-vitro experimental data could be achieved by performing standard compression tests. Although many complexities and difficulties in modeling arise due to deformation and non-homogeneity in tissue structure, process parameters and model can be exploited from experimental data of such in-vitro experiments. Deformation and non-homogeneity in tissue structure may lead to many potential sources of forces applied to surgical tools, which leads to an imperfect prediction of force (Okamura, et al., 2004). To have better prediction of both force and needle tip position, interactive medical imaging is useful in robotic surgery simulation (Dimaio, et al., 2005; Alterovitz, et al., 2005; Mahvash & Dupont, 2010). In addition to the real-time imaging, Schwartz (2005) provides an accurate pre-operation modeling of soft biological tissues to simulate surgery process. Nonetheless, in these procedures some complications have

arisen because of misplacement of surgical tools. While, less misplacement of end-effecter during target finding would lead to more accurate needle insertion (Nath, 2000). Analysis of deep penetration of the tissue was performed in friction force identification (Dimaio & Salcudean, 2003). Under specified condition, harmonic velocity experiments were conducted for a definite tissue thickness to determine the amount of friction force (Okamura, et al., 2004).

In other applications such as drug delivery, imprecise placement of surgical tools may lead to false dosage distribution or may damage delicate structures. The authors discuss about four phases for the process of needle insertion (Abolhassani, et al., 2007; Barbe, et al., 2007; TouficAzar & Hayward, 2008; and Mahvash & Dupont, 2010). It includes deformation, steady state penetration, tissue relaxation, and needle extraction phases. There are 4 different types of needle insertion:

- General quasi-static needle insertion (Dimaio & Salcudean, 2003; TouficAzar & Hayward, 2008)
- Fast needle insertion (Mahvash & Dupont, 2009)
- Rotational needle insertion (Alterovitz, et al., 2005; Yousefi, et al., 2010)
- Needle insertion with tapping (Lagerburg, et al., 2006)

In must be mentioned that Mahvash and Dupont (2009) used to describe the phenomena of fast needle insertion, in which their gauge for pain was variation in force-displacement diagram.

Overall, numerical simulation for better modeling of forces has been extensively studied by different researchers in recent years, which can be used in surgical simulations and robot-assisted surgeries. Furthermore, accurate modeling could be used in determination of tissue deformation during contact with surgical tools.

1.1. Literature Review on Needle Insertion Force Modeling

Many numerical methods from Okamura (2004), Barbe (2007), Misra (2009), Maurel (1999), and Kobayashi (2010) were employed for needle insertion force modeling. One of the numerical modeling methods recently developed in the work of Barbe (2007). Barbe (2007) uses Recursive Least Square with Covariance Resetting (RLS-CR) for the determination of coefficients of a non-linear viscoelastic Kelvin-Voigt model. Okamura (2004) describes the behaviour of soft tissue based on nonlinear models using springs in various functions against the insertion of external devices. Crouch (2007) reports a dynamic effect, which is gradual reduction in force during the insertion process. The modeling of tissue levels in needle insertion from skin to bone has been used as a discrete element combination method by Kesavades (2005).

Okamura (2004) determined a model for friction force in needle insertion process. They performed a sinusoidal stimulation of the tissue during needle insertion. This leaded to a hysteresis effect on force distribution. Nevertheless, more simple methods can be used for identification of friction force (See section 2.1 for details).

Both Okamura (2004) and Barbe (2007) achieved their numerical results using in-vivo experiments in force modeling. In addition, a tensor-mass method had been applied for fast computation of non-linear and viscoelastic mechanical forces and deformation of biological soft tissue (Schwartz, 2005). In some other works, using phantom soft tissues, complex non-linear models dependent on tissue deformation were studied (Dimaio & Salcudean, 2003). Other non-linear elastic models were employed to investigate the effect of velocity variation and deformation-velocity correlation on penetration force (Mahvash & Dupont, 2010). While Alterovitz (2005) estimated the tissue deformation with a steerable bevel-tip needle insertion. In this chapter, a highly accurate method for force modeling during needle insertion into the soft biological tissues is proposed. This would be useful for robotic operation with needle as end-effecter or can be used in robotic surgery simulations.

1.2. A Multi-Criteria Higher Order Neural Network

In recent years, applied artificial intelligence, including various types of Artificial Neural Networks (ANNs), has been extensively used in various scientific branches. Appropriate pattern recognition can provide an efficient perception of a system with complex behaviour. In artificial neural networks, many different structures from simple feedforward neural networks (e.g. back-propagation networks) to more complex networks (e.g. recurrent networks, multi agent systems, etc.) have been proposed, whereas each of which may have superiority depending on the subject problem. Different limitations of traditional neural networks have motivated the researchers to develop more efficient intelligent systems, one of which can be addressed to Higher Order Neural Networks (HONNs). It has been demonstrated that HONNs provide some superiority including the resolution of the dilemma of choosing the number of neurons and layers of network, better fitting specifications, less time-consuming processes, and open-box specificity compared to traditional ANNs.

In this chapter, we simulate the process of a quasi-static needle insertion into soft biological tissue. In order to provide needle insertion force model, we use polynomial structures of higher order neural networks. For configuration of polynomial network, a genetic-based programming is applied. One of the advantages of genetic algorithms compared to other search methods is its intelligent specificity. Since one of our main objectives of simulation is acquiring an open-box model, we use a multi-objective fitness function such that not only regression values but also the model simplicity can simultaneously increase;

however, the simplicity of network may be sacrificed. Multi-Objective Problems (MOPs) are usually used to find a suitable fitness function using good associations of several objective functions which may lead to trade-off between different objectives. These trade-off problems are usually referred to "Pareto optimum." To implement a Multi-Objective Evolutionary Algorithm (MOEA), diverse methods can be used, some of which has been mentioned as: Multi-Objective Genetic Algorithm (MOGA), MOMGA, NPGA, NSGA, NSGA-II, PAES, PESA, PESA-II, SPEA, and SPEA2 (Coello, 2007). A good example is presented by Huang and Wang (2006) where they introduce a single objective fitness function for support vector machines. In their work, a multi criteria problem formed as a combination of three goals including classification accuracy, number of selected features, and the feature cost. They plot the accuracy and feature number versus different weights for the German (credit card) data set to exploit the appropriate weighing. Similar to Huang & Wang work, in our study, model complexity (number of involved terms in model expression) and regression value are used as two main objectives.

2. SOFT TISSUE INSERTION METHODS AND FORMULATION

Proposed models suggest the allocation of sensible forces in the formulation of needle insertion force, which divide the forces of procedures into three major parts. In most studies, these sensible forces are divided to cutting, stiffness, and friction forces, where most authors such as Ra (2002), Okamura (2004), Abolhassani (2007), Barbe (2007), TouficAzar and Hayward (2008), Misra (2009), and Mahvash and Dupont (2010) accept the Equation (1) for force distribution.

$$f(x) = f_{cutting} + f_{friction} + f_{stiffness} \qquad (1)$$

Each term in Equation (1) can be measured with separate experiments. From separately-measured terms, general force term can be achieved.

Okamura (2004) showed that considering these three terms, direct modeling should entail a higher accuracy, especially for insertion stage after penetration where stiffness force disappears. With simple assumptions on the role of each term, TouficAzar and Hayward (2008) used Equation (1) for determination of soft tissue fracture toughness. They used two consequent penetrations in a single surgery site. Therefore, differences between these two consequent penetrations could be calculated as the amount of work conducted by cutting force. This would be possible by subtraction of force-displacement graph integral of two consequences. Complications are intensified when studying soft tissue fracture. Therefore, in order to derive an efficient model for exerted force, it is indispensable to develop a highly accurate method.

Needle insertion force procedure could be divided into different phases. These phases entail different mechanics of insertion. Most of the authors, such as Abolhassani (2007), Barbe (2007), TouficAzar and Hayward (2008), and Mahvash and Dupont (2010), mentioned more than three phases for the insertion process. In addition to withdrawal, they claimed at least three phases for the insertion task. These phases are divided as below:

1. Before penetration with a small puncture
2. Steady state penetration
3. Tissue Relaxation
4. Withdrawal (Extraction).

3. EXPERIMENTAL SETUP FOR SOFT TISSUE NEEDLE INSERTION

For determining tissue characteristics, various types of experiments can be employed. With respect to the application of the needle insertion, we preferably use constant velocities experiments for modeling of the needle insertion process. Using a 0.98 mm (diameter) and 22.5o (bevel tip angel) needle, we conducted different in-vitro experiments. In all of the experiments bovine liver were used as the soft tissue. The results of the experiments were acquired in seven different velocities from 5 mm/min to 300 mm/min that any of them was the result of insertion in a new location.

3.1. Effects of Dehydration and Temperature

Suitable porosity of bovine liver makes it an appropriate replacement of human liver simulation. Therefore, all the experiments were conducted with bovine liver. Oxygen and blood have better transfer in more porous organs. Haemmerich (2005) showed that under in-vitro conditions, the human body behaviour could be simulated for the experiments. Phantom tissue insertions in in-vitro cases include some problems in tissue fixation. The effects of temperature and dehydration on soft tissue were considered on experimental setup.

Due to high level of water supply in soft tissues, dehydration will have undesirable effect on mechanical characteristics. Increment in tensile of strength and module of elasticity are inevitable side effects of the dehydration on soft tissue. Bovine liver kept hydrated with normal saline solution (0.1 M Phosphate Buffered Saline). Soft tissue samples were acquired 5 hours after killing, while the liver was stored under protected thermal condition. All of the experiments were performed in laboratory temperature, which is between 20o-25o siliceous; however, some of the researchers stated that temperature variations do not affect these types of tests.

3.2. Standard Compression Tests

Needle tip position needs a manual setup at the initial steps of the insertion. A 5*5*3 cm3 fixture was designed which was used to make bone liver

balance. The fixture has flexibility to be regulated in desired height; therefore, the tissue could be fixed in a favorable pressure. It can provide a sufficiently good simulation environment for the soft tissue in the body. Relatively smooth walls of the fixture can confirm this purpose. Now for different sets of experiments, tissue samples needed to be incised in definite dimensions. Making out of Plexy-Glass materials and polyamide screws leads to have an MRI compatible fixture. Moreover, a needle holder was employed for the prevention of needle buckling during tests (Dimaio & Salcudean, 2003).

All the experiments were performed on a ZWICK/ROELL PC system (VERSION 5.1/17.01.92) which was equipped with a 20N load cell with the accuracy of digitizing 0.001 units. Therefore, 0.01 Newton is regarded as the minimum amount of force, which could be measured with this setup (see Figure 1).

Figure 1. All the experiments performed under a Zwick/Roell PC system equipped with a needle holder and a 20 N load cell

Exploiting accurate numerical methods, force model could be determined as a comprehensive polynomial equation. The results can be presented such as Equation (1) in part 2, which can be stated with velocity and position parameters. This approach established with the effect of velocity in the coefficients of non-linear models. In this chapter, a novel numerical model for this procedure is presented.

4. GENETIC-BASED POLYNOMIAL HIGHER ORDER NEURAL NETWORK

We use second-order and third-order polynomial neural networks to simulate the process of needle insertion. Although more complex structures or higher order networks can be used, we try to focus on simplicity of network as an important objective. Structure of network is being chosen by an automatic genetic algorithm.

4.1. Polynomial Higher Order Neural Networks

Polynomial Higher Order Neural Networks (also known as Polynomial Networks and Polynomial Neural Networks) can be divided to two main groups: Sigma-Pi Networks (also known as High-order Processing Unit, HPU) and Pi-Sigma Networks (PSN). The HPU model incorporates a higher number of learning parameters. It causes a longer running time but provides an investigation of all correlations among inputs. Homma and Gupta (2002) proposed a Sigma-Pi Artificial Second Order Neural Unit (ASONU) without losing the higher performance. PSNs are developed to comprise a high order correlation between inputs using lower number of weights than HPUs to provide a faster learning. At first, Shin and Ghosh (1991) introduced a higher-order neural network in the form of the PSN model to study several pattern recognitions. Although they claimed that a generalization of PSN can approximate any

measurable function, it is not a universally applicable estimation. In this regard, a generalization of PSN was developed as Ridge Polynomial Higher Order Neural Network (RPHONN) by Shin and Ghosh (1995).

In this study, we develop a Sigma-Pi model, which does not require large number of learning parameters. The genetic approach was used to select appropriate high-order terms automatically. This was expected to results in a diminution of the number of high-order terms and network weights.

Overall, Sigma-Pi Polynomial Higher Order Neural Networks incorporate productive inputs up to a predefined order next to the inputs. A general mathematical structure of Sigma-Pi polynomial neural network can be presented in Equation (2) as follows:

$$Z = w_0 + \sum_{i_1=1}^{P} w_{i_1} x(i_1) + \sum_{i_1=1}^{P} \sum_{i_2=i_1}^{P} w_{i_1 i_2} x(i_1) x(i_2) + ..$$

$$+ \sum_{i_1=1}^{P} .. \sum_{i_N=i_N-1}^{P} w_{i_1 i_N} x(i_1) .. x(i_N)$$

(2)

where is the input vector, P is the number of features of input, N is the maximum order of higher order network, and different indexes of w are adjustable weights of the network.

The given structure can be applied to model different pattern behaviour. One of the advantages of polynomial neural networks is their simplicity in pattern presentation. In fact, it presents complex behaviour of system via a polynomial combination of input features. In addition, in many pattern recognition cases, the main objective is to provide a mathematical model of the target behaviour of under-study process. It means that the main objectives would be simplicity and an open-box specificity of the model. In the general case, Pi-Sigma Higher Order Neural Network by Fallahnezhad (2011), presents a novel hybrid higher order neural structure (i.e. Hybrid Higher

Order Neural Classifier also known as HHONC) which has proven a superior open-box specificity next to its superior performance dealing pattern classifications.

In this part, two features including position and velocity of the needle are presented, which, in turn, could be the end-effecter of a robotic manipulator. Okamura (2004) and Barbe (2007) have shown that the relation between force and these parameters is kind of polynomial. This chapter aims to provide an open-box polynomial network of the model.

4.2. Structure and Algorithm of Genetic-Based Polynomial Network

Genetic programming is an intelligent approach, which can be used to optimize single- or multi-objective functions. Such evolutionary algorithms with faster running processes, more reliable and robust performance offer various advantages compared to other constructive methods. Output strings in genetic algorithms are generated with different ratios of reproduction, crossover, and mutation of previous strings. In first step, initial strings are randomly chosen. Reproduction is a procedure by which each string is selected based on the fitness function value of each chromosome and for each of which a roulette wheel is constructed. To create another offspring, a simple rotation of the weighted roulette wheel leads to the reproduction of previous strings. Therefore, more accurate strings, which lead to high values of fitness function, would have a higher probability to be chosen in a succeeding generation (Goldberg, 1998).

To optimize polynomial structure, strings indicating high-order terms inclusion in the model were used as the objective code. In the case of second order polynomial network, since the number of terms is only eight, genetic approach is not used to find the best model. All configurations with $2^8=256$ different states were convention-

ally checked in a few running processes via the constructive algorithm. Equation (3) contains the general terms of this network:

$$F = f(1, y, y^2, x, xy, xy^2, x^2, x^2y, x^2y^2) \qquad (3)$$

where, x is the position term and y is the velocity term. Therefore, the most complex structure of such second order polynomial indicates a 9-term additive formula.

For the Third Order Polynomial Network, genetic programming is employed focusing on two main objectives, fitness performance, and model complexity. To incorporate a higher fitness performance, the model may need to use higher order terms, that is, three in the case of Third Order Polynomial Network. This, however, may increase model complexity, which endangers the open-box specificity. Both fitness performance and model complexity can be optimized using multi-objective fitness functions. The general Third Order Polynomial Network structure has a general equation of (4), represented follows:

$$F = f(1, y, y^2, y^3, x, xy, xy^2xy^3, x^2, \\ x^2y, x^2y^2, x^2y^3, x^3, x^3y, x^3y^2, x^3y^3) \qquad (4)$$

Therefore, the code, which should be optimized, includes 15 terms. Each bit of this code can receive the values of 0 and 1 where 0 means that the model does not comprise that term. When a code (string/chromosome output given by GA) is formed, polynomial neurons which are a productive terms are formed, and learning weights are updated. To update network weights, back propagation method based on the Levenberg-Marquardt algorithm is implemented. In addition to training and testing samples, validation samples were used to prevent a well-known over-fitting problem. We have already shown that in a similar higher order neural network, results achieved for validation instances have similar trend to testing instances (Fallahnezhad, et al., 2011). Therefore, the main criterion for stop training is the results for the validation samples.

Briefly, the algorithm of the proposed method is described below:

- *Step 1.* Initialize 20 strings of code randomly. Set the model code to a random value of N = [N1... N15] (for third order polynomial network)
- *Step 2.* Initialize the weights of the current model.
- *Step 3.* Update the weights. Calculate the regression value of training, especially for the validation samples.
- *Step 4.* If the overall regression value of validation samples (fitness function for genetic approach) is getting worse stop; otherwise, proceed to the next step.
- *Step 5.* Select parents from the current generation by applying the roulette wheel selection method.
- *Step 6.* Generate a second population of solutions from those selected through genetic operators: crossover (also called recombination) and mutation; meanwhile the best

string would be copied to the next generation without any manipulations.
- *Step 7.* Replace the new generations with offspring obtained from Step 6, then go to Step 2.

Figures 2 and 3 illustrate the trend of genetic programming to the goal model for needle insertion force modeling during phase 1 and phase 2, respectively. To demonstrate the robustness of the GA algorithm, the program was allowed to continue operating up to 200 generation. It is known that, after 20 to 30 generations, the algorithm reaches the goal model, which in turn indicates a speedy running of the algorithm.

In this algorithm, in order to find the best model orders, the population size is composed of 20 strings where each string is 15 bits chromosome. These numbers exchange to the binary mode and vice versa in each algorithm loop to prepare them for the reproduction pool operations and the evaluation step, respectively. To avoid the more complex model and to guarantee convergence of the algorithm, the upper bound and the lower bound are selected for the search area. The lower bound and the higher bound are selected

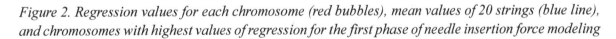

Figure 2. Regression values for each chromosome (red bubbles), mean values of 20 strings (blue line), and chromosomes with highest values of regression for the first phase of needle insertion force modeling

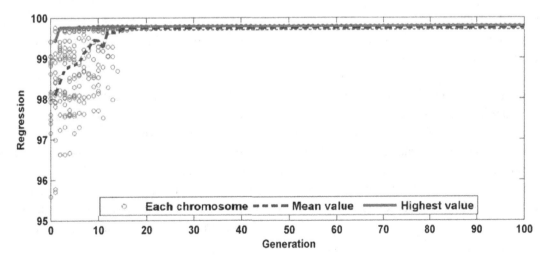

Figure 3. Regression values for each chromosome (red bubbles), mean values of 20 strings (blue line), and chromosomes with highest values of regression for the second phase of needle insertion force modeling

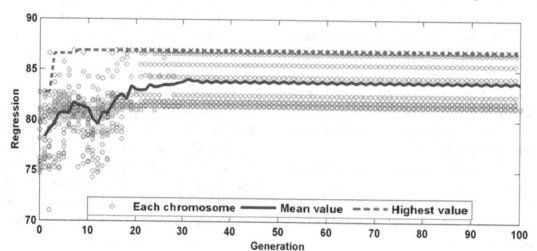

as all zero, and [h1, h2,... h15], respectively. The initial crossover and mutation parameters are chosen 80% and 4%, respectively.

5. RESULTS

Different reports reveal that if the needle reaches to the layer of skin in the first phase of insertion, it is needed to increase the exerted force massively to create a small puncture point in the tissue. This would be an inevitable irregularity in force-displacement diagram, which might be occurred in any experimental data (TouficAzar & Hayward, 2008).

In this section, firstly, some general information derived from the experimental data. Then, some necessary aspects of numerical modeling were highlighted, and the results of modeling in second and third order were presented in the two first phases, respectively. Second order polynomial neural network uses a constructive search method to find the higher orders; however, in the case of third order, we need to employ a genetic-based algorithm to find higher order terms.

Eventually, using a multi-objective fitness function, the best-fitted model is achieved. Regression value of validation samples next to the model simplicity are employed as the features of multi-objective approach and these are two main objective functions to be optimized.

5.1. Results of Experiments

Because of the tenacious behavior of the tissue, the puncture might occur with a relative distance from the tissue surface. Therefore, the assumed phases for the modeling process sufficiently satisfy this purpose. These assumptions lead to the employment of different models due to the turnover of biological tissue in the unloading phase, which has been mentioned by Dimaio and Salcudean (2003) and Okamura (2004) (see Figure 4).

The general format of the model is based on Equation 2. It is observed that the difference reduces as the open-box specificity is decreased from the high-order terms. Consequently, genetic programming is employed to choose the appropriate high-order terms considering the structure of force model that is present. Two different stages were used in force modeling of

Figure 4. Two first phases of insertion with puncture point in a definite distance from the tissue surface at the case of 50mm/min of velocity

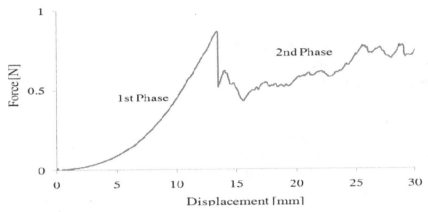

Table 1. Needle insertion tests information

Insertion Velocity	1st Phase Length(mm)	Final Force of 1st Phase (N)	Mean Force Value in 2nd Phase (N)
5 mm/min	1.02±0.27	1.22±0.10	1.04±0.24
25 mm/min	1.07±0.34	1.03±0.11	1.21±0.13
50 mm/min	1.08±0.45	1.21±0.21	0.97±0.21
100 mm/min	0.83±0.22	1.03±0.16	0.98±0.10
150 mm/min	0.72±0.31	0.98±0.12	0.73±0.14
200 mm/min	0.70±0.24	0.87±0.24	0.69±0.28
300 mm/min	0.76±0.13	0.93±0.22	0.74±0.23

needle insertion. The reaction of the tissue in each phase leads to different shapes in the force-displacement graph. For each phase, both the second and third order polynomial neural networks are utilized. In Table 1, some specific information such as the level of puncture from tissue surface, maximum force in the first phase, and mean value force of the second phase of needle insertion tests are provided from the experimental results.

5.2. Results of Numerical Modeling

In order to present a better scheme of the results, it may be considered necessary to summarize some criteria of numerical modeling beforehand:

1. In all of the following cases, two first phases were used separately, and a model for each phase is presented.

2. In the cases of second order polynomial neural networks, since the total number of models (model pool) is low enough, genetic programming is not employed. Therefore, a constructive search strategy has been implemented.

3. Samples have been divided to randomly selected categories: 80% of total as training samples; 10% as validation samples; and 10% as testing samples.

4. In all of the cases, validation samples have been used as the main criterion of stop

epoch. This was done in order to prevent well-known dilemma of over fitting on the training instances (Fallahnezhad, et al., 2011).

5. In the case of third order polynomial neural networks, two different experiments have been implemented. First, only regression value of the validation samples was chosen as the fitness function to be optimized by genetic programming. Second, since one main goal is to have an appropriate open-box model, a factor of model complexity to the fitness function is added.

6. For a comparison among the results of different models, a definition of regression over validation instances was used. The definition is given in Equation (5):

$$R^2 = 1 - \frac{\sum_{i-1}^{n}(f_i - \hat{f}_i)^2}{\sum_{i=1}^{n}(f_1 - \overline{f})^2} \tag{5}$$

where, is the mean value of output, is output of network and is the desired value.

5.2.1. Second Order Polynomial Modeling

Although Second Order Polynomial Neural Networks (SOPNN) may not excel on complex patterns, such simple structures provide simpler representation of behavior (higher open-box specificity). In this study, second order networks are applied first, and if the network did not meet the target expectation, the third order networks are employed.

Figure 5 exhibits different stages of the proposed SOPNN. From bottom up, the initial stage is a high-order term selection. For this stage, a constructive search strategy is used which enables testing of all possible models to find the

Figure 5. Structure of second order polynomial higher order neural network

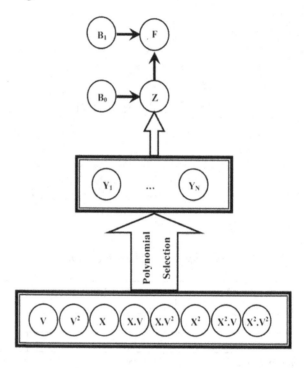

best fitted one. All possible second order inputs are shown in the initial step of the network. The chosen high-order terms are Y1... Yn. The next stage comprise one-layer back-propagation neural network. Equation (6) presents the mathematic notation of these stages:

$$Z = w_0^1 B_0 + w_1^1 Y_1 + ... + w_n^1 Y_n$$
$$F = w_0^2 B_1 + w_1^2 Z \tag{6}$$
$$\Rightarrow F = v_0 + v_1 Y_1 + ... + v_n Y_n$$

where Z is the output of the polynomial layer, B0 and B1 are the threshold values (usually set to 1) of the polynomial and scaling layers respectively; Y1, ..., Yn are the selected high-order terms; is the weight of layer jth and neuron ith; and F is the final output of the network.

From the equation demonstrated in (6), it seems clear that the learning algorithm of the network is similar to the back-propagation networks. Hagan

Table 2. Results of second order polynomial higher order neural networks: phase 1

Model terms	No. of Terms	Regression values (R2)		
		All samples	Validation	Testing
XV2, X2, X2V, X2V2	4	97.00	98.10	96.87
XV, X2, X2V, X2V2	4	97.17	98.06	96.99

Table 3. Results of second order polynomial higher order neural networks: phase 2

Model terms	No. of Terms	Regression values (R2)		
		All samples	Validation	Testing
X, XV, X2, X2V, X2V2	5	76.56	77.49	72.25
V, V2, X2V	3	76.15	77.20	76.68
V, V2, XV2, X2V	4	76.61	77.18	76.90

(1996) applied the Levenberg-Marquardt algorithm in order to optimize the error for all of the networks. Table 2 and Table 3 present details of the achieved best models for Phase 1 and Phase 2, respectively.

Equation (7) is the open box representation of Phase 1:

$$F = -0.084 -0.43(xy2) +0.23(x2) +1.55(x2y) -0.45(x2y2) = -0.084 - x(0.43y2) +x2 (0.23 +1.55y -0.45y2) \qquad (7)$$

From Table 3, it can be observed that the second order networks cannot properly interpret phase 2 of the insertion process. Therefore, the third order networks are introduced in the next section to improve these results. Nonetheless, a regression value of 77%, which in turn can be useful, is derived using three terms.

5.2.2. Third Order Polynomial Modeling

As stated previously, in order to improve the results of modeling, third order polynomial networks can be applied. Once the order is increased, it would be observed that the decision area of the input space may notably increase. As a result, the modeling performance may increase. In contrast,

increasing model terms affect the open-box specificity of the model. To overcome this dilemma, a multi-objective fitness function was employed to include both terms.

Similar to the second order networks, third order networks for both Phase 1 and Phase 2 are used, respectively. Since so many different models exist to be tested, genetic programming is utilized to find the best model from the existing pool. In this stage, regression value of validation samples as the sole fitness functions of the genetic algorithm are used. Results for phase 1 and 2 are provided in Table 4 and Table 5, respectively.

5.2.3. Multi-Objective Genetic-Based Third Order Polynomial Network

In this study, we focus on MOGA and use a single objective fitness function similar to the Goal-attainment algorithm used by Coello (2007), which has been described as the following:

$$F = \sum_{n=1}^{N_F} w_n F_n, \ \sum_{n=1}^{N_F} w_n = 1 \qquad (8)$$

where *NF* is the number of objective functions, *Fn* is the *nth* objective function, *wn* is the weight

Table 4. Results of third order polynomial higher order neural networks: phase 1

Model terms	No. Of Terms	Regression values (R2)		
		All samples	Validation	Testing
V, V2, X, XV, XV2, XV3, X2, X2V3, X3, X3V, X3V2, X3V3	12	99.80	99.79	99.79
V2, XV2, XV3, X2, X3, X3V, X3V2, X3V3	8	99.82	99.75	99.75

Table 5. Results of third order polynomial higher order neural networks: phase 2

Model terms	No. Of Terms	Regression values (R2)		
		All samples	Validation	Testing
V, V3, X, XV, XV2, XV3, X2V, X2V2, X2V3, X3, X3V, X3V2, X3V3	13	87.27	86.91	86.75
V, V2, V3, XV2, X2V, X2V2, X3V, X3V3	8	81.32	82.31	77.81

applied for *Fn* and *F* is the fitness function which must be applied to the genetic approach.

We use regression value of validation instances next to the model simplicity as two main objective functions to be optimized. We have normalized the model simplicity term to an objective function, which shows the percentage of simplicity. Formulas (9) cover the concept.

$$F = wF_1 + (1-w)F_2$$

$$F_2 = \frac{C_{max} - C}{C_{max} - 1} \times 100\%$$ (9)

where, *F1* and *F2*, respectively, are the regression value of validation samples and model simplicity, *w* defines the weight of each fitness function, *Cmax* and *C* are the values of model simplicity (number of terms) of the most complex and current models, respectively.

In the case of third order network, the most complex network including all high-order terms comprises 15 terms (i.e. Cmax=15). We can experimentally choose the value of *w* according to the desired result. Some sets of experiments were used with different magnitude for the *w*. Results of the experiment for this tests demonstrate the optimum weighting of 0.1 for *w*. Comparable results were shown in Table 6.

6. DISCUSSION

There are various parameters, which affect the amount of force during needle insertion process. The effects of these parameters were discussed in previous works. Some of these parameters are related to the geometrical conditions of the process, some to mechanical tissue models, and some others are related to the dynamic of needle insertion in the process (Misra, et al., 2009; Mahvash &

Table 6. Results for various applied weight in second phase for 3rd order modeling

Model terms	w	No. of Terms	Regression values (R2)		
			All samples	Validation	Testing
V, V2,V3, X2V	0.15	4	79.84	80.47	75.83
V3, XV, XV2, X2V, X2V2, X3V, X3V2	0.1	7	82.63	83.06	80.09

Dupont, 2010). In this study, we performed an in-vitro needle insertion to explore some of their effects in force-displacement diagram.

Several experiments were needed to investigate through the effects of different parameter in force-displacement diagram. These parameters can be divided in three main categories: geometrical parameters, such as needle length, needle diameter, and needle bevel tip angle; tissue combination model parameters, such as hyper-elastic or viscoelastic model parameters; and finally, dynamical parameters, which some of them are related to the kinematics of the process, such as needle directional velocity, needle rotational velocity, needle tip position, and frequency of insertion.

Results published by Barbe (2007) include specific tasks in order to study the effects of various parameters in the models, and all parameters involved in needle insertion process that might be contemplated. In addition to general parameters like needle diameter, velocity, length, tip bevel angle, and material elasticity which investigated by Misra (2009), method of insertion might be deemed to play a crucial role in force-displacement diagram. Kobayashi (2010) believes that these parameters might be considered in assumptions of symmetrical geometry.

Barbe (2007) declared that force modeling of experiments could be helpful in the identification of tissue characteristics and he showed the characteristics in the functions of the study. In order to investigate the effect of more parameters on tissue characteristics, the same methods could be applicable.

Before the main puncture (phase 1), the force-depth behavior can be mapped by a simple polynomial; thus, the performance of the network tabulated in Table 4 is perfect as expected. The main challenge of force modeling appears when the needle penetrates the tissue since a wide range of biomechanical phenomena come into play. Therefore, there is no need to complicate the model with higher orders in the first phase. In the second phase, we need to exploit from higher order polynomials to achieve more accuracy. By comparing the results of Table 3 and Table 5, it is easy to sense the differences of using 3rd order than 2nd order polynomial neural network. Because the increment in the number of possible structures for third order genetic algorithm can be used to detect the high-order terms. Here, some important points of the results of Table 4 and Table 5 must be taken in to account, and are as follows:

1. Next to the best result given by genetic algorithm, another model can present for a more precise study with multi-objective approach by considering the simplicity of model beside of its universality.

2. According to Table 4, the results of the third order networks compared to the second order networks in Phase 1 are somewhat improved; however, the best achieved model that has been formed appears to be much more complex. Therefore, the increment in the high-order terms may not be considered as a good option in Phase 1.

3. According to the results presented in Table 5, the regression in the best model is conspicuously improved, i.e., more than 10%. Nevertheless, the output of genetic programming is undoubtedly more black box while it includes 13 high-order terms. An investigation of the result reveals that some simple structures, which have considerable performance, are present. One of such structures includes 8 high-order terms. In this regard, model simplicity is employed as another important term of fitness function in multi-objective approach.

Unless Barbe (2007), the other related articles rarely discuss the effect of correlation in the viscoelastic models. Barbe (2007) departed all the equation terms perfectly in the linear Kelvin-Voigt model. In the non-linear model, one term between velocity and the position of needle tip was used. Based on the assumption of quasi-static motion, needle insertion occurs in low velocities. Due to the quasi-static insertion in the experiments, terms of inertia in the force equation disappears. This is depicted in the equation (10) presented by Barbe (2007):

$$f = -\mu p_s^n - \lambda p_s^n \left(\vartheta_s - \vartheta\right) + f_f + f_c \qquad (10)$$

A non-linear viscoelastic model describes the force in the first phase well; however, this might have some limitations in completing the insertion process modeling. As such, it might be better to use a model that depends on more aspects of these two parameters in the force-displacement diagram. In order to show the effects of these parameters through different experimental data, genetic programming structure has been applied.

7. CONCLUSION AND FUTURE WORK

In this chapter, a genetic programming polynomial neural network is employed to model needle insertion force. In previous works, some methodologies for the description of stiffness, friction, and cutting forces have been applied. Needle insertion into soft tissues has three or four phases; however, in this work, two first phases of insertion were studied in the modeling process; this approach was adopted in order to present a complete model which demonstrates the effect of the related parameters in force modeling of general needle insertion. Using bovine liver, needle insertion experiments with constant velocities were performed. In the process of medical needle insertion there might be many categories of parameters; some are geometrical parameters such as needle length, needle diameter, and needle bevel tip angle; some are soft biological tissue combination model parameters such as hyper-elastic model parameters or visco-elastic model parameters; and finally, some are related to the dynamic of insertion such as needle directional and rotational velocity and needle tip

position, which can affect in needle insertion force modeling. We were motivated to study the effects of dynamical parameters in force modeling. These parameters were included for investigation of the force modeling of the needle insertion process. With seven sets of experiments, in different velocities of 5, 25, 50, 100, 150, 200, and 300 mm/min, a force-displacement graph of the insertion was derived. These experiments were needed to have an investigation through the effects of position and velocity on force-displacement graph, which led to necessitation of employing a strong numerical method. With second order and third order of PHONN force modeling in two different phases was conducted. Both 2nd and 3rd order of PHONN can show a high regression value in modeling of the phase 1. However, 2nd order leads to more simple models of force. Optimized results revealed that the usage of third order of genetic programming could make an accurate formulation of needle insertion in force modeling at the phase 2. Eventually, multi-objective genetic-based third order of polynomial network was applied to have better open-box specificity in force models. Regression value of validation samples and the number of terms in model with an optimized weighting coefficient were applied as the features of multi-objective fitness function. Application of PHONN demonstrates the effect of displacement, velocity, as well as correlation of these two parameters in the force model formulation. Other terms such as rotational velocity (Alterovitz, et al., 2005; Yousefi, et al., 2010), accelerations, and tapping frequency might be regarded as a challenge in this field which is declared by Lagerburg (2006). It may be considered that in a near future, the researchers develop the idea of fast needle insertion, and receive efficient experimental results with the dynamic of fast needle insertion. However, it is clear that because of less displacement in tissue deformation, needle tapping might be considered even more expedient in prostate brachytherapy and other percutaneous therapies.

REFERENCES

Abolhassani, N., Patel, R., & Moallem, M. (2007). Needle insertion into soft tissue: A survey. *International Journal of Medicine and Engineering Physics*, *29*, 413–431. doi:10.1016/j.medengphy.2006.07.003

Alterovitz, R., Goldberg, K., & Okamura, A. (2005). Planning for steerable bevel-tip needle insertion through 2D soft tissue with obstacles. In *Proceedings of ICRA*, (pp. 1652-1657). Barcelona, Spain: ICRA.

Barbe, L., & Bayle, B., De Mathelin, et al. (2007). Needle insertions modeling: Identifiability and limitations. *International Journal of Biomedical Signal Processing and Control*, *2*, 191–198. doi:10.1016/j.bspc.2007.06.003

Bishoff, J. T. RCM-PAKY. (1998). Clinical application of a new robotic system for precise needle placement. *Journal of Endourology*. Retrieved from http://www.ncbi.nlm.nih.gov/pmc/articles/PMC3099458/

Coello, C. A., Lamont, G. B., & Veldhuizen, D. A. V. (2007). *Evolutionary algorithms for solving multi-objective problems* (2nd ed.). Berlin, Germany: Springer.

Crouch, J. R., Pizer, S. M., & Chaney, E. L. (2007). Automated finite-element analysis for deformable registration of prostate images. *IEEE Transactions on Medical Imaging*, *26*, 1379–1390. doi:10.1109/TMI.2007.898810

DiMaio, S. P., & Salcudean, S. E. (2003). Needle insertion modeling and simulation. *IEEE Transactions on Robotics and Automation*, *19*, 864–875. doi:10.1109/TRA.2003.817044

Fallahnezhad, M., Moradi, M. H., & Zaferanlouei, S. (2011). A hybrid higher order neural classifier for handling classification problems. *Expert Systems with Applications*, *38*, 386–393. doi:10.1016/j.eswa.2010.06.077

Gasser, T. C., Gudmundson, P., & Dohr, G. (2009). Failure mechanisms of ventricular tissue due to deep penetration. *Journal of Biomechanics*, *42*, 626–633. doi:10.1016/j.jbiomech.2008.12.016

Goldberg. (1998). *Genetic algorithms in search, optimization, and machine learning*. Reading, MA: Addison-Wesley.

Haemmerich, D., Lee, F. T., & Schutt, D. J. (2005). Large-volume radiofrequency ablation of ex-vivo bovine liver with multiple cooled cluster electrodes. *Journal de Radiologie*, *234*, 563–568.

Hagan, M. T., Demuth, H. B., & Beale, M. (1996). *Neural network design*. Boston, MA: PWS Publishing Company.

Homma, N., & Gupta, M. M. (2002). A general second order neural unit. *Bulleting of Collected Medical Science*, *11*, 1–6.

Huang, C. L., & Wang, C. J. (2006). A GA-based feature selection and parameters optimization for support vector machines. *International Journal of Experimental Systems Applications*, *31*, 231–240. doi:10.1016/j.eswa.2005.09.024

Kesavadas, T., Srimathveeravalli, G., & Arulesan, V. (2005). Parametric modeling and simulation of Trocar insertion. *Journal of Studies in Health Technologies and Informatics*, *119*, 252–254.

Kobayashi, Y., Onishi, A., & Watanabe, H. (2010). Development of an integrated needle insertion system with image guidance and deformation simulation. *Computerized Medical Imaging and Graphics*, *34*, 9–18. doi:10.1016/j.compmedimag.2009.08.008

Lagerburg Marinus, V., Moerland, A., & Vulpen, M. V. (2006). A new robotic needle insertion method to minimize attendant prostate motion, prostate brachytherapy. *Radiotherapy and Oncology*, *80*, 73–77. doi:10.1016/j.radonc.2006.06.013

Mahvash, M., & Dupont, P. E. (2009). Fast needle insertion to minimize tissue deformation and damage. In *Proceedings of the IEEE International Conference on Robotics and Automation,* (pp. 3097-3102). IEEE Press.

Mahvash, M., & Dupont, P. E. (2010). Mechanics of dynamic needle insertion into a biological material. *IEEE Transactions on Bio-Medical Engineering, 57,* 934–943. doi:10.1109/TBME.2009.2036856

Masamune, K., Kobayashi, E., & Masutani, Y. (1995). Development of an MRI-compatible needle insertion manipulator for stereotactic neurosurgery. *Computer Aided Surgery, 1*(4), 242–248. doi:10.3109/10929089509106330

Maurel, W. (1999). *3D modeling of the human upper limb including the biomechanics of joints, muscles and soft tissues.* (PhD Thesis). Laboratoire d'Infographie-Ecole Polytechnique Federale de Lausanne. Lausanne, Switzerland.

Misra, S., Macura, K., & Ramesh, K. (2009). The importance of organ geometry and boundary constraints for planning of medical interventions. *Medical Engineering & Physics, 31*(2), 195–206. doi:10.1016/j.medengphy.2008.08.002

Nath, S. (2000). Dosimetric effects of needle divergence in prostate seed implant using 125I and 103Pd radioactive seeds. *Medical Physics, 27,* 1058–1066. doi:10.1118/1.598971

Okamura, M., Simone, C., & O'Leary, M. D. (2004). Force modeling for needle insertion into soft tissue. *IEEE Transactions on Bio-Medical Engineering, 51,* 1707–1716. doi:10.1109/TBME.2004.831542

Ra, J. B., Kwon, S. M., & Kim, J. K. (2002). Spine needle biopsy simulator using visual and force feedback. *Computer Aided Surgery, 7,* 353–363. doi:10.3109/10929080209146524

Rizun, P. R. (2004). Robot-assisted neurosurgery. *Semin Laporasc Surgery, 11,* 99–106.

Rumelhart, D. E., Hinton, G. E., & Williams, R. (1986). Learning representation by back-propagation errors. *Nature, 323,* 533–536. doi:10.1038/323533a0

Schwartz, J. M., Denninger, M., & Rancourt, D. (2005). Modeling liver tissue properties using a non-linear visco-elastic model for surgery simulation. *Medical Image Analysis, 9,* 103–112. doi:10.1016/j.media.2004.11.002

Shin, Y., & Ghosh, J. (1991). The pi-sigma networks: An efficient higher-order neural network for pattern classification and function approximation. In *Proceedings of the IEEE IJCNN,* (pp. 13-18). IEEE Press.

Shin, Y., & Ghosh, J. (1995). Ridge polynomial networks. *IEEE Transactions on Neural Networks, 6,* 610–622. doi:10.1109/72.377967

Taylor, R. H., & Kazanzides, P. (2007). Medical robotics and computer-integrated interventional medicine. *International Journal of Advance in Computers, 73,* 219–260.

Tou☐cAzar, & Hayward, V. (2008). Estimation of the fracture toughness of soft tissue from needle insertion. *Lecture Notes in Computer Science, 5104,* 166-175.

Wei, Z., Wan, G., & Gardi, L. (2004). Robot-assisted 3D-TRUS guided prostate brachytherapy: System integration and validation. *Medical Physics, 31,* 539–548. doi:10.1118/1.1645680

Yousefi, H., Ramezanpour, H., & Rostami, M. (2010). Applications of needle insertion with rotating capability in manipulator. In *Proceedings of the ICBME 17th Iranian Conference on Biomedical Engineering,* (pp. 1-4). ICBME.

Zhang, M. (2008). *Artificial higher order neural networks for economics and business.* Hershey, PA: IGI Global. doi:10.4018/978-1-59904-897-0

Zivanovic, A., & Davies, B. L. (2000). A robotic system for blood sampling. *IEEE Transactions in Information Technology Biomedical Engineering*, *4*, 8–14. doi:10.1109/4233.826854

KEY TERMS AND DEFINITIONS

First Phase of Insertion: In the first phase of insertion there is no penetration of needle into soft tissue. It starts from an initial contact between needle tip and tissue surface. Then the tissue tends to deform from the center of initial contact. First phase of insertion continues until a small puncture occurs at the surface of the tissue. To rewrite the Equation (1) for this phase, it contains stiffness force in needle insertion process. Due to no penetration, there are no cutting and stiffness forces in process modeling. Under specified condition, such as standard compression test, the available viscoelastic models could be used for formulation of this phase.

Force Model: A mathematical model that could be used for the presentation of force magnitude during the process of needle insertion.

Fourth Phase of Insertion: The fourth and the final phase of insertion can be illustrated with an emphasis on the friction force. Similar to the second phase and with respect to the constant velocity insertion, the friction force can have a linear variation. In withdrawal phase, the effect of the cutting force disappears, and force terms can be only considered as stiffness and friction parts. The linear change of force in fourth phase is highly affected with extraction of friction force. To have a highly accurate needle insertion process, force modeling in two first phases of tissue insertion is more important. Two first phases of insertion highly depends on the penetration process. At the end of the second phase, needle reaches to the intended target; therefore, better modeling of these two phases leads to less misplacement in accessing the target. Under specific condition, a non-linear elastic behavior could be observed in the first phase of insertion. This elastic behavior can be discovered by pushing and drawing back of a device such as a probe, needle, or other minimally invasive surgery tools into the biological tissue. When exerting this type of external force, at first the tissue deforms and then returns to its initial state. These types of experiments could be used in determination of tissue characteristics (Okamura, et al., 2004). Due to large deformation, the tissue behavior could be regarded as non-linear elastic, viscoelastic, or hyper-elastic. This characteristic with definite formulation might be used in the description of tissue parameters. In order to investigate through the effects of variation in velocity and also impression of the needle tip position, seven different sets of experiment were conducted (See section 3.2, detail of experiments). These experiments aided in obtaining a comprehensive model for the two first phases of a quasi-static insertion. In order to make a mathematical model from this process, some terms might be considered. Friction force happens in needle-tissue interaction, which is related to needle diameter and linearly depth of insertion. Therefore, force-displacement equation may be stated incorporating the following terms: term of inertia, term of dampness (or viscosity), term of tissue deformation (which could be a simple elastic deformation), the effect of friction force (which could be related to the direction of motion), and finally, a first order macouli parenthesis for the description plastic deformation of the tissue with an elastic behavior. Due to very slow motion in quasi-static soft tissue insertion, term of inertia disappears in the force formulation. Other terms probably affect the insertion process in general quasi-static motion. Having a better mathematical formulation leads to a better numerical estimation of force in needle insertion. Therefore, most of the researchers are motivated to illustrate the mathematical description in force modeling procedure.

Multi-Objective Genetic-Algorithm (MOGA): Multi-objective genetic-based of polynomial neural network that is in third order for optimized force models.

Needle: A minimal invasive surgical device (tool) which is used for the insertion process for each kind of surgery, tissue sampling, seed implementing, etc.

Non-Linear Elastic Deformation Phase: The needle tip comes into contact with the tissue and deforms it without any penetration. It continues with puncture in the end of the first phase.

Phases of Insertion: A definite part of needle insertion process in which the tissue can reflect with a special mechanical behavior.

Polynomial Higher Order Neural Network (PHONN): A polynomial structure of higher order terms in fitness function.

Second Order Polynomial Neural Network (SOPNN): 2nd order of polynomial neural network which present a relatively simple and open box specification for force model.

Second Phase of Insertion: Second phase of insertion contains a steady-state penetration. This phase starts after a small puncture in tissue surface. During penetration, accurate insertion requires a complex study of tissue fracture. In addition to the fractures generated with needle tip, tissue deformation needs to be considered in calculation for the amount of dissipated energy. Cutting force, as the first term of Equation (1) appears in needle tip for tissue piercing. Obviously, stiffness force has a minimum effect on force distribution in this phase. Finally, friction force could be increased linearly when contact surface between needle shaft and ruptured area of tissue is increased. Distribution of these three forces will lead to more complicated force model in the second phase of insertion.

Soft Tissue: A relatively deformable human organic tissue such as liver, kidney, or any similar biological human or animal tissue.

Steady-State Visco-Plastic Penetration: Once energy is reached to a specific threshold, the liver capsule ruptures and a crack initiates. Then, steady state penetration initiates and the force increases with depth with an almost linear relation. This phase finishes when the needle tip stops at target point.

Third Phase of Insertion: The third phase of soft tissue needle insertion demonstrates the effects of tissue relaxation. After needle's stoppage in target point, third stage of insertion starts, and it will be finished when withdrawal phase starts. The effects of the third phase in a constant velocity insertion can be explained as a sudden decrement of force and a steady state of force, which is due to releasing of stored strain energy in the procedure.

Section 2
Artificial Higher Order Neural Networks for Simulation

Chapter 5
Artificial Polynomial and Trigonometric Higher Order Neural Network Group Models

Ming Zhang
Christopher Newport University, USA

ABSTRACT

Real world financial data is often discontinuous and non-smooth. Accuracy will be a problem, if we attempt to use neural networks to simulate such functions. Neural network group models can perform this function with more accuracy. Both Polynomial Higher Order Neural Network Group (PHONNG) and Trigonometric polynomial Higher Order Neural Network Group (THONNG) models are studied in this chapter. These PHONNG and THONNG models are open box, convergent models capable of approximating any kind of piecewise continuous function to any degree of accuracy. Moreover, they are capable of handling higher frequency, higher order nonlinear, and discontinuous data. Results obtained using Polynomial Higher Order Neural Network Group and Trigonometric polynomial Higher Order Neural Network Group financial simulators are presented, which confirm that PHONNG and THONNG group models converge without difficulty, and are considerably more accurate (0.7542% - 1.0715%) than neural network models such as using Polynomial Higher Order Neural Network (PHONN) and Trigonometric polynomial Higher Order Neural Network (THONN) models.

INTRODUCTION

HONN Models for Simulation

Artificial Higher Order Neural Network (HONN) is powerful technique to simulate data. Ghosh and Shin (1992) develop efficient higher-order neural networks for function approximation and classification. Zhang, Murugesan, and Sadeghi (1995) design polynomial higher order neural network for economic data simulation. Zhang, Fulcher, and Scofield (1996) study neural network group models for estimating rainfall from satellite images. Zhang, Zhang, and Fulcher (1997) explore financial simulation system using a higher order trigonometric polynomial neural network group model. Lu, Qi, Zhang, and Scofield (2000) provide PT-HONN models for multi-

DOI: 10.4018/978-1-4666-2175-6.ch005

polynomial function simulation. Zhang and Lu (2001) research financial data simulation by using Multi-Polynomial Higher Order Neural Network (M-PHONN) model. Zhang (2001) deliver a new model, called Adaptive Multi-Polynomial Higher Order Neural Network (A-PHONN), for financial data simulation. Qi and Zhang (2001) test the rainfall estimation using M-PHONN model and find that the M-PHONN model for estimating heavy convective rainfall from satellite data has 5% to 15% more accuracy than the polynomial higher order neural network. Zhang and Scofield (2001) expand an adaptive multi-polynomial high order neural network (A-PHONN) model for heavy convective rainfall estimation and find that the A-PHONN model has 6% to 16% more accuracy than the polynomial higher order neural network. Zhang (2003) intends PL-HONN model for financial data simulation. Rovithakis, Chalkiadakis, and Zervakis (2004) learn the high-order neural network structure selection for function approximation applications using genetic algorithms. Crane and Zhang (2005) discover the data simulation using SINCHONN Model. Zhang (2005) gives a data simulation system using sinx/x and sin x polynomial higher order neural networks. Zhang (2006) seeks a data simulation system using CSINC polynomial higher order neural networks. Zhang (2009a) delivers general format of Higher Order Neural Networks (HONNs) for nonlinear data analysis and six different HONN models. This chapter mathematically proves that HONN models could converge and have mean squared errors close to zero. This chapter illustrates the learning algorithm with update formulas. HONN models are compared with SAS Nonlinear (NLIN) models and results show that HONN models are 3 to 12% better than SAS Nonlinear models. Zhang (2009b) develops a new nonlinear model, Ultra high frequency Trigonometric Higher Order Neural Networks (UTHONN), for time series data analysis. Results show that UTHONN models are 3 to 12% better than Equilibrium Real Exchange Rates (ERER) model, and 4 − 9% better than

other Polynomial Higher Order Neural Network (PHONN) and Trigonometric Higher Order Neural Network (THONN) models. This study also uses UTHONN models to simulate foreign exchange rates and consumer price index with error approaching 0.0000%. Murata (2010) finds that a Pi-Sigma higher order neural network (Pi-Sigma HONN) is a type of higher order neural network, where, as its name implies, weighted sums of inputs are calculated first and then the sums are multiplied by each other to produce higher order terms that constitute the network outputs. This type of higher order neural networks has accurate function approximation capabilities.

The Motivations of Use of Artificial Higher Order Neural Network Group Theory

Accordingly, artificial higher order neuron network-based models are not yet sufficiently powerful to characterize complex systems. Moreover, a gap exists in the research literature between complex systems and general systems. Using artificial higher order neural network group theory is possible to bridge this gap.

If the function parameters being analyzed vary in a continuous and smooth fashion with respect to variable, then such functions can be effectively simulated by artificial higher order neural network. However, in the real world such variation can be discontinuous and non-smooth. Thus when using artificial higher order neural network to simulate the functions, accuracy will be a problem. In this case, artificial higher order neural network group can perform much better. Artificial higher order neural network group is possible to simulate discontinuous function to any degree accuracy using neural network group theory, even at the discontinuous points.

Artificial higher order neural networks are massively parallel architectures. Thus, by using parallel artificial higher order neural network based reasoning network, it can compute all rules, models, knowledge, and facts stored in different weights simultaneously. However, real world reasoning is always very complicated, nonlinear, and discontinuous. So simple artificial higher order neural network model cannot always give the correct reasoning, but artificial higher order neural network group potentially could.

The next logical step from artificial neuron-based and artificial neural network-based models is artificial neural network group-based models. Artificial higher order neural network group research is open-ended and holds considerable potential for developing complex systems. In order to develop artificial higher order neural network group-based models, an artificial higher order neural network group theory is required.

The key point of artificial Higher Order Neural Network Group Theory is of using group theory to study the structure of artificial higher order neural network groups. Contributions of the chapter are concerned with the following:

- To use group theory for building artificial higher order neural network group.
- To give the definitions of artificial higher order neural network groups.
- To describe the artificial higher order neural network group model features.
- To apply artificial higher order neural network group theory to build simulators.
- To give the test results of artificial polynomial higher order neural network group models and artificial trigonometric polynomial higher order neural network group models.

BACKGROUND

Dynamic HONN Models for Simulation

Kosmatopoulos, Ioannou, and Christodoulou (1992) study the stability and convergence prop-

erties of Recurrent High-Order Neural Networks (RHONNs) as models of nonlinear dynamical systems. The overall structure of the RHONN consists of dynamical elements distributed throughout the network for identification of nonlinear systems. Lee, Lee, and Park (1992) bring a neural controller of nonlinear dynamic systems using higher order neural networks. Kosmatopoulos, Polycarpou, Christodoulou, and Ioannou (1995) demonstrate several continuous-time and discrete-time recurrent high-order neural network models, and apply these models to various dynamic engineering problems. Draye, Pavisic, Cheron, and Libert (1996) build up dynamic recurrent neural networks for dynamic analysis. Kuroe, Ikeda, and Mori (1997) examine that recently high-order neural networks have been recognized to possess higher capability of nonlinear function representations. This chapter presents a method for identification of general nonlinear dynamical systems by recurrent high-order neural network. Ghazali, Hussain, and Nawi (2010) propose a novel Dynamic Ridge Polynomial Higher Order Neural Network (DRPHONN). The architecture of the new DRPHONN incorporates recurrent links into the structure of the ordinary Ridge Polynomial Higher Order Neural Network (RPHONN). RPHONN is a type of feedforward Higher Order Neural Network (HONN), which implements a static mapping of the input vectors. In order to model dynamical functions of the brain, it is essential to utilize a system that is capable of storing internal states and can implement complex dynamic system. Neural networks with recurrent connections are dynamical systems with temporal state representations. The dynamic structure approach has been successfully used for solving varieties of problems, such as time series forecasting, approximating a dynamical system, forecasting a stream flow, and system control.

HONN for Prediction

Fulcher and Brown (1994) offer a polynomial higher order neural network for predicting temperature distributions. Knowles, Hussain, Deredy, Lisboa, and Dunis (2005) consider higher-order neural network with Bayesian confidence measure for prediction of EUR/USD exchange rate. Saad, Prokhorov, and Wunsch (1998) look at the stock trend prediction using time delay recurrent and probabilistic Neural Networks. Zhang (2005) supplies polynomial full naïve estimated misclassification cost models for financial distress prediction using higher order neural network. Zhang and Fulcher (2004) discuss the higher order neural networks for satellite weather prediction. Christodoulou and Iliopoulos (2006) deal with the MAPK (mitogen-activated protein kinase), which is a three molecule module. This chapter also introduces higher order neural network models for prediction of steady state and dynamic behavior of MAPK cascade. Sanchez, Alanis, and Rico (2009) propose the use of Higher Order Neural Networks (HONNs) trained with an extended Kalman filter-based algorithm to predict the electric load demand as well as the electricity prices, with beyond a horizon of 24 hours. Due to the chaotic behavior of the electrical markets, it is not advisable to apply the traditional forecasting techniques used for time series; the results presented confirm that HONNs can very well capture the complexity underlying electric load demand and electricity prices. The proposed neural network model produces very accurate next day predictions and prognosticates with very good accuracy, a week-ahead of demand and price forecasts.

HONN for Time Series Data Predication

Tenti (1996) investigates forecasting foreign exchange rates using recurrent higher order neural networks. Kariniotakis, Stavrakakis, and Nogaret (1996) present wind power forecasting, the power output profile of a wind park, using advanced recurrent high order neural networks models. Tawfik and Liatsis (1997) go into prediction of non-linear time-series using higher order neural

networks. Zhang, Zhang, and Fulcher (1997) build up financial prediction system using higher order trigonometric polynomial neural network group model. Zhang, Zhang, and Keen (1999) extend to use THONN system for higher frequency non-linear data simulation and prediction. Foka (1999) offers time series prediction using evolving polynomial neural networks. Ghazali (2005) develops higher order neural network for financial time series prediction. Hussain, Knowles, Lisboa, El-Deredy, and Al-Jumeily (2006) study pipelined neural network and its application to financial time series prediction. Knowles, Ussain, Deredy, Lisboa, and Dunis (2009) present another type of Higher Order Neural Networks (HONN). These can be considered a 'stripped-down' version of MLPs, where joint activation terms are used, relieving the network of the task of learning the relationships between the inputs. The predictive performance of the network is tested with the EUR/USD exchange rate and evaluated using standard financial criteria including the annualized return on investment, showing 8% increase in the return compared with the MLP. Shi, Tan, and Ge (2009) address nonlinear problem by developing a technique consisting of a top-down part using an artificial Higher Order Neural Network (HONN) model and a bottom-up part based on a Bayesian Network (BN) model to automatically identify predictor variables for the stock return prediction from a large financial variable set. Chen, Wu, and Wu (2009) establish that forecasting exchange rates is an important financial problem that is receiving increasing attention especially because of its difficulty and practical applications. This chapter applies Higher Order Flexible Neural Trees (HOFNTs), which are capable of designing flexible Artificial Neural Network (ANN) architectures automatically, to forecast the foreign exchange rates. Liatsis, Hussain, and Milonidis (2009) concern with the development of novel artificial higher order neural networks architecture called the second-order pipeline recurrent neural network. The proposed artificial neural network consists of a linear and a nonlinear section, extracting relevant features from the input signal. The structuring unit of the proposed neural network is the second-order recurrent neural network. The architecture consists of a series of second-order recurrent neural networks, which are concatenated with each other. Simulation results in one-step ahead predictions of the foreign currency exchange rates demonstrate the superior performance of the proposed pipeline architecture as compared to other feed-forward and recurrent structures. Hussain and Liatsis (2009) introduce the development of novel artificial higher-order neural network architecture, called the recurrent Pi-sigma neural network. The proposed artificial neural network combines the advantages of both higher-order architectures in terms of the multi-linear interactions between inputs, as well as the temporal dynamics of recurrent neural networks, and produces highly accurate one-step ahead predictions of the foreign currency exchange rates, as compared to other feed-forward and recurrent structures. Selviah and Shawash (2009) provide a generalized correlation higher order neural network designs. Their performance is compared with that of first order networks, conventional higher order neural network designs, and higher order linear regression networks for financial time series prediction. The correlation higher order neural network design is shown to give the highest accuracy for prediction of stock market share prices and share indices. The simulations compare the performance for three different training algorithms, stationary versus non-stationary input data, different numbers of neurons in the hidden layer and several generalized correlation higher order neural network designs. Onwubolu (2009) describes real world problems of nonlinear and chaotic processes, which make them hard to model and predict. This chapter first compares the Neural Network (NN) and the artificial Higher Order Neural Network (HONN) and then presents commonly known neural network architectures and a number of HONN architectures. The Polynomial Neural Network (PNN) is then chosen as the HONN for application to the time series prediction problem. This research implies that the HONN model can be used as a feasible solution for exchange rate forecasting as well as for interest rate forecasting. Ghazali and Al-Jumeily (2009) discuss the use of two artificial Higher Order Neural Networks (HONNs) models, the Pi-Sigma Neural Networks and the Ridge Polynomial Neural Networks, in financial time series forecasting. From the simulation results, the predictions clearly demonstrated that HONNs models, particularly Ridge Polynomial Neural Networks generate higher profit returns with fast convergence, therefore show considerable promise as a decision making tool.

Adaptive HONN, Adaptive Group, and Other Models

Xu and Zhang (1999a) study approximation to continuous functions and operators using adaptive higher order neural networks. Xu and Zhang (2002) develop Adaptive Higher Order Neural Networks (AHONN) with a Neuron-adaptive Activation Function (NAF) to any nonlinear continuous functional and any nonlinear continuous operator. Xu (2009) introduces an adaptive Higher Order Neural Network (HONN) model and applies the adaptive model in business applications such as simulating and forecasting share prices. This adaptive HONN model offers significant advantages over traditional Standard ANN models such as much reduced network size, faster training, as well as much improved simulation and forecasting errors, due to their ability to better approximate complex, non-smooth, often discontinuous training data sets. Zhang, Zhang, and Fulcher (2000) develop higher order neural network group models for data approximation. Jiang, Gielen, and Wang (2010) investigate the combined effects of quantization and clipping on Higher Order Function Neural Networks (HOFNN) and Multi-Layer Feed-forward Neural Networks (MLFNN). Statistical models are used to analyze the effects of quantization in a digital implementation. Lu, song, and Shieh (2010) study the improving sparseness in kernel nonlinear feature extraction algorithms by Polynomial Kernel Higher Order Neural Networks.

Artificial Neural Network Group

Very little artificial neural network research has concentrated on such neuron network-based models as the integrated neural network (Matsuoka, et al., 1989) or holistic model (Pentland & Turk, 1989). Lumer (1992) proposed a new mechanism of selective attention among perceptual groups as part of his computational model of early vision. In this model, perceptual grouping is initially performed in connectionist networks by dynamically binding the neural activities triggered in response to related image features. Lie Groups were used in Tsao's (1989) group theory approach to the computer simulation of 3D rigid motion. More specifically, motion is expressed as an exponential mapping of the linear combination of six infinitesimal generators of the 1-parameter Lie subgroup. Hu (1992) proposed a level-by-level learning scheme for artificial neural groups. The learning process suggested by this method closely resembles the process of knowledge growth for human individuals and/or society, and can improve both network generalization and learning efficiency. The neural network hierarchical model devised by Willcox (1991) consists of binary-state neurons grouped into clusters, and can be analyzed using a Renormalization Group (RG) approach. Unlike the research previously described, Yang (1990) concerned himself with the activities of neuron *groups*. This work, together with Naimark's (1982) earlier theory of group representations, can be used as the basis for Neural Network Group Theory.

PHONNG GROUP

PHONNG Definition

A *set* (Waerden, 1970) is defined as a collection of *elements*, which possess the same properties. The symbol

$$a \in A$$

means:

A is a set, and a is an element of set A.

The *artificial polynomial higher order neural network set* is a set in which every element is a PHONN. The symbol

$$phonn \in PHONNS \text{ (where: } phonn = f : R^n \rightarrow R^m)$$

means:
PHONNS is a PHONN set, and *phonn*, which is one kind of artificial polynomial higher order neural network, is an element of set **PHONNS**. The domain of the artificial polynomial higher order neural network *phonn* inputs is the *n*-dimensional real number R^n. Likewise, the *phonn* outputs belong to the *m*-dimensional real number R^m. The artificial higher order neural network function *f* is a mapping from the inputs of *phonn* to its outputs.

The artificial polynomial higher order neural network set **PHONNS** is defined as the *union* of the **subsets** of **PHONN (order 2)**, **PHONN (order 3)**, **PHONN (order 4)**... and so on. In formal notation, we write:

PHONNS = **PHONN (order 2)**∪**PHONN(order 3)**∪**PHONN(order 3)**∪**PHONN(order 4)**∪.......

PHONN Generalized Sets (**PHONNGS**) are defined as the union of additive PHONN sets (**PHONN⁺**) and product PHONN sets (**PHONN***), as detailed, which is written as:

Algorithm 1.

---

a. $phonn^+_i \in PHONNS$;

or

if an addition $phonn^+_i + phonn^+_j$ is defined every two elements $phonn^+_i, phonn^+_j \in PHONNS$,

    then $phonn^+_i + phonn^+_j \in PHONN^+$, $\forall \, phonn^+_i, phonn^+_j \in PHONNS$;

or

if an addition $phonn^+_i + phonn^+_j$ is defined for every two elements

                  $phonn^+_i \in PHONNS$ and $phonn^+_j \in PHONN^+$,

then $phonn^+_i + phonn^+_j \in PHONN^+$, $\forall \, phonn^+_i \in PHONNS$ and $phonn^+_j \in PHONN^+$

or

if an addition $phonn^+_i + phonn^+_j$ is defined every two elements $phonn^+_i, phonn^+_j \in PHONN^+$,

then $phonn^+_i + phonn^+_j \in PHONN^+$, $\forall \, phonn^+_i, phonn^+_j \in PHONN^+$

b. $\exists$ an element $phonn^+_{i0}$ in $PHONN^+$ such that

$phonn^+_{i0} + phonn^+_i = phonn^+_i + phonn^+_{i0} = phonn^+_i \, \forall \, phonn^+_i \in PHONN^+$;

($phonn^+_{i0}$ is called the *identity* element of the set $PHONN^+$);

c. for every element $phonn^+_i \in PHONN^+$,

there exists a unique element, designated $phonn^+_i$,

for which $phonn^+_i + (-phonn^+_i) = (-phonn^+_i) + phonn^+_i = phonn^+_0$,

(the element $-phonn^+_i$ is called the *inverse* of $phonn^+_i$);

$PHONNGS = PHONN^* \cup PHONN^+$

Additive Generalized Artificial Higher Order Neural Network Sets

An *additive generalized* **PHONN set - PHONN⁺** - is a set in which element $phonn^+_i$ is either an artificial polynomial higher order neural network or an additive generalized polynomial higher order neural network, for which the following conditions in Algorithm 1 hold:

Product Generalised Artificial Higher Order Neural Network Sets

A *product generalized* **PHONN set - PHONN*** - is a set in which each element $phonn^*_i$ is either an artificial polynomial higher order neural network or a product generalized polynomial higher order neural network, for which the following conditions in Algorithm 2 hold:

The elements of set *PHONNS* are polynomial higher order neural networks; the elements of set *PHONNGS*, by contrast, are polynomial

Algorithm 2.

---

a. $phonn^*_i \in PHONNS$;

or

if the product $phonn^*_i phonn^*_j$ is defined for every two elements $phonn^*_i, phonn^*_j \in PHONNS$,

    then $phonn^*_i phonn^*_j \in PHONN^*$, $\forall \, phonn^*_i, phonn^*_j \in PHONNS$

or

if a product $phonn^*_i phonn^*_j$ is defined for every two elements

$phonn^*_i \in PHONNS$ and $phonn^*_j \in PHONN^*$,

then $phonn^*_i phonn^*_j \in PHONN^*$, $\forall \, phonn^*_i \in PHONNS$ and $phonn^*_j \in PHONN^*$;

or

if a product $phonn^*_i phonn^*_j$ is defined for every two elements $phonn^*_i, phonn^*_j \in PHONN^*$,

      then $phonn^*_i phonn^*_j \in PHONN^*$, $\forall \, phonn^*_i, phonn^*_j \in PHONN^*$;

b. $\exists$ an element $phonn^*_{ie}$ in $PHONN^*$ such that

$phonn^*_{ie} phonn^*_i = phonn^*_i phonn^*_{ie} = phonn^*_i \, \forall \, phonn^*_i \in PHONN^*$

($phonn^*_{ie}$ is called the *identity* element of the set $PHONN^*$);

c. For every element $phonn^*_i \in PHONN^*$, $\exists$ a unique element, designated $phonn^{*-1}_i$,

for which $phonn^*_i phonn^{*-1}_i = phonn^{*-1}_i phonn^*_i = phonn^*_e$,

(the element $phonn^{*-1}_i$ is called the *inverse* of $phonn^*_i$);

---

higher order neural network *groups*. The difference between a polynomial higher order neural network and a polynomial higher order neural network group was that, in which the polynomial higher order neural network generalized set **HONNGS** is a more generalized form of polynomial higher order neural network set **PHONNS**. Accordingly, polynomial higher order neural network groups should hold more potential for characterizing complex systems.

Following the group definitions by Inui (1978) and Naimark (1982), we have:

a nonempty set **PHONNG** is called a *polynomial higher order neural network group*, if **PHONNG** ⊂ P**HONNGS** (the polynomial higher order neural network generalized set), and either the product $h_i h_j$ or the sum $h_i + h_j$ is defined for every two elements $h_i, h_j \in PHONNG$.

Inference of Higher Order Neural Network Piecewise Function Groups

Hornik (1991) proved the following general result: "Whenever the activation function is continuous, bounded and non-constant, then for an arbitrary compact subset $X \subseteq R^n$, standard multilayer feed-forward networks can approximate any continuous function on X arbitrarily well with respect to uniform distance, provided that sufficiently many hidden units are available."

A more general result was proved by Leshno (1993): "A standard multilayer feed-forward network with a locally bounded piecewise continuous activation function can approximate *any* continuous function to *any* degree of accuracy if and only if the network's activation function is not a polynomial."

Zhang, Fulcher, and Scofield (1997) provided a general result for neural network group: "Consider a neural network Piecewise Function *Group*, in which each member is a standard multilayer feed-forward neural network, and which has a locally bounded, piecewise continuous (rather than polynomial) activation function and threshold.

Each such group can approximate *any* kind of piecewise continuous function, and to *any* degree of accuracy."

An inference is provided as follows: "Consider a higher order neural network Piecewise Function *Group*, in which each member is a standard multilayer feed-forward higher order neural network, and which has a locally bounded, piecewise continuous (rather than polynomial) activation function and threshold. Each such group can approximate *any* kind of piecewise continuous function, and to *any* degree of accuracy."

In the real world, if the function being analyzed varies in a discontinuous and non-smooth fashion with respect to input variables, then such functions cannot be effectively simulated by a higher order neural network. By contrast, if we use higher order neural network *groups* to simulate these functions, it *is* possible to simulate discontinuous functions to any degree accuracy, even at points of discontinuity

PHONN Models

Higher Order Neural Network models use trigonometric, linear, multiply, power and other neuron functions based on the following form in Box 1, where:

- **Output Layer Weights:** $(c_{k1k2}{}^o)$
- **Second Hidden Layer Weights:** $(c_{k1k2}{}^x)$ and $(c_{k1k2}{}^y)$
- **First Hidden Layer Weights:** $(c_{k1k2}{}^{hx})$ and $(c_{k1k2}{}^{hy})$

Choosing a different function f_i, results in a different higher order neural network model.

Polynomial Higher Order Neural Network (PHONN) model is shown in Box 2.

PHONG Model

The **PHONNG** model is a PHONN model *Group*. It is a piecewise function group of Polynomial

Table 1. Australian Dollar/US Dollar Exchange Rate. AUD$1.00 = USD$0.9083 on 2-Nov-2009, USA Federal Reserve Bank Data January 6th 2011.

USA Federal Reserve Bank Data				HONN Output				HONN Error Percentage			
Date	Rate de-sired output	Input 1 2 month ago	Input 2 1 month ago	PHONN	THONN	SPHONN	PHONNG	PHONN	THONN	SPHONN	PHONNG
11/2/2009	0.9083										
12/1/2009	0.9249										
1/4/2010	0.9133	0.9083	0.9249	0.9368	0.8708	0.9255	0.9192	2.5731	4.6535	1.3358	0.6460
2/1/2010	0.8877	0.9249	0.9133	0.9112	0.9096	0.9079	0.8758	2.6473	2.4670	2.2755	1.3405
3/1/2010	0.9001	0.9133	0.8877	0.9332	0.9252	0.8713	0.8379	3.6774	2.7886	3.1996	6.9103
4/1/2010	0.9212	0.8877	0.9001	0.8924	0.8876	0.9636	0.8609	3.1264	3.6474	4.6027	6.5458
5/3/2010	0.9255	0.9001	0.9212	0.9424	0.8913	0.9157	0.8739	1.8260	3.6953	1.0589	5.5754
6/1/2010	0.8396	0.9212	0.9255	0.8527	0.8856	0.8759	0.8242	1.5603	5.4788	4.3235	1.8342
7/1/2010	0.8380	0.9255	0.8396	0.8732	0.8632	0.8617	0.8407	4.2005	3.0072	2.8282	0.3222
8/2/2010	0.9135	0.8396	0.8380	0.9264	0.9547	0.9565	0.9366	1.4122	4.5101	4.7072	2.5287
9/1/2010	0.9093	0.8380	0.9135	0.8621	0.9428	0.9567	0.9082	5.1908	3.6842	5.2128	0.1188
10/1/2010	0.9710	0.9135	0.9093	0.8908	0.9541	0.9221	0.9522	8.2595	1.7405	5.0360	1.9361
11/1/2010	0.9878	0.9093	0.9710	0.9708	0.9544	0.9665	0.9681	1.7210	3.3813	2.1563	1.9943
12/1/2010	0.9675	0.9710	0.9878	0.9316	0.9872	0.9441	0.9839	3.7106	2.0362	2.4186	1.6951
Average Error (% Percentage)								3.3254	3.4242	3.2629	2.6206
Average Error of PHONN, THONN, and SPHONN(% percentage)								3.3748	PHONNG Better		0.7542

Box 1.

$$z = \sum_{\substack{k1,k2 \\ km=0}}^{n} c \prod_{j=1}^{m} \left[f_1\left(c_1 x_1\right) \right]^{k1} \left[f_2\left(c_2 x_2\right) \right]^{k2} \cdots \left[f_j\left(c_j x_j\right) \right]^{kj} \cdots \left[f_m\left(c_m x_m\right) \right]^{km}$$

$Let\ m = 2,\ c = c_{k1k2}, c_1 = c_{k1k2}{}^x,\ c_2 = c_{k1k2}{}^y,\ x_1 = x,\ and\ x_2 = y,\ we\ have:$

$$z = \sum_{k1,k2=0}^{n} c_{k1k2} \left[f_1\left(c_{k1k2}{}^x x\right) \right]^{k1} \left[f_2\left(c_{k1k2}{}^y y\right) \right]^{k2}$$

$$= \sum_{k1,k2=0}^{n} \left(c_{k1k2}{}^o\right) \left\{ c_{k1k2}{}^{hx} \left[f_1\left(c_{k1k2}{}^x x\right) \right]^{k1} \right\} \left\{ c_{k1k2}{}^{hy} \left[f_2\left(c_{k1k2}{}^y y\right) \right]^{k2} \right\}$$

$$where: c_{k1k2} = \left(c_{k1k2}{}^o\right) \left(c_{k1k2}{}^{hx} \right) \left(c_{k1k2}{}^{hy} \right)$$

Table 2. Australian Dollar/US Dollar Exchange Rate. AUD$1.00 = USD$0.9143 on 30-Nov-2009, USA Federal Reserve Bank Data January 6th 2011.

USA Federal Reserve Bank Data				HONN Output				HONN Error Percentage			
Date	Rate de-sired output	Input 1 2 month ago	Input 2 1 month ago	PHONN	THONN	SPHONN	THONNG	PHONN	THONN	SPHONN	THONNG
11/30/2009	0.9143										
12/31/2009	0.8978										
1/29/2010	0.8873	0.9143	0.8978	0.8975	0.8675	0.8704	0.8766	1.1496	2.2315	1.9047	1.2059
2/26/2010	0.8961	0.8978	0.8873	0.9254	0.8787	0.8484	0.8886	3.2697	1.9417	5.3231	0.8370
3/31/2010	0.9169	0.8873	0.8961	0.9464	0.8819	0.8629	0.8943	3.2174	3.8172	5.8894	2.4648
4/30/2010	0.9306	0.8961	0.9169	0.8775	0.8755	0.8937	0.9598	5.7060	5.9209	3.9652	3.1378
5/28/2010	0.8491	0.9169	0.9306	0.8621	0.8983	0.8567	0.8215	1.5310	5.7944	0.8951	3.2505
6/30/2010	0.8480	0.9306	0.8491	0.8125	0.8346	0.8226	0.8622	4.1863	1.5802	2.9953	1.6745
7/30/2010	0.9051	0.8491	0.8480	0.8695	0.9195	0.9335	0.9233	3.9333	1.5910	3.1378	2.0108
8/31/2010	0.8910	0.8480	0.9051	0.9405	0.9290	0.8734	0.9173	5.5556	4.2649	1.9753	2.9517
9/30/2010	0.9640	0.9051	0.8910	0.9758	0.9892	0.9075	0.9476	1.2241	2.6141	5.8610	1.7012
10/29/2010	0.9798	0.8910	0.9640	0.9915	0.9205	0.9451	0.9595	1.1941	6.0523	3.5415	2.0719
11/30/2010	0.9607	0.9640	0.9798	0.9806	0.9876	0.9834	0.9755	2.0714	2.8000	2.3629	1.5405
12/30/2010	1.0122	0.9798	0.9607	0.9913	0.9987	0.9616	0.9938	2.0648	1.3337	4.9990	1.8178
Average Error(% Percentage)								2.9253	3.3285	3.5708	2.0554
Average Error of PHONN, THONN, and SPHONN(% percentage)								3.1269	PHHONN Better		1.0715

Box 2.

$$
\text{Let}: \quad f_1\left(c_{k1k2}{}^{x}x\right) = \left(c_{k1k2}{}^{x}x\right); \text{and} f_2\left(c_{k1k2}{}^{y}y\right) = \left(c_{k1k2}{}^{y}y\right)
$$

$$
\text{then} \quad z = \sum_{k1,k2=0}^{n} c_{k1k2}\left[\, f_1\left(c_{k1k2}{}^{x}x\right)\right]^{k1}\left[\, f_2\left(c_{k1k2}{}^{y}y\right)\right]^{k2}
$$

$$
= \sum_{k1,k2=0}^{n}\left(c_{k1k2}{}^{o}\right)\left\{\, c_{k1k2}{}^{hx}\left(c_{k1k2}{}^{x}x\right)^{k1}\right\}\left\{c_{k1k2}{}^{hy}\left(c_{k1k2}{}^{y}y\right)^{k2}\right\}
$$

Box 3.

$$Z = \left\{ z_1,\ z_2,\ z_3,\ ...,\ z_i,\ z_{i+1},\ z_{i+2},\ ... \right\}$$

where : $\qquad z_i \in \mathbf{K}_i \subset \mathbf{R}^n, \mathbf{K}_i$ is a compact set

$$z_i = \sum_{k1,k2=0}^{n} \left(c_{ik1k2}{}^o\right)\left[\left(c_{ik1k2}{}^x\right)x\right]^{k1}\left[\left(c_{ik1k2}{}^y\right)y\right]^{k2} = \sum_{k1,k2=0}^{n} c_{ik1k2}x^{k1}y^{k2}$$

$$c_{ik1k2} = \left(c_{ik1k2}{}^o\right)\left[\left(c_{ik1k2}{}^x\right)^{k1}\right]\left[\left(c_{ik1k2}{}^y\right)^{k2}\right]$$

Higher Order Neural Networks, and is defined as shown in Box 3.

In the **PHONNG** Model (Piecewise Function Group), group *addition* is defined as the *piecewise* function:

$$Z = \begin{cases} z_1, z_1 & inputs \in \mathbf{K}_1 \\ z_2, z_2 & inputs \in \mathbf{K}_2 \\ z_i, z_i & inputs \in \mathbf{K}_i \\ z_{i+1}, z_{i+1} & inputs \in \mathbf{K}_{i+1} \end{cases}$$

where : $z_i inputs \in \mathbf{K}_i \subset \mathbf{R}^n, \mathbf{K}_i$ is a compact set

The **PHONNG** Model is an open and convergent model which can approximate any kind of piecewise continuous function *to any degree of accuracy*, even at discontinuous points (or regions).

An inductive proof of this inference is provided as follows:

Inference:

"Consider a artificial polynomial higher order neural network group as Piecewise Function Group, in which each member is a standard multilayer feedforward higher order neural network, and which has a locally bounded, piecewise continuous (rather than polynomial) activation function and threshold. Each such group can approximate any kind of piecewise continuous function, and to any degree of accuracy."

We use the following definitions in our proof:

- H_w: the higher order neural network with n input units, characterised by w;
- $\mathbf{P}$: the compact set, $\mathbf{P} \subset \mathbf{R}^n$;
- $C(\mathbf{R}^n)$: the family of "real world" functions one may wish to approximate with feedforward higher order neurl network architectures of the form H_w;
- s: every continuous function, $s \subset C(\mathbf{R}^n)$;
- $\mathbf{G}$: the family of all functions implied by the network's architecture - namely the family when w runs over all possible values;
- g: a good approximation to s on $\mathbf{P}$, $g \subset \mathbf{G}$;
- $\mathbf{L}^\infty(\mathbf{P})$: essentially bounded on $\mathbf{P}$ in $\mathbf{R}^n$ with respect to Lebesgue measurement;
- $\mathbf{L}^\infty_{loc}(\mathbf{P})$: locally essentially bounded on $\mathbf{P}$ in $\mathbf{R}^n$ with respect to Lebesgue measurement;

PHONNG is the higher order neural network group in which each addition $z_i + z_j$ is defined as the *Piecewise Function* for every two elements $z_i, z_j \in$ **PHONNG**.

$$z_i + z_j = \begin{cases} z_i, & I_i = (I \in P_1) \\ z_j, & I_j = (I \in P_2) \end{cases}$$

where I_i, I_j, and I (inputs to the higher order neural networks)

Proof

Step 1: $P_1 = P$

Based on the Leshno theorem (1993),

$$\lim_{j=\infty} \|s - z_j\| L\infty(P) = 0$$

So we have lim

$$\|s - g_j\| L\infty(_1) = 0$$
$$j = \infty$$

Step 2: $P_1 \cup P_2 = P$

$$s = \begin{cases} s_1, & \text{a continuous function on } P_1 \\ s_2, & \text{a continuous function on } P_2 \end{cases}$$

In P1, we have:

$$\lim_{j=\infty} \|s_1 - g_j^{(1)}\| L\infty(P_1) = 0$$

There exists a function $g^{(1)}$ which is a good approximation to s_1 on P_1.

In P_2, we have:

$$\lim_{j=\infty} \|s_2 - g_j^{(2)}\| L\infty(P_2) = 0$$

There exists a function $g^{(2)}$ which is a good approximation to s_2 on P_2.

Based on the earlier definition of Neural Network Piecewise Function Groups,

$$z_i + z_j = \begin{cases} z_1 = g^{(1)}, & I_1 = (I \in P1) \\ z_2 = g^{(2)}, & I_2 = (I \in P2) \end{cases}$$

where I1, I_2, and I (inputs to the higher order neural networks)

Step 3: $P_1 \cup P_2 \cup \ldots \cup P_m = P$,
m is an any integer and m $\rightarrow \infty$.

$$s = \begin{cases} s_1, & \text{a continuous function on } P_1 \\ s_2, & \text{a continuous function on } P_2 \\ s_m, & \text{a continuous function on } P_m \end{cases}$$

Based on the definition of Neural Network Piecewise Function Group, we have:

$$z_1 + z_2 + \ldots + z_m = \begin{cases} z_1 = g^{(1)}, & I = (I \in P_1) \\ z_2 = g^{(2)} & I = (I \in P_2) \\ z_m = g^{(m)} & I = (I \in P_m) \end{cases}$$

Step 4: $P_1 \cup P_2 \cup \ldots \cup P_m \cup P_{m+1} = P$

$$s = \begin{cases} s_1, & \text{a continuous function on } P_1 \\ s_2, & \text{a continuous function on } P_2 \\ s_m, & \text{a continuous function on } P_m \\ s_{m+1}, & \text{a continuous function on } P_{m+!} \end{cases}$$

In P_{m+1}, based on Leshno's (1993) Theorem, we have:

$$\lim_{j=\infty} \|s_{m+1} - g_j^{(m+1)}\| L\infty(P_{m+1}) = 0$$

There exists a function $g^{(m+1)}$ which is a good approximation to s_{m+1} on P_{m+1}.

Based on step 3, we have:

$$z_1 + z_2 + \ldots + z_m + z_{m+1} = \begin{cases} z_1 = g^{(1)}, & I = (I \in P_1) \\ z_2 = g^{(2)} & I = (I \in P_2) \\ z_m = g^{(m)} & I = (I \in P_m) \\ z_{m+1} = g^{(m+1)} & I = (I \in P_{m+!}) \end{cases}$$

In the real world, if the function being analyzed varies in a discontinuous and non-smooth fashion with respect to input variables, then such functions cannot be effectively simulated by a artificial polynomial higher order neural network. By contrast, if we use artificial polynomial higher order neural network *groups* to simulate these functions, it *is* possible to simulate discontinuous functions to any degree accuracy, even at points of discontinuity.

TRIGONOMETRIC POLYNOMIAL HIGHER ORDER NEURAL NETWORK GROUPS

THONNG Definition

A *set* (Waerden, 1970) is defined as a collection of *elements*, which possess the same properties. The symbol

$$a \in A$$

means:

A is a set, and a is an element of set A.

The *artificial trigonometric polynomial higher order neural network set* is a set in which every element is a THONN. The symbol

$$thonn \in THONNS \ (\text{where: } thonn = f : \mathbf{R}^n \rightarrow \mathbf{R}^m)$$

means:

THONNS is a THONN set, and *thonn*, which is one kind of artificial trigonometric polynomial higher order neural network, is an element of set *THONNS*. The domain of the artificial trigonometric polynomial higher order neural network *thonn* inputs is the *n*-dimensional real number $\mathbf{R}^n$. Likewise, the *thonn* outputs belong to the *m*-dimensional real number $\mathbf{R}^m$. The artificial higher order neural network function *f* is a mapping from the inputs of *thonn* to its outputs.

The artificial trigonometric polynomial higher order neural network set *THONNS* is defined as the *union* of the *subsets* of *THONN (order 2)*, *THONN (order 3)*, *THONN (order 4)*... and so on. In formal notation, we write:

THONNS = THONN (order 2)∪*THONN(order 3)*∪*THONN(order 3)*∪*THONN(order 4)*∪.......

Algorithm 3.

a. $thonn^+_i \in THONNS$;
or
if an addition $thonn^+_i + thonn^+_j$ is defined every two elements $thonn^+_i, thonn^+_j \in THONNS$,
    then $thonn^+_i + thonn^+_j \in THONN^+, \forall thonn^+_i, thonn^+_j \in THONNS$;
or
if an addition $thonn^+_i + thonn^+_j$ is defined for every two elements
    $thonn^+_i \in THONNS$ and $thonn^+_j \in THONN^+$,
then $thonn^+_i + thonn^+_j \in THONN^+, \forall thonn^+_i \in THONNS$ and $thonn^+_j \in THONN^+$;
or
if an addition $thonn^+_i + thonn^+_j$ is defined every two elements $thonn^+_i, thonn^+_j \in THONN^+$,
then $thonn^+_i + thonn^+_j \in THONN^+, \forall thonn^+_i, thonn^+_j \in THONN^+$;
b. $\exists$ an element $thonn^+_{i0}$ in $THONN^+$ such that
$thonn^+_{i0} + thonn^+_i = thonn^+_i + thonn^+_{i0} = thonn^+_i, \forall thonn^+_i \in \mathbf{THONN^+}$;
($thonn^+_{i0}$ is called the *identity* element of the set $THONN^+$);
c. for every element $thonn^+_i \in \mathbf{THONN^+}$,
there exists a unique element, designated $thonn^+_i$,
for which $thonn^+_i + (-thonn^+_i) = (-thonn^+_i) + thonn^+_i = thonn^+_0$,
(the element $-thonn^+_i$ is called the *inverse* of $thonn^+_i$);

Alogrithm 4.

---

a. *thonn** $_i$ ∈ *THONNS*;
or
if the product *thonn** $_i$ *thonn** $_j$ is defined for every two elements *thonn** $_i$, *thonn** $_j$ ∈ *THONNS*,
    then *thonn** $_i$ *thonn** $_j$ ∈ *THONN**, ∀ *thonn** $_i$, *thonn** $_j$ ∈ *THONNS*
or
if a product *thonn** $_i$ *thonn** $_j$ is defined for every two elements
thonn* $_i$ ∈ *THONNS* and *thonn** $_j$ ∈ *THONN**,
then *thonn** $_i$ *thonn** $_j$ ∈ *THONN**, ∀ *thonn** $_i$ ∈ *THONNS* and *thonn** $_j$ ∈ *THONN**;
or
if a product *thonn** $_i$ *thonn** $_j$ is defined for every two elements *thonn** $_i$, *thonn** $_j$ ∈ *THONN**,
    then *thonn** $_i$ *thonn** $_j$ ∈ *THONN**, ∀ *thonn** $_i$, *thonn** $_j$ ∈ *THONN**;
b. ∃ an element *thonn** $_{ie}$ in *THONN** such that
thonn* $_{ie}$ *thonn** $_i$ = *thonn** $_i$ *thonn** $_{ie}$ = *thonn** $_i$, ∀ *thonn** $_i$ ∈ **THONN***
(*thonn** $_{ie}$ is called the *identity* element of the set *THONN**);
c. For every element *thonn** $_i$ ∈ **THONN***, ∃ a unique element, designated *thonn* $^{*\text{-}1}$ $_i$,
for which *thonn** $_i$ *thonn* $^{*\text{-}1}$ $_i$ = *thonn* $^{*\text{-}1}$ $_i$ *thonn** $_i$ = *thonn** $_e$,
(the element thonn $^{*\text{-}1}$ $_i$ is called the *inverse* of *thonn** $_i$);

THONN Generalized Sets (*THONNGS)* are defined as the union of additive THONN sets (*THONN⁺*) and product THONN sets (*THONN**), as detailed, which we write as:

$$THONNGS = THONN^* \cup \textbf{THONN}^+$$

Additive Generalized Artificial Higher Order Neural Network Sets

An *additive generalized* **THONN** *set* - *THONN⁺* - is a set in which element *thonn⁺* $_i$ is either an artificial trigonometric polynomial higher order neural network or an additive generalized trigonometric polynomial higher order neural network, for which the following conditions in Algorithm 3 hold:

Product Generalised Artificial Higher Order Neural Network Sets

A *product generalized* **THONN** *set* - *THONN** - is a set in which each element *thonn** $_i$ is either an artificial trigonometric polynomial higher order neural network or a product generalized trigonometric polynomial higher order neural network, for which the following conditions in Algorithm 4 hold:

The elements of set *THONNS* are trigonometric polynomial higher order neural networks; the elements of set *THONNGS*, by contrast, are trigonometric polynomial higher order neural network *groups*. The difference between a trigonometric polynomial higher order neural network and a trigonometric polynomial higher order neural network group was that, in which the trigonometric polynomial higher order neural network generalized set **HONNGS** is a more generalized form of trigonometric polynomial higher order neural network set *THONNS*. Accordingly, trigonometric polynomial higher order neural network groups should hold more potential for characterizing complex systems.

Following the group definitions by Inui (1978) and Naimark (1982), we have: a nonempty set *THONNG* is called a *trigonometric polynomial higher order neural network group*, if **THONNG** ⊂ THONN**GS** (the trigonometric polynomial higher order neural network generalized set), and either the product $h_i h_j$ or the sum $h_i + h_j$ is defined for every two elements h_i, h_j ∈ *THONNG*.

Box 4.

$$\text{Let:} \quad f_1\left(c_{k1k2}{}^x x\right) = \sin\left(c_{k1k2}{}^x x\right); f_2\left(c_{k1k2}{}^y y\right) = \cos\left(c_{k1k2}{}^y y\right)$$

$$\text{then} \quad z = \sum_{k1,k2=0}^{n} c_{k1k2}\left[f_1\left(c_{k1k2}{}^x x\right) \right]^{k1}\left[f_2\left(c_{k1k2}{}^y y\right) \right]^{k2}$$

$$= \sum_{k1,k2=0}^{n}\left(c_{k1k2}{}^o\right)\left\{ c_{k1k2}{}^{hx}\left[\sin\left(c_{k1k2}{}^x x\right)\right]^{k1}\right\}\left\{c_{k1k2}{}^{hy}\left[\cos\left(c_{k1k2}{}^y y\right)\right]^{k2}\right\}$$

Trigonometric Polynomial Higher Order Neural Network (THONN) Model

When j is sufficiently large, this model is able to simulate higher order nonlinear data. (see Box 4)

Trigonometric Polynomial Higher Order Neural Network Group (THONNG) Model

In order to handle discontinuities in the input training data, the Trigonometric Polynomial Higher Order Neural Network *Group* (**THONNG**) model has also been developed. This is a model in which every element is a *trigonometric* polynomial higher order neural network - THONN (Zhang & Fulcher, 1996b). The domain of the THONN inputs is the *n*-dimensional real number $\boldsymbol{R}^n$. Likewise, the THONN outputs belong to the *m*-dimensional real number $\boldsymbol{R}^m$. The artificial trigonometric higher order neural network function *f* constitutes a mapping from the inputs of THONN to its outputs.

The **THONNG** model is a THONN model *Group*. It is a piecewise function group of Trigonometric Polynomial Higher Order Neural Networks, and is defined as shown in Box 5.

In the **THONNG** Model (Piecewise Function Group), group *addition* is defined as the *piecewise* function:

$$Z = \begin{cases} z_1, z_1 & \text{inputs} \in \mathbf{K}_1 \\ z_2, z_2 & \text{inputs} \in \mathbf{K}_2 \\ z_i, z_i & \text{inputs} \in \mathbf{K}_i \\ z_{i+1}, z_{i+1} & \text{inputs} \in \mathbf{K}_{i+1} \end{cases}$$

where : z_i inputs $\in \mathbf{K}_i \subset \mathbf{R}^n, \mathbf{K}_i$ is a compact set

The **THONNG** Model is an open and convergent model, which can approximate any kind of

Box 5.

$$Z = \left\{ z_1, \ z_2, \ z_3, \ ..., \ z_i, \ z_{i+1}, \ z_{i+2}, \ ...\right\}$$

where : $\quad z_i \in \mathbf{K}_i \subset \mathbf{R}^n, \mathbf{K}_i$ is a compact set

$$z_i = \sum_{k1,k2=0}^{n} c_{k1k2}\left[f_1\left(c_{k1k2}{}^x x\right) \right]^{k1}\left[f_2\left(c_{k1k2}{}^y y\right) \right]^{k2}$$

$$= \sum_{k1,k2=0}^{n}\left(c_{k1k2}{}^o\right)\left\{ c_{k1k2}{}^{hx}\left[\sin\left(c_{k1k2}{}^x x\right)\right]^{k1}\right\}\left\{c_{k1k2}{}^{hy}\left[\cos\left(c_{k1k2}{}^y y\right)\right]^{k2}\right\}$$

piecewise continuous function *to any degree of accuracy*, even at discontinuous points (or regions).

THONN ∈ *THONNG*

where: THONN = *f*: $R^n \rightarrow R^m$; THONNG is the group model.

Based on the inference of Zhang, Fulcher, and Scofield (1997), each such artificial higher order neural network group can approximate any kind of piecewise continuous function, and to any degree of accuracy. Hence, *THONNG* is also able to simulate discontinuous data.

An inductive proof of this inference is provided as follows:

Consider a artificial trigonometric polynomial higher order neural network group as Piecewise Function Group, in which each member is a standard multilayer feedforward higher order neural network, and which has a locally bounded, piecewise continuous (rather than polynomial) activation function and threshold. Each such group can approximate any kind of piecewise continuous function, and to any degree of accuracy.

HIGHER ORDER NEURAL NETWORK GROUP FINANCIAL SIMULATION SYSTEM

The above concepts have been incorporated into a Higher Order Neural network Group financial simulation system. This system comprises two parts, one being a Polynomial Higher Order Neural Network Simulator - *PHONNSim-*, and the other a Trigonometric polynomial Higher Order Neural Network Simulator - *THONNSim*. These *PHONNSim and THONNSim* financial simulation systems were written in the C language, runs under X-Windows on a SUN workstation, and incorporates a user-friendly Graphical User Interface. Any step, data or calculation can be reviewed and modified dynamically in different windows. At the top of the simulator main win-

dow, there are three pull-down menus, namely Data, Translators, and Neural Network. Each of these offers several options; selecting an option creates another window for further processing. For instance, once we have selected some data via the Data menu, two options are presented for data loading and graphical display.

PRELIMINARY TESTING OF PHONNG AND THONNG SIMULATOR

This chapter uses the monthly Australian Dollar and USA dollar exchange rate from November 2009 to December 2010 (See Table 1 and 2) as the test data for PHONNG and THONNG models. Rate and desired output data, R_t are from USA Federal Reserve Bank Data bank. Input1, R_{t-2} are the data at time t-2. Input 2, R_{t-1} are the data at time t-1. The values of R_{t-2}, R_{t-1}, and R_t are used as inputs and output in the PHONNG and THONNG models. PHONNG model is used for Table 1 and THONNG model is used in Table 2. The test data of PHONNG and THONNG orders 6 for using 10,000 epochs are shown on the tables.

In Table 1, AustralianDollar/USDollar Exchange Rate AUD\$1.00 = USD\$0.9083 on 2-Nov-2009, the average errors of PHONN, THONN, Sigmoid Polynomial Higher Order Neural Network (SPHONN), and PHONNG are 3.3254%, 3.4242%, 3.2629%, and 2.6206%, respectively. The average error of PHONN, THONN, and SPHONN is 3.3748%. Therefore, PHONNG error is 0.7542% better than the average error of PHONN, THONN, and SPHONN models. In Table 2, AustralianDollar/USDollar Exchange Rate AUD\$1.00 = USD\$0.9143 on 30-Nov-2009, the average errors of PHONN, THONN, SPHONN, and THONNG are 2.9253%, 3.3085%, 3.5708%, and 2.0554%, respectively. The average error of PHONN, THONN, and SPHONN is 3.1269%. Therefore, THONNG error is 1.0715% better than the average error of PHONN, THONN, and SPHONN models.

FUTURE RESEARCH DIRECTIONS

One of the topics for future research is to continue building models of higher order neural networks for different data series.

CONCLUSION

The details of open box and nonlinear higher order neural network models of PHONNG and THONNG are developed. The learning algorithm formulae for PHONNG and THONNG are provided based on the structures of PHONNG and THONNG. PHONNG and THONNG simulators are tested for the PHONNG and THONNG models using high frequency data. The running results are compared with Polynomial Higher Order Neural Network (PHONN), Trigonometric Higher Order Neural Network (THONN), and Sigmoid Polynomial Higher Order Neural Network (SPHONN) models. Test results show that errors of PHONNG, THONN, and SPHONNG models are 2.9253% to 3.5708%, and the average error of Polynomial Higher Order Neural Network Group (PHONNG) and Trigonometric Higher Order Neural Network Group (THONNG) models are from 2.0554% to 2.6206%. It means that PHONNG and THONNG models are 0.7542% to 1.0715% better than the average of the PHONN, THONN, and SPHONN models.

ACKNOWLEDGMENT

The author would like to acknowledge the financial assistance of the following organizations in the development of Higher Order Neural Networks: Fujitsu Research Laboratories, Japan (1995-1996), Australian Research Council (1997-1998), the US National Research Council (1999-2000), and the Applied Research Centers and Dean's Office Grants of our University, USA (2001-2011).

REFERENCES

Chen, Y., Wu, P., & Wu, Q. (2009a). Foreign exchange rate forecasting using higher order flexible neural tree. In Zhang, M. (Ed.), *Artificial Higher Order Neural Networks for Economics and Business* (pp. 94–112). Hershey, PA: IGI Global. doi:10.4018/978-1-59904-897-0.ch005

Christodoulou, M. A., & Iliopoulos, T. N. (2006a). Neural network models for prediction of steady-state and dynamic behavior of MAPK cascade. In *Proceedings of 14th Mediterranean Conference on Control and Automation*, (pp. 1 – 9). IEEE.

Crane, J., & Zhang, M. (2005). Data simulation using SINCHONN model. In *Proceedings of IASTED International Conference on Computational Intelligence*, (pp. 50-55). Calgary, Canada: IASTED.

Draye, J. S., Pavisic, D. A., Cheron, G. A., & Libert, G. A. (1996). Dynamic recurrent neural networks: A dynamic analysis. *IEEE Transactions SMC- Part B, 26*(5), 692-706.

Dunis, C. L., Laws, J., & Evans, B. (2006b). Modelling and trading the soybean-oil crush spread with recurrent and higher order networks: A comparative analysis. *Neural Network World, 3*(6), 193–213.

Foka, A. (1999). *Time series prediction using evolving polynomial neural networks*. (MSc Thesis). University of Manchester Institute of Science & Technology. Manchester, UK.

Fulcher, G. E., & Brown, D. E. (1994). A polynomial neural network for predicting temperature distributions. *IEEE Transactions on Neural Networks, 5*(3), 372–379. doi:10.1109/72.286909

Ghazali, R. (2005). *Higher order neural network for financial time series prediction*. Retrieved from http://www.cms.livjm.ac.uk/research/doc/ConfReport2005.doc

Ghazali, R., & Al-Jumeily, D. (2009). Application of pi-sigma neural networks and ridge polynomial neural networks to financial time series prediction. In Zhang, M. (Ed.), *Artificial Higher Order Neural Networks for Economics and Business* (pp. 271–294). Hershey, PA: IGI Global. doi:10.4018/978-1-59904-897-0.ch012

Ghazali, R., Hussain, A. J., & Nawi, N. M. (2010). Dynamic ridge polynomial higher order neural network. In Zhang, M. (Ed.), *Artificial Higher Order Neural Networks for Computer Science and Engineering – Trends for Emerging Application* (pp. 255–268). Hershey, PA: IGI Global.

Ghosh, J., & Shin, Y. (1992). Efficient higher-order neural networks for function approximation and classification. *International Journal of Neural Systems*, *3*(4), 323–350. doi:10.1142/S0129065792000255

Hornik, K. (1991). Approximation capabilities of multilayer feedforward networks. *Neural Networks*, *4*, 251–257. doi:10.1016/0893-6080(91)90009-T

Hu, S., & Yan, P. (1992). Level-by-level learning for artificial neural groups. *ACTA Electronica SINICA*, *20*(10), 39–43.

Hussain, A., Knowles, A., Lisboa, P., El-Deredy, W., & Al-Jumeily, D. (2006). Polynomial pipelined neural network and its application to financial time series prediction. *Lecture Notes in Artificial Intelligence*, *4304*, 597–606.

Hussain, A., & Liatsis, P. (2009). A novel recurrent polynomial neural network for financial time series prediction. In Zhang, M. (Ed.), *Artificial Higher Order Neural Networks for Economics and Business* (pp. 190–211). Hershey, PA: IGI Global. doi:10.4018/978-1-59904-897-0.ch009

Inui, T., Tanabe, Y., & Onodera, Y. (1978). *Group theory and its application in physics*. Heidelberg, Germany: Springer-Verlag. doi:10.1007/978-3-642-80021-4

Jiang, M., Gielen, G., & Wang, L. (2010). Analysis of quantization effects on higher order function and multilayer feedforward neural networks. In Zhang, M. (Ed.), *Artificial Higher Order Neural Networks for Computer Science and Engineering – Trends for Emerging Application* (pp. 187–222). Hershey, PA: IGI Global.

Kariniotakis, G. N., Stavrakakis, G. S., & Nogaret, E. F. (1996). Wind power forecasting using advanced neural networks models. *IEEE Transactions on Energy Conversion*, *11*(4), 762–767. doi:10.1109/60.556376

Knowles, A., Hussain, A., Deredy, W. E., Lisboa, P., & Dunis, C. L. (2009). Higher order neural networks with bayesian confidence measure for the prediction of the EUR/USD exchange rate. In Zhang, M. (Ed.), *Artificial Higher Order Neural Networks for Economics and Business* (pp. 48–59). Hershey, PA: IGI Global. doi:10.4018/978-1-59904-897-0.ch002

Knowles, A., Hussain, A., Deredy, W. E., Lisboa, P. G. J., & Dunis, C. (2005). *Higher-order neural network with bayesian confidence measure for prediction of EUR/USD exchange rate*. Paper presented at the Forecasting Financial Markets Conference. Marseilles, France.

Kosmatopoulos, E. B., Ioannou, P. A., & Christodoulou, M. A. (1992). Identification of nonlinear systems using new dynamic neural network structures. In *Proceedings of the 31st IEEE Conference on Decision and Control,* (vol. 1), (pp. 20 – 25). IEEE Press.

Kosmatopoulos, E. B., Polycarpou, M. M., Christodoulou, M. A., & Ioannou, P. A. (1995). High-order neural network structures for identification of dynamical systems. *IEEE Transactions on Neural Networks*, *6*(2), 422–431. doi:10.1109/72.363477

Kuroe, Y., Ikeda, H., & Mori, T. (1997). Identification of nonlinear dynamical systems by recurrent high-order neural networks. In *Proceedings of IEEE International Conference on Systems, Man, and Cybernetics,* (Vol. 1), (pp. 70 – 75). IEEE Press.

Lee, M., Lee, S. Y., & Park, C. H. (1992). Neural controller of nonlinear dynamic systems using higher order neural networks. *Electronics Letters, 28*(3), 276–277. doi:10.1049/el:19920170

Leshno, M., Lin, V., Ya, P. A., & Schocken, S. (1993). Multilayer feedforward networks with a nonpolynomial activation function can approximate any function. *Neural Networks, 6,* 861–867. doi:10.1016/S0893-6080(05)80131-5

Liatsis, P., Hussain, A., & Milonidis, E. (2009). Artificial higher order pipeline recurrent neural networks for financial time series prediction. In Zhang, M. (Ed.), *Artificial Higher Order Neural Networks for Economics and Business* (pp. 164–189). Hershey, PA: IGI Global. doi:10.4018/978-1-59904-897-0.ch008

Lu, B., Qi, H., Zhang, M., & Scofield, R. A. (2000). Using PT-HONN models for multi-polynomial function simulation. In *Proceedings of IASTED International Conference on Neural Networks,* (pp. 1-5). Pittsburgh, PA: IASTED.

Lu, Z., Song, G., & Shieh, L. (2010). Improving sparsity in kernel principal component analysis by polynomial kernel higher order neural networks. In Zhang, M. (Ed.), *Artificial Higher Order Neural Networks for Computer Science and Engineering – Trends for Emerging Application* (pp. 223–238). Hershey, PA: IGI Global.

Lumer, E. D. (1992). Selective attention to perceptual groups: The phase tracking mechanism. *International Journal of Neural Systems, 3*(1), 1–17. doi:10.1142/S0129065792000024

Matsuoka, T., Hamada, H., & Nakatsu, R. (1989). Syllable recognition using integrated neural networks. In *Proceedings of the International Joint Conference on Neural Networks*, (pp. 251-258). Washington, DC: IEEE.

Murata, J. (2010). Analysis and improvement of function approximation capabilities of pi-sigma higher order neural networks. In Zhang, M. (Ed.), *Artificial Higher Order Neural Networks for Computer Science and Engineering – Trends for Emerging Application* (pp. 239–254). Hershey, PA: IGI Global.

Naimark, M. A., & Stern, A. I. (1982). *Theory of group representations.* Berlin, Germany: Springer-Verlag. doi:10.1007/978-1-4613-8142-6

Onwubolu, G. C. (2009). Artificial higher order neural networks in time series prediction. In Zhang, M. (Ed.), *Artificial Higher Order Neural Networks for Economics and Business* (pp. 250–270). Hershey, PA: IGI Global. doi:10.4018/978-1-59904-897-0.ch011

Pentland, A., & Turk, M. (1989). Face processing: Models for recognition. In *Proceedings of SPIE - Intelligent Robots and Computer Vision VIII: Algorithms and Technology,* (pp. 20-35). SPIE.

Qi, H., & Zhang, M. (2001). Rainfall estimation using M-THONN model. In *Proceedings of International Joint Conference on Neural Networks,* (pp. 1620 – 1624). IJCNN.

Rovithakis, G. A., Chalkiadakis, I., & Zervakis, M. E. (2004). High-order neural network structure selection for function approximation applications using genetic algorithms. *IEEE Transactions on Systems, Man and Cybernetics. Part B, 34*(1), 150–158.

Saad, E. W., Prokhorov, D. V., & Wunsch, D. C. II. (1998). Comparative study of stock trend prediction using time delay recurrent and probabilistic neural networks. *IEEE Transactions on Neural Networks*, 9(6), 1456–1470. doi:10.1109/72.728395

Sanchez, E. N., Alanis, A. Y., & Rico, J. (2009). Electric load demand and electricity prices forecasting using higher order neural networks trained by kalman filtering. In Zhang, M. (Ed.), *Artificial Higher Order Neural Networks for Economics and Business* (pp. 295–313). Hershey, PA: IGI Global.

Selviah, D. R., & Shawash, J. (2009). Generalized correlation higher order neural networks for financial time series prediction. In Zhang, M. (Ed.), *Artificial Higher Order Neural Networks for Economics and Business* (pp. 212–249). Hershey, PA: IGI Global. doi:10.4018/978-1-59904-897-0.ch010

Shi, D., Tan, S., & Ge, S. S. (2009). Automatically identifying predictor variables for stock return prediction. In Zhang, M. (Ed.), *Artificial Higher Order Neural Networks for Economics and Business* (pp. 60–78). Hershey, PA: IGI Global. doi:10.4018/978-1-59904-897-0.ch003

Tawfik, H., & Liatsis, P. (1997). Prediction of non-linear time-series using higher-order neural networks. In *Proceeding IWSSIP 1997 Conference*. Poznan, Poland: IWSSIP.

Tenti, P. (1996). Forecasting foreign exchange rates using recurrent neural networks. *Applied Artificial Intelligence*, 10, 567–581. doi:10.1080/088395196118434

Tsao, T.-R. (1989). A group theory approach to neural network computing of 3D rigid motion. In *Proceedings of the International Joint Conference on Neural Networks*, (vol 2), (pp. 275-280). IJCNN.

Waerden, B. L. (1970). *Algebra*. New York, NY: Frederick Ungar Publishing Co.

Willcox, C. R. (1991). Understanding hierarchical neural network behavior: A renormalization group approach. *Journal of Physics. A. Mathematical Nuclear and General*, 24, 2655–2644. doi:10.1088/0305-4470/24/11/030

Xu, S. (2009). Adaptive higher order neural network models and their applications in business. In Zhang, M. (Ed.), *Artificial Higher Order Neural Networks for Economics and Business* (pp. 314–329). Hershey, PA: IGI Global. doi:10.4018/978-1-59904-897-0.ch014

Xu, S., & Zhang, M. (1999). Approximation to continuous functions and operators using adaptive higher order neural networks. In *Proceedings of International Joint Conference on Neural Networks 1999*. Washington, DC: IEEE.

Xu, S., & Zhang, M. (2002). An adaptive higher-order neural networks (AHONN) and its approximation capabilities. In *Proceedings of the 9th International Conference on Neural Information Processing*, (Vol. 2), (pp. 848 – 852). IEEE.

Yang, X. (1990). Detection and classification of neural signals and identification of neural networks (synaptic connectivity). *Dissertation Abstracts International - B, 50*(12), 5761.

Zhang, J. (2005). *Polynomial full naïve estimated misclassification cost models for financial distress prediction using higher order neural network*. Paper presented at the 14th Annual Research Work Shop on Artificial Intelligence and Emerging Technologies in Accounting, Auditing, and Ta. San Francisco, CA.

Zhang, J. C., Zhang, M., & Fulcher, J. (1997). Financial simulation system using a higher order trigonometric polynomial neural network group model. In *Proceedings of the IEEE/IAFE 1997 Computational Intelligence for Financial Engineering (CIFEr)*, (pp. 189 – 194). Houston, TX: IEEE Press.

Zhang, M. (2001). Financial data simulation using A-THONN model. *In Proceedings of International Joint Conference on Neural Networks,* (Vol 3), (pp. 1823 – 1827). IJCNN.

Zhang, M. (2001). Financial data simulation using A-PHONN model. In *Proceedings of the International Joint Conference on Neural Networks 2001,* (pp. 1823–1827). Washington, DC: IJCNN.

Zhang, M. (2003). Financial data simulation using PL-HONN model. In *Proceedings IASTED International Conference on Modelling and Simulation,* (pp. 229-233). Marina del Rey, CA: IASTED.

Zhang, M. (2005). A data simulation system using sinx/x and sinx polynomial higher order neural networks. In *Proceedings of IASTED International Conference on Computational Intelligence,* (pp. 56 – 61). Calgary, Canada: IASTED.

Zhang, M. (2006). A data simulation system using CSINC polynomial higher order neural networks. In *Proceedings of the 2006 International Conference on Artificial Intelligence,* (Vol. 1), (pp. 91-97). Las Vegas, NV: IEEE.

Zhang, M. (2009a). Artificial higher order neural network nonlinear model - SAS NLIN or HONNs. In Zhang, M. (Ed.), *Artificial Higher Order Neural Networks for Economics and Business* (pp. 1–47). Hershey, PA: IGI Global.

Zhang, M. (2009b). Ultra high frequency trigonometric higher order neural networks for time series data analysis. In Zhang, M. (Ed.), *Artificial Higher Order Neural Networks for Economics and Business* (pp. 133–163). Hershey, PA: IGI Global. doi:10.4018/978-1-59904-897-0.ch007

Zhang, M., & Fulcher, J. (2004). Higher order neural networks for satellite weather prediction. In Fulcher, J., & Jain, L. C. (Eds.), *Applied Intelligent Systems* (*Vol. 153,* pp. 17–57). Berlin, Germany: Springer.

Zhang, M., Fulcher, J., & Scofield, R. A. (1996). Neural network group models for estimating rainfall from satellite images. In *Proceedings of World Congress on Neural Networks,* (pp. 897-900). San Diego, CA: IEEE.

Zhang, M., & Lu, B. (2001). Financial data simulation using M-PHONN model. In *Proceedings of IJCNN 2001,* (vol. 3), (pp. 1828 – 1832). Washington, DC: IJCNN.

Zhang, M., Murugesan, S., & Sadeghi, M. (1995). Polynomial higher order neural network for economic data simulation. In *Proceedings of International Conference on Neural Information Processing,* (pp. 493-496). Beijing, China: IEEE.

Zhang, M., & Scofield, R. A. (2001). Rainfall estimation using A-PHONN model. In *Proceedings of International Joint Conference on Neural Networks,* (Vol. 3), (pp. 1583–1587). Washington, DC: IJCNN.

Zhang, M., Zhang, J. C., & Fulcher, J. (1997). Financial prediction system using higher order trigonometric polynomial neural network group model. In *Proceedings of the IEEE International Conference on Neural Networks,* (pp. 2231-2234). Houston, TX: IEEE Press.

Zhang, M., Zhang, J. C., & Fulcher, J. (2000). Higher order neural network group models for data approximation. *International Journal of Neural Systems, 10*(2), 123–142. doi:10.1016/S0129-0657(00)00011-9

Zhang, M., Zhang, J. C., & Keen, S. (1999). Using THONN system for higher frequency non-linear data simulation & prediction. In *Proceedings of IASTED International Conference on Artificial Intelligence and Soft Computing,* (pp. 320-323). Honolulu, HI: IASTED.

ADDITIONAL READING

Al-Rawi, M. S., & Al-Rawi, K. R. (2010). On the equivalence between ordinary neural networks and higher order neural networks. In Zhang, M. (Ed.), *Artificial Higher Order Neural Networks for Computer Science and Engineering – Trends for Emerging Application* (pp. 138–158). Hershey, PA: IGI Global.

Baldi, P., & Venkatesh, S. S. (1993). Random interactions in higher order neural networks. *IEEE Transactions on Information Theory, 39*(1), 274–283. doi:10.1109/18.179374

Boutalis, Y. S., Christodoulou, M. A., & Theodoridis, D. C. (2010). Identification of nonlinear systems using a new neuro-fuzzy dynamical system definition based on high order neural network function approximators. In Zhang, M. (Ed.), *Artificial Higher Order Neural Networks for Computer Science and Engineering – Trends for Emerging Application* (pp. 423–449). Hershey, PA: IGI Global.

Brucoli, M., Carnimeo, L., & Grassi, G. (1997). Associative memory design using discrete-time second-order neural networks with local interconnections. *IEEE Transactions on Circuits and Systems. I, Fundamental Theory and Applications, 44*(2), 153–158. doi:10.1109/81.554334

Burshtein, D. (1998). Long-term attraction in higher order neural networks. *IEEE Transactions on Neural Networks, 9*(1), 42–50. doi:10.1109/72.655028

Cao, J., Ren, F., & Liang, J. (2009). Dynamics in artificial higher order neural networks with delays. In Zhang, M. (Ed.), *Artificial Higher Order Neural Networks for Economics and Business* (pp. 389–429). Hershey, PA: IGI Global. doi:10.4018/978-1-59904-897-0.ch018

Chen, Y., Wu, P., & Wu, Q. (2009b). Higher order neural networks for stock index modeling. In Zhang, M. (Ed.), *Artificial Higher Order Neural Networks for Economics and Business* (pp. 113–132). Hershey, PA: IGI Global. doi:10.4018/978-1-59904-897-0.ch006

Das, A., Lewis, F. L., & Subbarao, K. (2010). Back-stepping control of quadrotor: A dynamically tuned higher order like neural network approach. In Zhang, M. (Ed.), *Artificial Higher Order Neural Networks for Computer Science and Engineering – Trends for Emerging Application* (pp. 484–513). Hershey, PA: IGI Global.

Dehuri, S., & Chao, S. (2010). A theoretical and empirical study of functional link neural networks (FLANNs) for classification. In Zhang, M. (Ed.), *Artificial Higher Order Neural Networks for Computer Science and Engineering – Trends for Emerging Application* (pp. 545–573). Hershey, PA: IGI Global.

Dunis, C. L., Laws, J., & Evans, B. (2009). Modeling and trading the soybean-oil crush spread with recurrent and higher order networks: A comparative analysis. In Zhang, M. (Ed.), *Artificial Higher Order Neural Networks for Economics and Business* (pp. 348–367). Hershey, PA: IGI Global.

Epitropakis, M. G., Plagianakos, V. P., & Vrahatis, M. N. (2010). Evolutionary algorithm training of higher order neural networks. In Zhang, M. (Ed.), *Artificial Higher Order Neural Networks for Computer Science and Engineering – Trends for Emerging Application* (pp. 57–85). Hershey, PA: IGI Global. doi:10.1016/j.asoc.2009.08.010

Giles, L., & Maxwell, T. (1987). Learning, invariance and generalization in high-order neural networks. *Applied Optics, 26*(23), 4972–4978. doi:10.1364/AO.26.004972

Gupta, M. M., Homma, N., Hou, Z., Solo, A. M. G., & Bukovsky, I. (2010). Higher order neural networks: Fundamental theory and applications. In Zhang, M. (Ed.), *Artificial Higher Order Neural Networks for Computer Science and Engineering – Trends for Emerging Application* (pp. 397–422). Hershey, PA: IGI Global.

Gupta, M. M., Homma, N., Hou, Z., Solo, A. M. G., & Goto, T. (2009). Fundamental theory of artificial higher order neural networks. In Zhang, M. (Ed.), *Artificial Higher Order Neural Networks for Economics and Business* (pp. 368–388). Hershey, PA: IGI Global. doi:10.4018/978-1-59904-897-0.ch017

Karnavas, Y. L. (2010). Electrical machines excitation control via higher order neural networks. In Zhang, M. (Ed.), *Artificial Higher Order Neural Networks for Computer Science and Engineering – Trends for Emerging Application* (pp. 366–396). Hershey, PA: IGI Global.

Lu, Z., Shieh, L., & Chen, G. (2009). A new topology for artificial higher order neural networks - Polynomial kernel networks. In Zhang, M. (Ed.), *Artificial Higher Order Neural Networks for Economics and Business* (pp. 430–441). Hershey, PA: IGI Global.

Najarian, S., Hosseini, S. M., & Fallahnezhad, M. (2010). Artificial tactile sensing and robotic surgery using higher order neural networks. In Zhang, M. (Ed.), *Artificial Higher Order Neural Networks for Computer Science and Engineering – Trends for Emerging Application* (pp. 514–544). Hershey, PA: IGI Global.

Neto, J. P. (2010). Higher order neural networks for symbolic, sub-symbolic and chaotic computations. In Zhang, M. (Ed.), *Artificial Higher Order Neural Networks for Computer Science and Engineering – Trends for Emerging Application* (pp. 37–56). Hershey, PA: IGI Global.

Ricalde, L., Sanchez, E., & Alanis, A. Y. (2010). Recurrent higher order neural network control for output trajectory tracking with neural observers and constrained inputs. In Zhang, M. (Ed.), *Artificial Higher Order Neural Networks for Computer Science and Engineering – Trends for Emerging Application* (pp. 286–311). Hershey, PA: IGI Global.

Rumelhart, D., Hinton, G., & McClelland, J. (1986). Learning internal representations by error propagation. In D. Rumelhart & J. McClelland (Eds.), *Parallel Distributed Processing: Explorations in the Microstructure of Cognition, Volume 1: Foundations*. Cambridge, MA: MIT Press.

Sanchez, E., Urrego, D. A., Alanis, A. Y., & Carlos-Hernandez, S. (2010). Recurrent higher order neural observers for anaerobic processes. In Zhang, M. (Ed.), *Artificial Higher Order Neural Networks for Computer Science and Engineering – Trends for Emerging Application* (pp. 333–365). Hershey, PA: IGI Global.

Seiffertt, J., & Wunsch, D. C. II. (2009). Higher order neural network architectures for agent-based computational economics and finance. In Zhang, M. (Ed.), *Artificial Higher Order Neural Networks for Economics and Business* (pp. 79–93). Hershey, PA: IGI Global.

Selviah, D. (2009). High speed optical higher order neural network for discovering data trends and patterns in very large databases. In Zhang, M. (Ed.), *Artificial Higher Order Neural Networks for Economics and Business* (pp. 442–465). Hershey, PA: IGI Global.

Selviah, D., & Shawash, J. (2010). Fifty years of electronic hardware implementations of first and higher order neural networks. In Zhang, M. (Ed.), *Artificial Higher Order Neural Networks for Computer Science and Engineering – Trends for Emerging Application* (pp. 269–285). Hershey, PA: IGI Global.

Shawash, J., & Selviah, D. (2010). Artificial higher order neural network training on limited precision processors. In Zhang, M. (Ed.), *Artificial Higher Order Neural Networks for Computer Science and Engineering – Trends for Emerging Application* (pp. 312–332). Hershey, PA: IGI Global.

Shin, Y. (1991). The pi-sigma network: An efficient higher-order neural network for pattern classification and function approximation. In *Proceedings of the International Joint Conference on Neural Networks*, (Vol. 1), (pp. 13-18). Seattle, WA: IJCNN.

Theodoridis, D. C., Christodoulou, M. A., & Boutalis, Y. S. (2010). Neuro-fuzzy control schemes based on high order neural network function aproximators. In Zhang, M. (Ed.), *Artificial Higher Order Neural Networks for Computer Science and Engineering – Trends for Emerging Application* (pp. 450–483). Hershey, PA: IGI Global.

Tseng, Y.-H., & Wu, J.-L. (1994). Constant-time neural decoders for some BCH codes. In *Proceedings of IEEE International Symposium on Information Theory*, (p. 343). IEEE Press.

Wang, Z., Liu, Y., & Liu, X. (2009). On complex artificial higher order neural networks: Dealing with stochasticity, jumps and delays. In Zhang, M. (Ed.), *Artificial Higher Order Neural Networks for Economics and Business* (pp. 466–483). Hershey, PA: IGI Global.

Xu, B., Liu, X., & Liao, X. (2005). Global asymptotic stability of high-order Hopfield type neural networks with time delays. *Computers & Mathematics with Applications (Oxford, England)*, *45*(10-11), 1729–1737. doi:10.1016/S0898-1221(03)00151-2

Xu, S. (2010). Adaptive higher order neural network models for data mining. In Zhang, M. (Ed.), *Artificial Higher Order Neural Networks for Computer Science and Engineering – Trends for Emerging Application* (pp. 86–98). Hershey, PA: IGI Global.

Young, S., & Downs, T. (1993). Generalisation in higher order neural networks. *Electronics Letters*, *29*(16), 1491–1493. doi:10.1049/el:19930996

Yu, W. (2010). Robust adaptive control using higher order neural networks and projection. In Zhang, M. (Ed.), *Artificial Higher Order Neural Networks for Computer Science and Engineering – Trends for Emerging Application* (pp. 99–137). Hershey, PA: IGI Global.

Zhang, L., Simoff, S. J., & Zhang, J. C. (2009). Trigonometric polynomial higher order neural network group models and weighted kernel models for financial data simulation and prediction. In Zhang, M. (Ed.), *Artificial Higher Order Neural Networks for Economics and Business* (pp. 484–503). Hershey, PA: IGI Global. doi:10.4018/978-1-59904-897-0.ch022

Zhang, M. (2010a). Higher order neural network group –based adaptive trees. In Zhang, M. (Ed.), *Artificial Higher Order Neural Networks for Computer Science and Engineering – Trends for Emerging Application* (pp. 1–36). Hershey, PA: IGI Global. doi:10.4018/978-1-61520-711-4.ch001

Zhang, M. (2010b). Rainfall estimation using neuron-adaptive artificial higher order neural networks. In Zhang, M. (Ed.), *Artificial Higher Order Neural Networks for Computer Science and Engineering – Trends for Emerging Application* (pp. 159–186). Hershey, PA: IGI Global. doi:10.4018/978-1-61520-711-4.ch007

Zhang, M., Xu, S., & Fulcher, J. (2002). Neuron-adaptive higher order neural-network models for automated financial data modeling. *IEEE Transactions on Neural Networks*, *13*(1), 188–204. doi:10.1109/72.977302

KEY TERMS AND DEFINITIONS

AHONUs: Artificial Higher Order Neural Units.

HONN: Artificial Higher Order Neural Network.

MPHONN: Multi-Polynomial Higher Order Neural Network models.

MPONNG: Multi-layer higher order neural network group model. It is combined the characteristics of PHONN, THONN, and SPHONN.

NAHONN: Neuron-Adaptive Higher Order Neural Network.

PHONN: Polynomial Higher Order Neural Network.

PHONNG: Polynomial Higher Order Neural Network Group.

SPHONN: Sigmoid Polynomial Higher Order Neural Network.

THONN: Trigonometric polynomial Higher Order Neural Network.

THONNG: Trigonometric polynomial Higher Order Neural Network.

Chapter 6
Fundamentals of Higher Order Neural Networks for Modeling and Simulation

Madan M. Gupta
University of Saskatchewan, Canada

Noriyasu Homma
Tohoku University, Japan

Ivo Bukovsky
Czech Technical University in Prague, Czech Republic

Ashu M. G. Solo
Maverick Technologies America Inc., USA

Zeng-Guang Hou
The Chinese Academy of Sciences, China

ABSTRACT

In this chapter, the authors provide fundamental principles of Higher Order Neural Units (HONUs) and Higher Order Neural Networks (HONNs) for modeling and simulation. An essential core of HONNs can be found in higher order weighted combinations or correlations between the input variables and HONU. Except for the high quality of nonlinear approximation of static HONUs, the capability of dynamic HONUs for the modeling of dynamic systems is shown and compared to conventional recurrent neural networks when a practical learning algorithm is used. In addition, the potential of continuous dynamic HONUs to approximate high dynamic order systems is discussed, as adaptable time delays can be implemented. By using some typical examples, this chapter describes how and why higher order combinations or correlations can be effective for modeling of systems.

1. INTRODUCTION

The human brain has more than 10 billion neurons, which have complicated interconnections, and these neurons constitute a large-scale signal processing and memory network. The mathematical study of a single neural model and its various extensions is the first step in the design of a complex neural network for solving a variety of problems in the fields of signal processing, pattern recognition, control of complex processes, neurovision systems, and other decision making processes. Neural network solutions for these problems can be directly used for computer science and engineering applications.

DOI: 10.4018/978-1-4666-2175-6.ch006

Figure 1. A simple neural model as a multiple-input (dendrites) and single-output (axon) processor

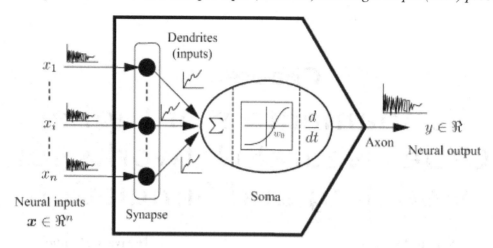

A simple neural model is presented in Figure 1. In terms of information processing, an individual neuron with dendrites as multiple-input terminals and an axon as a single-output terminal may be considered a Multiple-Input/Single-Output (MISO) system. The processing functions of this MISO neural processor may be divided into the following four categories:

1. **Dendrites:** They consist of a highly branching tree of fibers and act as input points to the main body of the neuron. On average, there are 10^3 to 10^4 dendrites per neuron, which form receptive surfaces for input signals to the neurons.

2. **Synapse:** It is a storage area of past experience (knowledge base). It provides Long-Term Memory (LTM) to the past accumulated experience. It receives information from sensors and other neurons and provides outputs through the axons.

3. **Soma:** The neural cell body is called the *soma*. It is the large, round central neuronal body. It receives synaptic information and performs further processing of the information. Almost all logical functions of the neuron are carried out in the soma.

4. **Axon:** The neural output line is called the *axon*. The output appears in the form of an action potential that is transmitted to other neurons for further processing.

The electrochemical activities at the synaptic junctions of neurons exhibit a complex behavior because each neuron makes hundreds of interconnections with other neurons. Each neuron acts as a parallel processor because it receives action potentials in parallel from the neighboring neurons and then transmits pulses in parallel to other neighboring synapses. In terms of information processing, the synapse also performs a crude pulse frequency-to-voltage conversion as shown in Figure 1.

1.1. Neural Mathematical Operations

In general, it can be argued that the role played by neurons in the brain reasoning processes is analogous to the role played by a logical switching element in a digital computer. However, this analogy is too simple. A neuron contains a sensitivity threshold, adjustable signal amplification or attenuation at each synapse and an internal structure that allows incoming nerve signals to be integrated over both space and time. From a mathematical point of view, it may be concluded that the processing of information within a neuron involves the following two distinct mathematical operations:

1. **Synaptic Operation:** The strength (weight) of the synapse is a representation of the storage of knowledge and thus the memory for previous knowledge. The synaptic operation assigns a relative weight (significance) to each incoming signal according to the past experience (knowledge) stored in the synapse.
2. **Somatic Operation:** The somatic operation provides various mathematical operations such as aggregation, thresholding, nonlinear activation, and dynamic processing to the synaptic inputs. If the weighted aggregation of the neural inputs exceeds a certain threshold, the soma will produce an output signal to its axon.

A simplified representation of the above neural operations for a typical neuron is shown in Figure 2. A biological neuron deals with some interesting mathematical mapping properties because of its nonlinear operations combined with a threshold in the soma. If neurons were only capable of

carrying out linear operations, the complex human cognition and robustness of neural systems would disappear.

Observations from both experimental and mathematical analysis have indicated that neural cells can transmit reliable information if they are sufficiently redundant in numbers. However, in general, a biological neuron has an unpredictable mechanism for processing information. Therefore, it is postulated that the collective activity generated by large numbers of locally redundant neurons is more significant than the activity generated by a single neuron.

1.2. Synaptic Operation

As shown in Figure 2, let us consider a neural memory vector of accumulated past experiences $\mathbf{w} = [w_1, w_2, \ldots, w_n]^T \in \Re^n$, which is usually called synapse weights, and a neural input vector $\mathbf{x} = [x_1, x_2, \ldots, x_n]^T \in \Re^n$ as the current external stimuli. Through the comparison process between the neural memory $\mathbf{w}$ and the input $\mathbf{x}$, the neuron can calculate a similarity between the usual (memory base) and current stimuli and thus know the current situation (Kobayashi, 2006). According to the similarity, the neuron can then derive its internal value as the membrane potential.

Figure 2. Simple model of a neuron showing (a) synaptic and (b) somatic operations

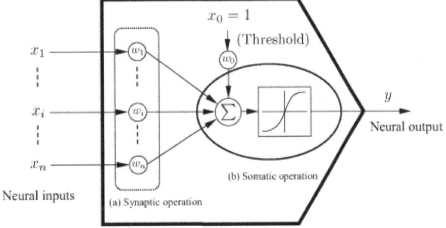

A similarity measure u can be calculated as an inner product of the neural memory vector $\mathbf{w}$ and the current input vector $\mathbf{x}$ given by

$$u = \mathbf{w} \cdot \mathbf{x} \ (= \mathbf{w}^T \mathbf{x})$$

$$= w_1 x_1 + w_2 x_2 + \cdots + w_n x_n = \sum_{i=1}^{n} w_i x_i \tag{1}$$

The similarity implies the linear combination of the neural memory and the current input, or correlation between them. This idea can be traced back to the milestone model proposed by McCulloch and Pitts (1943).

As shown in Figure 3, the inner product can also be represented as

$$u = \mid \mathbf{w} \mid\mid \mathbf{x} \mid \cos\theta \tag{2}$$

where |.| denotes the absolute value of the vector and θ is the angle between the vectors $\mathbf{w}$ and $\mathbf{x}$.

When a current input $\mathbf{x}$ points to the same or very similar direction of the neural memory $\mathbf{w}$, the similarity measure u becomes large and correlation between the memory $\mathbf{w}$ and the input $\mathbf{x}$ becomes positively strong due to $\cos\theta \approx 1$. If the input $\mathbf{x}$ points to the opposite or nearly opposite direction of the memory $\mathbf{w}$, the absolute value of the similarity measure $|u|$ also becomes large, but the negative correlation becomes strong because $\cos\theta \approx -1$. In these two cases, absolute

values of the memory $\mathbf{w}$ and the input $\mathbf{x}$ also influence the similarity measure. The other particular case is that the input $\mathbf{x}$ and the memory $\mathbf{w}$ are orthogonal with each other. In this case, the similarity measure u becomes very small due to $\cos\theta \approx 0$. If the two vectors are strictly orthogonal, the similarity measure u is equal to 0. Thus, the similarity measure is independent of the absolute values of the memory $\mathbf{w}$ and the input $\mathbf{x}$.

The inner product indicates how much the directions of two vectors are similar to each other. Indeed, in the case of normalized vectors $\mathbf{w}$ and $\mathbf{x}$, i.e., $\mid \mathbf{w} \mid = \mid \mathbf{x} \mid = 1$, the similarity measure is nothing but $\cos\theta$:

$$u = \mid \mathbf{w} \mid\mid \mathbf{x} \mid \cos\theta = \cos\theta \equiv u_\theta \tag{3}$$

Note that the linear combination can be extended to higher order combinations as in the following section.

1.2.1. Higher Order Terms of Neural Inputs

In the linear combination given in Equation (1), we considered a neural input vector consisting of only the first order terms of neural inputs in the polynomial. Naturally, we can extend the first order terms to the higher order terms of the neural inputs or any other nonlinear ones. To separate different classes of data with a nonlinear discriminant line, an HONN (Rumelhart, et al., 1986a; Giles & Maxwell, 1987; Softky & Kammen, 1991; Xu, et al., 1992; Taylor & Commbes, 1993; Homma & Gupta, 2002) is used. An HONN is composed of one or more HONUs.

Here let us consider the second order polynomial of the neural inputs. In this case, the extended neural input and memory vectors, $\mathbf{x}_a$ and $\mathbf{w}_a$, can be defined by

Figure 3. Inner product as a measure of similarity between a neural memory (past experience) $\mathbf{w}$ and a neural input (current experience) $\mathbf{x}$

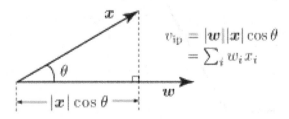

$$\mathbf{x}_a = [x_1, x_2, \ldots, x_n, x_1^2, x_1 x_2,$$
$$\ldots, x_1 x_n, x_2^2, \ldots, x_{n-1} x_n, x_n^2]^T \qquad (4)$$

$$\mathbf{w}_a = [w_{01}, w_{02}, \ldots, w_{0n}, w_{11}, w_{12},$$
$$\ldots, w_{1n}, w_{22}, \ldots, w_{(n-1)n}, w_{nn}]^T \qquad (5)$$

Then the similarity measure can be given with the same notation

$$u_a = \mathbf{w}_a \cdot \mathbf{x}_a = \mathbf{w}_a^T \mathbf{x}_a$$
$$= w_1 x_1 + w_2 x_2 + \cdots + w_n x_n + w_{11} x_1^2$$
$$+ w_{12} x_1 x_2 + \cdots + w_{1n} x_1 x_n$$
$$+ w_{22} x_2^2 + \cdots + w_{(n-1)n} x_{n-1} x_n + w_{nn} x_n^2$$
$$= \sum_{i=1}^{n} w_i x_i + \sum_{i=1}^{n} \sum_{j=i}^{n} w_{ij} x_i x_j \qquad (6)$$

The second order terms of $x_i x_j$ can be related to correlations between the two inputs x_i and x_j. That is, if the two inputs are statistically independent of each other, then the second order terms become 0 while absolute values of terms become large if there is a linear relation between them. The squared terms of neural inputs x_i^2 indicate the power of the inputs from the physical point of view.

Consequently, the similarity measure of general higher order terms can be defined as

$$u_a = \sum_{i=1}^{n} w_i x_i + \sum_{i=1}^{n} \sum_{j=i}^{n} w_{ij} x_i x_j + \cdots$$
$$+ \sum_{i_1=1}^{n} \sum_{i_2=i_1}^{n} \cdots \sum_{i_n=i_{n-1}}^{n} w_{i_1 i_2 \ldots i_n} x_{i_1} x_{i_2} \cdots x_{i_n} \qquad (7)$$

1.3. Somatic Operation

Typical neural outputs are generated by a sigmoidal activation function of the similarity measure

u of the inner product of neural memories (past experiences) and current inputs. In this case, the neural output y can be given as

$$y = \varphi(u) \in \Re^1 \qquad (8)$$

where φ is a neural activation function. An example of the activation function can be defined as a so-called sigmoidal function given by

$$\varphi(x) = \frac{1}{1 + \exp(-x)} \qquad (9)$$

and shown in Figure 4.

Note that the activation function is not limited to the sigmoid one. However, this type of sigmoid function has been widely used in various fields. Here if the similarity u is large—that is, the current input $\mathbf{x}$ is similar to the corresponding neural memory $\mathbf{w}$ —the neural output y is also large. On the other hand, if the similarity u is small, the neural output y is also small. This is a basic characteristic of biological neural activities. Note that the neural output is not proportional to the similarity u, but a nonlinear function of u with saturation characteristics. This nonlinearity might be a key mechanism to make the neural activities more complex as brains do.

Figure 4. A sigmoidal activation function

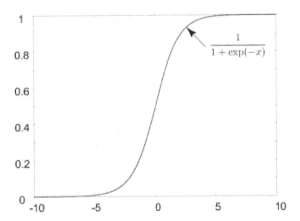

1.4. Learning from Experiences

From the computational point of view, we have discussed how neurons, which are elemental computational units in the brain, produce outputs y as the results of neural information processing based on comparison of current external stimuli $\mathbf{x}$ with neural memories of past experiences $\mathbf{w}$. Consequently, the neural outputs y are strongly dependent on the neural memories $\mathbf{w}$. Thus, how neurons can memorize past experiences is crucial for neural information processing. Indeed, one of the most remarkable features of the human brain is its ability to adaptively learn in response to knowledge, experience, and environment. The basis of this learning appears to be a network of interconnected adaptive elements by means of which transformation between inputs and outputs is performed.

Learning can be defined as the acquisition of new information. In other words, learning is a process of memorizing new information. Adaptation implies that the element can change in a systematic manner and in so doing alter the transformation between input and output. In the brain, transmission within the neural system involves coded nerve impulses and other physical chemical processes that form reflections of sensory stimuli and incipient motor behavior.

Many biological aspects are associated with such learning processes, including (Harston, 1990):

- Learning overlays hardwired connections
- Synaptic plasticity versus stability: a crucial design dilemma
- Synaptic modification providing a basis for observable organism behavior

Here, we have presented the basic foundation of neural networks starting from a basic introduction to the biological foundations, neural models, and learning properties inherent in neural networks. The rest of the chapter contains the following five sections:

In section 2, as the first step to understanding HONNs, we will develop a general matrix form of the Second Order Neural Units (SONUs) and the learning algorithm. Using the general form, it will be shown that, from the point of view of both the neural computing process and its learning algorithm, the widely used linear combination neural units described above are only a subset of the developed SONUs.

In section 3, we will conduct some simulation studies to support the theoretical development of Second Order Neural Networks (SONNs). The results will show how and why SONNs can be effective for many problems.

In section 4, HONUs and HONNs with a learning algorithm will be presented. Toward computer science and engineering applications, function approximation and time series analysis problems will be considered in section 5.

Concluding remarks and future research directions will be given in section 6.

2. SECOND ORDER NEURAL UNITS AND SECOND ORDER NEURAL NETWORKS

Neural networks, consisting of first order neurons which provide the neural output as a nonlinear function of the weighted linear combination of neural inputs, have been successfully used in various applications such as pattern recognition/ classification, system identification, adaptive control, optimization, and signal processing (Sinha, et al., 1999; Gupta, et al., 2003; Narendra & Parthasarathy, 1990; Cichochi & Unbehauen, 1993).

The higher order combination of the inputs and weights will yield higher neural performance. However, one of the disadvantages encountered in the previous development of HONUs is the larger number of learning parameters (weights) required (Schmidt, 1993). To optimize the features space, a learning capability assessment method has been proposed by Villalobos and Merat (1995).

In this section, in order to reduce the number of parameters without loss of higher performance, an SONU is presented (Homma & Gupta, 2002); A SONU is also sometimes denoted as a quadratic neural unit (Bukovsky, et al., 2010). Using a general matrix form of the second order operation, the SONU provides the output as a nonlinear function of the weighted second order combination of input signals. Note that the matrix form can contribute to high speed computing, such as parallel and vector processing, which is essential for scientific and image processing.

2.1. Formulation of the Second Order Neural Unit

A SONU with n-dimensional neural inputs, $\mathbf{x}(t) \in \Re^n$, and a single neural output, $y(t) \in \Re^1$, is developed in this section (Figure 5). Let $\mathbf{x}_a = [x_0, x_1, \ldots, x_n]^T \in \Re^{n+1}, x_0 = 1$ be an augmented neural input vector. Here a new second-order aggregating formulation is proposed by using an augmented weight matrix $\mathbf{W}_a(t) \in \Re^{(n+1) \times (n+1)}$ as

$$u = \mathbf{x}_a^T \mathbf{W}_a \mathbf{x}_a \qquad (10)$$

Then the neural output, y, is given by a nonlinear function of the variable u as

$$y = \varphi(u) \in \Re^1 \qquad (11)$$

Because both the weights w_{ij} and w_{ji}, $i, j \in \{0, 1, \ldots, n\}$ in the augmented weight matrix $\mathbf{W}_a$ yield the same second order term $x_i x_j$ (or $x_j x_i$), an upper triangular matrix or lower triangular matrix is sufficient to use. For instance, instead of separately determining values for w_{01} and w_{10}, both of which are weights for $x_0 x_1$, one can eliminate one of these weights and determine a value for either w_{01} or w_{10} that would be as much as both of these combined if they were computed separately. This saves time in the neural network's intensive procedure of computing weights. The same applies for other redundant weights. The equation for the discriminant line can be reexpressed as equal to transpose of the vector of neural inputs multiplied by the upper triangular matrix of neural weights multiplied by the vector of neural inputs again:

$$u = \mathbf{x}_a^T \mathbf{W}_a \mathbf{x}_a = \sum_{i=0}^{n} \sum_{j=i}^{n} w_{ij} x_i x_j, \quad x_0 = 1 \qquad (12)$$

The number of elements, $\mathbf{W}_n$, in the matrix of neural weights with redundant elements is equal to $(n+1) * (n+1)$. To calculate the number of elements in the final matrix of neural weights with

Figure 5. An SONU defined by Equations (10) and (11)

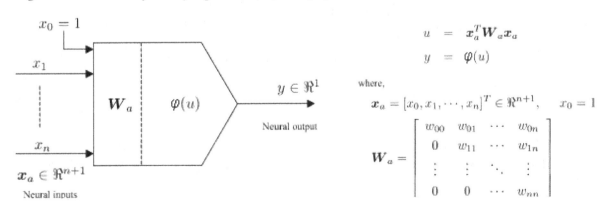

redundant elements eliminated, $\mathbf{W_a}$, first find the number of elements, which is $(n+1) * (n+1)$. Then subtract the number of diagonal elements in the matrix, which is $n+1$. Divide this by 2 and the result is the number of elements above or below the diagonal in the matrix. Then add back the number of diagonal elements in the matrix. Therefore, the number of elements in $\mathbf{W_a}$ with redundant elements eliminated is given as

$$\frac{(n+1) * (n+1) - (n+1)}{2} + (n+1) = \frac{n^2 + 3n + 2}{2}$$

Note that the conventional first order weighted linear combination is only a special case of this second order matrix formulation. For example, the special weight matrix (row vector). $\mathbf{W_a} \equiv Row[w_{00}, w_{01}, \ldots, w_{0n}] \in \Re^{(n+1) \times (n+1)}$, can produce the equivalent weighted linear combination, $u = \sum_{j=0}^{n} w_{0j} x_j$. Therefore, the proposed neural model with the second order matrix operation is more general and, for this reason, it is called an SONU.

2.2. Learning Algorithms for Second Order Neural Units

Here learning algorithms are developed for SONUs. Let k denote the discrete time steps, $k = 1, 2, \ldots$, and $y_d(k) \in \Re^1$ be the desired output signal corresponding to the neural input vector $\mathbf{x}(k) \in \Re^n$ at the k-th time step. A square error, $E(k)$, is defined by the error, $e(k) = y(k) - y_d(k)$, as

$$E(k) = \frac{1}{2} e(k)^2 \tag{13}$$

where $y(k)$ is the neural output corresponding to the neural input $\mathbf{x}(k)$ at the k-th time instant.

The purpose of the neural units is to minimize the error E by adapting the weight matrix $\mathbf{W_a}$ as

$$\mathbf{W}_a(k+1) = \mathbf{W}_a(k) + \Delta \mathbf{W}_a(k) \tag{14}$$

Here $\Delta \mathbf{W}_a(k)$ denotes the change in the weight matrix, which is defined as proportional to the gradient of the error function $E(k)$

$$\Delta \mathbf{W}_a(k) = -\eta \frac{\partial E(k)}{\partial \mathbf{W}_a(k)} \tag{15}$$

where $\eta > 0$ is a learning coefficient. Since the derivatives, $\partial E / \partial w_{ij}, i, j \in \{1, 2, \ldots, n\}$, are calculated by the chain rule as

$$\frac{\partial E(k)}{\partial w_{ij}(k)} = \frac{\partial E(k)}{\partial y(k)} \cdot \frac{\partial y(k)}{\partial u(k)} \cdot \frac{\partial u(k)}{\partial w_{ij}(k)}$$
$$= e(k)\varphi'(u(k)) x_i(k) x_j(k) \tag{16}$$

or

$$\frac{\partial E(k)}{\partial \mathbf{W}_a(k)} = e(k)\varphi'(u(k)) \mathbf{x}_a(k) \mathbf{x}_a^T(k) \tag{17}$$

The changes in the weight matrix are given by

$$\Delta \mathbf{W}_a(k) = -\eta e(k)\varphi'(u(k)) \mathbf{x}_a(k) \mathbf{x}_a^T(k) \tag{18}$$

Here $\varphi'(u)$ is the slope of the nonlinear activation function used in Equation (11). For activation functions such as sigmoidal function, $\varphi'(u) \geq 0$ and $\varphi'(u)$ can be regarded as a gain of the changes in weights. Then

$$\Delta \mathbf{W}_a(k) = -\gamma e(k) \mathbf{x}_a(k) \mathbf{x}_a^T(k) \tag{19}$$

where $\gamma = \eta\varphi'(u)$. Note that taking the average of the changes for some input vectors, the changes in the weights, $\Delta w_{ij}(k)$, implies the correlation between the error $e(k)$ and the corresponding inputs term $x_i(k)x_j(k)$.

Therefore, conventional learning algorithms such as the back propagation algorithm can easily be extended for multilayered neural network structures having the proposed SONUs.

In Table 1, fundamental learning rules of static and dynamic SONUs are summarized (for clarity with simplification of $\varphi(v)=v$) for the case of time series prediction. As an extension of the above static learning rule of SONUs, the update rule of dynamic SONUs includes the recurrently

calculated derivatives of neural output $\partial y_n(k+n_s)/\partial w_{ij}$ where $\mathbf{j}_{ij}$ denotes columns of a recurrently calculated Jacobian matrix (Table 1).

3. PERFORMANCE ASSESSMENT OF SECOND ORDER NEURAL UNITS

To evaluate the learning and generalization abilities of the proposed general SONUs, the XOR classification problem is used. The XOR problem will provide a simple example of how well an SONU works for the nonlinear classification problem.

Table 1. Summary of fundamental static and dynamic learning techniques for SONU for time series prediction where $\varphi(v) = v$ for simplicity

SONU	Mathematical Structure	Learning Rule
Static	y_n... neural output $x_1, x_2, ..., x_n$ ... external neural inputs W... upper triangular weight matrix $\mathbf{x_a} = \begin{bmatrix} 1 \\ x_1 \\ \vdots \\ x_n \end{bmatrix}, \mathbf{W} = \begin{bmatrix} w_{00} & w_{01} & \cdots & w_{0n} \\ 0 & w_{11} & \cdots & w_{1n} \\ \vdots & \ddots & \ddots & \vdots \\ 0 & \cdots & 0 & w_{nn} \end{bmatrix}$ $y_n = \sum_{i=0}^{n} \sum_{j=i}^{n} x_i x_j w_{ij} = \mathbf{x_a}^T \mathbf{W} \mathbf{x_a}$	**Levenberg-Marquardt (L-M)** N... number of samples (data length) $\Delta w_{ij} = -(\mathbf{j}_{ij}^T \cdot \mathbf{j}_{ij} + \frac{1}{\mu})^{-1} \cdot \mathbf{j}_{ij}^T \cdot \mathbf{e}$ $\mathbf{j}_{ij} = \frac{\partial \mathbf{y_n}}{\partial w_{ij}} = \begin{bmatrix} x_i(1) x_j(1) \\ x_i(2) x_j(2) \\ \vdots \\ x_i(N) x_j(N) \end{bmatrix}$ $\mathbf{e} = \begin{bmatrix} e(1) & e(2) & \cdots & e(N) \end{bmatrix}^T$ --- **Gradient Descent** k... sample number $w_{ij}(k+1) = w_{ij}(k) + \Delta w_{ij}(k)$ $\Delta w_{ij}(k) = -\frac{1}{2}\mu e(k)^2 = \mu e(k) x_i(k) x_j(k)$
Discrete Dynamic	$y_n(k+n_s) = \mathbf{x_a}^T \mathbf{W} \mathbf{x_a}$ $\mathbf{x_a} = \begin{bmatrix} 1 \\ y_n(k+n_s-1) \\ y_n(k+n_s-2) \\ \vdots \\ y_n(k+1) \\ x_1(k) \\ \vdots \\ x_m(k) \end{bmatrix},$ typically for prediction: $x_1(k) = y_r(k)$ $\vdots$ $x_m(k) = y_r(k-m+1)$ y_r... real value	**Recurrent Gradient Descent (RTRL)** $\Delta w_{ij}(k) = \mu e(k) \frac{\partial y_n(k+n_s)}{\partial w_{ij}}$ $\frac{\partial y_n(k+n_s)}{\partial w_{ij}} = \frac{\partial(\mathbf{x_a}^T \mathbf{W} \mathbf{x_a})}{\partial w_{ij}} = \mathbf{j}_{ij}^T \mathbf{W} \mathbf{x_a} + x_i x_j + \mathbf{x_a}^T \mathbf{W} \mathbf{j}_{ij}$ $\mathbf{j}_{ij} = \frac{\partial \mathbf{x_a}}{\partial w_{ij}} = \begin{bmatrix} 0 & \frac{\partial y_n(k+n_s-1)}{\partial w_{ij}} & \frac{\partial y_n(k+n_s-2)}{\partial w_{ij}} & \cdots & \frac{\partial y_n(k+1)}{\partial w_{ij}} & 0 \cdots 0 \end{bmatrix}^T$ --- Backpropagation Through Time (BPTT) BPTT learning technique may be implemented as the combination of: a) RTRL for recurrent calculation of neural outputs and their derivatives (with respect to weights) at every sample time k, and b) Levenberg-Marquardt algorithm for calculation of weight increments $\Delta \mathbf{W}$ when recurrent calculations are accomplished.

3.1. XOR Problem

Because the two-input XOR function is not linearly separable, it is one of the simplest logic functions that cannot be realized by a single linear combination neural unit. Therefore, it requires a multilayered neural network structure consisting of linear combination neural units.

On the other hand, a single SONU can solve this XOR problem by using its general second order functions defined in Equation (12). To implement the XOR function using a single SONU, the four learning patterns corresponding to the four combinations of two binary inputs

$$(x_1, x_2) \in \{(-1, -1), (-1, 1), (1, -1), (1, 1)\}$$

and the desired output

$$y_d = x_1 \oplus x_2 \in \{-1, 1\}$$

were applied to the SONU.

For the XOR problem, the neural output, y, is defined by the signum function as $y = \varphi(u) = \text{sgn}(u)$. The correlation learning algorithm with a constant gain, $\gamma = 1$, in Equation (19) was used in this case. The learning was terminated as soon as the error converged to 0. Because the SONU with the signum function classifies the neural input data by using the second order nonlinear function of the neural inputs $\mathbf{x}_a^T \mathbf{W}_a \mathbf{x}_a$ as in Equation (10), many nonlinear classification boundaries are possible such as a hyperbolic boundary and an elliptical boundary (Table 2).

Note that the results of the classification boundary are dependent on the initial weights (Table 2), and any classification boundary by the second order functions can be realized by a single SONU. This realization ability of the SONU is obviously superior to the linear combination neural unit, which cannot achieve such nonlinear classification using a single neural unit. At least three linear combination neural units in a layered structure are needed to solve the XOR problem.

Secondly, the number of parameters (weights) required for solving this problem can be reduced by using the SONU. In this simulation study, by using the upper triangular weight matrix, only six parameters including the threshold were required

Table 2. Initial weights ($k = 0$), final weights, and the classification boundaries for the XOR problem

k	w_{00}	w_{01}	w_{02}	w_{11}	w_{12}	w_{22}	Boundaries
	(A hyperbolic boundary)						
0	0.323	-0.870	-0.153	0.977	0.031	-0.332	
4	-0.177	0.630	0.347	0.477	-1.469	-0.832	
	(A hyperbolic boundary)						
0	-0.773	0.818	0.748	0.793	-0.525	0.369	
4	-1.023	0.568	0.498	0.543	-0.775	0.119	
	(An elliptical boundary)						
0	0.847	0.397	0.779	-0.996	-0.961	-0.803	
3	0.947	0.497	0.679	-0.896	-1.061	-0.703	

for the SONU whereas at least nine parameters were required for the layered structure with three linear combination neural units.

Each weight w_{ij} represents how the corresponding input correlation term $x_i x_j$ affects the neural output. If the absolute value of the weight is very small, then the effect of the corresponding input term on the output may also be very small. On the other hand, the corresponding term may be dominant or important if the absolute value of the weight is large compared to the other weights.

The weights in Table 2 suggest that the absolute value of w_{12} is always large independent of the initial values and the largest except for only one case (middle row where it is still the second largest). The absolute value of w_{00} is the largest in one case (middle row) among three cases, but the smallest in one case (top row). The input term corresponding to the weight w_{00} is nothing but the bias. Note that the large $|w_{12}|$ implies a large contribution of the correlation term $x_1 x_2$ to the output and that the contribution of the term may be negative because $w_{12} < 0$. Indeed, the target XOR function can be defined as $y = -x_1 x_2$.

Consequently, if the target (unknown) function involves a higher order combination of the input variables, the ability of the higher order neural units can be superior to neural units that do not have necessary higher order input terms. Of course, this is only a discussion on the synaptic operation, and somatic operation may create higher order terms in the sense of Taylor expansion of the nonlinear activation functions. However, such higher order terms by somatic operation may be limited or indirect. Thus, the direct effect of the higher order terms is a reason why the higher order neural units can be effective for such problems that may involve the higher order terms of the input variables.

3.2. Time Series Prediction

In this subsection, the time-series prediction performance of dynamic SONUs (Figure 7)

adapted by dynamic gradient descent (RTRL) is demonstrated and compared to single hidden layer perceptron-type recurrent neural networks with various numbers of sigmoid neurons in the hidden layer (from 3 to 10) and two recurrent configurations, recurrent hidden layer (RNN) and tapped delay feedbacks of neural output (TptDNN). For comparison of the performance, extensive simulation analysis was performed on theoretical and real data shown in Figure 6 and also white noise was added to training and testing data to compare generalization and overfitting of SONUs (see Tables 3-5).

4. HIGHER ORDER NEURAL UNITS AND HIGHER ORDER NEURAL NETWORKS

To capture the higher order nonlinear properties of the input pattern space, extensive efforts have been made by Rumelhart et al. (1986), Giles and Maxwell (1987), Softky and Kammen (1991), Xu et al. (1992), Taylor and Commbes (1993), and Homma and Gupta (2002) toward developing architectures of neurons that are capable of capturing not only the linear correlation between components of input patterns, but also the higher order correlation between components of input patterns. HONNs have proven to have good computational, storage, pattern recognition, and learning properties, and are realizable in hardware (Taylor & Commbes, 1993). Regular polynomial networks that contain the higher order correlations of the input components satisfy the Stone-Weierstrass theorem that is a theoretical background of universal function approximators by means of neural networks (Gupta, et al., 2003), but the number of weights required to accommodate all the higher order correlations increases exponentially with the number of the inputs. HONUs are the basic building block for such an HONN. For such an HONN as shown in Figure 8, the output is given by

$$y = \varphi(u) \tag{20}$$

Figure 6. All signals (clean data) that were used in the experimental study. The first 1000 samples were training data. Samples for k=1001-2000 were used as testing data.

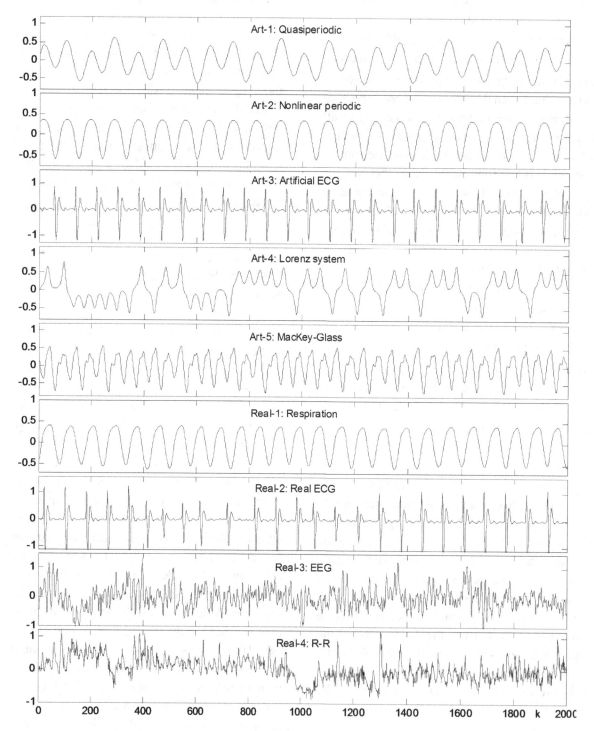

Figure 7. Schematics of the recurrent QNU with n_s-1 state feedbacks (recurrences) and n_r external inputs (real measured values) as used for time series prediction

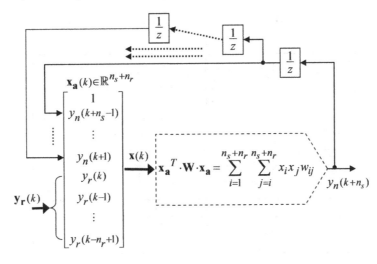

Table 3. Total counts of simulation experiments with SONU (QNU), recurrent perceptron-type neural networks (RNN), and tapped-delay neural networks (TptDNN) with a single hidden layer and various numbers of hidden neurons (3, 5, or 7)

| count all records | | G | | | | | OF | | | | | | Row Sum | | |
| | | pure | | | smooth | | | pure | | | smooth | | | | | |
data info		QNU	RNN	TptDNN	QNU	RNN	TptDNN	QNU	RNN	TptDNN	QNU	RNN	TptDNN	QNU	RNN	TptDNN
Art-1	Quasiperiodic	72	144	144	256	448	448	98	324	320	432	1296	1296	858	2212	2208
Art-2	NonlinPeriodic	68	144	144	256	448	448	94	324	320	432	1296	1296	850	2212	2208
Art-3	ECG_Art	72	144	144	256	448	448	104	324	323	432	1296	1296	864	2212	2211
Art-4	Lorenz	72	144	144	256	448	448	106	324	312	430	1296	1296	864	2212	2200
Art-5	MacKeyGlass	72	144	144	255	448	448	94	324	317	429	1296	1296	850	2212	2205
Real-1	Respiration	72	144	144	253	448	448	96	324	321	432	1296	1296	853	2212	2209
Real-2	ECG_Real	72	144	144	256	448	448	108	324	321	432	1296	1296	868	2212	2209
Real-3	EEG	72	144	144	256	448	448	106	324	324	432	1296	1296	866	2212	2212
Real-4	RR	72	144	144	256	448	448	96	324	324	361	1296	1296	785	2212	2212
Column Sum		644	1296	1296	2300	4032	4032	902	2916	2882	3812	11664	11664			

Table 4. The percentage of counts of neural architectures that were tested with better than average performance, measured with sum of square errors (SSE), of all neural architectures that were tested

| % J<Javer | | G | | | | | OF | | | | | | Row Average | | |
| | | pure | | | smooth | | | pure | | | smooth | | | | | |
data info		QNU	RNN	TptDNN	QNU	RNN	TptDNN	QNU	RNN	TptDNN	QNU	RNN	TptDNN	QNU	RNN	TptDNN
Art-1	Quasiperiodic	81%	46%	50%	89%	49%	59%	91%	85%	69%	89%	76%	67%	87%	64%	61%
Art-2	NonlinPeriodic	81%	46%	50%	84%	49%	56%	96%	75%	70%	90%	59%	57%	88%	57%	58%
Art-3	ECG_Art	100%	40%	33%	96%	43%	43%	93%	58%	59%	97%	48%	51%	97%	47%	46%
Art-4	Lorenz	76%	47%	46%	81%	48%	52%	81%	80%	69%	80%	79%	71%	80%	63%	59%
Art-5	MacKeyGlass	89%	51%	54%	76%	50%	50%	78%	65%	56%	82%	57%	55%	81%	56%	54%
Real-1	Respiration	82%	56%	51%	82%	50%	57%	97%	69%	59%	84%	59%	57%	86%	58%	56%
Real-2	ECG_Real	100%	33%	36%	97%	34%	36%	95%	55%	57%	97%	43%	42%	97%	41%	43%
Real-3	EEG	81%	63%	63%	61%	45%	46%	40%	73%	62%	37%	68%	59%	55%	62%	58%
Real-4	RR	89%	42%	49%	55%	44%	64%	83%	57%	57%	95%	52%	57%	81%	49%	56%
Column Average		86%	47%	48%	80%	46%	51%	84%	68%	62%	84%	60%	57%			

Table 5. Count of types of neural architectures that reached absolute minimum SSE for three predicting horizons (after averaging results over three levels of noise distortion)

data info		QNU	RNN	TptDNN	QNU	TptDNN
Art-1	Quasiperiodic	3			1	1
Art-2	NonlinPeriodic	3			2	
Art-3	ECG_Art	3			2	
Art-4	Lorenz		3			2
Art-5	MacKeyGlass	3			2	
Real-1	Respiration	2	1		2	
Real-2	ECG_Real	3			2	
Real-3	EEG	2		1	2	
Real-4	RR	3			2	
column count		22	4	1	15	3
percentage		81%	15%	4%	83%	17%
		100%			100%	

Figure 8. Block diagram of the HONU, Equations (20) and (21)

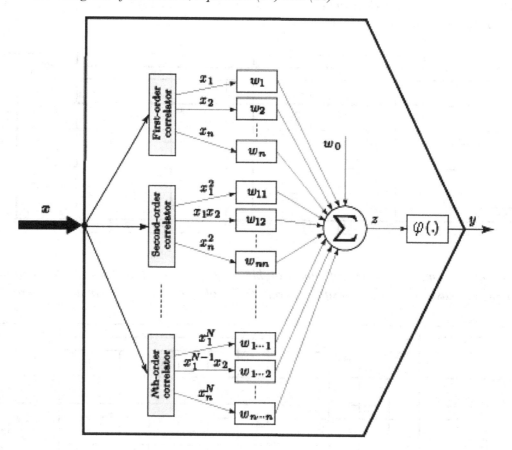

$$u = w0$$
$$+\sum_{i_1}^{n} w_{i_1} x_{i_1} + \sum_{i_1,i_2}^{n} w_{i_1 i_2} x_{i_1} x_{i_2} + \cdots + \sum_{i_1,\ldots,i_N}^{n} w_{i_1 \cdots i_N} x_{i_1} \cdots x_{i_N}$$
$$(21)$$

where $\mathbf{x} = [x_1, x_2, \ldots, x_n]^T$ is a vector of neural inputs, y is an output, and $\varphi(.)$ is a strictly monotonic activation function such as a sigmoidal function whose inverse, $\varphi^{-1}(.)$, exists. The summation for the kth-order correlation is taken on a set $C(i_1 \cdots i_j), (1 \leq j \leq N)$, which is a set of the combinations of j indices $1 \leq i_1 \cdots i_j \leq n$ defined by

$$C(i_1 \cdots i_j)$$
$$\equiv \{< i_1 \cdots i_j >: 1 \leq i_1 \cdots i_j \leq n, i_1 \leq i_2 \leq \cdots \leq i_j\},$$
$$1 \leq j \leq N$$

Also, the number of the Nth-order correlation terms is given by

$$\binom{n+j-1}{j} = \frac{(n+j-1)!}{j!(n-1)!}, \qquad 1 \leq j \leq N$$

The introduction of the set $C(i_1 \cdots i_j)$ is to absorb the redundant terms due to the symmetry of the induced combinations. In fact, Equation (21) is a truncated Taylor series with some adjustable coefficients. The Nth-order neural unit needs a total of

$$\sum_{j=0}^{N} \binom{n+j-1}{j} = \sum_{j=0}^{N} \frac{(n+j-1)!}{j!(n-1)!}$$

weights including the basis of all of the products up to N components.

Example 1. In this example, we consider a case of the third order ($N = 3$) neural network with two neural inputs ($n = 2$). Here

$$C(i) = \{0,1,2\}$$

$$C(i_1 i_2) = \{11,12,22\}$$

$$C(i_1 i_2 i_3) = \{111,112,122,222\}$$

and the network equation is

$$y = \varphi \begin{pmatrix} w0 + w_1 x_1 + w_2 x_2 + w_{11} x_1^2 \\ + w_{12} x_1 x_2 + w_{22} x_2^2 + w_{111} x_1^3 \\ + w_{112} x_1^2 x_2 + w_{122} x_1 x_2^2 + w_{222} x_2^3 \end{pmatrix}$$

The HONUs may be used in conventional feedforward neural network structures as hidden units to form HONNs. In this case, however, consideration of the higher correlation may improve the approximation and generalization capabilities of the neural networks. Typically, only SONNs are usually employed in practice to give a tolerable number of weights as discussed in sections 2 and 3. On the other hand, if the order of the HONU is high enough, Equations (20) and (21) may be considered as a neural network with n inputs and a single output. This structure is capable of dealing with the problems of function approximation and pattern recognition.

To accomplish an approximation task for given input-output data $\{\mathbf{x}(k), y(k)\}$, the learning algorithm for the HONN can easily be developed on the basis of the gradient descent method. Assume that the error function is formulated as

$$E(k) = \frac{1}{2}[d(k) - y(k)]^2 = \frac{1}{2} e^2(k)$$

where $e(k) = d(k) - y(k)$, $d(k)$ is the desired output, and $y(k)$ is the output of the neural network. Minimization of the error function by a standard steepest descent technique yields the following set of learning equations:

$$w_0^{new} = w_0^{old} + \eta(d - y)\varphi'(u) \qquad (22)$$

$$w_{ij}^{new} = w_{ij}^{old} + \eta(d-y)\varphi'(u)x_{i_1}x_{i_2}\cdots x_{i_j} \qquad (23)$$

where $\varphi'(u) = d\varphi/du$. Like the backpropagation algorithm for a Multilayered Feedforward Neural Network (MFNN), a momentum version of the above is easily obtained.

Alternatively, because all the weights of the HONN appear linearly in Equation (21), one may use the method for solving linear algebraic equations to carry out the preceding learning task if the number of patterns is finite. To do so, one has to introduce the following two augmented vectors

$$\mathbf{w} \equiv \begin{bmatrix} w_0, w_1, \ldots, w_n, w_{11}, w_{12}, \ldots, \\ w_{nn}, \ldots, w_{1\ldots1}, w_{2\ldots2}, \ldots, w_{n\ldots n} \end{bmatrix}^T$$

and

$$\mathbf{u}(\mathbf{x}) \equiv \begin{bmatrix} x_0, x_1, \ldots, x_n, x_1^2, x_1x_2, \ldots, \\ x_n^2, \ldots, x_1^N, x_1^{N-1}x_2, \ldots, w_n^N \end{bmatrix}^T$$

where $x_0 \equiv 1$, so that the network equations, Equations (20) and (21), may be rewritten in the following compact form:

$$y = \varphi(\mathbf{w}^T\mathbf{u}(\mathbf{x})) \qquad (24)$$

For the given p pattern pairs $\{\mathbf{x}(k), d(k)\}$, ($1 \le k \le p$), define the following vectors and matrix

$$\mathbf{U} = \begin{bmatrix} u^T(1), u^T(2), \ldots, u^T(p) \end{bmatrix}^T,$$

$$\mathbf{d} = \begin{bmatrix} \varphi^{-1}(d(1)), \varphi^{-1}(d(2)), \ldots, \varphi^{-1}(d(p)) \end{bmatrix}^T$$

where $\mathbf{u}(k) = \mathbf{u}(\mathbf{x}(k)), 1 \le k \le p$. Then, the learning problem becomes one that finds a solution of the following linear algebraic equation

$$\mathbf{U}\mathbf{w} = \mathbf{d} \qquad (25)$$

If the number of the weights is equal to the number of the data and the matrix $\mathbf{U}$ is nonsingular, then Equation (25) has a unique solution

$$\mathbf{w} = \mathbf{U}^{-1}\mathbf{d}$$

A more interesting case occurs when the dimension of the weight vector $\mathbf{w}$ is less than the number of data p. Then the existence of the exact solution for the above linear equation is given by

$$rank[\mathbf{U} \vdots \mathbf{d}] = rank[\mathbf{U}]$$

In case this condition is not satisfied, the pseudoinverse solution is usually an option and gives the best fit.

The following example shows how to use the HONN presented in this section to deal with pattern recognition problems that are also typical applications in computer science and engineering situations. It is of interest to show that solving such problems is equivalent to finding the decision surfaces in the pattern space such that the given data patterns are located on the surfaces.

Example 2. Consider a three-variable XOR function defined as

$$\begin{aligned} y &= f(x_1, x_2, x_3) = (x_1 \oplus x_2) \oplus x_3 \\ &= x_1 \oplus (x_2 \oplus x_3) = (x_3 \oplus x_1) \oplus x_2 \\ &= x_1 \oplus x_2 \oplus x_3 \end{aligned}$$

The eight input pattern pairs and corresponding outputs are given in Table 6. This is a typical nonlinear pattern classification problem. A single linear neuron with a nonlinear activation function is unable to form a decision surface such that the patterns are separated in the pattern space. Our objective here is to find all the possible solutions using the third order neural network to realize the logic function.

Table 6. Truth table of XOR function $x_1 \oplus x_2 \oplus x_3$

Pattern	Input x_1	Input x_2	Input x_3	Output y
A	−1	−1	−1	−1
B	−1	−1	1	1
C	−1	1	−1	1
D	−1	1	1	−1
E	1	−1	−1	1
F	1	−1	1	−1
G	1	1	−1	−1
H	1	1	1	1

A third order neural network is designed as

$$y = w_0 + w_1 x_1 + w_2 x_2$$
$$+ w_3 x_3 + w_{12} x_1 x_2 + w_{13} x_1 x_3$$
$$+ w_{23} x_2 x_3 + w_{123} x_1 x_2 x_3$$

where $x_1, x_2, x_3 \in \{-1, 1\}$ are the binary inputs, and the network contains eight weights. To implement the above mentioned logic XOR function, one may consider the solution of the following set of linear algebraic equations:

$$\begin{cases} w_0 - w_1 - w_2 - w_3 + w_{12} + w_{13} + w_{23} - w_{123} = -1 \\ w_0 - w_1 - w_2 + w_3 + w_{12} - w_{13} - w_{23} + w_{123} = 1 \\ w_0 - w_1 + w_2 - w_3 - w_{12} + w_{13} - w_{23} + w_{123} = 1 \\ w_0 - w_1 + w_2 + w_3 - w_{12} - w_{13} + w_{23} - w_{123} = -1 \\ w_0 + w_1 - w_2 - w_3 - w_{12} - w_{13} + w_{23} + w_{123} = 1 \\ w_0 + w_1 - w_2 + w_3 - w_{12} + w_{13} - w_{23} - w_{123} = -1 \\ w_0 + w_1 + w_2 - w_3 + w_{12} - w_{13} - w_{23} - w_{123} = -1 \\ w_0 + w_1 + w_2 + w_3 + w_{12} + w_{13} + w_{23} + w_{123} = 1 \end{cases}$$

The coefficient matrix **U** is given by

$$U = \begin{bmatrix} 1 & -1 & -1 & -1 & 1 & 1 & 1 & -1 \\ 1 & -1 & -1 & 1 & 1 & -1 & -1 & 1 \\ 1 & -1 & 1 & -1 & -1 & 1 & -1 & 1 \\ 1 & -1 & 1 & 1 & -1 & -1 & 1 & -1 \\ 1 & 1 & -1 & -1 & -1 & -1 & 1 & 1 \\ 1 & 1 & -1 & 1 & -1 & 1 & -1 & -1 \\ 1 & 1 & 1 & -1 & 1 & -1 & -1 & -1 \\ 1 & 1 & 1 & 1 & 1 & 1 & 1 & 1 \end{bmatrix}$$

which is nonsingular. The equations have a unique set of solutions:

$$w_0 = w_1 = w_2 = w_3 = w_{12} = w_{13} = w_{23} = 0, \quad w_{123} = 1$$

Therefore, the logic function is realized by the third order polynomial $y = x_1 x_2 x_3$. This solution is unique in terms of the third order polynomial.

Xu et al. (1992) as well as Taylor and Combes (1993) also demonstrated that HONNs may be effectively applied to problems using a model of a curve, surface, or hypersurface to fit a given data set. This problem, called *nonlinear surface fitting*, is often encountered in many computer science and engineering applications. Some learning algorithms for solving such problems can be found in their papers. Moreover, if one assumes $\varphi(x) = x$ in the HONU, the weight exhibits linearity in the networks and the learning algorithms for the HONNs may be characterized as a linear least square (LS) procedure. Then the well-known local minimum problems existing in many nonlinear neural learning schemes may be avoided.

4.1. Representation of Higher Order Neural Network Discriminant Using Multidimensional Matrix Product

The discriminant of a HONN is a summation of quadratic terms. This can be alternatively represented using multidimensional matrix multiplication (Solo, 2010).

For example,

$$\sum_{i=1}^{3}\sum_{j=1}^{3} w_{ij} x_i x_j$$

$$= w_{11}x_1^2 + w_{12}x_1x_2 + w_{13}x_1x_3 + w_{21}x_2x_1 + w_{22}x_2^2 + w_{23}x_2x_3 + w_{31}x_3x_1 + w_{32}x_3x_2 + w_{33}x_3^2$$

$$= w_{11}x_1^2 + w_{22}x_2^2 + w_{33}x_3^2 + x_1x_2(w_{12} + w_{21}) + x_1x_3(w_{13} + w_{31}) + x_2x_3(w_{23} + w_{32})$$

This weighted summation is easily represented using classical matrices multiplied together:

$$\sum_{i=1}^{3}\sum_{j=1}^{3} w_{ij} x_i x_j =$$

$$\begin{bmatrix} x_1 & x_2 & x_3 \end{bmatrix} * \begin{bmatrix} w_{11} & w_{12} & w_{13} \\ w_{21} & w_{22} & w_{23} \\ w_{31} & w_{32} & w_{33} \end{bmatrix} * \begin{bmatrix} x_1 \\ x_2 \\ x_3 \end{bmatrix}$$

It is extremely useful to express these weighted summations as matrices multiplied together to eliminate unnecessary terms in neural network designs. Because both the weights w_{ij} and w_{ji} in the matrix above correspond to the same second-order term $x_i x_j$, it is sufficient to use only an upper triangular or lower triangular matrix. For instance, instead of separately determining values for w_{12} and w_{21}, both of which are weights for $x_1 x_2$, one can eliminate one of these weights and determine a value for either w_{12} or w_{21} that would be as much as both of these combined if they were computed separately. The same applies for other redundant weights. This saves time in the neural network's intensive procedure of computing weights.

However, the following equation and more complicated equations used for neural network applications cannot be expressed using classical matrices. Variables x_i, x_j, and x_k are inputs and w_{ijk} are weights for these inputs.

$$\sum_{i=1}^{2}\sum_{j=1}^{2}\sum_{k=1}^{2} w_{ijk} x_i x_j x_k$$

$$= w_{111}x_1^3 + w_{112}x_1^2x_2 + w_{121}x_1^2x_2 + w_{122}x_1x_2^2 + w_{211}x_1^2x_2 + w_{212}x_1x_2^2 + w_{221}x_1x_2^2 + w_{222}x_2^3$$

$$= w_{111}x_1^3 + x_1^2x_2(w_{112} + w_{121} + w_{211}) + x_1x_2^2(w_{122} + w_{212} + w_{221}) + w_{222}x_2^3$$

This weighted summation can be alternatively represented using multidimensional matrices (Solo, 2010) multiplied together. Premultiply the 2 * 2 * 2 weight matrix by a 1 * 2 * 2 input matrix in the first dimension and second dimension. Then postmultiply the 2 * 2 * 2 weight matrix by a 2 * 1 * 2 input matrix in the first dimension and second dimension. Premultiply this entire product by a 1 * 2 input matrix in the first dimension and second dimension. Note that because the first dimension and second dimension of these multidimensional matrices are being multiplied, this does not need to be indicated in the equations below.

$$\sum_{i=1}^{2}\sum_{j=1}^{2}\sum_{k=1}^{2} w_{ijk} x_i x_j x_k =$$

$$\begin{bmatrix} x_1 & x_2 \end{bmatrix} * \left(\begin{bmatrix} \begin{bmatrix} x_1 & x_2 \end{bmatrix} \\ \begin{bmatrix} x_1 & x_2 \end{bmatrix} \end{bmatrix} * \begin{bmatrix} \begin{bmatrix} w_{111} & w_{121} \\ w_{211} & w_{221} \end{bmatrix} \\ \begin{bmatrix} w_{112} & w_{122} \\ w_{212} & w_{222} \end{bmatrix} \end{bmatrix} * \begin{bmatrix} \begin{bmatrix} x_1 \\ x_2 \end{bmatrix} \\ \begin{bmatrix} x_1 \\ x_2 \end{bmatrix} \end{bmatrix} \right)$$

The multidimensional matrix product (Solo, 2010) of the first dimension and second dimension of the 1 * 2 * 2 input matrix and the 2 * 2 * 2 weight matrix results in a 1 * 2 * 2 matrix.

$$\sum_{i=1}^{2}\sum_{j=1}^{2}\sum_{k=1}^{2} w_{ijk} x_i x_j x_k =$$

$$\begin{bmatrix} x_1 & x_2 \end{bmatrix} * \left(\begin{bmatrix} \begin{bmatrix} w_{111}x_1 + w_{211}x_2 & w_{121}x_1 + w_{221}x_2 \end{bmatrix} \\ \begin{bmatrix} w_{112}x_1 + w_{212}x_2 & w_{122}x_1 + w_{222}x_2 \end{bmatrix} \end{bmatrix} * \begin{bmatrix} \begin{bmatrix} x_1 \\ x_2 \end{bmatrix} \\ \begin{bmatrix} x_1 \\ x_2 \end{bmatrix} \end{bmatrix} \right)$$

The multidimensional matrix product of the first dimension and second dimension of the 1 * 2 * 2 matrix and the 2 * 1 * 2 input matrix results in a 1 * 1 * 2 matrix.

$$\sum_{i=1}^{2}\sum_{j=1}^{2}\sum_{k=1}^{2} w_{ijk} x_i x_j x_k =$$

$$\begin{bmatrix} x_1 & x_2 \end{bmatrix} * \begin{bmatrix} \begin{bmatrix} w_{111}x_1^2 + w_{211}x_1x_2 + w_{121}x_1x_2 + w_{221}x_2^2 \end{bmatrix} \\ \begin{bmatrix} w_{112}x_1^2 + w_{212}x_1x_2 + w_{122}x_1x_2 + w_{222}x_2^2 \end{bmatrix} \end{bmatrix}$$

The 1 * 1 * 2 matrix can be simplified into a 1-D matrix with 2 elements, so it can be premultiplied by the 1 * 2 input matrix in the first dimension and second dimension.

$$\sum_{i=1}^{2}\sum_{j=1}^{2}\sum_{k=1}^{2} w_{ijk} x_i x_j x_k =$$

$$\begin{bmatrix} x_1 & x_2 \end{bmatrix} * \begin{bmatrix} w_{111}x_1^2 + w_{211}x_1x_2 + w_{121}x_1x_2 + w_{221}x_2^2 \\ w_{112}x_1^2 + w_{212}x_1x_2 + w_{122}x_1x_2 + w_{222}x_2^2 \end{bmatrix} =$$

$$w_{111}x_1^3 + w_{112}x_1^2x_2 + w_{121}x_1^2x_2 + w_{122}x_1x_2^2 + w_{211}x_1^2x_2 + w_{212}x_1x_2^2 + w_{221}x_1x_2^2 + w_{222}x_2^3 =$$

$$w_{111}x_1^3 + x_1^2x_2(w_{112} + w_{121} + w_{211}) + x_1x_2^2(w_{122} + w_{212} + w_{221}) + w_{222}x_2^3$$

Thus, this multidimensional matrix multiplication yields the same result as the summation of quadratic terms above.

4.2. Modified Polynomial Neural Networks

4.2.1. Sigma-Pi Neural Networks

Note that an HONU contains all the linear and nonlinear correlation terms of the input components to the order n. A slightly generalized structure of the HONU is a polynomial network that includes weighted sums of products of selected input components with an appropriate power. Mathematically, the input-output transfer function of this network structure is given by

$$u_i = \prod_{j=1}^{n} x_j^{w_{ij}} \tag{26}$$

$$y = \varphi\left(\sum_{i=1}^{N} w_i u_i\right) \tag{27}$$

where $w_i, w_{ij} \in \Re$, N is the order of the network and u_i is the output of the i-th hidden unit. This type of feedforward network is called a *sigma-pi network* (Rumelhart, et al., 1986). It is easy to show that this network satisfies the Stone-Weier-strass theorem if $\varphi(x)$ is a linear function. More-over, a modified version of the sigma-pi network, as proposed by Hornik et al. (1989) and Cotter (1990), is

$$u_i = \prod_{j=1}^{n} \left(p\left(x_j \right) \right)^{w_{ij}} \tag{28}$$

$$y = \varphi \left(\sum_{i=1}^{N} w_i u_i \right) \tag{29}$$

where $w_i, w_{ij} \in \Re$ and $p\left(x_j \right)$ is a polynomial of x_j. It is easy to verify that this network satisfies the Stone-Weierstrass theorem, and thus, it can be an approximator for problems of functional approximations. The sigma-pi network defined in Equations (26) and (27) is a special case of the above network while $p\left(x_j \right)$ is assumed to be a linear function of x_j. In fact, the weights w_{ij} in both the networks given in Equations (26) and (28) may be restricted to integer or nonnegative integer values.

4.2.2. Ridge Polynomial Neural Networks

To obtain fast learning and powerful mapping capabilities, and to avoid the combinatorial increase in the number of weights of HONNs, some modified polynomial network structures have been introduced. One of these is the *pi-sigma network* (Shin & Ghosh, 1991), which is a regular higher order structure and involves a much smaller number of weights than sigma-pi networks. The mapping equation of a pi-sigma network can be represented as

$$u_i = \sum_{j=1}^{n} w_{ij} x_j + \theta_i \tag{30}$$

$$y = \varphi \left(\prod_{i=1}^{N} u_i \right) = \varphi \left(\prod_{i=1}^{N} \left[\sum_{j=1}^{n} w_{ij} x_j + \theta_i \right] \right) \tag{31}$$

The total number of weights for an Nth-order pi-sigma network with n inputs is only $(n+1)N$. Compared with the sigma-pi network structure, the number of weights involved in this network is significantly reduced. Unfortunately, when $\varphi(x) = x$, the pi-sigma network does not match the conditions provided by the Stone-Weierstrass theorem because the linear subspace condition is not satisfied (Gupta, et al., 2003). However, some studies have shown that it is a good network model for smooth functions (Shin & Ghosh, 1991).

To modify the structure of the above mentioned pi-sigma networks such that they satisfy the Stone-Weierstrass theorem, Shin and Ghosh (1991) suggested considering the *Ridge Polynomial Neural Network* (RPNN). For the vectors

$$\mathbf{w}_{ij} = \left[w_{ij1}, w_{ij2}, ..., w_{ijn} \right]^{T}$$

and

$$\mathbf{x} = \left[x_1, x_2, ..., x_n \right]^{T},$$

let

$$< \mathbf{x}, \mathbf{w}_{ij} > = \sum_{k=1}^{n} w_{ijk} x_k$$

which represents an inner product between the two vectors. A one-variable continuous function f of the form $< \mathbf{x}, \mathbf{w}_{ij} >$ is called a *ridge function*. A *ridge polynomial* is a ridge function that can be represented as

Table 7. The number of weights in the polynomial networks

Order of network	Number of weights					
	Pi-sigma		RPNN		Sigma-pi	
N	n=5	n=10	n=5	n=10	n=5	n=10
2	12	22	18	33	21	66
3	18	33	36	66	56	286
4	24	44	60	110	126	1001

$$\sum_{i=0}^{N}\sum_{j=0}^{M}a_{ij}<\mathbf{x},\mathbf{w}_{ij}>^{i}$$

for some $a_{ij}\in\Re$ and $\mathbf{w}_{ij}\in\Re^{n}$. The operation equation of a RPNN is expressed as

$$y=\varphi\left(\sum_{j=1}^{N}\prod_{i=1}^{n}\left(<\mathbf{x},\mathbf{w}_{ij}>+\theta_{ji}\right)\right)$$

where $\varphi(x)=x$. The *denseness*, which is a fundamental concept for universal function approximators described in the Stone-Weierstrass theorem, of this network can be verified (Gupta, et al., 2003).

The total number of weights involved in this structure is $N(N+1)(n+1)/2$. A comparison of the number of weights of the three types of polynomial network structures is given in Table 7. The results show that when the networks have the same higher-order terms, there are significantly less weights for a RPNN than for a sigma-pi network. This is a very attractive improvement offered by RPNNs.

5. ENGINEERING APPLICATIONS

Function approximation problems are typical examples in many computer science and engineering situations. The capability to approximate nonlinear complex functions can be a basis of the complex pattern classification ability as well.

Furthermore, the neural network approach with high approximation ability can be used for time series analysis by introducing time delay features into the neural network structure. Time series analysis or estimation is one of the most important problems in computer science and engineering applications. In this section, we will explain the function approximation ability of HONNs first. Neural network structures to represent time delay features will then be introduced for time series analysis.

5.1. Function Approximation Problem

For evaluating the function approximation ability of HONNs, an example was taken from Klassen et al. (1988). The task consists of learning a representation for an unknown, one-variable nonlinear function, $F(x)$, with the only available information being the 18 sample patterns (Villalobos & Merat, 1995).

For this function approximation problem, a two-layered neural network structure was composed of two SONUs in the first layer and a single SONU in the output layer (Figure 9). The nonlinear activation function of the SONUs in the first layer was defined by a bipolar sigmoidal function as

$$\varphi(u)=(1-\exp(-u))/(1+\exp(-u)),$$

but for the single output SONU, instead of the sigmoidal function, the linear function was used:

Figure 9. A two-layered neural network structure with two SONUs in the first layer and a single SONU in the output layer for the function approximation problem

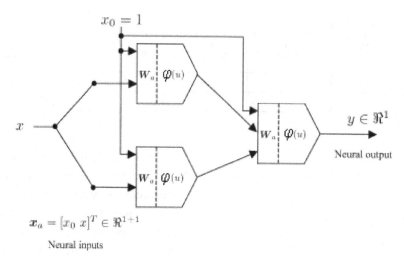

Figure 10. Training pairs and outputs estimated by the network with SONUs for the Klassen's function approximation problem (Klassen, et al., 1988)

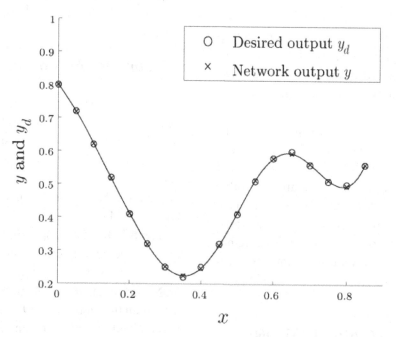

$y = \varphi(u) = u$. The gradient learning algorithm with $\eta = 0.1$ was used for this problem.

The mapping function obtained by the SONU network after 10^7 learning iterations appears in Figure 10. In this case, the average square error taken over 18 patterns was 4.566E-6. The fact that the approximation accuracy shown in Figure 10 is extremely high is evidence of the high approximation ability of the SONN.

Five particular trigonometric functions,

$\sin(\pi x)$, $\cos(\pi x)$, $\sin(2\pi x)$, $\cos(2\pi x)$,

and $\sin(4\pi x)$, were used as special features of the extra neural inputs (Klassen, et al., 1988). In addition, it has been reported (Villalobos & Merat, 1995) that the term $\cos(\pi x)$ is not necessary to achieve a lower accuracy within the error tolerance 1.125E-4, but still four extra features were required.

On the other hand, in this study, the high approximation accuracy of the proposed SONU network was achieved by only two SONUs with the sigmoidal activation function in the first layer and a single SONU with the linear activation function in the output layer, and no special features were required for high accuracy. These are remarkable advantages of the proposed SONN structure.

To highlight the superiority of HONN over the simple first-order neural networks in capturing nonlinear correlations among multiple inputs, we show another example of function approximation. For simplicity and to even more emphasize the strength of concept of HONN, we will demonstrate the example using a single higher-order neural unit of various orders N = 2, 3, 4, 5.

We consider a multiple-input static function

$$f(x,y,z) = \frac{x + y^2 - |x \cdot y \cdot z|}{0.1 + x^2 + y^2 + z^2}, \qquad (32)$$

where x, y, and z are normally distributed random variables (*stdev*=1) that represent the input pattern data, and $f()$ represent the target data. The length of training data was 300. For training both MLP and HONU, a basic version of the Levenberg-

Figure 11. The upper plot shows training performance of static MLP neural network with 10 sigmoidal neurons in a hidden layer and a linear output neuron. MLP needs many epochs; the bottom plot shows that training performance of HONU improves with increasing order N. HONUs are trained in very few epochs with the same Levenberg-Marquardt algorithm.

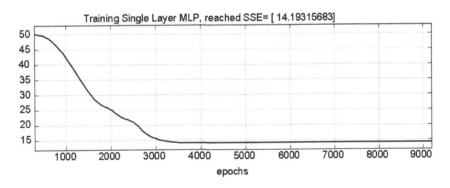

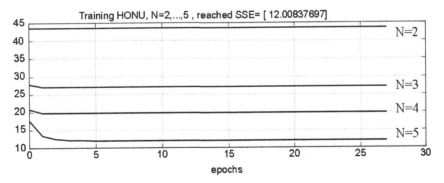

Figure 12. Testing for trained MLP network and HONU from Figure 11 on different data than training data. The upper plot shows testing of static MLP network from upper part of Figure 11. The bottom plot shows testing of the best trained HONU for N=5. Mean average error of HONU is better than the one of MLP.

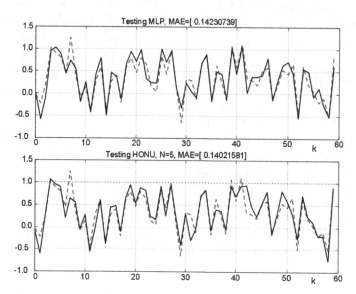

Figure 13. Simulation run from different initial weights than in Figure 11. Again, the upper plot shows training performance of a static MLP and the bottom one shows very similar training performance of a HONU for initial weights different from Figure 11. This time, the MLP typically got stuck in a worse local minimum (SSE=36.75) than in Figure 12 (SSE=14.19). The convergence of HONUs in Figure 11 and Figure 13 is almost identical; this is because pure HONU (a polynomial neural unit) is linear in its parameters, but it performs strong nonlinear mapping.

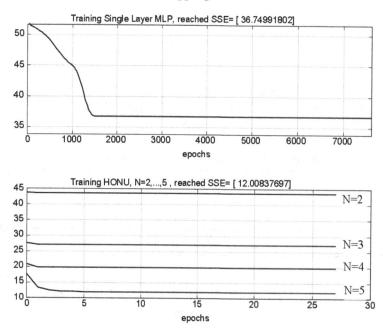

Figure 14. Testing for trained MLP network and HONU from Figure 13 on different data. The upper plot shows testing of a static MLP network from the upper part of Figure 13. The bottom plot shows that testing of the best trained HONU (N = 5). HONU is pervasively more often precise then MLP. However, its MAE is this time worse because the three outliers of the HONU become very imprecise. This may occasionally happen with pure HONUs without output sigmoid function and it relates to a lack of training data.

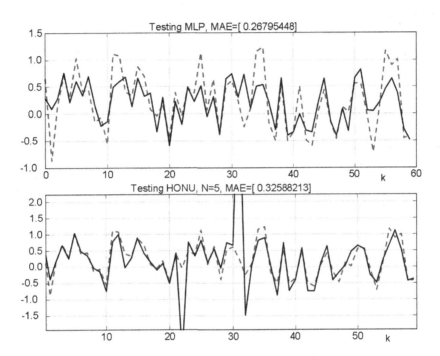

Marquardt algorithm was implemented using a decreasing learning rate when training performance, Sum of Square Errors (SSE), stopped decreasing in two consequent training epochs (see Figures 11-14).

6. CONCLUDING REMARKS AND FUTURE RESEARCH DIRECTIONS

In this chapter, the basic foundation of neural networks, starting from a basic introduction to biological foundations, neural unit models, and learning properties, has been introduced. Then as the first step to understanding HONNs, a general SONU was developed. Simulation studies for both the pattern classification and function approximation problems demonstrated that the learning and generalization abilities of the proposed SONU

and neural networks having SONUs are greatly superior to that of the widely used linear combination neural units and their networks. Indeed, from the point of view of both the neural computing process and its learning algorithm, it has been found that linear combination of neural units that are widely used in multilayered neural networks are only a subset of the proposed SONUs. Some extensions of these concepts to Radial Basis Function (RBF) networks, fuzzy neural networks, and dynamic neural units will be interesting future research projects.

To further strengthen the readers' interest in HONUs and HONNs, it should be mentioned that HONUs are powerful nonlinear approximators that are linear in their parameters. That is, if we look at the fundamental HONU representations, such as Equation (21) in this chapter, we clearly see that when input variables are substituted with training data, the weight optimization of many fundamental HONN architectures yields a linear optimization problem that is uniquely solvable by the Levenberg-Marquardt algorithm or even by the least squares method. We believe that HONNs represent a very big opportunity for many researchers, as the need for more advanced optimization methods is not so urgent for many HONUs that are basic polynomials, yet nonlinearly powerful architectures. Therefore, rather than search for some complicated optimization techniques, neural networks researchers and practitioners may spend more effort with proper data selection and signal processing that plays a crucial role in performance of neural networks including HONNs of course.

There is certainly rapidly growing research interest in the field of HONNs. There are increasing complexities in applications not only in the fields of aerospace, process control, ocean exploration, manufacturing, and resource-based industry, but also in computer science and engineering. This chapter deals with the theoretical foundations of HONNs and will help readers to develop or apply the methods to their own modeling and simulation problems. Most of the book deals with real modeling and simulation applications.

We hope that our efforts in this chapter will stimulate research interests, provide some new challenges to its readers, generate curiosity for learning more in the field, and arouse a desire to seek new theoretical tools and applications. We will consider our efforts successful if this chapter raises one's level of curiosity.

ACKNOWLEDGMENT

Dr. Madan M. Gupta wishes to acknowledge support from the Natural Sciences and Engineering Research Council of Canada through the Discovery Grant. Dr. Ivo Bukovsky's research is supported by grants SGS12/177/OHK2/3T/12 and SGS10/252/OHK2/3T/12. Dr. Zeng-Guang Hou's research is partially supported by the National Natural Science Foundation of China (Grant 61175076).

REFERENCES

Bukovsky, I., Bila, J., & Gupta, M. M. (2005). Linear dynamic neural units with time delay for identification and control. *Automatizace, 48*(10), 628–635.

Bukovsky, I., Bila, J., & Gupta, M. M. (2006). Stable neural architecture of dynamic neural units with adaptive time delays. In *Proceedings of the 7th International FLINS Conference on Applied Artificial Intelligence*, (pp. 215-222). FLINS.

Bukovsky, I., Bila, J., Gupta, M. M., Hou, Z.-G., & Homma, N. (2010a). Foundation and classification of nonconventional neural units and paradigm of nonsynaptic neural interaction . In Wang, Y. (Ed.), *Discoveries and Breakthroughs in Cognitive Informatics and Natural Intelligence* (pp. 508–523). Hershey, PA: IGI Global. doi:10.4018/978-1-60566-902-1.ch027

Bukovsky, I., Homma, N., Smetana, L., Rodriguez, R., Mironovova, M., & Vrana, S. (2010b). Quadratic neural unit is a good compromise between linear models and neural networks for industrial applications. In *Proceedings of the ICCI 2010: the 9th IEEE International Conference on Cognitive Informatics*. Beijing, China: IEEE Press.

Bukovsky, I., & Simeunovic, G. (2006). Dynamic-order-extended time-delay dynamic neural units. In *Proceedings of the 8th Seminar on Neural Network Applications in Electrical Engineering NEUREL-2006*. IEEE Press.

Cichochi, A., & Unbehauen, R. (1993). *Neural networks for optimization and signal processing*. Chichester, UK: Wiley.

Cotter, N. (1990). The stone-weierstrass theorem and its application to neural networks. *IEEE Transactions on Neural Networks, 1*(4), 290–295. doi:10.1109/72.80265

Giles, C. L., & Maxwell, T. (1987). Learning invariance, and generalization in higher-order networks. *Applied Optics, 26,* 4972–4978. doi:10.1364/AO.26.004972

Gupta, M. M., Jin, L., & Homma, N. (2003). *Static and dynamic neural networks: From fundamentals to advanced theory.* Hoboken, NJ: IEEE & Wiley. doi:10.1002/0471427950

Harston, C. T. (1990). The neurological basis for neural computation . In Maren, A. J., Harston, C. T., & Pap, R. M. (Eds.), *Handbook of Neural Computing Applications* (*Vol. 1,* pp. 29–44). New York, NY: Academic.

Homma, N., & Gupta, M. M. (2002). A general second order neural unit. *Bulletin of Collected Medical Science, 11*(1), 1–6.

Hornik, K., Stinchcombe, M., & White, H. (1989). Multilayer feedforward networks are universal approximators. *Neural Networks, 2*(5), 359–366. doi:10.1016/0893-6080(89)90020-8

Klassen, M., Pao, Y., & Chen, V. (1988). Characteristics of the functional link net: A higher order delta rule net. In *Proceedings of IEEE 2nd Annual International Conference on Neural Networks.* IEEE Press.

Kobayashi, S. (2006). *Sensation world made by the brain – Animals do not have sensors.* Tokyo, Japan: Corona.

Matsuba, I. (2000). *Nonlinear time series analysis.* Tokyo, Japan: Asakura-syoten.

McCulloch, W. S., & Pitts, W. H. (1943). A logical calculus of the ideas imminent in nervous activity. *The Bulletin of Mathematical Biophysics, 5,* 115–133. doi:10.1007/BF02478259

Narendra, K., & Parthasarathy, K. (1990). Identification and control of dynamical systems using neural networks. *IEEE Transactions on Neural Networks, 1,* 4–27. doi:10.1109/72.80202

Pao, Y. H. (1989). *Adaptive pattern recognition and neural networks.* Reading, MA: Addison-Wesley.

Rumelhart, D. E., Hinton, G. E., & Williams, R. J. (1986). Learning internal representations by error propagation . In Rumelhart, D. E., & McClelland, J. L. (Eds.), *Parallel Distributed Processing: Explorations in the Microstructure of Cognition* (*Vol. 1,* pp. 318–362). Cambridge, MA: MIT Press.

Schmidt, W., & Davis, J. (1993). Pattern recognition properties of various feature spaces for higher order neural networks. *IEEE Transactions on Pattern Analysis and Machine Intelligence, 15,* 795–801. doi:10.1109/34.236250

Shin, Y., & Ghosh, J. (1991). The pi-sigma network: An efficient higher-order neural network for pattern classification and function approximation. In *Proceedings of the International Joint Conference on Neural Networks,* (pp. 13-18). IEEE.

Sinha, N., Gupta, M. M., & Zadeh, L. (1999). *Soft computing and intelligent control systems: Theory and applications.* New York, NY: Academic.

Softky, R. W., & Kammen, D. M. (1991). Correlations in high dimensional or asymmetrical data sets: Hebbian neuronal processing. *Neural Networks, 4,* 337–347. doi:10.1016/0893-6080(91)90070-L

Solo, A. M. G. (2010). Multidimensional matrix algebra and multidimensional matrix calculus: Part 1 of 5. In *Proceedings of the 2010 International Conference on Scientific Computing* (*CSC 2010*), (pp. 353-359). CSREA Press.

Solo, A. M. G. (2010). Multidimensional matrix algebra and multidimensional matrix calculus: Part 2 of 5. In *Proceedings of the 2010 International Conference on Scientific Computing* (*CSC 2010*), (pp. 360-366). CSREA Press.

Solo, A. M. G. (2010). Multidimensional matrix algebra and multidimensional matrix calculus: Part 3 of 5. In *Proceedings of the 2010 International Conference on Scientific Computing (CSC 2010)*, (pp. 367-372). CSREA Press.

Solo, A. M. G. (2010). Multidimensional matrix algebra and multidimensional matrix calculus: Part 4 of 5. In *Proceedings of the 2010 International Conference on Scientific Computing (CSC 2010)*, (pp. 373-378). CSREA Press.

Solo, A. M. G. (2010). Multidimensional matrix algebra and multidimensional matrix calculus: Part 5 of 5. In *Proceedings of the 2010 International Conference on Scientific Computing (CSC 2010)*, (pp. 379-381). CSREA Press.

Taylor, J. G., & Commbes, S. (1993). Learning higher order correlations. *Neural Networks, 6*, 423–428. doi:10.1016/0893-6080(93)90009-L

Villalobos, L., & Merat, F. (1995). Learning capability assessment and feature space optimization for higher-order neural networks. *IEEE Transactions on Neural Networks, 6*, 267–272. doi:10.1109/72.363427

Werbos, P. J. (1990). Backpropagation through time: What it is and how to do it. *Proceedings of the IEEE, 78*(10), 1550–1560. doi:10.1109/5.58337

Williams, R. J., & Zipser, D. (1989). A learning algorithm for continually running fully recurrent neural networks. *Neural Computation, 1*, 270–280. doi:10.1162/neco.1989.1.2.270

Xu, L., Oja, E., & Suen, C. Y. (1992). Modified Hebbian learning for curve and surface fitting. *Neural Networks, 5*, 441–457. doi:10.1016/0893-6080(92)90006-5

ADDITIONAL READING

Amari, S. (1971). Characteristics of randomly connected threshold-element networks and network systems. *Proceedings of the IEEE, 59*(1), 35–47. doi:10.1109/PROC.1971.8087

Amari, S. (1972). Characteristics of random nets of analog neuron-like elements. *IEEE Transactions on Systems, Man, and Cybernetics, 2*, 643–654. doi:10.1109/TSMC.1972.4309193

Amari, S. (1972). Learning patterns and pattern sequences by self-organizing nets of threshold elements. *IEEE Transactions on Computers, 21*, 1197–1206. doi:10.1109/T-C.1972.223477

Amari, S. (1977). A mathematical approach to neural systems. In Metzler, J. (Ed.), *Systems Neuroscience* (pp. 67–118). New York, NY: Academic.

Amari, S. (1977). Neural theory of association and concept formation. *Biological Cybernetics, 26*, 175–185. doi:10.1007/BF00365229

Amari, S. (1990). Mathematical foundations of neurocomputing. *Proceedings of the IEEE, 78*(9), 1443–1462. doi:10.1109/5.58324

Amit, D. J., Gutfreund, G., & Sompolinsky, H. (1985). Spin-glass model of neural networks. *Physical Review A., 32*, 1007–1018. doi:10.1103/PhysRevA.32.1007

Anagun, A. S., & Cin, I. (1998). A neural-network-based computer access security system for multiple users. In *Proceedings of the 23rd International Conference on Computers and Industrial Engineering*, (Vol. 35), (pp. 351-354). IEEE Press.

Anderson, J. A. (1983). Cognition and psychological computation with neural models. *IEEE Transactions on Systems, Man, and Cybernetics, 13*, 799–815.

Anninos, P. A., Beek, B., Csermel, T. J., Harth, E. E., & Pertile, G. (1970). Dynamics of neural structures. *Journal of Theoretical Biology, 26*, 121–148. doi:10.1016/S0022-5193(70)80036-4

Aoki, C., & Siekevltz, P. (1988, December). Plasticity in brain development. *Scientific American*, 56–64. doi:10.1038/scientificamerican1288-56

Churchland, P. S., & Sejnowski, T. J. (1988). Perspectives on cognitive neuroscience. *Science, 242*, 741–745. doi:10.1126/science.3055294

Ding, M.-Z., & Yang, W.-M. (1997). Stability of synchronous chaos and on-off intermittency in coupled map lattices. *Physical Review E: Statistical Physics, Plasmas, Fluids, and Related Interdisciplinary Topics, 56*(4), 4009–4016. doi:10.1103/PhysRevE.56.4009

Durbin, R. (1989). On the correspondence between network models and the nervous system . In Durbin, R., Miall, C., & Mitchison, G. (Eds.), *The Computing Neurons*. Reading, MA: Addison-Wesley.

Engel, K., Konig, P., Kreiter, A. K., & Singer, W. (1991). Interhemispheric synchronization of oscillatory neuronal responses in cat visual cortex. *Science, 252*, 1177–1178. doi:10.1126/science.252.5009.1177

Ersu, E., & Tolle, H. (1984). A new concept for learning control inspired by brain theory. In *Proceedings of the 9th World Congress IFAC,* (pp. 245-250). IFAC.

Forbus, K. D., & Gentner, D. (1983). Casual reasoning about quantities. In *Proceedings of the 5th Annual Conference of the Cognitive Science Society,* (pp. 196-206). Cognitive Science Society.

Fujita, M. (1982). Adaptive filter model of the cerebellum. *Biological Cybernetics, 45*, 195–206. doi:10.1007/BF00336192

Garliaskas, A., & Gupta, M. M. (1995). A generalized model of synapse-dendrite-cell body as a complex neuron. In *Proceedings of the World Congress on Neural Networks,* (Vol. 1), (pp. 304-307). IEEE.

Gupta, M. M. (1988). Biological basis for computer vision: Some perspective. In *Proceedings of the SPW Conference on Intelligent Robots and Computer Vision,* (pp. 811-823). SPW.

Gupta, M. M., & Knopf, G. K. (1992). A multitask visual information processor with a biologically motivated design. *Journal of Visual Communication and Image Representation, 3*(3), 230–246. doi:10.1016/1047-3203(92)90020-T

Hiramoto, M., Hiromi, Y., Giniger, E., & Hotta, Y. (2000). The drosophila netrin receptor frazzled guides axons by controlling netrin distribution. *Nature, 406*(6798), 886–888. doi:10.1038/35022571

Holmes, C. C., & Mallick, B. K. (1998). Bayesian radial basis functions of variable dimension. *Neural Computation, 10*(5), 1217–1233. doi:10.1162/089976698300017421

Honma, N., Abe, K., Sato, M., & Takeda, H. (1998). Adaptive evolution of holon networks by an autonomous decentralized method. *Applied Mathematics and Computation, 9*(1), 43–61. doi:10.1016/S0096-3003(97)10008-X

Hopfield, J. (1990, April). Artificial neural networks are coming: An interview by W. Myers. *IEEE Expert*, 3–6.

Joshi, A., Ramakrishman, N., Houstis, E. N., & Rice, J. R. (1997). On neurobiological, neuro-fuzzy, machine learning, and statistical pattern recognition techniques. *IEEE Transactions on Neural Networks, 8.*

Kaneko, K. (1994). Relevance of dynamic clustering to biological networks. *Physica D. Nonlinear Phenomena, 75*, 55–73. doi:10.1016/0167-2789(94)90274-7

Kaneko, K. (1994). Relevance of dynamic clustering to biological networks. *Physica D. Nonlinear Phenomena*, *75*, 55–73. doi:10.1016/0167-2789(94)90274-7

Kaneko, K. (1997). Coupled maps with growth and death: An approach to cell differentiation. *Physica D. Nonlinear Phenomena*, *103*, 505–527. doi:10.1016/S0167-2789(96)00282-5

Knopf, G. K., & Gupta, M. M. (1993). Dynamics of antagonistic neural processing elements. *International Journal of Neural Systems*, *4*(3), 291–303. doi:10.1142/S0129065793000237

Kohara, K., Kitamura, A., Morishima, M., & Tsumoto, T. (2001). Activity-dependent transfer of brain-derived neurotrophic factor to postsynaptic neurons. *Science*, *291*, 2419–2423. doi:10.1126/science.1057415

Kohonen, T. (1988). An introduction to neural computing. *Neural Networks*, *1*(1), 3–16. doi:10.1016/0893-6080(88)90020-2

Kohonen, T. (1990). The self-organizing map. *Proceedings of the IEEE*, *78*(9), 1464–1480. doi:10.1109/5.58325

Kohonen, T. (1991). Self-organizing maps: Optimization approaches . In Kohonen, T., Makisara, K., Simula, O., & Kangas, J. (Eds.), *Artificial Neural Networks* (pp. 981–990). Amsterdam, The Netherlands: Elsevier.

Kohonen, T. (1993). Things you haven't heard about the self-organizing map. In *Proceedings of the International Conference of Neural Networks 1993*, (pp. 1147-1156). IEEE.

Kohonen, T. (1998). Self organization of very large document collections: State of the art. In *Proceedings of the 8th International Conference on Artificial Neural Networks*, (Vol. 1), (pp. 65-74). IEEE.

LeCun, Y., Boser, B., & Solla, S. A. (1990). In Touretzky, D. (Ed.), *Optimal brain damage* (*Vol. 2*, pp. 598–605). Advances in Neural Information Processing Systems San Francisco, CA: Morgan Kaufmann.

LeCun, Y., Boser, B., & Solla, S. A. (1990). In Touretzky, D. (Ed.), *Optimal brain damage* (*Vol. 2*, pp. 598–605). Advances in Neural Information Processing Systems San Francisco, CA: Morgan Kaufmann.

Lippmann, R. P. (1987). An introduction to computing with neural networks. *IEEE Acoustics . Speech and Signal Processing Magazine*, *4*(2), 4–22.

Lovejoy, C. O. (1981). The origin of man. *Science*, *211*, 341–350. doi:10.1126/science.211.4480.341

Maire, M. (2000). On the convergence of validity interval analysis. *IEEE Transactions on Neural Networks*, *11*(3), 799–801. doi:10.1109/72.846751

Mantere, K., Parkkinen, J., Jaasketainen, T., & Gupta, M. M. (1993). Wilson-Cowan neural network model in image processing. *Journal of Mathematical Imaging and Vision*, *2*, 251–259. doi:10.1007/BF00118593

McCarthy, J., & Hayes, P. J. (1969). Some philosophical problems from the standpoint of artificial intelligence. In Meltzer & Michie (Eds.), *Machine Intelligence*, (pp. 463-502). Edinburgh, UK: Edinburgh University Press.

McCulloch, W. S., & Pitts, W. H. (1943). A logical calculus of the ideas imminent in nervous activity. *The Bulletin of Mathematical Biophysics*, *5*, 115–133. doi:10.1007/BF02478259

McDermott, D. (1982). A temporal logic for reasoning about processes and plans. *Cognitive Science*, *6*, 101–155. doi:10.1207/s15516709cog0602_1

Melkonian, D. S. (1990). Mathematical theory of chemical synaptic transmission. *Biological Cybernetics*, *62*, 539–548. doi:10.1007/BF00205116

Pecht, O. Y., & Gur, M. (1995). A biologically-inspired improved MAXNET. *IEEE Transactions on Neural Networks, 6,* 757–759. doi:10.1109/72.377981

Petshe, T., & Dickinson, B. W. (1990). Trellis codes, receptive fields, and fault-tolerance self-repairing neural networks. *IEEE Transactions on Neural Networks, 1*(2), 154–166. doi:10.1109/72.80228

Poggio, T., & Koch, C. (1987, May). Synapses that compute motion. *Scientific American,* 46–52. doi:10.1038/scientificamerican0587-46

Poggio, T., & Koch, C. (1987, May). Synapses that compute motion. *Scientific American,* 46–52. doi:10.1038/scientificamerican0587-46

Rao, D. H., & Gupta, M. M. (1993). A generic neural model based on excitatory - inhibitory neural population. [IJCNN.]. *Proceedings of IJCNN, 1993,* 1393–1396.

Rosenblatt, F. (1958). The perceptron: A probabilistic model for information storage and organization in the brain. *Psychological Review, 65,* 386–408. doi:10.1037/h0042519

Sandewall, E. (1989). Combining logic and differential equations for describing real-world systems. In *Proceedings of the 1st International Conference on Principles of Knowledge Representation and Reasoning,* (pp. 412-420). San Francisco, CA: Morgan Kaufmann.

Setiono, R., & Liu, H. (1996). Symbolic representation of neural networks. *Computer, 29*(3), 71–77. doi:10.1109/2.485895

Skarda, C. A., & Freeman, W. J. (1987). How brains make chaos in order to make sense of the world. *The Behavioral and Brain Sciences, 10,* 161–195. doi:10.1017/S0140525X00047336

Stevens, C. F. (1968). Synaptic physiology. *Proceedings of the IEEE, 79*(9), 916–930. doi:10.1109/PROC.1968.6444

Wilson, H. R., & Cowan, J. D. (1972). Excitatory and inhibitory interactions in localized populations of model neurons. *Biophysical Journal, 12,* 1–24. doi:10.1016/S0006-3495(72)86068-5

Chapter 7
High Order Neuro–Fuzzy Dynamic Regulation of General Nonlinear Multi–Variable Systems

Dimitris C. Theodoridis
Democritus University of Thrace, Greece

Yiannis S. Boutalis
Democritus University of Thrace, Greece

Manolis A. Christodoulou
Technical University of Crete, Greece

ABSTRACT

The direct adaptive dynamic regulation of unknown nonlinear multi variable systems is investigated in this chapter in order to address the problem of controlling non-Brunovsky and non-square systems with control inputs less than the number of states. The proposed neuro-fuzzy model acts as a universal approximator. While with the careful selection of a Lyapunov-like function, the authors prove the stability of the proposed control algorithm. Weight updating laws derived from the Lyapunov analysis assure the boundedness of the closed-loop signals incorporating the well-known modified parameter hopping. In addition, the proposed algorithm shows robustness when facing modelling errors, and therefore, the state trajectories present uniform ultimate boundedness. The proposed dynamic controller proved to control those general nonlinear systems, which are difficult or even impossible to control with other algorithms. Simulation results on well-known benchmark problems demonstrate the applicability and effectiveness of the method.

DOI: 10.4018/978-1-4666-2175-6.ch007

INTRODUCTION

Nonlinear dynamical systems are generally represented by nonlinear dynamical equations of the form:

$$\dot{x} = f(x, u) \tag{1}$$

or, after appropriate transformation if it is possible, by its equivalent affine in the control form:

$$\dot{x} = f(x) + G(x) \cdot u . \tag{2}$$

The mathematical description of the above system is required, so that we are able to control it. Unfortunately, the exact mathematical model of the plant, especially when this is highly nonlinear and complex is rarely known and thus appropriate identification schemes have to be applied in order to provide an approximate model of the plant. The problem becomes more complex when the system, apart from being "unknown," is also time varying. Adaptive systems and consequently adaptive control is one of the active approaches in the control theory that gives answers in this kind of problems since 1950 (Aseltine, Mancini, & Sartune, 1958; Ioannou & Sun, 1996).

In this framework, adaptive control approaches rely on adequate approximates of the system parameters (indirect control approaches) or on estimates of the controller parameters incorporated to the system dynamics (direct control approaches), as they described accurately in Ioannou and Fidan (2006). Neural networks and fuzzy inference systems in their neuro-fuzzy approach, being universal approximators, are effectively used to approximate the unknown functions involved in system dynamics (Hornik, Stinchcombe, & White, 1989; Passino & Yurkovich, 1998).

However, the remarkable capabilities of neural networks to learn (identification) and control (adaptively) nonlinear dynamical systems (Narendra & Parthasarathy, 1990; Chen & Narendra,

2002; Plett, 2003; Zhan & Wan, 2006) together with the human like thinking of fuzzy logic is leading to their use for a wide class of applications. Therefore, the tracking accuracy depends mainly on neural networks structure, which should be chosen appropriately from the designer (Li, Chen, & Yuan, 2002; Kumar, Panwar, Sukavanam, Sharma, & Borm, 2011; Pedro & Dahunsi, 2011; Thammano & Ruxpakawong, 2010).

Fully connected Recurrent Neural Networks (RNN) (Tsoi & Back, 1994; Rashid, Huang, & Kechadi, 2007) contains interlink between neurons to reflect the dynamics of the nonlinear system but it suffers both by structure complexity and the poor performance accuracy (Rashid, Huang, & Kechadi, 2007). Many researchers focused in Dynamic Recurrent Neural Networks (DRNN), such as Higher Order Neural Networks (HONNs), which doesn't contain interlink between hidden layer neurons leading in this way to the network structure complexity reduction (Pearlmutter, 1995; Rashid, Huang, & Kechadi, 2007). Thus, among neural networks, HONNs, especially in their recurrent form have been shown to be particularly effective in modelling and controlling dynamical nonlinear systems (Rovithakis & Christodoulou, 2000). In control applications, researchers often assume that the states of the system are all measurable. In practise, however, this is not always the case and one should consider state estimation first. Discrete time Recurrent Higher Order Neural Networks (RHONN) have been recently proposed (Alanis, Sanchez, Loukianov, & Perez-Cisneros, 2010; Alanis, Sanchez, Loukianov, & Perez-Cisneros, 2011; Alanis, Leon, Sanchez, & Ruiz-Velazquez, 2011), where the NN weights learning is performed using Kalman filtering discrete-time schemes. Those schemes proved to be very useful for real-time applications.

The neural and fuzzy approaches are most of the time equivalent, differing between each other mainly in the structure of the approximator chosen. In order to bridge the neural and fuzzy approaches several researchers introduce adaptive schemes using a class of parameterized functions that include both neural networks and fuzzy systems (Cho & Wang, 1996; Juang & Lin, 1998; Li & Mukaidono, 1995; Lin & Cunningham, 1995; Jang & Lin, 1998; Mitra & Hayashi, 2000).

Recently (Theodoridis, Boutalis, & Christodoulou, 2009; Boutalis, Christodoulou, & Theodoridis, 2010), High Order Neural Network Function approximators (HONNFs) have been proposed for the identification of nonlinear dynamical systems of the form (1) or (2), approximated by a Fuzzy Dynamical System. One of the main characteristic of this neuro-fuzzy blending is that, distinct from other approaches, the required a-priori experts information is kept quite law and is reduced only to some initial guess of the centres of the membership functions of the fuzzy output variables. In addition, by following this approach, the global approximation problem is transformed to many simpler ones, each one associated with a specific region of the fuzzy output variables. This way, the approximation abilities of this scheme are significantly enhanced when compared to other approaches. In this chapter, HONNFs are also used for the neuro fuzzy identification of unknown nonlinear dynamical systems. This approximation depends on the fact that fuzzy rules could be identified with the help of HONNFs. The same rationale has been employed (Theodoridis, Christodoulou, & Boutalis, 2008; Boutalis, Theodoridis, & Christodoulou, 2009; Theodoridis, Christodoulou, & Boutalis, 2010), where this neuro-fuzzy approach (Fuzzy Recurrent High Order Neural Networks, F-RHONNs) is used for direct and indirect control schemes.

One difficulty, often encountered in control approaches of affine in the control systems using static feedback, is that each state variable has to be affected by at least one input in order the system to be regulated. This requirement is debunked in special system classes such as the feedback linearizable Brunovsky canonical form or systems that can be treated by the "backstepping" approach, where a multivariable system can be controlled by a single input (Ioannou & Fidan,

2006). Unfortunately, many systems cannot be transformed to these forms rendering the respective control approaches inapplicable. One solution to this problem is to abandon static feedback and use a control law that is governed by a dynamic equation (Rovithakis & Christodoulou, 2000).

In this chapter, a new method is proposed for designing dynamic controllers with arbitrarily small tracking error for uncertain, mismatched nonlinear systems. Thus, we present a direct control approach, which uses a HONN based neuro-fuzzy approximator. The proposed approach uses the combination of high human thinking expressed with fuzzy logic and the adaptation abilities of higher order neural systems. The control inputs are calculated dynamically and combined with the accurate estimates of the neuro-fuzzy approximator leading to a better controller for the general nonlinear system. The dynamic controller is designed in such a way that it can be valid both for square (number of states = number of inputs) or non-square systems using dynamic inputs, while also it leads to the regulation of the real system states to zero.

Recently, a great deal of attention has been given in robust nonlinear control where many methods apply a synthetic approach which uses the controlled variable and the weighting factors in order to make the time derivative of the Lyapunov candidate function negative definite. Here, we also follow the classical Lyapunov stability analysis in order to adjust the weighting factors in F-RHONNs by solving a simple nonlinear differential equation of weighting factor. The new method of parameter hopping that has been already introduced by the authors in Boutalis, Theodoridis, and Christodoulou (2009) is suitably adapted to the new control structure, reassuring in this way that the control input and all other signals in the closed-loop remain bounded making the system Lyapunov stable. Moreover, the controller that is being proposed is designed in such a way that the closed-loop error dynamics become linear as well as stable.

Several simulation studies of nonlinear systems have been conducted to show the effectiveness of this new approach. In comparison with the robust control using a feed-forward static Fuzzy Neural Network (FNN), this new approach does not require the uncertain fuzzy rules with its defuzification process. Therefore, real time coding is simplified which will reduce the cost of hardware platform for the real world implementations of F-RHONN robust controller. Thus, the industrial impact of this new approach will be the feasibility of cheaper hardware implementation to reduce the cost of building intelligent control systems using this innovative approach, i.e., the robust control of robotic arm, inverted pendulum, chaotic systems, etc.

This chapter is organized as follows: Section 2 presents the problem formulation and some background concerning the neuro-fuzzy approximation capabilities, Section 3 introduces the new architecture and its associated direct dynamic regulation properties as well as its stability analysis. Simulation results are shown in Section 4, and finally, conclusion and future work is shown in Section 5.

PROBLEM FORMULATION AND NEURO-FUZZY APPROXIMATION

Problem Formulation

The mathematical description of many engineering applications is non-Brunovsky and non-square with the number of control inputs being less than the system states. Those systems have affine in the control form or they are transformed into affine and in general are given by Equation (2), where $x \in R^n$ the number of system states, which is assumed to be completely measured, $u \in R^m$ the number of control inputs, $f \in R^n$ is an unknown smooth vector field called the drift term, and $G \in R^{n \times m}$ is a matrix with its rows represent-

ing the unknown smooth controlled vector fields g_{ij}, $i = 1, \ldots, n$, $j = 1, 2, \ldots, m$.

Following the analysis presented in Theodoridis, Boutalis, and Christodoulou (2009), we are using an affine in the control neuro-fuzzy dynamical modelling which approximates the system in (2) and uses at least two fuzzy subsystem blocks for the description of $f(x)$ and $G(x)$ as follows:

$$\dot{\hat{x}}_i = -a_i \hat{x}_i + \overline{x}_{f_i} W_{f_i} s_f(x) + \sum_{j=1}^{m} \overline{x}_{g_{ij}} W_{g_{ij}} s_{g_j}(x) u_j$$

$$(3)$$

where $a_i > 0$ a positive real constant, $\overline{x}_{f_i}$, $\overline{x}_{g_{ij}}$ are vectors containing the output fuzzy centres extracted from the f_i, g_{ij} function terms, respectively. Also, W_{f_i}, $W_{g_{ij}}$ are matrices containing neural weights according to (3) and $s_f(x)$, $s_{g_j}(x)$ are vectors containing high order combinations of sigmoid functions of the states.

The problem we are facing is to force system states of Equation (2) to zero from an arbitrarily initial value by applying dynamical control inputs to the plant. In this case, and having in our mind that the plant is considered unknown, we propose its approximation by the following neuro-fuzzy dynamic algorithm described in the next section plus a modelling error term $\mu(x, u)$:

$$\dot{x}_i = -a_i x_i + \overline{x}_{f_i} W_{f_i}^* s_f(x)$$
$$+ \sum_{j=1}^{m} \overline{x}_{g_{ij}} W_{g_{ij}}^* s_{g_j}(x) u_j + \mu_i(x, u)$$

$$(4)$$

where the optimal weights $W_{f_i}^*$, $W_{g_{ij}}^*$ are unknown. Therefore, the state regulation problem is analyzed for the system (4) instead of (2). Since the optimal weights are unknown, we propose a dynamic controller and appropriate updating laws for W_{f_i}, $W_{g_{ij}}$ derived with the help of Lyapunov stability analysis, which guarantee convergence of the system states to zero together with boundedness of all signal in the closed-loop. It is also important to make additional assumptions to assure the controllability of our plant or to guarantee the uniqueness and existence of solution for any finite initial condition with $u \in U_c$.

- **Assumption 1:** For any admissible input and any finite initial condition, the state trajectories are uniformly ultimate bounded UUB for any finite time period $T > 0$. Hence, $|x(T)| < \infty$.

- **Assumption 2:** Functions $f_i(\bullet)$, $g_{ij}(\bullet)$ are assumed to be unknown continuous nonlinear functions with respect to x and satisfy a local Lipschitz condition so that the solution $x(t)$ of (2) is unique for any finite initial condition and admissible input.

In addition, we make the following assumption about the modelling errors.

- **Assumption 3:** We assume that the modelling error term $\mu_i(x, u)$ satisfies:

$$\mu_i(x, u) = \mu_{ix}(x) + \mu_{iu}(x)u$$

with

$$\left|\mu_{ix}(x)\right| \le k_1 + k_2'\left|x\right|, \ \left|\mu_{iu}(x)\right| \le k_2''$$

where k_1, k_2', k_2'' are known positive constants. Therefore, we can write:

$$\left|\mu_i(x, u)\right| \le \left|\mu_{ix}(x)\right| + \left|\mu_{iu}(x)\right| \le k_1 + k_2'\left|x\right| + k_2''\left|u\right| \tag{5}$$

Neuro-Fuzzy Approximation

Let us consider a nonlinear function $f(x, u)$, where $f : R^{n+m} \to R^n$ is a smooth vector field defined

on a compact set $\Psi \subset R^{n+m}$, with input space $u \in U \subset R^m$ and state-space $x \in X \subset R^n$, where $n > m$. In addition, we assume that the dynamic equation that describes the I/O behaviour of a system has the following form:

$$\dot{x}_i(t) = f_i\left(x(t), u(t)\right) \tag{6}$$

where $f_i(\bullet)$, $i = 1, 2, ..., n$, is a continuous function and t denotes the temporal variable.

- **Assumption 4:** *Notice that since $\Psi \subset R^{n+m}$ then Ψ is closed and bounded set. Also, it is noted that even if Ψ is not compact we may assume that there is a time instant T such that $\left(x(t), u(t)\right)$ remain in a compact subset of Ψ for all $t < T$; i.e. if $\Psi_T := \left\{\left(x(t), u(t)\right) \in \Psi, t < T\right\}$. The interval Ψ_T represents the time period over which the approximation is to be performed.*

In the sequel, we consider that the function $f(x, u)$ is approximated by a fuzzy system using appropriate fuzzy rules. In this framework, let Ω_f be defined as the universe of discourse of $(x, u) \in X \cup U \subset R^{n+m}$ belonging to the $(j_1, j_2, ..., j_{n+m})^{th}$ input fuzzy patch and pointing - through the vector field $f(\bullet)$ to the subset which belong to the $(l_1, l_2, ..., l_{n+m})^{th}$ output fuzzy patch. Also, Ω_{f_i} is a subset of Ω_f containing input pair values associated with f_i.

Furthermore, $\Omega_{f_i}^p$, with $p = 1, 2, ..., q$ the number of fuzzy partitions of the $i - th$ state variable, is defined as the $p - th$ sub region of Ω_{f_i} such that $\Omega_{f_i} = \bigcup_{p=1}^q \Omega_{f_i}^p$.

Thus, we are now ready to state the following definitions.

Definition 1: According to the above notation the Indicator Function (INF) connected to $\Omega_{f_i}^p$ is defined as follows:

$$I_i^p\left(x\left(t\right),u\left(t\right)\right)$$
$$=\begin{cases}\alpha_i^p\left(x\left(t\right),u\left(t\right)\right) & if\ \left(x\left(t\right),u\left(t\right)\right)\in\Omega_{f_i}^p\\ 0 & otherwise\end{cases}$$

(7)

where $\alpha_i^p\left(x\left(t\right),u\left(t\right)\right)$ denotes the firing strength of the rule.

Then, assuming a standard defuzzification procedure (e.g. Centroid of area or weighted average), the functional representation of the fuzzy system that approximates the real one (6) can be written as:

$$\hat{f}_i\left(x\left(t\right),u\left(t\right)\right)=\frac{\displaystyle\sum_{p=1}^{q}I_i^p\cdot\overline{x}_{f_i}^p}{\displaystyle\sum_{p=1}^{q}I_i^p}$$

(8)

where the summation is carried over all the available fuzzy rules and $\overline{x}_{f_i}^p$ is the $p-th$ fuzzy centre of f_i.

Definition 2: We can define the weighted INF (WINF) by the following equation:

$$\left(I_w\right)_i^p=\frac{I_i^p}{\displaystyle\sum_{p=1}^{q}I_i^p}$$

(9)

which is the INF defined in (7) and divided by the sum of all INF participating in the summation of (8).

Thus, Equation (8) can be rewritten as:

$$\hat{f}_i\left(x\left(t\right),u\left(t\right)\right)=\sum_{p=1}^{q}\left(I_w\right)_i^p\ \overline{x}_{f_i}^p$$

(10)

Based on the fact that functions of high order neurons are capable of approximating discontinuous functions (Christodoulou, 2007; Kosmatopoulos, 1996), we use High Order Neural Networks (HONN's) in order to approximate an $\left(I_w\right)_i^p$. Thus, we have the following definition.

Definition 3: A HONN is defined as (Rovithakis, 2000):

$$N_i^p\left(x\left(t\right),u\left(t\right);w,k\right)=\sum_{l=1}^{k}w_{f_i}^{pl}\prod_{j\in I_l}\Phi_j^{d_j(l)}$$

(11)

where $I_l=\left\{I_1,I_2,...,I_k\right\}$ is a collection of k not-ordered subsets of $\left\{1,2,...,n+m\right\}$, $d_j\left(l\right)$ are non-negative integers. Φ_j are the elements of the following vector:

$$\Phi=\left[\Phi_1\cdots\Phi_n\Phi_{n+1}\cdots\Phi_{n+m}\right]^T$$
$$=\left[s\left(x_1\right)\cdots s\left(x_n\right)s\left(u_1\right)\cdots s\left(u_m\right)\right]^T$$

where s denotes the sigmoid function defined as:

$$s\left(x\right)=\frac{\alpha}{1+e^{-\beta x}}-\gamma$$

(12)

with α,β being positive real numbers and γ being a real number.

Special attention has to be given in the selection of parameters α,β,γ so that $s\left(x\right)$ fulfill the persistency of excitation condition ($s\in\left[-\gamma,-\gamma+\alpha\right]$ when $\gamma<0$) required in some system identification tasks. Also, $w_{f_i}^{pl}$ is the HONN weights with $i=1,2,...,n,\quad p=1,2,...,q$ and $l=1,2,...,k$ the number of high order terms.

Thus, Equation (11) can be written as:

$$N_i^p\left(x\left(t\right),u\left(t\right);w,k\right)=\sum_{l=1}^{k}w_{f_i}^{pl}s_l\left(x\left(t\right),u\left(t\right)\right)$$

(13)

Figure 1. Fuzzy partitioning of the system output

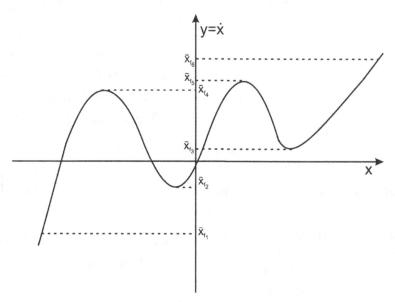

where $s_l\left(x(t), u(t)\right)$ are high order terms of sigmoid functions of the state and/or input.

The next lemma (Kosmatopoulos, 1996) states that a HONN of the form in Equation (13) can approximate the Weighted Indicator Function (WINF), $\left(I_w\right)_i^p$ with arbitrarily small approximation error depending on the careful selection of the high order terms.

Lemma 1: Consider the WINF $\left(I_w\right)_i^p$ and the family of the HONN's $N_i^p\left(x(t), u(t); w, k\right)$. Then for any $\varepsilon_i^p > 0$, there is a vector of weights w and a number of k high order connections such that:

$$\sup_{(x(t), u(t)) \in \Psi} \left\{ \begin{array}{l} \left(I_w\right)_i^p\left(x(t), u(t)\right) \\ -\sum_{l=1}^{k} w_{f_i}^{pl} s_l\left(x(t), u(t)\right) \end{array} \right\} < \varepsilon_i^p .$$

The magnitude of approximation error $\varepsilon_i^p > 0$ depends on the choice of the number of high order terms.

Furthermore, someone can say that we are provided with rules of the form:

R_i^p : IF $\left(x(t), u(t)\right) \in \Omega_{f_i}^p$ THEN $HONN_p$ is $\left(I_w\right)_i^p$.

Following the above analysis, actually we give a membership value according to the output fuzzy partitioning, as shown in Figure 1, to every HONN which participates to the estimation of $f_i\left(x, u\right)$.

As a consequence we have the following definition.

Definition 4: The Center Membership Value (CMV) $\overline{x}_{f_i}^p$ which is the $p - th$ fuzzy center of the $i - th$ state variable activates a HONN to a degree of implementation $\overline{x}_{f_i}^p$.

Therefore, the rules are modified after all as:

R_i^p : IF $\left(x(t), u(t)\right) \in \Omega_{f_i}^p$ THEN $HONN_p$ is $\left(I_w\right)_i^p$ with (CMV) $\overline{x}_{f_i}^p$.

Now, we can group those rules which participate to the construction of the $i - th$ state variable output according to the following form:

R_i: IF $\left(x(t), u(t) \right) \in \Omega_{f_i}$ THEN $HONN_1$ is $\left(I_w \right)_i^1 (t)$ with (CMV) $\overline{x}_{f_i}^1$ and $HONN_2$ is $\left(I_w \right)_i^2 (t)$ with (CMV) $\overline{x}_{f_i}^2$ and ... and $HONN_q$ is $\left(I_w \right)_i^q (t)$ with (CMV) $\overline{x}_{f_i}^q$.

As it is evident by the above definition, the $i-th$ state variable of the system output can be determined as follows:

R_i: IF $\left(x(t), u(t) \right) \in \Omega_{f_i}$ THEN

$$\begin{aligned} \hat{f}_i(x,u) &= \left(I_w \right)_i^1 (t) \cdot \overline{x}_{f_i}^1 \\ &+ \left(I_w \right)_i^2 (t) \cdot \overline{x}_{f_i}^2 + \cdots + \left(I_w \right)_i^q (t) \cdot \overline{x}_{f_i}^q \end{aligned},$$

where it is clear enough that the information about the antecedent partitioning and membership functions as well as the number of rules is not necessary here to be determined.

Following the above notation Equation (10) in conjunction with Equation (13) can be rewritten as:

$$\hat{f}_i \left(x(t), u(t) \right) = \sum_{p=1}^{q} \overline{x}_{f_i}^p \cdot \left(\sum_{l=1}^{k} w_{f_i}^{pl} \cdot s_l \left(x(t), u(t) \right) \right) \tag{14}$$

Based on the above analysis and Equation (14) one may easily detect the distinct characteristics of the proposed approximation approach; namely, the minimal a-priori information's requirements (only an estimate of $\overline{x}_{f_i}^p$) and the split of the global approximation problem to q simpler ones (with q being the number of the involved HONN approximators).

Equation (14) can be written in a more compact form as:

$$\dot{\hat{x}} = X_f W_f s_f(x,u) \tag{15}$$

where X_f is a matrix containing the centres of the partitions of every fuzzy output variable of $f(x,u)$, $s_f(x,u)$ is a vector containing high order combinations of sigmoid functions of the state x and control input u. In addition, W_f is a matrix containing respective neural weights according to (14). For notational simplicity we assume that all output fuzzy variables are partitioned to the same number, q, of partitions.

Under these specifications X_f is a $n \times n \cdot q$ block diagonal matrix of the form $X_f = diag \left(\overline{x}_{f_1}, \overline{x}_{f_2}, ..., \overline{x}_{f_n} \right)$ with $\overline{x}_{f_i}$ being a q-dimensional row vector of the form:

$$\overline{x}_{f_i} = \begin{bmatrix} \overline{x}_{f_i}^1 & \overline{x}_{f_i}^2 & \cdots & \overline{x}_{f_i}^q \end{bmatrix}$$

or in a more detailed form:

$$X_f = \begin{bmatrix} \overline{x}_{f_1}^1 & \cdots & \overline{x}_{f_1}^q & 0 & \cdots & 0 & 0 & \cdots & 0 \\ 0 & \cdots & 0 & \overline{x}_{f_2}^1 & \cdots & \overline{x}_{f_2}^q & 0 & \cdots & 0 \\ \cdots & \cdots & \cdots & \cdots & \cdots & \cdots & \cdots & \cdots & \cdots \\ 0 & \cdots & 0 & 0 & \cdots & 0 & \overline{x}_{f_n}^1 & \cdots & \overline{x}_{f_n}^q \end{bmatrix}.$$

Also, $s_f(x) = \begin{bmatrix} s_1(x) & \cdots & s_k(x) \end{bmatrix}^T$, where each $s_l(x)$ with $l = \{1, 2, ..., k\}$, is a high order combination of sigmoid functions of the state variables and the inputs and W_f is a $n \cdot q \times k$ matrix with neural weights. W_f assumes the form $W_f = \begin{bmatrix} W_{f_1} & \cdots & W_{f_n} \end{bmatrix}^T$, where each W_{f_i} is a matrix $\left[W_{f_i}^{pl} \right]_{q \times k}$.

An alternative, recurrent NF form of Equation (15) which will be used in the subsequent analysis of this chapter is:

$$\dot{\hat{x}} = A\hat{x} + \hat{f} \tag{16}$$

Considering that f is approximated by the NF model described above, Equation (16) can be rewritten as:

$$\dot{\hat{x}} = A\hat{x} + X_f W_f s_f (x, u) \qquad (17)$$

where A is a $n \times n$ stable matrix which for simplicity can be taken to be diagonal as: $A = diag[-a_1, -a_2, ..., -a_n]$, with $a_i > 0$.

From the above definitions and Equation (14) it is obvious that the accuracy of the approximation of $f_i(x, u)$ depends on the approximation abilities of HONN's and on an initial estimate of the centres of the output membership functions. It has to be mentioned here that the neuro-fuzzy representation, finally given by (17), offers some advantages over other fuzzy or neural adaptive representations. Considering the proposed approach from the Adaptive Fuzzy Systems (AFS) point of view, the main advantage is that the proposed approach is much less vulnerable in initial AFS design assumptions because there is no need for a priori information related to the IF part of the rules (type and centers of membership functions, number of rules). This information is replaced by the existence of HONNF. Considering the proposed approach from the NN point of view, the final representation of the dynamic equations is actually a combination of high-order neural networks, each one being specialized in approximating a function related to a corresponding center of output state membership function. This way, instead of having one large HONN trying to approximate "everything," we have many, probably smaller, specialized HONNs. Conceptually, this strategy is expected to present better approximation results; this is also verified in the simulations of the relevant references. Moreover, as it has be shown in Boutalis, Theodoridis, and Christodoulou (2009), due to the particular bond of each HONN with one centre of an output state membership function, the existence of the control law is assured by introducing the novel technique of parameter "hopping" in the corresponding weight updating laws.

Direct Dynamic Regulation

We choose a positive definite function $z(x, u, W_f)$ of class C^2 from $R^n \times R^m \times R^{n \times k_f} \to R^+$ as follows:

$$z = \frac{1}{2} x^T x + \frac{1}{2} u^T u + \frac{1}{2} tr\left\{ \left(\overline{x}_f W_f\right)^T \left(\overline{x}_f W_f\right) \right\} \qquad (18)$$

where the derivative with respect to time is written as:

$$\dot{z} = \frac{\vartheta z}{\vartheta x}^T \dot{x} + \frac{\vartheta z}{\vartheta u}^T \dot{u} + \frac{\vartheta z}{\vartheta W_f}^T \dot{W}_f$$

$$= \frac{\vartheta z}{\vartheta x}^T \left(\begin{array}{c} -Ax + \overline{x}_f W_f^* s_f(x) \\ + \sum_{j=1}^{m} \overline{x}_{g_j} W_{g_j}^* s_{g_j}(x) u_j + \mu(x, u) \end{array} \right)$$

$$+ \frac{\vartheta z}{\vartheta u}^T \dot{u} + \frac{\vartheta z}{\vartheta W_f}^T \dot{W}_f \qquad (19)$$

In the sequel, we define the filtered error equation as:

$$r = \dot{e}_s + \kappa e_s \qquad (20)$$

where κ is a positive definite constant number chosen appropriately from the designer and $e_s = \zeta - z$. In addition, the filtered version of r taking into account the function z can be written as:

$$r = \frac{\vartheta z}{\vartheta x}^T \overline{x}_f W_f s_f(x) + \frac{\vartheta z}{\vartheta x}^T \overline{x}_g W_g S_g(x) u - \dot{z}$$

$$- \frac{\vartheta z}{\vartheta x}^T Ax + \frac{\vartheta z}{\vartheta u}^T \dot{u} + \frac{\vartheta z}{\vartheta W_f}^T \dot{W}_f - \sum_{i=1}^{n} \sum_{l=1}^{k_f} \sigma_{f_i}^l tr\left\{ H_{f_i}^T W_{f_i}^l \right\} \qquad (21)$$

where H_f is the hopping magnitude (Boutalis, Theodoridis, & Christodoulou, 2009), the form of which is given below. Also, $\bar{x}_g \in R^{n \times q_g}$ with q_g the number of fuzzy partitions of $G(x)$, W_g is a $q_g \times k_g$ matrix of synaptic weights and $S_g(x)$ is a $k_g \times m$ matrix of high order sigmoidal terms. After substituting (19) to the above equation we result to:

$$r = x^T \bar{x}_f \tilde{W}_f s_f(x) + x^T \bar{x}_g \tilde{W}_g S_g(x) u - x^T \mu(x, u)$$
$$-\sum_{i=1}^{n} \sum_{l=1}^{k_f} \sigma_{f_i}^l tr\left\{ H_f^T W_{f_i}^l \right\}$$
(22)

Thus, employing e_s in conjunction with (20), Equation (21) becomes:

$$\dot{\zeta} + \kappa\zeta = \kappa z + x^T \bar{x}_f W_f s_f(x) + x^T \bar{x}_g W_g S_g(x) u$$
$$-x^T A x + \dot{u}^T u + tr\left\{ \dot{W}_f^T W_f \right\} - \sum_{i=1}^{n} \sum_{l=1}^{k_f} \sigma_{f_i}^l tr\left\{ H_f^T W_{f_i}^l \right\}$$

And taking into account Equation (1) we result to equation ζ as follows:

$$\dot{\zeta} = -\kappa\zeta + \frac{1}{2}\kappa\left[x^T x + u^T u + tr\left\{ \left(\bar{x}_f W_f\right)^T \left(\bar{x}_f W_f\right)\right\}\right]$$
$$+x^T \bar{x}_f W_f s_f(x) + x^T \bar{x}_g W_g S_g(x) u$$
$$-x^T A x + \dot{u}^T u + tr\left\{ \dot{W}_f^T W_f \right\} - \sum_{i=1}^{n} \sum_{l=1}^{k_f} \sigma_{f_i}^l tr\left\{ H_f^T W_{f_i}^l \right\}$$
(23)

where $\sigma_{f_i}^l = 0$ when no hopping occurs and $\sigma_{f_i}^l = 1$ when the hopping action is activated. Thus, we select the following cases, which will help in the remaining chapter analysis to examine the effect of activating (or not) the hopping condition.

- **Case 1:** When $\sigma_{f_i}^l = 0$.

We notice that if we choose appropriately the control law from the above equation such as:

$$\dot{u}^T = -\frac{1}{2}\kappa u^T - x^T \bar{x}_g W_g S_g(x)$$
(24)

Also, taking into account the relation $\frac{1}{2}\kappa I = aI$ and creating the updating law as:

$$\dot{W}_f = -\bar{x}_f^T x s_f^T - \frac{1}{2}\kappa\bar{x}_f^T \bar{x}_f W_f,$$

or in a more detailed form as:

$$\dot{W}_{f_i}^l = -\bar{x}_{f_i}^T x_i s_{f_i}^T - \frac{1}{2}\kappa\bar{x}_{f_i}^T \bar{x}_{f_i} W_{f_i}^l,$$
(25)

for every state and high order term, we result to:

$$\dot{\zeta} = -\kappa\zeta.$$
(26)

Equation (26) denotes that ζ converges to zero exponentially fast with a rate of convergence κ.

- **Case 2:** When $\sigma_{f_i}^l = 1$.

In this special case, when the hopping condition is valid then the updating law for the W_f weights in a detailed form becomes as shown in Box 1.where H_f in Equation (21) and after is the hopping term and equals to

$$H_f = \kappa_{f_i}^{outer} \frac{\bar{x}_{f_i} W_{f_i}^l \left(\bar{x}_{f_i}\right)^T}{tr\left\{ \left(\bar{x}_{f_i}\right)^T \bar{x}_{f_i} \right\}}$$

After substituting this hopping term to Equation (23) we notice that ζ continues as previously in case 1 to converge to zero exponentially

Box 1.

$$\dot{W}_{f_i}^l = \begin{cases} -\overline{x}_{f_i}^T x_i s_{f_i}^T - \dfrac{1}{2}\kappa \overline{x}_{f_i}^T \overline{x}_{f_i} W_{f_i}^l & \begin{aligned} & if\ \overline{x}_{f_i} \cdot W_{f_i}^l \in P_{f,MIMO} \\ & or\ \overline{x}_{f_i} \cdot W_{f_i}^l = \pm \varepsilon_i\ and\ \overline{x}_{f_i} \cdot \dot{W}_{f_i}^l >< 0 \end{aligned} \\[2em] -\overline{x}_{f_i}^T x_i s_{f_i}^T - \dfrac{1}{2}\kappa \overline{x}_{f_i}^T \overline{x}_{f_i} W_{f_i}^l - \kappa_{f_i}^{outer}\dfrac{\overline{x}_{f_i} W_{f_i}^l \left(\overline{x}_{f_i}\right)^T}{tr\left\{\left(\overline{x}_{f_i}\right)^T \overline{x}_{f_i}\right\}} & otherwise \end{cases} \tag{27}$$

fast. In the sequel, the main analysis focuses on stability issues by selecting firstly a suitable Lyapunov-like function and proving later the negativity of its time derivative according to some appropriate restrictions. Stability plays a crucial role in system theory and control engineering, and has been investigated extensively in the past century. Some of the most fundamental concepts of stability were introduced by the Russian mathematician and engineer Alexandr Lyapunov (1992). The work of Lyapunov was extended and brought to the attention of the larger control engineering and applied mathematics community by LaSalle and Lefschetz, Krasovskii, Hahn, Massera, Malkin, Kalman and Bertram, and many others (Ioannou & Sun, 1996). In the approach used here, which is standard in stability analysis of adaptive schemes, the Lyapunov candidate function is selected to be a positive definite one. It usually incorporates the "energy" of the approximation and weight error signals. By selecting the weight adaptation laws so that its time derivative remains negative definite we assure the approximation error convergence to zero.

STABILITY ANALYSIS

We consider the Lyapunov-like function with the following form:

$$V_g = \frac{1}{2}e_s^2 + \frac{1}{2}tr\left\{\tilde{W}_g^T D_g^{-1}\tilde{W}_g\right\} \tag{28}$$

where $\tilde{W}_g = W_g^* - \hat{W}_g$. Taking the derivative of (28) we have:

$$\dot{V}_g = \dot{e}_s e_s + tr\left\{\dot{W}_g^T D_g^{-1}\tilde{W}_g\right\},$$

And after substituting (21) to the above equation we result to:

$$\dot{V}_g = -\kappa e_s^2 + e_s \begin{vmatrix} -\dot{z} - x^T A x + x^T \overline{x}_f W_f s_f(x) \\ +x^T \overline{x}_g W_g S_g(x) u + \dot{u}^T u \end{vmatrix} +$$
$$e_s tr\left\{\dot{W}_f^T W_f\right\} - e_s \sum_{i=1}^n \sum_{l=1}^{k_f} \sigma_{f_i}^l tr\left\{H_f^T W_{f_i}^l\right\}$$
$$+tr\left\{\dot{W}_g^T D_g^{-1}\tilde{W}_g\right\}$$

Continuing, we use the derivative of z given by Equation (19) and making the appropriate operations to the above equation becomes:

$$\dot{V}_g = -\kappa e_s^2 + e_s \begin{vmatrix} x^T \overline{x}_f \tilde{W}_f s_f(x) + x^T \overline{x}_g \tilde{W}_g S_g(x) u \\ -x^T \mu(x,u) \end{vmatrix}$$
$$-e_s \sum_{i=1}^n \sum_{l=1}^{k_f} \sigma_{f_i}^l tr\left\{H_f^T W_{f_i}^l\right\} + tr\left\{\dot{W}_g^T D_g^{-1}\tilde{W}_g\right\}$$

Hence, if we choose:

$$tr\left\{\dot{W}_g^T D_g^{-1}\tilde{W}_g\right\} = -x^T \overline{x}_g \tilde{W}_g S_g(x) u$$

we obtain:

$$\dot{W}_g = -\overline{x}_g^T x u^T S_g^T D_g$$

or in a more detailed form:

$$\dot{W}_{g_{ij}}^l = -\overline{x}_{g_{ij}}^T x_i u_{ij} s_{g_{ij}}^l d_{g_{ij}}. \tag{29}$$

Thus, the derivative of Lyapunov-like function can be written once again as:

$$\dot{V}_g = -\kappa e_s^2 + e_s x^T \overline{x}_f \tilde{W}_f s_f(x) - e_s x^T \mu(x, u)$$
$$-e_s \sum_{i=1}^{n} \sum_{l=1}^{k_f} \sigma_{f_i}^l tr\left\{H_f^T W_{f_i}^l\right\} \tag{30}$$

Moving further, in order to prove the negativity of Lyapunov-like function we have to state the following lemmas.

Lemma 1: The control law:

$$\dot{u}^T = -\frac{1}{2}\kappa u^T - x^T \overline{x}_g W_g S_g(x)$$

together with the update law in Box 2.and $\frac{1}{2}\kappa I = aI$ guarantees that:

$$\zeta(t) \leq 0, \quad \forall t \geq 0$$

$\lim_{t \to \infty} \zeta(t) = 0$ exponentially fast provided that $\zeta(0) < 0$

$\left\|\overline{x}_f W_f\right\| \leq \overline{w}_f, \quad \forall t \geq 0$ provided that $\overline{x}_f W_f(0) \in X_{W_f}$ and $\overline{x}_f W_f^* \in X_{W_f}$.

Proof: Motivated from Equation (26), we conclude that ζ goes to zero exponentially fast with convergence rate depending of the appropriate selection of constant κ. More precisely, we have $\dot{\zeta}(t) = -\kappa\zeta(t), \quad \forall t \geq 0$ which the solution is:

$$\zeta(t) = \zeta(0)e^{-\kappa t}, \quad \forall t \geq 0.$$

Since $\kappa > 0$, if we choose the initial condition $\zeta(0) < 0$, we have that $\zeta(t) \leq 0, \quad \forall t \geq 0$.

In order to prove the restriction of the weights during their adaptation we only need to show that

$$\frac{d\left(\left\|\overline{x}_f W_f(t)\right\|\right)^2}{dt} \leq 0$$

whenever $\left\|\overline{x}_f W_f(t)\right\| = \overline{w}_f, \quad \forall t \geq 0$. The proof of this argument can be found in (Theodoridis, Boutalis, & Christodoulou, 2010) and for that reason it is omitted.

From the above analysis, we have not said anything about the boundedness of the weight estimates of W_g. It is crucial in order to prevent the well known from the adaptive control literature parameter drift phenomenon to apply a restrictive method such as projection or parameter hopping. Therefore, the weight estimates W_g are confined

Box 2.

$$\dot{W}_{f_i}^l = \begin{cases} -\overline{x}_{f_i}^T x_i s_{f_i}^T - \frac{1}{2}\kappa\overline{x}_{f_i}^T \overline{x}_{f_i} W_{f_i}^l & \begin{array}{l} if\ \overline{x}_{f_i} \cdot W_{f_i}^l \in P_{f,MIMO} \\ or\ \overline{x}_{f_i} \cdot W_{f_i}^l = \pm\varepsilon_i\ and\ \overline{x}_{f_i} \cdot \dot{W}_{f_i}^l > < 0 \end{array} \\ -\overline{x}_{f_i}^T x_i s_{f_i}^T - \frac{1}{2}\kappa\overline{x}_{f_i}^T \overline{x}_{f_i} W_{f_i}^l - \kappa_{f_i}^{outer} \dfrac{\overline{x}_{f_i} W_{f_i}^l (\overline{x}_{f_i})^T}{tr\left\{(\overline{x}_{f_i})^T \overline{x}_{f_i}\right\}} & otherwise \end{cases}$$

Box 3.

$$\dot{W}_{g_{ij}}^{l} = \begin{cases} -\overline{x}_{g_{ij}}^{T} x_i u_{ij} s_{g_{ij}}^{l} d_{g_{ij}} & \text{if } \overline{x}_{g_{ij}} \cdot W_{g_{ij}}^{l} \in P_{g,MIMO} \\ & \text{or } \overline{x}_{g_{ij}} \cdot W_{g_{ij}}^{l} = \pm \varepsilon_{g_{ij}} \text{ and } \overline{x}_{g_{ij}} \cdot \dot{W}_{g_{ij}}^{l} >< 0 \\ -\overline{x}_{g_{ij}}^{T} x_i u_{ij} s_{g_{ij}}^{l} d_{g_{ij}} - \kappa_{g_{ij}}^{outer} H_{g_{ij}}^{l} & \text{otherwise} \end{cases} \tag{31}$$

to the set $P_{g,MIMO} = \left\{ W_g : \|W_g\| \leq \overline{w}_g \right\}$, through the use of a hopping algorithm (Theodoridis, Boutalis, & Christodoulou, 2010) with $\overline{w}_g$ a known positive constant. Thus, the standard updating law is modified to as shown in Box 3.

Furthermore, in the following Lemma some useful properties proved to be valid.

Lemma 2: We can apply the following properties to our system:

$$e_s(t) \leq 0, \quad \forall t \geq 0$$

$$|x(t)|^2 \leq 4|e_s(t)|, \quad \forall t \geq 0$$

$$|u(t)|^2 \leq 4|e_s(t)|, \quad \forall t \geq 0$$

Proof: We have defined that $z = \zeta - e_s$. Since $z \geq 0, \forall t \geq 0$, we conclude that $\zeta(t) \geq e_s(t), \forall t \geq 0$ but from Lemma 1 we have that $\zeta(t) \leq 0, \forall t \geq 0$. Thus, $e_s(t) \leq 0, \forall t \geq 0$. Furthermore, it is clear that since the above inequalities hold, the following must be true also:

$$|\zeta(t)| \leq |e_s(t)|, \quad \forall t \geq 0.$$

Once again,

$$z = \frac{1}{2}\left(|x|^2 + |u|^2 + tr\left\{ \left(\overline{x}_f W_f\right)^T \left(\overline{x}_f W_f\right) \right\} \right) \geq \frac{1}{2}|x|^2$$

and

$$z \leq |\zeta(t)| + |e_s(t)| \leq 2|e_s(t)|.$$

From those inequalities we result to $|x(t)|^2 \leq 4|e_s(t)|, \forall t \geq 0$. In addition, if we take the inequality $z \geq \frac{1}{2}|u|^2$ with the same analysis we have $|u(t)|^2 \leq 4|e_s(t)|, \forall t \geq 0$.

Lemma 3: The negativity of the Lyapunov-like function is actually strengthened due to the hopping term when the outer hopping condition is activated ($\sigma_{f_i}^{l} = 1$). Therefore:

$$\sum_{i=1}^{n} \sum_{l=1}^{k_f} tr\left\{ H_f^T W_{f_i}^l \right\} \geq 0.$$

Proof: Starting again from the Lyapunov-like function V_g in (28), we study the effect of the additional term of the update law $W_{f_i}^l$ when the outer hopping condition is activated ($\sigma_{f_i}^l = 1$), in the negativity of $\dot{V}_g$. The additional term is given by:

$$V_{g_{outer}} = \frac{1}{2} \sum_{i=1}^{n} \sum_{l=1}^{k_f} \left[\left(\overline{x}_{f_i} \tilde{W}_{f_i}^l\right)^T d_{f_i}^{-1} \left(\overline{x}_{f_i} \tilde{W}_{f_i}^l\right) \right] \tag{32}$$

where n together with k_f determine all possible combinations of weight vectors that require hopping.

Taking the time derivative (32) and taking into account (27), we obtain:

$$\dot{V}_{g_{outer}} = \sum_{i=1}^{n}\sum_{l=1}^{k_f}\left[\left(\overline{x}_{f_i}\dot{W}_{f_i}^l\right)^T d_{f_i}^{-1}\left(\overline{x}_{f_i}\tilde{W}_{f_i}^l\right)\right]$$

$$= -\sum_{i=1}^{n}\sum_{l=1}^{k_f}\frac{\kappa_{f_i}^{outer}d_{f_i}\overline{x}_{f_i}W_{f_i}^l\overline{x}_{f_i}\left(\overline{x}_{f_i}\right)^T d_{f_i}^{-1}\overline{x}_{f_i}\tilde{W}_{f_i}^l}{\left|\overline{x}_{f_i}\right|^2}$$

$$= -\sum_{i=1}^{n}\sum_{l=1}^{k_f}\left[\kappa_{f_i}^{outer}\left(\overline{x}_{f_i}W_{f_i}^l\right)\left(\overline{x}_{f_i}\tilde{W}_{f_i}^l\right)\right].$$

Since $\tilde{W}_{f_i}^l = W_{f_i}^l - \left(W_{f_i}^l\right)^*$, we have that:

$$\left(\overline{x}_{f_i}W_{f_i}^l\right)\left(\overline{x}_{f_i}\tilde{W}_{f_i}^l\right) = \overline{x}_{f_i}\left(\tilde{W}_{f_i}^l + \left(W_{f_i}^l\right)^*\right)\left(\overline{x}_{f_i}\tilde{W}_{f_i}^l\right)$$

$$= \left(\overline{x}_{f_i}\tilde{W}_{f_i}^l\right)\left(\overline{x}_{f_i}\tilde{W}_{f_i}^l\right) + \left(\overline{x}_{f_i}\left(W_{f_i}^l\right)^*\right)\left(\overline{x}_{f_i}\tilde{W}_{f_i}^l\right)$$

$$= \left|\overline{x}_{f_i}\tilde{W}_{f_i}^l\right|^2 + \left(\overline{x}_{f_i}\left(W_{f_i}^l\right)^*\right)\left(\overline{x}_{f_i}\tilde{W}_{f_i}^l\right)$$

$$= \frac{1}{2}\left|\overline{x}_{f_i}\tilde{W}_{f_i}^l\right|^2 + \frac{1}{2}\left|\overline{x}_{f_i}\tilde{W}_{f_i}^l\right|^2 + 2\left(\overline{x}_{f_i}\left(W_{f_i}^l\right)^*\right)\left(\overline{x}_{f_i}\tilde{W}_{f_i}^l\right)$$

$$= \frac{1}{2}\left|\overline{x}_{f_i}\tilde{W}_{f_i}^l\right|^2 + \frac{1}{2}\left|\overline{x}_{f_i}W_{f_i}^l\right|^2 - \frac{1}{2}\left|\overline{x}_{f_i}\left(W_{f_i}^l\right)^*\right|^2.$$

Since, by definition, $\left|\overline{x}_{f_i}\left(W_{f_i}^l\right)^*\right| \leq \varepsilon_i$ and $\left|\overline{x}_{f_i}W_{f_i}^l\right| > \varepsilon_i$ for $\sigma_{f_i}^l = 1$, we have that:

$$\dot{V}_{g_{outer}} \leq -\sum_{i=1}^{n}\sum_{l=1}^{k_f}\left[\frac{\kappa_{f_i}^{outer}}{2}\left|\overline{x}_{f_i}\tilde{W}_{f_i}^l\right|^2\right].$$

$$\leq -\sum_{i=1}^{n}\sum_{l=1}^{k_f}\kappa_{f_i}^{outer}\varepsilon_i^2 \leq -\kappa_f\varepsilon^2 \leq 0$$

According to lemmas 2 and 3, we conclude that: $e_s\sum_{i=1}^{n}\sum_{l=1}^{k_f}tr\left\{H_f^T W_{f_i}^l\right\} \geq 0$. The same lines of proof examine the negativity of the Lyapunov like function is followed for the case of parameter hopping term for the weight updating law $\dot{W}_{g_{ij}}^l$.

Therefore, further investigation of the Lyapunov-like function negativity concerns the following equation:

$$\dot{V}_g = -\kappa e_s^2 + e_s x^T \overline{x}_f \tilde{W}_f s_f(x) - e_s x^T \mu(x,u) \tag{33}$$

Continuing our analysis, we can assume also that the weight estimation error $\tilde{W}_f$ and the sigmoid function $s_f(x)$ are bounded by known positive constants $\overline{w}_f$, k_0, respectively, as follows:

$\left\|\tilde{W}_f\right\| \leq \overline{w}_f$ and $\left|s_f(x)\right| \leq k_0$. Employing those inequalities to $\dot{V}_g$, we have:

$$\dot{V}_g \leq -\kappa\left|e_s\right|^2 + \left|e_s\right|\left|x\right|\left|\overline{x}_f\right|\overline{w}_f k_0 + \left|e_s\right|\left|x\right|\left|\mu(x,u)\right| \tag{34}$$

Thus, we are now ready to investigate two main cases for the modeling errors.

The Modeling Error at Zero Case

In the following, taking into account assumption 3 we examine the negativity of $\dot{V}_g$ when we have modeling error at zero case. This implies that the modeling error remain non-zero $\mu(x,u)_{x=0,u=0} = k_1 \neq 0$ when $\left|x\right| = 0$ and $\left|u\right| = 0$.

In the sequel, using lemma 2 and after substituting in assumption 3 we result to:

$$\left|\mu_{z0}(x,u)\right| \leq k_1 + 2k_2'\sqrt{\left|e_s\right|} + 2k_2''\sqrt{\left|e_s\right|} = k_1 + 2k_2\sqrt{\left|e_s\right|} \tag{35}$$

where $k_2 = k_2' + k_2''$. Employing (35) and using lemma 2, (34) becomes:

$$\dot{V}_g \leq -\kappa\left|e_s\right|^2 + 2\left|\overline{x}_f\right|\overline{w}_f k_0\left|e_s\right|\sqrt{\left|e_s\right|} + 2k_1\left|e_s\right|\sqrt{\left|e_s\right|} + 4k_2\left|e_s\right|^2$$

$$\leq 4k_2\left|e_s\right|^2 - \kappa\left|e_s\right|^2 + 2\left|\overline{x}_f\right|\overline{w}_f k_0\left|e_s\right|\sqrt{\left|e_s\right|} + 2k_1\left|e_s\right|\sqrt{\left|e_s\right|}$$

$$\leq -\left[(\kappa - 4k_2)\sqrt{\left|e_s\right|} - 2k_1 - 2k_0\left|\overline{x}_f\right|\overline{w}_f\right]\left|e_s\right|\sqrt{\left|e_s\right|}$$

$$\leq 0$$

provided that:

147

$$\sqrt{|e_s|} > \frac{2\left(k_1 + k_0 \left|\overline{x}_f\right| \overline{w}_f\right)}{\kappa - 4k_2}$$

and

$$\kappa > 4k_2 > 0$$

or

$$|e_s| > \frac{4\left(k_1 + k_0 \left|\overline{x}_f\right| \overline{w}_f\right)^2}{\left(\kappa - 4k_2\right)^2},$$

and

$$\kappa > 4k_2 > 0.$$

Those inequalities together with Lemma 2 demonstrate that the trajectories of $e_s(t)$ and $x(t)$ are Uniformly Ultimately Bounded (UUB) with respect to the arbitrarily small (since κ can be chosen sufficiently large) sets E and X shown below:

$$\mathrm{E} = \left\{ e_s(t) : \left|e_s(t)\right| \leq \frac{4\left(k_1 + k_0 \left|\overline{x}_f\right| \overline{w}_f\right)^2}{\left(\kappa - 4k_2\right)^2} \right\},$$

and

$$\mathrm{X} = \left\{ x(t) : \left|x(t)\right| \leq \frac{4\left(k_1 + k_0 \left|\overline{x}_f\right| \overline{w}_f\right)}{\kappa - 4k_2} \right\}.$$

Since if we start for example from inside of E then $e_s(t)$ is bounded by $\dfrac{4\left(k_1 + k_0 \left|\overline{x}_f\right| \overline{w}_f\right)^2}{\left(\kappa - 4k_2\right)^2}$ owing to the definition of E but if we start from outside the set, then $\dot{V}_g \leq 0$ and hence the solu-

tion $e_s(t)$ is forced towards the boundary of E. Thus, we have the following theorem.

Theorem 1. Consider the plant model (4) with modeling errors satisfying assumption 3, then the dynamic controller:

$$\dot{u}^T = -\frac{1}{2}\kappa u^T - x^T \overline{x}_g W_g S_g(x)$$

together with

$$\dot{\zeta} = -\kappa \zeta,$$

$$z = \zeta - e_s,$$

a positive definite function:

$$z = \frac{1}{2}\left(|x|^2 + |u|^2 + tr\left\{\left(\overline{x}_f W_f\right)^T \left(\overline{x}_f W_f\right)\right\}\right),$$

the hopping term:

$$H_{f_i}^l = \frac{\overline{x}_{f_i} W_{f_i}^l \left(\overline{x}_{f_i}\right)^T}{tr\left\{\left(\overline{x}_{f_i}\right)^T \overline{x}_{f_i}\right\}},$$

and the updating laws in Box 4.guarantee the UUB of the trajectories of $e_s(t)$ and $x(t)$ with respect to the arbitrarily small sets E and X:

a. $\mathrm{E} = \left\{ e_s(t) : \left|e_s(t)\right| \leq \dfrac{4\left(k_1 + k_0 \left|\overline{x}_f\right| \overline{w}_f\right)^2}{\left(\kappa - 4k_2\right)^2} \right\}$

b. $\mathrm{X} = \left\{ x(t) : \left|x(t)\right| \leq \dfrac{4\left(k_1 + k_0 \left|\overline{x}_f\right| \overline{w}_f\right)}{\kappa - 4k_2} \right\}$

provided that $\kappa > 4k_2 > 0$. Also, the closed loop system mentioned above together with the modified updating laws guarantees:

Box 4.

$$\dot{W}_{f_i}^l = \begin{cases} -\overline{x}_{f_i}^T x_i s_{f_i}^T - \dfrac{1}{2}\kappa \overline{x}_{f_i}^T \overline{x}_{f_i} W_{f_i}^l & \begin{array}{l} if \ \overline{x}_{f_i} \cdot W_{f_i}^l \in P_{f,MIMO} \\[4pt] or \ \overline{x}_{f_i} \cdot W_{f_i}^l = \pm \varepsilon_i \ and \ \overline{x}_{f_i} \cdot \dot{W}_{f_i}^l > < 0 \end{array} \\[14pt] -\overline{x}_{f_i}^T x_i s_{f_i}^T - \dfrac{1}{2}\kappa \overline{x}_{f_i}^T \overline{x}_{f_i} W_{f_i}^l - \kappa_{f_i}^{outer} H_{f_i}^l & otherwise \end{cases}$$

$$\dot{W}_{g_{ij}}^l = \begin{cases} -\overline{x}_{g_{ij}}^T x_i u_{ij} s_{g_{ij}}^l d_{g_{ij}} & \begin{array}{l} if \ \overline{x}_{g_{ij}} \cdot W_{g_{ij}}^l \in P_{g,MIMO} \\[4pt] or \ \overline{x}_{g_{ij}} \cdot W_{g_{ij}}^l = \pm \varepsilon_{g_{ij}} \ and \ \overline{x}_{g_{ij}} \cdot \dot{W}_{g_{ij}}^l > < 0 \end{array} \\[14pt] -\overline{x}_{g_{ij}}^T x_i u_{ij} s_{g_{ij}}^l d_{g_{ij}} - \kappa_{g_{ij}}^{outer} H_{g_{ij}}^l & otherwise \end{cases}$$

c. $u \in L_\infty$

d. $\dot{e}_s \in L_\infty$

Proof: The cases (a) and (b) have been proved previously.

The case (c) is proved as follows.

We have found that the control signal is given by:

$$\dot{u}^T = -\frac{1}{2}\kappa u^T - x^T \overline{x}_g W_g S_g(x),$$

which is a Bounded Input Bounded Output (BIBO) ordinary differential equation. Hence, since the term $x^T \overline{x}_g W_g S_g(x)$ is bounded, we conclude that $u \in L_\infty$.

As concerning case (d) we have that:

$$\dot{e}_s = -\kappa e_s + x^T \overline{x}_f \tilde{W}_f s_f(x) + x^T \overline{x}_g \tilde{W}_g S_g(x) u$$
$$-x^T \mu(x,u) - \sum_{i=1}^{n}\sum_{l=1}^{k_f} \sigma_{f_i}^l tr\left\{H_f^T W_{f_i}^l\right\}$$

with $\tilde{W}_f, \tilde{W}_g$ bounded according to (27) and (31), respectively, $s_f(x), S_g(x)$ are bounded by definition, e_s, x are bounded according to Theorem 1 and $\mu(x,u)$ is also bounded according to assumption 3 and Theorem 1. Therefore, $\dot{e}_s$ is a function of bounded signals and hence $\dot{e}_s \in L_\infty$. Furthermore, we have notice the following remarks.

- **Remark 1:** In this chapter, we ensure the robustness of our adaptive regulation system when we have modeling errors by applying the well known from other previous works method called parameter hopping. This is not the only algorithm which ensures the stability of our adaptive control scheme in the presence of modeling errors but with other modifications such as switching parameter hopping (Theodoridis, Boutalis, & Christodoulou, 2010), switching σ-modification (Ioannou & Fidan, 2006), ε-modification (Ioannou & Fidan, 2006), and dead-zone (Ioannou & Fidan, 2006). The parameter hopping modification is used due its smoothness property and the fact that when external disturbances are affecting the system dynamics then an a priori known bound of W_g is needed.

- **Remark 2:** Theorem 1 shows how the design constant κ should be selected, in order to guarantee the UUB of the state x, even in the presence of modeling error terms are not uniformly bounded a priori, as assumption 3 implies. In general, the value of κ becomes large as we allow large model imperfections. Nevertheless, κ is implemented as gain in the construction of $\dot{\zeta}$ and for practical reasons it cannot take arbitrarily large values, leading to a compromise between the value of κ and the maximum allowable modeling error.

In the sequel, we present two special subcases, which are of particular interest, since we will prove the convergence of state x to zero.

No Modeling Error at Zero Case

We start by formulating the following assumption.

- **Assumption 4:** The modeling error term $\mu(x, u)$ satisfies the following inequality:

$$\left|\mu(x, u)\right| \le k_2' \left|x\right|.$$

Notice that assumption 4, which is actually assumption 3 with $k_1 = 0$, $k_2'' = 0$, assign that both the unknown system and the F-RHONN model should have the same origin. Employing assumption 4 and following the same analysis as previously, $\dot{V}_g$ becomes:

$$\dot{V}_g \le -\kappa \left|e_s\right|^2 + 4\left|\overline{x}_f\right|\left|\overline{w}_f\right| k_0 \left|e_s\right|^2 + 4k_2' \left|e_s\right|^2$$
$$\le -\left[\left(\kappa - 4k_2' - 4k_0 \left|\overline{x}_f\right|\left|\overline{w}_f\right|\right)\sqrt{\left|e_s\right|}\right]\left|e_s\right|^2$$
$$\le 0$$

$$(36)$$

Provided that the design constant κ is chosen such as:

$$\kappa > 4\left(k_2' + k_0 \left|\overline{x}_f\right|\left|\overline{w}_f\right|\right) > 0,$$

and the following inequality holds:

$$\left|s_f(x)\right| \le k_0 \left|x\right|. \tag{37}$$

Therefore, we can state and prove the following Theorem.

Theorem 2. Consider the plant model:

$$\dot{x}_i = -a_i x_i + \overline{x}_{f_i} W_{f_i}^* s_f(x)$$
$$+ \sum_{j=1}^m \overline{x}_{g_{ij}} W_{g_{ij}}^* s_{g_j}(x) u_j + \mu_i(x, u)$$

with modeling errors satisfying assumption 4, then the dynamic controller:

$$\dot{u}^T = -\frac{1}{2}\kappa u^T - x^T \overline{x}_g W_g S_g(x)$$

together with

$$\dot{\zeta} = -\kappa\zeta,$$

$$z = \zeta - e_s,$$

a positive definite function:

$$z = \frac{1}{2}\left(\left|x\right|^2 + \left|u\right|^2 + tr\left\{\left(\overline{x}_f W_f\right)^T \left(\overline{x}_f W_f\right)\right\}\right),$$

the hopping term:

$$H_{f_i}^l = \frac{\overline{x}_{f_i} W_{f_i}^l \left(\overline{x}_{f_i}\right)^T}{tr\left\{\left(\overline{x}_{f_i}\right)^T \overline{x}_{f_i}\right\}},$$

and the updating laws in Box 5 guarantee the following properties:

a. $e_s, \dot{e}_s, \left|x\right|, \left|u\right|, W_{f_i}^l, W_{g_{ij}}^l, \zeta \in L_\infty$, $\left|e_s\right| \in L_2$
b. $\lim_{t \to \infty} e_s(t) = 0$, $\lim_{t \to \infty} \left|x(t)\right| = 0$
c. $\lim_{t \to \infty} \left\|W_f(t)\right\| = 0$, $\lim_{t \to \infty} \left|u(t)\right| = 0$

Box 5.

$$
\dot{W}_{f_i}^l = \begin{cases} -\overline{x}_{f_i}^T x_i s_{f_i}^T - \dfrac{1}{2}\kappa \overline{x}_{f_i}^T \overline{x}_{f_i} W_{f_i}^l & \begin{array}{l} if \ \overline{x}_{f_i} \cdot W_{f_i}^l \in P_{f,MIMO} \\ or \ \overline{x}_{f_i} \cdot W_{f_i}^l = \pm \varepsilon_i \ and \ \overline{x}_{f_i} \cdot \dot{W}_{f_i}^l > < 0 \end{array}, \\ -\overline{x}_{f_i}^T x_i s_{f_i}^T - \dfrac{1}{2}\kappa \overline{x}_{f_i}^T \overline{x}_{f_i} W_{f_i}^l - \kappa_{f_i}^{outer} H_{f_i}^l & otherwise \end{cases}
$$

$$
\dot{W}_{g_{ij}}^l = -\overline{x}_{g_{ij}}^T x_{ij} u_{ij} s_{g_{ij}}^l d_{g_{ij}}
$$

d. $\quad \lim_{t \to \infty} \dot{W}_g(t) = 0$

provided that $\kappa > 4\left(k_2' + k_0 |\overline{x}_f| \overline{w}_f\right) > 0$ and (37) holds.

Proof. From (36), we have that $V_g \in L_\infty$; therefore, $e_s, \tilde{W}_g \in L_\infty$. Furthermore, $W_g = \tilde{W}_g + W_g^* \in L_\infty$. Since $e_s = \zeta - z$ and $\zeta(t) \le 0 \quad \forall t \ge 0$, we also have $\zeta, z \in L_\infty$ which in turn implies $|x|, |u|, \|W_f\| \in L_\infty$. Moreover, since V_g is a monotone decreasing function of time and bounded from below, the $\lim_{t \to \infty} V_g(t) = \left(V_g\right)_\infty$ exists so by integrating $\dot{V}_g$ from 0 to ∞ we have:

$$
\int_0^\infty |e_s|^2 \, dt \le \frac{1}{\kappa - 4\left(k_2' + k_0 |\overline{x}_f| \overline{w}_f\right)},
$$

$$
\left[V_g(0) - \left(V_g\right)_\infty\right] < \infty
$$

which implies that $|e_s| \in L_2$. Furthermore,

$$
\dot{e}_s = -\kappa e_s + x^T \overline{x}_f \tilde{W}_f s_f(x) + x^T \overline{x}_g \tilde{W}_g S_g(x) u
$$
$$
-x^T \mu(x,u) - \sum_{i=1}^{n} \sum_{l=1}^{k_f} \sigma_{f_i}^l tr\left\{H_f^T W_{f_i}^l\right\}.
$$

Since $\dot{e}_s \in L_\infty$ and $|x|, u \in L_\infty$, the sigmoidals are bounded by definition, $\tilde{W}_f, \tilde{W}_g \in L_\infty$ and Assumption 4 holds.

Therefore and since $e_s \in L_2 \bigcap L_\infty$ and $\dot{e}_s \in L_\infty$, applying Barbalat's Lemma, we con-

clude that $\lim_{t \to \infty} e_s(t) = 0$. In the sequel, having that $u, s_f(x), S_g(x), x$ are bounded and the convergence of $e_s(t)$ to zero, we conclude that $\dot{W}_g$ also converge to zero. Furthermore, since $e_s(t), \zeta(t)$ converge to zero, we also have:

$$
\lim_{t \to \infty} z\left(x(t), u(t), W_f(t)\right)
$$
$$
= \lim_{t \to \infty} \zeta(t) - \lim_{t \to \infty} e_s(t) = 0.
$$

Finally, we result to:

$$
\lim_{t \to \infty} |x(t)| = 0,
$$

$$
\lim_{t \to \infty} |u(t)| = 0,
$$

$$
\lim_{t \to \infty} \|W_f(t)\| = 0.
$$

We are now ready to state the following remark.

- **Remark 3:** From the above analysis, we conclude that the accuracy of the dynamic neural network model is restricted into a specific origin. This means, that if we have complete model matching at zero case, our modified adaptive regulator can guarantee the stability properties of the closed loop system. In addition, Theorem 2 clearly indicates that there is no need uniformly to bound the weight estimates W_g through the use of the hopping algorithm (31), in order to simplify the implementation issue.

No Modeling Error Case

In this case, we state the following assumption.

- **Assumption 5:** The modeling error term $\mu(x, u)$ satisfies the following inequality:

$|\mu(x, u)| = 0$ denoting that there is no modeling error.

Employing assumption 5 and following the same analysis as in the previous section, $\dot{V}_g$ becomes:

$$
\begin{aligned}
\dot{V}_g &\leq -\kappa |e_s|^2 + 4|\overline{x}_f||\overline{w}_f|k_0 |e_s|^2 \\
&\leq -\left(\kappa - 4k_0 |\overline{x}_f||\overline{w}_f|\right)|e_s|^2 \qquad (38) \\
&\leq 0
\end{aligned}
$$

provided that the design constant κ is chosen such as:

$$
\kappa > 4k_0 |\overline{x}_f||\overline{w}_f|,
$$

and (37) holds.

Therefore, we can state and prove the following Theorem.

Theorem 3. Consider the plant model:

$$
\dot{x}_i = -a_i x_i + \overline{x}_{f_i} W_{f_i}^* s_f(x) + \sum_{j=1}^{m} \overline{x}_{g_{ij}} W_{g_j}^* s_{g_j}(x) u_j
$$

with the dynamic controller:

$$
\dot{u}^T = -\frac{1}{2}\kappa u^T - x^T \overline{x}_g W_g S_g(x)
$$

together with

$$
\dot{\zeta} = -\kappa \zeta,
$$

$$
z = \zeta - e_s,
$$

a positive definite function:

$$
z = \frac{1}{2}\left(|x|^2 + |u|^2 + tr\left\{\left(\overline{x}_f W_f\right)^T \left(\overline{x}_f W_f\right)\right\}\right),
$$

the hopping term:

$$
H_{f_i}^l = \frac{\overline{x}_{f_i} W_{f_i}^l \left(\overline{x}_{f_i}\right)^T}{tr\left\{\left(\overline{x}_{f_i}\right)^T \overline{x}_{f_i}\right\}},
$$

and the updating laws in Box 6.guarantee the following properties:

a. $e_s, \dot{e}_s, |x|, |u|, W_{f_i}^l, W_{g_{ij}}^l, \zeta \in L_\infty, \quad |e_s| \in L_2$

b. $\lim_{t \to \infty} e_s(t) = 0, \quad \lim_{t \to \infty} |x(t)| = 0$

Box 6.

$$
\dot{W}_{f_i}^l = \begin{cases}
-\overline{x}_{f_i}^T x_i s_{f_i}^T - \dfrac{1}{2}\kappa \overline{x}_{f_i}^T \overline{x}_{f_i} W_{f_i}^l & \text{if } \overline{x}_{f_i} \cdot W_{f_i}^l \in P_{f,MIMO} \\
& \text{or } \overline{x}_{f_i} \cdot W_{f_i}^l = \pm\varepsilon_i \text{ and } \overline{x}_{f_i} \cdot \dot{W}_{f_i}^l >< 0, \\
-\overline{x}_{f_i}^T x_i s_{f_i}^T - \dfrac{1}{2}\kappa \overline{x}_{f_i}^T \overline{x}_{f_i} W_{f_i}^l - \kappa_{f_i}^{outer} H_{f_i}^l & \text{otherwise}
\end{cases}
$$

$$
\dot{W}_{g_{ij}}^l = -\overline{x}_{g_{ij}}^T x_i u_{ij} s_{g_{ij}}^l d_{g_{ij}}
$$

c. $\lim_{t\to\infty}\left\|W_f(t)\right\|=0,\quad \lim_{t\to\infty}\left|u(t)\right|=0$

d. $\lim_{t\to\infty}\dot{W}_g(t)=0$

provided that $\kappa > 4k_0\left|\bar{x}_f\right|\bar{w}_f$ and (36) holds.

Proof. From (38) we have that $V_g \in L_\infty$, therefore, $e_s, \tilde{W}_g \in L_\infty$. Furthermore, $W_g = \tilde{W}_g + W_g^* \in L_\infty$. Since $e_s = \zeta - z$ and $\zeta(t)\le 0 \quad \forall t\ge 0$, we also have $\zeta, z \in L_\infty$ which in turn implies $\left|x\right|,\left|u\right|,\left\|W_f\right\| \in L_\infty$. Moreover, since V_g is a monotone decreasing function of time and bounded from below, the $\lim_{t\to\infty}V_g(t)=\left(V_g\right)_\infty$ exists so by integrating $\dot{V}_g$ from 0 to ∞ we have:

$$\int_0^\infty \left|e_s\right|^2 dt \le \frac{1}{\kappa - 4k_0\left|\bar{x}_f\right|\bar{w}_f}\left[V_g(0)-\left(V_g\right)_\infty\right]<\infty,$$

which implies that $\left|e_s\right| \in L_2$. Furthermore,

$$\dot{e}_s = -\kappa e_s + x^T\bar{x}_f\tilde{W}_f s_f(x) + x^T\bar{x}_g\tilde{W}_g S_g(x)u$$
$$-\sum_{i=1}^{n}\sum_{l=1}^{k_f}\sigma_{f_i}^l tr\left\{H_f^T W_{f_i}^l\right\}.$$

Since $\dot{e}_s \in L_\infty$ and $\left|x\right|, u \in L_\infty$, the sigmoidals are bounded by definition, $\tilde{W}_f, \tilde{W}_g \in L_\infty$; therefore and since $e_s \in L_2 \cap L_\infty$ and $\dot{e}_s \in L_\infty$, applying Barbalat's Lemma, we conclude that $\lim_{t\to\infty}e_s(t)=0$. In the sequel, having that $u, s_f(x), S_g(x), x$ are bounded and the convergence of $e_s(t)$ to zero, we conclude that $\dot{W}_g$ also converge to zero. Furthermore, since $e_s(t), \zeta(t)$ converge to zero, we also have:

$$\lim_{t\to\infty}z\left(x(t),u(t),W_f(t)\right)$$
$$=\lim_{t\to\infty}\zeta(t)-\lim_{t\to\infty}e_s(t)=0.$$

And finally, we result to:

$$\lim_{t\to\infty}\left|x(t)\right|=0,$$

$$\lim_{t\to\infty}\left|u(t)\right|=0,$$

$$\lim_{t\to\infty}\left\|W_f(t)\right\|=0.$$

From the above Theorem 3, it is clear enough that if we choose appropriately the control constant κ as to fulfill the requirement of $\kappa > 4k_0\left|\bar{x}_f\right|\bar{w}_f$ then there is a time period after which the algorithm provides a suitable set of constant weights for which the control signal and the system states converge to zero. Also, Theorem 3 clearly indicates that there is no need to uniformly bound the weight estimates W_g through the use of the hopping algorithm (31), something that is expected due to the no modeling error assumption. Therefore, in this case, the implementation of the algorithm is simplified.

Simulation Examples

To demonstrate the potency of the proposed control scheme we present simulation results with well known benchmark problems. The full potential of the method is demonstrated in the simulations, when the proposed method regulates a Dc Motor described by nonlinear equations under the presence of modeling errors at the zero case.

In addition, the well known benchmark problem of controlling the Lorenz system is considered showing also a very good performance. We test the regulation abilities of our controller in several different cases (in regard to the number of control inputs) taking once again into account the presence of modeling errors. In this case both examples are controlled by a dynamic controller.

Example 1: DC Motor

In this example, we present simulations, where the proposed approach is applied to solve the problem of regulating the speed of a 1 KW DC motor with a normalized model described by the following dynamical equations (Leonhard, 1985)

$$
\begin{bmatrix} \dot{x}_1 \\ \dot{x}_2 \\ \dot{x}_3 \end{bmatrix} = \begin{bmatrix} -\dfrac{1}{T_a} x_1 - \dfrac{1}{T_a} x_2 x_3 \\ \dfrac{1}{T_m} x_1 x_3 - \dfrac{K_0}{T_m} x_2 \\ -\dfrac{1}{T_f} \dfrac{x_3}{a - b x_3} \end{bmatrix} + \begin{bmatrix} \dfrac{1}{T_a} & 0 \\ 0 & 0 \\ 0 & \dfrac{1}{T_f} \end{bmatrix} \cdot \begin{bmatrix} u_1 \\ u_2 \end{bmatrix}
$$

(39)

which is of a nonlinear, affine in the control form where the states are chosen to be the armature current $x_1 = I_a$, the angular speed $x_2 = \Omega$ and the stator flux $x_3 = \Phi$. As control inputs the armature $u_1 = V_a$ and the field voltages $u_2 = V_f$ are used. With this choice, the regulation problem of a DC motor is translated as follows: Find a dynamic controller to force the angular velocity and the armature current to go to zero, while the magnetic flux varies.

We simulated a 1kw DC motor with parameter values that can be seen in Table 1.

In the following, we chose the number of fuzzy partitions in X_f as $q = 5$ in the range of:

$$f_1 = [-182.5667, 0], \; f_2 = [-19.3627, 30.0566]$$

and the number of fuzzy partitions in X_g as $q = 1$ in the range of:

$$g_1 = [148, 150], \; g_2 = [42, 44].$$

In addition, the depth of high order terms is selected as $k_f = k_g = 2$ (only first order sigmoidal terms $s(x_1)$, $s(x_2)$ were used) and the general form of sigmoid functions is given in Equation (12). The parameters of the sigmoidal that have been used in this simulation are $\alpha_1 = 0.1, \alpha_2 = 6$, $\beta_1 = 1, \beta_2 = 0.1$, and $\gamma_1 = \gamma_2 = 0$. The parameters used in the updat-

Table 1. Parameter values for the DC motor

Parameter	Value
$1/T_a$	148.88 sec^{-1}
$1/T_m$	42.91 sec^{-1}
K_0/T_m	0.0129 sec^{-1}
T_f	31.88 sec
a	2.6
b	1.6

ing laws (27), (31) for the external bounds chosen as $|\varepsilon_i| = 5$ and the constant values used for the appropriate hopping as $\kappa_{f_i}^{outer} = 0.8$ and $\kappa_{g_{ij}}^{outer} = 0.6$.

In the simulations carried out, the actual system is simulated with sampling time $t = 10^{-3}$ sec by using the complete set of Equations (39). The produced control law (24) is applied on this system with $\kappa = 64$, which in turn produces states x_1, x_2, which in the sequel are used for the computation of the estimation errors. We select the initial weights as $W_f(0) = W_g(0) = 0$ and the learning rate $d_{g_{ij}} = 10$. In the control phase, we assumed that the system variables have the initial values $\begin{bmatrix} \Omega & I_a & \Phi \end{bmatrix} = \begin{bmatrix} 0.9 & 0.8 & 0.98 \end{bmatrix}$.

Figure 2 gives the evolution of the armature current (blue line) and angular speed (red line) under the presence of modeling errors at zero case having the following form:

$$\mu_1(x, u) = 2x_1 + \sin(0.1x_2) + \sin(0.1u_1) + 0.1$$

and

$$\mu_2(x, u) = 3x_2 + \sin(10x_1) + \sin(10u_2) + 0.3$$

It can be clearly seen from the above figure, that the regulation of the angular velocity and the

Figure 2. Convergence of the armature current and angular speed to a small region (-0.05, 0.05) around zero under the presence of modeling errors at zero case

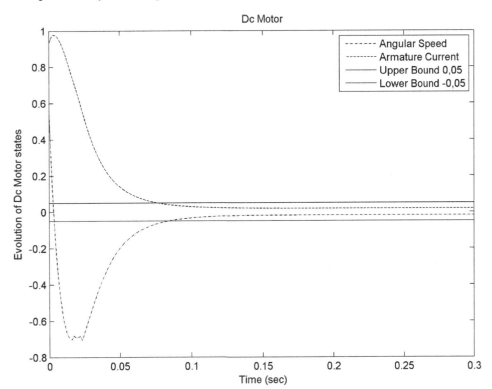

armature current keeps their values near to a small set around zero, where its bounds (upper and lower) are calculated with respect to the scheme of modeling errors and other simulation parameters mentioned before, as $-0.1 < x(t) < 0.1$.

Figure 3 presents the evolution of the control inputs, while Figures 4 and 5 demonstrate the effectiveness of the parameter hopping method to the weight evolution, which prevents the drift phenomenon.

Once again, from the above dc motor regulation scheme we notice that, despite the realization of parameter hopping, the evolution of all signals in the controlled closed loop system presents smoothness.

Example 2: Direct Dynamic Control of Lorenz System with Modeling Errors

The Lorenz system was derived to model the two-dimensional convection flow of a fluid layer heated from below and cooled from above. The model represents the Earth's atmosphere heated by the ground's absorption of sunlight and losing heat into space. It can be described by the following dynamical equations:

$$\dot{x}_1 = \sigma\left(x_2 - x_1\right)$$
$$\dot{x}_2 = \rho x_1 - x_2 - x_1 x_3 \qquad (40)$$
$$\dot{x}_3 = -\beta x_3 + x_1 x_2$$

where x_1, x_2 and x_3 represent measures of fluid velocity, horizontal and vertical temperature variations, correspondingly. The parameters

Figure 3. Evolution of control inputs under the presence of modeling errors at zero case

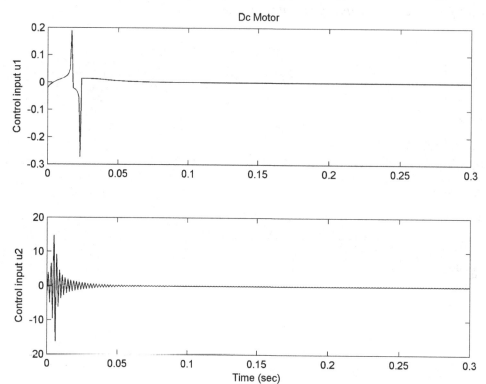

Figure 4. Evolution of $\overline{x}_{f_2} \cdot W_{f_2}$ without the activation of parameter hopping

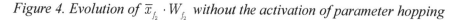

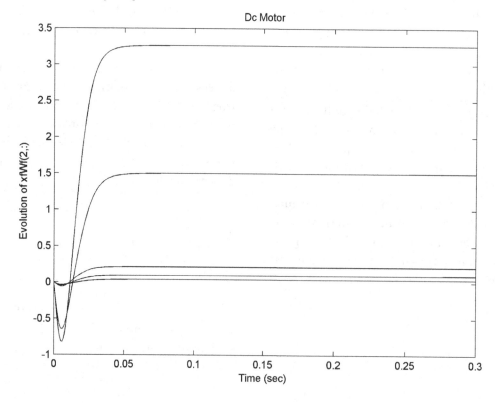

Figure 5. Evolution of $\overline{x}_{f_1} \cdot W_{f_1}^l$ with $l = 3, 4, 5$ when the parameter hopping condition is activated

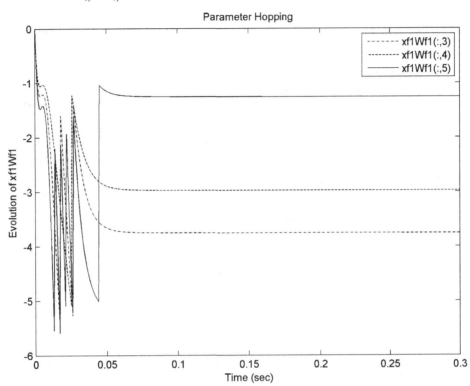

σ, ρ, and β are positive and represent the Prandtl number, Rayleigh number and geometric factor, correspondingly. Selecting $\sigma = 10$, $\rho = 28$ and $\beta = \dfrac{8}{3}$ the system presents three unstable equilibrium points and the system trajectory wanders forever near a strange invariant set called strange attractor presenting thus a chaotic behavior (Yeap & Ahmed, 1994).

However, the Lorenz system including control inputs (Yeap & Ahmed, 1994) can be expressed as:

$$\begin{aligned}
\dot{x}_1 &= \sigma\left(x_2 - x_1\right) + u_1 \\
\dot{x}_2 &= \rho x_1 - x_2 - x_1 x_3 + u_2 \\
\dot{x}_3 &= -\beta x_3 + x_1 x_2 + u_3
\end{aligned} \qquad (41)$$

The control objective is to derive appropriate dynamic control law to regulate the system to one of its equilibrium, which is $(0,0,0)$ when we have only one or two control inputs. In particular, we consider that Equations (41) has the following initial condition:

$$x_0 = \left[0.3, -0.8, 2\right]^T$$

The main parameters for the control law (24) and the learning laws (27), (29) are selected as: a) The constant of the dynamic controller $\kappa = 44$, b) the parameters of the sigmoidals that have been used $a_1 = a_2 = a_3 = 1$, $\beta_1 = \beta_2 = \beta_3 = 1$, and $\gamma_1 = \gamma_2 = \gamma_3 = 0$, c) the number of fuzzy partitions being $q = 5$ for $f_i(x)$ (in the range of $f_1 = [-102, 143]$, $f_2 = [-147, 322]$ and $f_3 = [-139, 350]$), $q = 3$ for $g_i(x)$ around the number one, and d) the depth of high order sigmoid terms $k_f = 9$ where in this case $s_i(x)$ assume high order connections up to the second order and $k_g = 3$ where we assume for the $g_i(x)$ term first order connections.

The parameters used in the updating laws for the external bounds chosen as $|\varepsilon_i| = 25$ and the constant values used for the appropriate hopping $\kappa_{f_i}^{outer} = 0.6$. Furthermore, we select the initial weights as $W_f(0) = W_g(0) = 0$ and the learning rate $d_{g_{ij}} = 1$. Finally, the sampling time was chosen as $t = 10^{-3} \sec$.

Figure 6 shows the convergence of states x_1, x_2, and x_3 to zero exponentially fast when we have control inputs only at x_2, x_3, and no modeling errors at zero case which have the following form:

$$\mu_1(x,u) = x_1 + \sin(0.5x_2) + 3 \cdot \sin(0.1u_2)$$

and

$$\mu_2(x,u) = 2x_3 + 3 \cdot \sin(10x_1) + \sin(u_3)$$

CONCLUSION

A direct dynamic control scheme was considered in this chapter, aiming at the regulation of nonlinear (non-Brunovsky non-square form) general unknown plants. The approach is based on a new Neuro-Fuzzy Dynamical Systems (NFDS) definition, which uses the concept of Adaptive Fuzzy Systems (AFS) operating in conjunction with High Order Neural Network Functions (F-HONNFs). Since the plant is considered unknown, we proposed its approximation by a special form of a NFDS, which, however, may assume a smaller number of control inputs than the original unknown model. In the sequel, three different cases concerning the scheme of modelling errors were investigated. The first one is the general case where the modelling error involves and a not necessarily known positive number except the system states and the control inputs. In the next case, the above positive number was

Figure 6. Convergence of Lorenz states to zero when we have no modeling error at zero case

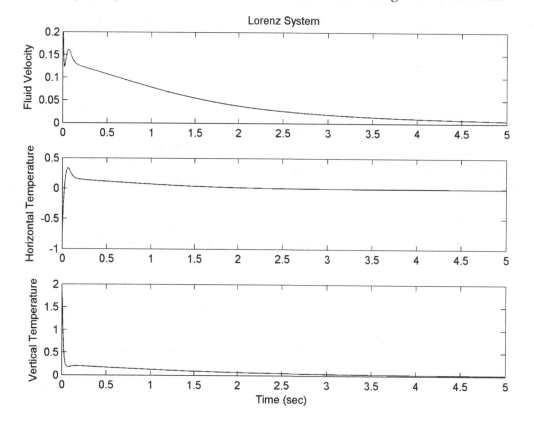

assumed zero and finally in the last case, which is the simplest, the modelling error depends only on system states.

In each case, weight updating laws for the synaptic weights of the involved HONNs were provided, which assure that the system states reach zero or a small region around zero exponentially fast, keeping at the same time all signals in the closed loop bounded. A method of parameter hopping, incorporated in the weight updating law, assures the existence of the control signal and the existence of solutions. Simulations in matlab environment were presented, illustrating the advantages of the developed neuro-fuzzy dynamic controller.

FUTURE TRENDS

In the future, the proposed algorithm could be extended to cope with the problem of trajectory tracking of unknown nonlinear dynamical systems in a non-square form. Also, it can be considered in specific real time applications, such as control of motors or robot manipulators (Theodoridis, Boutalis, & Christodoulou, 2010), provided that its computational requirements are kept low in order to be programmable in conventional microcontrollers.

REFERENCES

Alanis, A. Y., Leon, B. S., Sanchez, E. N., & Ruiz-Velazquez, E. (2011). Blood glucose level neural model for type 1 diabetes mellitus patients. *International Journal of Neural Systems, 21*(6), 491–504. doi:10.1142/S0129065711003000

Alanis, A. Y., Sanchez, E. N., Loukianov, A. G., & Perez-Cisneros, M. A. (2010). Real-time discrete neural block control using sliding modes for electric induction motors. *IEEE Transactions on Control Systems Technology, 18*(1), 11–21. doi:10.1109/TCST.2008.2009466

Alanis, A. Y., Sanchez, E. N., Loukianov, A. G., & Perez-Cisneros, M. A. (2011). Real-time neural-state estimation. *IEEE Transactions on Neural Networks, 22*(3), 497–505. doi:10.1109/TNN.2010.2103322

Aseltine, J. A., Mancini, A. R., & Sartune, C. W. (1958). A survey of adaptive control systems. *I.R.E. Transactions on Automatic Control, 3*(6), 102–108. doi:10.1109/TAC.1958.1105168

Boutalis, Y. S., Christodoulou, M. A., & Theodoridis, D. C. (2010). Identification of nonlinear systems using a new neuro-fuzzy dynamical system definition based on high order neural network function approximators. In Zhang, M. (Ed.), *Artificial Higher Order Neural Networks for Computer Science and Engineering: Trends for Emerging Applications* (pp. 423–449). Hershey, PA: IGI Global.

Boutalis, Y. S., Theodoridis, D. C., & Christodoulou, M. A. (2009). A new neuro FDS definition for indirect adaptive control of unknown nonlinear systems using a method of parameter hopping. *IEEE Transactions on Neural Networks, 20*(4), 609–625. doi:10.1109/TNN.2008.2010772

Chen, L., & Narendra, K. S. (2002). Nonlinear adaptive control using neural networks and multiple models. In *Proceedings of the 2000 American Control Conference,* (pp. 4199-4203). Chicago, IL: IEEE.

Cho, K. B., & Wang, B. H. (1996). Radial basis function based adaptive fuzzy systems and their applications to system identification and prediction. *Fuzzy Sets and Systems, 83*, 325–339. doi:10.1016/0165-0114(95)00322-3

Diao, Y., & Passino, K. M. (2002). Adaptive neural/fuzzy control for interpolated nonlinear systems. *IEEE Transactions on Fuzzy Systems, 10*(5), 583–595. doi:10.1109/TFUZZ.2002.803493

Hornik, K., Stinchcombe, M., & White, H. (1989). Multilayer feed forward networks are universal approximators. *International Journal of Neural Networks, 2*, 359–366. doi:10.1016/0893-6080(89)90020-8

Ioannou, P., & Fidan, B. (2006). *Adaptive control tutorial*. SIAM. doi:10.1137/1.9780898718652

Ioannou, P., & Sun, J. (1996). *Robust adaptive control*. Upper Saddle River, NJ: Prentice Hall.

Juang, C. F., & Lin, C. T. (1998). An on-line self-constructing neural fuzzy inference network and its applications. *IEEE Transactions on Fuzzy Systems, 6*(1), 12–32. doi:10.1109/91.660805

Kumar, N., Panwar, V., Sukavanam, N., Sharma, S. P., & Borm, J. H. (2011). Neural network-based nonlinear tracking control of kinematically redundant robot manipulators. *Mathematical and Computer Modelling, 53*(9), 1889–1901. doi:10.1016/j.mcm.2011.01.014

Li, R. P., & Mukaidono, M. (1995). A new approach to rule learning based on fusion of fuzzy logic and neural networks. *IEICE Transactions on Information and Systems, 78*(11), 1509–1514.

Li, X., Chen, Z. Q., & Yuan, Z. Z. (2002). Simple recurrent neural network-based adaptive predictive control for nonlinear systems. *Asian Journal of Control, 4*(2), 231–239. doi:10.1111/j.1934-6093.2002.tb00350.x

Lin, Y. H., & Cunningham, G. A. (1995). A new approach to fuzzy-neural system modelling. *IEEE Transactions on Fuzzy Systems, 3*(2), 190–198. doi:10.1109/91.388173

Lyapunov, A. M. (1992). *The general problem of the stability of motion* (Fuller, A. T., Trans.). New York, NY: Taylor and Francis.

Mitra, S., & Hayashi, Y. (2000). Neuro-fuzzy rule generation: Survey in soft computing framework. *IEEE Transactions on Neural Networks, 11*(3), 748–768. doi:10.1109/72.846746

Narendra, K. S., & Parthasarathy, K. (1990). Identification and control of dynamical systems using neural networks. *IEEE Transactions on Neural Networks, 1*(1), 4–27. doi:10.1109/72.80202

Passino, K. M., & Yurkovich, S. (1998). *Fuzzy control*. Menlo Park, CA: Addison Wesley Longman.

Pearlmutter, B. A. (1995). Gradient calculation of recurrent neural networks: A survey. *IEEE Transactions on Neural Networks, 6*(5), 1212–1228. doi:10.1109/72.410363

Pedro, J., & Dahunsi, O. (2011). Neural network based feedback linearization control of a servo-hydraulic vehicle suspension system. *International Journal of Applied Mathematics and Computer Science, 21*(1), 137–147. doi:10.2478/v10006-011-0010-5

Plett, G. L. (2003). Adaptive inverse control of linear and nonlinear systems using dynamic neural networks. *IEEE Transactions on Neural Networks, 14*(2), 360–376. doi:10.1109/TNN.2003.809412

Poznyak, A. S., Yu, W., Sanchez, E. N., & Perez, J. P. (1999). Nonlinear adaptive trajectory tracking using dynamic neural networks. *IEEE Transactions on Neural Networks, 10*(6), 1402–1411. doi:10.1109/72.809085

Rashid, T., Huang, B. Q., & Kechadi, T. (2007). Auto regressive recurrent neural network approach for electricity load forecasting. *International Journal of Computational Intelligence, 3*(1), 66–71.

Rovithakis, G. A., & Christodoulou, M. A. (2000). Adaptive control with recurrent high order neural networks. In Grible, M. A., & Johnson, M. A. (Eds.), *Advances in Industrial Control*. London, UK: Springer Verlag. doi:10.1007/978-1-4471-0785-9

Thammano, A., & Ruxpakawong, P. (2010). Nonlinear dynamic system identification using recurrent neural network with multi-segment piecewise-linear connection weight. *Memetic Computing, 2*(4), 273–282. doi:10.1007/s12293-010-0042-7

Theodoridis, D. C., Boutalis, Y. S., & Christodoulou, M. A. (2009). A new neuro-fuzzy dynamical system definition based on high order neural network function approximators. In *Proceedings of the European Control Conference ECC 2009,* (pp. 3305-3310). Budapest, Hungary: ECC.

Theodoridis, D. C., Boutalis, Y. S., & Christodoulou, M. A. (2010). A new adaptive neuro-fuzzy controller for trajectory tracking of robot manipulators. *International Journal of Robotics and Automation, 26*(1), 1–12.

Theodoridis, D. C., Christodoulou, M. A., & Boutalis, Y. S. (2010). Neuro – fuzzy control schemes based on high order neural network function aproximators. In Zhang, M. (Ed.), *Artificial Higher Order Neural Networks for Computer Science and Engineering: Trends for Emerging Applications* (pp. 450–483). Hershey, PA: IGI Global.

Tsoi, A. C., & Back, A. D. (1994). Locally recurrent feed forward networks: A critical review of architectures. *IEEE Transactions on Neural Networks, 5*(2), 229–239. doi:10.1109/72.279187

Wang, L. (1994). *Adaptive fuzzy systems and control*. Englewood Cliffs, NJ: Prentice Hall.

Yeap, T. H., & Ahmed, N. U. (1994). Feedback control of chaotic systems. *Dynamics and Control, 4*(1), 97–114. doi:10.1007/BF02115741

Yih, G. L., Wei, Y. W., & Tsu, T. L. (2005). Observer-based direct adaptive fuzzy-neural control for nonaffine nonlinear systems. *IEEE Transactions on Neural Networks, 16*(4), 853–861. doi:10.1109/TNN.2005.849824

Zhan, R., & Wan, J. (2006). Neural network-aided adaptive unscented Kalman filter for nonlinear state estimation. *IEEE Signal Processing Letters, 13*(7), 445–448. doi:10.1109/LSP.2006.871854

Chapter 8
Modeling and Simulation of Alternative Energy Generation Processes using HONN

Salvador Carlos Hernández
Cinvestav del IPN, Unidad Saltillo, México

Rocío Carrasco Navarro
Cinvestav del IPN, Unidad Guadalajara, México

Edgar Nelson Sanchez Camperos
Cinvestav del IPN, Unidad Guadalajara, México

Joel Kelly Gurubel Tun
Cinvestav del IPN, Unidad Guadalajara, México

José Andrés Bueno García
Cinvestav del IPN, Unidad Guadalajara, México

ABSTRACT

This chapter deals with the application of Higher Order Neural Networks (HONN) on the modeling and simulation of two processes commonly used to produce gas with energy potential: anaerobic digestion and gasification. Two control strategies for anaerobic digestion are proposed in order to obtain high biomethane flow rate from degradation of organic wastes such as wastewater. A neurofuzzy scheme which is composed by a neural observer, a fuzzy supervisor, and two control actions is presented first. After that, a speed-gradient inverse optimal neural control for trajectory tracking is designed and applied to an anaerobic digestion model. The control law calculates dilution rate and bicarbonate in order to track a methane production reference trajectory under controlled conditions and avoid washout. A nonlinear discrete-time neural observer (RHONO) for unknown nonlinear systems in presence of external disturbances and parameter uncertainties is used to estimate the biomass concentration, substrate degradation, and inorganic carbon. On the other side, a high order neural network structure is developed for the process identification in a gasification reactor; the gas, composed mainly of hydrogen and carbon monoxide (synthesis gas or syngas), is produced from thermo chemical transformation of solid organic wastes. The identifier is developed in order to reproduce a kinetic model of a biomass gasifier. In both cases (biological and thermo chemical processes), the Extended Kalman Filter (EKF) is used as a training algorithm. The proposed methodologies application is illustrated via numerical simulations.

DOI: 10.4018/978-1-4666-2175-6.ch008

INTRODUCTION

The energy and environmental situation around the world makes the power generation system based on renewable sources take more relevance. These systems have many advantages since they allow the energy diversification reducing dependence on oil; using renewable raw material it is possible to decrease CO_2 global emissions. Processes using organic wastes allow environmental risks to be minimized by the valorization of that kind of materials.

Biomass is a resource with high energy potential and represents an opportunity area for both, developed and emerging countries. Then, study of processes for wastes transformation is an important topic all around the world. Biological and thermo chemical systems are well identified to take advantage of biomass potential for energy generation.

Anaerobic digestion is a biological process very efficient to transform organic wastes. It is widely used to treat wastewater with high organic load. The organic materials are progressively transformed by different bacteria populations in successive stages. The final products are treated effluents and a biogas mainly composed of methane and carbon dioxide, which can be used as an alternative energy source (Roos, 1991). This bioprocess is sensitive to variations on the operating conditions, such as pH, temperature, overloads, etc. In addition, some variables and parameters are hard to measure due to economic or technical constraints, e.g. biomass sensors are expensive or designed on the basis of physic-chemical principles and they are not reliable for an automatic control perspective; also, substrate (that means, organic load) is determined off-line by chemical analysis requiring at least two hours; this situation affects the efficiency of supervision and control strategies. State observers are an alternative to estimate that kind of variables; several reported works focus on this topic. Bastin and Dochain (1990) developed an observer using

a non-linear model; it is robust in presence of parameter uncertainties, but its convergence rate depends on operating conditions. The interval observer (Gouze, et al., 2000) takes into account model uncertainties; the estimation is done over defined intervals; this observer gives good estimations but the interval selection and estimation convergence need to be improved. The observer developed by Teillol et al. (2003) is devoted to estimate unmeasured inputs and also unknown state variables and shows good performances. It is designed on the basis of a tangent linearization which could limit the operation range; moreover, the observer requires on-line measures hard to have with standard methods e.g. substrate, which can be indirectly measured off-line using Chemical Oxygen Demand (COD) values. In addition, a Takagi-Sugeno observer was proposed (Carlos Hernandez, et al., 2009); the main idea is to design several local observers and implement a fuzzy interpolation to obtain the global state estimation. The advantage of this approach is that the estimation convergence can be easily tuned since only linear systems techniques are required and a wide operating range can be considered if necessary. On the other hand, several control techniques have been already implemented in order to improve performances of anaerobic digestion processes. In example, linearizing control is devoted to obtain a linear mapping between the outputs (or states) and a new control input, this technique can be used to deal with some goals such as tracking and regulation in presence of disturbances (Kendi & Doyle, 1996; Simeonov & Queinnec, 2006). The L/A technique (Lakrori, 1989) considers positivity restrictions of the process variables and also the actuators saturation. The empirical knowledge of the process can be incorporated to the control design considering intelligent approaches: fuzzy control (Mendez Acosta, et al., 2003; Garcia, et al., 2007) and artificial neural networks (Holubar, et al., 2002; Baruch, et al., 2008). Different works have been developed on the topic of adaptive control for anaerobic reactors.

Simulations results are reported in some works where the authors consider an adaptive algorithm to control the substrate concentration manipulating the dilution rate, good performances are obtained but measures of substrate are required, which are usually done off-line (Bastin & Dochain, 1990). Adaptive linearizing control (Dochain & Perrier, 1997) is proposed in order to incorporate in the controller structure the on-line estimation of the component concentrations and parameters such as reaction rates and yield coefficients. An important research was developed in order to unify the advantages of optimal and adaptive approaches; the resulting structure is an optimal heuristic controller embedded within a non-linear linearizing control, the states and parameters, which are not available on-line, are estimated using adaptive control techniques (Van Impe & Bastin, 1995). In addition, an adaptive control law has been developed to perform an exact regulation towards a set point despite of parameter uncertainty obtaining interesting results in simulation and real time (Mailleret, et al., 2004). In other work, the authors propose an adaptive linearizing feedback controller complemented by an asymptotic state observer and a linear regressive parameter estimator in order to regulate the output pollution; good results are obtained in simulations (Petre, et al., 2008). Artificial neural networks have been proposed as an interesting alternative to solve several problems on anaerobic processes (Baruch, 2008), such as modelling, state estimation, supervision and control. In example, a neural observer is based on a recurrent high order neural network, which is trained by an extended Kalman filter (Sanchez, 2008; Rovithakis, 2000). The main objective of the observer is to detect the biological activity inside the bioreactor. Methane production, biomass growth, and substrate degradation are good indicators of the biological activity inside the bioreactor. In addition, a control strategy including a neural observer is implemented in Carlos Hernandez (2010). The control strategy allows the process to reject large disturbances; this implies the treatment of high quantities of substrate and to obtain a high biogas production.

Concerning thermo-chemical processes, biomass gasification allows generation of thermal and electric energy through low cost technologies (Klass, 1998). The principle of this process is to transform a solid fuel into a mixture of gases by applying high temperature in an oxygen controlled atmosphere. With this incomplete combustion, the gases with energy potential such as synthesis gas (H_2 + CO) and methane can be used in different systems for electricity generation (Reed, 1981; Bridgwater, 2003). In addition, the harmful components before they are released to the atmosphere can be captured and used for synthesize chemical substance with high added value. Finally, the residual heat obtained from the thermo chemical reactions can be used in cogeneration systems. The gasification process and the integration to cogeneration devices have been studied mainly from the mechanical engineering point of view. The combination with other disciplines such as automatic control can bring higher profits for such processes; for example, it is possible to obtain appropriate mathematical models for the analysis of properties (stability, controllability, operation regions, etc.) and to design and validate control systems which improve efficiency, allowing selective production of a specific component an ease the effective coupling with cogeneration devices. There are few reports concerning biomass gasification with an automatic control perspective. For example, in Gobel et al. (2007), the development of a mathematical model for a fixed-bed gasifier is presented. The model was used for studies of the stationary performance and to identify an efficient control strategy for the operation during load changes. The results show that controlling the addition of air as well as the addition of biomass in order to maintain a constant bed height, even when the operating conditions are changed significantly, implies a reduction of time constant of the system. The potential advantage of applying this control strategy was demonstrated in a mathematical simulation where the plant was taken from full load to half load 1 h after the start of the simulation by reducing the rate of biomass feeding to half. In Paes (2005), an interesting study was performed in order to develop a model for the prediction of (dynamic) behavior for a small-scale gasifier. A mass-flow controller was proposed to manipulate the inflow of air to control the outgoing gas flow. A cascade control setup with a temperature controller that can overrule the mass flow controller was needed in order to reach a better control of temperature. In other research (Karppanen, 2000), a fuzzy control system was designed and tested in an industrial circulating fluidized bed boiler. Fuzzy Logic Control was shown to be suitable for implementing non-linear control cases in an industrial fullscale CFB boiler. Implemented applications gave better control performance than PID when non-symmetric control like steam (header) pressure is needed. In addition, in Sagues (2007), a fuzzy control for a biomass gasifier was proposed. The airflow rate (F_A) and the frequency of motion of the grate (f_g) were selected as the action variables; the temperature profile inside the gasifier (T) and the CO/CO_2 ratio were considered as controlled variables. In addition the moisture content (or humidity Hp) and the elemental composition of the biomass (e_c) were taken as disturbances (D) since they could not be manipulated by the controller and depended on the processed biomass. Two fuzzy algorithms were evaluated obtaining good performances.

Most of reported models for gasification processes are based on thermodynamic equilibrium, process kinetics, and neural networks (Puig Arnavat, et al., 2010; Basu & Kaushal, 2009). Equilibrium models allow predicting the maximum achievable yield of a desired product; they imply low computational cost and are an important tool for preliminary studies. However, they cannot give highly accurate results in all cases.

Equilibrium models usually overestimate the yields of H_2 and CO, underestimate those of CO_2 and predict an outlet stream free from CH_4, tars and char (Puig-Arnavat, et al., 2010). There exist two methods for thermodynamic equilibrium modeling: stoichiometric and non-stoichiometric method. First one is based on stoichiometric reactions and it requires a clearly defined reaction mechanism that incorporates all chemical reactions and species involved; to simplify the process modeling, those species that are present in the largest amounts (those which have the lowest value of free energy of formation) are selected to be represented (Puig-Arnavat, et al., 2010). The non-stoichiometric approach is based on the minimization of the total Gibbs free energy in the system, and no particular reaction mechanisms or species are involved in the numerical simulation. The only required data is the elemental composition of the raw material (Li, et al., 2004). Several works have been developed on the basis of thermodynamic equilibrium models for biomass gasification (Schuster, et al., 2001; Mountouris, et al., 2006; Melgar, et al., 2007; Jarungthammachote & Dutta, 2007). A model applicable to various gasifiers has been developed, with and without considering char (Huang & Ramaswamy, 2009). The equilibrium models were then modified closely matching the CH_4 or both CH_4 and CO compositions from experimental data. The thermodynamic equilibrium model without considering char provides a good description of a downdraft gasifier at high temperature when there is no formation of char. The modified equilibrium model matching the methane yield in the produced gas is closer to its average experimental value. The thermodynamic equilibrium model considering char is more general and widely applicable. However, the predictions do not match well with experimental data. The modified equilibrium model considering char closely matching both methane and carbon monoxide yields in the produced gas can better describe the downdraft gasifier. In addition to equilibrium considerations, other operating conditions such as the complex fluid flow, heat and mass transfer properties and their influence on local equilibrium, can be lumped into the model as a first approximation, by modifying the model gasification temperature to improve the model accuracy in prediction of syngas composition. This provides a viable tool for the process simulation and optimization (Huang & Ramaswamy, 2009). A model based on minimization of the Gibbs free energy was developed to predict the composition of produced gas in different reactors (Jarungthammachote & Dutta, 2007); the energy balance was used to calculate the reaction temperature, and this temperature was employed in the minimization of the Gibbs free energy calculation. The model was validated by numerical simulation and using experimental data. Some other works are developed considering thermodynamic equilibrium (Lu, et al., 2007; Kaushal, et al., 2010; Detournay, et al., 2011; Sekhar, et al., 2012). On the other side, kinetic models predict the degradation progress and the product composition at different positions in a reactor; then, they are obtained from the study of kinetic mechanisms. The main objective is to describe the conversion of the solid fuels during the gasification process. This information is very important in order to design, evaluate, and improve gasification reactors. This kind of models allows a better simulation of the experimental data where the residence time of gas and biomass is relatively short (Puig-Arnavat, et al., 2010). One the first kinetic models was proposed by (Wang & Kinoshita, 1993), that model is based on the description of surface reactions in the reduction zone considering four reactions; the Langmuir-Hinshelwood mechanism was used to represent the reactions rates, and a given residence time and specific reaction temperature were supposed. The resulting model was validated comparing the simulation performance with experimental data. A good approximation was observed, and then, the main process behavior was predicted adequately. After that, the model was improved,

complemented and modified by different authors. Giltrap et al. (2003) developed a model of the reduction zone of a downdraft biomass gasifier to predict the composition of the produced gas under steady-state operation, the kinetic rate expressions were similar as the ones used by Wang and Kinoshita. Other reaction mechanism, such as exponential one, was used in order to improve the simulation of the temperature profile in the reduction reaction zone (Babu & Sheth, 2006). Chen (1987) developed a model to study the dependence of the reactor performance on operating conditions, such as feedstock moisture content, chip size, reactor insulation, input air temperature and gasifier load. The model is composed of a section to determine the amount of oxygen needed for a fixed input of fuel at a specific operating condition. This estimation is used as an input for the drying, pyrolysis and combustion zones. The outputs from this zone (product concentrations and its temperature) are used to predict the temperature profile along the axis of the gasification zone, the gas composition, the conversion efficiency and the length of the gasification zone at any given time interval. In other reported work (Jayah, et al., 2003), the Chen model was modified in order to minimize the over-prediction related to the temperature of the produced gas; also a gasification zone with variable diameter was considered. Other works were performed focusing on the development of kinetic models of biomass gasification processes (Puig Arnavat, et al., 2010; Basu & Kaushal, 2009; Cuoci, et al., 2009; Gordillo & Belghit, 2011; Dupont, et al., 2011). Finally, artificial neural networks representing simplified models of biological neural networks. It constitute a parallel, distributed, and massively interconnected processor which stores experimental knowledge and has a large number of applications, such as, financial and economic modeling, medical applications, industrial process optimization and quality control, etc. There are different topologies, among which recurrent higher order neural networks allow the development of robust control algorithms, an efficient models of complex dynamic systems, easy implementation and the ability to adjust parameters on-line (Sanchez, et al., 2008). These are important characteristics for complex process such as biological and thermo chemical processes for energy generation. For example, an Artificial Neural Networks (ANN) model is developed to predict gasification characteristics (Xiao, et al., 2008); the model is validated with experimental data and it is applied to the degradation of municipal wastes by thermo chemical processes. The training and validating relative errors are within ±15% and ±20%, respectively, and predicting relative errors of an industrial sample are below ±25%. In other work (Guo, et al., 2001), a model based on multilayer feedforward neural networks was developed to simulate biomass gasification in a steam fluidized bed gasifier; the validation is done with experimental data considering arboreal and herbaceous biomass. Some deviations are obtained for CO, CO_2, and H_2; nevertheless, the performance of the neural model is very close to real behavior. Brown et al. (2006) developed an equilibrium reaction modeling approach for the design of biomass gasifiers. A nonlinear regression, with an artificial neural network, related changes in temperature differences to fuel composition and operational variables. This approach was applied to a fluidized bed improving the accuracy of equilibrium calculations and reducing the amount of data required by preventing the NN from learning atomic and heat balances. Other research was focused on the development of neural network based models that correlated the yields of the gases produced with both the characteristics of the biomass and the operational conditions of the gasifier (De Souza, et al., 2010). Multilayer perceptrons were trained and validated using data from the literature for different biomasses and for circulating and bubbling fluidized bed gasifiers. High correlations values (ranging from 0.94 to 0.99) between predicted and observed values were obtained and sensitivity techniques were used in order to

evaluate and discard input variables. The neural network models were further used together with the Particle Swarm Optimization technique (PSO) to calculate the conditions that allowed the maximization in the yield of a desired gas. The results obtained indicate that the developed approach provides a valuable tool to help in the efficient design, operation and control of fluidized bed gasifiers.

The work presented in this chapter illustrates the potential of artificial neural networks to be applied in modeling, identification, and state estimation of waste transformation for energy generation processes. Anaerobic digestion and gasification are used as examples for neural networks applications in this scientific and technological field.

HIGHER ORDER NEURAL NETWORKS

Structure

Recurrent neural networks have at least one feedback loop; this structure allows the neural network to improve its learning capability and then to enhance performances for a specific application (Haykin, 1999; Zhang, 2007). Then, this kind of neural networks represents a better alternative to deal with model and control of nonlinear systems (16), since control algorithms can be developed to be robust to uncertainties and modeling errors (Gao, 2008; Haidar, 2009). Recurrent Higher Order Neural Networks (RHONN) are a generalization of the first-order Hopfield networks (Rovithakis, 2000), and have some important characteristics such as properties for efficient modeling of complex dynamic systems, on-line parameters adaptation, simple structure and easy implementation.

In next lines, the neural networks structure used in this work is described. First at all, the nonlinear MIMO system represented by (1) is considered:

$$x_i(k+1) = F\big(x(k), u(k)\big) \qquad (1)$$

where $x \in \Re^n, u \in \Re^m$ y $F \in \Re^n \times \Re^m \to \Re^n$ is a nonlinear function. Now, a discrete time recurrent higher order neural network (RHONN) can be represented as:

$$x_i(k+1) = w_i^T z_i\big(x(k), u(k)\big), \quad i = 1, ..., n \qquad (2)$$

with $x_i \ (i = 1, 2, ..., n)$ is the state of the ith neuron, n is the number of neural units, $w_i \ (1, 2, ..., n)$ is the respective on-line adapted weight vector, and $z_i\big(x(k), u(k)\big)$ is given by:

$$z_i\big(x(k), u(k)\big) = \begin{bmatrix} z_{i1} \\ z_{i2} \\ \vdots \\ z_{iLi} \end{bmatrix} = \begin{bmatrix} \Pi_{j \in I_1} y_i^{di\,j(1)} \\ \Pi_{j \in I_2} y_i^{di\,j(2)} \\ \vdots \\ \Pi_{j \in I_{L1}} y_i^{di\,j(Li)} \end{bmatrix} \qquad (3)$$

where L_i is the respective number of higher-order connections, $\{I_1, I_2, ..., I_{Li}\}$ is a collection of non ordered subsets of $\{1, 2, ..., n\}$, $d_{ij}(k)$ are non-negative integers and y_i is defined as follows:

$$y_i = \begin{bmatrix} y_{i_1} \\ \vdots \\ y_{i_n} \\ y_{i_{n+1}} \\ \vdots \\ y_{i_{n+m}} \end{bmatrix} = \begin{bmatrix} s(x_1) \\ \vdots \\ s(x_n) \\ u_1 \\ \vdots \\ u_n \end{bmatrix} \qquad (4)$$

In (4), $u = [u_1, u_2, ..., u_m]^T$ is the input vector to the neural network (NN) and $S(\bullet)$ is defined by:

$$S(x) = \frac{1}{1 + \exp(-\beta x)} \qquad (5)$$

where β is the function slope.

We consider the problem to approximate the general time nonlinear system (1), by the following discrete-time RHONN, introducing the modeling error:

$$x_i(k+1) = w_i^{*T} z_i\big(x(k), u(k)\big) + \varepsilon_{zi}, \quad i = 1, ..., n \qquad (6)$$

where x_i is the ith plant state, ε_{zi} is a bounded approximation error, which can be reduced by increasing the number of adjustable weights. Assume that exist an ideal weight vector w_i^T such that $\|\varepsilon_z\|$ can be minimized on a compact set $\Omega_{zi} \subset \Re^{Li}$ (Rovithakis, 2000). In general, it is assumed that this vector exists and is constant but unknown (Sanchez, et al., 2007). Let us define its estimate as w_i, and the estimation error as:

$$\tilde{w}_i(k) = w_i^* - w_i(k) \qquad (7)$$

Training Algorithm

The well-known Kalman Filter (KF) is a set of mathematical Equations which provides an efficient computational recursive solution to estimate the estates of a perturbed linear system with additive noise in the estates and the outputs (Song, 1995). For the Kalman filter based neural network training, the network weights become the states to be estimated and the neural network output is the measurement. In this case, the error between the neural network output and the plant output can be considered as additive white noise. Due to the fact that the neural network mapping is nonlinear, an EKF-type is required. The training goal is to find the optimal weights that minimize the prediction error. The weights estimation is done recursively, so that each update of the estimated weight is made from a previous weight and the current data; this implies that updating of all estimated weights is not required. This is the most important reason

Figure 1. RHONN trained with the extended Kalman filter scheme

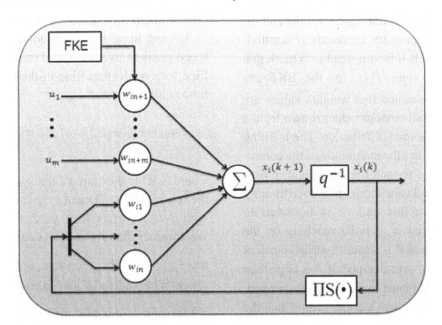

why the EKF is used as neural networks training algorithm. Figure 1 is a schematic representation of the EKF training algorithm.

The EKF as training algorithm is given by:

$$w_i\left(k+1\right) = w_i\left(k\right) + \eta_i K_i\left(k\right) e\left(k\right)$$
$$K_i\left(k\right) = P_i\left(k\right) H_i\left(k\right) M_i\left(k\right) \qquad i = 1,...,n$$
$$P_i\left(k+1\right) = P_i\left(k\right) - K_i\left(k\right) H_i^T\left(k\right) P_i\left(k\right) + Q_i\left(k\right)$$
(8)

where

$$M_i\left(k\right) = \left[R_i\left(k\right) + H_i^T\left(k\right) P_i\left(k\right) H_i\left(k\right)\right]^{-1}$$
$$e\left(k\right) = y\left(k\right) - \hat{y}\left(k\right)$$
(9)

with $e\left(k\right) \in \Re^p$ is the output estimation error and $P_i\left(k\right) \in \Re^{Li \times Li}$ is the weight estimation error covariance matrix at step k, $w_i \in \Re^{Li}$ is the weight vector, L_i is the respective number of neural network weights, $y \in \Re^p$ is the plant output, $\hat{y} \in \Re^p$ is the neural network output, n is the number of neural network states, $K_i \in \Re^{Li \times p}$ is the Kalman gain matrix, $Q_i \in \Re^{Li \times Li}$ is the NN weight estimation noise covariance matrix, $R_i \in \Re^{p \times p}$ is the error noise covariance, and $H_i \in \Re^{Li \times p}$ is the measurement matrix, in which each entry $\left(H_{ij}\right)$ is the derivative of the ith neural output with respect to ijth NN weight, $\left(w_{ij}\right)$, given as follows:

$$H_{ij}\left(k\right) = \left[\frac{\partial \hat{y}\left(k\right)}{\partial w_{ij}\left(k\right)}\right]^T$$
(10)

where $i = 1,...,n$ and $j = 1,...,L_i$. Usually P_i and Q_i are initialized as a diagonal matrices verifying the condition: $P_i(0) > R_i(0) > Q_i(0)$. This condition implies that *a priori* knowledge is not required to initialize the vector weights. In fact, higher entries in $P_i(0)$ correspond to a higher uncertainty in the *a priori* knowledge. It is advisable to set $P_i(0)$ between 100–1000 and so on for the other covariance matrices. An arbitrary scaling can be applied to $P_i(0)$, $R_i(0)$, and

$Q_i(0)$ without altering the evolution of the weight vector. Since the NN outputs do not depend directly on the weight vector, the matrix H is initialized as $H(0) = 0$. It is important to remark that $H_i(k)$, $K_i(k)$, and $P_i(k)$ for the EKF are bounded. It is assumed that weights values are initialized to small random values drawn from a zero mean and normal distribution. The learning rate (η) determines the magnitude of the correction term applied to each neuron weight; it usually requires small values to achieve good training performance, to this end, it is bounded to $0 < \eta < 1$; moreover, η is far reaching on the convergence. Thus, if η is small then the transient estimated state is over-damped; if η is large then the transient estimated state is under-damped; finally if η is larger than a critical value then the estimated state is unstable. Therefore, it is better to set η to a small value and edge it upward if necessary. The Luenberger-like observer gain (g) is set by trial and error; unfortunately there is a shortage of clear scientific rationale to define it. However, it is bounded to $0 < g < 0.1$ for a good performance on the basis of training experience.

Speed-Gradient Inverse Optimal Neural Control

Speed-gradient inverse optimal neural control is an adequate and novel algorithm easy to implement. This control stabilizes a feedback control where asymptotic convergence to a state reference trajectory is guaranteed. Then, it is shown that this control optimize a cost functional. The proposed controller is based on a discrete-time RHONN model and discrete-time inverse optimal control that have been applied successfully in mechanical (Ornelas, et al., 2010) and biological (Leon, et al., 2011) systems. Therefore, the speed-gradient inverse optimal neural control is a method adapted for the control of the anaerobic process. Methane production, biomass growth, and substrate degradation are good indicators of the biological activity inside the reactor. Therefore, reference

trajectories of these variables can be designed in order to obtain a maximum production of methane.

In next lines, the methodology to design a speed-gradient inverse optimal neural is described. First, let consider the affine-in-the-input discrete-time nonlinear system:

$$x(k+1) = f(x(k)) + g(x(k))u(k) \qquad (11)$$

where $\in R^n$ is the state of the system, $u \in R^m$ is the control input, $f(x)$ and $g(x)$ are smooth maps with $f(x) \in R^n$, $g(x) \in R^{n \times m}$, $k \in Z_+ = \{0, 1, 2, \dots\}$. We consider that x is an isolated fixed point of $f(x) + g(x)\,\overline{u}$ with $\overline{u}$ constant, that is, $f(x) + g(x)u = x$. Without loss of generality, we consider x $= 0$ for some $\overline{u}$ constant, $f(0) = 0$ and rank$\{g(x)\}$ $= m \; \forall x_k = 0$.

For system (11), the control law

$$u_k^* = -\frac{1}{2} R^{-1}(x_k) g^T(x_k) \frac{\partial V(x_{k+1})}{\partial x_{k+1}} \qquad (12)$$

is defined to be inverse optimal (globally) stabilizing if:

1.   It achieves (global) asymptotic stability of $x = 0$ for system (11);
     $V(x_k)$ is (radially unbounded) positive definite function such that inequality

$$\overline{V} := V(x_{k+1}) - V(x_k) + u_k^{*T} R(x_k) u_k^* \le 0 \qquad (13)$$

is satisfied. When , then $V(x_k)$ is a solution for the HJB partial-differential Equation (14), which is directly related to a classic optimal control:

$$l(x_k) + V(x_{k+1}) - V(x_k)$$
$$+ \frac{1}{4} \frac{\partial V^T(x_{k+1})}{\partial x_{k+1}} g(x_k) R^{-1}(x_k) g^T(x_k) \frac{\partial V(x_{k+1})}{\partial x_{k+1}} = 0$$
$$(14)$$

As it is established in the definition of (12), the inverse optimal control problem is based on the knowledge of $V(x_k)$. Thus, we propose a CLF, $V(x_k)$, such that (1) and (2) are guaranteed. That is, instead of solving (14) for $V(x_k)$, we propose a control Lyapunov function $V_c(x_k)$ with the form:

$$V_c\left(x_k, x_{\delta,k}\right) = \frac{1}{2}\left(x_{\delta,k} - x_k\right)^T P_k \left(x_{\delta,k} - x_k\right)$$
$$P_k = P_k^T > 0$$

$$(15)$$

for the control law (20) in order to ensure stability of the fixed point of system (11). This will be achieved by defining an appropriate matrix P_k. $x_{\delta,k} \in R_+^n$ is the desired trajectory for the considered system. Moreover, it will be established that the control law (12) with (15), which is referred to as the inverse optimal control law, optimizes a meaningful cost functional of the form:

$$V\left(x_k\right) = \sum_{n=k}^{\infty}\left(l\left(x_n\right) + u_n^T R\left(x_n\right)u_n\right). \quad (16)$$

Consequently, by considering $V\left(x_k\right) = V_c(x_k)$ as in (15), the control law (12) takes the following form:

$$u_k^* = -\frac{1}{2}\left[R\left(x_k\right) + \frac{1}{2}g^T\left(x_k\right)P_k g\left(x_k\right)\right]^{-1}$$
$$g^T\left(x_k\right)P_k g\left(x_k\right)f\left(x_k, x_{\delta,k+1}\right)$$

$$(17)$$

It is worth to point out that P_k and R are positive definite and symmetric matrices; thus, the existence of the inverse in (17) is ensured. To compute P_k, which ensures stability of the fixed point of system (11) with (17), the Speed-Gradient (SG) algorithm is used. This algorithm is described in next lines.

Fradkov and Pogromsky (1998) formulate a discrete-time application of the SG algorithm with the objective to find a control law u_k which ensures the control goal:

$$Q\left(x_{k+1}\right) \le \Delta, \qquad for\, k \ge k^*, \quad (18)$$

$\Delta > 0$ where Q is a control goal function, a constant , and is the time step at which the control goal is achieved. Q ensures stability if it is a positive definite function.

Control law (17) at every time step depends on the matrix P_k. Let define the matrix P_k at every time step k as:

$$P_k = p_k P' \quad (19)$$

where $P' = P'^T > 0$ is a given constant matrix and p_k is a scalar parameter to be adjusted by the SG algorithm. Then, (17) is transformed into:

$$u_k^* = -\frac{p_k}{2}\left[R\left(x_k\right) + \frac{p_k}{2}g^T\left(x_k\right)P'g\left(x_k\right)\right]^{-1}$$
$$g^T\left(x_k\right)P'g\left(x_k\right)f\left(x_k, x_{\delta,k+1}\right)$$

$$(20)$$

The SG algorithm is now reformulated for the inverse optimal control problem.

Proposition.- Consider a discrete-time nonlinear system of the form (11) with (20) as input. Let Q be a SG goal function as defined as $Q\left(x_k, p_k\right) = V_{sg}\left(x_{k+1}\right)$, and denoted by $Q_k(p)$. Let $\bar{p}, p^* \in \Pi$ (Π , is the set of admissible values for p_k) be positive constant values and $\Delta\left(x_k\right)$ be a positive definite function with $\Delta\left(0\right) = 0$ and $\in^*$ be a sufficiently small positive constant. Assume that: There exist p^* and $\in^*$ such that

$$Q_k\left(p^*\right) \le \in^* << \Delta\left(x_k\right) \quad and \quad 1 - \in^* /\Delta\left(x_k\right) \approx 1. \quad (21)$$

For all $p_k \in \Pi$:

$$\left(p^* - p_k\right)^T \nabla_p Q_k\left(p\right) \le \in^* -\Delta\left(x_k\right) < 0 \quad (22)$$

where $\nabla_p Q_k\left(p\right)$ denotes the gradient of $Q_k(p)$ with respect to p_k. Then, for any initial condition

$p_0 > 0$, there exists a $k^* \in Z_+$ such that the SG Control Goal (18) is achieved by means of the following dynamic variation of parameter p_k:

$$p_{k+1} = p_k - \gamma_{d,k} \nabla_p Q_k(p), \qquad (23)$$

with

$$\gamma_{d,k} = \gamma_c \delta_k \left| \nabla_p Q_k(p) \right|^{-2} \qquad (24)$$

and

$$\delta_k = \begin{cases} 1 & for \quad Q(p_k) > \Delta(x_k) \\ 0 & otherwise. \end{cases} \qquad (25)$$

Finally, for $k \geq k^*$, p_k becomes a constant value denoted by $\bar{p}$ and the SG algorithm is completed.

With $Q(x_k, p_k)$ defined as before, the dynamic variation of parameter p_k in (11) results in

$$p_{k+1} = p_k + 8\gamma_{d,k} \frac{f^T(x_k) P'g(x_k) R(x_k)^2 g^I(x_k) f(x_k)}{\left(2R(x_k) + p_k g^I(x_k) P'g(x_k)\right)^3} \qquad (26)$$

which is positive for all time step k if $p_0 > 0$. Therefore positiveness for p_k is ensured and requirement $P_k = P_k^T > 0$ for (15) is guaranteed.

When the SG control goal (18) is achieved, then $P = \bar{p} P'$ for $k \geq k^*$. Thus, matrix P_k in (17) is considered constant and $Pk = P$ where P is computed as $p_k = \bar{p}$, with P' a design positive definite matrix. Under these constraints, we obtain:

$$u_k^* = -\frac{1}{2} \left(R(x_k) + \frac{1}{2} g^T(x_k) Pg(x_k) \right)^{-1}$$
$$g^T(x_k) Pg(x_k) f(x_k, x_{\delta,k+1}). \qquad (27)$$

The proof that control law (27) ensures stability and optimality for (11) without solving the HJB Equation (14) is shown in (Ornelas, et al., 2011). The control law (27) is inverse optimal in the sense that it minimizes the meaningful functional given by

$$J = \sum_{k=0}^{\infty} \left(l(x_k) + u_k^T R(x_k) u_k \right). \qquad (28)$$

BIOMETHANE GENERATION PROCESS

Description

Anaerobic digestion is a complex and sequential process, which occurs in four basic stages: hydrolysis, acidogenesis, acetogenesis, and methanogenesis (Belmonte-Izquierdo, 2010). Each stage has a specific dynamics: hydrolysis, acidogenesis, and acetogenesis are fast stages in comparison with methanogenesis, which is the slowest one; it imposes the dynamics of the process and is considered as the limiting stage. There are two ways in order to synthesize CH_4; the first one by acid acetic cleavage, which produces CH_4 and CO_2; and the second one by CO_2 reduction with hydrogen, which generates CH_4 and water. The acetate reaction is the primary producer of CH_4 because of the limited amount of hydrogen available (Monnet, 2003). Then, special attention is focused on methanogenesis. In this work, it is supposed that anaerobic digestion is developed in a Completely Stirred Tank Reactor (CSTR) with biomass filter. A variety of factors affect the rate of digestion and biogas production, such as pH, temperature, overloads, etc. A detailed comparative summary of research on the inhibition of anaerobic processes is presented in Chen (2007) and Cheng and Creamer (2007). In addition, some variables and parameters are hard to measure due to economical or technical constraints. Then, estimation and control strategies are required in order to guarantee adequate performance.

A functional diagram of an anaerobic digestion is proposed in Beteau (1992) as shown in Figure 2. Biomass is classified as: X_1, corresponding to hydrolytic,

Figure 2. Functional diagram of the anaerobic digestion

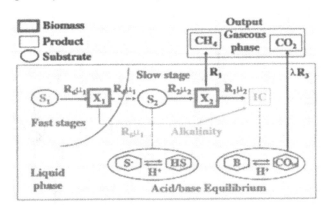

acidogenic and acetogenic bacteria and X_2, corresponding to methanogenic bacteria. On the other hand, the organic load is classified in S_1, the components equivalent glucose, which model complex molecules and S_2, the components equivalent acetic acid, which represent the molecules transformed in acetic acid directly. This classification allows the process to be represented by a fast stage, which involves hydrolysis, acidogenesis, and acetogenesis, and a slow stage, which corresponds mainly to methanogenesis.

Thus, a mathematical model representing both stages is deduced as follows (Belmonte-Izquierdo, et al., 2009). On one side, the biological phenomena are modeled by ordinary differential Equations (29), which represent the dynamical part of the process as:

$$\frac{dX_1}{dt} = \left(\mu_1 - k_{d1}\right) X_1,$$

$$\frac{dS_1}{dt} = -R_6 \mu_1 X_1 + D_{in}\left(S_{1in} - S_1\right),$$

$$\frac{dX_2}{dt} = \left(\mu_2 - k_{d2}\right) X_2,$$

$$\frac{dS_2}{dt} = -R_3 \mu_2 X_2 + R_4 \mu_1 X_1 + D_{in}\left(S_{2in} - S_2\right),$$

$$\frac{dIC}{dt} = R_2 R_3 \mu_2 X_2 + R_5 \mu_1 X_1 - \lambda R_1 R_3 \mu_2 X_2 +$$
$$D_{in}\left(IC_{in} - IC\right),$$

$$\frac{dZ}{dt} = D_{in}\left(Z_{in} - Z\right)$$

$$(29)$$

where μ_1 is the growth rate (Haldane type) of X_1 (h^{-1}), μ_2 the growth rate (Haldane type) of X_2 (h^{-1}), k_{d1} the death rate of X_1 (mol L^{-1}), k_{d2} the death rate of X_2 (mol L^{-1}), D_{in} the dilution rate (h^{-1}), S_{1in} the fast degradable substrate input (mol L^{-1}), S_{2in} the slow degradable substrate input (mol L^{-1}), IC inorganic carbon (mol L^{-1}), Z the total of cations (mol L^{-1}), IC_{in} the inorganic carbon input (mol L^{-1}), Z_{in} the input cations (mol L^{-1}), λ is a coefficient considering law of partial pressure for the dissolved CO_2 and $R_1, ..., R_6$ are the yield coefficients. On the other side, the physical-chemical phenomena (acid-base equilibria and material conservation) are modeled by algebraic Equations (30).

$$HS + S^- - S_2 = 0,$$
$$H^+ S^- - K_a HS = 0,$$
$$H^+ B - K_b CO_{2d} = 0, \qquad (30)$$
$$B + CO_{2d} - IC = 0,$$
$$B + S^- - Z = 0,$$

where HS is non ionized acetic acid (mol L^{-1}), S^- ionized acetic acid (mol L^{-1}), H^+ ionized hydrogen (mol L^{-1}), B measured bicarbonate (mol L^{-1}), Z the total of cations (mol L^{-1}), CO_{2d} dissolved carbon dioxide (mol L^{-1}), K_a is an acid-base equilibrium constant, K_b is an equilibrium constant between B and CO_{2d}. Finally, the gaseous phase (CH_4 and CO_2) is considered as the process output:

Figure 3. Observer scheme

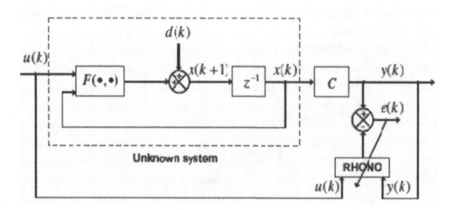

$$Y_{CH_4} = R_1 R_2 \mu_2 X_2$$
$$Y_{CO_2} = \lambda R_2 R_3 \mu_2 X_2 \qquad (31)$$

Biomass growth, substrate degradation, and CH_4 production are good indicators of biological activity inside the reactor. These variables will be used for monitoring the process and to design an inverse optimal neural controller.

Application of Neural Networks on a Biomethane Production Process

A discrete time Recurrent High Order Neural Observer (RHONO) is proposed in order to estimate variables hard to measure due to technical or economical constraints: biomass X_2, substrate S_2, and inorganic carbon.

After that, a neurofuzzy control strategy and a speed-gradient inverse optimal neural control to improve methane production are described.

Discrete Time RHONO

The discrete-time RHONO estimates the variables of the methanogenesis stage: biomass (X_2), substrate (S_2), and inorganic carbon (IC). The observability property of this anaerobic digestion process is analyzed in a previous work (Carlos Hernandez, 2004; Alcaraz-Gonzalez & Gonzalez-Alvarez,

2007). It is concluded that substrates (S_1 and S_2), biomasses (X_1 and X_2) and inorganic carbon (IC) are observable states. In Figure 3, the proposed observer scheme is displayed and the structure of RHONO composed of a parallel configuration is shown in Equations (32).where k is a real number representing a time sample, $X \in R^n$ is the state vector, $u \in R^m$ the input vector, $y \in R^p$ the output vector, $d \in R^n$ a disturbance vector, e the output error and $F(\bullet, \bullet)$ a smooth vector field.

$$\hat{X}_{2,k+1} = w_{11}S\left(\hat{X}_{2,k}\right) + w_{12}S^2\left(\hat{X}_{2,k}\right) + w_{13}S\left(\hat{IC}_k\right)$$
$$+w_{14}S^2\left(\hat{X}_{2,k}\right)D_{in,k} + w_{15}S^2\left(\hat{X}_{2,k}\right)IC_{in,k} + g_1 e_k,$$

$$\hat{S}_{2,k+1} = w_{21}S\left(\hat{S}_{2,k}\right) + w_{22}S^2\left(\hat{S}_{2,k}\right) + w_{23}S\left(\hat{IC}_k\right)$$
$$+w_{24}S^2\left(\hat{S}_{2,k}\right)D_{in,k} + w_{25}S^2\left(\hat{S}_{2,k}\right)S_{2in,k} + g_2 e_k,$$

$$\hat{IC}_{k+1} = w_{31}S\left(\hat{IC}_k\right) + w_{32}S^2\left(\hat{IC}_k\right) + w_{33}S\left(\hat{X}_{2,k}\right)$$
$$+w_{34}S^2\left(\hat{IC}_k\right)D_{in,k} + w_{35}S^2\left(\hat{IC}_k\right)IC_{in,k} + g_3 e_k,$$

$$(32)$$

where w_{ij} is the respective on-line adapted weight vector; $\hat{X}_2, \hat{S}_2$ and $\hat{IC}$ are the estimated states; $S(\bullet)$ is the sigmoid function defined as $S(x) = \alpha \tanh(\beta x)$; ($g_1, g_2, g_3$) are the Luenberger-like observer gains, e_k is the output error, D_{in}, S_{2in}, and IC_{in} are defined as before. The neural network is trained with an Extended Kalman Filter (EKF), which provides an efficient computational solution to estimate the state of a non-linear dynamic system with additive state and output white noises (Song & Grizzle, 1995). For KF-based neural network training, the network weights become the states to be estimated. The error between the neural network output and the measured plant output can be considered as additive white noise.

The RHONO is trained with the EKF algorithm described on previous section (Equations 8 – 10). The performance of the RHONO is shown in Figure 4.

As can be seen, the estimation of the three variables of methanogenesis is done adequately. A step on input substrate is used to test the observer performances. In addition, the three variables are initialized randomly in order to evaluate the convergence, which is remarked at the beginning of the simulation. Different initial conditions were tested and in all cases, the convergence time is short. After that, the estimation is well done for each variable even in presence of the step on input substrate.

Neurofuzzy Control Strategy

The control scheme is represented in Figure 5 (Sanchez, et al., 2001; Carlos Hernandez, et al., 2010). It is an integrated control strategy since it is composed by a fuzzy supervisor, a neural observer and two control laws. The main idea is to detect the process state by means of the supervisor, which uses the information from the process and from the RHONO to select the most adequate control action in order to avoid washout in presence of disturbances and to enhance methane production.

For small disturbances, the process is able to operate in open loop. For closed loop, two PI L/A control actions (Lakrori, 1989; Dantigny, 1989) could be applied in order to regulate bicarbonate inside the reactor: a) adding a base (33), which

allows the process to have high methane production, but rejecting only small disturbances (bigger than for open loop), and b) dilution rate (34), which causes low methane production but allows large disturbances to be rejected.

$$b_{inc\_k} = (b_{inck-1} - b_{inc})\left(\frac{B_{k-1}}{B_k}\right)^{K_{1b}}\left(\frac{B_k^*}{B_k}\right)^{K_{2b}} + b_{inc\_min} \tag{33}$$

$$D_k = D_{k-1}\left(\frac{B_{k-1}}{B_k}\right)^{K_{1D}}\left(\frac{B_k^*}{B_k}\right)^{K_{2D}} \tag{34}$$

where k is an integer which represent a sample time, b_{inc} is the added base, B is the measured bicarbonate, B^* is the reference, b_{inc_min} is the minimal value for the bicarbonate, D is the dilution rate, K_{1b} (K_{1D}) and K_{2b} (K_{2D}) are the proportional and integral gains respectively for each control action.

The supervisor uses two variables in order to determine when and which control action apply. The organic daily load per biomass unit (ODL/X_2) defined as in (35) is important regarding process operation limits due to its relation with disturbances amplitude on input substrate.

$$ODL / X_2 = \frac{DA_2 S_{2\_0}}{\hat{X}_2} \tag{35}$$

where A_2 is the disturbance amplitude on the substrate input S_{2in}, S_{2-0} the initial value of the substrate S_2 and $\hat{X}_2$ is the observed biomass. In presence of a disturbance on S_{2in}, ODL/X_2 can abruptly increase up to a value, which exceeds the conditions of stability limits (critical value); therefore, the process tends to washout. If ODL/X_2 is above its critical value then a control law must be applied in order to allow biomass growth, and hence, diminishing ODL/X_2 and leading the process to the functioning region. In contrast, if ODL/X_2 is under its critical value then the system can work in open loop. On the other hand, disturbances on input substrate affect methane produc-

Figure 4. Estimation of methanogenesis stage by using the proposed RHONO: a) biomass X_2, b) substrate S_2, c) inorganic carbon

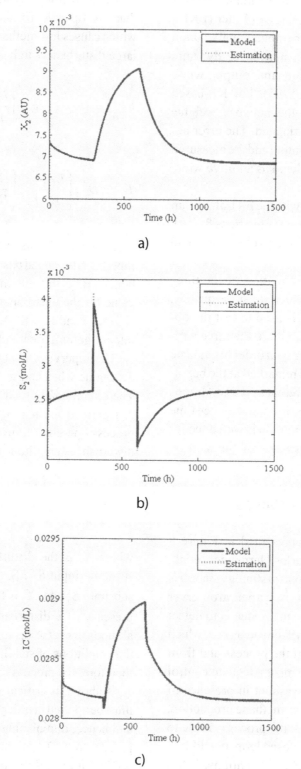

a)

b)

c)

Figure 5. Neurofuzzy control strategy

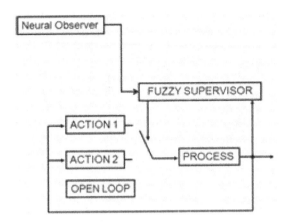

tion (ΔQCH_4): a small variation on the methane production could be caused by small disturbances, which can be rejected by the process without a control action; meanwhile, a high variation is caused by a larger disturbance, which requires a control action. From this information, six fuzzy rules having the next form are deduced:

If ODL/X_2 is (δ) and ΔQCH_4 is (φ) then u_i where (δ) can be SMALL, AVERAGE or BIG; (φ) can be LOW or HIGH, and u_i can be b_{inc}, D or open loop.

Deffuzzyfication is done as follows:

$$u = \frac{\sum_{j=1}^{R} \gamma_j u_j}{\gamma_j} \qquad (36)$$

where $\gamma_j = \gamma_{ODL/X2} * \gamma_{\Delta QCH4}$ and $\sum_{j=1}^{R} \gamma_j = 1$; R is the number of rules, l and k are stand for the lst and the kst fuzzy sets of COJ/X_2 and ΔQCH_4, respectively.

The performance of the process with this control strategy is illustrated in Figure 6.

A disturbance is incepted at time $t=50h$; the process behavior is shown in Figure 6a. ΔQCH_4 belongs to LOW and $ODL/X2$ belongs to SMALL; both fuzzy sets are associated to OPEN LOOP; then a control action is not required. For this reason, the supervisor allows the process to operate in open loop (b_{inc} and D constants at equilibrium values).

A disturbance $A_2=2.2$ is considered at time $t=50$ h; the obtained results are shown in Figure 6b. The control strategy induces the next behavior: ΔQCH_4 belongs to HIGH (associated to closed loop) meanwhile ODL/X_2 belongs to LARGE (associated to D action). Then, the supervisor allows the D action to be applied; consequently, B starts to be regulated and X_2 tends to a new equilibrium value. As the action is applied, ΔQCH_4 continues to belong to HIGH, meanwhile ODL/X_2 decreases and belongs to AVERAGE (associated to b_{inc} action). Then, action D is progressively stopped and b_{inc} starts to be applied. Consequently, X_2 and B decrease when D is stopped; when b_{inc} is applied X_2 and B increase again leading to a new equilibrium point. Finally, ΔQCH_4 leaves HIGH and belongs to LOW (associated to open loop); meanwhile ODL/X_2 decreases and belongs to SMALL (associated to open loop). That means, the disturbance has been rejected. Then, the supervisor stops b_{inc} action and the process operates in open loop again. On the other side, large disturbances affect the neural estimation of X_2; nevertheless, the control strategy is able to keep the process in the operating point attraction region.

Speed-Gradient Inverse Optimal Neural Control for Anaerobic Digestion

The methodology introduced in section 2 is now applied to an anaerobic process. A speed-gradient inverse optimal neural control law is designed in order to track the optimal trajectories of the system described by (29-31).

The first step is to represent the RHONO (32) as an affine system; after that, it is possible to apply the methodology of the speed-gradient inverse optimal control. The RHONO is then written as required by the described methodology; the resulting expressions are illustrated on Equations (37), where f and g are the respective functions of the compatible system.

Figure 6. Process performance considering the neurofuzzy control strategy: a) small disturbance, b) large disturbance

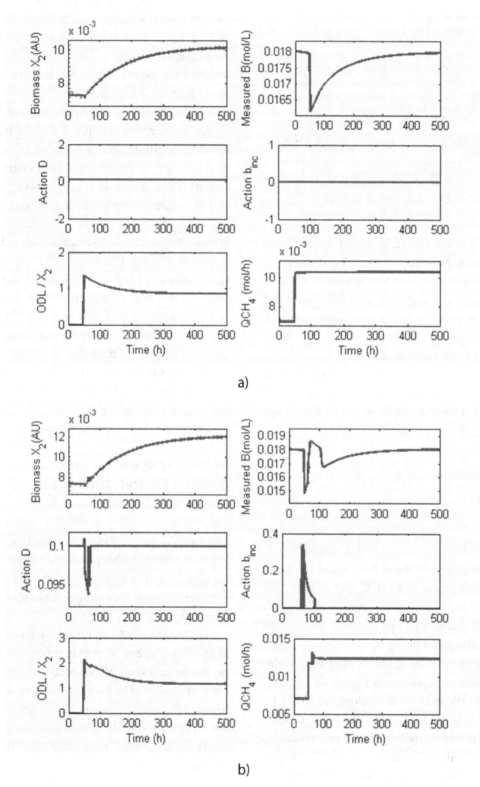

a)

b)

$$f_1\left(\hat{X}_{2,k}, \hat{IC}_k\right) = w_{11}S\left(\hat{X}_{2,k}\right) + w_{12}S^2\left(\hat{X}_{2,k}\right)$$

$$+ w_{13}S\left(\hat{IC}_k\right) + g_1 e_k,$$

$$G_{11}(\hat{X}_{2,k}) = w_{14}S^2\left(\hat{X}_{2,k}\right) \qquad G_{12}(\hat{X}_{2,k}) = w_{14}S^2\left(\hat{X}_{2,k}\right)$$

$$f_2\left(\hat{S}_{2,k}, \hat{IC}_k\right) = w_{21}S\left(\hat{S}_{2,k}\right) + w_{22}S^2\left(\hat{S}_{2,k}\right) + w_{23}S\left(\hat{IC}_k\right)$$

$$+ w_{25}S^2\left(\hat{S}_{2,k}\right)S_{2in,k} + g_2 e_k,$$

$$G_{21}(\hat{S}_{2,k}) = w_{24}S^2\left(\hat{S}_{2,k}\right)$$

$$(37)$$

$$f_3\left(\hat{X}_{2,k}, \hat{IC}_k\right) = w_{31}S\left(\hat{IC}_k\right)$$

$$+ w_{32}S^2\left(\hat{IC}_k\right) + w_{33}S\left(\hat{X}_{2,k}\right) + g_3 e_k$$

$$G_{31}(\hat{IC}_k) = + w_{34}S^2\left(\hat{IC}_k\right)$$

$$G_{32}(\hat{IC}_k) = w_{35}S^2\left(\hat{IC}_k\right)$$

Then, the Equation (37) is represented in a matrix form as illustrated by Equation (38). The functions f, g as well as the vector of reference trajectories f_{ref} are included. The matrix P' which will be used for the control law is defined also as shown below.

$$g\left(x_k\right) = \begin{bmatrix} G_{11} & G_{12} \\ G_{21} & 0 \\ G_{31} & G_{32} \end{bmatrix} \qquad P' = \begin{bmatrix} P_{11} & P_{12} & P_{13} \\ P_{21} & P_{22} & P_{23} \\ P_{31} & P_{32} & P_{33} \end{bmatrix}$$

$$f\left(x_k\right) = \begin{bmatrix} f_1 \\ f_2 \\ f_3 \end{bmatrix}$$

$$f_{ref}\left(x_{\delta,k+1}\right) = \begin{bmatrix} X_{2ref} \\ S_{2ref} \\ IC_{ref} \end{bmatrix}.$$

$$(38)$$

According to (27) and considering the different restrictions described in the methodology, the next inverse optimal control law can be formulated for the anaerobic process:

$$u_k^* = -\frac{1}{2}\left[R\left(x_k\right) + \frac{1}{2}g^T\left(x_k\right)P_k g\left(x_k\right)\right]^{-1}$$

$$g^T\left(x_k\right)P_k g\left(x_k\right)f\left(x_k, x_{\delta,k+1}\right).$$

$$(39)$$

where the positive definite matrix $P_k = p_k P'$ is calculated by the SG algorithm, $R(x_k)$ is a constant matrix $g(x_k)$ and $f(x_k)$ are matrices as in (38) and $f\left(x_k, x_{\delta,k+1}\right) = f\left(x_k\right) - f_{ref}\left(x_{\delta,k+1}\right)$. The other parameters selection is done according to the recommendations of the RHONO design, such as described in the respective section of this chapter.

The inverse optimal neural control algorithm requires reference trajectories to force the system to track them. The proposed reference trajectories were taken from (Belmonte-Izquierdo, 2010); those trajectories are obtained from a system controlled and considering the presence of maximum disturbance in the inlet substrate S_{2in}. In this work, the proposed control algorithm is tested in presence of disturbance of 200% S_{2in} at t=200 hours, as is illustrated in Figure 7. As can be seen, tracking performance of trajectories is efficient and the error approaches zero in the steady state. The YCH_4 is calculated with the Equation (24) which is based on the observed states; then, possibly the tracking error is due to the tracking error obtained in the variables estimation.

HYDROGEN GENERATION PROCESS

Kinetic Model of Biomass Gasification

The transformation from solid to gas is developed in several stages: drying, pyrolysis, combustion, and reduction; each one takes place in different

Figure 7. Process performance with the speed-gradient inverse optimal neural control: a) tracking performance, b) control inputs

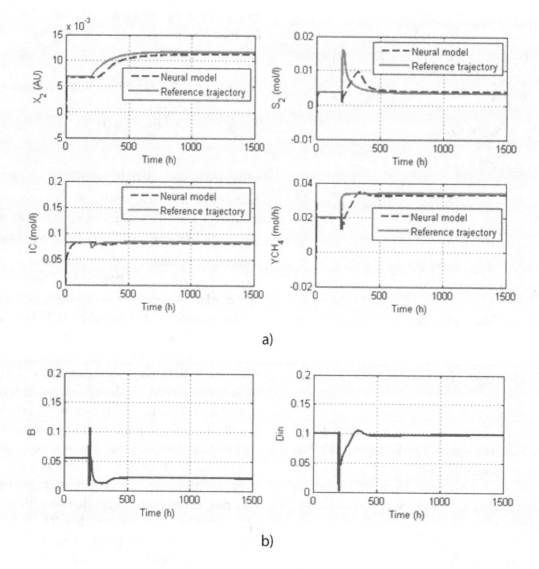

a)

b)

reaction zones (Wang & Kinoshita, 1993). Since combustion reaction in the pyrolysis zone is faster than the gasification reaction in the reduction zone (Wang & Kinoshita, 1993; Reed, 1981), all biomass gasification rates are controlled by kinetics in the char reduction zone. Figure 8 displays a simplified scheme of a fluidized bed gasifier, including the different reaction zones.

Biomass enters the high temperature Flaming Pyrolysis (FP) zone where it is converted into char and volatiles. Combustion takes place when the volatiles react with oxidant. The pyrolysis-combustion process in the FP zone is dominated by exothermic reactions where biomass is converted into char, CO_2, and H_2O. It is assumed that part of the volatiles is cracked into methane in the FP zone. The products from the FP zone then

Figure 8. General scheme of a fluidized bed gasification process

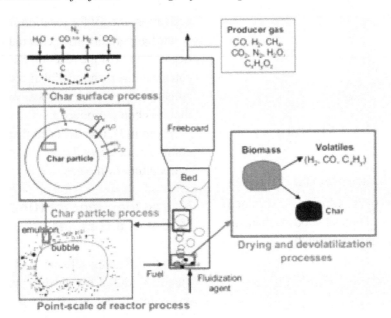

move into the Char Reduction (CR) zone, where endothermic reactions dominate and the thermal energy generated by the pyrolysis combustion process is transformed into chemical energy in combustible gas species such as H_2 and CO, this mixture is known as synthesis gas or syngas. The concentrations of the products exiting the FP zone become the initial concentrations of the reactants in the CR zone. Thus, in the CR zone, the initial amounts of H_2 and CO are zero and the amount of nitrogen remains constant.

A general Equation for biomass gasification is presented in Equation (40).

$$CH_\alpha O_\beta + yO_2 + zN_2 + wH_2O = x_1C + x_2H_2$$
$$+x_3CO + x_4H_2O + x_5CO_2 + x_6CH_4 + x_7N_2$$
$$(40)$$

where $CH_\alpha O_\beta$ is the chemical representation of biomass, and y, z, w, and x_i are the molar numbers of the different components in the reaction. The subscripts α and β are determined from ultimate analysis of the biomass feedstock.

Temperature in the CR zone ranges from 700-900°C. At temperatures below 900°C, mass transfer and pore diffusion are much faster than chemical reactions; thus, the rate-controlling factor is chemical kinetics (Reed, 1981; Reed, et al., 1988). In the CR zone, the following reactions take place:

$$C + CO_2 \leftrightarrow 2CO \text{ b. } C + 2H_2 \leftrightarrow CH_4 \qquad (41)$$

$$C + H_2O \leftrightarrow H_2 + CO \text{ d. } H_2O + CH_4 \leftrightarrow CO + 3H_2$$

The production ratio of the different components is given by the following differential Equations:

$$\frac{dx_1}{dt} = v_1(X) + v_2(X) + v_3(X)$$

$$\frac{dx_2}{dt} = -v_2(X) + 2v_3(X) - 3v_4(X)$$

$$\frac{dx_3}{dt} = -2v_1\left(X\right) - v_2\left(X\right) - v_4\left(X\right)$$

$$\frac{dx_4}{dt} = v_2\left(X\right) + v_4\left(X\right) \tag{42}$$

$$\frac{dx_5}{dt} = v_1\left(X\right),\ \frac{dx_6}{dt} = -v_3\left(X\right) + v_4\left(X\right)$$

with $v_i\left(X\right)$ the net reaction rate of the char reduction zone reactions (41), which are obtained considering Langmuir-Hinshelwood mechanism (Laurendeau, 1978), and are given by:

$$-v_1\left(X\right) = k_{a1}\frac{x_5 - x_3^2/\left(P_X K_{p1}\right)}{\sum\left(K_i + 1/p\right)x_i}\left(\frac{x_1,0}{x_1}\right)^{1/3}\frac{x_1}{\rho d_p}$$

$$-v_2\left(X\right) = k_{a2}\frac{x_4 - x_3 x_2/\left(P_X K_{p2}\right)}{\sum\left(K_i + 1/p\right)x_i}\left(\frac{x_1,0}{x_1}\right)^{1/3}\frac{x_1}{\rho d_p} \tag{43}$$

$$-v_3\left(X\right) = k_{a3}\frac{x_2^2 - x_6/\left(P_X K_{p3}\right)}{\sum\left(K_i + 1/p\right)x_i}\left(\frac{x_1,0}{x_1}\right)^{1/3}\frac{x_1}{\rho d_p}$$

$$-v_4\left(X\right) = k_{a4}\frac{x_4 x_6 - x_3 x_2^3/\left(P_X^2 K_{p4}\right)}{\sum\left(K_i + 1/p\right)x_i}\left(\frac{x_1,0}{x_1}\right)^{1/3}\frac{x_1}{\rho d_p}$$

where K_i is the adsorption constant for species i, p is the pressure in the gasifier, ρ is char density, d_p is the initial diameter of the char sphere, K_{pi} es is the equilibrium constant for each reaction in the char reduction zone and k_{ai} is the apparent rate constant for reaction i. The apparent rate constant is the product of a pre-exponential factor A_i and an exponential factor, according to the Arrhenius Equation:

$$k_{ai} = A_i\exp\left(-E_{ai}/RT\right) \tag{44}$$

where R is the universal gas constant, E_{ai} is the activation energy for reaction i and T is the absolute temperature in the char reduction zone. The negative sign of the reaction rate Equations indicates that the reaction global component is being consumed, whereas the positive sign indicates that it is being produced.

From (43), it is deduced that the gas product composition depends on the pressure and the temperature of the gasifier.

Neural Identifier for Kinetic Model of a Gasifier

The identification scheme used to reproduce the kinetic model of the gasifier presented in previous point (Equations 41-43) is described in this section. A recurrent high order neuronal network with n=6, considering that all the state variables are measured, is considered for this task. The parameters identification and the states identification are related in the sense of how the measurements of the sensors can be used to obtain an approximated model of the plant to be controlled. For many control applications, it is advisable to identify the state of the system or at least a part of it. The aim of this work is to reproduce the behavior of the gasifier considering different operation conditions with the neuronal identifier. This approach allows the user to obtain a better understanding of the reaction mechanisms during the solid biomass transformation, as well as to analyze the properties of the process. Thus, the acquired knowledge of the process by means of the identification will facilitate the instrumentation and the development of control strategies in order to optimize the operation of this kind of processes.

The neuronal identifier proposed for the gasifier represented by (41 - 43) is described by next discrete time expressions, as shown in Box 1: where x_1, x_2, x_3, x_4, x_5, and x_6 represent the concentrations of carbon (C), hydrogen (H_2), carbon monoxide (CO), water (H_2O), carbon

Box 1.

$$\hat{x}_1(k+1) = w_{11}S(x_1) + w_{12}S(x_1)S(x_5)S(x_3) + w_{13}S(x_4) + w_{14}S(x_3)S(x_4)$$
$$\qquad + w_{15}S(x_2)S(x_6) + w_{16}u_T$$

$$\hat{x}_2(k+1) = w_{21}S(x_2) + w_{22}S(x_4) + w_{23}S(x_3)S(x_4) + w_{24}S(x_6)S(x_1)$$
$$\qquad + w_{25}u_T$$

$$\hat{x}_3(k+1) = w_{31}S(x_3) + w_{32}S(x_5) + w_{33}S(x_3)S(x_1) + w_{34}S(x_3)S(x_2)S(x_1)$$
$$\qquad + w_{35}S(x_4)S(x_6) + w_{36}u_T \qquad (45)$$

$$\hat{x}_4(k+1) = w_{41}S(x_4) + w_{42}S(x_3)S(x_2) + w_{43}S(x_6) + w_{44}S(x_3)S(x_2)S(x_1)$$
$$\qquad + w_{45}u_T$$

$$\hat{x}_5(k+1) = w_{51}S(x_5) + w_{52}S(x_3)S(x_1) + w_{53}u_T$$

$$\hat{x}_6(k+1) = w_{61}S(x_6) + w_{62}S(x_2) + w_{63}S(x_6)S(x_1) + w_{64}S(x_4)S(x_6)$$
$$\qquad + w_{65}S(x_3)S(x_2)S(x_1) + w_{66}u_T$$

dioxide (CO_2), and methane (CH_4), respectively; u_T and u_p are control inputs (temperature and pressure, respectively). The initial conditions are defined by next Equations system, which is obtained from (46):

$$x_2 = x_3 = 0$$
$$x_1 + x_5 + x_6 = 1$$
$$2x_4 + 4x_6 = \alpha + 2w \qquad (46)$$
$$x_4 + 2x_5 = 2y + \beta + w$$
$$x_7 = z$$

Figure 9. Identification scheme

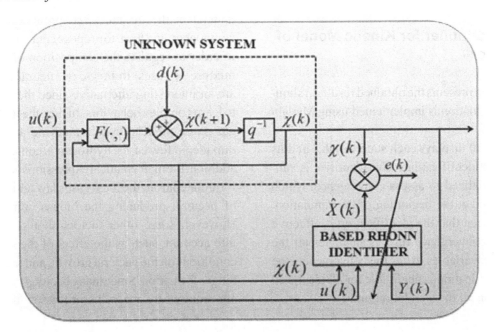

Table 1. RHONN covariance matrices in identification process

$P_i(0)$	$Q_i(0)$	$R_i(0)$
$\left[P_1(0)\right]_{7\times7} = diag\{9e6\}$	$\left[Q_1(0)\right]_{7\times7} = diag\{0.1\}$	$\left[R_1(0)\right]_{1\times1} = 9e2$
$\left[P_2(0)\right]_{6\times6} = diag\{9e7\}$	$\left[Q_2(0)\right]_{6\times6} = diag\{0.01\}$	$\left[R_2(0)\right]_{1\times1} = 8e3$
$\left[P_3(0)\right]_{7\times7} = diag\{2e6\}$	$\left[Q_3(0)\right]_{7\times7} = diag\{0.1\}$	$\left[R_3(0)\right]_{1\times1} = 2e3$
$\left[P_4(0)\right]_{6\times6} = diag\{9e7\}$	$\left[Q_4(0)\right]_{6\times6} = diag\{0.001\}$	$\left[R_4(0)\right]_{1\times1} = 7e2$
$\left[P_5(0)\right]_{4\times4} = diag\{9e9\}$	$\left[Q_5(0)\right]_{4\times4} = diag\{0.01\}$	$\left[R_5(0)\right]_{1\times1} = 8e3$
$\left[P_6(0)\right]_{7\times7} = diag\{9e5\}$	$\left[Q_6(0)\right]_{7\times7} = diag\{0.01\}$	$\left[R_6(0)\right]_{1\times1} = 5e2$

The training method is performed on-line, using a series-parallel configuration as displayed in Figure 9.

All the neural networks states are initialized randomly as well as the initial weight vectors. The EKF covariance matrices are initialized as diagonal, with nonzero elements. These values are determined by test and error as appear in Table 1.

Neural Identifier for Kinetic Model of a Gasifier

This section presents the obtained results in simulation. Simulation is implemented using Matlab/Simulink ®.

Figure 10 displays each state variable and its respective identification. The identifier is randomly initialized to assess convergence, which is illustrated at the beginning of the simulation. It can be seen that the identification is effective since the convergence time is small for all the considered variables. After the convergence, the error identification is negligible for all identified variables in all the simulation time.

FUTURE RESEARCH DIRECTIONS

Processes generating gases with energy potential require deep studies in order to maximize the obtained products. In the case of anaerobic digestion, the development of specific models of gaseous phase, which include the effect of operating conditions, is an interesting topic. With this kind of models, it would be possible to better understand the mechanisms to produce a specific component, and then, to propose control strategies in order to regulate the composition of the final mixture of gases. In this topic, neural networks are an interesting alternative since they are able to learn complex behaviors. In fact, the traditional gas phase models involve methane and carbon dioxide; in few cases, hydrogen is considered. In addition, the mathematical expressions are usually formulated from the ideal gases law and the yield of bacteria producing the biogas components. However, some other factors should be taken into account, such as the effect of the operating conditions on the bacteria growth, and then on the biogas formation. Since many bacteria population are required by anaerobic processes, the neural

Figure 10. Identification of the kinetic model of a gasifier

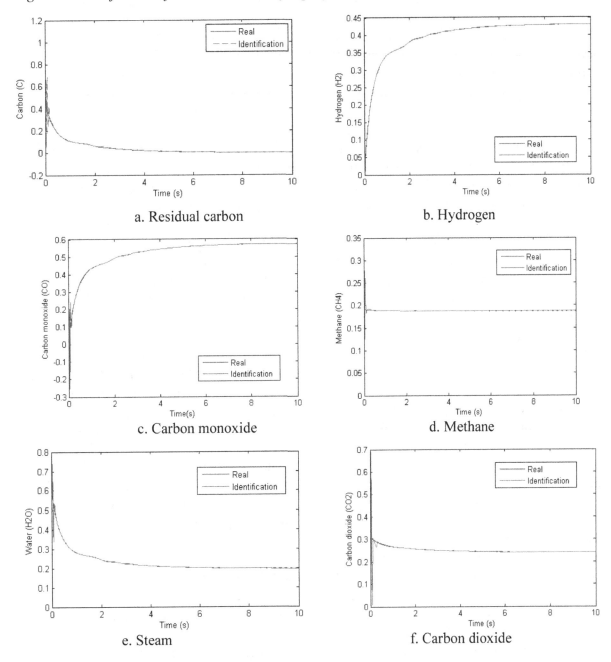

a. Residual carbon

b. Hydrogen

c. Carbon monoxide

d. Methane

e. Steam

f. Carbon dioxide

networks are an interesting tool in order to identify and reproduce a specific organism metabolism. In addition, neural networks are able to predict the whole process behavior in face of different operating conditions. The state observation is an aspect to be improved in biological processes, specifically for the efficient estimation of the substrate degradation. The implementation of virtual sensors requires a good processing of the available signals (outputs and inputs) which have high nonlinearities. An alternative to this situation is the design of neural observers. On the other side, the maximization of biomethane production is a main objective on anaerobic processes. It implies the implementation of control strategies, which guarantee the adequate operation even in presence of disturbances and change on the parameters and operating conditions. Neural networks approach is an alternative to design efficient and relatively simple control structures achieving the biomethane maximization.

Concerning gasification, a research direction is the study of the effect of different operating conditions on the process performances, mainly, on the composition of the final gas mixture. From the structure of chemical reactions, the manipulation of some variables such as temperature, pressure and air input, it is possible to promote the formation of a specific component. Then, it is important to develop control strategies in order to improve the process operation and to ease the manipulation that kind of variables. As for biological processes, neural networks are an important alternative to reach these objectives. For example, the identification of the complex thermo chemical reactions occurring during the wastes transformation can be done by neural networks with a structure relatively simple. The prediction of the process behavior in face on different scenarios can be also performed by neural networks. Modeling of gasification using neural networks is very important since it is possible to study this kind of processes in a simulation stage, then, to minimize risks and costs on future real experimentation. Neural networks can be also an alternative to replace certain sensors minimizing costs and enhancing the process supervision. An example of this situation is the implementation of a neural supervision system, which allows the waste degradation to be estimated in-line at each instant. With this system, it would be possible to identify immediately the formation of a specific component and also to detect eventual problems on the waste transformation. Related to the process control, there are many factors, which can be solved using neural networks, such as the feed of raw materials, the regulation of internal tempera-

ture, the kinetics of reactions, the performance of the process regardless of the raw material, etc.

The real time experimentation is indeed an important topic in order to validate the proposed topologies and control structures. The idea is to get some feedbacks from real processes in order to evaluate the developed algorithms in real scenarios.

The integration of a complete chain to valorize organic wastes is also a main future direction. Nowadays, there exist a lot of examples of generating energy from wastes; however, a multidisciplinary collaboration is not systematic in this kind of applications. The global system of energy generation from wastes is composed by several stages (preparation of raw materials, transformation, supervision and control, recovery and cleaning of gases, transformation of gases into energy). Usually, each step is studied individually without consider the previous and future stage. Then, integral studies are required. In this sense, again, neural networks are a powerful tool to deal with this topic.

On the other side, the proposed algorithms imply the tuning of a large number of parameters. A future research direction concerns the development of algorithms which can be self-tuned or algorithms which can control the increase of the number of parameters.

CONCLUSION

In this chapter, the application of high order neural networks on two processes for gases generation from organic wastes transformation was described: anaerobic digestion for biomethane production and gasification for hydrogen production. A nonlinear discrete-time Recurrent High Order Neural Observer (RHONO) is used to estimate the biomass concentration, substrate degradation and inorganic carbon in an anaerobic digestion process considering a CSTR with biomass filter, which is operated in continuous mode. This RHONO is based on a discrete-time recurrent high-order neural network trained with an Extended Kalman Filter (EKF)-based algorithm. The variables are estimated from CH_4 and CO_2 flow rates, which are commonly measured in this kind of processes. Also, pH and system inputs measurements are assumed. Simulation results illustrate the effectiveness of model adaptation to system disturbance and robustness of the proposed RHONO. Two control strategies are evaluated to enhance methane production: a neurofuzzy strategy, which uses the RHONO estimation and some other physic variables in order to detect the process state and to determine the application of a control action according to the operating conditions. The neurofuzzy strategy allows the process to improve performances in presence of disturbances on the input substrate; at the same time, the methane production is also improved. On the other hand, an affine mathematical model is obtained with the aim of applying speed-gradient inverse optimal neural control. Once the neural model is obtained, an inverse control law, based on this model, is developed. The goal is to force the system to track desired reference signals, which is achieved by designing a control law as was described. Simulation results show how the control law is able to stabilize the methane production along a desired trajectory in presence of disturbances and avoid washout. Thus, this control action fulfills the objectives of reject disturbances; obtain a high efficiency of the process that is reflected in a good production of biogas and to avoid that the process be blocked or stopped. The observer is efficient because it estimate very well the important variables. Thus, it satisfies the necessity to monitoring variables of the process in substitution of sensors expensive or not reliable for control purposes.

In the case of gasification, a first approximation of an identification system is developed. The idea is to reproduce the process behavior, mainly the products formation, by means of a high order neural network. The neural identification is evaluated for carbon (C), hydrogen (H2), carbon monoxide (CO), water (H2O), carbon dioxide (CO2), and methane (CH4) concentrations. At this stage of the study, a discrete recurrent high order neuronal network considering that all the states are measurable is used; the neuronal identifier is trained with the extended Kalman filter algorithm which is implemented on line. As for the other cases, simulation results illustrate the effectiveness of the proposed identification scheme. Research is being performed to use the proposed identifier to sinthetize an adequate control law, which would be able to enhance the transformation of wastes and the production of gases with energy potential.

REFERENCES

Alcaraz-Gonzalez, V., & Gonzalez-Alvarez, V. (2007). Robust nonlinear observers for bioprocesses: Application to wastewater treatment. In *Selected Topics in Dynamics and Control of Chemical and Biological Processes* (pp. 119–164). Berlin, Germany: Springer-Verlag. doi:10.1007/978-3-540-73188-7_5

Babu, B. V., & Sheth, P. N. (2006). Modeling and simulation of reduction zone of downdraft biomass gasifier: Effect of char reactivity factor. *Energy Conversion and Management, 47*(15–16), 2602–2611. doi:10.1016/j.enconman.2005.10.032

Baruch, I. S., Galvan-Guerra, R., & Nenkova, B. (2008). Centralized indirect control of an anaerobic digestion bioprocess using recurrent neural identifier. *Lecture Notes in Computer Science*, 297–310. doi:10.1007/978-3-540-85776-1_25

Bastin, G., & Dochain, D. (1990). *On-line estimation and adaptive control of bioreactors*. Amsterdam, The Netherlands: Elsevier Science Publications. doi:10.1016/S0003-2670(00)82585-4

Basu, P., & Kaushal, P. (2009). Modeling of pyrolysis and gasification of biomass in fluidized beds: A review. *Chemical Product and Process Modeling, 4*(1).

Belmonte-Izquierdo, R., Carlos-Hernandez, S., & Sanchez, E. N. (2009). Hybrid intelligent control scheme for an anaerobic wastewater treatment process. In *Proceedings of the Second International Workshop on Advanced Computational Intelligence (IWACI 2009)*. Mexico City, Mexico: IWACI.

Belmonte-Izquierdo, R., Carlos-Hernandez, S., & Sanchez, E. N. (2010). A new neural observer for an anaerobic bioreactor. *International Journal of Neural Systems, 20*(1), 75–86. doi:10.1142/S0129065710002267

Beteau, J. F. (1992). *An industrial wastewater treatment bioprocess modelling and control.* (Unpublished Doctoral Dissertation). INPG. France.

Bridgwater, A. V. (2003). Renewable fuels and chemicals by thermal processing of biomass. *Chemical Engineering Journal, 91*, 87–102. doi:10.1016/S1385-8947(02)00142-0

Brown, D., Fuchino, T., & Marechal, F. (2006). Solid fuel decomposition modelling for the design of biomass gasification systems. In W. Marquardt & C. Pantelides (Eds.), *Proceedings of the 16th European Symposium on Computer Aided Process Engineering and 9th International Symposium on Process Systems Engineering*, (pp. 1661–1666). Garmisch-Partenkirchen, Germany: IEEE.

Carlos-Hernandez, S., Oudaak, N., Beteau, J. F., & Sanchez, E. N. (2004). Fuzzy observer for the anaerobic digestion process. In *Proceedings of IFAC Symposium on Structures Systems and Control*. Oaxaca, Mexico: IFAC.

Carlos-Hernandez, S., Sanchez, E. N., & Beteau, J.-F. (2009). Fuzzy observers for anaerobic wwtp: Synthesis and implementation. *Control Engineering Practice, 17*(6), 690–702. doi:10.1016/j.conengprac.2008.11.008

Carlos-Hernandez, S., Sanchez, E. N., & Bueno, J. A. (2010). *Neurofuzzy control strategy for an abattoir wastewater treatment process*. Paper presented at the 11th IFAC Symposium on Computer Applications in Biotechnology. Leuven, Belgica.

Chen, J. S. (1987). *Kinetic engineering modelling of co-current moving bed gasification reactors for carbonaceous material*. (Unpublished Doctoral Dissertation). Ithaca, NY: Cornell University.

Chen, Y., Cheng, J. J., & Creamer, K. S. (2007). Inhibition of anaerobic digestion process: A review. *Bioresource Technology, 99*(10), 4044–4064. doi:10.1016/j.biortech.2007.01.057

Cuoci, A., Faravelli, T., Frassoldati, A., Grana, R., Pierucci, S., Ranzi, E., & Sommariva, S. (2009). Mathematical modelling of gasification and combustión of solid fuels and wastes. *Chemical Engineering Transactions, 18*, 989–994.

Dantigny, P., Ninow, J. L., & Lakrori, M. (1989). A new control strategy for yeast production based on the L/A* approach. *Applied Microbiology and Biotechnology, 36*(3), 352–357.

De Souza, M. B., Jr., Barreto, A. G., Jr., Nemer, L. C., Soares, P. O., & Quitete, C. P. B. (2010). A study on modeling and operational optimization of biomass gasification processes using neural networks. In *Proceedings of 2010 Annual Meeting of AIChE*. Salt Lake City, UT: AIChE.

Detournay, M., Hemati, M., & Andreux, R. (2011). Biomass steam gasification in fluidized bed of inert or catalytic particles: Comparison between experimental results and thermodynamic equilibrium predictions. *Powder Technology, 208*, 558–567. doi:10.1016/j.powtec.2010.08.059

Dochain, D., & Perrier, M. (1997). Dynamical modelling, analysis, monitoring and control design for nonlinear bioprocesses. *Advances in Biochemical Engineering/Biotechnology, 56*, 147–197. doi:10.1007/BFb0103032

Dupont, D., Nocquet, T., Da Costa, J. A. Jr., & Verne-Tournon, C. (2011). Kinetic modelling of steam gasification of various woody biomass chars: Influence of inorganic elements. *Bioresource Technology, 102*, 9743–9748. doi:10.1016/j.biortech.2011.07.016

Fradkov, A. L., & Pogromsky, A. Y. (1998). *Introduction to control of oscillations and chaos.* Singapore: World Scientific Publishing Co. doi:10.1142/9789812798619

Gao, M. (2008). Robust exponential stability of Markovian jumping neural networks with time-varying delay. *International Journal of Neural Systems, 18*(3), 207–218. doi:10.1142/S0129065708001531

Garcia, C., Molina, F., Roca, E., & Lema, J. M. (2007). Fuzzy-based control of an anaerobic reactor treating wastewaters containing ethanol and carbohydrates. *Industrial & Engineering Chemistry Research, 46*(21), 6707–6715. doi:10.1021/ie0617001

Giltrap, D. L., McKibbin, R., & Barnes, G. R. G. (2003). A steady state model of gas–char reactions in a downdraft gasifier. *Solar Energy, 74*, 85–91. doi:10.1016/S0038-092X(03)00091-4

Gøbel, B., Henriksen, U., Jensen, T. K., Qvale, B., & Houbak, N. (2007). The development of a computer model for a fixed bed gasifier and its use for optimization and control. *Bioresource Technology, 98*, 2043–2052. doi:10.1016/j.biortech.2006.08.019

Gordillo, E. D., & Belghit, A. (2011). A two phase model of high temperature steam-only gasification of biomass char in bubbling fluidized bed reactors using nuclear heat. *International Journal of Hydrogen Energy, 36*, 374–381. doi:10.1016/j.ijhydene.2010.09.088

Gouze, J. L., Rapaport, A., & Hadj-Sadok, Z. (2000). Interval observers for uncertain biological systems. *Ecological Modelling, 133*(1–2), 45–56. doi:10.1016/S0304-3800(00)00279-9

Guo, B., Li, D., Cheng, C., Lu, Z. A., & Shen, Y. (2001). Simulation of biomass gasification with a hybrid neural network model. *Bioresource Technology, 76*, 77–83. doi:10.1016/S0960-8524(00)00106-1

Haidar, A. M. A. (2009). An intelligent load shedding scheme using neural networks and neuro-fuzzy. *International Journal of Neural Systems, 19*(6), 473–479. doi:10.1142/S0129065709002178

Haykin, S. (1999). *Neural networks: A comprehensive foundation* (2nd ed.). Upper Saddle River, NJ: Prentice Hall.

Holubar, P., Zani, L., Hager, M., Froschl, W., Radak, Z., & Braun, R. (2002). Advanced controlling of anaerobic digestion by means of hierarchical neural networks. *Water Research, 36*, 2582–2588. doi:10.1016/S0043-1354(01)00487-0

Huang, H. J., & Ramaswamy, S. (2009). Modeling biomass gasification using thermodynamic equilibrium approach. *Applied Biochemistry and Biotechnology, 154*, 193–204. doi:10.1007/s12010-008-8483-x

Jarungthammachote, S., & Dutta, A. (2007). Thermodynamic equilibrium model and second law analysis of a downdraft waste gasifier. *Energy, 32*, 1660–1669. doi:10.1016/j.energy.2007.01.010

Jayah, T. H., Aye, L., Fuller, R. J., & Stewart, D. F. (2003). Computer simulation of a downdraft wood gasifier for tea drying. *Biomass and Bioenergy, 25*, 459–469. doi:10.1016/S0961-9534(03)00037-0

Karppanen, E. (2000). *Advanced control of an industrial circulating fluidized bed boiler using fuzzy logic.* (Doctoral Dissertation). University of Oulu. Oulu, Finland.

Kaushal, P., Abedi, J., & Mahinpey, N. (2010). A comprehensive mathematical model for biomass gasification in a bubbling fluidized bed reactor. *Fuel, 89*, 3650–3661. doi:10.1016/j.fuel.2010.07.036

Kendi, T. A., & Doyle, F. J. (1996). Nonlinear control of a fluidized bed reactor using approximate feedback linearization. *Industrial & Engineering Chemistry Research, 35*, 746–757. doi:10.1021/ie950334a

Klass, D. L. (1998). Biomass for renovable energy. In *Fuels and Chemicals* (pp. 225–256). Longon, UK: Elsevier.

Lakrori, M. (1989). Control of a continuous bio-process by simple algorithms of P and L/A types. In *Proceedings of International IFAC Symposium on Nonlinear Control System Design*. Capri, Italy: IFAC.

Laurendeau, M. (1978). Kinetics of coal char gasification and combustion. *Journal of Energy Combustion, 4,* 221–270. doi:10.1016/0360-1285(78)90008-4

Leon, B. S., Alanis, A. Y., Sanchez, E. N., Ornelas, F., & Ruiz-Velazquez, E. (2011). Inverse optimal trajectory tracking for discrete time nonlinear positive systems. In *Proceedings of 50th IEEE Conference on Decision and Control and European Control Conference (IEEE CDC-ECC)*. Orlando, FL: IEEE Press.

Li, X. T., Grace, J. R., Lim, C. J., Watkinson, A. P., Chen, H. P., & Kim, J. R. (2004). Biomass gasification in a circulating fluidized bed. *Biomass and Bioenergy, 26,* 171–193. doi:10.1016/S0961-9534(03)00084-9

Lu, Y., Guo, L., Zhang, X., & Yan, Q. (2007). Thermodynamic modeling and analysis of biomass gasification for hydrogen production in supercritical water. *Chemical Engineering Journal, 131,* 233–244. doi:10.1016/j.cej.2006.11.016

Mailleret, L., Bernard, O., & Steyer, J. P. (2004). Nonlinear adaptive control for bioreactors with unknown kinetics. *Automatica, 40,* 1379–1385. doi:10.1016/j.automatica.2004.01.030

Melgar, A., Pérez, J. F., Laget, H., & Horillo, A. (2007). Thermochemical equilibrium modelling of a gasifying process. *Energy Conversion and Management, 48,* 59–67. doi:10.1016/j.enconman.2006.05.004

Mendez-Acosta, H. O., Campos-Delgado, D. U., & Femat, R. (2003). Intelligent control of an anaerobic digester: Fuzzy-based gain scheduling for a geometrical approach. In *Proceeding of IEEE International Symposium on Intelligent Control*, (pp. 298–303). Houston, TX: IEEE Press.

Monnet, F. (2003). *An introduction to anaerobic digestion of organic wastes. Technical Report*. Edinburgh, UK: Remade Scotland.

Mountouris, A., Voutsas, E., & Tassios, D. (2006). Plasma gasification of sewage sludge: Process development and energy optimization. *Energy Conversion and Management, 47,* 1723–1737. doi:10.1016/j.enconman.2005.10.015

Ornelas, F., Sanchez, E. N., & Loukianov, A. G. (2010). Discrete-time inverse optimal control for nonlinear systems trajectory tracking. In *Proceedings of the 49th IEEE Conference on Decision and Control*. Atlanta, GA: IEEE Press.

Paes, T. (2005). *Modeling for control of a biomass gasifier*. (Unpublished Doctoral Dissertation). Technische Universiteit Eindhoven. Eindhoven, The Netherlands.

Petre, E., Selisteanu, D., & Sendrescu, D. (2008). Adaptive control strategies for a class of anaerobic depollution bioprocesses. In *Proceedings of the IEEE Automation, Quality and Testing, Robotics,* (vol 2), (pp. 159–164). Cluj-Napoca, Romania: IEEE Press.

Puig-Arnavat, M., Carles Bruno, J., & Coronas, A. (2010). Review and analysis of biomass gasification models. *Renewable & Sustainable Energy Reviews, 14,* 2481–2851. doi:10.1016/j.rser.2010.07.030

Reed, T. B. (1981). *Biomass gasification principle and technology*. Upper Saddle River, NJ: Noyes Data Corporation.

Reed, T. B., Levie, B., & Graboski, M. S. (1988). *Fundamentals, development and scaleup of the air-oxygen stratified downdraft gasifier*. Columbus, OH: Battelle.

Roos, K. F. (1991). *Profitable alternatives for regulatory impacts on livestock waste management*. Paper presented at the National Livestock, Poultry and Aquacultural Waste Management National Workshop. Kansas City, MO.

Rovithakis, G. A., & Chistodoulou, M. A. (2000). *Adaptive control with recurrent high-order neural networks*. Berlin, Germany: Springer Verlag. doi:10.1007/978-1-4471-0785-9

Sagüés, C., García-Bacaicoa, P., & Serrano, S. (2007). Automatic control of biomass gasifiers using fuzzy inference systems. *Bioresource Technology*, *98*, 845–855. doi:10.1016/j.biortech.2006.03.004

Sanchez, E. N., Alanis, A. Y., & Chen, G. R. (2006). Recurrent neural networks trained with the Kalman filtering for discrete chaos reconstruction. *Continuous Discrete Impulsive Systems B*, *13*, 1–18.

Sanchez, E. N., Alanis, A. Y., & Loukianov, A. G. (2007). Discrete-time recurrent high order neural observer for induction motors. In Melin, P. (Eds.), *Foundations of Fuzzy Logic and Soft Computing*. Berlin, Germany: Springer-Verlag. doi:10.1007/978-3-540-72950-1_70

Sanchez, E. N., Alanis, A. Y., & Loukianov, A. G. (2008). *Discrete time high order neural control trained with Kalman filtering*. Berlin, Germany: Springer-Verlag. doi:10.1007/978-3-540-78289-6

Schuster, G., Löffler, G., Weigl, K., & Hofbauer, H. (2001). Biomass steam gasification--An extensive parametric modeling study. *Bioresource Technology*, *77*, 71–79. doi:10.1016/S0960-8524(00)00115-2

Sekhar Barman, N., Ghosh, S., & De, S. (2012). Gasification of biomass in a fixed bed downdraft gasifier – A realistic model including tar. *Bioresource Technology*, *107*, 505–511. doi:10.1016/j.biortech.2011.12.124

Simeonov, I., & Queinnec, I. (2006). Linearizing control of the anaerobic digestion with addition of acetate (control of the anaerobic digestion). *Control Engineering Practice*, *14*, 799–810. doi:10.1016/j.conengprac.2005.04.011

Song, Y., & Grizzle, J. W. (1995). The extended Kalman filter as a local asymptotic observer for discrete-time nonlinear systems. *Journal of Mathematical Systems. Estimation and Control*, *5*(1), 59–78.

Theilliol, D., Ponsart, J. C., Harmand, J., Join, C., & Gras, P. (2003). On-line estimation of unmeasured inputs for an aerobic wastewater treatment processes. *Control Engineering Practice*, *11*(9), 1007–1019. doi:10.1016/S0967-0661(02)00230-7

Van Impe, J. F., & Bastin, G. (1995). Optimal adaptive control of fed-batch fermentation processes. *Control Engineering Practice*, *3*(7), 939–954. doi:10.1016/0967-0661(95)00077-8

Wang, Y., & Kinoshita, C. M. (1993). Kinetic model of biomass gasification. *Solar Energy*, *51*(1), 19–25. doi:10.1016/0038-092X(93)90037-O

Xiao, G., Ni, M. J., Chi, Y., Jin, B. S., Xiao, R., Zhong, Z. P., & Huang, Y. J. (2008). Gasification characteristics of MSW and an ANN prediction model. *Waste Management (New York, N.Y.)*, *29*(1), 240–244. doi:10.1016/j.wasman.2008.02.022

Zhang, B. (2007). Delay-dependent robust exponential stability for uncertain recurrent neural networks with time-varying delays. *International Journal of Neural Systems*, *17*(3), 207–218. doi:10.1142/S012906570700107X

ADDITIONAL READING

Chynoweth, D. P., Owens, J. M., & Legrand, R. (2001). Renewable methane from anaerobic digestion of biomass. *Renewable Energy, 22*(1-3), 1–8. doi:10.1016/S0960-1481(00)00019-7

de Baere, L. (2000). Anaerobic digestion of solid waste: state-of-the-art. *Water Science and Technology, 41*(3), 283–290.

de Souza-Santos, M. L. (2004). *Solid fuels combustion and gasification: Modeling, simulation and equipment operation.* New York, NY: Marcel Dekker Inc. doi:10.1201/9780203027295

Faaij, A., van Ree, R., Waldheim, L., Olsson, E., Oudhuis, A., & van Wijk, A. (1997). Gasification of biomass wastes and residues for electricity production. *Biomass and Bioenergy, 12*(6), 387–407. doi:10.1016/S0961-9534(97)00010-X

Gunaseelan, V. N. (1997). Anaerobic digestion of biomass for methane production: A review. *Biomass and Bioenergy, 13*(1), 83–114. doi:10.1016/S0961-9534(97)00020-2

Kirubakaran, V., Sivaramakrishnan, V., Nalini, R., Sekar, T., Premalatha, M., & Subramanian, P. (2009). A review on gasification of biomass. *Renewable and Sustainable Energy, 13*, 179–186. doi:10.1016/j.rser.2007.07.001

Lim, K. O., & Sims, R. E. H. (2003). Liquid and gaseous biomass fuels. In *Bioenergy Options for a Cleaner Environment* (pp. 103–140). Dordrecht, The Netherlands: Elsevier.

McCarty, P. L. (1964). Anaerobic waste treatment fundamentals. *Public Works, 95*(9), 107–112.

Moylan, P. J., & Anderson, B. D. O. (1973). Nonlinear regulator theory and an inverse optimal control problem. *IEEE Transactions on Automatic Control, 18*(5), 460–465. doi:10.1109/TAC.1973.1100365

Pind, P. F., Angelidaki, I., Ahring, B. K., Stamatelatou, K., & Lyberato, G. (2003). Monitoring and control of anaerobic reactors. *Advances in Biochemical Engineering/Biotechnology, 82*, 135–182. doi:10.1007/3-540-45838-7_4

Ricalde, L. J., & Sanchez, E. N. (2005). *Inverse optimal nonlinear high order recurrent neural observer.* Paper presented at the International Joint Conference on Neural Networks. Montreal, Canada.

Van Lier, J. B., Tilche, A., Ahring, B. K., Macarie, H., Moletta, R., & Dohanyos, M. (2001). New perspectives in anaerobic digestion. *Water Science and Technology, 43*(1), 1–18.

Wang, L., Weller, C. L., Jones, D. D., & Hanna, M. A. (2008). Contemporary issues in thermal gasification of biomass and its application to electricity and fuel production. *Biomass and Bioenergy, 32*, 573–581. doi:10.1016/j.biombioe.2007.12.007

Willems, J. L., & Voorde, H. V. D. (1977). Inverse optimal control problem for linear discrete-time systems. *Electronics Letters, 13*, 493. doi:10.1049/el:19770361

Williams, R. J., & Zipser, D. (1989). A learning algorithm for continually running fully recurrent neural networks. *Neural Computation, 1*, 270–280. doi:10.1162/neco.1989.1.2.270

Yang, H., Li, J., & Ding, F. (2007). A neural network learning algorithm of chemical process modeling based on the extended Kalman filter. *Neurocomputing, 70*(4), 625–632. doi:10.1016/j.neucom.2006.10.033

Section 3
Artificial Higher Order Neural Networks for Control and Predication

Chapter 9
Distributed Adaptive Control for Multi–Agent Systems with Pseudo Higher Order Neural Net

Abhijit Das
Automation and Robotics Research Institute, USA

Frank Lewis
Automation and Robotics Research Institute, USA ·

ABSTRACT

The idea of using multi-agent systems is becoming more popular every day. It not only saves time and resources but also eliminates much of the human workload. These ideas are especially effective in the combat zone, where multiple unmanned aerial vehicles can achieve simultaneous objectives or targets. The evolution of distributed control started with a simple integrator systems, and then different control methodologies have been adopted for more and more complex nonlinear systems. In addition, from a practical standpoint, the dynamics of the agents involved in networked control architecture might not be identical. Therefore, an ideal distributed control should accommodate multiple agents that are nonlinear systems associated with unknown dynamics. In this chapter, a distributed control methodology is presented where nonidentical nonlinear agents communicate among themselves following directed graph topology. In addition, the nonlinear dynamics are considered unknown. While the pinning control strategy has been adopted to distribute the input command among the agents, a Pseudo Higher Order Neural Net (PHONN)-based identification strategy is introduced for identifying the unknown dynamics. These two strategies are combined beautifully so that the stability of the system is assured even with minimum interaction among the agents. A detailed stability analysis is presented based on the Lyapunov theory, and a simulation study is performed to verify the theoretical claims.

INTRODUCTION

Coordination and consensus of distributed groups of agents is inspired by naturally occurring phenomena such as flocking in birds, swarms in insects, circadian rhythms in nature, synchronization and phase transitions in physical and chemical systems, and the laws of thermodynamics (Hui & Haddad, 2008). Early work has been done in the control systems community by Fax & Murray (2004), Jadbabaie, Lin, and Morse (2003), Olfati-Saber and Murray (2004), Ren and Beard (2005), and Tsitsiklis (1984), which by now are

DOI: 10.4018/978-1-4666-2175-6.ch009

well known. Consensus has been studied for systems on communication graphs with fixed or varying topologies and communication delays. The average consensus problem has garnered much interest. Synchronization to time-varying trajectories has been studied based on physical or natural systems by Chopra and Spong (2009), Kuramoto (1975), Strogatz (2000), and Vicsek, Czirok, Jacob, Cohen, and Schochet (1995). Synchronization of nonlinear passive dynamic systems has been studied by Chopra and Spong (2006). Consensus using nonlinear protocols has been considered there and in Hui and Haddad (2008).

Convergence of consensus to a virtual leader or header node has been studied in Jadbabaie et al. (2003) and Jiang and Baras (2009). Dynamic consensus for tracking of time-varying signals has been presented in Spanos, Olfati-Saber, and Murray (2005). Recently, the pinning control has been introduced for synchronization control of coupled complex dynamical systems (Li, Wang, & Chen, 2004; Li, Duan, & Chen, 2009; Lu & Chen, 2005; Wang & Chen, 2002). Pinning control is a powerful technique that allows controlled synchronization of interconnected dynamic systems by adding a control or leader node that is connected (pinned) into a small percentage of nodes in the network. These pinned or controlled nodes view the control node simply as another neighbor, and consider the control node's state value in computing their local protocols. Analysis shows that all nodes converge to the state of the control node, which may be time varying. Analysis has been done using Lyapunov techniques by assuming either a Jacobian linearization of the nonlinear node dynamics or a Lipschitz condition. A related idea is soft control (Han, Li, & Guo, 2006) where a shill node moves through the network, and is perceived by existing nodes simply as another neighbor for purposes of computation of their own averaging protocols. Proper placement and motion of the shill agent results in consensus to the state of the shill.

Consensus and collective motion of distributed agents has been analyzed using the theory of graphs and/or Markov processes. Recent publications allow analysis using traditional control theory notions including matrix analysis, Lyapunov theory, etc., upon the introduction of certain key definitions including irreducibility, M-matrices, Frobenius form, special Lyapunov forms, etc. Notable are the books by Qu (2009) and Wu (2007). Such techniques allow one to bring in the machinery of matrix analysis (Bernstein, 2005). Instrumental in this analysis are the techniques employed in Khoo, Xie, and Man, 2012).

Distributed multiagent systems with unknown nonlinear dynamics and disturbances were studied in Hou, Cheng, and Tan (2009) where distributed adaptive controllers were designed to achieve robust consensus. That treatment assumed undirected graphs and solved the consensus problem, that is, the nodes reach a steady-state consensus that depends on the initial conditions. Expressions for the consensus value were not given.

The study of control protocols on digraphs is significantly more involved than their study on undirected graphs, where the graph Laplacian potential can be taken as a Lyapunov function. In this research, we present a Lyapunov-based technique embedded with PHONN for design of protocols for robust synchronization to tracking of a leader or control node. Design techniques are developed for general digraphs. The leader has unknown nonlinear dynamics, and the nodes have unknown, non-identical, nonlinear dynamics and disturbances. Suitable control protocols are derived using a Lyapunov function that is carefully crafted to depend on a special local synchronization error that can be computed in a distributed fashion. The control laws thus derived are distributed in nature and can be implemented locally by each node. They consist of a linear protocol plus a nonlinear adaptive learning component, which is derived from HONN like neural net (PHONN). These protocols are robust to uncertain disturbances and dynamics, and to modeling errors in a sense to be made precise. It is shown that the synchronization error converges to a residual set. Singular value analysis is used. It is shown that the singular values of certain key matrices are intimately related to structural properties of the graph. Simulation results are given to show the effectiveness of the proposed method.

NEURAL NET AND FUNCTION APPROXIMATION

Figure 1 shows a schematic diagram of two-layer Neural Network (NN) with n inputs and m outputs. Assuming the linear activation functions in the output layer one can write the output as (Lewis, et al., 1999):

$$p = W^T \sigma(V^T l) \tag{1}$$

where, V and W are the first and second layer weight matrices and $\sigma(\cdot)$ is defined as the activa-

tion function for first layer. Now if the first-layer weights and thresholds V in are predetermined by some *a priori* method, then only the second-layer weights and thresholds W are to be determined to define the NN. Define, $\mu(l) \equiv \sigma(V^T l) \in \Re^X$ with X = number of hidden first layer so that

$$p = W^T \mu(l) \tag{2}$$

This NN is *linear* in the parameter W.

The basic universal approximation result (Hornik, Stinchombe, & White, 1989) says that any smooth function $a(s)$ can be approximated arbitrarily closely on a compact set using two-layer NN with appropriate weights. If, $a(s) : \Re^n \to \Re^m$ be a smooth function, then given a compact set $S \in \Re^n$ and a positive number ε_N, there exist a two-layer NN such that

$$a(s) = W^T \mu(s) + \varepsilon \tag{3}$$

Figure 1. A typical two-layer neural network

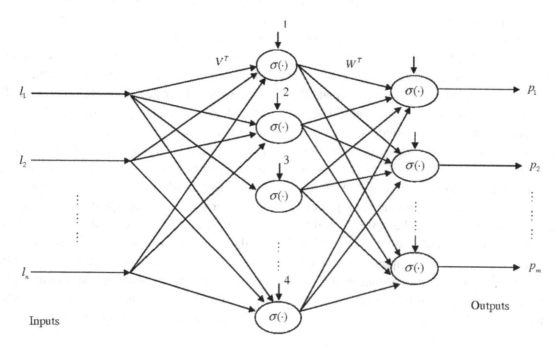

with $\|\varepsilon\| < \varepsilon_N \forall s \in S$ and for some large X. The term ε often known as the *NN function approximation error* and it is decreases as X increases.

Predetermination of V is sometimes become difficult. This problem is addressed by selecting the matrix V in randomly. It is shown in Igelnik and Pao (1995) that, for Random Vector Functional Link (RVFL) nets, the resulting function $\mu(s) = \sigma(V^T s)$ is a basis, so that the RVFL NN has the universal approximation property. The NN described in is a feed-forward NN. However, it is shown subsequently that the weights in NN must be tuned online to achieve closed loop control stability and desired controller performance. The tuning functions are often nonlinear and contain higher order state variables. Therefore, in real applications, the NN is in fact a dynamically higher order.

Higher Order Neural Net (HONN) and Pseudo Higher Order Neural Net (PHONN)

Higher order neural nets are the extension of the single layer neural net described in the previous section. Higher order generally describes any order of the neural net, which is greater than one (Kosmatopoulos, Polycarpou, Christodoulou, & Ioannou, 1995). For example, the response of a second order neural net to the input pattern $X = \left[l_1, l_2, \ldots, l_{n_i} \right]$ is given by (Karayiannis & Venetsanopoulos, 1993):

$$p_i = \text{sgn}\left(\sum_{j_1=1}^{n_i} \sum_{j_2=1}^{n_i} w_{i;j_1,j_2} l_{j_1} l_{j_2} \right) \qquad (4)$$

where $w_{i;j_1,j_2}$ are the weights of the network. So we can see that in higher (second) order neural net, the network response depends on the weighted summation of the quadratic terms $l_{j_1} l_{j_2}$ for $1 \le j_1, j_2 \le n_i$. So the total input to the neuron is not only a linear combination of the components

l_j, but also their product $l_{j_1} l_{j_2}$. Like this, one can go further higher order interactions represented by $l_{j_1} l_{j_2} l_{j_3} \ldots$ etc. This is the basic structure of a higher order neural network. Interestingly, it can be shown that higher order neural network of any order can be trained by any of the learning algorithms developed for first order neural net.

In contrast to the HONN, the structure of Pseudo Higher Order Neural Net (PHONN) is different in the sense that PHONN has the basic structure of first order neural net

$$p_i = \text{sgn}\left(\sum_{j=1}^{n_i} w_{i,j} l_j \right) \qquad (5)$$

Now, when this first order neural net is used in adaptive control loop simulation, then each time step the value of the weights $w_{i,j}$ can be derived from some weight tuning dynamics which involves different components of X and thus $w_{i,j} = w_{i,j}(l_1, l_2, \ldots, l_{n_i})$ are also the functions of different components of X. So if we look into the each time step of the dynamic simulation of the adaptive control involving first order neural network, the Equation (5) can be seen as

$$p_i = \text{sgn}\left(\sum_{j=1}^{n_i} w_{i,j}(X) l_j \right) \qquad (6)$$

which is more like the HONN response in (4). So (6) reveals the fact that a single layer neural net in the dynamic loop of adaptive control simulation involving dynamic weight tuning laws work similar to a higher order neural net. We will call it as Pseudo Higher Order like Neural Net (PHONN).

SYNCHRONIZATION CONTROL FORMULATION

Consider a graph $G = (V, E)$ with a nonempty finite set of N nodes $V = \{v_1, \cdots, v_N\}$ and a set of edges or arcs $E \subseteq V \times V$. We assume the graph is simple, e.g. no repeated edges and $(v_i, v_i) \notin E, \forall i$ no self loops. General directed graphs are considered. Denote the connectivity matrix as $A = [a_{ij}]$ with $a_{ij} > 0$ if $(v_j, v_i) \in E$ and $a_{ij} = 0$ otherwise. Note $a_{ii} = 0$. The set of neighbors of a node v_i is $N_i = \{v_j : (v_j, v_i) \in E\}$, i.e. the set of nodes with arcs incoming to v_i. Define the in-degree matrix as a diagonal matrix $D = [d_i]$ with $d_i = \sum_{j \in N_i} a_{ij}$ the weighted in-degree of node i (i.e. i-th row sum of A). Define the graph Laplacian matrix as $L = D - A$, which has all row sums equal to zero. Define $d_i^o = \sum_j a_{ji}$, the (weighted) out-degree of node i, that is the i-th column sum of A.

We assume the communication digraph is strongly connected, i.e. there is a directed path from v_i to v_j for all distinct nodes $v_i, v_j \in V$. Then A and L are irreducible (Qu, 2009). That is they are not cogredient to a lower triangular matrix, i.e., there is no permutation matrix U such that

$$L = U \begin{bmatrix} * & 0 \\ * & * \end{bmatrix} U^T \qquad (7)$$

The results of this research can easily be extended to graphs having a spanning tree (i.e. not necessarily strongly connected) using the Frobenius form Bernstein (2005) in (7).

Synchronization Control Problem

Consider node dynamics defined for the i-th node as

$$\dot{x}_i = f_i(x_i) + u_i + w_i(t) \qquad (8)$$

where $x_i(t) \in R$ is the state of node i, $u_i(t) \in R$ is the control input, and $w_i(t) \in R$ is a disturbance

acting upon each node. Note that each node may have its own distinct dynamics. Standard assumptions for existence of unique solutions are made, e.g. $f_i(x_i)$ either continuously differentiable or Lipschitz. The overall graph dynamics is

$$\dot{x} = f(x) + u + w \qquad (9)$$

where the overall (global) state vector is

$$x = \begin{bmatrix} x_1 & x_2 & \cdots & x_N \end{bmatrix}^T \in R^N,$$

global node dynamics vector is

$$f(x) = \begin{bmatrix} f_1(x_1) & f_2(x_2) & \cdots & f_N(x_N) \end{bmatrix}^T \in R^N,$$

input $u = \begin{bmatrix} u_1 & u_2 & \cdots & u_N \end{bmatrix}^T \in R^N$, and

$$w = \begin{bmatrix} w_1 & w_2 & \cdots & w_N \end{bmatrix}^T \in R^N.$$

- *Definition 1.* The *local neighborhood synchronization error* for node *i is* defined as (Khoo, et al., 2012; Li, et al., 2004):

$$e_i = \sum_{j \in N_i} a_{ij}(x_j - x_i) + b_i(x_0 - x_i) \qquad (10)$$

with pinning gains $b_i \geq 0$, and $b_i > 0$ for at least one i with $x_0 =$ leader node state. Then, $b_i \neq 0$ if and only if there exist an arc from the control node to the i-th node in G. We refer to the nodes *i* for which $b_i \neq 0$ as the pinned or controlled nodes.

Note that (10) represents the information that is available to any node *i* for control purposes.

The state of the leader or control node is $x_0(t)$ which satisfies the (generally nonautonomous) dynamics

$$\dot{x}_0 = f(x_0, t) \qquad (11)$$

A special case is the standard constant consensus value with $\dot{x}_0 = 0$. The drift term could represent, e.g. motion dynamics of the control node. That is, we assume that the control node can have a time-varying state.

The distributed control design problem confronted herein is as follows: Design control protocols for all the nodes in G to synchronize to the state of the control node, i.e. one requires $x_i(t) \to x_0(t)$, $\forall i$. It is assumed that the dynamics of the control node is unknown to any of the nodes in G. It is assumed further that both the node nonlinearities $f_i(.)$ and the node disturbances $w_i(t)$ are unknown. Thus, the synchronization protocols must be robust to unmodeled dynamics and unknown disturbances.

In fact, (11) is a command generator. Therefore, we are considering a distributed command generator tracker problem with unknown node dynamics and unknown command generator dynamics.

Synchronization Error Dynamics

From (10), the global error vector for network G is given by

$$e = -(L+B)(x - \underline{1}x_0) = -(L+B)(x - \underline{x}_0) \tag{12}$$

where,

$$e = \begin{bmatrix} e_1 & e_2 & \cdots & e_N \end{bmatrix}^T \in R^N$$

and $\underline{x}_0 = \underline{1}x_0 \in R^N$. $B \in R^{N \times N}$ is a diagonal matrix with diagonal entries b_i and $\underline{1}$ is the N-vector of ones.

Differentiating (12),

$$\dot{e} = -(L+B)(\dot{x} - \dot{\underline{x}}_0) = \\ -(L+B)\big[f(x) - \underline{f}(x_0,t) + u + w(t)\big] \tag{13}$$

where $\underline{f}(x_0,t) = \underline{1}f(x_0(t),t) \in R^N$.

Remark 1. *If the node states are vectors $x_i(t) \in R^n$ and $x_0(t) \in R^n$, then $x, e \in R^{nN}$ and (12) becomes*

$$\dot{e} = -\big[(L+B) \otimes I_n\big]\big[f(x) - \underline{f}(x_0,t) + u + w(t)\big] \tag{14}$$

with $\otimes$ the Kronecker product. To avoid obscuring the essentials, throughout the research we take the node states as scalars, $x_i(t) \in R$. If they are vectors, all of the following development is easily modified by introducing the Kronecker product terms as appropriate. In fact, a simulation example is presented for the case $x_i(t) \in R^2$, namely 1-D motion control for coupled inertial agents.

Remark 2. *Note that*

$$\delta = (x - \underline{x}_0) \tag{15}$$

is the disagreement vector in (Olfati-Saber & Murray, 2004). We do not use this error herein because it is a global quantity that cannot be computed locally at each node, in contrast to the local neighborhood error (10). As such, it is suitable for analysis but not for distributed controls design using Lyapunov techniques.

Remark 3. We take the communication digraph as strongly connected. Therefore, if $b_i \neq 0$ for at least one i then $(L+B)$ is an irreducibly diagonally dominant M-matrix and hence nonsingular (Qu, 2009).

An M-matrix is a square matrix having its off-diagonal entries nonpositive and all principal minors nonnegative. Based on Remark 3, the next result is therefore obvious from (12) and the Cauchy Schwartz inequality (see also Khoo et al., 2012).

Lemma 1. Let the graph be strongly connected and $B \neq 0$. Then

$$\|\delta\| \leq \|e\| / \underline{\sigma}(L+B) \tag{16}$$

with $\underline{\sigma}(L+B)$ the minimum singular value of $(L+B)$, and $e = 0$ if and only if the nodes synchronize, that is

$$x(t) = \underline{x}_0(t) \qquad (17)$$

Synchronization Control Design

The control problem confronted in this research is to design a control strategy so that local neighborhood error $e(t)$ is bounded to a small residual set. Then according to Lemma 1 all nodes synchronize so that $\|x_i(t) - x_0(t)\|$ is small $\forall i$. It is assumed that the dynamics $f(x_0, t)$ of the control node is unknown to any of the nodes in G. It is assumed further that both the node nonlinearities $f_i(.)$ and the node disturbances $w_i(t)$ are unknown. As such, the synchronization protocols must be robust to unmodeled dynamics and unknown disturbances.

To achieve this goal, define the input u_i for node i as

$$u_i = v_i - \hat{f}_i(x_i) \qquad (18)$$

where, $\hat{f}_i(x_i)$ is an estimate of $f_i(x_i)$ and $v_i(t)$ is an auxiliary control signal to be designed via Lyapunov techniques in Theorem 1. This can be written in vector form for the overall network of N nodes as

$$u = v - \hat{f}(x) \qquad (19)$$

where

$$v = \begin{bmatrix} v_1 & v_2 & \cdots & v_N \end{bmatrix}^T \in R^N.,$$

$$\hat{f}(x) = \begin{bmatrix} \hat{f}_1(x_1) & \hat{f}_2(x_2) & \cdots & \hat{f}_N(x_N) \end{bmatrix}^T \in R^N.$$

Then from (13) one gets

$$\dot{e} = -(L+B)\left[f(x) - \underline{f}(x_0, t) - \hat{f}(x) + v + w\right] \qquad (20)$$

Following the techniques in Khalil (2002), assume that the unknown nonlinearities in (8) are locally smooth and thus can be approximated on a compact set $\Omega_i \in R$ by

$$f_i(x_i) = W_i^T \varphi_i(x_i) + \varepsilon_i \qquad (21)$$

with $\varphi_i(x_i) \in R^{\nu_i}$ a suitable basis set of ν_i functions at each node i and $W_i \in R^{\nu_i}$ a set of unknown coefficients. According to the Neural Network (NN) approximation literature (Ge & Wang, 2004), a variety of basis sets can be selected, including sigmoids, gaussians, etc. There $\varphi_i(x_i) \in R^{\nu_i}$ is known as the NN activation function vector and $W_i \in R^{\nu_i}$ as the NN weight matrix. The ideal approximating weights $W_i \in R^{\nu_i}$ in (21) are assumed unknown. The intention is to select only a small number ν_i of NN neurons at each node (see Simulations).

To compensate for unknown nonlinearities, each node will maintain a neural network locally to keep track of the current estimates for the nonlinearities. The idea is to use the information of the states from the neighbors of node i to evaluate the performance of the current control protocol along with the current estimates of the nonlinear functions. Therefore, select the local node's approximation $\hat{f}_i(x_i)$ as

$$\hat{f}_i(x_i) = \hat{W}_i^T \varphi_i(x_i) \qquad (22)$$

where $\hat{W}_i \in R^{\nu_i}$ is a current estimate of the NN weights for node i, and ν_i is the number of NN neurons maintained at each node i. It will be shown in Theorem 1 how to select the estimates of the parameters $\hat{W}_i \in R^{\nu_i}$ using the local neighborhood synchronization errors (10) and it will also be discussed that the choice of $\hat{W}_i$ based on a proposed dynamic weight tuning law is a function of higher order states. Therefore, Equation (22) is true representation of pseudo higher order neural net.

The global node nonlinearity $f(x)$ for G is now written as

$$f(x) = W^T \varphi(x) + \varepsilon \qquad (23)$$

where $W^T = diag\{W_i^T\}$,

$$\varphi(x) = \left[\varphi_1^T(x_1) \quad \varphi_2^T(x_2) \quad \cdots \quad \varphi_N^T(x_N) \right]^T,$$

$$\varepsilon = \left[\varepsilon_1 \quad \varepsilon_2 \quad \cdots \quad \varepsilon_N \right]^T \in R^N.$$

The estimate $\hat{f}(x)$ is

$$\hat{f}(x) = \hat{W}^T \varphi(x) \qquad (24)$$

with $\hat{W}^T = diag\{\hat{W}_i^T\}$. Now, the error dynamics (20) takes the form $v(t)$

$$\dot{e} = -(L+B)\left[\tilde{f}(x) + v + w(t) - \underline{f}(x_0, t) \right] \qquad (25)$$

where the parameter estimation error is $\tilde{W}_i = W_i - \hat{W}_i$ and the function estimation error is

$$\tilde{f}(x) = f(x) - \hat{f}(x) = \tilde{W}^T \varphi(x) + \varepsilon \qquad (26)$$

with $\tilde{W}^T = W^T - \hat{W}^T$. Therefore, one obtains finally the error dynamics

$$\dot{e} = -(L+B)\left[\tilde{W}^T \varphi(x) + v + \varepsilon + w(t) - \underline{f}(x_0, t) \right] \qquad (27)$$

with $v(t)$ an auxiliary control yet to be designed.

LYAPUNOV DESIGN FOR NETWORKED SYSTEMS: DISTRIBUTED NN TUNING PROTOCOLS

Now we show how to select the auxiliary control and NN weight tuning laws such as to guarantee that all nodes synchronize to the desired control node signal, i.e., $x_i(t) \to x_0(t)$, $\forall i$. It is assumed that the dynamics $f(x_0, t)$ of the control node (which could represent its motion) are unknown to any of the nodes in G. It is assumed further that the node disturbances $w_i(t)$ are unknown. The Lyapunov analysis technique approach of Khalil (2002) is used, though there are some complications arising from the fact that $v(t)$ and the NN weight tuning laws must be implemented as distributed protocols. This entails a careful selection of the Lyapunov function.

The singular values of a matrix M are denoted $\sigma_i(M)$ with $\bar{\sigma}(M)$ the maximum singular value and $\underline{\sigma}(M)$ the minimum singular value. The Frobenius norm is $\|M\|_F = \sqrt{tr\{M^T M\}}$ with $tr\{\cdot\}$ the trace. The Frobenius inner product of two matrices is $\langle M_1, M_2 \rangle_F = \sqrt{tr\{M_1^T M_2\}}$.

The following Fact gives two standard results used in neural adaptive control (Khalil, 2002).

Fact 1. Let the nonlinearities $f(x)$ in (23) be smooth on a compact set $\Omega \in R^N$. Then:

- The NN estimation error $\varepsilon(x)$ is bounded by $\|\varepsilon\| \leq \varepsilon_M$ on Ω, with ε_M a fixed bound (Ge & Wang, 2004).
- *Weierstrass higher-order approximation theorem.* Select the activation functions $\varphi(x)$ as a complete independent basis (e.g. polynomials). Then NN estimation error $\varepsilon(x)$ converges uniformly to zero on Ω as $\nu_i \to \infty$, $i = 1, N$. That is $\forall \xi > 0$ there

exist $\bar{\nu}_i$, $i = 1, N$ such that $\nu_i > \bar{\nu}_i$, $\forall i$ implies $\sup_{x \in \Omega} \|\varepsilon(x)\| < \xi$ (Stone, 1948).

The following standard assumptions are required. Although the bounds mentioned are assumed to exist, they are not used in the design and do not have to be known. They appear in the error bounds in the proof of Theorem 1 (Though not required, if desired, standard methods can be used to estimate these bounds including [Rovithakis, 2000]).

Assumption 1.

- The unknown disturbance w_i is bounded for all i. Thus the overall disturbance vector w is also bounded by $\|w\| \le w_M$ with w_M a fixed bound.
- The unknown consensus variable dynamics $\underline{f}(x_0, t)$ is bounded so that $\|\underline{f}(x_0, t)\| \le F_M$, $\forall t$.
- The target trajectory is in a bounded region, e.g. $\|x_0(t)\| < X_0$, $\forall t$, with X_0 a constant bound.
- Unknown ideal NN weight matrix W is bounded by $\|W\|_F \le W_M$.
- NN activation functions φ_i are bounded $\forall i$, so that one can write for the overall network that $\|\varphi\| \le \phi_M$.

Assumption 1b means that the maximum velocity of the leader node is unknown but bounded above.

The next definitions extend standard notions (Khalil, 2002; Lewis, Jagannathan, & Yesildirek, 1999) to synchronization for distributed systems.

- *Definition 2.* The global neighborhood error $e(t) \in R^N$ is Uniformly Ultimately Bounded (UUB) if there exists a compact set

$\Omega \subset R^N$ so that $\forall e(t_0) \in \Omega$ there exists a bound B and a time $t_f(B, e(t_0))$, both independent of $t_0 \ge 0$, such that $\|e(t)\| \le B$ $\forall t \ge t_0 + t_f$.

- *Definition 3.* The control node trajectory $x_0(t)$ given by (11) is cooperative UUB with respect to solutions of node dynamics (8) if there exist a compact set $\Omega \subset R$ so that $\forall (x_i(t_0) - x_0(t_0)) \in \Omega$ there exist a bound B and a time $t_f(B, (x_i(t_0) - x_i(t_0)))$, both independent of $t_0 \ge 0$, such that $\|x_i(t) - x_0(t)\| \le B$ $\forall i$, $\forall t \ge t_0 + t_f$.

The next key constructive result is needed. An M − matrix is a square matrix having nonpositive off-diagonal elements and all principal minors nonnegative.

Lemma 2. (Qu, 2009) *Let* L be irreducible and B have at least one diagonal entry $b_i > 0$. Then $(L + B)$ is a nonsingular M − matrix. Define

$$q = \begin{bmatrix} q_1 & q_2 & \cdots & q_N \end{bmatrix}^T = (L + B)^{-1} \underline{1} \qquad (28)$$

$$P = \operatorname{diag}\{p_i\} \equiv \operatorname{diag}\{1 / q_i\} \qquad (29)$$

Then $P > 0$ and the matrix Q defined as

$$Q = P(L + B) + (L + B)^T P \qquad (30)$$

is positive definite.

The main result of this research is given by the following theorem, which shows how to design the control protocols (18) and tune the NN weights such that the local neighborhood cooperative errors for all nodes are UUB, which implies consensus variable $x_0(t)$ is cooperative UUB, thereby showing synchronization and cooperative stability for the whole network G.

Theorem 1: Distributed Adaptive Control Protocol for Synchronization. Consider the networked systems given by (8), (9) under Assumption 1. Let the communication digraph be strongly connected. Select the auxiliary control signals in (18) as $v_i(t) = ce_i(t)$ with the neighborhood synchronization errors $e_i(t)$ defined in (10) so that the local node control protocols are given by

$$u_i = ce_i - \hat{f}_i(x_i) = c \sum_{j \in N_i} a_{ij} (x_j - x_i)$$
$$+ cb_i (x_0 - x_i) \quad - \hat{W}_i^T \varphi_i(x_i) \tag{31}$$

or

$$u = ce - \hat{W}^T \varphi(x) \tag{32}$$

with control gains $c > 0$. Let local node NN tuning laws be given by

$$\dot{\hat{W}}_i = -F_i \varphi_i e_i^T p_i (d_i + b_i) - \kappa F_i \hat{W}_i \tag{33}$$

with $F_i = \Pi_i I_{\nu_i}$, the $\nu_i \times \nu_i$ identity matrix, $\Pi_i > 0$ and $\kappa > 0$ scalar tuning gains, and $p_i > 0$ defined in (29). Select $\kappa = \frac{1}{2} c\underline{\sigma}(Q)$ and the control gain c so that

$$c\underline{\sigma}(Q) > \frac{1}{2} \phi_M \bar{\sigma}(P) \bar{\sigma}(A) \tag{34}$$

with P>0, Q>0 the matrices in Lemma 2 and A the graph adjacency matrix. Then there exist numbers of neurons $\bar{\nu}_i, i = 1, N$ such that for $\nu_i > \bar{\nu}_i, \forall i$ the overall local cooperative error vector $e(t)$ and the NN weight estimation errors $\tilde{W}$ are UUB, with practical bounds given by (52) and (53), respectively. Therefore, the control node trajectory $x_0(t)$ is cooperative UUB and all nodes synchronize to $x_0(t)$. Moreover, the bounds on local consensus errors (10) can be made small by increasing the control gains c.

Proof

Part a. We claim that for a fixed $\varepsilon_M > 0$, there exist numbers of neurons $\bar{\nu}_i, i = 1, N$ such that for $\nu_i > \bar{\nu}_i, \forall i$ the NN approximation error is bounded by $\|\varepsilon\| \leq \varepsilon_M$. The claim is proven in Part b of the proof. Consider now the Lyapunov function candidate

$$V = \frac{1}{2} e^T P e + \frac{1}{2} tr \left\{ \tilde{W}^T F^{-1} \tilde{W} \right\} \tag{35}$$

with *e(t)* the vector of local neighborhood cooperative errors (10), $0 < P = P^T \in R^{N \times N}$ the diagonal matrix defined in (29), and F^{-1} a block diagonal matrix defined in terms of $F = diag\{F_i\}$. Then,

$$\dot{V} = e^T P \dot{e} + tr \left\{ \tilde{W}^T F^{-1} \dot{\tilde{W}} \right\} \tag{36}$$

and from (27)

$$\dot{V} = -e^T P(L+B) \left[\tilde{W}^T \varphi(x) + ce + \varepsilon + w - \underline{f}(x_0, t) \right]$$
$$+ tr \left\{ \tilde{W}^T F^{-1} \dot{\tilde{W}} \right\} \tag{37}$$

$$\dot{V} = -ce^T P(L+B)e - e^T P(L+B) \left\{ \varepsilon + w - \underline{f}(x_0, t) \right\}$$
$$- e^T P(L+B) \tilde{W}^T \varphi(x) + tr \left\{ \tilde{W}^T F^{-1} \dot{\tilde{W}} \right\} \tag{38}$$

$$\dot{V} = -ce^T P(L+B)e - e^T P(L+B) \left\{ \varepsilon + w - \underline{f}(x_0, t) \right\}$$
$$+ tr \left\{ \tilde{W}^T \left(F^{-1} \dot{\tilde{W}} - \varphi e^T P(L+B) \right) \right\} \tag{39}$$

$$\dot{V} = -ce^T P(L+B)e - e^T P(L+B) \left\{ \varepsilon + w - \underline{f}(x_0, t) \right\}$$
$$+ tr \left\{ \tilde{W}^T \left(F^{-1} \dot{\tilde{W}} - \varphi e^T P(D+B-A) \right) \right\} \tag{40}$$

Since L is irreducible and B has at least one diagonal entry $b_i > 0$, then $(L+B)$ is a nonsingular M − matrix. Defining therefore Q according to (30) one has

$$\dot{V} = -\frac{1}{2}ce^T Qe - e^T P(L+B)\{\varepsilon + w - \underline{f}(x_0, t)\}$$
$$+tr\left\{\tilde{W}^T\left(F^{-1}\dot{\hat{W}} - \varphi e^T P(D+B)\right)\right\} + tr\left\{\tilde{W}^T \varphi e^T PA\right\}$$

$$(41)$$

Adopt now the NN weight tuning law (33) or $\dot{\hat{W}}_i = F_i \varphi_i e_i^T p_i (d_i + b_i) + \kappa F_i \hat{W}_i$. Since P and $(D+B)$ are diagonal and $\dot{\hat{W}}$ has the form in (24), one has

$$\dot{V} = -\frac{1}{2}ce^T Qe - e^T P(L+B)\{\varepsilon + w(t) - \underline{f}(x_0, t)\}$$
$$+\kappa tr\left\{\tilde{W}^T(W - \tilde{W})\right\} + tr\left\{\tilde{W}^T \varphi e^T PA\right\}$$

$$(42)$$

Therefore, for fixed $\varepsilon_M > 0$

$$\dot{V} \leq -\frac{1}{2}c\underline{\sigma}(Q)\|e\|^2 + \|e\|\bar{\sigma}(P)\bar{\sigma}(L+B)(\varepsilon_M + w_M + F_M)$$
$$+\kappa W_M\|\tilde{W}\|_F - \kappa\|\tilde{W}\|_F^2 + \|\tilde{W}\|_F\|e\|\phi_M\bar{\sigma}(P)\bar{\sigma}(A)$$

$$(43)$$

Then

$$\dot{V} \leq -\begin{bmatrix}\|e\| & \|\tilde{W}\|_F\end{bmatrix}$$
$$\begin{bmatrix}\frac{1}{2}c\underline{\sigma}(Q) & -\frac{1}{2}\phi_M\bar{\sigma}(P)\bar{\sigma}(A) \\ -\frac{1}{2}\phi_M\bar{\sigma}(P)\bar{\sigma}(A) & \kappa\end{bmatrix}\begin{bmatrix}\|e\| \\ \|\tilde{W}\|_F\end{bmatrix}$$
$$+\begin{bmatrix}B_M\bar{\sigma}(P)\bar{\sigma}(L+B) & \kappa W_M\end{bmatrix}\begin{bmatrix}\|e\| \\ \|\tilde{W}\|_F\end{bmatrix}$$

with $B_M \equiv \varepsilon_M + w_M + F_M$. Write this as

$$\dot{V} \leq -z^T Rz + r^T z \qquad (44)$$

Then $\dot{V} \leq 0$ if R is positive definite and

$$\|z\| > \frac{\|r\|}{\underline{\sigma}(R)} \qquad (45)$$

According to (35) one has

$$\frac{1}{2}\underline{\sigma}(P)\|e\|^2$$
$$+\frac{1}{2\Pi_{max}}\|\tilde{W}\|_F^2 \leq V \leq \frac{1}{2}\bar{\sigma}(P)\|e\|^2 + \frac{1}{2\Pi_{min}}\|\tilde{W}\|_F^2$$

$$(46)$$

$$\frac{1}{2}\begin{bmatrix}\|e\| & \|\tilde{W}\|_F\end{bmatrix}\begin{bmatrix}\underline{\sigma}(P) & 0 \\ 0 & \frac{1}{\Pi_{max}}\end{bmatrix}\begin{bmatrix}\|e\| \\ \|\tilde{W}\|_F\end{bmatrix} \leq V \leq$$
$$\frac{1}{2}\begin{bmatrix}\|e\| & \|\tilde{W}\|_F\end{bmatrix}\begin{bmatrix}\bar{\sigma}(P) & 0 \\ 0 & \frac{1}{\Pi_{min}}\end{bmatrix}\begin{bmatrix}\|e\| \\ \|\tilde{W}\|_F\end{bmatrix}$$

$$(47)$$

with Π_{min}, Π_{max} the minimum and maximum values of Π_i. Define variables to write $\frac{1}{2}z^T \underline{S}z \leq V \leq \frac{1}{2}z^T \bar{S}z$. Then

$$\frac{1}{2}\underline{\sigma}(\underline{S})\|z\|^2 \leq V \leq \frac{1}{2}\bar{\sigma}(\bar{S})\|z\|^2 \qquad (48)$$

Therefore

$$V > \frac{1}{2}\frac{\bar{\sigma}(\bar{S})\|r\|^2}{\underline{\sigma}^2(R)} \qquad (49)$$

implies (45).

One can write the minimum singular values of R as

$$\underline{\sigma}(R)$$

$$=\frac{\left(\frac{1}{2}c\underline{\sigma}(Q)+\kappa\right)-\sqrt{\left[\frac{1}{2}c\underline{\sigma}(Q)-\kappa\right]^2+\frac{1}{4}\varphi_M^2\bar{\sigma}^2(P)\bar{\sigma}^2(A)}}{2} \tag{50}$$

To obtain a cleaner form for $\underline{\sigma}(R)$, select $\kappa=\frac{1}{2}c\underline{\sigma}(Q)$. Then

$$\underline{\sigma}(R)=\frac{c\underline{\sigma}(Q)-\frac{1}{2}\varphi_M\bar{\sigma}(P)\bar{\sigma}(A)}{2} \tag{51}$$

which is positive under condition (34). Therefore, $z(t)$ is UUB (Khalil, 2002).

In view of the fact that, for any vector z, one has $\|z\|_1\geq\|z\|_2\geq\cdots\geq\|z\|_\infty$, sufficient conditions for (45) are

$$\|e\|>\frac{B_M\bar{\sigma}(P)\bar{\sigma}(L+B)+\kappa W_M}{\underline{\sigma}(R)} \tag{52}$$

or

$$\|\tilde{W}\|>\frac{B_M\bar{\sigma}(P)\bar{\sigma}(L+B)+\kappa W_M}{\underline{\sigma}(R)} \tag{53}$$

Now Lemma 1 shows that the consensus errors $\delta(t)$ are UUB. Then $x_0(t)$ is cooperative UUB. Note that increasing gain c decreases the bound in (52).

Part b. According to (44)
$\dot{V}\leq-\underline{\sigma}(R)\|z\|^2+\|r\|\|z\|$ and according to (48)

$$\dot{V}\leq-\alpha V+\beta\sqrt{V} \tag{54}$$

with $\alpha\equiv 2\underline{\sigma}(R)/\bar{\sigma}(\bar{S})$, $\beta\equiv\sqrt{2}\|r\|/\sqrt{\underline{\sigma}(S)}$. Thence

$$\sqrt{V(t)}\leq\sqrt{V(0)}e^{-\alpha t/2}+\tfrac{\beta}{\alpha}(1-e^{-\alpha t/2})\leq\sqrt{V(0)}+\tfrac{\beta}{\alpha}$$

Using (48) one has

$$\|e(t)\|\leq\|z(t)\|\leq\sqrt{\frac{\bar{\sigma}(\bar{S})}{\underline{\sigma}(S)}}\sqrt{\|e(0)\|^2+\|\tilde{W}(0)\|_F^2}+\frac{\bar{\sigma}(\bar{S})}{\underline{\sigma}(S)}\frac{\|r\|}{\underline{\sigma}(R)}$$

Then (12) shows that

$$\|x(t)\|\leq\frac{1}{\underline{\sigma}(L+B)}\|e(t)\|+\sqrt{N}\|x_0(t)\|$$

$$\|x(t)\|\leq\frac{1}{\underline{\sigma}(L+B)}\left[\sqrt{\frac{\bar{\sigma}(\bar{S})}{\underline{\sigma}(S)}}\sqrt{\|e(0)\|^2+\|\tilde{W}(0)\|_F^2}+\frac{\bar{\sigma}(\bar{S})}{\underline{\sigma}(S)}\frac{\|r\|}{\underline{\sigma}(R)}\right]+\sqrt{N}X_0\equiv r_0 \tag{55}$$

where $\|r\|\leq B_M\bar{\sigma}(P)\bar{\sigma}(L+B)+\kappa W_M$. Therefore, the state is contained for all times $t\geq 0$ in a compact set $\Omega_0=\{x(t)\mid\|x(t)\|\leq r_0\}$. According to the Weierstrass approximation theorem, given any NN approximation error bound ε_M there exist numbers of neurons $\bar{\nu}_i, i=1,N$ such that $\nu_i>\bar{\nu}_i, \forall i$ implies $\sup_{x\in\Omega}\|\varepsilon(x)\|<\varepsilon_M$.

Discussion

If either (52) or (53) holds, the Lyapunov derivative is negative and V decreases. Therefore, these provide practical bounds for the neighborhood synchronization error and the NN weight estimation error.

Part a of the proof contains the new material relevant to cooperative control of distributed systems. Part b of the proof is standard in the neural adaptive control literature (Ge & Wang, 2004; Lewis, et al., 1999). Note that the set defined by (55) depends on the initial errors and the graph structural properties. Therefore, proper accommodation of large initial errors requires a larger number of neurons in the NN. The proof also reveals that, for a given number of neurons, the admissible initial condition set is bounded (Lewis, et al., 1999).

It is important to select the Lyapunov function candidate V in (35) in terms of locally available variables, e.g. the local neighborhood synchronization error $e(t)$ in (10) and (12). This means that any local control signals $v_i(t)$ and NN tuning laws developed in the proof are distributed and hence implementable at each node. The use of the Frobenius norm in the Lyapunov function is also instrumental, since it gives rise to Frobenius inner products in the proof that only depend on trace terms, where only the diagonal terms are important. In fact, the Frobenius norm is ideally suited for the design of distributed protocols. Equation (29) shows that P in (35) is chosen diagonal. This is important in allowing selection of the NN tuning law (33) that leads to expression (42).

The result of this Lyapunov design is the local node NN tuning law (33) which depends on the local cooperative error $e_i(t)$. By contrast, standard NN tuning laws (Lewis, et al., 1999) depend on a global tracking error, equivalent to the disagreement error vector $\delta = \left(x - \underline{x}_0 \right)$ which is not available at each node. Note that (33) is a distributed version of the sigma-mod tuning law of P. Ioannou. The parameters p_i in (33) are computed as in Lemma 2, which requires global information of the graph. As such, they are not known locally at the nodes. However, NN tuning parameters $f_i > 0$ are arbitrary, so that $p_i f_i > 0$ can be arbitrary.

Each node maintains a local NN to provide estimates of its nonlinear dynamics. The local nature of the NNs, as reflected in the distributed

tuning protocols (33), means that the number of neurons ν_i at each node can be selected fairly small (see the Simulations). It is not necessary to select a large centralized NN to approximate the full global vector of nonlinearities $f(x)$ in (20). The total number of neurons in the network is

$$\nu = \sum_{i=1}^{N} \nu_i \ .$$

The unknown dynamics of the control node $f(x_0, t)$ in (11) (which could be, e.g., motion) are treated as a disturbance to be rejected. The proof shows that even though these dynamics are unknown, synchronization of all nodes to the generally time-varying control node state $x_0(t)$ is guaranteed, within a small error. The simulations corroborate this.

Note that the node control gains c are similar to the pinning gain parameters defined in Wang and Chen (2002). According to (52) and (51) increasing these gains results in a smaller synchronization error.

Corollary 1. Given the setup in Theorem 1, suppose the NN estimation errors are equal to zero. Then under the protocol (31) the local neighborhood errors converge to the residual set defined by

$$\|e\| \geq 2B_M \frac{\overline{\sigma}(P)\overline{\sigma}(L+B)}{c \ \underline{\sigma}(Q)} \tag{56}$$

with $B_M = d_M + F_M$ the sum of the disturbance bound and the bound on the consensus variable (control node) dynamics (Assumption 1) and P, Q defined in Lemma 2. The synchronization error norm $\|e(t)\|$ convergences to this set exponentially as $\|e(0)\| e^{-\alpha t/2}$ with convergence rate

$$\alpha = c \frac{\underline{\sigma}(Q)}{\overline{\sigma}(P)} \tag{57}$$

The speed of synchronization can be increased by increasing the control gains c in protocol (31).

Proof: If the NN estimation errors are zero, then according to the proof of Theorem 1 one has

$$V = \tfrac{1}{2} e^T P e$$

$$\dot{V} \le -\tfrac{1}{2} c \, \underline{\sigma}(Q) \|e\|^2 + \|e\| \bar{\sigma}(P) \bar{\sigma}(L+P) B_M$$

which is negative if (56) holds. One has for large $\|e(t)\|$, approximately

$$V = \tfrac{1}{2} e^T P e$$

$$\dot{V} \le -\tfrac{1}{2} c \, \underline{\sigma}(Q) \|e\|^2$$

So that using standard techniques one has

$$\dot{V} \le -\alpha V$$

with α given by (57). Therefore $V(t) \le V(0) e^{-\alpha t}$ and the errors converge at the rate $\|e(0)\| e^{-\alpha t/2}$.

According to this corollary, the upper bounds on the residual local neighborhood errors depend graph properties through the inequalities of Lemma 3 involving $\bar{\sigma}(L+B)$.

Remark 4. If the node states are vectors $x_i \in R^n$ and $x_0 \in R^n$, the control protocols (31) and the error bounds given by (52) or (53) will remain unaltered. The NN weight tuning protocols will then be given by

$$\dot{\hat{W}}_i = -F_i \varphi_i e_i^T \left(p_i (d_i + b_i) \otimes I_n \right) - \kappa F_i \hat{W}_i$$
(58)

Remark 5. It is easy to extend the Theorem 1 to the case where the digraph only contains a spanning tree using the Frobenius form Qu (2009).

Relation of Error Bounds to Graph Structural Properties

According to the bounds (52) and (53) both the synchronization error and the NN weight estima-

tion error increase with the maximum singular values $\bar{\sigma}(A)$, $\bar{\sigma}(L+B)$, and $\bar{\sigma}(P)$. It is desired to obtain bounds on these singular values in terms of graph properties. Recall that $d_i = \sum_{j \in N_i} a_{ij}$ is the (weighted) in-degree of node i, that is, the i-*th* row sum of adjacency matrix A, and $d_i^o = \sum_j a_{ji}$, the (weighted) out-degree of node i, that is the i-*th* column sum of A. It is direct to obtain upper bounds on these singular values in terms of graph properties. Recalling several results from (Bernstein, 2005) one can easily show the following.

Lemma 3: Bounds on Maximum Singular Values of A and *(L+B)*

$$\bar{\sigma}(A) \le \sum_{i=1}^{N} d_i \equiv vol(G)$$

$$\bar{\sigma}(A) \le \sqrt{\max_i(d_i) \times \max_i(d_i^o)}$$

$$\bar{\sigma}(L+B) \le \sum_{i-1}^{N} (b_i + d_i + d_i^o)$$

$$\bar{\sigma}(L+B) \le \sqrt{\max_i(b_i + d_i + d_i^o) \times \max_i(b_i + 2d_i)}$$

∎

These results show that the residual synchronization error is bounded above in terms of the graph complexity expressed in terms of volumes and maximum degree sums.

SIMULATION RESULTS

This section will show the effectiveness of the distributed adaptive protocol of Theorem 1 on several fronts. First, it is compared to standard pinning control (Li, et al., 2004; Wang & Chen, 2002). Next, it is shown that the protocol effectively enforces synchronization, using only a few NN nodes at each node, for unknown nonlinear control node dynamics, unknown nonlinear node dynamics, and unknown disturbances at each node.

For this set of simulations, consider the 5-node strongly connected digraph structure in Figure 2 with a leader node connected to node 3. The edge weights and the pinning gain in (10) were taken equal to 1.

Case 1: Nonlinear Node Dynamics and Disturbances

For Figure 2, consider the following node dynamics

$$
\begin{aligned}
\dot{x}_1 &= x_1^3 + u_1 + d_1 \\
\dot{x}_2 &= x_2^2 + u_2 + d_2 \\
\dot{x}_3 &= x_3^4 + u_3 + d_3 \\
\dot{x}_4 &= x_4 + u_4 + d_4 \\
\dot{x}_5 &= x_5^5 + u_5 + d_5
\end{aligned}
\tag{59}
$$

which has nonlinearities and disturbances at each node, all assumed unknown. The disturbance at i-th node is $w_i = 0.1 \times \mathrm{randn}(1) \times \cos(t)$ (we use MATLAB symbology).

Consider now the control protocol of Theorem 1. Take the desired consensus value of $x_0 = 2$, i.e. $\dot{x}_0 = f(x_0, t) = 0$. The following parameters are used in the simulation. Control gain $c = 300$, number of neurons at each node:

Figure 2. Five node SC digraph with one leader node

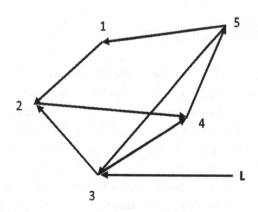

$\nu_i = 3$, $\kappa = 0.8$, $F_i = 1500$. Figure 3 plots the disagreement vector $\delta = (x - \underline{x}_0)$ and the NN estimation errors $f_i(x_i) - \hat{f}_i(x_i)$. The steady-state consensus error is approximately zero. Table 1 shows that at steady-state, the NNs closely estimate the nonlinearities (That is, the nonlinearities in [59] evaluated at the consensus value of $x_0 = 2$. Recall there are small random disturbances $w_i(t)$ present).

Case 2: Synchronization of Second-Order Dynamics

Consider the node dynamics for node i given by the second-order dynamics

$$
\begin{aligned}
\dot{q}_{1_i} &= q_{2_i} + u_{1i} \\
\dot{q}_{2_i} &= J_i^{-1}\left[u_{2i} - B_i^r q_{2_i} - M_i g l_i \sin(q_{1_i})\right]
\end{aligned}
\tag{60}
$$

where $q_i = \left[q_{1_i}, q_{2_i}\right]^T \in R^2$ is the state vector, J_i is the total inertia of the link and the motor, B_i^r is overall damping coefficient, M_i is total mass, g is gravitational acceleration and l_i is the distance from the joint axis to the link center of mass for node. J_i, B_i^r, M_i, g and l_i are considered unknown and may be different for each node. This is similar to the inertial agent dynamics $J_i \ddot{q}_i + B_i^r \dot{q}_i + M_i g l_i \sin(q_i) = u_i$; however, here we take an input into each state component, so it

Table 1. Steady-state values

$f(x)$	$\hat{f}(x) = \mathrm{Est}\left(f(x)\right)$
8	7.9835
4	3.8701
16	15.8063
2	1.8051
32	31.5649

Figure 3. Consensus errors and NN weight estimation errors with distributed adaptive control

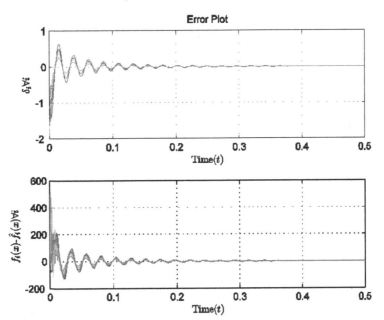

is not the same as second-order consensus. It is easy to treat second-order consensus using the method of this research and it will be done in another research.

The desired target node dynamics is taken as the inertial system

$$m_0 \ddot{q}_0 + d_0 \dot{q}_0 + k_o q_0 = u_0 \qquad (61)$$

with known m_0, d_0, k_0. Select the feedback linearization input

$$u_0 = -\left[K_1 \left(q_0 - \sin(\beta t) \right) + K_2 \left(\dot{q}_0 - \beta \cos(\beta t) \right) \right]$$
$$+ d_0 \dot{q}_0 + k_0 q_0 + \beta^2 m_0 \sin(\beta t)$$
$$(62)$$

for a constant $\beta > 0$. Then, the target motion $q_0(t)$ tracks the desired reference trajectory $\sin(\beta t)$.

The cooperative adaptive control law of Theorem 1 was simulated, including the Kronecker product, with I_2 as in Figure 4 verifies the fact that every node dynamics synchronizes to the

target node dynamics. Figure 5 is the phase plane plot for all the nodes along with the target node. It can be seen that the phase plane trajectories of all the nodes, started with different initial conditions, synchronize to the target node phase plane trajectory, finally forming a lissajous pattern.

CONCLUSION

A nonlinear adaptive control technique using pseudo higher order neural network has been adopted for designing distributed control for generalized multiagent system with unknown dynamics. The tracker dynamics are also considered unknown. Pinning control is used for defining the distributed neighborhood error, which assures that the connected agents only need to use limited information for overall system stability. In addition, each agent including the tracker has its own pseudo higher order neural net identification strategy to determine the associated unknown dynamics. Using the Lyapunov theory, a thorough discussion on state boundedness is also established. Based on

Figure 4. State synchronization errors δ_i and NN estimation errors

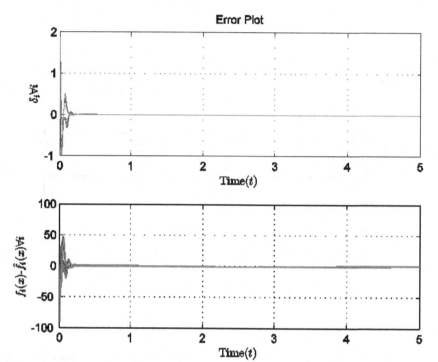

Figure 5. Synchronized motion phase plane plot

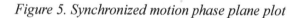

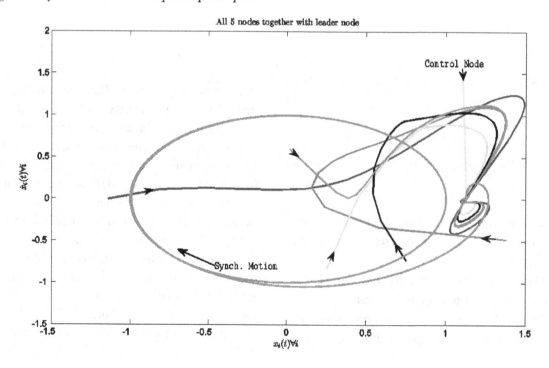

the theory and information provided in this chapter, one can easily draw the roadmap for second order and then higher order multiagent systems with unknown dynamics while communicating via directed graph topology.

ACKNOWLEDGMENT

This work was supported by the National Science Foundation ECS-0801330, the Army Research Office W91NF-05-1-0314, and the Air Force Office of Scientific Research FA9550-09-1-0278.

REFERENCES

Bernstein, D. S. (2005). *Matrix mathematics*. Princeton, NJ: Princeton University Press.

Chopra, N., & Spong, M. W. (2006). Passivity-based control of multi-agent systems. In *Advances in Robot Control* (pp. 107–134). Berlin, Germany: Springer. doi:10.1007/978-3-540-37347-6_6

Chopra, N., & Spong, M. W. (2009). On exponential synchronization of Kuramoto oscillators. *IEEE Transactions on Automatic Control, 54*(2), 353–357. doi:10.1109/TAC.2008.2007884

Fax, J. A., & Murray, R. M. (2004). Information flow and cooperative control of vehicle formations. *IEEE Transactions on Automatic Control, 49*(9), 1465–1476. doi:10.1109/TAC.2004.834433

Ge, S. S., & Wang, C. (2004). Adaptive neural control of uncertain MIMO nonlinear systems. *IEEE Transactions on Neural Networks, 15*(3), 674–692. doi:10.1109/TNN.2004.826130

Han, J., Li, M., & Guo, L. (2006). Soft control on collective behavior of a group of autonomous agents by a shill agent. *Journal of Systems Science and Complexity, 19*, 54–62. doi:10.1007/s11424-006-0054-z

Hornik, K., Stinchombe, M., & White, H. (1989). Multilayer feedforward networks are universal approximations. *Neural Networks, 20*, 359–366. doi:10.1016/0893-6080(89)90020-8

Hou, Z.-G., Cheng, L., & Tan, M. (2009). Decentralized robust adaptive control for the multiagent system consensus problem using neural networks. *IEEE Transactions on Systems, Man, and Cybernetics . Part B, 39*(3), 636–647.

Hui, Q., & Haddad, W. M. (2008). Distributed nonlinear control algorithms for network consensus. *Automatica, 44*, 2375–2381. doi:10.1016/j.automatica.2008.01.011

Igelnik, B., & Pao, Y. H. (1995). Stochastic choice of basis functions in adaptive function approximation and the functional-link net. *IEEE Transactions on Neural Networks, 6*, 1320–1329. doi:10.1109/72.471375

Jadbabaie, A., Lin, J., & Morse, S. (2003). Coordination of groups of mobile autonomous agents using nearest neighbor rules. *IEEE Transactions on Automatic Control, 48*(6), 988–1001. doi:10.1109/TAC.2003.812781

Jiang, T., & Baras, J. S. (2009). *Graph algebraic interpretation of trust establishment in autonomic networks. Preprint Wiley Journal of Networks*. New York, NY: Wiley.

Karayiannis, N. B., & Venetsanopoulos, A. N. (1993). *Artificial neural networks: Learning algorithms, performance evaluation, and applications*. Berlin, Germany: Springer.

Khalil, H. K. (2002). *Nonlinear systems* (3rd ed.). Upper Saddle River, N.J: Prentice Hall.

Khoo, S., Xie, L., & Man, Z. (2009). Robust finite-time consensus tracking algorithm for multirobot systems. *IEEE Transaction on Mechatronics, 14*(2), 219–228. doi:10.1109/TMECH.2009.2014057

Kosmatopoulos, E. B., Polycarpou, M. M., Christodoulou, M. A., & Ioannou, P. A. (1995). High-order neural network structures for identification of dynamical systems. *IEEE Transactions on Neural Networks*, 6(2), 422–431. doi:10.1109/72.363477

Kuramoto, Y. (1975). Self-entrainment of a population of coupled non-linear oscillators. *Lecture Notes in Physics*, 39, 420–422. doi:10.1007/BFb0013365

Lewis, F., Jagannathan, S., & Yesildirek, A. (1999). *Neural network control of robot manipulators and nonlinear systems*. London, UK: Taylor and Francis.

Li, X., Wang, X., & Chen, G. (2004). Pinning a complex dynamical network to its equilibrium. *IEEE Transactions on Circuits and Systems*, 51(10), 2074–2087. doi:10.1109/TCSI.2004.835655

Li, Z., Duan, Z., & Chen, G. (2009). Consensus of multi-agent systems and synchronization of complex networks: A unified viewpoint. *IEEE Transactions on Circuits and Systems*, 57(1), 213–224.

Lu, J., & Chen, G. (2005). A time-varying complex dynamical network model and its controlled synchronization criteria. *IEEE Transactions on Automatic Control*, 50(6), 841–846. doi:10.1109/TAC.2005.849233

Olfati-Saber, R., & Murray, R. M. (2004). Consensus problems in networks of agents with switching topology and time-delays. *IEEE Transactions on Automatic Control*, 49(9), 1520–1533. doi:10.1109/TAC.2004.834113

Qu, Z. (2009). *Cooperative control of dynamical systems: Applications to autonomous vehicles*. New York, NY: Springer-Verlag. doi:10.1109/TAC.2008.920232

Ren, W., & Beard, R. W. (2005). Consensus seeking in multiagent systems under dynamically changing interaction topologies. *IEEE Transactions on Automatic Control*, 50(5), 655–661. doi:10.1109/TAC.2005.846556

Rovithakis, G. A. (2000). Paper. In *Proceedings of the IEEE International Symposium on Intelligent Control*, (pp. 7-12). Patras, Greece: IEEE Press.

Spanos, D. P., Olfati-Saber, R., & Murray, R. M. (2005). *Dynamic consensus on mobile networks*. Paper presented at the 2005 IFAC World Congress. Prague, Czech Republic.

Stone, M. H. (1948). The generalized weierstrass approximation theorem. *Mathematics Magazine*, 21(4-5), 167–184, 237–254. doi:10.2307/3029750

Strogatz, S. (2000). From Kuramoto to Crawford: Exploring the onset of synchronization in populations of coupled oscillators. *Physica D. Nonlinear Phenomena*, 143, 1–20. doi:10.1016/S0167-2789(00)00094-4

Tsitsiklis, J. N. (1984). *Problems in decentralized decision making and computation*. (Ph.D. Dissertation). Massachusetts Institute of Technology. Cambridge, MA.

Vicsek, T., Czirok, A., Jacob, E. B., Cohen, I., & Schochet, O. (1995). Novel type of phase transitions in a system of self-driven particles. *Physical Review Letters*, 75, 1226–1229. doi:10.1103/PhysRevLett.75.1226

Wang, X. F., & Chen, G. (2002). Pinning control of scale-free dynamical networks. *Physica A*, 310(3), 521–531. doi:10.1016/S0378-4371(02)00772-0

Wu, C. W. (2007). *Synchronization in complex networks of nonlinear dynamical systems*. Singapore: World Scientific. doi:10.1142/6570

KEY TERMS AND DEFINITIONS

Agreement: Nodes v_i, v_j in a network agree if $x_i = x_j$.

Asymptotic χ-Consensus: A protocol asymptotically solves the χ-Consensus problem if there exists an asymptotically stable equilibrium x^* of the closed-loop system satisfying $x_i^* = \chi(x(0))$ for all i.

Asymptotic Consensus Problem: Nodes achieve consensus asymptotically if, for all initial conditions $x_i(0)$, $\lim_{t \to \infty} \left\| x_i(t) - x_j(t) \right\| = 0, \forall i, j$.

Average Consensus Problem: Find a distributed protocol to compute

$$\chi(x(0)) = Ave(x(0)) = \frac{1}{N} \sum_{i=1, N} x_i(0).$$

χ-Consensus Problem: Let $\chi(x_1, x_2, \cdots, x_N) : R^N \to R$. The χ-Consensus problem is to find a way to compute the global quantity $\chi(x(0))$ using a distributed (local) protocol.

Consensus Problem: Nodes have reached consensus if $x_i = x_j, \forall i, j$. Usually refers to constant steady-state value.

Diagonally Dominant Matrix: A $n \times n$ matrix (may be complex) $\bar{L} = (l_{ij})$ is diagonally dominant if $|l_{ii}| \geq \sum_{\substack{j=1 \\ i \neq j}}^{n} |l_{ij}|, \forall 0 \leq i \leq n$. When the equality sign goes away, then $\bar{L}$ can be called as strictly diagonally dominant.

Doubly Diagonally Dominant Matrix: The matrix $\bar{L} \in \Re^{n \times n}$ is a doubly diagonally dominant matrix (defined as $\bar{L} \in G^{n \times n}$) if

$$|l_{ii}||l_{jj}| \geq \sum_{k \neq i} l_{ik} \sum_{k \neq j} l_{jk}, \forall i, j \in \langle n \rangle, i \neq j.$$

Synchronization Problem: Nodes are said to synchronize if $\lim_{t \to \infty} \left\| x_i(t) - x_j(t) \right\| = 0, \forall i, j$.

Chapter 10
Cooperative Control of Unknown Networked Lagrange Systems using Higher Order Neural Networks

Gang Chen
Chongqing University, China

Frank L. Lewis
University of Texas at Arlington, USA

ABSTRACT

This chapter investigates the cooperative control problem for a group of Lagrange systems with a target system to be tracked. The development is suitable for the case that the desired trajectory of the target node is only available to a portion of the networked systems. All the networked systems can have different dynamics. The dynamics of the networked systems, as well as the target system, are all assumed unknown. A higher-order neural network is used at each node to approximate the distributed unknown dynamics. A distributed adaptive neural network control protocol is proposed so that the networked systems synchronize to the motion of the target node. The theoretical analysis shows that the synchronization error can be made arbitrarily small by appropriately tuning the design parameters.

INTRODUCTION

The topic of distributed cooperative control of multi-agent systems has gained great interest in recent years due to the advent of powerful embedded systems and communication networks. Cooperative control of multi-agent systems has

broad applications in such areas as distributed reconnaissance and surveillance, multi-robot search and rescue, multi-sensor location and identification, air traffic control, and so on. Compared with the centralized cooperative control method, the distributed cooperative control strategy enjoys many advantages, such as scalability, robustness, and reliability. From the control point of view, the cooperative control of multi-agent systems can

DOI: 10.4018/978-1-4666-2175-6.ch010

be categorized into two classes: the cooperative regulator problem and the cooperative tracking problem. For the cooperative regulator problem, by using the fundamental 'nearest neighbor rule,' each agent eventually synchronizes to an unprescribed common value, which is generally a function of the initial states of the systems. For the distributed tracking problem, there exists a leader or control node in the networked systems. The control node acts as a command generator, which generates the desired reference trajectory. All other systems are required to follow the trajectory of the control node. The distributed tracking control of multi-agent systems has a wide range of applications in industry. For example, in cooperative tele-operation systems, multiple remote robot arms are required to track the trajectory of the local dominant or master robot arm. Manipulator robots are widely used in the complex and integrated production process where the flexibility, reliability, manipulability, and scalability are highly required. It is a typical example for a group of robots to transport a large-size work-piece, where the cooperative robotic manipulators are required to follow the same trajectory. The case of a group of mobile robots following a leader robot, where only the leader robot is mounted with a camera to decide the moving route, is another example where the distributed tracking control is needed.

The purpose of this chapter is to provide analysis/design techniques for the cooperative tracking control of multiple nonlinear Lagrange systems, which may include manipulator robots, ships, underwater vehicles, helicopters, or satellites. In the design of classical tracking controller, the external signal, such as the coupling information, is considered as a disturbance and its effect is minimized by the controller. However, for the distributed tracking control problem of networked Lagrange systems, the interactions between the systems generate the necessary information to achieve the purpose of tracking control. The distributed tracking control problem considered in this chapter is also different from the usual path-following problem since we consider the case where only a few of the networked Lagrange systems have access to the desired time-varying trajectory of the target system. In other words, to achieve the trajectory tracking for some Lagrange systems, which have no access to the desired trajectory information, the decision-making is only based on the neighbors' information. Moreover, many existing results in the context of multi-agent cooperative control require that the model parameters of the agents are perfectly known or known with a small degree of uncertainty. In practice, it is hard to acquire the model parameters accurately. Therefore, we need to study the cooperative control problem in the presence of uncertain dynamics. In this chapter, we assume that the dynamics of the networked systems, as well as the target system, are all assumed unknown. Based on the universal approximation capability of Neural Networks (NN), a Higher Order Neural Network (HONN) is used at each node to approximate the distributed unknown dynamics. The design and analysis of control algorithms are provided by applying the Lyapunov stability theory.

BACKGROUND

The study of cooperative control of multi-agent systems has been ongoing for many years. Jadbabaie, Lin, and Morse (2003) provided a theoretical explanation for the consensus behavior of the Vicsek model. This paper initiated a great deal of interest in research on consensus problem of multi-agent systems. A general framework of the consensus problem for the fixed or switching topologies was established in Olfati-Saber and Murray (2004). Ren and Beard (2005) extended the results in Jadbabaie, et al. (2003), Olfati-Saber and Murray (2004) by providing more relaxed conditions. In particular, the use of graph theory and matrix theory produced many interesting results, such as those in Qu (2009), Chopra and Spong (2006), Ren and Beard (2008), and Wu (2007), to name just a few. Based on certain key definitions such as irreducibility, M-matrix, Frobenius form, etc., recent publications allow for the analysis using traditional control theory notions (see, for example, Qu, Wang, & Hull, 2008).

Most existing works focused on the consensus problem of multiple vehicles with single-integrator or double-integrator dynamics (see, for example, Olfati-Saber, Fax, & Murray, 2007; Ren, Beard, & Atkins, 2007). Recently, some attempts have been made to consider the tracking control of networked Lagrange systems. Rodriguez-Angeles and Nijmeijer (2004) studied the position synchronization problem for a group of manipulator robots. There, it is assumed that each robot has access to the desired common trajectory. By using a cross-coupling technique, Sun, Shao, and Feng (2007) investigated the position synchronization problem of multi-axis motions. The results depend on a bidirectional communication topology. Chung and Slotine (2009) used contraction analysis method to study the synchronization problems of networked Lagrange systems. Synchronization of the systems in a leader-following configuration can be considered as a tracking problem where the desired trajectory is given by the leader. The achieved results rely on undirected or directed ring communication topology. Chopra and Spong (2006) studied passivity-based tracking control of networked Lagrange systems. The results required that the graph was balanced and that the dynamics of the systems were known. Ren (2009) studied distributed consensus algorithms for networked Lagrange systems. They only considered the undirected communication topology. The work in Khoo, Xie, and Man (2009) considered finite-time consensus tracking algorithms for multi-robot systems with directed communication topology, where the dynamics of the Lagrange systems were needed. Hou, Cheng, and Tan (2009) considered the Lagrange systems, which include model uncertainties and external disturbances. The uncertain dynamics were compensated by the adaptive NN scheme. The proposed algorithms rely on undi-

rected communication topology. Hong, Chen, and Bushnell (2008) investigated observer-based tracking control of multi-agent systems with an active leader. Here, the leader's nominal control input was required to be known to all the agents. The graph formed by the followers was undirected.

This chapter focuses on the distributed tracking control problem for the networked Lagrange systems with directed communication topology. We assume that the inertia matrix, the Coriolis/Centripetal matrix, the friction term, and the gravity term are all unknown for all nodes as well as for the target system. In contrast to the synchronization approaches given in Rodriguez-Angeles and Nijmeijer (2004), Sun, Shao, and Feng (2007), Chung and Slotine (2009), Ren (2009), Hou, Cheng, and Tan (2009), the proposed methods in this chapter do not rely on all-to-all, ring, or undirected communication topologies but allow for general directed communication topologies, which is only required to have a spanning tree. In contrast to the passivity-based approach shown in Chopra and Spong (2006), the proposed approach does not depend on the passivity property, the balanced graph, and the dynamic model. Since the dynamics of the robots are unknown, the algorithm in Khoo, Xie, and Man (2009) is not suitable for our case.

NNs can uniformly approximate any continuous function over a compact domain, provided the network has sufficient number of neurons (Hornik, Stinchombe, & White, 1989). This powerful property inspires a great number of neural network-based control algorithms for a large class of unknown nonlinear systems (see, for example, Lewis, Yesildirek, & Liu 1996; Lewis, Jagannathan, & Yesildirek, 1998; Narendra & Parthasarathy, 1990; Polycarpou, 1996; Chen & Khalil, 1992; Zhang, Ge, & Hang, 1999). Based on the Lyapunov stability theory, many novel NN online learning algorithms have been developed. Rigorous proofs of convergence and stability have been presented (see, for example, Lewis, Jagannathan, & Yesildirek, 1998). Although the traditional

NN models are recognized for their performance in system identification or identification-based control, they function as "black boxes" and are unable to provide explanations for their behavior (Zhang, Xu, & Fulcher, 2002). In addition, traditional NN cannot deal with discontinuities in the input data and the higher order nonlinearity of the systems being estimated. In order to overcome these deficiencies, HONNs receive some researchers' attention. HONNs utilize higher combinations of their inputs. They are able to capture higher-order correlations and show impressive computational, storage, and learning capabilities (Giles & Maxwell, 1987). Typically, NONNs contain multiplication operation such that they are able to manage complex mappings in system identification or identification based control. Redding, Kowalczyk, and Downs (1993) showed that the HONNs are as powerful as any other feed-forward NN architecture when the orders of the networks are the same. Various kinds of NONN structures have been proposed. Rumelhart and McClelland (1986) developed Sigma-pi NN where the hidden units calculate a product of the inputs. Shin and Ghosh (1991) introduced pi-sigma network which consists of an input layer, a single hidden layer of linear summation units and products units in the output layer. In function link NNs, the input vector can be augmented with a suitably enhanced representation of the inputs to generate the NONN. Durbin and Rumelhart (1989) introduced product-unit neural networks in which the product unit can automatically learn the higher-order term in the systems. NNs are also effective tools for the cooperative control of multi-agent systems with unknown dynamics. Neural adaptive control has not been fully explored for control of multi-agent systems. For the networked nonlinear systems, Chen and Lewis (2011) presented a distributed tracking controller based on the functional-link NN with one layer of tunable weights. However, using a functional-link NN requires one to select the suitable basis functions first. To solve this deficiency, multilayer higher-order NNs with

arbitrary activation functions (as long as the functions satisfy an approximation property and their derivatives are bounded) are employed in this chapter. This higher-order NN requires no pre-selection of a basis set. The approximation property is generally better in multilayer higher-order NN than the functional-link NN. However, the HONN-based cooperative control becomes more challenging. The proposed scheme should be distributed because the controller for each Lagrange system only uses the state information of itself and its neighbors. Moreover, the distributed scheme is amenable to parallel computing within a distributed processing architecture. In order to allow for a trade-off between the NN complexity and the NN reconstruction error bound, we also discuss the distributed robust adaptive control of the networked Lagrange systems. In the final part of this chapter, illustrative design and simulation are provided.

PRELIMINARIES

Consider a directed graph or digraph $G = (V, E, A)$ with a nonempty finite set of nodes or vertices $V = \{v_1, v_2, \cdots, v_n\}$, a set of edges or arcs $E \subseteq V \times V$, and an adjacency matrix $A = [a_{ij}]$ with weights $a_{ij} > 0$ if $(v_j, v_i) \in E$ and $a_{ij} = 0$ if otherwise. We assume that the graph is simple, i.e., $(v_i, v_i) \notin E$, $\forall i$, with no self loops and no multiple edges in same direction between the same pairs of nodes. Thus, $a_{ii} = 0$. Define the in-degree of node v_i as the i-th row sum of A, i.e., $d_{in}(v_i) = \sum_{j=1}^{n} a_{ij}$. Define the diagonal in-degree matrix $D = diag\{d_{in}(v_i)\}$ and the graph Laplacian matrix $L = D - A$. The set of neighbors of a node v_i is $N_i = \{v_j : (v_j, v_i) \in E\}$, i.e., the set of nodes with edges incoming to v_i. A directed path is a sequence of nodes $v_1, v_2, \cdots, v_r$ such that $(v_i, v_{i+1}) \in E$, $i \in \{1, 2, \cdots, r-1\}$. A directed tree is a directed graph, where every node except the root node has exactly one parent. A spanning tree of a digraph is a directed tree that connects all the nodes of the graph.

The systems considered here consist of $n+1$ manipulator robots, where an robot indexed by 0 is assigned as the leader and the other robots indexed by 1, 2, $\cdots$, n are referred to as the followers.

The Euler-Lagrange equations of motion for the leader robot and the followers are described as

$$M_0(q_0)\ddot{q}_0 + C_0(q_0, \dot{q}_0)\dot{q}_0 + h_0(\dot{q}_0) + g_0(q_0) = \tau_0 \quad (1)$$

and

$$M_i(q_i)\ddot{q}_i + C_i(q_i, \dot{q}_i)\dot{q}_i + h_i(\dot{q}_i) + g_i(q_i) = \tau_i + \delta_i,$$

$$i = 1, 2, \cdots, n \quad (2)$$

respectively, where $q_j \in R^m$ ($j = 0, 1, \cdots, n$) is the generalized configuration coordinates; $M_j(q_j) \in R^{m \times m}$ is the symmetric, positive definite inertia matrix; $C_j(q_j, \dot{q}_j) \in R^{m \times m}$ is the Coriolis/Centrifugal matrix; $h_j(\dot{q}_j) \in R^m$ is the friction term; $g_j(q_j) \in R^m$ is the gravity vector; τ_i is the vector of control input torques; δ_i represents the input disturbance. The inertia, Coriolis, friction, and gravity terms are all assumed unknown.

System (2) can be written in global form as

$$M\ddot{Q}_N + C\dot{Q}_N + H + G_r = \tau + \delta \quad (3)$$

where

$$M = diag\{M_1, M_2, \cdots, M_n\},$$

$$C = diag\{C_1, C_2, \cdots, C_n\},$$

$$Q_N = (q_1^T, q_2^T, \ldots, q_n^T)^T,$$

$$H = \left(h_1^T, h_2^T, \cdots, h_n^T\right)^T,$$

$$G_r = \left(g_1^T, g_2^T, \cdots, g_n^T\right)^T,$$

$$\tau = \left(\tau_1^T, \tau_2^T, \cdots, \tau_n^T\right)^T, \text{ and}$$

$$\delta = \left(\delta_1^T, \delta_2^T, \cdots, \delta_n^T\right)^T.$$

The following assumption is needed to facilitate the development of the subsequent results.

Assumption 1. The input disturbance δ_i is bounded, i.e., there exists a fixed bound $\varsigma_{B,i}$ such that $\|\delta_i\| \leq \varsigma_{B,i}$.

The dynamic model (2) has the following useful properties (Lewis, Jagannathan, & Yesildirek, 1998).

Property 1: The inertia matrix $M_i(q_i)$ is symmetric and positive definite.

Property 2: The Coriolis/Centrifugal matrix can always be selected so that the matrix $\left(\dot{M}_i(q_i) - 2C_i(q_i, \dot{q}_i)\right)$ is skew symmetric. Therefore, $x^T \left(\dot{M}_i(q_i) - 2C_i(q_i, \dot{q}_i)\right)x = 0$ for all vector x. This is a statement of the fact that the fictitious forces in the robot systems do not work.

The communication topology among the $n+1$ robots is a directed graph $G = (V, E, A)$ with $V = \{v_0, v_1, \cdots, v_n\}$ and the adjacency matrix

$$A = \begin{bmatrix} 0 & 0 & 0 & \cdots & 0 \\ b_1 & 0 & a_{12} & \cdots & a_{1n} \\ b_2 & a_{21} & 0 & & \\ \vdots & \vdots & \ddots & \ddots & \vdots \\ b_{n-1} & a_{(n-1)1} & & 0 & a_{(n-1)n} \\ b_n & a_{n1} & \cdots & a_{n(n-1)} & 0 \end{bmatrix} \in R^{(n+1)(n+1)}$$

$$(4)$$

Denote the adjacency matrix of the subgraph $\bar{G} = (\bar{V}, \bar{E}, \bar{A})$ formed by the followers by

$$\bar{A} = \begin{bmatrix} 0 & a_{12} & \cdots & & a_{1n} \\ a_{21} & 0 & \cdots & & \vdots \\ \vdots & \ddots & \ddots & \ddots & \vdots \\ a_{(n-1)1} & \cdots & \ddots & 0 & a_{(n-1)n} \\ a_{n1} & & \cdots & a_{n(n-1)} & 0 \end{bmatrix} \in R^{n \times n}. \tag{5}$$

Let

$$\bar{D} = diag\{d_1, d_2, \cdots, d_n\}$$

with $d_i = \sum_{j=1}^{n} a_{ij}$ ($i \in \{1, 2, \cdots, n\}$). Thus, the Laplacian matrix of the subgraph $\bar{G}$ can be defined as

$$\bar{L} = \bar{D} - \bar{A}. \tag{6}$$

Denote

$$B = diag\{b_1, b_2, \cdots, b_n\}$$

and $b = (b_1, b_2, \cdots, b_n)^T$ with $b_i > 0$ ($i \in \{1, 2, \cdots, n\}$) if $0 \in N_i$ and $b_i = 0$ if otherwise. Thus, for the digraph $G = (V, E, A)$, we have

$$L = \begin{bmatrix} 0 & 0_{1 \times n} \\ -b & \bar{L} + B \end{bmatrix}. \tag{7}$$

If the graph G has a spanning tree, then $Rank(L) = n$ (Ren & Beard, 2008). In light of (7), it follows that $Rank[-b, \bar{L} + B] = n$ and $(\bar{L} + B)1_n = b$, where 1_n is the n-vector of all ones. Thus, $Rank(\bar{L} + B) = n$. An important special case is that $\bar{G}$ is strongly connected. In this situation, $\bar{L}$ is irreducible. Then $\bar{L} + B$ is irreducibly diagonally dominant as long as one pinning gain $b_i \neq 0$ and, hence, nonsingular.

The distributed tracking control problem confronted here is as follows: Design the control protocols for each node so that all the nodes in $\bar{G}$ synchronize to the states of the leader node, i.e., $q_i \to q_0$, $\dot{q}_i \to \dot{q}_0$, $\forall i$. It is assumed that the dynamics of each node are unknown.

Definition 1. The local neighborhood position error and velocity error for robot i are defined as

$$e_i^1 = \sum_{j=1}^{n} a_{ij}(q_j - q_i) + b_i(q_0 - q_i), \tag{8}$$

$$e_i^2 = \sum_{j=1}^{n} a_{ij}(\dot{q}_j - \dot{q}_i) + b_i(\dot{q}_0 - \dot{q}_i), \tag{9}$$

respectively.

Note that (8) and (9) represent the information that is available for node *i*. Thus, they can be used for control purpose.

From (8) and (9), the overall local neighborhood position and velocity error vectors for the networked systems are given by

$$E_1 = ((\bar{L} + B) \otimes I_m)(1_n \otimes q_0 - Q_N), \tag{10}$$

$$E_2 = ((\bar{L} + B) \otimes I_m)(1_n \otimes \dot{q}_0 - \dot{Q}_N), \tag{11}$$

respectively, where $E_1 = ((e_1^1)^T, (e_2^1)^T, \cdots, (e_n^1)^T)^T$ and $E_2 = ((e_1^2)^T, (e_2^2)^T, \cdots, (e_n^2)^T)^T$. Define the global position and velocity disagreement vectors as

$$\zeta = 1_n \otimes q_0 - Q_N, \tag{12}$$

$$\dot{\zeta} = 1_n \otimes \dot{q}_0 - \dot{Q}_N, \tag{13}$$

respectively. Thus,

$$E_1 = ((\bar{L} + B) \otimes I_m)\zeta,$$

$$E_2 = ((\bar{L} + B) \otimes I_m)\dot{\zeta}.$$

Note that (12) and (13) are the disagreement vectors in Olfati-Saber and Murray (2004). In contrast to the local neighborhood vectors, the global vectors cannot be calculated locally at each node. Thus they are suitable for the analysis but not for the distributed controller design using Lyapunov techniques.

The following result is very useful in the subsequent analysis.

Lemma 1. If the graph G has a spanning tree, then

$$\|\zeta\| \le \|E_1\|/\underline{\sigma}(\bar{L} + B), \qquad (14)$$

$$\|\dot{\zeta}\| \le \|E_2\|/\underline{\sigma}(\bar{L} + B), \qquad (15)$$

with $\underline{\sigma}(\bar{L} + B)$ denoting the minimum singular value of $(\bar{L} + B)$, and $E_1 = 0$, $E_2 = 0$ if and only if the nodes synchronize, that is $\zeta = 0$ and $\dot{\zeta} = 0$.

Proof. If the graph G has a spanning tree with the root node being the target node (1), then $\bar{L} + B$ is a nonsingular M-matrix (Qu, 2009). All eigenvalues of $\bar{L} + B$ have positive real part (Horn & Johnson, 1987). Noticing (10) and (11), one gets that $\zeta = ((\bar{L} + B) \otimes I_m)^{-1} E_1$ and $\dot{\zeta} = ((\bar{L} + B) \otimes I_m)^{-1} E_2$. Thus, the claim follows.

By appropriately choosing information states on which synchronization is reached, the results proposed in this chapter have applications in formation control. For example, if the desired offsets between the vehicles i and j are $\Delta_{ij} \in R^m$, the equation (8) can be redefined as

$$e_i^1 = \sum_{j=1}^n a_{ij}((q_j - \Delta_j) - (q_i - \Delta_i))$$
$$+ b_i((q_0 - \Delta_0) - (q_i - \Delta_i))$$

with $\Delta_{ij} = \Delta_i - \Delta_j$. In fact, if the graph G has a spanning tree and $E_1 = 0$, then

$$\begin{bmatrix} q_1 \\ q_2 \\ \vdots \\ q_n \end{bmatrix} = 1_n \otimes q_0 + \begin{bmatrix} \Delta_{10} \\ \Delta_{20} \\ \vdots \\ \Delta_{n0} \end{bmatrix}.$$

Define the sliding-mode error

$$S = E_2 + \Lambda E_1, \qquad (16)$$

where $S = (s_1^T, s_2^T, \cdots, s_n^T)^T$, $\Lambda = \eta \otimes I_m$, and $\eta = diag\{\eta_1, \eta_2, \cdots, \eta_n\}$ with η_i ($1 \le i \le n$) being the positive design parameters.

The i-th sub-vector of S in (16) can be written into the following form

$$s_i = e_i^2 + \eta_i e_i^1, \ i = 1, 2, \cdots, n. \qquad (17)$$

For follower i, the error dynamics is given by

$$M_i \dot{s}_i + C_i s_i = M_i \dot{e}_i^2 + M_i \eta_i e_i^2 + C_i (e_i^2 + \eta_i e_i^1). \qquad (18)$$

The term $C_i s_i$ is added to use a skew symmetry property in the proof of the main theorem.

Taking the time derivative on both sides of (9) yields

$$\dot{e}_i^2 = -(d_i + b_i)\ddot{q}_i + \sum_{j=1}^n a_{ij}\ddot{q}_j + b_i \ddot{q}_0. \qquad (19)$$

Substituting (19) into (18) and applying (2), one gets

$$M_i \dot{s}_i + C_i s_i = -(d_i + b_i)(\tau_i + \delta_i) + f_i(x_i), \qquad (20)$$

where

$$f_i(x_i) = M_i \left(\sum_{j \in N_i} a_{ij}\ddot{q}_j + b_i \ddot{q}_0 \right) + M_i \eta_i e_i^2$$

$$+C_i \left(\sum_{j \in N_i} a_{ij} \dot{q}_j + b_i \dot{q}_0 \right) + C_i \eta_i e_i^1 + (d_i + b_i)(h_i + g_i)$$
$$(21)$$

with

$$x_i = (q_i^T, \dot{q}_i^T, q_j^T, \dot{q}_j^T, \ddot{q}_j^T, b_i q_0^T, b_i \dot{q}_0^T, b_i \ddot{q}_0^T)^T,$$

$j \in N_i$, N_i being the neighbor set of robot i in the graph formed by the follower robots, and $b_i > 0$ if $0 \in N_i$ and $b_i = 0$ if otherwise.

According to the approximation property of NNs, the unknown dynamics for each node can be approximated arbitrarily closely on an appropriate compact set by using a multilayer NN with appropriate weights. Specially, let Γ be a compact, simple connected set and $f_i(\bullet) : \Gamma \to R^m$. Define $C^m(\Gamma)$ as the space of continuous function $f_i(\bullet)$. Then, for all $f_i(\bullet) \in C^m(\Gamma)$, there exist weights W_i and V_i such that

$$f_i(x_i) = W_i^T \sigma_i(V_i^T \overline{x}_i) + \varepsilon_i,$$
$$(22)$$

where $V_i = \begin{bmatrix} V_{1,i} & V_{2,i} & \cdots & V_{l,i} \end{bmatrix}$ ($l > 1$ denoting the NN node number);

$$\sigma_i(V_i^T \overline{x}_i) = (\sigma_i(V_{1,i}^T \overline{x}_i), \sigma_i(V_{2,i}^T \overline{x}_i), \cdots,$$

$\sigma_i(V_{l,i}^T \overline{x}_i))^T$; Typical selections for $\sigma_i(\cdot)$ include sigmoid, hyperbolic tangent, or radial basic functions; $\overline{x}_i$ denotes the input vector which is augmented with a suitably enhanced representation of the input data x_i. The elements of the vector $\overline{x}_i$ include the higher-order representation of the input x_i so that the NN does not have to learn these terms. That is to say that the higher-order NN is used in this chapter. If the multi-layer HONNs are used in the networked Lagrange systems, the design of HONN based control protocol as well as the NN weights tuning laws be-

comes more challenging. In what follows, we will show how to implement multi-layer HONN in the networked Lagrange system and how to guarantee the stability and performance of the networked systems.

For further analysis, we need the following assumptions.

Assumption 2. The NN approximation error ε_i is bounded, i.e., there exists a fixed constant bound $\varepsilon_{B,i}$ such that $\|\varepsilon_i\| \leq \varepsilon_{B,i}$.

For notational convenience define the matrix of all the NN weights as $Z_i = \begin{bmatrix} W_i & 0 \\ 0 & V_i \end{bmatrix}$.

Assumption 3. NN weight matrix is bounded by

$$\|Z_i\|_F \leq Z_{B,i}, \forall i$$
$$(23)$$

with positive constant $Z_{B,i}$.

To compensate for unknown nonlinearities, each node will maintain a HONN locally. The approximation of $f_i(x_i)$ is given by

$$\hat{f}_i(x_i) = \hat{W}_i^T \sigma_i(\hat{V}_i^T \overline{x}_i),$$
$$(24)$$

where $\hat{W}_i$, $\hat{V}_i$ are the current estimates of the NN weights for robot i. For each follower robot, define the weight deviations or weight estimation errors as $\tilde{W}_i = W_i - \hat{W}_i$, $\tilde{V}_i = V_i - \hat{V}_i$, and $\tilde{Z}_i = Z_i - \hat{Z}_i$.

Let $\sigma_i = \sigma_i(V_i^T \overline{x}_i)$, $\hat{\sigma}_i = \sigma_i(\hat{V}_i^T \overline{x}_i)$. For (24), the estimation error can be expressed as

$$W_i^T \sigma_i - \hat{W}_i^T \hat{\sigma}_i = \tilde{W}_i^T (\hat{\sigma}_i - \hat{\sigma}_i' \hat{V}_i^T \overline{x}_i)$$
$$+ \hat{W}_i^T \hat{\sigma}_i' \tilde{V}_i^T \overline{x}_i + \omega_i(x_i)$$
$$(25)$$

where $\hat{\sigma}_i' = \left. \frac{d\sigma_i(z)}{dz} \right|_{z = \hat{V}_i^T \overline{x}_i}$,
$$\omega_i(x_i) = \tilde{W}_i^T \hat{\sigma}_i' V_i^T \overline{x}_i + W_i^T o(\tilde{V}_i^T \overline{x}_i)^2,$$

$o(\tilde{V}_i^T \bar{x}_i)^2$ denotes the sum of the high-order terms of the Taylor series expansion.

Lemma 2. For (25), the residual term $\omega_i(x_i)$ is bounded by

$$\|\omega_i(x_i)\| \leq c_{1,i} + c_{2,i} \|\hat{\sigma}_i' \hat{V}_i^T \bar{x}_i\| + c_{3,i} \|\hat{W}_i^T \hat{\sigma}_i'\|_F \|\bar{x}_i\|, \quad (26)$$

where $c_{1,i}$, $c_{2,i}$, and $c_{3,i}$ are computable positive constants.

Proof. According (25), one has

$$\omega(x_i) = W_i^T(\sigma_i - \hat{\sigma}_i) + W_i^T \hat{\sigma}_i' \hat{V}_i^T \bar{x}_i - \hat{W}_i^T \hat{\sigma}_i' V_i \bar{x}_i.$$

Thus,

$$\|\omega_i(x_i)\| \leq \|W_i\|_F \sqrt{l} + \|W_i\|_F \|\hat{\sigma}_i' \hat{V}_i^T \bar{x}_i\|$$
$$+ \|V_i\|_F \|\hat{W}_i^T \hat{\sigma}_i'\|_F \|\bar{x}_i\|.$$

By letting $c_{1,i} = \|W_i\|_F \sqrt{l}$, $c_{2,i} = \|W_i\|_F$, and $c_{3,i} = \|V_i\|_F$, we get (26).

DISTRIBUTED ADAPTIVE CONTROLLER DESIGN

The next definition extends the standard definition of uniform ultimate boundedness to the distributed tracking control system.

Definition 2. The position and velocity tracking errors for each manipulator robot are said to be cooperatively Uniformly Ultimately Bounded (UUB) if there exist compact sets $\Omega_1 \in R^m$ and $\Omega_2 \in R^m$ such that for all $q_i(t_0) \in \Omega_1$ and $\dot{q}_i(t_0) \in \Omega_2$, there exist bounds B_1 and B_2 and a time $T(B_1, B_2, q_i(t_0), \dot{q}_i(t_0))$ such that $\|q_i(t) - q_0(t)\| \leq B_1$, $\|\dot{q}_i(t) - \dot{q}_0(t)\| \leq B_2$ for all $t \geq t_0 + T$.

Now we show how to design the control protocol and tune the NN weights such that the global tracking errors are UUB for the networked Lagrange systems.

Theorem 1. Consider the networked Lagrange systems (1) and (2). Assume that the uni-directed graph G has a spanning tree. Make Assumptions 1-3. Design the distributed adaptive controller as

$$\tau_i = \frac{1}{d_i + b_i}\left(K_i s_i + \hat{W}_i^T \sigma_i(\hat{V}_i^T \bar{x}_i) + u_i\right) \quad (27)$$

with

$$u_i = \frac{\text{sgn}(s_i)}{\upsilon_i}\left(\|\hat{\sigma}_i' \hat{V}_i^T \bar{x}_i\|^2 + \|\hat{W}_i^T \hat{\sigma}_i'\|_F^2 \|\bar{x}_i\|^2\right),$$

$\upsilon_i > 0$, and $K_i = K_i^T > 0$. Let the distributed adaptive tuning laws be given by

$$\dot{\hat{W}}_i = F_i(\hat{\sigma}_i - \hat{\sigma}_i' \hat{V}_i^T \bar{x}_i)s_i^T - \kappa_i F_i \|s_i\| \hat{W}_i, \quad (28)$$

$$\dot{\hat{V}}_i = L_i \bar{x}_i s_i^T \hat{W}_i^T \hat{\sigma}_i' - \kappa_i L_i \|s_i\| \hat{V}_i \quad (29)$$

with constant matrices $F_i = F_i^T > 0$, $L_i = L_i^T > 0$, and scalar design parameter $\kappa_i > 0$. Then the tracking errors (16) and the NN weight estimation errors are all UUB. Moreover, the local neighborhood position and velocity errors (8), (9) are UUB, and the global position and velocity disagreement vectors (12), (13) are cooperatively UUB.

Proof. Consider the Lyapunov function candidate

$$V = \frac{1}{2}S^T M S + \frac{1}{2}\sum_{i=1}^{n} tr\{\tilde{W}_i^T F_i^{-1} \tilde{W}_i\}$$
$$+ \frac{1}{2}\sum_{i=1}^{n} tr\{\tilde{V}_i^T L_i^{-1} \tilde{V}_i\} \quad (30)$$

Differentiating (30) yields

$$\dot{V} = \frac{1}{2} S^T \dot{M} S + S^T M \dot{S} - \sum_{i=1}^{n} tr\{\tilde{W}_i^T F_i^{-1} \dot{\hat{W}}_i\}$$
$$- \sum_{i=1}^{n} tr\{\tilde{V}_i^T L_i^{-1} \dot{\hat{V}}_i\} \tag{31}$$

Taking the time derivative on both sides of (16), one has

$$\dot{S} = \dot{E}_2 + \Lambda \dot{E}_1. \tag{32}$$

Substituting (32) into (31) yields

$$\dot{V} = \frac{1}{2} S^T \dot{M} S - S^T C S + S^T M \left(\dot{E}_2 + \Lambda \dot{E}_1 \right)$$
$$+ S^T C \left(E_2 + \Lambda E_1 \right) - \sum_{i=1}^{n} tr\{\tilde{W}_i^T F_i^{-1} \dot{\hat{W}}_i\} ,$$
$$- \sum_{i=1}^{n} tr\{\tilde{V}_i^T L_i^{-1} \dot{\hat{V}}_i\} \tag{33}$$

where, in order to apply Property 2, we first add the term $-S^T C S$ and then subtract it. Thus,

$$\dot{V} = S^T M \left(\dot{E}_2 + \Lambda \dot{E}_1 \right) + S^T C \left(E_2 + \Lambda E_1 \right)$$
$$- \sum_{i=1}^{n} tr\{\tilde{W}_i^T F_i^{-1} \dot{\hat{W}}_i\} - \sum_{i=1}^{n} tr\{\tilde{V}_i^T L_i^{-1} \dot{\hat{V}}_i\} \tag{34}$$

We first calculate the term $S^T M \dot{E}_2$. From (11), we have,

$$S^T M \dot{E}_2 = -S^T M \left(\left(\bar{L} + B \right) \otimes I_m \right) \ddot{Q}_N$$
$$+ S^T M \left(B \otimes I_m \right) \left(1_n \otimes \ddot{q}_0 \right) \tag{35}$$

According to the fact that

$$\bar{L} + B = \left(\bar{D} + B \right) - \bar{A}, \tag{36}$$

one has

$$S^T M \dot{E}_2 = -S^T M \left(\left(\bar{D} + B \right) \otimes I_m \right) \ddot{Q}_N$$
$$+ S^T M \left(\bar{A} \otimes I_m \right) \ddot{Q}_N + S^T M (B \otimes I_m)(1_n \otimes \ddot{q}_0)$$

Noticing that

$$(B \otimes I_m)(1_n \otimes \ddot{q}_0) = b \otimes \ddot{q}_0$$

with $b = B 1_n$, and applying (3), i.e.,

$$\ddot{Q}_N = M^{-1}(\tau + \delta - H - G_r - C \dot{Q}_N),$$

one has

$$S^T M \dot{E}_2 = -S^T \left(\left(\bar{D} + B \right) \otimes I_m \right)(\tau + \delta - H - G_r)$$
$$+ S^T C \left(\left(\bar{D} + B \right) \otimes I_m \right) \dot{Q}_N + S^T M (\bar{A} \otimes I_m) \ddot{Q}_N$$
$$+ S^T M (b \otimes \ddot{q}_0) \tag{37}$$

Next we calculate the term $S^T C E_2$. According to (11) and (36), one has

$$S^T C E_2 = S^T C \left(\left(\bar{L} + B \right) \otimes I_m \right)(1_n \otimes \dot{q}_0 - \dot{Q}_N)$$

$$= S^T C \left(\left(\bar{D} + B \right) \otimes I_m \right)(1_n \otimes \dot{q}_0 - \dot{Q}_N)$$
$$- S^T C (\bar{A} \otimes I_m)(1_n \otimes \dot{q}_0 - \dot{Q}_N)$$

$$= -S^T C \left(\left(\bar{D} + B \right) \otimes I_m \right) \dot{Q}_N + S^T C (\bar{A} \otimes I_m) \dot{Q}_N$$
$$+ S^T C (b \otimes \dot{q}_0) \tag{38}$$

Substituting (37) and (38) into (34) yields

$$\dot{V} = -S^T\left((\bar{D}+B)\otimes I_m\right)(\tau + \delta - H - G_r)$$
$$+S^T M(\bar{A}\otimes I_m)\ddot{Q}_N + S^T M(b\otimes \ddot{q}_0)$$

$$+S^T M\Lambda\dot{E}_1 + S^T C(\bar{A}\otimes I_m)\dot{Q}_N + S^T C(b\otimes \dot{q}_0)$$
$$+S^T C\Lambda E_1 - \sum_{i=1}^n tr\{\tilde{W}_i^T F_i^{-1}\dot{\hat{W}}_i\} - \sum_{i=1}^n tr\{\tilde{V}_i^T L_i^{-1}\dot{\hat{V}}_i\} \qquad (39)$$

Define

$$F(x) = \left((\bar{D}+B)\otimes I_m\right)(H+G_r) + M(\bar{A}\otimes I_m)\ddot{Q}_N$$
$$+M(b\otimes \ddot{q}_0) + M\Lambda\dot{E}_1$$

$$+C(\bar{A}\otimes I_m)\dot{Q}_N + C(b\otimes \dot{q}_0) + C\Lambda E_1$$

with $F(x) = (f_1^T(x_1), f_2^T(x_2), \cdots, f_n^T(x_n))^T$ and $f_i(x_i)$ defined in (21).

According to (22), the global nonlinearity $F(x)$ is now written as

$$F(x) = W^T\sigma(V^T\bar{x}) + \varepsilon$$
$$= \begin{bmatrix} W_1^T & & & \\ & W_2^T & & \\ & & \ddots & \\ & & & W_n^T \end{bmatrix}\begin{bmatrix} \sigma_1(V_1^T\bar{x}_1) \\ \sigma_2(V_2^T\bar{x}_2) \\ \vdots \\ \sigma_n(V_n^T\bar{x}_n) \end{bmatrix} + \begin{bmatrix} \varepsilon_1 \\ \varepsilon_2 \\ \vdots \\ \varepsilon_n \end{bmatrix}. \quad (40)$$

Substituting (40) into (39) yields

$$\dot{V} = -S^T\left((\bar{D}+B)\otimes I_m\right)(\tau+\delta) + S^T W^T\sigma(V^T\bar{x})$$
$$-\sum_{i=1}^n tr\{\tilde{W}_i^T F_i^{-1}\dot{\hat{W}}_i\} - \sum_{i=1}^n tr\{\tilde{V}_i^T L_i^{-1}\dot{\hat{V}}_i\} + S^T\varepsilon \qquad .$$

From (25) and (27), we have

$$\dot{V} = \sum_{i=1}^n(-s_i^T K_i s_i - s_i^T\hat{W}_i^T\hat{\sigma}_i - s_i^T u_i) + \sum_{i=1}^n s_i^T W_i^T\sigma_i$$
$$-\sum_{i=1}^n tr\{\tilde{W}_i^T F_i^{-1}\dot{\hat{W}}_i\} - \sum_{i=1}^n tr\{\tilde{V}_i^T L_i^{-1}\dot{\hat{V}}_i\}$$

$$-S^T\left((\bar{D}+B)\otimes I_m\right)\delta + S^T\varepsilon$$

$$= \sum_{i=1}^n(-s_i^T K_i s_i - s_i^T u_i) + \sum_{i=1}^n s_i^T\tilde{W}_i^T(\hat{\sigma}_i - \hat{\sigma}_i'\hat{V}_i^T\bar{x}_i)$$
$$+\sum_{i=1}^n s_i^T\hat{W}_i^T\hat{\sigma}_i'\tilde{V}_i^T\bar{x}_i + \sum_{i=1}^n s_i^T\omega_i(x_i)$$
$$-\sum_{i=1}^n tr\{\tilde{W}_i^T F_i^{-1}\dot{\hat{W}}_i\} - \sum_{i=1}^n tr\{\tilde{V}_i^T L_i^{-1}\dot{\hat{V}}_i\} \qquad .$$
$$-S^T\left((\bar{D}+B)\otimes I_m\right)\delta + S^T\varepsilon$$

Furthermore,

$$\dot{V} \le \sum_{i=1}^n(-\lambda_{\min}(K_i)\|s_i\|^2 - s_i^T u_i)$$
$$-\sum_{i=1}^n tr\{\tilde{W}_i^T F_i^{-1}(\dot{\hat{W}}_i - F_i(\hat{\sigma}_i - \hat{\sigma}_i'\hat{V}_i^T\bar{x}_i)s_i^T)\}$$

$$-\sum_{i=1}^n tr\{\tilde{V}_i^T L_i^{-1}(\dot{\hat{V}}_i - L_i\bar{x}_i s_i^T\hat{W}_i^T\hat{\sigma}_i')\} + \sum_{i=1}^n\|s_i\|\|\omega_i(x_i)\|$$
$$+\sum_{i=1}^n(d_i + b_i)\|s_i\|\varsigma_{B,i} + \sum_{i=1}^n\|s_i\|\varepsilon_{B,i} \qquad (41)$$

Applying Lemma 2 and using Young's inequality yield

$$\|\omega_i(x_i)\| \le c_{0,i} + \frac{1}{\upsilon_i}\left\|\hat{\sigma}_i'\hat{V}_i^T\bar{x}_i\right\|^2 + \frac{1}{\upsilon_i}\left\|\hat{W}_i^T\hat{\sigma}_i'\right\|_F^2\|\bar{x}_i\|^2 \qquad (42)$$

with $c_{0,i} = c_{1,i} + \frac{1}{4}c_{2,i}^2\upsilon_i + \frac{1}{4}c_{3,i}^2\upsilon_i$.

Substituting (42) into (41) yields

$$\dot{V} \le \sum_{i=1}^n(-\lambda_{\min}(K_i)\|s_i\|^2)$$
$$-\sum_{i=1}^n tr\{\tilde{W}_i^T F_i^{-1}(\dot{\hat{W}}_i - F_i(\hat{\sigma}_i - \hat{\sigma}_i'\hat{V}_i^T\bar{x}_i)s_i^T)\}$$

$$-\sum_{i=1}^{n} tr\{\tilde{V}_i^T L_i^{-1}(\dot{\tilde{V}}_i - L_i \bar{x}_i s_i^T \hat{W}_i^T \hat{\sigma}_i')\} + \sum_{i=1}^{n} c_{0,i} \|s_i\|$$

$$+\sum_{i=1}^{n}(d_i + b_i)\|s_i\|\varsigma_{B,i} + \sum_{i=1}^{n}\|s_i\|\varepsilon_{B,i} .$$

According to (28) and (29), one has

$$\dot{V} \leq -\sum_{i=1}^{n}\lambda_{\min}(K_i)\|s_i\|^2 + \sum_{i=1}^{n}\kappa_i\|s_i\|tr\{\tilde{W}_i^T\hat{W}_i\}$$

$$+\sum_{i=1}^{n}\kappa_i\|s_i\|tr\{\tilde{V}_i^T\hat{V}_i\} + \sum_{i=1}^{n}c_{0,i}\|s_i\|$$

$$+\sum_{i=1}^{n}(d_i + b_i)\|s_i\|\varsigma_{B,i} + \sum_{i=1}^{n}\|s_i\|\varepsilon_{B,i}$$

$$\leq -\sum_{i=1}^{n}\lambda_{\min}(K_i)\|s_i\|^2 + \sum_{i=1}^{n}\kappa_i\|s_i\|tr\{\tilde{Z}_i^T(Z_i - \tilde{Z}_i)\}$$

$$+\sum_{i=1}^{n}\|s_i\|(c_{0,i} + (d_i + b_i)\varsigma_{B,i} + \varepsilon_{B,i}) .$$

Since

$$tr\{\tilde{Z}_i^T(Z_i - \tilde{Z}_i)\} = \langle \tilde{Z}_i, Z_i \rangle$$

$$-\|\tilde{Z}_i\|_F^2 \leq \|\tilde{Z}_i\|_F \|Z_i\|_F - \|\tilde{Z}_i\|_F^2 ,$$

we have

$$\dot{V} \leq -\sum_{i=1}^{n}\lambda_{\min}(K_i)\|s_i\|^2 + \sum_{i=1}^{n}\kappa_i\|s_i\|\|\tilde{Z}_i\|_F (Z_{B,i} - \|\tilde{Z}_i\|_F)$$

$$+\sum_{i=1}^{n}\|s_i\|(c_{0,i} + (d_i + b_i)\varsigma_{B,i} + \varepsilon_{B,i})$$

$$\leq -\sum_{i=1}^{n}\|s_i\|\begin{bmatrix}\lambda_{\min}(K_i)\|s_i\| - \kappa_i\|\tilde{Z}_i\|_F(Z_{B,i} - \|\tilde{Z}_i\|_F)\\ -c_{0,i} - (d_i + b_i)\varsigma_{B,i} - \varepsilon_{B,i}\end{bmatrix} .$$

Thus $\dot{V}$ is negative as long as the term in braces is positive. Completing the square yields

$$\lambda_{\min}(K_i)\|s_i\| - \kappa_i\|\tilde{Z}_i\|_F (Z_{B,i} - \|\tilde{Z}_i\|_F)$$

$$-c_{0,i} - (d_i + b_i)\varsigma_{B,i} - \varepsilon_{B,i}$$

$$= \kappa_i\left(\|\tilde{Z}_i\|_F - Z_{B,i}/2\right)^2 + \lambda_{\min}(K_i)\|s_i\| - c_{0,i},$$

$$-(d_i + b_i)\varsigma_{B,i} - \varepsilon_{B,i} - \kappa_i Z_{B,i}^2/4$$

which is guaranteed positive as long as either

$$\|s_i\| > \frac{c_{0,i} + (d_i + b_i)\varsigma_{B,i} + \varepsilon_{B,i} + \kappa_i Z_{B,i}^2/4}{\lambda_{\min}(K_i)} \tag{43}$$

or

$$\|\tilde{Z}_i\|_F > Z_{B,i}/2 + \sqrt{(c_{0,i} + (d_i + b_i)\varsigma_{B,i} + \varepsilon_{B,i})/\kappa_i + Z_{B,i}^2/4} . \tag{44}$$

Thus, $\dot{V}$ is negative outside a compact set.

Now it is desired to show UUB of the local neighbor errors. In light of (16), we consider the Lyapunov function

$$V_0 = \frac{1}{2} E_1^T E_1 .$$

The time derivative of V_0 is given by

$$\dot{V}_0 = -E_1^T \Lambda E_1 + E_1^T S \leq -\underline{\sigma}(\Lambda)\|E_1\|^2 + \|E_1\|\|S\|$$

$$\leq -\underline{\sigma}(\Lambda)\|E_1\|^2 + \|E_1\|\sum_{i=1}^{n}\|s_i\|$$

which is negative as long as

$$\|E_1\| > \frac{1}{\underline{\sigma}(\Lambda)}\sum_{i=1}^{n}\|s_i\|,$$

or if

$$\|E_1\| \geq \frac{1}{\underline{\sigma}(\Lambda)}\sum_{i=1}^{n}\|s_i\| + \upsilon \equiv \mu$$

with $\upsilon > 0$ being any positive constant.

The residual set $\|E_1\| \leq \dfrac{1}{\underline{\sigma}(\Lambda)} \displaystyle\sum_{i=1}^{n} \|s_i\| + \upsilon \equiv \mu$

is equivalent to the set $\{E_1 : V_0(E_1) \leq \dfrac{1}{2}\mu^2\}$ and so is a level curve of $V_0(E_1)$ (Khalil, 2002) and outside this ball one has the Lyapunov derivative bounded above according to

$$\dot{V}_0 \leq -\underline{\sigma}(\Lambda)\|E_1\|^2 + \|E_1\|\sum_{i=1}^{n}\|s_i\| \leq -\underline{\sigma}(\Lambda)\upsilon^2 .$$

Integrating yields

$$V_0(t) - V_0(t_0) \leq -\underline{\sigma}(\Lambda)\upsilon^2(t - t_0)$$

so that $V_0(t)$ reduces to $\dfrac{1}{2}\mu^2$ within a finite time of

$$t - t_0 \leq \dfrac{V_0(t_0) - \mu^2/2}{\underline{\sigma}(\Lambda)\upsilon^2} .$$

According to (16), one can get the bound on $\|E_2\|$, i.e.,

$$\|E_2\| \leq \overline{\sigma}(\Lambda)\|E_1\| + \|S\| .$$

Thus, we know that $\|E_1\|$ and $\|E_2\|$ are UUB. In light of Lemma 1, one can get that $\|\zeta\|$ and $\|\dot{\zeta}\|$ are UUB, i.e., the position and velocity-tracking errors for each follower robot are cooperatively UUB. Moreover, the position q_i and velocity $\dot{q}_i$ signals for each follower i are bounded. According to the boundedness of s_i, $\hat{W}_i$, and $\hat{V}_i$, one can get that the distributed adaptive control input (27) is bounded. Furthermore, in light of the boundedness of the position and velocity signals, the boundedness of the external disturbances, and the boundedness of the control input, one can get that the acceleration signal $\ddot{q}_i$ is also bounded for each follower i. Since all the signals in the systems are bounded, there exists a compact set such that

the approximation property holds throughout. Thus, the claim follows.

It is important to select the Lyapunov function candidate V in (30) in terms of the local neighborhood position and velocity errors in (10) and (11). This means that the protocols and the tuning laws developed in the proof are distributed in nature and hence can be implemented at each robot. By contrast, standard NN tuning laws (Lewis, Yesildirek, & Liu, 1996) depend on the global tracking errors ζ and $\dot{\zeta}$, which are not available at each node.

According to a standard Lyapunov theorem extension (Lewis, Jagannathan, & Yesildirek, 1998), the filtered tracking errors and the NN weight estimates are UUB with practical bounds given respectively by the right-hand sides of (43) and (44).

For the protocol (27), the information of the states of the neighbors is used to evaluate the performance of the current control protocol along with the current estimates of the nonlinearities. Due to the protocol's distribution structure, the proposed scheme can be implemented on parallel processors for distributed concurrent computing. Due to the adaptive nature of the protocol (27), knowledge of manipulator dynamic model is not required. This is a highly desirable feature in practical applications where some dynamics effects such as friction cannot be modeled accurately. The directed adaptive control approach used is based on forcing the tracking errors to be UUB without requiring convergence of the weight estimates of the system model to their true values.

The difference between standard adaptive control and the adaptive NN approach proffered here is significant. The tedium of analysis and computation of regression matrices, as required in standard adaptive approaches, is avoided. The first terms of (28) and (29) are the standard unsupervised back-propagation algorithm. The last terms correspond to the e-modification to guarantee the bounded parameter estimates. There is no preliminary off-line learning phase. Moreover, initializing the NN weights is very easy.

For each robot, we assume that its neighbor's position and velocity information are available. In practice, the position and velocity measurements can be obtained by means of optical encoder and tachometer, respectively. The acceleration information, which is used as input signals of NN, can be indirectly calculated by the numerical differentiation of the velocities.

From (43), we can see that arbitrarily small tracking errors can be achieved by selecting large control gain matrix K_i. On the other hand, the NN weight error is fundamentally bounded by $Z_{B,i}$ for each i. The tuning parameter κ_i offers a design tradeoff between the relative eventual magnitudes of $\|s_i\|$ and $\|\tilde{Z}_i\|_F$; a smaller κ_i yields a smaller $\|s_i\|$ and a larger $\|\tilde{Z}_i\|_F$, and vice versa.

In light of (43), we find that the larger the in-degree is for robot i, the bigger the influence of the disturbance to the eventual tracking error is. Thus, for the case that each follower robot has only one in-degree, the disturbance has the smallest influence to the tracking errors.

The discontinuous control term u_i in (27) may produce chattering dynamics. The chattering can be eliminated by introducing a boundary layer in the vicinity of the sliding surface and using a continuous approximation of the sign function in the layer. The switching functions in the control are replaced by the saturation functions defined as

$$sat(s_{j,i}) \begin{cases} 1, \text{if } s_{j,i}/\varphi_i \geq 1 \\ s_{j,i}/\varphi_i \text{ if } -1 < s_{j,i}/\varphi_i < 1 \\ -1 \text{ if } s_{j,i}/\varphi_i \leq -1 \end{cases}$$

where $s_{j,i}$ denotes the j-th element of the vector s_i; φ_i is the boundary layer thickness. The saturation function is the same as the sign function whenever the variable $s_{j,i}$ is outside of the bound-

ary layer. Thus, we can expect that the systems are driven to the boundary of the layer of the sliding surface. Define $\bar{s}_i = s_i - \varphi_i sat(s_i)$ with $sat(s_i)$ defined element-wise for the vector s_i. Thus, the control protocol (27) can be modified as

$$\tau_i = \frac{1}{d_i + b_i} \begin{pmatrix} K_i \bar{s}_i + \hat{W}_i^T \sigma_i (\hat{V}_i^T \bar{x}_i) \\ + \frac{sat(s_i)}{v_i} \left(\left\| \hat{\sigma}_i' \hat{V}_i^T \bar{x}_i \right\|^2 + \left\| \hat{W}_i^T \hat{\sigma}_i' \right\|_F^2 \left\| \bar{x}_i \right\|^2 \right) \end{pmatrix}$$

with the adaptive tuning laws

$$\dot{\hat{W}}_i = F_i (\hat{\sigma}_i - \hat{\sigma}_i' \hat{V}_i^T \bar{x}_i) \bar{s}_i^T - \kappa_i F_i \|\bar{s}_i\| \hat{W}_i,$$

$$\dot{\hat{V}}_i = L_i \bar{x}_i \bar{s}_i^T \hat{W}_i^T \hat{\sigma}_i' - \kappa_i L_i \|\bar{s}_i\| \hat{V}_i.$$

ROBUST DISTRIBUTED CONTROLLER DESIGN

In this section, we discuss the case that the NN reconstruction error in (22) does not satisfy Assumption 2, i.e., the error bound is not a constant.

In particular, we assume that

$$\|\varepsilon_i(x_i)\| \leq \theta_i p_i(x_i) \tag{45}$$

with $p_i(x_i) > 0$ being a known function and $\theta_i \geq 0$ being a constant parameter, and the NN weight matrices are constrained to the following compact sets

$$\Omega_{1,i} = \{W_i : tr\{W_i^T W_i\} \leq W_{\max,i}\}, \tag{46}$$

$$\Omega_{2,i} = \{V_i : tr\{V_i^T V_i\} \leq V_{\max,i}\}. \tag{47}$$

As in (40), the global nonlinearity $F(x)$ can be rewritten as

$$F(x) = W^T \sigma(V^T \overline{x}) + \varepsilon(x)$$

$$= \begin{bmatrix} W_1^T & & & \\ & W_2^T & & \\ & & \ddots & \\ & & & W_n^T \end{bmatrix} \begin{bmatrix} \sigma_1(V_1^T \overline{x}_1) \\ \sigma_2(V_2^T \overline{x}_2) \\ \vdots \\ \sigma_n(V_n^T \overline{x}_n) \end{bmatrix} + \begin{bmatrix} \varepsilon_1(x_1) \\ \varepsilon_2(x_2) \\ \vdots \\ \varepsilon_n(x_n) \end{bmatrix}.$$

Consider a control law of the form

$$\tau_i = \frac{1}{d_i + b_i}(K_i s_i + \hat{W}_i^T \sigma_i(\hat{V}_i^T \overline{x}_i) + u_{i1} + u_{i2}),$$

(48)

with

$$u_{i1} = (d_i + b_i)\varsigma_{B,i} \tanh((d_i + b_i)\varsigma_{B,i} s_i / \overline{\varepsilon}_1),$$

(49)

$$u_{i2} = \hat{\phi}_i \psi_i(x_i) \tanh(s_i \psi_i(x_i)/\overline{\varepsilon}_2),$$

(50)

where the function $\tanh(\cdot)$ performs the element-wise operation;

$$\phi_i = \max\{\|V_i\|_F, \sqrt{l}\|W_i\|_F, \theta_i\};$$

$$\psi_i(x_i) = 1 + \left\|\hat{\sigma}_i' \hat{V}_i^T \overline{x}_i\right\| + \left\|\hat{W}_i^T \hat{\sigma}_i'\right\|_F \|\overline{x}_i\| + p_i(x_i);$$

$\hat{W}_i$, $\hat{V}_i$ and $\hat{\phi}_i$ are parameter estimates of W_i, V_i and ϕ_i, respectively; u_{i1} and u_{i2} are two smooth robustness signals; u_{i1} is utilized to eliminate the effect of the external disturbances; u_{i2} is utilized to suppress the effect of NN approximation error; $\overline{\varepsilon}_1 > 0$ and $\overline{\varepsilon}_2 > 0$ are design parameters which control the tracking precision.

Let the distributed adaptive tuning laws be given by

$$\dot{\hat{W}}_i = \begin{cases} \alpha_i(\hat{\sigma}_i - \hat{\sigma}_i'\hat{V}_i^T\overline{x}_i)s_i^T & \text{if } tr\{\hat{W}_i^T\hat{W}_i\} < W_{\max,i} \\ \text{or } tr\{\hat{W}_i^T\hat{W}_i\} \\ = W_{\max,i} \text{ and } s_i^T\hat{W}_i^T(\hat{\sigma}_i - \hat{\sigma}_i'\hat{V}_i^T\overline{x}_i) \le 0 \\ \alpha_i(\hat{\sigma}_i - \hat{\sigma}_i'\hat{V}_i^T\overline{x}_i)s_i^T \\ -\alpha_i \frac{s_i^T\hat{W}_i^T(\hat{\sigma}_i - \hat{\sigma}_i'\hat{V}_i^T\overline{x}_i)}{tr\{\hat{W}_i^T\hat{W}_i\}}\hat{W}_i, \text{ if } tr\{\hat{W}_i^T\hat{W}_i\} \\ = W_{\max,i} \\ \text{and } s_i^T\hat{W}_i^T(\hat{\sigma}_i - \hat{\sigma}_i'\hat{V}_i^T\overline{x}_i) > 0 \end{cases}$$

(51)

$$\dot{\hat{V}}_i = \begin{cases} \beta_i \overline{x}_i s_i^T \hat{W}_i^T \hat{\sigma}_i' & \text{if } tr\{\hat{V}_i^T\hat{V}_i\} < V_{\max,i} \\ \text{or } tr\{\hat{V}_i^T\hat{V}_i\} = V_{\max,i} \text{ and } s_i^T\hat{W}_i^T\hat{\sigma}_i'\hat{V}_i^T\overline{x}_i \le 0 \\ \beta_i \overline{x}_i s_i^T \hat{W}_i^T \hat{\sigma}_i' \\ -\beta_i \frac{s_i^T\hat{W}_i^T\hat{\sigma}_i'\hat{V}_i^T\overline{x}_i}{tr\{\hat{V}_i^T\hat{V}_i\}}\hat{V}_i, \text{ if } tr\{\hat{V}_i^T\hat{V}_i\} = V_{\max,i} \\ \text{and } s_i^T\hat{W}_i^T\hat{\sigma}_i'\hat{V}_i^T\overline{x}_i > 0 \end{cases}$$

(52)

and

$$\dot{\hat{\phi}}_i(t) = \mu_i\left(s_i^T\psi_i(x_i)\tanh(\psi_i(x_i)s_i/\overline{\varepsilon}_2) - \gamma_i(\hat{\phi}_i - \phi_{0,i})\right)$$

(53)

with constants $\alpha_i, \beta_i, \mu_i, \gamma_i, \phi_{0,i} > 0$.

Here we employ the projection method for the adaptive law of parameter matrices $\hat{W}_i$ and $\hat{V}_i$ (Goodwin & Mayne, 1987) and incorporate a leakage term based on a variant of the σ modification (Polycarpou & Ioannou, 1995) for the adaptive law of $\hat{\phi}_i$. With the projection method, it warrants that the adaptive parameters are kept bounded within some closed ellipsoids. Assume that $\hat{W}_i(0) \in \Omega_{1,i}$ and $\hat{V}_i(0) \in \Omega_{2,i}$. Then it is straightforward to prove that the closed ellipsoids are invariant (Goodwin & Mayne, 1987), i.e., $\forall t > 0$, $tr\{\hat{W}_i^T\hat{W}_i\} < W_{\max,i}$, $tr\{\hat{V}_i^T\hat{V}_i\} < V_{\max,i}$,

$i = 1, 2, \cdots, n$. With the leakage term, it is guaranteed that the estimate $\hat{\phi}_i$ remains bounded.

The following technical Lemma (Polycarpou & Ioannou, 1995) is needed for further analysis.

Lemma 3. The following inequality holds for any $\varepsilon > 0$ and for any $\eta \in R$

$$0 \leq |\eta| - \eta \tanh(\eta/\varepsilon) \leq \varepsilon/2.$$

Theorem 2. Consider the networked Lagrange systems (1) and (2). Assume that the uni-directed graph G has a directed spanning tree. Let the distributed controller be designed as (48) and the adaptive laws for the parameters $\hat{W}_i$, $\hat{V}_i$, and $\hat{\phi}_i$ be chosen as (51), (52), and (53), respectively. Then the global position and velocity tracking errors are cooperatively UUB.

Proof. Let $\tilde{W}_i = W_i - \hat{W}_i$, $\tilde{V}_i = V_i - \hat{V}_i$, and $\tilde{\phi}_i = \phi_{B,i} - \hat{\phi}_i$ with $\phi_{B,i} = \max\{\phi_i, \phi_{0,i}\}$. Consider the Lyapunov function

$$V = \frac{1}{2} S^T M S$$

$$+ \frac{1}{2} \sum_{i=1}^{n} \frac{1}{\alpha_i} tr\{\tilde{W}_i^T \tilde{W}_i\} + \frac{1}{2} \sum_{i=1}^{n} \frac{1}{\beta_i} tr\{\tilde{V}_i^T \tilde{V}_i\}.$$

$$+ \frac{1}{2} \sum_{i=1}^{n} \frac{1}{\mu_i} \tilde{\phi}_i^2$$

$$(54)$$

Proceeding as in the proof of Theorem 1, one has

$$\dot{V} = -S^T((\bar{D} + B) \otimes I_m)(\tau + \delta) + S^T W^T \sigma(V^T \bar{x})$$

$$+ S^T \varepsilon(x) - \sum_{i=1}^{n} \frac{1}{\alpha_i} tr\{\tilde{W}_i^T \dot{\hat{W}}_i\}$$

$$- \sum_{i=1}^{n} \frac{1}{\beta_i} tr\{\tilde{V}_i^T \dot{\hat{V}}_i\} - \sum_{i=1}^{n} \frac{1}{\mu_i} \tilde{\phi}_i \dot{\hat{\phi}}_i$$

$$= -\sum_{i=1}^{n} (d_i + b_i) s_i^T \tau_i + \sum_{i=1}^{n} s_i^T W_i^T \sigma_i - \sum_{i=1}^{n} \frac{1}{\alpha_i} tr\{\tilde{W}_i^T \dot{\hat{W}}_i\}$$

$$- \sum_{i=1}^{n} \frac{1}{\beta_i} tr\{\tilde{V}_i^T \dot{\hat{V}}_i\} - \sum_{i=1}^{n} \frac{\tilde{\phi}_i \dot{\hat{\phi}}_i}{\mu_i}$$

$$- \sum_{i=1}^{n} (d_i + b_i) s_i^T \delta_i + \sum_{i=1}^{n} s_i^T \varepsilon_i(x_i). \qquad (55)$$

Substituting (48) into (55) yields

$$\dot{V} = -\sum_{i=1}^{n} s_i^T (K_i s_i + u_{1,i} + u_{2,i}) + \sum_{i=1}^{n} s_i^T (W_i^T \sigma_i - \hat{W}_i^T \hat{\sigma}_i)$$

$$- \sum_{i=1}^{n} \frac{1}{\alpha_i} tr\{\tilde{W}_i^T \dot{\hat{W}}_i\} - \sum_{i=1}^{n} \frac{1}{\beta_i} tr\{\tilde{V}_i^T \dot{\hat{V}}_i\}$$

$$- \sum_{i=1}^{n} \frac{\tilde{\phi}_i \dot{\hat{\phi}}_i}{\mu_i} - \sum_{i=1}^{n} (d_i + b_i) s_i^T \delta_i + \sum_{i=1}^{n} s_i^T \varepsilon_i(x_i)$$

$$= -\sum_{i=1}^{n} s_i^T (K_i s_i + u_{1,i} + u_{2,i})$$

$$+ \sum_{i=1}^{n} s_i^T (\tilde{W}_i^T \hat{\sigma}_i - \tilde{W}_i^T \hat{\sigma}_i' \hat{V}_i^T \bar{x}_i + \hat{W}_i^T \hat{\sigma}_i' \tilde{V}_i^T \bar{x}_i)$$

$$- \sum_{i=1}^{n} \frac{1}{\alpha_i} tr\{\tilde{W}_i^T \dot{\hat{W}}_i\}$$

$$- \sum_{i=1}^{n} \frac{1}{\beta_i} tr\{\tilde{V}_i^T \dot{\hat{V}}_i\} - \sum_{i=1}^{n} \frac{\tilde{\phi}_i \dot{\hat{\phi}}_i}{\mu_i} + \sum_{i=1}^{n} s_i^T \omega_i(x_i)$$

$$- \sum_{i=1}^{n} (d_i + b_i) s_i^T \delta_i + \sum_{i=1}^{n} s_i^T \varepsilon_i(x_i)$$

$$(56)$$

According to the proof of Lemma 2 and the definitions of ϕ_i and $\psi_i(x_i)$, we have

$$\|\omega_i(x_i) + \varepsilon_i(x_i)\| \leq \phi_i \psi_i(x_i).$$

Thus

$$\dot{V} \leq -\sum_{i=1}^{n} \lambda_{\min}(K_i) \|s_i\|^2 - \sum_{i=1}^{n} s_i^T (u_{1,i} + u_{2,i})$$

$$-\sum_{i=1}^{n} tr\{\tilde{W}_i^T (\dot{\hat{W}}_i / \alpha_i - (\hat{\sigma}_i - \hat{\sigma}_i' \hat{V}_i^T \overline{x}_i) s_i^T)\}$$

$$-\sum_{i=1}^{n} tr\{\tilde{V}_i (\dot{\hat{V}}_i / \beta_i - \overline{x}_i s_i^T \hat{W}_i^T \hat{\sigma}_i')\} - \sum_{i=1}^{n} \frac{\tilde{\phi}_i \dot{\hat{\phi}}_i}{\mu_i}$$

$$+\sum_{i=1}^{n} (d_i + b_i) \|s_i\| \varsigma_{B,i} + \sum_{i=1}^{n} \phi_i \psi_i(x_i) \|s_i\| \tag{57}$$

According to (51)-(53), one has

$$\dot{V} \leq -\sum_{i=1}^{n} \lambda_{\min}(K_i) \|s_i\|^2$$

$$+\sum_{i=1}^{n} I_{pi} \frac{s_i^T \hat{W}_i^T (\hat{\sigma}_i - \hat{\sigma}_i' \hat{V}_i^T \overline{x}_i)}{tr\{\hat{W}_i^T \hat{W}_i\}} tr\{\tilde{W}_i^T \hat{W}_i\}$$

$$+\sum_{i=1}^{n} I_{pi} \frac{s_i^T \hat{W}_i^T \hat{\sigma}_i' \hat{V}_i^T \overline{x}_i}{tr\{\hat{V}_i^T \hat{V}_i\}} tr\{\tilde{V}_i^T \hat{V}_i\}$$

$$+\sum_{i=1}^{n} \gamma_i \tilde{\phi}_i (\hat{\phi}_i - \phi_{0,i})$$

$$+\sum_{i=1}^{n} \|s_i\| \phi_i \psi_i(x_i) - \sum_{i=1}^{n} \phi_i \psi_i(x_i) s_i^T \tanh(s_i \psi_i(x_i) / \overline{\varepsilon}_2)$$

$$+\sum_{i=1}^{n} (d_i + b_i) \|s_i\| \varsigma_{B,i}$$

$$-\sum_{i=1}^{n} (d_i + b_i) \varsigma_{B,i} s_i^T \tanh((d_i + b_i) \varsigma_{B,i} s_i / \overline{\varepsilon}_1)$$

with $I_{pi} = 0$ if the first group of conditions in (51) (or [52]) is satisfied and $I_{pi} = 1$ if otherwise. Applying Lemma 3 yields

$$\dot{V} \leq -\sum_{i=1}^{n} \lambda_{\min}(K_i) \|s_i\|^2$$

$$+\sum_{i=1}^{n} I_{pi} \frac{s_i^T \hat{W}_i^T (\hat{\sigma}_i - \hat{\sigma}_i' \hat{V}_i^T \overline{x}_i)}{tr\{\hat{W}_i^T \hat{W}_i\}} tr\{\tilde{W}_i^T \hat{W}_i\}$$

$$+\sum_{i=1}^{n} I_{pi} \frac{s_i^T \hat{W}_i^T \hat{\sigma}_i' \hat{V}_i^T \overline{x}_i}{tr\{\hat{V}_i^T \hat{V}_i\}} tr\{\tilde{V}_i^T \hat{V}_i\}$$

$$+\sum_{i=1}^{n} \gamma_i \tilde{\phi}_i (\hat{\phi}_i - \phi_{0,i}) + \frac{1}{2} \sum_{i=1}^{n} \phi_{B,i} m \overline{\varepsilon}_2 + \frac{1}{2} \sum_{i=1}^{n} m \overline{\varepsilon}_1.$$

If $I_{pi} \neq 0$, in light of the projection property (Goodwin & Mayne, 1987), one has

$$tr\{\tilde{W}_i^T \hat{W}_i\} = tr\left\{\frac{1}{2}(W_i - \hat{W}_i)^T \hat{W}_i + \frac{1}{2} \tilde{W}_i^T (W_i - \tilde{W}_i)\right\}$$

$$= tr\left\{\frac{1}{2} W_i^T W_i - \frac{1}{2} \hat{W}_i^T \hat{W}_i - \frac{1}{2} \tilde{W}_i^T \tilde{W}_i\right\}$$

$$= \frac{1}{2} tr\{W_i^T W_i\} - \frac{1}{2} tr\{\hat{W}_i^T \hat{W}_i\} - \frac{1}{2} tr\{\tilde{W}_i^T \tilde{W}_i\} \leq 0.$$

Similarly, we can get that $tr\{\tilde{V}_i^T \hat{V}_i\} \leq 0$ for the case $I_{pi} \neq 0$. Thus,

$$I_{pi} \frac{s_i^T \hat{W}_i^T (\hat{\sigma}_i - \hat{\sigma}_i' \hat{V}_i^T \overline{x}_i)}{tr\{\hat{W}_i^T \hat{W}_i\}} tr\{\tilde{W}_i^T \hat{W}_i\} \leq 0, \tag{58}$$

and

$$I_{pi} \frac{s_i^T \hat{W}_i^T \hat{\sigma}_i' \hat{V}_i^T \overline{x}_i}{tr\{\hat{V}_i^T \hat{V}_i\}} tr\{\tilde{V}_i^T \hat{V}_i\} \leq 0. \tag{59}$$

Note that

$$\tilde{\phi}_i (\hat{\phi}_i - \phi_{0,i}) = \tilde{\phi}_i (\hat{\phi}_i - \phi_{B,i} + \phi_{B,i} - \phi_{0,i})$$

$$= -\tilde{\phi}_i^2 + \tilde{\phi}_i (\phi_{B,i} - \phi_{0,i})$$

$$\leq -\frac{1}{2}\tilde{\phi}_i^2 + \frac{1}{2}(\phi_{B,i} - \phi_{0,i})^2 . \qquad (60)$$

According to (58)-(60), we have

$$\dot{V} \leq -\sum_{i=1}^{n}\lambda_{\min}(K_i)\|s_i\|^2 - \frac{1}{2}\sum_{i=1}^{n}\gamma_i\tilde{\phi}_i^2$$

$$+ \frac{1}{2}\sum_{i=1}^{n}\gamma_i(\phi_{B,i} - \phi_{0,i})^2 + \frac{1}{2}\sum_{i=1}^{n}\phi_{B,i}m\bar{\varepsilon}_2 + \frac{1}{2}\sum_{i=1}^{n}m\bar{\varepsilon}_1$$

$$\leq -\sum_{i=1}^{n}\lambda_{\min}(K_i)\|s_i\|^2 - \frac{1}{2}\sum_{i=1}^{n}\frac{1}{\alpha_i}tr\{\tilde{W}_i^T\tilde{W}_i\}$$

$$- \frac{1}{2}\sum_{i=1}^{n}\frac{1}{\beta_i}tr\{\tilde{V}_i^T\tilde{V}_i\} - \frac{1}{2}\sum_{i=1}^{n}\gamma_i\tilde{\phi}_i^2 + \sum_{i=1}^{n}\frac{2}{\alpha_i}W_{\max,i}$$

$$+ \sum_{i=1}^{n}\frac{2}{\beta_i}V_{\max,i} + \frac{1}{2}\sum_{i=1}^{n}\gamma_i(\phi_{B,i} - \phi_{0,i})^2$$

$$+ \frac{1}{2}\sum_{i=1}^{n}\phi_{B,i}m\bar{\varepsilon}_2 + \frac{1}{2}\sum_{i=1}^{n}m\bar{\varepsilon}_1$$

Let $c_0 = \min\left\{\dfrac{2\lambda_{\min}(K_i)}{\bar{\sigma}(M_i)}, \gamma_i\mu_i, 1\right\}$ and

$$\rho_0 = \sum_{i=1}^{n}\frac{2}{\alpha_i}W_{\max,i} + \sum_{i=1}^{n}\frac{2}{\beta_i}V_{\max,i} + \frac{1}{2}\sum_{i=1}^{n}\gamma_i(\phi_{B,i} - \phi_{0,i})^2$$

$$+ \frac{1}{2}\sum_{i=1}^{n}\phi_{B,i}m\bar{\varepsilon}_2 + \frac{1}{2}\sum_{i=1}^{n}m\bar{\varepsilon}_1$$

Then one has

$$\dot{V}(t) \leq -c_0V(t) + \rho_0 .$$

According to the well known comparison principle (Khalil, 2002), one can further get that

$$V(t) \leq V(0)e^{-c_0t} + \frac{\rho_0}{c_0}(1 - e^{-c_0t}) .$$

Thus,

$$\|S\| \leq \sqrt{\frac{2V(0)}{\underline{\sigma}(M)}e^{-c_0t} + \frac{2\rho_0}{\underline{\sigma}(M)c_0}(1 - e^{-c_0t})} .$$

The remainder of the proof mimics that of Theorem 1.

Through the use of projection mapping in the tuning laws, the weight estimates are always bounded and the parameter drift phenomenon in the presence of disturbances is avoided. By introducing the robust control terms in the design of control laws, the transient performance and the final tracking accuracy can be guaranteed. In this section, the proposed algorithms do not need to know the bounds of the NN approximation errors in the robust term. An adaptive scheme is used to estimate the bounds of the NN approximation errors. In order to avoid high-frequency chattering phenomena, no discontinuous control law is used in the protocol.

ILLUSTRATIVE DESIGN AND SIMULATION

As an example of networked Lagrange systems, a group of robot manipulators is considered in this section. For ease of plotting, we simulate a multi-manipulator systems composed of six two-link revolute manipulators. The profile of the two-link planar manipulator is shown in Figures 1 and 2 show the communication topology among the manipulators, which has a spanning tree.

The adjacency matrix of the graph can be written as

$$A = \begin{bmatrix} 0 & 0 & 0 & 0 & 0 & 0 \\ 1 & 0 & 0 & 0 & 0 & 0 \\ 1 & 0 & 0 & 0 & 0 & 0 \\ 0 & 0 & 1 & 0 & 0 & 0 \\ 0 & 1 & 0 & 1 & 0 & 0 \\ 0 & 1 & 0 & 0 & 0 & 0 \end{bmatrix} .$$

Figure 1. Two-link revolute manipulator

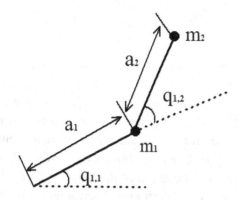

Figure 2. The communication topology

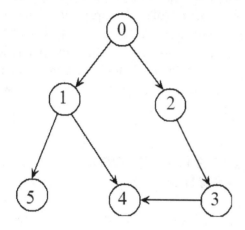

The Laplacian matrix of the subgraph $\bar{G}$ formed by the follower manipulators can be written as

$$\bar{L} = \begin{bmatrix} 0 & 0 & 0 & 0 & 0 \\ 0 & 0 & 0 & 0 & 0 \\ 0 & -1 & 1 & 0 & 0 \\ -1 & 0 & -1 & 2 & 0 \\ -1 & 0 & 0 & 0 & 1 \end{bmatrix}.$$

and the diagonal matrix B which describes the interaction relationship between the leader manipulator and the follower manipulators is

$$B = diag\begin{pmatrix} 1 & 1 & 0 & 0 & 0 \end{pmatrix}.$$

The manipulator dynamics satisfy some important physical properties as a consequence of the fact that they are Lagrange systems. By employing these properties, we can preprocess the NN input signals so that they can explicitly introduce some of the nonlinearities inherent to manipulator dynamics. Thus, it reduces the burden of expectation on the NN and, in fact, also reduces the NN approximation error. The following properties are very important for the preprocessing of NN input signals.

P1: For revolute joints, the occurrences of the joint variables q_i in the inertia matrix $M_i(q_i)$ are as $\sin(q_i)$, $\cos(q_i)$.

P2: As in (Hensen, et al., 2000), friction forces $h_i(\dot{q}_i)$ can be modeled as

$$h_i(\dot{q}_i) = c_{v,i}\dot{q}_i + c_{h1,i}\left(1 - \frac{2}{1 + e^{2w_{1,i}\dot{q}_i}}\right)$$
$$+ c_{h2,i}\left(1 - \frac{2}{1 + e^{2w_{2,i}\dot{q}_i}}\right),$$

where $c_{v,i}$ denotes the viscous friction coefficient and the remaining terms with coefficients $c_{h1,i}$, $c_{h2,i}$, $w_{1,i}$, and $w_{2,i}$ model the Coulomb and Stribeck friction.

P3: For revolute joints, the occurrences of the joint variable q_i in gravity vector $g_i(q_i)$ are as $\sin(q_i)$, $\cos(q_i)$.

P4: The occurrences of the neighbors' input information for manipulator i are as $\left(\sum_{j \in N_i} a_{ij}\ddot{q}_j + b_i\ddot{q}_0\right)$, $\left(\sum_{j \in N_i} a_{ij}\dot{q}_j + b_i\dot{q}_0\right)$, e_i^1, and e_i^2.

According to the physical properties of the manipulator, the input signals of the NN for node i can be taken as

$$\bar{x}_i = \left[\sin^T(q_i), \cos^T(q_i), \dot{q}_i^T, \cos^T(q_i)\left(\sum_{j \in N_i} a_{ij}\ddot{q}_j + b_i\ddot{q}_0\right)\right.$$
$$\left. , \sin^T(q_i)\left(\sum_{j \in N_i} a_{ij}\ddot{q}_j + b_i\ddot{q}_0\right),\right.$$

$$\left. \sin^T(q_i)\left(\sum_{j \in N_i} a_{ij}\dot{q}_j + b_i\dot{q}_0\right) , \cos^T(q_i)e_i^2, \sin^T(q_i)e_i^2, \sin^T(q_i)e_i^1, 1\right]^T.$$

The activation function for the neuron is chosen as sigmoid function. In the simulation, the dynamic model of two-link revolute manipulator is given as follows.

$$M_i(q_i) = \begin{bmatrix} M_{i11} & M_{i12} \\ M_{i21} & M_{i22} \end{bmatrix},$$

$$C_i(q_i, \dot{q}_i) = \begin{bmatrix} C_{i11} & C_{i12} \\ C_{i21} & 0 \end{bmatrix},$$

$$h_i(\dot{q}_i) = \begin{bmatrix} h_{i1}(\dot{q}_{i1}) \\ h_{i2}(\dot{q}_{i2}) \end{bmatrix},$$

$$g_i(q_i) = \begin{bmatrix} g_{i1} \\ g_{i2} \end{bmatrix},$$

$$M_{i11} = (m_1 + m_2)a_1^2 + m_2 a_2^2 + 2m_2 a_1 a_2 \cos(q_{i2}),$$

$$M_{i12} = m_2 a_2^2 + m_2 a_1 a_2 \cos(q_{i2}),$$

$$M_{i22} = m_2 a_2^2,$$

$$C_{i11} = -\dot{q}_{i2} m_2 a_1 a_2 \sin(q_{i2}),$$

$$C_{i12} = -(\dot{q}_{i1} + \dot{q}_{i2})m_2 a_1 a_2 \sin(q_{i2}),$$

$$C_{i21} = \dot{q}_{i1} m_2 a_1 a_2 \sin(q_{i2}),$$

$$h_{i1}(\dot{q}_{i1}) = c_{v,i1}\dot{q}_{i1} + c_{h1,i1}\left(1 - \frac{2}{1 + e^{2w_{1,i1}\dot{q}_{i1}}}\right) + c_{h2,i1}\left(1 - \frac{2}{1 + e^{2w_{2,i1}\dot{q}_{i1}}}\right),$$

$$h_{i2}(\dot{q}_{i2}) = c_{v,i2}\dot{q}_{i2} + c_{h1,i2}\left(1 - \frac{2}{1 + e^{2w_{1,i2}\dot{q}_{i2}}}\right) + c_{h2,i2}\left(1 - \frac{2}{1 + e^{2w_{2,i2}\dot{q}_{i2}}}\right),$$

$$g_{i1} = (m_1 + m_2)ga_1\cos(q_{i1}) + m_2 ga_2\cos(q_{i1} + q_{i2}),$$

$$g_{i2} = m_2 ga_2\cos(q_{i1} + q_{i2}).$$

For simplicity, we assume that each manipulator has the same parameters. The parameters of manipulators are set as follows. The masses of links 1 and 2 are $m_1 = m_2 = 1kg$; the link lengths are $a_1 = a_2 = 1m$. We assume that the joint trajectories of the leader manipulator 0 are $q_0 = (\sin(t), \cos(t))^T$. Let the initial conditions of the five follower manipulators be

$$q_1 = q_2 = q_3 = q_4 = q_5 = 0,$$

$$\dot{q}_1 = \dot{q}_2 = \dot{q}_3 = \dot{q}_4 = \dot{q}_5 = 0.$$

The external disturbances are assumed to be $\delta_i = 0.1\sin(q_i)$, $\forall i$. In simulation, we let

$$\Lambda = diag\left(7, \quad 20, \quad 7, \quad 20, \quad 7\right) \otimes I_2,$$

$$K_i = diag\left(20, \quad 10\right), \kappa_i = 1, \text{ and}$$
$$F_i = L_i = 10I.$$

$$c_{v,i1} = c_{v,i2} = c_{h1,i1} = c_{h1,i2} = 2,$$

$$c_{h2,i1} = c_{h2,i2} = 1, w_{1,i1} = w_{1,i2} = 2,$$
$$w_{2,i1} = w_{2,i2} = -1.$$

We simulate the networked systems under the control protocol (27). Figures 3 and 4 show the tracking trajectories. It turns out that the simulation results coincide with the theoretical analysis.

Figure 3. Trajectories for joint 1

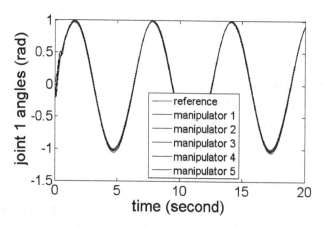

Figure 4. Trajectories for joint 2

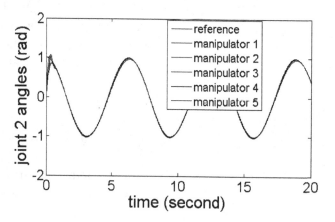

CONCLUSION

This chapter has given and analyzed the distributed tracking control scheme for networked Lagrange systems with a target system to be tracked. All the systems can have different dynamics and the dynamics are all nonlinear and unknown. Higher-order NNs were used at each subsystem to approximate the unknown dynamics. Based on the Lyapunov techniques, an adaptive synchronization control protocol was presented. The proposed scheme was distributed since the controller for each Lagrange system only used the information of itself and its neighbors. Due to the distributed structure, the scheme was amenable to parallel computing within a distributed processing architecture. Moreover, the algorithms were

suitable for the case that the desired trajectory of the target node was only available to a portion of the systems. Under the given control protocol, it was shown that the synchronization errors can be reduced as small as possible. Finally, by using a networked two-link manipulator system, we illustrated the distributed control scheme derived in this chapter.

ACKNOWLEDGMENT

This work was supported by the National Natural Science Foundation of China under Grant No. 61273108, CQ CSTC 2011 BB2056, SRFDP-09-0191120025, CDJZR11170003, FA9550-09-1-0278, and ECCS-0801330.

REFERENCES

Chen, F. C., & Khalil, H. K. (1992). Adaptive control of nonlinear systems using neural networks. *International Journal of Control*, *55*(6), 1299–1317. doi:10.1080/00207179208934286

Chen, G., & Lewis, F. L. (2011). Distributed adaptive tracking control for synchronization of unknown networked Lagrangian systems. *IEEE Transactions on Systems, Man, and Cybernetics, Part B, 41*(3).

Chopra, N., & Spong, M. W. (2006). Passivity-based control of multi-agent systems . In Kawamura, S., & Svinin, M. (Eds.), *Advances in Robot Control: From Everyday Physics to Human-Like Movements* (pp. 107–134). New York, NY: Springer-Verlag.

Chung, S., & Slotine, J. J. E. (2009). Cooperative robot control and concurrent synchronization of Lagrangian systems. *IEEE Transactions on Robotics*, *25*(3), 686–700. doi:10.1109/TRO.2009.2014125

Durbin, R., & Rumelhart, D. E. (1989). Product units: A computationally powerful and biologically plausible extension to backpropagation networks. *Neural Computation*, *1*(1), 133–142. doi:10.1162/neco.1989.1.1.133

Giles, G. L., & Maxwell, T. (1987). Learning, invariance, and generalization in high-order neural networks. *Applied Optics*, *26*(23), 4972–4978. doi:10.1364/AO.26.004972

Goodwin, G. C., & Mayne, D. Q. (1987). A parameter estimation perspective of continuous time model reference adaptive control. *Automatica*, *23*(1), 57–70. doi:10.1016/0005-1098(87)90118-X

Hensen, R. H. A., Angelis, G. Z., van de Molengraft, M. J. G., de Jager, A. G., & Kok, J. J. (2000). Grey-box modeling of friction: An experimental case-study. *European Journal of Control*, *6*(3), 258–267.

Hong, Y., Chen, G. R., & Bushnell, L. (2008). Distributed observers design for leader following control of multi-agent networks. *Automatica*, *44*(3), 846–850. doi:10.1016/j.automatica.2007.07.004

Horn, R. A., & Johnson, C. R. (1987). *Matrix analysis*. Cambridge, UK: Cambridge University Press.

Hornik, K., Stinchombe, M., & White, H. (1989). Multilayer feedforward networks are universal approximations. *Neural Networks*, *2*(5), 359–366. doi:10.1016/0893-6080(89)90020-8

Hou, Z. G., Cheng, L., & Tan, M. (2009). Decentralized robust adaptive control for the multiagent system consensus problem using neural networks. *IEEE Transactions on Systems, Man, and Cybernetics . Part B*, *39*(3), 636–647.

Jadbabaie, A., Lin, J., & Morse, A. S. (2003). Coordination of groups of mobile autonomous agents using nearest neighbor rules. *IEEE Transactions on Automatic Control*, *48*(6), 988–1001. doi:10.1109/TAC.2003.812781

Khalil, H. K. (2002). *Nonlinear systems*. Upper Saddle River, NJ: Prentice-Hall.

Khoo, S., Xie, L., & Man, Z. (2009). Robust finite-time consensus tracking algorithm for multirobot systems. *IEEE/ASME Transactions on Mechatronics*, *14*(2), 219–228. doi:10.1109/TMECH.2009.2014057

Lewis, F. L., Jagannathan, S., & Yesildirek, A. (1998). *Neural network control of robot manipulators and non-linear systems*. New York, NY: Taylor & Francis.

Lewis, F. L., Yesildirek, A., & Liu, K. (1996). Multilayer neural-net robot controller with guaranteed tracking performance. *IEEE Transactions on Neural Networks*, *7*(2), 388–399. doi:10.1109/72.485674

Narendra, S., & Parthasarathy, K. (1990). Identification and control of dynamical systems using neural networks. *IEEE Transactions on Neural Networks*, *1*(1), 4–27. doi:10.1109/72.80202

Olfati-Saber, R., Fax, A. J., & Murray, R. M. (2007). Consensus and cooperation in networked multi-agent systems. *Proceedings of the IEEE, 95*(1), 215–233. doi:10.1109/JPROC.2006.887293

Olfati-Saber, R., & Murray, R. M. (2004). Consensus problems in networks of agents with switching topology and time-delays. *IEEE Transactions on Automatic Control, 49*(9), 1520–1533. doi:10.1109/TAC.2004.834113

Polycarpou, M. M. (1996). Stable adaptive neural control scheme for nonlinear systems. *IEEE Transactions on Automatic Control, 41*(3), 447–451. doi:10.1109/9.486648

Polycarpou, M. M., & Ioannou, P. A. (1996). A robust adaptive nonlinear control design. *Automatica, 32*(3), 423–427. doi:10.1016/0005-1098(95)00147-6

Qu, Z. (2009). *Cooperative control of dynamical systems: Applications to autonomous vehicles.* New York, NY: Springer-Verlag. doi:10.1109/TAC.2008.920232

Qu, Z., Wang, J., & Hull, R. A. (2008). Cooperative control of dynamical systems with application to autonomous vehicles. *IEEE Transactions on Automatic Control, 53*(4), 894–911. doi:10.1109/TAC.2008.920232

Redding, N. J., Kowalczyk, A., & Downs, T. (1993). Constructive higher-order network algorithm that is polynomial time. *Neural Networks, 6*(7), 997–1010. doi:10.1016/S0893-6080(09)80009-9

Ren, W. (2009). Distributed leaderless consensus algorithms for networked Euler–Lagrange systems. *International Journal of Control, 82*(11), 2137–2149. doi:10.1080/00207170902948027

Ren, W., & Beard, R. W. (2005). Consensus seeking in multiagent systems under dynamically changing interaction topologies. *IEEE Transactions on Automatic Control, 50*(5), 655–661. doi:10.1109/TAC.2005.846556

Ren, W., & Beard, R. W. (2008). *Distributed consensus in multi-vehicle cooperative control.* New York, NY: Springer-Verlag.

Ren, W., Beard, R. W., & Atkins, E. M. (2007). Information consensus in multivehicle cooperative control. *IEEE Control Systems Magazine, 27*(2), 71–82. doi:10.1109/MCS.2007.338264

Rodriguez-Angeles, A., & Nijmeijer, H. (2004). Mutual synchronization of robots via estimated state feedback: A cooperative approach. *IEEE Transactions on Control Systems Technology, 12*(4), 542–554. doi:10.1109/TCST.2004.825065

Rumelhart, D. E., & McClelland, J. L. (1986). *Parallel distributed computing: Exploration in the microstructure of cognition.* Cambridge, MA: MIT Press.

Shin, Y., & Ghosh, J. (1991). *The pi-sigma network: An efficient higher-order neural network for pattern classification and function approximation.* Paper presented at International Joint Conference on Neural Network. Seattle, WA.

Sun, D., Shao, X., & Feng, G. (2007). A model-free cross-coupled control for position synchronization of multi-axis motions: Theory and experiments. *IEEE Transactions on Control Systems Technology, 15*(2), 306–314. doi:10.1109/TCST.2006.883201

Wu, C. W. (2007). *Synchronization in complex networks of nonlinear dynamical systems.* Singapore: World Scientific. doi:10.1142/6570

Zhang, M., Xu, S., & Fulcher, J. (2002). Neuron-adaptive higher order neural-network models for automated financial data modeling. *IEEE Transactions on Neural Networks, 13*(1), 188–204. doi:10.1109/72.977302

Zhang, T., Ge, S. S., & Hang, C. C. (1999). Design and performance analysis of a direct adaptive controller for nonlinear systems. *Automatica, 35*(11), 1809–1817. doi:10.1016/S0005-1098(99)00098-9

Chapter 11
Symbolic Function Network:
Application to Telecommunication Networks Prediction

George S. Eskander
ETS, Quebec University, Canada

Amir Atiya
Cairo University, Egypt

ABSTRACT

Quality of Service (QoS) of telecommunication networks could be enhanced by applying predictive control methods. Such controllers rely on utilizing good and fast (real-time) predictions of the network traffic and quality parameters. Accuracy and recall speed of the traditional Neural Network models are not satisfactory to support such critical real time applications. The Symbolic Function Network (SFN) is a HONN-like model that was originally motivated by the current needs of developing more enhanced and fast predictors for such applications. In this chapter, the authors use the SFN model to design fast and accurate predictors for the telecommunication networks quality control applications. Three predictors are designed and tested for the network traffic, packet loss, and round trip delay. This chapter aims to open a door for researchers to investigate the applicability of SFN in other prediction tasks and to develop more accurate and faster predictors.

INTRODUCTION

Delivering real-time multi-media across the Internet has become a challenge to multimedia providers, as it is an essential element in offering some advanced services as distance learning, digital libraries, video conferencing, and video on demand. These services could not be delivered across the Internet in a guaranteed quality of service due the heterogeneous makeup of the Internet that leads to unspecified bandwidth available for each application. The lack of available bandwidth, especially during periods of high demand, creates traffic jams on the Internet that result in packet loss, transmission delay, and bad quality.

DOI: 10.4018/978-1-4666-2175-6.ch011

Predicting the network state and conditions like traffic generated by multimedia sources (Adas, 1998), packet loss ratio (Parlos, 2002), and packet delay time (Atiya, Yoo, Chong, & Kim, 2007) can be utilized to develop the so-called predictive controllers that control the network and provide better performance. Such prediction process needs accurate and very fast (real-time) predictors.

Symbolic Function Network (SFN) is designed with the goal to impart more flexibility than the traditional Neural Networks (NNs) (Eskander & Atiya, 2009). While traditional Higher Order Neural Networks (HONNs) use higher order terms to model complex nonlinearities and correlations between system inputs and features, SFN use basic building blocks like power, logarithm, and exponential functions to model the system nonlinearities. By concatenating these terms, the features correlation can be also modeled. The wider range of available activation functions, and the evolutionary structure of SFN, is expected to permit higher modeling power with sparser structure when compared to traditional NNs and even HONNs.

The symbolic function network can be represented as a tree based neural network. The terminals of the tree are the most relevant features that affect the system output, and the weights of the neural tree are the parameters that determine its overall functionality. SFN model showed encouraging results in the field of communication networks prediction (Eskander, Atiya, Chong, Kim, & Yoo, 2007). Accordingly, we believe that more improvement can be achieved by applying more advanced optimization to the SFN model.

This chapter aims to give a background of the application of SFN to model the behavior of communication networks. Through the chapter, a background of computer networks prediction strategies is introduced followed by an overview on the SFN model. Three different predictors for traffic of MPEG video, Packet Loss Ratio (PLR) and Round-Trip-Time (RTT) are proposed based on the SFN modeling approach.

BACKGROUND

There are many problems faced in transporting multimedia streams, such as real-time video or audio over networks that offer no service guarantees. The majority of these problems originate from the delay-sensitive nature of multimedia content. Irrespective of the method used to transport media content over an IP network, there is a strict timing sequence that must be used by the decoder during playback. For acceptable playback experience, all relevant packets must be available at the destination for assembly when needed and in the correct sequence. An obvious and simple solution to this problem is destination-side buffering and more recently, edge-caching. The trade-off of this approach is that the media content is not delivered to the destination in real-time or even in near real-time. Even though many media applications, such as streaming and on-demand video and audio, are tolerant to such large delays in delivery, there are numerous applications that require real-time or near real-time media delivery, such as gaming, conferencing, and telephony applications.

Predicting traffic generated by multimedia sources is needed for effective dynamic bandwidth allocation and for multimedia Quality-of-Service (QoS) control strategies implemented at the network edges which is called "End To End quality-of-service control." These techniques are needed in both QoS supporting networks, which offer a guaranteed quality of service level like ATM networks, and in the best effort Networks which doesn't guarantee any specific quality of service levels like IP "Internet protocol" networks. For the networks that support QoS, there are many models that supporting Variable Bit Rate (VBR) applications. For example, Renegotiated Constant Bit Rate network service model (RCBR) network service model that gives applications the option to renegotiate their rate (bandwidth) after the connections have been accepted. Renegotiating for less bandwidth will always succeed, but renegotiations for more bandwidth might fail. When renegotiations fail, applications must reduce their output bit rate to avoid network congestion and buffer overflow. For on-line (real-time) VBR video applications, the video encoder can trade the output bit rate with perceptual quality. For the Best effort networks like IP networks, there is much work have been done to deign control mechanisms that controls the traffic and hence support quality of services. One of the problems encountered in efforts to design and implement such edge-based QoS control in IP network, for applications requiring real-time or near real-time content delivery, is the need to know the source traffic bit-rate time-series. To this end, future values of this time-series are needed.

Besides the need to predict network traffic, prediction of other network conditions like Packet Loss Rate (PLR), and Round Trip Time (RTT) is needed to support these QoS controllers. The motivation for predicting PLR and RTT arises from the introduction of several TCP (Transmission Control Protocol)-friendly rate control mechanisms that can adjust the traffic rate based on these key quantities. Rather than using previously measured values of PLR and RTT, a better approach is to use predictions of these quantities. Such a predictive approach will be quicker to track congestion conditions than the typically used reactive approach. The other motivation for predicting PLR is that for real time multimedia traffic transmitted using UDP (User Datagram Protocol), a procedure to recover lost packets is by adding redundancy using Forward Error Correction (FEC). These are extra packets that can be used to reconstruct lost packets. The FEC packets, however, represent a bandwidth overhead, and it is therefore imperative to send only as much of these as needed. The estimate of the packet loss rate is needed to estimate the amount of such redundancy and hence lessening the overhead.

Two main properties must be fulfilled when one design a real-time predictor for such communication networks predictive controllers. First, prediction accuracy so that the controller produces suitable control signals, and second, prediction speed so that the control signal arises before needed. In this context, sparse and accurate modeling tools are needed.

Symbolic Function Network (SFN) is an evolutionary neural tree networks that permits more flexibility in modeling than traditional neural networks. Evolving neural trees are special case of neural networks category known as evolutionary neural networks that search for best basis functions in a greedy manner, hence facilitate sparse representation (Yao, 1999). Moreover, symbolic reduction techniques can be applied on the final evolved tree to reduce the model expression. In SFN, a set of elementary functions are searched and selected in a way that their connectivity, structure, and parameters are being adapted to the modeled system. Development of the SFN model was motivated by the aim of achieving sparse models that can predict systems behavior to attain real time constraints. Accordingly, SFN is ideal for the real-time communication networks prediction tasks. Some communication networks predictors are developed based on the SFN approach like Round Trip Time (RTT), MPEG video traffic, and Packet Loss Ratio (PLR) predictors.

OVERVIEW OF SFN MODEL

SFN network is composed of some basic functions (building blocks). These functions can operate on pure system inputs, or affects other basic functions in a cascading way. To this end, a constructive training algorithm is applied to build the network in a top down strategy. Elementary functions are added to the tree one by one in some way so as to achieve as best fitting performance as possible for the given training data. By having several layers of the

Figure 1. Example of a constructed symbolic network

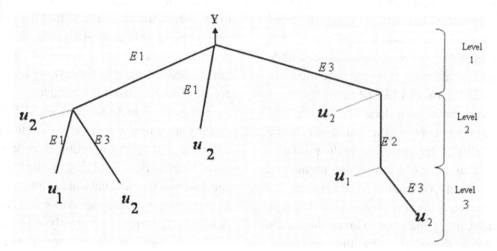

tree several levels of function concatenations can be achieved. The elementary functions used in SFN are the power, exponential, and logarithmic functions. The mathematical form of these functions can be represented as follows:

$$E1(u) = w(u^2 + 1)^v$$
$$E2(u) = qe^{\alpha u} \qquad\qquad (1)$$
$$E3(u) = p \log(u^2 + 1)$$

Where u is a scalar input, and $w, v, q, \alpha,$ and p are the free parameters to be tuned by the optimization algorithm. Figure 1 represents an example of a SFN network that constructed by the training algorithm. The constructed network contains 3 layers, 7 nonlinear links and 3 linear dummy links.

This network represents a nonlinear Symbolic function Y of two inputs u_1 and u_2 where

$$Y = E1(u_2 + E1(u_1) + E3(u_2)) + E1(u_2)$$
$$+ E3(u_2 + E2(u_1 + E3(u_2))).$$

Example of using the SFN approach in systems modelling is shown here. Input-output data are generated from a sinusoidal signal

$Y(u) = \sin(2\pi u)$, and then delivered to the SFN training algorithm. The system could be modelled using only seven elementary functions and twelve parameters. Figure 2 shows the SFN realization of the sinusoidal signal. The SFN model is given by:

$$Y = \sin(u) = E1(u + E2(u)) + E2(u + E1(u))$$
$$+ E3(u + E2(u) + E3(u)).$$
$$Y = 0.3304 \left(1 + [u - 0.0009\, e^{4.5983u}]^2\right)^{4.6275}$$
$$+ 10.0713\, e^{(-4.4452[u + 0.3396(u^2 + 1)^{1.3831}])}$$
$$- 3.7065 \log(1 + [u - 1.0049\, e^{-3.3430u}$$
$$+ 1.1832 \log(u^2 + 1)]^2)$$

Figure 2. SFN realization of a sinusoidal signal

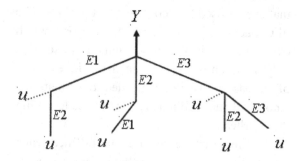

SFN Network Design

SFN networks are designed through applying two processes: weights optimization and structure optimization. In weight optimization process, all free network parameters are updated in order minimize the modeling error. The network structure can be optimized by adding new items to the network, or through removing some of the already admitted terms (pruning).

For the weights optimization process, a back propagation of modeling error is derived to compute the impact of parameters gradients on the fitness. The computed gradient values are then used to update the network parameters by applying steepest descent methodology.

To briefly describe this parameter optimization process, consider the particular path along the SFN network shown in Figure 3. Consider a particular path along the tree: Y- Z1- Z2- Z3- ---- where the functions encountered along the path are: $E_{i_1} - E_{i_2} - E_{i_3} ----- $

Then,

$$z_{j-1} = E_{i_j}(z_j) + E_{oth}(z_{oth}) \qquad (2)$$

Figure 3. Particular path along the SFN network

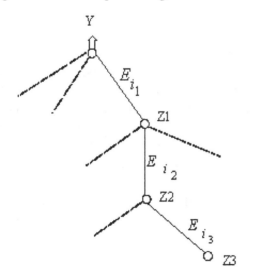

Where $E_{oth}(z_{oth})$ is the sum of other transformations that are affecting z_{oth} which are the brothers of z_j.

The backward computations are derived to compute the matrix of gradients in a recursive manner.

Let the error function be

$$J = \sum_{m=1}^{M}(y(m)-d(m))^2 = \sum_{m=1}^{M} e(m)^2 \qquad (3)$$

Where $y(m)$ and $d(m)$ are the actual network output and the target output for training example (m) respectively, and M is the size of the training set.

The instantaneous gradient w.r.t some weight ω is

$$\frac{\delta J}{\delta \omega}(m) = 2\,e(m)\,\frac{\delta y(m)}{\delta \omega} \qquad (4)$$

However the total gradient for the whole training set is

$$\frac{\delta J}{\delta \omega} = 2\sum_{m=1}^{M} e(m)\,\frac{\delta y(m)}{\delta \omega} \qquad (5)$$

To obtain $\frac{\delta y}{\delta \omega}$ (we skipped the index m for ease notations), a key quantity has to be evaluated namely $\frac{\delta y}{\delta z_j}$. It is obtained using the chain rule by starting up the tree with j=1, and tracing the tree going downward as follows:

$$\frac{\delta y}{\delta z_j} = \frac{\delta y}{\delta z_{j-1}}\,\frac{\delta z_{j-1}}{\delta z_j} \qquad (6)$$

The above equation is used to compute the partial derivative of the network output w.r.t any hidden node in a recursive manner.

Using Equation (2) and Equation (6) we get:

$$\frac{\delta y}{\delta z_j} = \frac{\delta y}{\delta z_{j-1}} \ E'_{i_j}(z_j) \qquad (7)$$

Where $E'_{i_j}(z_j)$ is obtained by differentiating the basic functional forms (Equation 1) w.r.t its argument u and evaluated at $u = z_j$. Once $\frac{\delta y}{\delta z_j}$'s are evaluated for all the tree, the gradient can be obtained.

Let ω be the weight associated with node, i.e.

$$z_j = E_{i_{j+1}}(z_{j+1}, \omega) + E_{oth}(z_{oth}) \qquad (8)$$

$$\frac{\delta y}{\delta \omega} = \frac{\delta y}{\delta z_j} \ \frac{\delta E_{i_{j+1}}}{\delta \omega} \qquad (9)$$

$\frac{\delta E_{i_{j+1}}}{\delta \omega}$ Can be evaluated by differentiating the basic functional forms Equation (1) w.r.t the weights w, v, q, α, p whatever ω represents.

To optimize the SFN network structure three model variants are designed namely, forward (F-SFN), backward (B-SFN), and forward-backward (FB-SFN) model. In the forward method (F-SFN), the network components are added to the network in an incremental way. The network component can be a single link (FLK-SFN) or a complete layer (FLY-SFN). The algorithm builds the network incrementally from top to down. It starts with an empty network then adds the network elements one by one. After adding each element, and training the network, it measures the network performance and decides based on that to keep this added item or to restore the previous network configurations. In the backward training method (B-SFN), a complete layer of links is added and its parameters are tuned, a pruning algorithm is applied to remove the redundant weights from the network. In forward Backward Algorithm (FB-SFN [K]), a pruning algorithm runs in parallel with the constructive algorithm. To this end, links are added incrementally as done in the forward method until having a specific number (K) of admitted links, and then pruning algorithm starts to remove the least worth link. This process of forward-backward network construction continues until the performance reaches acceptable level.

SFN for Time Series Prediction

The SFN approach could be applied to model systems for the time series prediction task. To this end, old measurements of the system are fed to the SFN model and the network produces the predicted values. To show the applicability of SFN for the time series prediction task, and especially when the time series is noisy as it is the case of communication networks time series, the following synthetic system is used:

$$y(k+1) = 0.4y(k) + 0.4y(k)y(k-1) + 0.6u(k)^3 + 0.1.$$

We generated two sequences of 200 points each by considering the input signal as an independent random noise (uniform in [0, 0.5]). The first sequence is used for learning and the second sequence is used for testing the network performance. Figure 4 shows the SFN network testing performance for the B-SFN (1) (i.e. a single layer backward-algorithm SFN). The designed SFN contained only 10 weights with mean square prediction error (MSE) of 5.89E-05.

Figure 4. SFN performance for the time series forcasting probelm

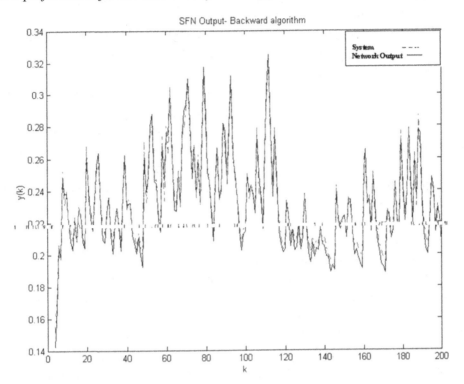

This result is very encouraging as a very light predictor could model the system with an acceptable fitness in presence of a noise signal added to the system. Consequently, we expect that SFN could be applied to design fast and accurate predictors for the communication networks predictive controllers.

MPEG VIDEO CODED TRAFFIC PREDICTION

As aforementioned, predicting traffic generated by multimedia sources is needed for effective dynamic bandwidth allocation and for multimedia Quality-of-Service (QoS) control strategies implemented at the network edges. As a special case of quality of service assurance application, we consider here the delivery of real- time video across the Internet. We report here the design SFN predictors for Single-Step (SS) and Multi-Step (MS) traffic prediction of video streams coded in MPEG format. Simulation results for eleven Mpeg Video files have shown compromising results when compared to the literature.

MPEG Video Coding

Mpeg is a video compression standard. The Mpeg video file is a compression of the video stream into a number of pictures called frames. There are two types of frames; intra frames, and none intra frames. An intra-frame or I-frame is a frame that is encoded using only information from within that frame only. None intra frames use information from outside the frame, i.e., from the frames that have already been encoded. There are two types of none intra frames; predicted frames (P-frames), and bidirectional frames (B-frames). The P-frames are predicted from I-frames and other P-frames. The B-frames are encoded using P-frames and I-frames.

The Mpeg File consists of a repeated sequence of frames called Group of pictures "GOPs." A regular MPEG GOP can be represented by the sequence of frames IBBPBBPBBPBB. GOP sequence is characterized by two parameters; M, and N. where M represents the distance between two successive I-frames, and N represents the distance between two successive P-frames. For the regular GOP, M=12, and N=3.

Simulations Setup

The time-series representing frame or Visual Object Plane (VOP) sizes of an MPEG-coded stream is extremely noisy, and it has very long-range time dependencies. Many research works have been done to develop new approaches for developing MPEG-coded real-time video traffic predictors for use in Single-Step (SS) and Multi-Step (MS) prediction horizons (Adas, 1998; Yoo, 2002; Doulamis, Doulamis, & Kollias, 2000a, 2000b, 2003; Frost & Melamed, 1994). We applied SFN on this problem in order to test the model ability in these time series prediction problems. SFN results are compared with the most performing predictors (Atiya, Aly, & Parlos, 2005; Bhattacharya, Parlos, & Atyia, 2003). Atiya, Aly, and Parlos (2005) designed a traffic predictor based on traditional MLP, and recurrent neural networks. However, Bhattacharya, Parlos, and Atyia (2003) designed a traffic predictor based on the sparse basis selection concept.

We used the same data used in above papers, which is the time series of eleven Mpeg Video files (Fitzek & Reisslein, 1998). Each series consists of 89 998 VOPs. The number of I-VOPs in each trace is 7 500, the number of P-frames in each trace is 22 500, and the number of B-frames in each trace is 59 998. For all trials, we used NMSE% as the performance measure to be minimized where:

$$NMSE\% = \frac{\sum_{m=1}^{M}(y(m) - d(m))^2}{\sum_{m=1}^{M} d(m)^2}$$

$*100 ; y(m), d(m)$ *are the network output and the desired output at any sample* $"m"$ *respectively, and* M *is the length of the testing set.*

Simulation Results

Prediction of I-VOPs Size Time Series

The model is trained using the first 1500 I-VOP sizes of the data trace of *Aladdin* video, while the designed predictor is tested on the remaining unused segment of the entire *Aladdin* video stream, as well as on the entire video traces of all other video streams. The results are listed in Table 1, and sample predicted trace is represented in Figure 5.

As shown in the results, most of SFN results outperform the Bhattacharya results; and some outperform the sparse results. Although most of the sparse results outperform SFN results, the difference is not that high. The good point here is that, while the sparse basis selection method based on using very large dictionary of pre-processed inputs, and then generation of a pool of nonlinear transformation of that extracted inputs; that must be generated based on some experience and maybe by trials; the SFN model does not need that. Therefore, to be fair in comparing the above results, we have to notice that in SFN we used only the most recent three pure values of the packet size to predict the next one. It is up to the algorithm to choose the best nonlinear transformations that represent the system and to optimize the weights of them. By other means, to make a formal comparison among the competing models, we have to build all of them using the same input dictionary. Surely, if we try the sparse basis selection model and the Bhattacharya techniques by just using the latest three pure values of the time series, it would give worse results and the SFN would be the best.

Comparison between SFN and Bhattacharya's Model Performance

Bhattacharya used a 15-7-1 recurrent network; for sure it is none constructive network that makes the resultant model is too complex; on the other hand, SFN model is a constructive one that results in a very sparse model representation. While the re-

Table 1. Testing error (in NMSE%) for single step ahead prediction of I-VOPS size time series for the some of the proposed model variants B-SFN, and FB-SFN, and the most recent published related work

s	Trace	SFN		Sparse	Bhattacharya
		B-SFN	FB-SFN (K=5)		
1	Aladdin	3.07	3.13	2.5	2.6
2	Die Hard III	2.92	2.95	1.89	2.9
3	Jurassic Park I	1.09	1.16	0.75	0.8
4	Lecture Room	0.15	0.14	58.3	0.2
5	Mr. Bean	2.01	2.1	2.22	-
6	Silence of the Lambs	2.58	2.42	1.61	3.6
7	Simpson's	1.04	1.11	1.33	-
8	Skiing	1.84	1.89	1.12	2
9	Star wars	1.63	1.79	1.27	1.5
10	The Firm	1.69	1.73	1.28	-
11	ARD Talk	0.79	0.86	-	0.9

Figure 5. Single step ahead predicted sizes of I-VOPs of lecture room

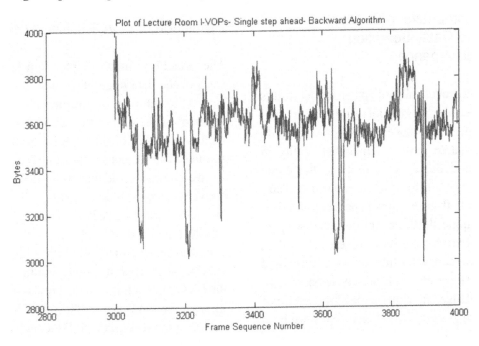

current network consists of about 120 parameters, the SFN network that build using the backward algorithm consists of 12 parameters, and that was built using the forward-backward algorithm consists of just 9 parameters. In addition, training the recurrent network consumed about 100 hours of real time while the SFN network are designed in just 2 hours. As referred to above, in the recurrent network design, the designer chose 15 inputs to be entered the network; those inputs are extracted from the predicted time series and other correlated time series, such as P-VOPs time series. Moreover, the designer had the role of not only chose that pure inputs but pre-process them based on his experience in modeling such systems. Surely, if this choice process has done in a wrong way, the network would not approximate the system in such good performance. Therefore, we can say that the overall network design time is much more than the computer processing time. However, in SFN all these processes are automated, the designer has just the role of choosing the number of the delayed inputs—that is three in these simulations—and let the constructive algorithm to do all tasks. At last, in addition of all above strong points of SFN rather than the recurrent networks, most of SFN performance results are better than the recurrent network performance.

Comparison between SFN and the Sparse Basis Selection Model Performance

As above, however, most of sparse model results are better than the SFN model results with a small difference in performance; the SFN model could be considered to have much higher ability in nonlinear modeling than the first one, that could be found when we look at the input dictionary that used in both cases. In the sparse basis selection based mode, the designer has chose 96 inputs extracted from the predicted time series (I-VOPs), and other two correlated time series (P-VOPs and B-VOPs). Those 96 inputs are chose based on a prior knowledge and experience of the nature of the modeled system. However, in SFN we built the network using just the latest three values of the predicted time series; neither input are extracted from other external time series, nor input pre-processing task is done. So, the SFN model itself could capture most of the nonlinearities of the modeled system without the need of preparing some of them manually and passing to it as done

in the sparse basis selection based linear model. Surely, it is expected that if we pass other pure inputs from the correlated time series or the predicted time series to the SFN model, it would give the best results. Finally, in the sparse basis selection technique, there was a case of encountering ill-conditioning problem that is due to the matrix computation which may results in very close to singular matrices. This problem could be overcome by starting the prediction from an initial time $n_0 > 1$; however n_0 must be large enough to avoid the ill-conditioning problem. Surely, the time series for all points $< n_0$ could not be predicted; if any traffic control mechanism is running and based on the predicted time series, it could not work in the time period before n_0. Such problem is not applicable for the SFN model design, while the prediction is available for all of the time series.

Prediction of P-VOPs Size Time Series

The model is trained using the first 1500 P-VOP sizes of the data trace of *Aladdin*, while the designed predictor is tested on the remaining unused segment of the entire *Aladdin* video stream, As well as on the entire video traces of all other video streams. The results are listed in Table 2.

We tried to build the P-Predictor using the forward link-by-link algorithm. The resulted predictor performance is worse than the I-predictors designed in the above section; this result was expected because the P-VOPs time series is found to be noisier and having higher nonlinearities than the I-VOPs; that is due to the previous work done in Atiya, Aly, and Parlos (2005) and Bhattacharya, Parlos, and Atyia (2003). By comparing the I-VOPs predictor performance and the P-VOPs predictor performance in the sparse and Bhattacharya work, we can notice that the first is much better.

However, in designing the SFN I-VOPs predictor we have results that outperform the recurrent

Table 2. Testing error (in NMSE%) for single step ahead prediction of P-VOPs size time series for one of the proposed model variants FLK-SFN, and the most recent published related work. In addition, the table shows the performance of using the I-VOPs predictor in predicting the P-VOPs time series.

s	Trace	SFN		Sparse	Bhattacharya
		FLK-SFN	Network trained by I VOPs data		
1	Aladdin	12.8214	10.6298	9.67	10.3
2	Die Hard III	8.3116	5.0294	4.1	9
3	Jurassic Park I	6.1566	3.7102	3.36	4
4	Lecture Room	6.0146	1.4704	1.36	6.9
5	Mr. Bean	9.5674	8.6198	6.15	
6	Silence of the Lambs	12.0746	4.2349	4.05	11
7	Simpsons	6.5117	6.1094	25.2	
8	Skiing	5.0078	2.6347	2.33	6.2
9	Starwars	10.4832	9.6073	9.05	9.2
10	The Firm	13.0989	9.9736	7.71	
11	ARD Talk	6.6909	5.4386		5.9

network results given by Bhattacharya; the SFN P-VOPs predictor is comparable with that given by Bhattacharya but not better. The reason is that we designed the I-VOPs predictor using the backward and the Forward-backward algorithms; both applying pruning algorithms in parallel with the constructive algorithms. However, in designing the P-VOPs predictor we used the forward link-by-link algorithm that does not run any pruning algorithm; so, the network is getting stuck with any previously admitted link.

The interesting thing we found is that when using the I-VOPs predictor designed in the above section in predicting the P-VOPs time series, it resulted in a very good performance, which outperforms the work of Bhattacharya and for most traces is nearly the same as the performance of the sparse basis selection based model. Therefore, it could be noticed that both of I-VOPs and P-VOPs time series prediction models nearly have the same nonlinearities and could replace each other. Hence, no need to design a separate predictor for each time series; considering that, for both predictors,

the same input pool must be used, which is, in this simulations, the latest three values.

Prediction of B-VOPs Size Time Series

The model is trained using the first 5000 B-VOP sizes of the data trace of *Aladdin*, while the designed predictor is tested on the remaining unused segment of the entire *Aladdin* video stream, as well as on the entire video traces of all other video streams. The results are listed in Table 3.

As the results have shown, the SFN performance of the B-VOPs predictor, for almost all traces, is better than the Forward MLP Network predictor designed by Bhattacharya. However, it is comparable with the performance of the sparse model. In addition, when using the I-VOPs predictor in prediction the B-VOPs time series we got nearly the same performance results; that means the B-VOPs time series prediction model is nearly the same as that of I-VOPs and P-VOPs. Hence, we can use just one predictor in predicting all of these the time series.

Table 3. Testing error (in NMSE%) for single step ahead prediction of B-VOPs size time series for one of the proposed model variants FLK-SFN, and the most recent published related work. In addition, the table shows the performance of using the I-VOPs predictor in predicting the b-vops time series.

| s | Trace | SFN | | Sparse | Bhattacharya |
		FLK-SFN	Network trained by I VOPs		
1	Aladdin	11.844	13.6145	9.25	8.2
2	Die Hard III	2.0644	2.0752	1.51	4
3	Jurassic Park I	2.0528	2.134	1.7	2.2
4	Lecture Room	1.2161	1.2242	0.72	28.3
5	Mr. Bean	6.3731	5.6191	3.08	
6	Silence of the Lambs	2.3426	2.2926	1.53	27.8
7	Simpsons	3.8354	3.9865	10.95	
8	Skiing	1.3818	1.4157	1.1	14.7
9	Starwars	2.7521	2.8682	2.97	3.5
10	The Firm	1.6999	1.7062	1.23	
11	ARD Talk	1.4632	1.465		3.2

PACKET LOSS RATIO PREDICTION

The quality of multimedia communicated through the Internet is highly sensitive to packet loss. It can severely degrade the quality of especially delay-sensitive multimedia applications. This delay usually occurs during periods of heavy congestion as packets have to be discarded when the buffers of the intermediate routers become full. Therefore, any mechanism that leads to reduce the packet loss rate would be a significant achievement. The motivation for predicting the Packet Loss Rate (PLR) arises from several considerations generally real-time applications use UDP-based transmission, as the TCP protocol is based on a complex retransmission algorithm that is not suitable for the real-time nature of such applications. The problem, however, is that if congestion occurs on a link carrying TCP as well as UDP traffic, TCP will react by reducing the traffic rate, while UDP will not. This will aggravate the congestion situation and also violate the fairness issue. It has therefore been recommended that UDP traffic use similar traffic reduction mechanisms as TCP and

several TCP-friendly rate control mechanisms have been developed. The rate adjustment is based on the key quantities: Packet Loss Rate (PLR) and the Round Trip Time (RTT). Rather than using previously measured values of PLR and RTT, a better approach is to use predictions of these quantities. Such a predictive approach will be quicker to track congestion conditions than the typically used reactive approach. The other motivation for predicting PLR is that for real time multimedia traffic transmitted using UDP a procedure to recover lost packets is by adding redundancy using Forward Error Correction (FEC). These are extra packets that can be used to reconstruct lost packets. The FEC packets, however, represent a bandwidth overhead, and it is therefore imperative to send only as much of these as needed. The estimate of the packet loss rate is needed to estimate the amount of such redundancy and hence lessening the overhead.

Due to above, an accurate prediction would therefore be very valuable. We found that much work have been done to develop reliable time series prediction models for the end-to-end Packet Loss

Rate (PLR); and we tried The SFN model to design PLR predictors and compared the performance with some competing models found in literature (Atiya, Yoo, Chong, & Kim, 2007).

PLR Simulation Setup

We have used the same data found in Atiya, Yoo, Chong, and Kim (2007). The data is collected by installing a transmission Processor at Chonbuk National University in South Korea, and a receiving retransmission processor at Seoul National University. The transmission processor transmitted packets using the TCP-friendly mechanism. The packet size is 625 bytes, and that includes 64 bytes reserved for Probe header. The probe header keeps track of the transmission time and order of the packet. This information is used to estimate PLR and RTT (Round Trip Time). The basic time unit is 2 seconds, so the time series of PLR and RTT values represents the measurement over each 2 Sec time interval. The RTT within each interval is the average of the individual packets' RTT. The resulted time PLR time series consists of 13,158 data points. In designing the SFN model, we used the first 2000 points in training the network and the remaining data as an out-of- samples test data.

For all trials, we used NMSE as the performance measure to be minimized where:

$$NMSE = \frac{\sum_{m=1}^{M}\left(y(m) - d(m)\right)^2}{\sum_{m=1}^{M} d(m)^2} \; ; y(m), d(m)$$

are the network output and the desired output
at any sample " m " respectively,
and M is the length of the testing set.

In addition, we used just the latest three data points as inputs to the network in order to predict the next data point.

PLR Simulation Results

The model results are listed in Table 4 and Figure 6.

As shown in the above results, SFN performance outperforms the performance of both SVM (Support Vector Machine) regression model, and ANN (Artificial Neural Network) prediction model. However, the sparse basis selection based prediction model gave a little better performance. As we explained in the previous section, the sparse model depends on the art of choosing and extracting the inputs to be passed to the training algorithm. The designer has to make some pre-processing task on the inputs. Unless this process is done in a right way, the model will not give such good performance. However, for the SFN model, this process is done automatically by the training al-

Table 4. Testing error (in NMSE) for single step ahead prediction of PLR time series for some of the proposed model variants FLK-SFN, and B-SFN, and the most recent published related work ANN, SVM, KNN, and the sparse basis selection model

Method	NMSE
Sparse (PLR & RTT- INP)	0.342
SPRSE (PLR INP)	0.337
ANN	0.406
SVM	0.54
KNN	0.377
B-SFN	0.456
FLK-SFN	0.392

Figure 6. SFN performance of single step ahead predicted PLR

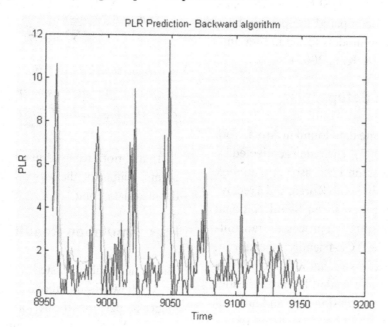

gorithm and such art and knowledge is not needed to guarantee the good results.

For the sparse model, an input dictionary has been generated before starting the training process; it consists of 51 extracted inputs. However, in the new model "SFN" we used just the latest three PLR values to predict the next one. May future trial have to be done in order to choose more pure inputs to be passed to the SFN learning algorithm; we expect it may outperform the sparse model.

PREDICTION OF ROUND TRIP TIME (RTT)

As discussed in the previous section, there are many TCP-friendly rate control mechanisms have been developed. These mechanisms are adjusting the rate based on the key quantities: packet loss rate and the Round Trip Time (RTT). Hence, the prediction of both PLR and RTT time series are highly needed and in good accuracy to support such mechanisms. In the previous section, we designed a SFN PLR-Predictor; in this section, we designed

a SFN RTT-Predictor. In addition, we used the first 2000 RTT values to design the network and tested it on the remaining time series. A segment of the Out-Of-Sample data is represented in Figure 7. The Constructed SFN network consists of 10 weights and gave the performance NMSE about 0.065 using the forward algorithm. Details of the simulations are published in Eskander, Atiya, Chong, Kim, and Yoo (2007).

FUTURE RESEARCH DIRECTIONS

This work opened the door for many interesting research points that need further investigation. The only obvious limitation of the current SFN design methodology is the relatively high computational training time, as it needs re-optimization of network parameters whenever the network structure changes. To improve the network design process, following research directions might need investigation:

Figure 7. SFN performance of single step ahead predicted RTT

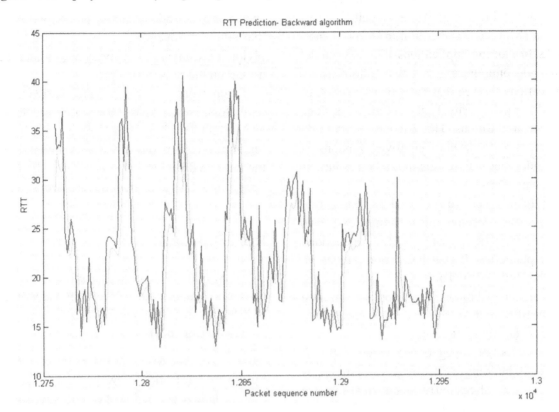

- Develop new evolutionary learning algorithms and using them to optimize the SFN network structure and weights in order to get sparser, and more fitting symbolic functions through a much faster training process. The evolutionary algorithms can be designed based on one or a combination of population based and evolutionary methods like: Genetic Algorithms (GA), Genetic Programming (GP), Particle Swarm Optimization (PSO), and Evolutionary Programming (EP).
- Improve the symbolic expressions represented by the SFN network by getting sparser symbolic representation through applying symbolic reduction procedures.

Moreover, the SFN model might be improved by trying other basic nonlinear transformations.

In addition, more accurate and sparser predictors might be proposed for the communication networks time series.

CONCLUSION

SFN model is a HONN-like model that is motivated by the current needs of developing more enhanced predictors. The accuracy and the recall speed of solutions of some critical applications such as the telecommunications network time series forecasting are still not enough to support the developing of reliable quality control strategies. Therefore, new neural networks models with higher approximation ability will help improving such applications.

SFN is approved to have high ability in function approximation, regression, and time series forecasting problems compared with some of the traditional neural networks models as Feed-Forward Multilayer perceptron and recurrent networks. In addition, applications of the new model to the telecommunications networks forecasting applications showed that the primary version of the SFN model compete the recent work done in these applications. This encourages us to do further work to develop improved versions of the model that may results in the best solutions to such problems.

In this chapter, we reviewed the application of SFN to the telecommunications networks forecasting applications such as MPEG coded video traffic prediction, Packet loss ration prediction, and the Round Trip Time prediction problems. Comparisons of the most recent work performance and the SFN model performance have been done and gave encouraging results.

Prediction of Mpeg coded video traffic is needed for building of effective control strategies and bandwidth allocation techniques that improve the quality of service. We used the SFN model to build traffic predictors for the different types of Mpeg frames. The results are very encouraging. Although, we built all the predictors using just three time lags, we got better performance than most of the predictors designed by the traditional neural networks (Recurrent and MLP Neural networks), and very close and sometimes better performance than those designed by the sparse basis selection adaptive algorithm . Considering that these methods used to do the performance comparison use a much larger input pool than used in training the SFN network; hence, we expect that better results could be obtained by SFN in case of using deeper networks and trying other input pools.

Prediction of the packet loss ratio and round trip time series is a hard task because the noisy and nonlinear nature of such time series. However, the SFN model gave encouraging results that outperforms many of the traditional forecasting models such as; SVM, and ANN. In addition, it

gave comparable performance with that of the sparse basis selection adaptive model. We expect that more improvement can be achieved by applying more advanced evolving algorithms such as; GP on the SFN design process.

Future work needed to enhance MPEG traffic predictors, Packet Loss Ratio (PLR) predictors, and Round Trip Time (RTT) predictors; by using improved versions of the SFN model. Since the improved versions may make it easier to try deeper networks and larger feature search space.

REFERENCES

Adas, A. N. (1998). Using adaptive linear prediction to support real – time VBR video under RCBR network service model. *IEEE Transactions on Networking, 6*(5).

Atiya, A. F., Aly, M. A., & Parlos, A. G. (2005). Sparse basis selection: New results and application to adaptive prediction of video source traffic. *IEEE Transactions on Neural Networks, 16*(5), 1136–1146. doi:10.1109/TNN.2005.853426

Atiya, A. F., Yoo, S. G., Chong, K. T., & Kim, H. (2007). Packet loss rate prediction using the sparse basis prediction model. *IEEE Transactions on Neural Networks, 18*(3), 950–954. doi:10.1109/TNN.2007.891681

Bhattacharya, A., Parlos, A. G., & Atyia, A. F. (2003). Prediction of MPEG-coded source traffic using recurrent neural networks. *IEEE Transactions on Signal Processing, 51*(8). doi:10.1109/TSP.2003.814470

Doulamis, A. D., Doulamis, N. D., & Kollias, S. D. (2000a). Recursive nonlinear models for online traffic prediction of VBR MPEG coded video sources. In *Proceeding of IEEE-INNS-ENNS International Joint Conference on Neural Networks IJCNN*, (pp. 114-119). IEEE Press.

Doulamis, A. D., Doulamis, N. D., & Kollias, S. D. (2000b). Nonlinear traffic modeling of VBR MPEG-2 video sources. In *Proceedings IEEE International Conference on Multi Media, ICME*, (pp. 1318-1321). IEEE Press.

Doulamis, A. D., Doulamis, N. D., & Kollias, S. D. (2003). An adaptable neural network model for recursive nonlinear traffic prediction and modeling of MPEG video sources. *IEEE Transactions on Neural Networks, 14*(1), 150–166. doi:10.1109/TNN.2002.806645

Eskander, G., & Atiya, A. (2009). Symbolic function network. *Neural Networks, 22*(4), 395–404. doi:10.1016/j.neunet.2009.02.003

Eskander, G. S., Atiya, A., Chong, K. T., Kim, H., & Yoo, S. G. (2007). Round trip time prediction using the symbolic function network approach. In *Proceedings of the 2007 International Symposium on Information Technology Convergence (ISITC 2007)*. Jeonju, South Korea: IEEE Press.

Fitzek, F., & Reisslein, M. (1998). *MPEG-4 and h.236 video traces for network performance evaluation*. Berlin, Germany: Technical University of Berlin.

Frost, V. S., & Melamed, B. (1994, March). Traffic modeling for telecommunications networks. *IEEE Communications Magazine*, 70–81. doi:10.1109/35.267444

Parlos, A. G. (2002). *Identification of the internet end to end delay dynamics using multi - step neuro – predictors*. New York, NY: IEEE Press. doi:10.1109/IJCNN.2002.1007528

Yao, X. (1999). Evolving artificial neural networks. *Proceedings of the IEEE, 87*(9), 1423–1447. doi:10.1109/5.784219

Yoo, S.-J. (2002). Efficient traffic prediction scheme for real time VBR MPEG video transmission over high speed networks. *IEEE Transactions on Broadcasting, 48*(1).

Chapter 12

Time Series Forecasting via a Higher Order Neural Network trained with the Extended Kalman Filter for Smart Grid Applications

Luis J. Ricalde
Universidad Autonoma de Yucatan, Mexico

Alma Y. Alanis
Universidad de Guadalajara, Mexico

Glendy A. Catzin
Universidad Autonoma de Yucatan, Mexico

Edgar N. Sanchez
Universidad de Guadalajara, Mexico

ABSTRACT

This chapter presents the design of a neural network that combines higher order terms in its input layer and an Extended Kalman Filter (EKF)-based algorithm for its training. The neural network-based scheme is defined as a Higher Order Neural Network (HONN), and its applicability is illustrated by means of time series forecasting for three important variables present in smart grids: Electric Load Demand (ELD), Wind Speed (WS), and Wind Energy Generation (WEG). The proposed model is trained and tested using real data values taken from a microgrid system in the UADY School of Engineering. The length of the regression vector is determined via the Lipschitz quotients methodology.

1. INTRODUCTION

In recent years, there has been an increasing attention on renewable energy generation and management due to the environmental and economic concerns. The first steps on integrating renewable

DOI: 10.4018/978-1-4666-2175-6.ch012

energy sources began with hybrid wind and solar systems as complementing sources and as solution for rural applications and weak grid interconnections. Further research have implemented hybrid systems including several small scale renewable energy sources as solar thermal, biomass, fuel cells and tidal power. Since the production costs for photovoltaic and wind turbine applications have considerably reduced, they have become the primary choice for hybrid energy generation systems. The future of energy production is headed towards the scheme of integration of renewable energy sources with existing conventional generation systems (coal, natural gas, oil). This integration is defined as a smart grid. This new scheme increases the power quality since the production becomes decentralized and is the main reason for which Institutions have increased the research on this concept (Meiqin, et al., 2008). Microgrids integrate small-scale energy generation systems mainly from renewable energy and implementing complex control technologies to improve the flexibility and reliability of the power system (Wu, et al., 2009). The smart grids can be connected to the public network to support it or can be operated autonomously. The design of these systems integrates a distributed power generation system and a management unit composed of a communication network, which monitors and controls the interconnection between energy sources, storage devices and electrical loads with the aid of sensors to enhance the overall functionality of the electric power delivery system (Gellings, 2009).

Among renewable energy sources, wind energy is the one with the lowest cost of electricity production (Welch, et al., 2009), for this reason the interest in the study of wind energy as a source of electricity production is increased. However, integration of the wind energy into the grid of supply of electric energy is a real challenge mainly due to that the generated energy depends on meteorological conditions (wind speed, particularly) present at certain moment and those cannot be modified by human intervention (Lange, 2003); therefore it is necessary to have an adequate intelligent control to accomplish that integration (Werbos, 2009). To utilize this renewable energy in a large scale without fierce impact to the grid, in addition to apply energy storage to regular wind power output, accurate wind power output forecasting is an effective mean (Shi, et al., 2011). The forecast of wind power is a good

way to improve the energy management of a wind power farm (Wu, et al., 2009). Integration of wind resource into the electricity transmission systems has as direct consequence environmental benefits because carbon dioxide emissions derived from electricity generation by traditional media are decreased; therefore, our planet is preserved for future generations.

Wind power prediction is also an essential process for (El-Fouly, et al., 2008):

1. Wind farms units maintenance.
2. Optimal power flow between conventional units and wind farms.
3. Electricity marketing bidding.
4. Power system generators scheduling.
5. Energy reserves and storages planning and scheduling.

Many factors affect wind power prediction, including the presence of an accurate forecasting model for wind speed and direction at the farm site, the presence of accurate technique for wind speed simulation all over the farm layout and the existence of sufficient information about the farm characteristic and layout. The required forecasting horizon for wind farms output power depends on the required application, which can be unit maintenance, control, small power systems operation, interconnected power systems operation and maintenance planning (El-Fouly, et al., 2008). As for wind speed prediction, previous work has shown temperature is the most important meteorological parameter. Humidity and current wind speed have also been identified as key indicators (Welch, et al., 2009).

Over the last decade or so there has been considerable activity and progress in the development of wind power forecasting. However, there is still much scope for improvement. Two broad strands can be identified in the systems that have been developed so far: those using predominantly physical modeling techniques; and those using predominantly statistical modeling techniques.

In the physical modeling approach the physical atmospheric processes involved are represented, in as far as this is possible. The statistical modeling approach is based on the time series of wind farm power measurements, which are typically available on-line. If purely statistical modeling techniques are used, good forecast results can be achieved for the short-term look-ahead times (from 0 to 6 hours) only. Beyond this horizon and especially in the 12- to 48-hour range of look-ahead times, it is essential to use an input from a Numerical Weather Prediction (NWP) model if successful results are to be achieved. As the development of wind power forecasting techniques has progressed over the last decade there have been significant interactions between the physical and statistical approaches, which result in advanced wind power forecasting systems (Fox, et al., 2007). Another salient technique that has been used recently in the task of wind forecasting are the Artificial Neural Networks (ANN) which are excellent approximators for nonlinear and stochastic models and have been implemented in several practical applications which require identification and control of unknown dynamic systems. In a smart grid that mainly uses the energy coming from the wind resource, it is important to have predictions of load demand in addition to wind speed and power forecasts. High accuracy of the load forecasting is required to give the exact information about the power purchasing and generation in electricity market, prevent more energy from wasting and maintaining the electricity price in a reasonable range. Factors such as season differences, climate changes, weekends, holidays, disasters and political reasons, operation scenarios of the power plants and faults occurring on the network lead to changes of the load demand and generation (Zhang, et al., 2010).

Over the last several years, many works have proven the great potential of the ANN to predict time series. Two important aspects when neural networks are employed are the architecture selection and the learning algorithm. The architecture considers the number of inputs, units in the hidden and output layers and if feedback loops are presented or not. The learning algorithm allows the network to acquire the knowledge of the task for which is being used. The main architecture used to deal with temporal sequences is the recurrent neural network, which presents feedback loops. The recurrent networks are based on the Hopfield model, they are considered as good candidates for nonlinear systems applications which deal with uncertainties and are attractive due to their easy implementation, simple relatively structure, robustness and the capacity to adjust their parameters on-line (Ricalde, 2005). The extensions of the first order model of Hopfield are called Recurrent Higher Order Neural Networks (RHONN) and present more interactions among the neurons.

In Sanchez et al. (2004), a Recurrent Multilayer Perceptron (RMLP) was used to forecast electric load demand with a 24 hours horizon. Two algorithms were employed to train this neural architecture: the Extended Kalman Filter (EKF) and the Extended Kalman Filter Derivative Free (EKFDF). The input vector was composed by a regression vector of length 7 and two external inputs corresponding to the hour and the day. During the training stage, the delayed outputs were taken from the electric load demand (series-parallel configuration) and in the testing stage were taken from the neural network output (parallel configuration). The number of neurons in the hidden layer was 15 units with logistic activation functions and the output layer was composed by just one neuron with a linear activation function. The Mean Square Error (MSE) was used to measure the performance of the neural network. Despite of the EKFDF algorithm was simpler to code, the EKF one required less iterations to obtain the specified prediction error, while the first algorithm never reached this error, therefore for this specific application the best solution was to use the EKF training. In Senjyu et al. (2006), a Recurrent Neural Network (RNN) was applied to forecast the output power of wind generators based on wind speed prediction using one year of historical data achieving from hour-ahead to day-ahead predictions with errors ranging from 5% for one hour horizon to 20% for one day ahead forecasting. In Barbounis et al. (2006), local recurrent neural networks were implemented to forecast wind speed and electrical power in a wind park with a 72 hours ahead forecast and obtaining a better performance in comparison with static network approaches. In Chen et al. (2007), a new adaptive model was specially designed to predict time series. The proposed model was based on a neural network whose input size was changed in a dynamic way during the prediction process. The network training was made by means of the Particle Swarm Optimization (PSO) algorithm and its performance was evaluated in terms of the Mean Absolute Percentage Error (MAPE) or the MSE. With this approach, Box-Jenkis and Mackey-Glass chaotic time series were used to validate the developed model. Application results prove the higher precision and generalization capacity obtained by this new method than the static models.

In Aquino et al. (2009) were generated models for wind speed forecasting, using structures based on Multilayer Perceptron (MLP) for horizons ranging from 1 to 4 hours ahead or from 1 to 24 hours ahead, with 2 different arrangements: the first one (called from here in advance as simple model) used as inputs to the network the previous 4 or 24 hours of the wind speed means that precede the forecasting horizon and in the second arrangement, based on wavelet functions, the inputs to the neural network were the wavelet coefficients from the multiresolution analysis using the Daubechies wavelet family at level 3. The neural networks outputs are 4 for the prediction horizon up to 4 hours and 24 in the case of the horizon extended to 24 hours. The number of neurons in the hidden layer was experimentally determined and was different for each prediction horizon and for each input arrangement to the network. In the case of the forecasting up to 4

hours in the simple model, the neural network final architecture was 4-14-4, where the first number points out the inputs number, the second refers to neurons number in the hidden layer and the last one is the outputs number from the network. For the same prediction horizon, but using the model based on wavelets, the final disposition was 16-19-4. For the second prediction horizon, the simple model had the architecture 24-26-24 and the model based on wavelets 96-15-24. In addition to these models, models by specialized neural networks that use the seasonality of the days with a forecasting horizon from 17 to 24 hours ahead were developed too. To create the inputs to these models, the wind speed time series was divided into 3 series: 1) from 1 to 8 hours, 2) from 9 to 16 hours, and 3) from 17 to 24 hours; these intervals defined 3 models of specialist neural networks. All of these models had 8 inputs and 8 outputs. The inputs to the specialized models correspond to the hourly mean wind speeds in the previous day in the time interval defined by the previously mentioned series and the outputs correspond to the hourly mean speeds forecasted in the same time interval but in the actual day. The number of hidden neurons for the specialist models was 15 for the first, 19 for the second and 18 for the third. The data used to create the models were taken from the wind park of Olinda, Pernambuco, Brazil, measured in intervals of 10 minutes at a height of 20 meters and were averaged to have them in 1 hour intervals. The error in the wind speed forecasting was assessed with the MAPE. The training algorithm was the resilient back-propagation. The results obtained with the model based on wavelets presented a superior performance compared with the simple MLP, while the results obtained with the specialized models did not yield any significant improvement than the simple MLP.

In the work accomplished by Welch et al. (2009), 3 types of neural networks were compared and trained using the PSO in order to provide the best prediction of 80 meters wind speed fifteen minutes into the future. The 3 types of neural networks compared were the MLP neural network, Elman Recurrent Neural Network (ERNN) and Simultaneous Recurrent Neural Network (SRNN). Each neural network was trained and tested using meteorological data of one week measured at the National Renewable Energy Laboratory (NREL) of the National Wind Technology Center (NWTC) located near of Boulder, Colorado. The inputs for all the architectures were wind speed measured at 80 meters, temperature at 2 meters and percent relative humidity. The training data included values for each of these inputs in one-minute intervals, with each data point representing the mean of readings taken every 2 seconds during that minute. An additional input was included in all of the architectures, corresponding to the bias, therefore total inputs were 4. The recurrent networks had an additional layer, called context layer, where fed back values taken from the hidden layer were stored, which allowed the networks to retain an internal memory. All of the neural networks had one neuron in the output layer (with a linear activation function) and the number of neurons in the hidden layer (with a logistic sigmoid activation function) was 10 for the MLP and 5 for the recurrent networks, being that these in the context layer had 5 neurons. Keeping the number of neurons pointed out for each architecture, the number of synaptic weights was the same in all of them. The performance of the neural networks was evaluated using the Absolute Relative Error (ARE). After training the neural networks, data that did not belong to the training data set were presented to them and the results were better for the recurrent networks. However, with the increase in accuracy came an increase in compute time due to the feedback loop of these networks.

In Zhang et al. (2010), a MLP was created and trained using the Matlab Neuron Network Toolbox to make the load forecast in Ontario Province, Canada. The work was focused on the behaviors of different training algorithms for the task previously pointed out. Due to several factors that affect the load changing (temperature, atmospheric pressure, relative humidity), two year of hourly weather and load data were collected to train the MLP. Neurons in the hidden layer employed the tangent sigmoid as activation functions and the neuron in the output layer used a linear function. The used training algorithms were the Levenberg-Marquardt and the Bayesian Regularization, where the best performance was the last one. Higher Order Neural Network (HONN) has been previously implemented for wind power short-term predictions, outperforming other classical methods due to the fast learning algorithm, which enables on-line implementations and the versatility to vary the prediction horizon (Kariniotakis, et al., 1996).

In this chapter, we propose the use of higher order terms in the input layer of the neural network with a logistic sigmoid as activation functions for the units in the hidden layer in addition to an EKF-based algorithm for training this structure. The length of the regression vector is determined using the Lipschitz quotients method proposed in He and Asada (1993). Here, the applicability of this architecture is illustrated via simulation for three time series: Electric Load Demand (ELD), Wind Speed (WS), and Wind Energy Generation (WEG), all of them from real data values. The chapter's main result is to show the potential applications of higher order neural networks in forecasting for energy generation in smart grid schemes.

2. MATHEMATICAL PRELIMINARIES

2.1. Artificial Neural Networks

A neural network is a massively parallel distributed processor made up of simple processing units (neurons) which has a natural propensity for storing experiential knowledge and making it available for later use. Knowledge is acquired by the network through a learning process and the interneuron connection strengths, known as synaptic weights, are used to store the acquired knowledge. The used process to accomplish the learning process is called training algorithm and its function is to modify the synaptic weights to attend a desired desing objective (Haykin, 1999).

The output of a neuron is obtained as follows: once that the inputs and the weights connecting each input to the neuron are linearly combined, they are pased through an activation function, which limits the output amplitude of a neuron to a finite value. There are four basic activations functions (Haykin, 1999; Sanchez & Alanis, 2006):

1. Step function

$$\varphi(v) = \begin{cases} 1 & \text{if} \quad v \geq 0 \\ 0 & \text{if} \quad v < 0 \end{cases} \tag{1}$$

2. Logistic sigmoid function

$$\varphi(v) = \frac{1}{1 + \exp(-av)} \tag{2}$$

3. Piecewise linear function

$$\varphi(v) = \begin{cases} 1 & \text{if} \quad v \geq 1 \\ v & \text{if} \quad -1 < v < 1 \\ -1 & \text{if} \quad v \leq -1 \end{cases} \tag{3}$$

4. Tangent sigmoid function

$$\varphi(v) = \frac{2}{1 + \exp(-2av)} - 1 \tag{4}$$

For identification and control, the most used structures are:

Feedforward Networks: In feedforward networks, the neurons are grouped into layers. Signals flow from the input to the output via unidirectional connections. The network exhibits high degree of connectivity, contains one or more hidden layers of neurons and the activation function of each neuron is smooth, generally a sigmoid function.

Recurrent Networks: In a recurrent neural network, the outputs of the neuron are fed back to the same neuron or neurons in the preceding layers. Signals flow in forward and backward directions.

2.2. Recurrent Higher Order Neural Networks

A recurrent network responds temporally to an external input signal. The feedback allow to recurrent neural networks to have a representation in state space, which made them convenient for diverse applications. The word order refers to the form in which the neuron activation potential is defined. (Sanchez & Alanis, 2006). When the local activation potential is combined with products of signals coming from the feedback of the network or when products are made between the fed back signals and the external input ones to the network, a neural network of order r emerges, where r represents the number of multiplied signals. The phrase higher order is employed when the input to a neuron includes the product of more than two signals.

Consider the next discrete RHONN (Sanchez, et al., 2008):

$$\hat{x}_i(k+1) = w_i^T z(\hat{x}(k), u(k)) \quad i = 1, ..., A \tag{5}$$

where x_i $(i = 1, ..., A)$ is the i-th neuron state at iteration k, L is the number of higher-order connections, $\{I_1, I_2, ..., I_L\}$ is a collection of non-ordered subsets of $\{1, 2, ..., A + m\}$, A is the state dimension, m is the number of external inputs, w_i $(i = 1, ..., A)$ are the on-line and adjustable weights of the neural network and $z(\hat{x}(k), u(k))$ is a vector defined by

$$z\left(\hat{x}\left(k\right),u\left(k\right)\right)=\left[z_1,z_2,...,z_L\right]^T$$

$$=\left[\Pi_{j\varepsilon I_1}\xi_j^{d_j(1)},\Pi_{j\varepsilon I_2}\xi_j^{d_j(2)},...,\Pi_{j\varepsilon I_L}\xi_j^{d_j(L)}\right]^T \quad (6)$$

with $d_j\left(l\right)$ representing nonnegative integers, and ξ is a vector constructed by the inputs to each neuron, defined as

$$\xi=\left[\xi_1,...,\xi_A,\xi_{A+1},...,\xi_{A+m}\right]^T$$

$$=\left[S\left(x_1\right),...,S\left(x_A\right),S\left(u_1\right),...,S\left(u_m\right)\right]^T \quad (7)$$

where $u=\left[u_1,u_2,...,u_m\right]^T$ being the external inputs vector to the neural network, and $S\left(\cdot\right)$ is the logistic sigmoid function formulated by

$$S(x)=\frac{1}{1+\exp(-ax)} \quad (8)$$

For the sigmoid function, a is a positive constant. From (5) three models can be derived:

• Parallel model

$$\hat{x}_i\left(k+1\right)=w_i^T z\left(\hat{x}\left(k\right),u\left(k\right)\right) \quad i=1,...,A \quad (9)$$

• Series-Parallel model

$$\hat{x}_i\left(k+1\right)=w_i^T z\left(x\left(k\right),u\left(k\right)\right) \quad i=1,...,A \quad (10)$$

• Feedforward model, Higher Order Neural Network (HONN)

$$\hat{x}_i\left(k+1\right)=w_i^T z\left(u\left(k\right)\right) \quad i=1,...,A \quad (11)$$

In (9)-(11), $\hat{x}$ is the neural network state vector, x is the plant state vector and u is the external inputs vector to the neural network. The model used to develop this work is the HONN.

2.2.1. Higher Order Neural Networks

As can be seen from (11), HONN model only uses the external inputs vector to the neural network to estimate neuron states. However, the input vector to the neural network can include, in addition to external inputs to the network, past outputs taken from it (known as regressors), so that in the next equation we denote ρ to the vector applied to the input of a HONN, which includes regressors and also external inputs to the neural network. The output of a HONN formed by A units can be represented by (Güler, 1999):

$$\sigma_i\left(\rho\right)$$

$$=S\left[\begin{array}{c}w_i^0\\+\sum_{j_1}w_i^1\left(j_1\right)\rho_{j_1}+\sum_{j_1}\sum_{j_2}w_i^2\left(j_1,j_2\right)\rho_{j_1}\rho_{j_2}+...\\\sum_{j_1}...\sum_{j_r}w_i^r\left(j_1,...,j_r\right)\rho_{j_1}...\rho_{j_r}\end{array}\right],$$

$$i=1,...,A$$

$$\hat{y}\left(\rho\right)=\sum_{i=1}^A w_i\sigma_i\left(\rho\right) \quad (12)$$

where $w_i^r\left(j_1,...,j_r\right)$ is the weight connecting the product $\rho_{j_1}...\rho_{j_r}$ to the i-th unit. The higher-order weights capture higher-order correlations. A unit that includes terms up to degree r will be called a r-th order unit (Giles & Maxwell, 1987). In (12), $S\left(\cdot\right)$ represents, again, the logistic sigmoid activation function defined in (8).

2.3. Kalman Filter

This section closely follows (Haykin, 2001). Kalman Filter (KF) estimates the state of a linear system with additive state and output white noise. Kalman filter algorithm is developed for a linear, discrete-time dynamical system described by the block diagram shown in Figure 1.

The block diagram of Figure 1 embodies the following pair of equations:

$$w\left(k+1\right)=F_{k+1,k}w\left(k\right)+v_1\left(k\right) \quad (13)$$

Figure 1. Block diagram of a linear, discrete-time dynamical system.

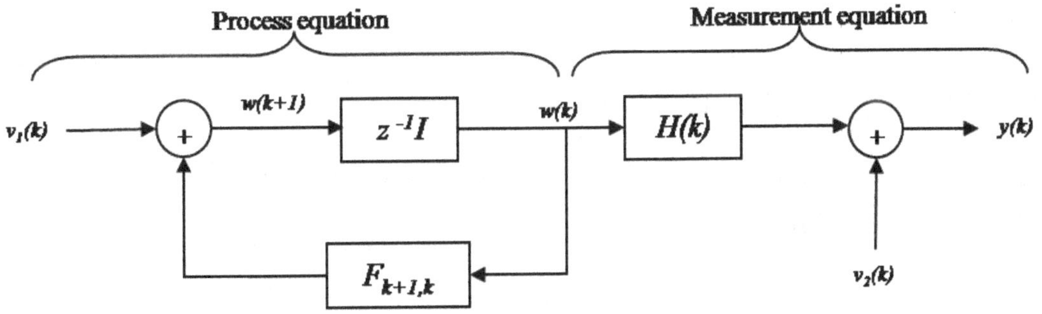

$$y(k) = H(k)w(k) + v_2(k) \qquad (14)$$

$$y(k) = h(k, w(k)) + v_2(k) \qquad (16)$$

The system (13) is known as the process equation where $F_{k+1,k} \in \Re^{N \times N}$ is the transition matrix taking the state $w(k) \in \Re^N$ from iteration k to iteration $k+1$ and $v_1(k) \in \Re^N$ is the process noise. Equation (14) is known as the observation or measurement, which represents the observable $y(k) \in \Re^O$ at iteration k, $H(k) \in \Re^{O \times N}$ is the measurement matrix and $v_2(k) \in \Re^O$ is the measurement noise. The measurement noise $v_2(k)$ is typically characterized as zero-mean, white noise with covariance matrix given by $E\left[v_2(l)v_2^T(l)\right] = \delta_{k,l}R(k)$. Similarly, the process noise $v_1(k)$ is also characterized as zero-mean, white noise with covariance matrix given by $E\left[v_1(l)v_1^T(l)\right] = \delta_{k,l}Q(k)$. $Q(k) \in \Re^{N \times N}$ and $R(k) \in \Re^{O \times O}$, respectively. Due to the fact that the neural network mapping is nonlinear, an EKF-type of algorithm is required and is explained at once.

2.3.1. Extended Kalman Filter

Consider a nonlinear dynamic system described by the next model in state space:

$$w(k+1) = f(k, w(k)) + v_1(k) \qquad (15)$$

As before, $v_1(k)$ and $v_2(k)$ are zero-mean, white noises with covariance matrices given by $Q(k)$ and $R(k)$, respectively. $f(k, w(k))$ denotes the nonlinear transition matrix function that is possibly time variant and $h(k, w(k))$ denotes a nonlinear measurement matrix that may be time variant too.

The basic idea of the extended Kalman filter is to linearize the state space model of (15) and (16) at each time instant around the most recent state estimate, which is taken to be either $\hat{w}(k)$ or $\hat{w}^-(k)$. The approximation proceeds in two stages:

Stage 1. The following two matrices are constructed:

$$F_{k+1,k} = \left. \frac{\partial f(k, w(k))}{\partial w} \right|_{w = \hat{w}(k)} \qquad (17)$$

$$H(k) = \left. \frac{\partial h(k, w(k))}{\partial w} \right|_{w = \hat{w}^-(k)} \qquad (18)$$

Stage 2. Once the matrices $F_{k+1,k}(\cdot)$ and $H(\cdot)$ are evaluated, they are then employed in a first-order Taylor approximation of the nonlinear functions $f(k, w(k))$ and $h(k, w(k))$ around

$\hat{w}(k)$ and $\hat{w}^-(k)$, respectively. Specifically, those matrices are approximated as follows:

$$f\left(k, w\left(k\right)\right) \approx F\left(w, \hat{w}\left(k\right)\right) + F_{k+1,k}\left(w, \hat{w}\left(k\right)\right)$$
(19)

$$h\left(k, w\left(k\right)\right) \approx H\left(w, \hat{w}^-\left(k\right)\right) + H_{k+1,k}\left(w, \hat{w}^-\left(k\right)\right)$$
(20)

With (19) and (20), the nonlinear state Equations (15) and (16) are approximated like:

$$w\left(k+1\right) \approx F_{k+1,k} w\left(k\right) + v_1\left(k\right) + d\left(k\right)$$
(21)

$$\bar{y}\left(k\right) \approx H\left(k\right) w\left(k\right) + v_2\left(k\right)$$
(22)

where

$$\bar{y}\left(k\right) \approx y\left(k\right) - \left(h\left(w, \hat{w}^-\left(k\right)\right) - H\left(k\right)\hat{w}^-\left(k\right)\right)$$
(23)

$$d\left(k\right) \approx f\left(w, \hat{w}\left(k\right)\right) - F_{k+1,k}\hat{w}\left(k\right)$$
(24)

The EKF equations are:

- State estimate propagation

$$\hat{w}^-\left(k\right) = f\left(k, \hat{w}\left(k-1\right)\right)$$

- Error covariance propagation

$$P^-\left(k\right) = F_{k,k-1} P\left(k-1\right) F_{k,k-1}^T + Q\left(k-1\right)$$

- Kalman gain matrix

$$K\left(k\right)$$
$$= P^-\left(k\right) H^T\left(k\right)\left[H\left(k\right) P^-\left(k\right) H^T\left(k\right) + R\left(k\right)\right]^{-1}$$

- State estimate update

$$\hat{w}\left(k\right) = \hat{w}^-\left(k\right) + K\left(k\right) y\left(k\right) - h\left(k, \hat{w}^-\left(k\right)\right)$$

- Error covariance update

$$P\left(k\right) = \left(I - K\left(k\right) H\left(k\right)\right) P^-\left(k\right)$$

2.4. Lipschitz Quotients

Lipschitz quotients are a useful tool in time series analysis for estimating the system order. By means of this algorithm, proposed in He and Asada (1993), it is possible to determine the vector regression size at the neural network input. Let it be

$$\left(g_1, g_2, ..., g_c\right)$$
$$= \left(y\left(n - n_k\right), y\left(n - 2n_k\right), ..., y\left(n - cn_k\right)\right)$$

where $y\left(n\right)$ represents the time series with M samples number, c increases consecutively from initial value 1 and n_k is the delay parameter (usually is chosen as 1). Maximum values for c are 15 or 20, due to if c exceeds these limits, the run time for the algorithm increases. In the input-output model formulation, vector g represents the input variables and y represents the output variable. It is assumed that sufficient input-output pairs $\left(g_i, y_i\right)$, $i = 1, 2, ..., M$ are available. With these notations, Lipschitz quotient $q_{ij}^{(c)}$ is given by

$$q_{ij}^{(c)} = \frac{\left|y_i - y_j\right|}{\sqrt{\left(g_{1i} - g_{1j}\right)^2 + ... + \left(g_{ci} - g_{cj}\right)^2}}, \quad i \neq j$$
(25)

where the superscript c in the Equation (25) represents the number of input variables in the input-output model. The following index is called Lipschitz number and is used to identify the optimal number of input variables:

$$q^{(c)} = \left(\sqrt{c} \prod_{l=1}^{p} q^{(c)}(l) \right)^{1/p} \tag{26}$$

where $q^{(c)}(l)$ is the l-th largest Lipschitz quotient among all $q_{ij}^{(c)}$ $(i \neq j; i, j = 1, 2, ..., M)$ with the c input variables $(g_1, g_2, ..., g_c)$. Parameter p is a positive number usually selected as $p = 0.01 \sim 0.02M$. Plotting $q^{(c)}$ *vs.* c, the optimal number of the regressors is determined, because $q^{(c)}$ enters to a saturated range from some value c_0.

3. FORECASTING PROBLEM IN WIND GENERATION SYSTEMS

Due to random variations in weather conditions, power generation from renewable sources is constantly changing. Combining the forecast of wind speed and output power is a good way to improve the performance in scheduling of wind power (Wu, et al., 2009).

The wind turbine obtains power from wind currents and converts it into mechanical energy leading the shaft rotation. The obtained energy is proportional to the sweep area, the air density, the wind speed, and the power coefficient as

$$P_m = 0.5 \varrho \pi R^2 V_w^3 C_p (\theta, \lambda) \tag{27}$$

where ϱ is the air density, R is the turbine radius, V_w the wind speed and $C_p(\theta, \lambda)$ is the coefficient of power conversion efficiency which depends on the blade pitch angle θ and the tip speed ratio λ. The tip speed ratio is defined as

$$\lambda = \frac{R \omega_m}{V_m} \tag{28}$$

where ω_m is the rotor speed. The relationship of C_p and λ can be generated by experimentation. The parameter C_p can be determined with the following relationship:

$$C_p = 0.22 \left(\frac{116}{\beta} - 0.4\theta - 5 \right) \exp\left(-\frac{12.5}{\beta} \right) \tag{29}$$

and β is obtained from

$$\beta = \frac{1}{\dfrac{1}{\lambda + 0.08\theta} - \dfrac{0.035}{\theta^3 + 1}} \tag{30}$$

As can be seen, for each wind speed, the maximum power available corresponds to one value of the turbine rotor speed. The aerodynamic power extracted from the wind is related with the torque by $P_w = T_w \omega_m$, then

$$T_w = 0.5 \varrho \pi R^3 V_w^2 \frac{C_p(\theta, \lambda)}{\lambda} \tag{31}$$

The generator in small wind turbines is typically a Permanent Magnet Synchronous Generator (PMSG). This synchronous generator connected to a power converter can operate at low speeds and does not require a gear transmission and a DC excitation system, which gives the advantage of the high efficiency where its performance highly depends on how it is controlled; the control scheme depends on the variation of the wind speed.

4. NEURAL NETWORK DESIGN

In order to carry out the time series forecasting, a multilayer neural network is designed. The structure is a HONN, which is composed by an input vector, one hidden layer and an output layer composed of just one neuron with a linear activa-

Figure 2. Designed higher order neural network

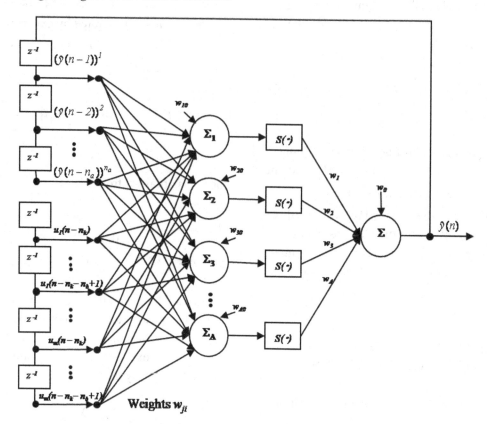

tion function. In Figure 2, the designed HONN architecture is depicted.

Before presenting details about the input and hidden layers, we define the next notation: n represents discrete time, k identifies the iteration, $y(n)$ is the time series with M samples, $\rho_i(k)$ is the input i to the neural network, $v_j(k)$ is the neuron j activation potential, $y_j(k)$ represents the neuron j output, $v(k)$ is the output neuron activation potential, $\hat{y}(k)$ is the neuron output in the output layer (neural network output), $\varphi(v_j(k))$ represents the neuron j activation function, $\varphi(v(k))$ is the activation function of the output layer neuron, $w_{ji}(k)$ is the weight connecting the input i to the neuron j input, $w_j(k)$ is the weight connecting neuron j output to the neuron input

in the output layer, s and A are the inputs total number to the neurons in the hidden and output layers, respectively.

4.1. Input Layer

The input vector in this architecture is a vector formed by delayed signals taken from the network output and delayed external inputs, which is called regression vector and it obeys to known model like Neural Network Output Error (NNOE), mathematically represented in (Norgaard, et al., 2000):

$$\phi(k) = \begin{bmatrix} \hat{y}(n-1),...,\hat{y}(n-n_a), u_1(n-n_k),..., \\ u_1(n-n_k-n_b+1), \\ ...,u_m(n-n_k),...,u_m(n-n_k-n_b+1) \end{bmatrix}^T$$

$$(32)$$

where $\hat{y}(n)$ is the time series produced by the neural network, $u_m(n)$ are the external input signals corresponding to time (hours and days), n_a and n_b represent the number of delayed output and external inputs to determine the prediction, respectively, and n_k is the number of delays employed (in this work was chosen the unit). The high order terms are implemented in the z vector defined as

$$z_i\big(\alpha_i(k)\big) = \big(\alpha_i(k)\big)^i, \qquad i = 1,...,n_a \tag{33}$$

where $\alpha_i(k)$ represents the neural network output delayed by the i number, i.e.:

$$\alpha_i(k) = \hat{y}(n-i) \tag{34}$$

Note from (33) and (34) that at each iteration k up to the delay $\hat{y}(n-n_a)$ is calculated, taken from the neural network output. This configuration receives the parallel name (Sanchez, et al., 2004). Following the model (32) and with (33), the input vector to the neural network remains represented as

$$\rho(k) = \begin{bmatrix} z\big(\alpha(k)\big), u_1\big(n-n_k\big),...,u_1\big(n-n_k-n_b+1\big), \\ ..., u_m\big(n-n_k\big),...,u_m\big(n-n_k-n_b+1\big) \end{bmatrix}^T \tag{35}$$

4.2. Hidden Layer

It is formed by A units whose activation function is the logistic sigmoid defined in (8). Having in mind the notation defined at the Section beginning and remembering that only exists a neuron with linear activation function in the output layer, we present the equations of the hidden and output layers of this neural network:

$$v_j(k) = \sum_{i=0}^{s} w_{ji}(k)\rho_i(k)$$

$$y_j(k) = \varphi\big(v_j(k)\big) = \frac{1}{1 + \exp\big(-av_j(k)\big)}$$

$$v(k) = \sum_{j=0}^{A} w_j(k)y_j(k)$$

$$\hat{y}(k) = \varphi\big(v(k)\big) = v(k) \tag{36}$$

5. LEARNING ALGORITHM BASED ON EKF

Neural network behaviour can be described by the following model (Sanchez & Alanis, 2006):

$$w(k+1) = w(k)$$
$$\hat{y}(k) = h\big(w(k), \rho(k)\big) \tag{37}$$

which is a simplification of the state space model given by (15) and (16). In (37), $w(k)$ is the synaptic weights vector, $\hat{y}(k)$ is the neural network output vector, $\rho(k)$ represents the input vector to the network and $h(\cdot)$ is the network output nonlinear function. Considering the model (37) and the EKF of the Section 2.3.1, the next equations set emerges, by means of them the synaptic weights of the neural network are updated at each iteration:

$$K(k) = P(k)H^T(k)\big[R + H(k)P(k)H^T(k)\big]^{-1}$$
$$w(k+1) = w(k) + K(k)\big[y(k) - \hat{y}(k)\big]$$
$$P(k+1) = P(k) - K(k)H(k)P(k) + Q \tag{38}$$

where $P(k) \in \Re^{N \times N}$ and $P(k+1) \in \Re^{N \times N}$ are the prediction error covariance matrices at iteration k and $k+1$, respectively, N represents the total number of neural network weights, $w(k) \in \Re^{N}$ is the weight vector (states), $y(k) \in \Re^{O}$ is the desired network output vector, O is the total number of outputs, $\hat{y}(k) \in \Re^{O}$ is the network output, $K(k) \in \Re^{N \times O}$ is the Kalman gain matrix, $Q \in \Re^{N \times N}$ is the process noise co-variance matrix, $R \in \Re^{O \times O}$ is the measurement noise covariance matrix, and $H(k) \in \Re^{O \times N}$ is a matrix where each entry is the derivative of one of the neural network output, $\hat{y}_i$, with respect to one neural network weight, w_j, as follows:

$$H_{ij}(k) = \left. \frac{\partial \hat{y}_i(k)}{\partial w_j(k)} \right|_{w(k) = \hat{w}(k+1)}, \tag{39}$$

$$i = 1, ..., O; \quad j = 1, ..., N$$

Usually P, Q and R are initialized as di-agonal matrices, with entries P_0, Q_0 and R_0, respectively. During the entire learning process, matrices Q and R remain constant.

5.1. EKF for the HONN

Once we have defined Equations (36), we can proceed to obtain matrix $H(k)$, for it we denote $H_1(k)$ as the derivative of the neural network output with respect to the weights in the hidden layer and $H_2(k)$ as the derivative of the neural network output with respect to the weights in the output layer of itself. There exists only one neural network output, so we omit subscript i from $\hat{y}_i$ in the next equations. By the chain rule, the values of $H_1(k)$ and $H_2(k)$ are calculated as:

$$H_1(k) = \frac{\partial \hat{y}(k)}{\partial w_{ji}(k)} = \frac{\partial \hat{y}(k)}{\partial v(k)} \frac{\partial v(k)}{\partial y_j(k)} \frac{\partial y_j(k)}{\partial v_j(k)} \frac{\partial v_j(k)}{\partial w_{ji}(k)}$$

$$H_2(k) = \frac{\partial \hat{y}(k)}{\partial w_j(k)} = \frac{\partial \hat{y}(k)}{\partial v(k)} \frac{\partial v(k)}{\partial w_j(k)} \tag{40}$$

The partial derivatives values are given by:

$$\frac{\partial \hat{y}(k)}{\partial v(k)} = 1$$

$$\frac{\partial v(k)}{\partial y_j(k)} = w_j(k)$$

$$\frac{\partial y_j(k)}{\partial v_j(k)} = \frac{a \exp\left(-a v_j(k)\right)}{\left(1 + \exp\left(-a v_j(k)\right)\right)^2}$$

$$\frac{\partial v_j(k)}{\partial w_{ji}(k)} = \rho_i(k)$$

$$\frac{\partial v(k)}{\partial w_j(k)} = y_j(k)$$

Substituting into (40) the partial derivatives values, we obtain:

$$H_1(k) = \frac{w_j(k) \cdot a \exp\left(-a v_j(k)\right) \cdot \rho_i(k)}{\left(1 + \exp\left(-a v_j(k)\right)\right)^2}$$

$$H_2(k) = y_j(k)$$

$$\tag{41}$$

Finally, $H(k)$ is formed like:

$$H(k) = \begin{bmatrix} H_1(k) \\ H_2(k) \end{bmatrix} \tag{42}$$

6. SIMULATION RESULTS

In this section, we implement the HONN previ-ously designed and trained with the EKF to predict three important variables in smart grids: ELD, WS, and WEG. The training is performed using data taken from UADY, Faculty of Engineering. We first present the results emerged from the applica-tion of the Lipschitz quotients algorithm and then the simulation results of one step ahead prediction carried out by the HONN for each time series. The equation that allows us to compute the MSE is

$$\text{MSE} = \frac{1}{2M} \sum_{i=1}^{M} \left(y_i(n) - \hat{y}_i(n) \right)^2 \qquad (43)$$

where $y(n)$ is the real time series and $\hat{y}(n)$ is the time series produced by the neural network. The ARE was used to measure the performance of the neural network in the prediction of the variables and is defined as

$$\text{ARE} = \left| \frac{y(n) - \hat{y}(n)}{y(n)} \right| \qquad (44)$$

6.1. System Order Determination

As first stage, we determine the optimal dimension of the regression vector applying the Lipschitz quotient algorithm using 300 samples of each time series, this stage is known as system's order determination. To determine system's order means to find the optimal number of regressors that must be included into the input vector of the HONN. If too many past signals are included in the regression vector, it will contain redundant information, which implies that the computation time is increased and if too small number of terms are included, system's essential dynamics will not be modeled. Lipschiz quotients algorithm can be applied by following the next steps for each time series:

1. Delay the time series from value 1 up to value 15 or 20. These variables will be the inputs for the algorithm.
2. Apply Equation (25) considering from 1 input up to c inputs.

3. Sort from major to minor the Lipschitz quotients $q_{ij}^{(c)}$ obtained from step 2.
4. Take the first p Lipschitz quotients previously sorted (remind: $p = 0.01 \sim 0.02M$, where M is the samples number).
5. Apply Equation (26).
6. Plot the Lipschitz number $q^{(c)}$ versus the number of input variables c into a semi-logarithmic scale.

The results for this stage are depicted in Figure 3, starting from which we select 8 regressors to be included into the neural network input vector for the ELD, 14 for the WS and 12 for WEG time series.

6.2. Results for the HONN

To train the HONN for each variable, we kept the following design parameters: 2 external inputs corresponding to hours and days, 25 units in the hidden layer, 1 neuron in the output layer, 300 iterations maximum, initial values for synaptic weights randomly selected in the range $(-0.5, 0.5)$ and MSE required to end the training less than 1×10^{-4}. The training was performed off-line, using a parallel configuration; for this case the delayed output is taken from the neural network output. The initial values for the covariance matrices (P, Q, R) were $P_0 = 40000$, $Q_0 = 4000$, and $R_0 = 5000$ for the ELD and $P_0 = Q_0 = R_0 = 10000$ for the WS and WEG. The data for the ELD was collected every 5 minutes and averaged each 15 minutes, in the case of the WS was taken every minute and without average, while that for the WEG, data was taken every minute and averaged each 15 minutes; therefore, we have all time series in a different time basis and this is the reason why we plot each variable as function of the sample. For the ELD we used 240 samples to accomplish the network training. In order to verify if the proposed scheme is ad-

Figure 3. Order of the system for different time series

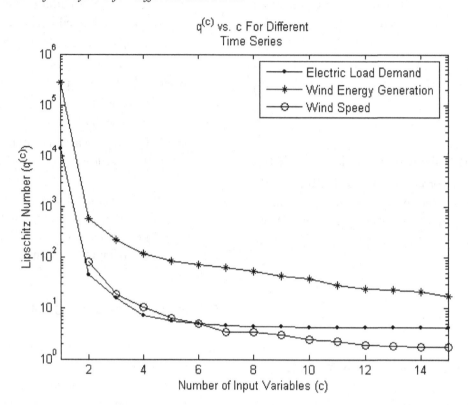

equate using less samples, we employed 192 samples for the WS and like good results were obtained using this samples number, the data to train the HONN for WEG forecasting was 192 too. The results for the ELD, WS, and WEG time series forecasting are shown in Figures 4, 5, and 6, respectively. The MSE reached for the ELD was 9.69×10^{-5} at iteration 123, for the WS was 9.27×10^{-5} at iteration 73 and for the WEG was 8.91×10^{-5} at iteration 29.

The ARE for each time series is presented in Figure 7. The upper graph corresponds to the ELD time series, the middle to WS and the bottom to WEG. Table 1 presents the MSE reached and the mean ARE for each time series.

The mean ARE for the wind speed time series can be compared with the mean ARE presented in the work of Welch et al. (2009), where three different neural networks architectures were used

to predict the same variable: the MLP had a mean ARE of 0.3847, the ERNN had a value of 0.3892 and the mean ARE for the SRNN was 0.3795. As can be seen from Table 1 and the values listed, the HONN architecture has a lesser value than the others architectures.

7. FUTURE RESEARCH DIRECTIONS

Future work on implementing higher order neural networks aims for the design of optimal operation algorithms for smart grids composed of wind and photovoltaic generation systems interconnected to the utility grid. This management system can use the forecasting data to operate the global system, fulfilling the load demand, minimizing the power supplied by the utility grid, and maximizing the one supplied by renewable sources.

Figure 4. Electric load demand time series forecasting

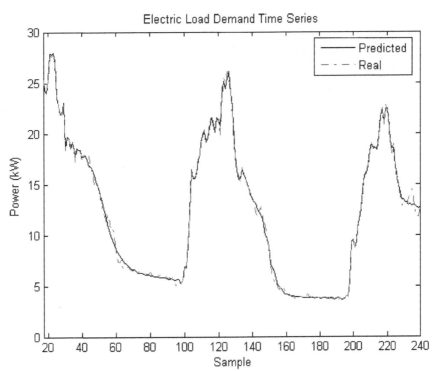

Figure 5. Wind speed time series forecasting

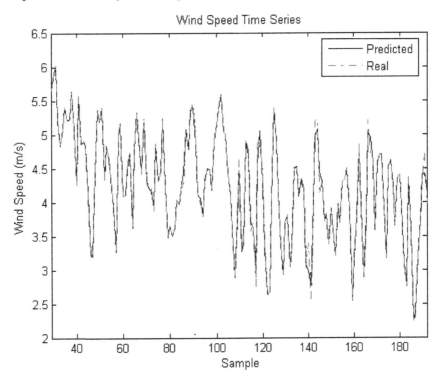

Figure 6. Wind energy generation time series forecasting

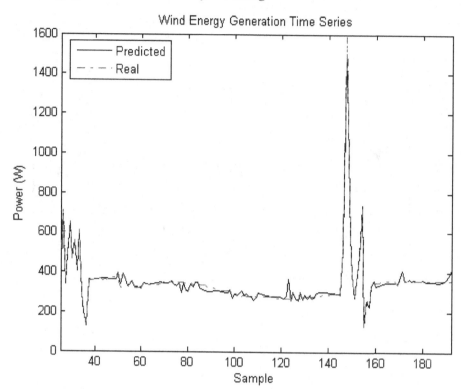

Figure 7. ARE for different time series

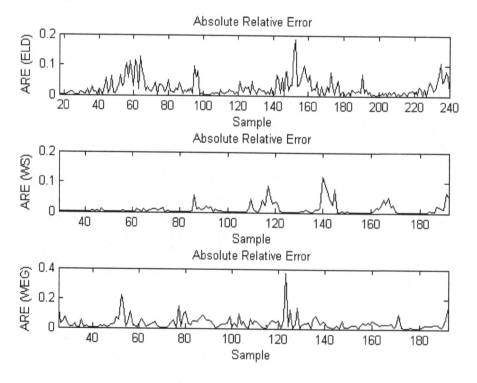

Table 1. Mean square error and mean absolute relative error

Time Series	MSE	ARE
ELD	9.69×10^{-5}	0.0254
WS	9.27×10^{-5}	0.0106
WEG	8.91×10^{-5}	0.0351

8. CONCLUSION

This chapter proposes the use of a HONN trained with an EKF-based algorithm to predict minutely data for smart grid variables with good results as shown by the ARE. The proposed method has a compact structure but taking into account the dynamic nature of the systems which behavior is needed to predict. The HONN proves in our experiments to be a model that captures very well the complexity associated with wind forecasting. Fewer neural units and faster training processes are required when using HONN than in first order applications. Performance comparisons for the WS time series have also been made between our proposed architecture and those presented by Welch et al. (2009) using the mean ARE, and we had a lesser value for this type of error than the ones shown in that reference, which confirms the efficiency of the developed method. The positive aspects in this new approach are that the neural network is adequate for highly nonlinear systems, relatively easy to code, and the training is also fast.

REFERENCES

Aquino, R. R. B., Lira, M. M. S., Oliveira, J. B., Carvalho, M. A., Jr., & Neto, O. N. (2009). Application of wavelet and neural network models for wind speed forecasting and power generation in a Brazilian experimental wind park. In *Proceedings of the IEEE International Joint Conference on Neural Networks,* (pp. 172-178). Atlanta, GA: IEEE Press.

Barbounis, T. G., Theocaris, J. B., Alexiadis, M. C., & Dokoupoulos, P. S. (2006). Long-Term wind speed and power forecasting using local recurrent neural network models. *IEEE Transactions on Energy Conversion, 21*(1), 273–284. doi:10.1109/TEC.2005.847954

Chen, Y., Chen, F., & Wu, Q. (2007). An artificial neural networks based dynamic decision model for time-series forecasting. In *Proceedings of the IEEE International Joint Conference on Neural Networks,* (pp. 696-699). Orlando, FL: IEEE Press.

El-Fouly Tarek, H. M., El-Saadany Ehab, F., & Salama Magdy, M. A. (2008). One day ahead prediction of wind speed and direction. *IEEE Transactions on Energy Conversion, 23*(1), 191–201. doi:10.1109/TEC.2007.905069

Fox, B., Flynn, D., Bryans, L., Jenkis, N., Milborrow, D., & O'Malley, M. ... Anaya-Lara, O. (2007). *Wind power integration: Connection and system operational aspects.* London, UK: The Institution of Engineering and Technology.

Gellings, C. W. (2009). *The smart grid: Enabling energy efficiency and demand response.* Boca Raton, FL: CRC Press.

Giles, C. L., & Maxwell, T. (1987). Learning, invariance, and generalization in high-order neural networks. *Applied Optics, 26*(23), 4972–4978. doi:10.1364/AO.26.004972

Güler, M. (1999). Neural classifiers for learning higher-order correlations. *Transactions Journal of Physics, 23*, 39–46.

Haykin, S. (1999). *Neural networks: A comprehensive foundation.* Upper Saddle River, NJ: Prentice Hall.

Haykin, S. (Ed.). (2001). *Kalman filtering and neural networks.* New York, NY: John Wiley & Sons, Inc. doi:10.1002/0471221546

He, X., & Asada, H. (1993). A new method for identifying orders of input-output models for nonlinear dynamic systems. In *Proceedings of the IEEE American Control Conference,* (pp. 2520-2523). San Francisco, CA: IEEE Press.

Kariniotakis, G. N., Stavrakakis, G. S., & Nogaret, E. F. (1996). Wind power forecasting using advanced neural networks models. *IEEE Transactions on Energy Conversion, 11*(4), 762–767. doi:10.1109/60.556376

Lange, M. (2003). *Analysis of the uncertainty of wind power predictions.* (Unpublished Doctoral Dissertation). Carl von Ossietzky Universität Oldenburg. Oldenburg, Germany.

Meiqin, M., Ming, D., Jianhui, S., Chang, L., Min, S., & Guorong, Z. (2008). *Testbed* for microgrid with multi-energy generators. In *Proceedings of the Canadian Conference on Electrical and Computer Engineering CCECE,* (pp. 637-640). CCECE.

Norgaard, M., Ravn, O., Poulsen, N. K., & Hansen, L. K. (2000). *Neural networks for modelling and control of dynamic systems: A practitioner's handbook.* London, UK: Springer-Verlag. doi:10.1007/978-1-4471-0453-7

Ricalde Castellanos, L. J. (2005). *Inverse optimal adaptive recurrent neural control with constrained inputs.* (Unpublished Doctoral Dissertation). Centro de Investigación y de Estudios Avanzados (CINVESTAV) del Instituto Politécnico Nacional (IPN). Guadalajara, México.

Sanchez, E. N., Alanis, A. Y., & Loukianov, A. G. (2008). *Discrete-time high order neural control trained with Kalman filtering.* Berlin, Germany: Springer-Verlag. doi:10.1007/978-3-540-78289-6

Sanchez, E. N., Alanis, A. Y., & Rico, J. (2004). Electric load demand prediction using neural networks trained by Kalman filtering. In *Proceedings of the IEEE International Joint Conference on Neural Networks,* (pp. 2771-2775). Budapest, Hungary: IEEE Press.

Sanchez Camperos, E. N., & Alanis Garcia, A. Y. (2006). *Redes neuronales: Conceptos fundamentales y aplicaciones a control automatico.* Madrid, Spain: Pearson-Prentice Hall.

Senjyu, T., Yona, A., Urasaki, N., & Funabashi, T. (2006). Application of recurrent neural network to long-term-ahead generating power forecasting for wind speed generator. In *Proceedings of the Power Systems Conference and Exposition PSCE,* (pp. 1260-1265). PSCE.

Shi, J., Lee, W. J., Liu, Y., Yang, Y., & Wang, P. (2011). Short term wind power forecasting using Hilbert-Huang transform and artificial neural network. In *Proceedings of the Fourth International Conference on Electric Utility Deregulation and Restructuring and Power Technologies,* (pp. 162-167). Weihai, China: IEEE.

Welch, R. L., Ruffing, S. M., & Venayagamoorthy, G. K. (2009). Comparison of feedforward and feedback neural network architectures for short term wind speed prediction. In *Proceedings of the IEEE International Joint Conference on Neural Networks,* (pp. 3335-3340). Atlanta, GA: IEEE Press.

Werbos, P. J. (2009). Putting more brain-like intelligence into the electric power grid: What we need and how to do it. In *Proceedings of the IEEE International Joint Conference on Neural Networks,* (pp. 3356-3359). Atlanta, GA: IEEE Press.

Wu, J., Chen, S., Zeng, J., & Gao, L. (2009). Control technologies in distributed generation systems based on renewable energy. *Asian Power Electronics Journal, 3*(1), 39–52.

Zhang, H. T., Xu, F. Y., & Zhou, L. (2010). Artificial neural network for load forecasting in smart grid. In *Proceedings of the Ninth Conference on Machine Learning and Cybernetics,* (pp. 3200-3205). Qingdao, China: IEEE.

ADDITIONAL READING

Al-Hamadi, H. M., & Soliman, S. A. (2004). Short-term electric load forecasting based on Kalman filtering algorithm with moving window weather and load model. *Electric Power Systems Research, 68*(1), 47–59. doi:10.1016/S0378-7796(03)00150-0

Alanis, A., Sanchez, E., & Ricalde, L. (2010). Discrete time reduced order neural observers for uncertain nonlinear systems. *International Journal of Neural Systems, 20*(1), 29–38. doi:10.1142/S0129065710002218

Alanis, A. Y., Sanchez, E. N., Loukianov, A. G., & Hernandez, E. A. (2010). Discrete-time recurrent high order neural networks for nonlinear identification. *Journal of the Franklin Institute, 347*(7), 1253–1265. doi:10.1016/j.jfranklin.2010.05.018

Artyomov, E., & Yadid-Pecht, O. (2005). Modified high-order neural network for invariant pattern recognition. *Pattern Recognition Letters, 26*(6), 843–851. doi:10.1016/j.patrec.2004.09.029

Azoff, E. M. (1994). *Neural network time series forecasting of financial markets.* New York, NY: John Wiley & Sons.

Chatfield, C. (2000). *Time-series forecasting.* Boca Raton, FL: Chapman & Hall/CRC. doi:10.1201/9781420036206

Farret, F., & Simoes, G. (2006). *Integration of alternative sources of energy.* New York, NY: John Wiley.

Gavrilas, M., & Gavrilas, G. (2010). An enhanced ANN wind power forecast model based on a fuzzy representation of wind direction. In *Proceedings of the Tenth Symposium on Neural Network Applications in Electrical Engineering,* (pp. 31-36). IEEE.

Hu, X., & Balasubramaniam, P. (Eds.). (2008). *Recurrent neural networks.* In-Tech. doi:10.5772/68

Kani, S. A. P., & Riany, G. H. (2008). A new ANN-based methodology for very short-term wind speed prediction using Markov chain approach. In *Proceedings of the IEEE Electric Power Conference,* (pp. 1-6). IEEE Press.

Karayiannis, N. B., & Venetsanopoulos, A. N. (1995). On the training and performance of high-order neural networks. *Mathematical Biosciences, 129*(2), 143–168. doi:10.1016/0025-5564(94)00057-7

Kosmatopoulos, E. B., Christodoulou, M. A., & Ioannou, A. P. (1997). Dynamic neural networks that ensure exponential identification error convergence. *Neural Networks, 10*(2), 299–314. doi:10.1016/S0893-6080(96)00060-3

Lubitz, W. D. (2005). *Near real time wind energy forecasting incorporating wind tunnel modeling.* (Unpublished Doctoral Dissertation). University of California. Davis, CA.

Mandal, P., Senjyu, T., & Funabashi, T. (2006). Neural networks approach to forecast several hour ahead electricity prices and loads in deregulated market. *Energy Conversion and Management, 47*(15-16), 2128–2142. doi:10.1016/j.enconman.2005.12.008

Manwell, J. F., McGowan, J. G., & Rogers, A. (2010). *Wind energy explained: Theory, design and application.* New York, NY: Wiley. doi:10.1260/030952406778055054

Patel, M. (2006). *Wind and solar power systems: Design, analysis and operation.* Boca Raton, FL: CRC Press Taylor & Francis Group. doi:10.1260/030952406778606197

Poznyak, A. S., Sanchez, E. N., & Yu, W. (2000). *Differential neural networks for robust nonlinear control*. Singapore, Singapore: World Scientific.

Poznyak, A. S., Yu, W., Sanchez, E. N., & Perez, J. P. (1999). Nonlinear adaptive trajectory tracking using dynamic neural networks. *IEEE Transactions on Neural Networks*, *10*(6), 1402–1411. doi:10.1109/72.809085

Sanchez, E. N., Alanis, A. Y., & Chen, G. (2006). Recurrent neural networks trained with Kalman filtering for discrete chaos reconstruction. *Dynamics of Continuous . Discrete and Impulsive Systems Series B: Applications and Algorithms*, *6*(13), 1–17.

Shafie-Khah, M., Parsa Moghaddam, M., & Sheikh-El-Eslami, M. K. (2011). Price forecasting of day-ahead electricity markets using a hybrid forecast method. *Energy Conversion and Management*, *52*(5), 2165–2169. doi:10.1016/j.enconman.2010.10.047

Shi, K. L., & Li, H. (2004). A novel control of a small wind turbine driven generator based on neural networks. *IEEE Power Engineering Society General Meeting*, *2*, 1999-2005.

Tai, H. M., & Jong, T. L. (1990). Information storage in high-order neural networks with unequal neural activity. *Journal of the Franklin Institute*, *327*(1), 129–141. doi:10.1016/0016-0032(90)90061-M

Weidong, X., Yubing, L., & Xingpei, L. (2010). Short-term forecasting of wind turbine power generation based on genetic neural network. In *Proceedings of the Eighth World Congress on Intelligent Control and Automation* (pp. 5943-5946). IEEE.

Xu, S., & Chen, L. (2009). Adaptive higher order neural networks. In *Proceedings of the WRI Global Congress on Intelligent Systems,* (Vol. 4), (pp. 26-30). WRI.

Zheng, T., Girgis, A. A., & Makram, E. B. (2000). A hybrid wavelet-Kalman filter method for load forecasting. *Electric Power Systems Research*, *54*(1), 11–17. doi:10.1016/S0378-7796(99)00063-2

KEY TERMS AND DEFINITIONS

Electric Load Demand: Power demanded from the utility grid.

Higher Order Neural Network: An artificial neural network where some input node contains products of more than two signals.

Kalman Filter: A method to estimate the state of an unknown dynamic system.

Time Series Forecasting: A task whose goal is to know the future value(s) of the interest variable from its present and past values.

Lipschitz Quotients: An algorithm to find the optimal number of regressors to model a dynamic system.

Wind Energy: A type of renewable energy to produce electrical power. The source for this type of electrical generation is the kinetic energy of the wind.

Smart Grid: An electrical energy generation system which involves both renewable and fossil resources to produce electricity. Also includes the control laws to synchronize both types of generation sources.

Section 4
Artificial Higher Order Neural Network Models and Applications

Chapter 13
HONNs with Extreme Learning Machine to Handle Incomplete Datasets

Shuxiang Xu
University of Tasmania, Australia

ABSTRACT

An Extreme Learning Machine (ELM) randomly chooses hidden neurons and analytically determines the output weights (Huang, et al., 2005, 2006, 2008). With the ELM algorithm, only the connection weights between hidden layer and output layer are adjusted. The ELM algorithm tends to generalize better at a very fast learning speed: it can learn thousands of times faster than conventionally popular learning algorithms (Huang, et al., 2006). Artificial Neural Networks (ANNs) have been widely used as powerful information processing models and adopted in applications such as bankruptcy prediction, predicting costs, forecasting revenue, forecasting share prices and exchange rates, processing documents, and many more. Higher Order Neural Networks (HONNs) are ANNs in which the net input to a computational neuron is a weighted sum of products of its inputs. Real life data are not usually perfect. They contain wrong, incomplete, or vague data. Hence, it is usual to find missing data in many information sources used. Missing data is a common problem in statistical analysis (Little & Rubin, 1987). This chapter uses the Extreme Learning Machine (ELM) algorithm for HONN models and applies it in several significant business cases, which involve missing datasets. The experimental results demonstrate that HONN models with the ELM algorithm offer significant advantages over standard HONN models, such as faster training, as well as improved generalization abilities.

INTRODUCTION

Artificial Neural Networks (ANNs) have been providing significant benefits in many business applications. They have been actively used for applications such as bankruptcy prediction, predicting costs, forecast revenue, processing documents, and more (Kurbel, et al., 1998; Atiya, et al., 2001; Baesens, et al., 2003). Almost any neural network model would fit into at least one business area or financial analysis. Traditional statistical methods have been used for business applications with many limitations (Azema-Barac, et al., 1997; Blum, et al., 1991; Park, et al., 1993).

DOI: 10.4018/978-1-4666-2175-6.ch013

This chapter addresses using ANNs for handling business data for the following reasons. First, although usually considered a black-box approach, ANNs are a natural technology for data mining. ANNs are non-linear models that resemble biological neural networks in structure and learn through training. ANNs present a model based on the massive parallelism and the pattern recognition and prediction abilities of the human brain. ANNs learn from examples in a way similar to how the human brain learns. Then ANNs take complex and noisy data as input and make educated guesses based on what they have learned from the past, like what the human brain does. Given the requirements of data mining within large databases of historical data, ANNs are a natural technology for this application (McCue, et al., 2007). Next, ANNs (especially higher order ANNs) are able to handle incomplete or noisy data (Peng, et al., 2007; Wang, 2003). Databases usually contain noise in the form of inaccuracies and inconsistencies. Lack of data validation procedures may allow a user to enter incorrect data. Data can also become corrupt during migration from one system to another. Missing data is a common problem especially when data is collected from many different sources. Finally, ANNs hold superior predictive capability, compared with other data mining approaches (Xu, 2009; Zhang, et al., 2007; Fulcher, et al., 2006; Browne, et al., 2004; Kohonen, et al., 2000). The predictive accuracy of a data mining approach strongly influences its effectiveness and popularity. Higher predictive accuracy with real data is an obviously desirable feature.

Many of the important business data mining functions performed by ANNs are mirrored by those of the human brain. These include classification, clustering, associative memory, modeling, time-series forecasting, and constraint satisfaction (Cios, et al., 2007; Bigus, 1996). These tasks, which are important for human survival as a species, involve simultaneous processing of large amounts of data, where fast and accurate pattern recognition and responses are required. Classifica-

tion refers to making distinctions between items, the most basic function performed by the human brain. We are able to analyse objects using the finest features to assess their similarities and differences. In the business environment, there is also a need for making classifications. Examples are: should a loan application for a new house be approved? Should an application for extending a line of credit to a growing business be approved? Should the new catalog of a company be mailed to this set of customers or to another set? All of these decisions are made based on classification. Clustering refers to the ability to group like things together. The business applications of clustering are mainly in the marketing arena. By clustering customers into groups based on similar attributes such as which products they buy or demographics they share, we can understand the markets in finer detail. Such information can be used to target specific groups of customers with products that many of them have previously purchased, or add-on services, which might appeal to the groups. Associative memory refers to associating two or more items. In business, many products are closely related to each other so when a customer purchases one of them he is likely to also buy the others. ANNs such as Bidirectional Associative Memories and Hopfield networks have been shown to be of such capabilities (Han, et al., 2006). Modeling refers to learning to predict outcomes based on existing examples. An experienced stock trader watches the changes of leading economic indicators to know when to buy or sell. With learning algorithms, ANNs are able to learn the existing examples and then, given new inputs, make predictions. Such ability to generalize on novel cases is one of the greatest strength of ANNs. An important variation of modeling is time-series forecasting, which looks at what has happened for some period back through time and predicts for some point in the future, a more difficult but more rewarding task. Finally, constraint satisfaction refers to solving complex problems that involve multiple simultaneous constraints. Having multiple conflicting goals is a natural part of life. ANNs with their weighted connections between neurons have proven themselves extremely adept at solving constraint satisfaction and optimization problems.

Recent international progress in the field of ANNs for business applications include the following. A Self-Organising Map (SOM) ANN model is designed in Peng et al. (2007) in an attempt to handle incomplete datasets for data mining. In Malone et al. (2006), a technique which can be used to extract propositional if-then type rules from an ANN model has been presented. Browne et al. (2004) design ANN algorithms to mine bioinformatics datasets, including the prediction of splice site junctions in Human DNA sequences. Wang (2003) proposes a SOM-based ANN model for data mining with incomplete data sets. Hansen et al. (2002) reports an extension of ANN methods for planning and budgeting in the State of Utah in the USA. Kohonen et al. (2000) have demonstrated the utility of a huge SOM with more than one million nodes to partition a little less than seven million patent abstracts where the documents are represented by 500-dimensional feature vectors. Kim et al. (1997) report an integrated ANN system for forecasting interest rates for corporate bonds and treasury bills. Brachman et al. (1996) use an ANN-based approach to identify suspicious credit card transactions.

While conventional ANN models have been bringing huge profits to many financial institutions, they suffer from several drawbacks. First, conventional ANNs cannot handle discontinuities in the input training data set (Zhang, et al., 2002). Next, they do not perform well on complicated business data with high frequency components and high order nonlinearity, and finally, they have difficulty handling incomplete data sets (data sets with missing values) (Kros, et al., 2006; Zhang, et al., 2002; Burns, 1986).

To overcome these limitations some researchers have proposed the use of Higher Order Neural Networks (HONNs) (Redding, et al., 1993; Zhang,

et al., 1999; Zhang, et al., 2000). HONNs are able to provide some explanation for the simulation they produce and thus can be considered as 'open box' rather than 'black box.' HONNs can simulate high frequency and high order nonlinear business data, and can handle discontinuities in the input training data set (Zhang, et al., 2002).

HONNs (Higher Order Neural Networks) (Lee, et al., 1986) are networks in which the net input to a computational neuron is a weighted sum of products of its inputs. Such neuron is called a Higher-order Processing Unit (HPU) (Lippman, 1989). It was known that HONN's can implement invariant pattern recognition (Psaltis, et al., 1988; Reid, et al., 1989; Wood, et al., 1996). Giles (Giles, et al., 1987) showed that HONN's have impressive computational, storage and learning capabilities. In Redding et al. (1993), HONN's were proved to be at least as powerful as any other FNN (Feedforward Neural Network) architecture when the orders of the networks are the same. Kosmatopoulos et al. (1995) studied the approximation and learning properties of one class of recurrent HONNs and applied these architectures to the identification of dynamical systems. Thimm et al. (1997) proposed a suitable initialization method for HONN's and compared this method to weight initialization techniques for FNNs. A large number of experiments were performed which leaded to the proposal of a suitable initialization approach for HONNs.

In Xu (2007), HONN models have been used in several business applications. The results demonstrate significant advantages of HONNs over conventional ANNs such as much reduced network size, faster training, as well as improved forecasting errors. In Ramanathan et al. (2007), HONNs are used for data clustering which offer significant improvement when compared to the results obtained from using self-organising maps. In Ho et al. (2006), global exponential stability and exponential convergence issues of HONNs are studied. In Fulcher et al. (2006), HONNs have been used for dealing with non-linear and discontinuous financial time-series data, and are able to offer roughly twice the performance of conventional ANNs on financial time-series prediction. Zhang et al. (2002) employ HONNs for financial data auto-modeling. Their algorithms are further shown to be capable of automatically finding an optimum model, given a specific application. In Abdelbar (1998), a HONN model is applied to the classification into age-groups of abalone shellfish, a difficult benchmark to which previous researchers have tried to handle using different ANN architectures.

Adaptive HONNs are HONNs with adaptive neuron activation functions. The idea of setting a few free parameters in the neuron activation function (or transfer function) of an ANN is relatively new. Such activation functions are adaptive because the free parameters can be adjusted (in the same way as connection weights) to adapt to different applications. ANNs with adaptive activation function provide better fitting properties than classical architectures with fixed activation functions (such as sigmoid function). Zhang et al. (2007) propose using an adaptive ANN for estimating rainfall by mining satellite data, which reduces the average errors of rainfall estimates for the total precipitation event to less than 10 per cent. Mishra (2006) uses an adaptive radial basis function neural network as a control scheme for a unified power flow controller to improve the transient stability performance of a multi-machine power system. Fiori (2003) presents adaptive ANNs and adjusts the free parameters in their activation functions in an unsupervised way by information-theoretic adapting rules. Zhang et al. (2002) uses adaptive HONNs for automated financial data mining.

Unlike traditional ANN learning algorithms, Extreme Learning Machine (ELM) randomly chooses hidden neurons and analytically determines the output weights (Huang, et al., 2005, 2006, 2008). With ELM algorithm, only the connection weights between hidden layer and output layer are adjusted. Many types of hidden nodes including additive nodes, RBF (radial basis function) nodes, multiplicative nodes, and other non neural alike nodes can be used as long as they are piecewise nonlinear. ELM algorithm tends to generalize better at very fast learning speed: it can learn thousands of times faster than conventionally popular learning algorithms (Huang, et al., 2006).

Real life data are not usually perfect. They contain wrong data, incomplete or vague. Hence, it is usual to find missing data in many information sources used. Missing data is a common problem in statistical analysis (Little & Rubin, 1987). Percentages of missing data less than 1% are usually considered trivial, 1% - 5% considered manageable. However, a percentage of 5% - 15% can have severe impact on any kind of analysis and damage the model's results. Missing data have a similar impact on neural networks as it does on other algorithms or models, such as K-Nearest Neighbor. These similarities include variance underestimation, distribution distortion, and correlation depression. By training a neural network with samples containing missing values, connection weights between neurons learned through training cannot be accurately applied to a test set, especially when the test set contains missing values itself (Kros, et al., 2006).

This chapter proposes an ELM algorithm for HONNs and applies it in benchmark datasets with missing values. An overview of ELM algorithms will be given. An ELM algorithm for HONNs will be developed. Benchmark datasets with missing values will be downloaded from the UCI Machine Learning Repository (Asuncion, et al., 2007). Experiments will be conducted to apply the developed algorithm on the selected datasets. For comparison studies, standard HONN algorithms (without ELM) will also be applied on the selected datasets. Such comparison studies will reveal the advantages and disadvantages of HONN with ELM against standard HONN models.

ELM ALGORITHM

Huang et al first proposed the use of ELM algorithm (Huang, et al., 2004a), based on the observations that the learning speed of feedforward neural networks is generally slow, largely because of the slow gradient-based learning algorithms as well as the large number of free parameters which need to be adjusted during the training process. The authors then proposed a new learning algorithm, ELM algorithm, for Single-hidden-layer Feedforward Neural Networks (SFNNs), which randomly chooses hidden layer neurons and only adjusts the output weights (between the hidden layer and the output layer). The proposed algorithm has been proved extremely fast in handling real world benchmark problems related to function approximation and classification tasks. Their experimental results also revealed a better generalization performance of the ELM algorithm. In a related paper (Huang, et al., 2004b), it was shown that the algorithm could be extended to RBF (Radial Basis Function) networks, which allows the centers and impact widths of RBF kernels to be randomly generated, with the output weights simply calculated rather than iteratively tuned. The ELM algorithm was soon extended from real domain to complex domain to become complex ELM algorithm (C-ELM) for non-linear channel equalization applications (Li, et al., 2005), which outperformed other ANN equalizers such as the complex minimal resource allocation network, complex RBF network, and complex backpropagation equalizers. In the mean time, Zhu et al. (2005) showed that, due to the nature of ELM algorithm (random determination of hidden neurons), ANNs with ELM algorithm generally require higher number of hidden meurons which increases the sizes of such ANNs; therefore, they proposed a hybrid training algorithm to determine input weights and to adjust output weights, with experimental results revealing better generalization performance as well as much more compact ANN configuration.

Several artificial as well as real benchmark function approximation and classification tasks have been tested using ELM algorithm (Huang, et al., 2006a) with outstanding results. In Huang et al. (2006b), ELM was extended to become a new algorithm for single hidden layer feedforward networks with randomly generated additive or radial basis function hidden neurons, which can work as universal approximators. The algorithm was named as Incremental Extreme Learning Machine (I-ELM) which outperforms many other learning algorithms. However, I-ELM does not recalculate the output weights of all the existing neurons when a new neuron is added. In Huang et al. (2007), it was shown that the convergence rate of I-ELM could be further improved by recalculating output weights of all the existing neurons based on a convex optimization approach when a new neuron is added.

In Zhang et al. (2007), ELM was used for directing multi-category classification problems in a cancer diagnosis research. Three benchmark microarray data sets were used for cancer diagnosis, with results indicating that ELM produced comparable or better classification accuracies with reduced learning times and reduced configuration when compared against conventional back-propagation ANNs and Support Vector Machines. In Huang et al. (2008a), I-ELM was extended from real domain to complex domain, and was shown that it could approximate any target functions in complex domain. An enhanced approach for I-ELM was proposed in Huang et al. (2008b): for each learning step some hidden neurons were randomly generated—among them, the hidden neuron leading to the largest residual error decreasing would be added to the existing configuration and the output weight was calculated in the same simple was as in the original I-ELM algorithm. In Lan et al. (2008) ELM was used to predict the sub-cellular localization of proteins based on frequent subsequences. The results showed that ELM was extremely fast and provided good generalization outcomes.

Feng et al. (2009) proposed an efficient ELM approach to automatically determine the number of hidden layer neurons in generalized Single hidden Layer Feedforward Networks (SLFNs). The algorithm was named Error Minimized Extreme Learning Machine (EM-ELM), which could add random hidden neurons to SLFNs one by one or group by group (with different group size). Experimental results demonstrated that EM-ELM had better generalization ability and was much faster than other sequential/incremental algorithms. Rong et al. (2009) proposed an Online Sequential fuzzy Extreme Learning Machine (OS-fuzzy-ELM) for function approximation and classification tasks. With OS-fuzzy-ELM the training process could be conducted with feeding the input training pairs in a one-by-one mode or a chunk-by-chunk mode with fixed or varying chunk size. All the antecedent parameters of membership functions were randomly assigned first, followed by adjusting the corresponding consequent parameters through learning. Performance of the OS-fuzzy-ELM algorithm against other existing algorithms was made on real world benchmark problems related to nonlinear system identification, indicating that the proposed algorithm produced better accuracies with at least an order of magnitude reduction in the training time.

Cao et al. (2010) introduced a new Wavelet Neural Network (WNN) with extreme learning machine, which used composite functions for the hidden neurons. The algorithm was tested on regression problems of some nonlinear functions as well as on real world problems, achieving better performance in most cases with significantly faster training process. Huang et al. (2010) studied ELM for classification problems specifically in the aspect of standard optimization to extend ELM to a type of Support Vector Machine (SVM). It was shown that ELM for classification tended to achieve better performance than traditional SVMs with simpler implementation. Miche et al. (2010) proposed an Optimally Pruned Extreme Learning Machine (OP-ELM) based on the original ELM,

with additional steps to make it more robust and generic. Results for both computational time and accuracy are compared against the original ELM based on three widely used methodologies: Multilayer Perceptron (MLP), Support Vector Machine (SVM), and Gaussian Process (GP). The proposed algorithm performed several orders of magnitude faster than the other algorithms while maintaining an accuracy that is comparable to the performance of the SVM.

HONN MODELS WITH ELM ALGORITHM

HONNs (Lee, et al., 1986) are networks in which the net input to a computational neuron is a weighted sum of products of its inputs. Such neuron is called a Higher-order Processing Unit (HPU) (Lippman, 1989). The network structure of an HONN is the same as that of a multi-layer Feedforward Neural Network (FNN). That is, it consists of an input layer with some input units, an output layer with some output units, and at least one hidden layer consisting of intermediate processing units. Usually there is no activation function for neurons in the input layer and the output neurons are summing units, the activation function for hidden layer neurons can be any nonlinear piecewise continuous ones.

Based on a one-dimensional HONN defined in Zhang et al. (2002), this chapter proposes the following ELM algorithm for HONNs. The main idea of ELM lies in the random selection of hidden neurons with random initialization of the Single Layer Feedforward Network (SLFN) weights and biases. Then, the input weights and biases do not need to be adjusted during training, only the output weights are learned. The training of the SLFN can be achieved with a few steps and very low computational costs.

Consider a set of S distinct training samples (X_i, Y_i) with $X_i \in R^n$ and $Y_i \in R^m$, where n and *m* are positive integers. Then a Single Layer Feedforward Network (SLFN) with *N* hidden neurons can be mathematically represented by

$$\sum_{i=1}^{N} O_i f(w_i X_j + b_i),\ 1 \leq j \leq S \qquad (1)$$

with *f* being the randomly selected neuron activation function, w_i the input weights, b_i the biases, and O_i the output weights.

In case of two-dimensional HONN with a single hidden layer, Equation (1) becomes

$$\sum_{i=1}^{NP} O_i f\left(w_i \begin{bmatrix} X_j \\ H(X_j) \end{bmatrix} + b_i\right),\ 1 \leq j \leq S \qquad (2)$$

where

$$NP = N + C_N^2 \qquad (3)$$

$$H(X_j) = X_j \otimes X_j^T,\ 1 \leq j \leq S \qquad (4)$$

Assume that the single layer HONN approximates the training samples perfectly, then the errors between the estimated outputs are the actual outputs are zero, which means

$$\sum_{i=1}^{NP} O_i f\left(w_i \begin{bmatrix} X_j \\ H(X_j) \end{bmatrix} + b_i\right) = Y_j,\ 1 \leq j \leq S$$
$$(5)$$

Then the ELM algorithm, when applies to a HONN, states that with randomly initialized input weights and biases, and with the condition that the randomly selected neuron activation function is infinitely differentiable, then the output weights can be determined so that the single layer HONN provides an approximation of the sample values to any degree of accuracy. The way to calculate the output weights from the hidden layer output

matrix and the target values is proposed with the use of a Moore-Penrose generalized inverse of the matrix generated from (5).

HONN MODEL APPLICATIONS

In this section, the HONN model with ELM algorithm as defined in Section 3 has been used in several business applications. The algorithm has been implemented in Java, based on a HONN implementation in Matlab version R2009b, run on a standard Windows XP operating system (professional version). The results are given and discussed.

Automobile Quality Determination

The first experiment uses an automobile dataset to determine automobile quality. This automobile dataset (Asuncion, et al., 2007) is made of 205 instances, with 25 attributes (inputs) and 1 class attribute (output). This data set consists of three types of attributes: (a) the various characteristics of automobiles, (b) its assigned insurance risk rating, and (c) its normalized losses in use as compared to other cars. The second attribute (insurance rating) corresponds to the degree to which the auto is more risky than its price indicates. Cars are initially assigned a risk factor symbol associated with its price. Then, if it is more risky (or less), this symbol is adjusted by moving it up (or down) the scale. A value of 3 indicates that the auto is risky, -3 that it is pretty safe. The third attribute is the relative average loss payment per insured vehicle year. This value is normalized for all autos within a particular size classification (two-door small, station wagons, sports, etc.), and represents the average loss per car per year. This third factor is considered the output (class) attribute. The 26 attributes are shown in Table 1.

The following are examples of instances from the dataset:

Table 1. 26 Attributes

Attribute	Attribute Range.
A1. symboling	-3, -2, -1, 0, 1, 2, 3.
A2. normalized-losses	continuous from 65 to 256.
A3. make	Alfa-Romero, Audi, BMW, Chevrolet, Dodge, Honda, Isuzu, Jaguar, Mazda, Mercedes-Benz, Mercury, Mitsubishi, Nissan, Peugot, Plymouth, Porsche, Renault, Saab, Subaru, Toyota, Volkswagen, Volvo.
A4. fuel-type	diesel, gas.
A5. aspiration	std, turbo.
A6. num-of-doors	four, two.
A7. body-style	hardtop, wagon, sedan, hatchback, convertible.
A8. drive-wheels	4wd, fwd, rwd.
A9. engine-location	front, rear.
A10. wheel-base	continuous from 86.6 to 120.9.
A11. length	continuous from 141.1 to 208.1.
A12. width	continuous from 60.3 to 72.3.
A13. height	continuous from 47.8 to 59.8.
A14. curb-weight	continuous from 1488 to 4066.
A15. engine-type	dohc, dohcv, l, ohc, ohcf, ohcv, rotor.
A16. num-of-cylinders	eight, five, four, six, three, twelve, two.
A17. engine-size	continuous from 61 to 326.
A18. fuel-system	1bbl, 2bbl, 4bbl, idi, mfi, mpfi, spdi, spfi.
A19. bore	continuous from 2.54 to 3.94.
A20. stroke	continuous from 2.07 to 4.17.
A21. compression-ratio	continuous from 7 to 23.
A22. horsepower	continuous from 48 to 288.
A23. peak-rpm	continuous from 4150 to 6600.
A24. city-mpg	continuous from 13 to 49.
A25. highway-mpg	continuous from 16 to 54.
A26. price	continuous from 5118 to 45400.

```
3,?,alfaromero, gas,std,two,
convertible,rwd,front, 88.60,168.80,
64.10, 48.80,2548,dohc,
four,130, mpfi,3.47,2.68,9.00,
111,5000,21,27,13495
3,?,alfaromero,
gas,std,two,convertible,
rwd,front,88.60,168.80,
64.10,48.80, 2548,dohc,four,
130,mpfi,3.47,2.68,9.00,
```

```
111,5000,21,27, 16500
1,?,alfaromero,
gas,std,two,hatchback,rwd, fro
nt,94.50,171.20,65.50,52.40,2823,
ohcv,six,152,mpfi,
2.68,3.47,9.00,154,5000, 19,26,16500
2,164,audi,gas,std,four,
sedan,fwd,front,99.80, 176.60,66.20,
54.30,2337,ohc, four,109,mpfi,
3.19,3.40,10.00,102,5500, 24,30,13950
```

```
1,110,dodge,gas,std,
four,wagon,fwd,front,
103.30,174.60,64.60, 59.80,2535,ohc,
four,122,2bbl, 3.34,3.46,8.50,88,
5000,24,30,8921
2,103, volvo,gas,std,four, sedan,rwd,
front,104.30,188.80,67.20,
56.20,2912,ohc,four,
141,mpfi,3.78,3.15,9.50,
114,5400,23,28,12940
1,74,volvo,gas,std,
four,wagon,rwd,front,
104.30,188.80,67.20,
57.50,3034,ohc,four, 141,mpfi,
3.78,3.15,9.50,114, 5400,23,28,13415
0,?,volkswagen,gas,std,
four,sedan,fwd,front,100.40,
180.20,66.90,55.10,
2661,ohc,five,136,
mpfi,3.19,3.40,8.50,110,
5500,19,24,13295
0,?,volkswagen,diesel, turbo,
four,sedan,fwd,front,100.40,
180.20,66.90,55.10, 2579,ohc,four,97,
idi,3.01,3.40,23.00,68,
4500,33,38,13845
2,94,volkswagen,gas,
std,four,sedan,fwd,front,
97.30,171.70,65.50,
55.70,2275,ohc,four,
109,mpfi,3.19,3.40, 9.00,85,5250,27,
34,8495
```

There are missing values in this dataset. For this experiment, the data set is divided into a training set made of 70% of the original set and a test set made of 20% of the original set. The final 10% is used for generalisation purpose for evaluating the performance. To verify the advantages of the ELM HONN model the following ANNs have also been applied on the data set for comparison studies: a standard HONN model with one hidden layer; a Multi-Layer Perceptron (MLP) with the sigmoid activation function (and one hidden layer); An RBF Neural Network with the Gaussian activation function (and one hidden layer). For all of these ANNs the number of hidden layer neurons has been determined using an approach from (Xu, 2010). The experimental results are displayed in Table 2. It is worth noting that, while ELM HONN and standard HONN produce similar correctness rates, ELM HONN is considerably faster than standard HONN. Due to the nature of HONN models, training takes longer time because of the significantly increased number of input neurons (compared with conventional MLP and RBF neural networks). However, the correctness rates produced by these conventional ANNs are significantly lower.

Credit Card Approval

The second application uses a credit card dataset (Asuncion, et al., 2007) to approve or reject a credit card application from a new client. The dataset contains examples representing positive and negative instances of clients who were and were not granted credit. All attribute names and values have been modified to become meaningless symbols for protecting confidentiality of the data. This dataset is interesting because there is a good mix of attributes, which are either continuous or nominal with small numbers of values, or nominal with larger numbers of values. There are also a few missing values. The dataset is made of 690 instances with 15 factor attributes plus one class attribute, which indicates approval or denial. The attributes information are as follows:

A1. b, a.
A2. continuous.
A3. continuous.
A4. u, y, l, t.
A5. g, p, gg.
A6. c, d, cc, i, j, k, m, r, q, w, x, e, aa, ff.
A7. v, h, bb, j, n, z, dd, ff, o.
A8. continuous.
A9. t, f.

Table 2. Comparing ELM HONN against standard HONN, MLP, RBF neural networks

ANN	Dataset	# HL	TT (sec)	Correctness
ELM HONN	Automobile	1	13.9	94.3%
Standard HONN	Automobile	1	27.8	93.5%
MLP	Automobile	1	8.2	75.7%
RBF	Automobile	1	7.4	76.9%

HL: Hidden Layer, TT: Training Time

A10. t, f.
A11. continuous.
A12. t, f.
A13. g, p, s.
A14. continuous.
A15. continuous.
A16. +,- (class attribute)

The following are examples of instances from the dataset:

```
b,30.83,0,u,g,w,v,1.25,t,t,01,f
,g,00202,0,+
a,58.67,4.46,u,g,q,h,3.04,t,t,06,f
,g,00043,560,+
a,24.50,0.5,u,g,q,h,1.5,t,f,0,f
,g,00280,824,+
b,27.83,1.54,u,g,w,v,3.75,t,t,05,t
,g,00100,3,+
b,20.17,5.625,u,g,w,v,1.71,t,f,0,f
,s,00120,0,+
b,37.17,4,u,g,c,bb,5,t,f,0,t
,s,00280,0,-
b,?,0.375,u,g,d,v,0.875,t,f,0,t
,s,00928,0,-
```

```
b,25.67,2.21,y,p,aa,v,4,t,f,0,f
,g,00188,0,-
b,34.00,4.5,u,g,aa,v,1,t,f,0,t,g,002
40,0,-
a,49.00,1.5,u,g,j,j,0,t,f,0,t
,g,00100,27,-
```

For this experiment, the dataset is divided into a training set made of 75% of the original set and a test set made of 15% of the original set. The final 10% is used for generalisation purpose for evaluating the ELM HONN performance.

To verify the advantages of the ELM HONN model the following ANNs have also been trained on the data set for comparison studies: a standard HONN model with one hidden layer; a Multi-Layer Perceptron (MLP) with the sigmoid activation function (and one hidden layer); An RBF Neural Network with the Gaussian activation function (and one hidden layer).

For all of these ANNs the number of hidden layer neurons has been determined using an approach for determining a near optimal number of hidden layer neurons from Xu (2010). The experimental results are displayed in Table 3. It

Table 3. Comparing ELM HONN against standard HONN, MLP, RBF neural networks

ANN	Dataset	# HL	TT (sec)	Correctness
ELM HONN	Credit Card	1	25.8	95.8%
Standard HONN	Credit Card	1	49.8	94.8%
MLP	Credit Card	1	14.2	70.4%
RBF	Credit Card	1	13.4	72.9%

HL: Hidden Layer, TT: Training Time

can be observed that ELM HONN and standard HONN produce similar correctness rates, but ELM HONN is considerably faster than standard HONN. Again, due to the nature of HONN models, training takes longer time because of the significantly increased number of input neurons (compared with conventional MLP and RBF neural networks).

Wine Quality Recognition

The last experiment uses a wine quality recognition dataset (Asuncion, et al., 2007) to train several neural networks for determining the quality of new wines. Each wine is put into one of three classes (based on its quality information). These data are the results of a chemical analysis of wines grown in the same region in Italy but derived from three different cultivars. The chemical analysis determined the quantities of 13 constituents (attributes) found in each of the three types of wines. The attributes are:

A1. Alcohol
A2. Malic acid
A3. Ash
A4. Alcalinity of ash
A5. Magnesium
A6. Total phenols
A7. Flavanoids
A8. Nonflavanoid phenols
A9. Proanthocyanins
A10. Color intensity
A11. Hue
A12. OD280/OD315 of diluted wines
A13. Proline

All attributes are continuous. Some values have been deliberated removed to create challenges. There are a total of 178 instances in this dataset. The following are examples of instances from the dataset:

```
1,14.22,1.7,2.3,16.3,118,3.2,3,.26,2.
03,6.38,.94,3.31,970
1,13.29,1.97,2.68,16.8,102,3,3.23,.31
,1.66,6,1.07,2.84,1270
1,13.72,1.43,2.5,16.7,108,3.4,3.67,.1
9,2.04,6.8,.89,2.87,1285
2,12.37,.94,1.36,10.6,88,1.98,.57,.28
,.42,1.95,1.05,1.82,520
2,12.33,1.1,2.28,16,101,2.05,1.09,.63
,.41,3.27,1.25,1.67,680
2,12.64,1.36,2.02,16.8,100,2.02,1.41,
.53,.62,5.75,.98,1.59,450
3,13.23,3.3,2.28,18.5,98,1.8,.83,.61,
1.87,10.52,.56,1.51,675
3,12.58,1.29,2.1,20,103,1.48,.58,.53,
1.4,7.6,.58,1.55,640
3,13.17,5.19,2.32,22,93,1.74,.63,.61,
1.55,7.9,.6,1.48,725
3,13.84,4.12,2.38,19.5,89,1.8,.83,.48
,1.56,9.01,.57,1.64,480
```

For this experiment, the dataset is divided into a training set made of 80% of the original set and a test set made of 10% of the original set. The final 10% is used for generalisation purpose for observing the ELM HONN performance.

To verify the advantages of the ELM HONN model the following ANNs have also been trained on the data set for comparison studies: a standard HONN model with one hidden layer; a Multi-Layer Perceptron (MLP) with the sigmoid activation function (and one hidden layer); An RBF Neural Network with the Gaussian activation function (and one hidden layer).

For all of these ANNs the number of hidden layer neurons has been determined using the approach for determining a near optimal number of hidden layer neurons from Xu (2010). The experimental results are displayed in Table 4. We can see that ELM HONN and standard HONN produce similar correctness rates, but ELM HONN is considerably faster than standard HONN. Again

Table 4. Comparing ELM HONN against standard HONN, MLP, RBF neural networks

ANN	Dataset	# HL	TT (sec)	Correctness
ELM HONN	Wine Quality	1	8.8	93.6%
Standard HONN	Wine Quality	1	15.3	88.2%
MLP	Wine Quality	1	5.1	74.8%
RBF	Wine Quality	1	5.7	75.2%

HL: Hidden Layer, TT: Training Time

due to the nature of HONN models, training takes longer time because of the significantly increased number of input neurons (compared with conventional MLP and RBF neural networks).

CONCLUSION

Extreme Learning Machine (ELM) randomly chooses hidden neurons and analytically determines the output weights. With ELM algorithm, only the connection weights between hidden layer and output layer are adjusted. Many types of hidden nodes including additive nodes, RBF (Radial Basis Function) nodes, multiplicative nodes, and other non neural alike nodes can be used as long as they are piecewise nonlinear. ELM algorithm tends to generalize better at very fast learning speed.

HONNs (Higher Order Neural Networks) are networks in which the net input to a computational neuron is a weighted sum of products of its inputs. HONNs are able to provide some explanation for the simulation they produce and thus can be considered as 'open box' rather than 'black box.' HONNs can simulate high frequency and high order nonlinear business data, and can handle discontinuities in the input training data set.

Real life data are not usually perfect. They contain wrong data, incomplete or vague. Hence, it is usual to find missing data in many information sources used. By training a neural network with samples containing missing values, connection weights between neurons learned through training cannot be accurately applied to a test set, especially when the test set contains missing values itself.

In this chapter, a HONN with ELM algorithm has been introduced and applied in several significant business cases. Experiments demonstrated that such model offers significant advantages over standard HONN models such as significantly faster training as well as improved simulation and forecasting errors. It appears that HONN with ELM model works faster than the standard HONN models due to the nature of the ELM algorithm. As part of the future research, some current cross-validation approaches may be adopted so that the forecasting errors could be reduced further down to a more satisfactory level. Another direction for future research would be the use of an ensemble of HONN models with ELM algorithm for modeling and simulation.

REFERENCES

Abdelbar, A. M. (1998). Achieving superior generalisation with a high order neural network. *Neural Computing & Applications*, 7(2), 141–146. doi:10.1007/BF01414166

Arai, M., Kohon, R., & Imai, H. (1991). Adaptive control of a neural network with a variable function of a unit and its application. *Transactions on Institutional Electronic Information Communication Engineering, 74*(A), 551-559.

Asuncion, A., & Newman, D. J. (2007). *UCI machine learning repository*. Irvine, CA: University of California. Retrieved from http://www.ics.uci. edu/~mlearn/MLRepository.html

Atiya, A. F. (2001). Bankruptcy prediction for credit risk using neural networks: A survey and new results. *IEEE Transactions on Neural Networks, 12*(4), 929–935. doi:10.1109/72.935101

Azema-Barac, M., & Refenes, A. (1997). Neural networks for financial applications . In Fiesler, E., & Beale, R. (Eds.), *Handbook of Neural Computation*. Oxford University Press. doi:10.1887/0750303123/b365c125

Baesens, B., Setiono, R., Mues, C., & Vanthienen, J. (2003). Using neural network rule extraction and decision tables for credit-risk evaluation. *Management Science, 49*(3). doi:10.1287/mnsc.49.3.312.12739

Barron, A. R. (1994). Approximation and estimation bounds for artificial neural networks. *Machine Learning, 14*, 115–133. doi:10.1007/BF00993164

Bigus, J. P. (1996). *Data mining with neural networks*. New York, NY: McGraw-Hill.

Blum, E., & Li, K. (1991). Approximation theory and feed-forward networks. *Neural Networks, 4*, 511–515. doi:10.1016/0893-6080(91)90047-9

Brachman, R. J., Khabaza, T., Kloesgen, W., Piatetsky-Shapiro, E., & Simoudis, E. (1996). Mining business databases. *Communications of the ACM, 39*(11), 42–48. doi:10.1145/240455.240468

Browne, A., Hudson, B. D., Whitley, D. C., Ford, M. G., & Picton, P. (2004). Biological data mining with neural networks: Implementation and application of a flexible decision tree extraction algorithm to genomic problem domains. *Neurocomputing, 57*, 275–293. doi:10.1016/j.neucom.2003.10.007

Burns, T. (1986). The interpretation and use of economic predictions. *Proceedings of the Royal Society A*, 103-125.

Campolucci, P., Capparelli, F., Guarnieri, S., Piazza, F., & Uncini, A. (1996). Neural networks with adaptive spline activation function. [Bari, Italy: IEEE Press.]. *Proceedings of IEEE MELECON, 1996*, 1442–1445.

Cao, J., Lin, Z., & Huang, G. B. (2010). Composite function wavelet neural networks with extreme learning machine. *Neurocomputing, 73*(7–9), 1405–1416. doi:10.1016/j.neucom.2009.12.007

Chen, C. T., & Chang, W. D. (1996). A feed-forward neural network with function shape autotuning. *Neural Networks, 9*(4), 627–641. doi:10.1016/0893-6080(96)00006-8

Cios, K. J., Pedrycz, W., Swiniarski, R. W., & Kurgan, L. A. (2007). *Data mining: A knowledge discovery approach*. Berlin, Germany: Springer.

Dayhoff, J. E. (1990). *Neural network architectures: An introduction*. New York, NY: Van Nostrand Reinhold.

Feng, G., Huang, G.-B., Lin, Q., & Gay, R. (2009). Error minimized extreme learning machine with growth of hidden nodes and incremental learning. *IEEE Transactions on Neural Networks, 20*(8), 1352–1357. doi:10.1109/TNN.2009.2024147

Fiori, S. (2003). Closed-form expressions of some stochastic adapting equations for nonlinear adaptive activation function neurons. *Neural Computation, 15*(12), 2909–2929. doi:10.1162/089976603322518795

Fulcher, J., Zhang, M., & Xu, S. (2006). Application of higher-order neural networks to financial time-series prediction. In Kamruzzaman, J., Begg, R., & Sarker, R. (Eds.), *Artificial Neural Networks in Finance and Manufacturing*. Hershey, PA: IGI Global. doi:10.4018/978-1-59140-670-9.ch005

Gallant, A. R., & White, H. (1988). There exists a neural network that does not make avoidable mistakes. In *Proceedings of the IEEE Second International Conference on Neural Networks*, (pp. 657-665). San Diego, CA: SOS Printing.

Giles, C. L., & Maxwell, T. (1987). Learning, invariance, and generalization in higher order neural networks. *Applied Optics*, *26*(23), 4972–4978. doi:10.1364/AO.26.004972

Grossberg, S. (1986). Some nonlinear networks capable of learning a spatial pattern of arbitrary complexity. *Proceedings of the National Academy of Sciences of the United States of America*, *59*, 368–372. doi:10.1073/pnas.59.2.368

Hammadi, N. C., & Ito, H. (1998). On the activation function and fault tolerance in feedforward neural networks. *IEICE Transactions on Information & Systems . E (Norwalk, Conn.)*, *81D*(1), 66–72.

Han, J., & Kamber, M. (2006). *Data mining: Concepts and techniques*. Amsterdam, The Netherlands: Elsevier.

Hansen, J. V., & Nelson, R. D. (1997). Neural networks and traditional time series methods: A synergistic combination in state economic forecasts. *IEEE Transactions on Neural Networks*, *8*(4), 863–873. doi:10.1109/72.595884

Hansen, J. V., & Nelson, R. D. (2002). Data mining of time series using stacked generalizers. *Neurocomputing*, *43*, 173–184. doi:10.1016/S0925-2312(00)00364-7

Haykin, S. S. (1994). *Neural networks: A comprehensive foundation*. New York, NY: Macmillan.

Hinton, G. E. (1989). Connectionist learning procedure. *Artificial Intelligence*, *40*, 251–257. doi:10.1016/0004-3702(89)90049-0

Ho, D. W. C., Liang, J. L., & Lam, J. (2006). Global exponential stability of impulsive high-order BAM neural networks with time-varying delays. *Neural Networks*, *19*(10), 1581–1590. doi:10.1016/j.neunet.2006.02.006

Holden, S. B., & Rayer, P. J. W. (1995). Generalisation and PAC learning: Some new results for the class of generalised single-layer networks. *IEEE Transactions on Neural Networks*, *6*(2), 368–380. doi:10.1109/72.363472

Hu, Z., & Shao, H. (1992). The study of neural network adaptive control systems. *Control and Decision*, *7*, 361–366.

Huang, G. B., & Chen, L. (2007). Convex incremental extreme learning machine. *Neurocomputing*, *70*, 3056–3062. doi:10.1016/j.neucom.2007.02.009

Huang, G.-B., & Chen, L. (2008b). Enhanced random search based incremental extreme learning machine. *Neurocomputing*, *71*, 3460–3468. doi:10.1016/j.neucom.2007.10.008

Huang, G. B., Chen, L., & Siew, C.-K. (2006b). Universal approximation using incremental constructive feedforward networks with random hidden nodes. *IEEE Transactions on Neural Networks*, *17*(4), 879–892. doi:10.1109/TNN.2006.875977

Huang, G.-B., Ding, X., & Zhou, H. (2010). Optimization method based extreme learning machine for classification. *Neurocomputing*, *74*, 155–163. doi:10.1016/j.neucom.2010.02.019

Huang, G. B., Li, M. B., Chen, L., & Siew, C. K. (2008a). Incremental extreme learning machine with fully complex hidden nodes. *Neurocomputing*, *71*, 576–583. doi:10.1016/j.neucom.2007.07.025

Huang, G. B., & Siew, C.-K. (2004b). Extreme learning machine: RBF network case. In *Proceedings of the Eighth International Conference on Control, Automation, Robotics and Vision (ICARCV 2004)*, (vol. 2), (pp. 1029-1036). Kunming, China: ICARCV.

Huang, G. B., & Siew, C. K. (2005). Extreme learning machine with randomly assigned RBF kernels. *International Journal of Information Technology, 11*(1), 16–24.

Huang, G. B., Zhu, Q.-Y., & Siew, C.-K. (2004a). Extreme learning machine: A new learning scheme of feedforward neural networks. In *Proceedings of International Joint Conference on Neural Networks (IJCNN2004)*, (vol. 2), (pp. 985-990). Budapest, Hungary: IJCNN.

Huang, G. B., Zhu, Q. Y., & Siew, C. K. (2006a). Extreme learning machine: Theory and applications. *Neurocomputing, 70*, 489–501. doi:10.1016/j.neucom.2005.12.126

Kawato, M., Uno, Y., Isobe, M., & Suzuki, R. (1987). A hierarchical model for voluntary movement and its application to robotics. In *Proceedings of the IEEE International Conference Network*, (vol 4), (pp. 573-582). IEEE Press.

Kay, A. (2006). Artificial neural networks. *Computerworld*. Retrieved on 27 November 2006 from http://www.computerworld.com/softwaretopics/software/appdev/story/0,10801,57545,00.html

Kim, S. H., & Noh, H. J. (1997). Predictability of interest rates using data mining tools: a comparative analysis of Korea and the US. *Expert Systems with Applications, 13*(2), 85–95. doi:10.1016/S0957-4174(97)00010-9

Kohonen, T., Kaski, S., Lagus, K., Salojarvi, J., Honkela, J., Paatero, V., & Saarela, A. (2000). Self organization of a massive document collection. *IEEE Transactions on Neural Networks, 11*, 574–585. doi:10.1109/72.846729

Kosmatopoulos, E. B., Polycarpou, M. M., Christodoulou, M. A., & Ioannou, P. A. (1995). High-order neural network structures for identification of dynamical systems. *IEEE Transactions on Neural Networks, 6*(2), 422–431. doi:10.1109/72.363477

Kros, J. F., Lin, M., & Brown, M. L. (2006). Effects of neural networks s-sigmoid function on KDD in the presence of imprecise data. *Computers & Operations Research, 33*, 3136–3149. doi:10.1016/j.cor.2005.01.024

Kurbel, K., Singh, K., & Teuteberg, F. (1998). Search and classification of "interesting" business applications in the world wide web using a neural network approach. In *Proceedings of the 1998 IACIS Conference*. Cancun, Mexico: IACIS.

Lan, Y., Soh, Y. C., & Huang, G.-B. (2008). Extreme learning machine based bacterial protein subcellular localization prediction. In *Proceedings of the IEEE International Joint Conference on Neural Networks 2008*, (pp. 1859–1863). IEEE Press.

Lee, Y. C., Doolen, G., Chen, H., Sun, G., Maxwell, T., Lee, H., & Giles, C. L. (1986). Machine learning using a higher order correlation network. *Physica D. Nonlinear Phenomena, 22*, 276–306.

Li, M. B., Huang, G.-B., Saratchandran, P., & Sundararajan, N. (2005). Fully complex extreme learning machine. *Neurocomputing, 68*, 306–314. doi:10.1016/j.neucom.2005.03.002

Lippman, R. P. (1989). Pattern classification using neural networks. *IEEE Communications Magazine, 27*, 47–64. doi:10.1109/35.41401

Little, R. J., & Rubin, D. B. (1987). *Statistical analysis with missing data*. New York, NY: John Wiley and Sons.

Machine Learning Repository, U. C. I. (2007). *Website*. Retrieved from ftp://ftp.ics.uci.edu/pub/machine-learning-databases/auto-mpg/auto-mpg.data

Malone, J., McGarry, K., Wermter, S., & Bowerman, C. (2006). Data mining using rule extraction from Kohonen self-organising maps. *Neural Computing & Applications*, *15*(1), 9–17. doi:10.1007/s00521-005-0002-1

McCue, C. (2007). *Data mining and predictive analysis: Intelligence gathering and crime analysis*. London, UK: Butterworth-Heinemann.

Miche, Y., Sorjamaa, A., Bas, P., Simula, O., Jutten, C., & Lendasse, A. (2010). OP-ELM: Optimally pruned extreme learning machine. *IEEE Transactions on Neural Networks*, *21*(1).

Mishra, S. (2006). Neural-network-based adaptive UPFC for improving transient stability performance of power system. *IEEE Transactions on Neural Networks*, *17*(2), 461–470. doi:10.1109/TNN.2006.871706

Park, J., & Sandberg, I. W. (1993). Approximation and radial-basis-function networks. *Neural Computation*, *5*, 305–316. doi:10.1162/neco.1993.5.2.305

Peng, H., & Zhu, S. (2007). Handling of incomplete data sets using ICA and SOM in data mining. *Neural Computing & Applications*, *16*(2), 167–172. doi:10.1007/s00521-006-0058-6

Picton, P. (2000). *Neural networks*. Basingstoke, UK: Palgrave.

Psaltis, D., Park, C. H., & Hong, J. (1988). Higher order associative memories and their optical implementations. *Neural Networks*, *1*, 149–163. doi:10.1016/0893-6080(88)90017-2

Ramanathan, K., & Guan, S. U. (2007). Multiorder neurons for evolutionary higher-order clustering and growth. *Neural Computation*, *19*(12), 3369–3391. doi:10.1162/neco.2007.19.12.3369

Redding, N., Kowalczyk, A., & Downs, T. (1993). Constructive high-order network algorithm that is polynomial time. *Neural Networks*, *6*, 997–1010. doi:10.1016/S0893-6080(09)80009-9

Reid, M. B., Spirkovska, L., & Ochoa, E. (1989). Simultaneous position, scale, rotation invariant pattern classification using third-order neural networks. *International Journal of Neural Networks*, *1*, 154–159.

Rong, H. J., Huang, G.-B., Sundararajan, N., & Saratchandran, P. (2009). Online sequential fuzzy extreme learning machine for function approximation and classification problems. *IEEE Transactions on Systems, Man, and Cybernetics. Part B, Cybernetics*, *39*(4), 1067–1072. doi:10.1109/TSMCB.2008.2010506

Rumelhart, D. E., & McClelland, J. L. (1986). *Parallel distributed computing: Exploration in the microstructure of cognition*. Cambridge, MA: MIT Press.

Thimm, G., & Fiesler, E. (1997). High-order and multilayer perceptron initialization. *IEEE Transactions on Neural Networks*, *8*(2), 349–359. doi:10.1109/72.557673

Vecci, L., Piazza, F., & Uncini, A. (1998). Learning and approximation capabilities of adaptive spline activation function neural networks. *Neural Networks*, *11*, 259–270. doi:10.1016/S0893-6080(97)00118-4

Wang, S. H. (2003). Application of self-organising maps for data mining with incomplete data sets. *Neural Computing & Applications*, *12*(1), 42–48. doi:10.1007/s00521-003-0372-1

Wood, J., & Shawe-Taylor, J. (1996). A unifying framework for invariant pattern recognition. *Pattern Recognition Letters*, *17*, 1415–1422. doi:10.1016/S0167-8655(96)00103-1

Xu, S. (2009). Adaptive higher order neural network models and their applications in business. In Zhang, M. (Ed.), *Artificial Higher Order Neural Networks for Economics and Business* (pp. 314–329). Hershey, PA: IGI Global. doi:10.4018/978-1-59904-897-0.ch014

Xu, S. (2009). A novel higher order artificial neural networks. In *Proceedings of the Second International Symposium on Computational Mechanics (ISCM II)*, (pp. 1507-1511). Hong Kong, China: ISCM.

Xu, S. (2010). Data mining using higher order neural network models with adaptive neuron activation functions. *International Journal of Advancements in Computing Technology*, 2(4), 168–177. doi:10.4156/ijact.vol2.issue4.18

Xu, S., & Chen, L. (2009). Adaptive higher order neural networks for effective data mining. In *Proceedings of the Sixth International Symposium on Neural Networks (ISNN 2009)*, (pp. 165-173). Wuhan, China: ISNN.

Yamada, T., & Yabuta, T. (1992). Remarks on a neural network controller which uses an auto-tuning method for nonlinear functions. In *Proceedings of IJCNN*, (vol 2), (pp. 775-780). IJCNN.

Zhang, M., Xu, S., & Lu, B. (1999). Neuron-adaptive higher order neural network group models. In *Proceedings of the International Joint Conference on Neural Networks – IJCNN 1999*. Washington, DC: IJCNN.

Zhang, M., Xu, S. X., & Fulcher, J. (2002). Neuron-adaptive higher order neural-network models for automated financial data modeling. *IEEE Transactions on Neural Networks*, 13(1), 188–204. doi:10.1109/72.977302

Zhang, M., Xu, S. X., & Fulcher, J. (2007). ANSER: An adaptive-neuron artificial neural network system for estimating rainfall using satellite data. *International Journal of Computers and Applications*, 29(3), 215–222. doi:10.2316/Journal.202.2007.3.202-1585

Zhang, M., Zhang, J., & Fulcher, J. (2000). Higher order neural network group models for financial simulation. *International Journal of Neural Systems*, 12(2), 123–142. doi:10.1016/S0129-0657(00)00011-9

Zhang, R., Huang, G.-B., & Sundararajan, N. P. (2007). Multi-category classification using an extreme learning machine for microarray gene expression cancer diagnosis. *IEEE/ACM Transactions on Computational Biology and Bioinformatics*, 4(3), 485–495. doi:10.1109/tcbb.2007.1012

Zhu, Q. Y., Qin, P. N., & Huang, G.-B. (2005). Evolutionary extreme learning machine. *Pattern Recognition*, 38, 1759–1763. doi:10.1016/j.patcog.2005.03.028

KEY TERMS AND DEFINITIONS

Artificial Neural Networks (ANNs): A computational model that simulates the functional aspects of biological neural networks. ANNs are adaptive systems that change their behaviour based on external and/or internal information that flows through the networks during a learning process.

Data Mining: The process of discovering new patterns from large data sets.

Extreme Learning Machine: An algorithm for ANNs which randomly chooses hidden neurons and analytically determines the output weights. With ELM algorithm, only the connection weights between hidden layer and output layer are adjusted.

Feedforward Neural Networks: ANNs where connections between the neurons do not form a directed cycle.

Higher Order Neural Networks: ANNs in which the net input to a computational neuron is a weighted sum of products of its inputs.

Chapter 14
Symbolic Function Network:
Theory and Implementation

George S. Eskander
ETS, Quebec University, Canada

Amir Atiya
Cairo University, Egypt

ABSTRACT

This chapter reviews a recent HONN-like model called Symbolic Function Network (SFN). This model is designed with the goal to impart more flexibility than both traditional and HONNs neural networks. The main idea behind this scheme is the fact that different functional forms suit different applications and that no specific architecture is best for all. Accordingly, the model is designed as an evolving network that can discover the best functional basis, adapt its parameters, and select its structure simultaneously. Despite the high modeling capability of SFN, it is considered as a starting point for developing more powerful models. This chapter aims to open a door for researchers to propose new formulations and techniques that impart more flexibility and result in sparser and more accurate models. Through this chapter, the theoretical basis of SFN is discussed. The model optimization computations are deeply illustrated to enable researchers to easily implement and test the model.

1. INTRODUCTION

Symbolic Function Network (SFN) is designed with the goal to impart more flexibility than the traditional neural networks (Eskander & Atiya, 2009). It is related to Higher Order Neural Networks (HONN) in the sense that both aim to model the complex nonlinearities as early as possible, so avoid the need of having huge connectivity between simple networks inputs (like the first order elements in ordinary NNs), by using more complex network inputs (like the higher order elements in HONNs). The difference between traditional HONNs and SFNs appears in the methodology to achieve this aim.

In HONNs, the complex correlations among system inputs are modeled early in the network so permits simple synaptic and somatic activa-

DOI: 10.4018/978-1-4666-2175-6.ch014

tions able to model the complex system. In this case, modeling operation starts with discovering the correlation between either linear or simple nonlinear terms (powers) of system inputs, and then applies simple synaptic and somatic activations on these complex terms. On the other hand, SFN design operation starts by learning suitable, and somehow complex, somatic activations that affects individual system inputs, and then correlation between these complex terms is modeled by cascading them in a tree-based network structure. The wider range of available activation functions, and the evolutionary structure of SFN, is expected to permit higher modeling power with sparser structure when compared to traditional NNs and even HONNs.

The symbolic function network can be represented as a tree based neural network. The terminals of the tree are the most relevant features that affect the system output, and the weights of the neural tree are the parameters that determine its overall functionality. Through the training phase, the best fitting symbolic function of the training data is discovered. There are two main goals that have to be achieved simultaneously: goodness of fit and sparsity. Sparse representation of a system is motivated by two aims: achieving good generalization performance, and achieving a simple and concise presentation of the modeled system that result in fast recall speed.

Although the concept of representing systems in a flexible evolving symbolic form is realized in the SFN scheme, we believe that this realization has just opened a door to design of more reliable models. In SFN, small range of elementary functions such as powers, the exponential function, and the logarithm are used as building blocks. However, a very large pool of basic functions can be rather investigated. Moreover, the tree structure of the SFN scheme can be replaced by various evolving network structures. Finally, the forward-backward evolving mechanisms and the steepest-descent-based optimization methods used in building the Symbolic Function Network are just samples from a huge pool of candidate methodologies.

Through this chapter, we introduce some of the topics related to the SFN model and some implementations of them. We represent a survey on the literature related to this work. Then, we discuss the evolutionary neural networks techniques as the SFN model has some aspects of evolving construction. A special case of such evolving networks is the tree-based networks; we presented some models that follow this type of structures. Then, the model implementation details have been discussed and clearly explained. These details include the elementary functions used in the model, the network structure, the model notations and computations, the network optimization techniques, and the constructive algorithms used to build the network. Finally, SFN power in system modeling is investigated by considering some approximation, regression, and time series prediction problems.

2. BACKGROUND

The evolving tree structure of SFN is motivated by the aim of achieving sparse models. Evolving neural trees search for best basis functions in a greedy manner hence facilitate sparse representation. Moreover, symbolic reduction techniques can be applied on the final evolved tree to reduce the model expression. Evolving neural trees are special case of neural networks category known as Evolutionary neural networks. There have been a number of attempts to design of such networks; the early methods include constructive and pruning algorithms (Fahlman & Lebiere, 1990). The main disadvantage of these methods is that the topological subsets are often searched using structural hill climbing methods instead of the complete class of ANN architectures available in the search space (Angeline, Sunders, & Pollack, 1994). For such type of nonlinear evolved systems, the optimization task must be split into two optimization problems; the structure and weights optimization problems. These problems could not be solved simultaneously. As above, the constructive and pruning algorithms can be used to find the optimal structure, in these cases; the traditional gradient based optimization algorithms can be used to tune the network weights. Recent tendency to optimize ANN architecture and weights; is to apply evolutionary programming (Yao, 1999; Yao, Ling, & Lin, 1999; Yao, 1997; Zhang & Muhlenbein, 1994).

Neural tree network concept had many implementations like the Competitive Neural Tree model (CNeT) (Behnke & Karayiannis, 1998), Neural Tree Network model (NTN), sparse neural trees (Zhang, 1997, 2002; Sanger, 1991), recursive neural network model (Gori, Kuchler, & Sperduti, 1999), Additive Tree model (EAT) (Chen, Yang, Zhang, & Dong, 2005), and Flexible Neural Tree model (FNT) (Chen, Yang, & Abraham, 2006; Chen, 2005; Chen, Yang, & Dong, 2004; Chen, Yang, Dong, & Abraham, 2004; Chen, Yang, & Dong, 2004; Chen & Zhang, 2003). Evolving neural tree networks can be done through structure and weights optimization problems. For structure optimization problem, various methods have been applied, such as GP (Chen, Yang, & Abraham, 2006; Chen, 2005; Chen & Zhang, 2003), ant programming (Chen, Yang, & Dong, 2004), Probabilistic Incremental Program Evolution (PIPE) (Chen, Yang, & Dong, 2004; Chen, Yang, Dong, & Abraham, 2004). For parameter optimization problem, various methods have been applied, such as Particle Swarm Optimization (PSO) (Chen, Yang, & Abraham, 2006; Chen, 2005; Chen, Yang, & Dong, 2004; Chen & Zhang, 2003), a random search algorithm (Chen, Yang, & Dong, 2004), and a variant of simulated annealing called degraded ceiling (Chen, Yang, Dong, & Abraham, 2004). Many complicated nonlinear models are additive models of a number of linear and nonlinear terms. A single linear term or

a nonlinear term such as neural network has its limitation in approximating this class of models. Recently, a tendency for combining linear and nonlinear models in solving nonlinear problems, such as nonlinear time series forecasting, has been an active research area. An example of applying this idea is to build a hybrid ARIMA and Neural network model (Zhang, 2003). A reliable tree based additive model has been designed based on the above idea (Chen, Yang, Zhang, & Dong, 2005). In addition, a similar work has been done to model an economic system by discovering the model symbolic expression using an evolving approach (Koza, 1991). Neural Tree Network model (NTN) (Sankar & Mammone, 1991a, 1991b, 1993; Adas, 1998; Yoo, 2002) is introduced in an attempt to combine the advantages of the neural networks and the decision trees. Decision trees have been used to perform pattern recognition. Since the nineties, much work has been done to map the decision trees into multilayer neural networks (Sethi, 1990; Sethi & Jan, 1991). Competitive Neural Trees (CNeT) (Behnke & Karaviannis, 1998) are another type of neural trees where competitive learning principle is combined with structural adaptation through learning.

SFN is related to aforementioned evolutionary neural tree networks while it permits more flexibility through selection from a set of elementary functions in a way that their connectivity, structure, and parameters are being adapted to the modeled system. This model is also related to the feature subset concept (John, Kohavi, & Pfleger, 1994; Narendra & Fuknaga, 1997), where the most relevant features that affect the system output are selected for the modeling task. Also, Sparse Basis Selection Approach (Chen, Donoho, & Saunders, 1998; Cotter, Delgado, & Rao, 2001; Coinfman & Wickerhauser, 1992; Natarjan, 1995; Narendra & Fuknaga, 1997; Poggio & Girosi, 1998; Reeves, 1999; Suykend, Lukas, & Vandewalls, 2000; Atiya, Aly, & Parlos, 2005) is related to SFN where a certain family of basic functions with varying parameters is used to represent signals.

3. SFN MODEL

SFN network is built in a constructive way in a top down fashion. Elementary functions are added to the tree one by one in some way so as to achieve as best fitting performance as possible for the given training data. By having several layers of the tree several levels of function concatenations can be achieved. The elementary functions used in SFN are: $u^v, \exp(u),$ and $\log(u)$. These functions are selected because most models encountered in practice involve these basic functions. Instead of generating a very large number of fixed parameter transformations and let the training process to choose the best smallest set; a set of flexible transformations are generated and the training process tune their parameters using a suitable optimization technique. The three basic elements are defined as E1, E2, and E3.

$$E1(u) = w(u)^v$$
$$E2(u) = qe^{\alpha u} \qquad (1)$$
$$E3(u) = p\log(u)$$

Where u is a scalar input. These elements are tunable; where $w, v, q, \alpha,$ and p are the free parameters to be tuned by the optimization algorithm. In the training algorithm, the derivatives of the basic functions are evaluated with respect to u. If u is close to zero we could encounter numerical problems as the derivatives will be very large in magnitude. Also for $u < 0$, $E3$ is not defined. To avoid these issues, $E1$ and $E3$ are modified as follows:

$$E1(u) = w(u^2 + 1)^v$$
$$E2(u) = qe^{\alpha u} \qquad (2)$$
$$E3(u) = p\log(u^2 + 1)$$

3.1. Network Structure

The SFN concept is realized in a top-down tree-based structure. Other structures are tried like down-top network trees, while experiments have shown that a structure in the form of a tree constructed in a top-down fashion gives the best performance and the sparsest networks. The experimental results reported in Section 5 showed low complexity of the designed SFN models when compared to other NNs like multi-layer perceptron. It is open for future research to try other structures, algorithms, and optimization techniques.

The tree structure gives a compact representation. It is the practice in symbolic computation models to model any symbolic expression in the form of a tree. The input signals enter the terminal nodes to be transformed by the basic transformation functions; only the useful transformations that reduce the error are selected. Then, the nonlinear transformations are added linearly. We call the nonlinear transformations: 'Links' and the group of links that have the same parent node are called: 'Band.' Therefore, the Band is a linear function of the selected links. Each selected terminal node is candidate to be a hidden node by affecting new child links; again, only the useful child links are added to the child Band. Actually, the child Band consists of the new added links besides the baseline input signal that was being affected by the parent link. This base line input is transferred to the above node by a unity weight called: 'dummy link'; that is because it has no effect on the input. To understand this process let us consider the illustrative example as in Figure 1.

Assume the process of training the first network layer resulted in a single Band network that consists of just two links: E1, and E3, respectively; the network output:

$$Y = E1(u_2) + E3(u_1)$$

Figure 1. Link admission process

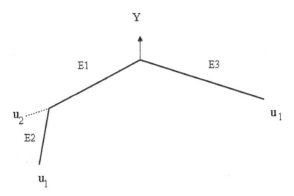

Note that for every link there is a baseline input variable on which it operates. For example at the parent node where we added the new link it used to be $E1(u_2)$, i.e. the baseline variable is u_2. After adding the link the baseline variable is kept in addition to the added link so that $E1(u_2)$ is replaced by $E1(u_2 + E2(u_1))$. The reason for that is that by adding a link we do not want to "disrupt" much the overall function of the network. By keeping u_2 it is like the old function plus some added term. At least theoretically if the multiplier weight w, p, or q of the new link is zero then we get the same error performance as the old network, thus having possibly a smooth transition when adding the link.

For simplicity, assume that $E1(u_2) = w\, u_2^v$. Assume the residual error after ending this training stage is E_{res}, where $E_{res} = d - y$ and d is the target. Therefore, $E_{res} = d - (w\, u_2^v + E3(u_1))$. Assume the training goal is to design a network with an error precision Egoal. Let Etot be the sum of the square Eres of all the training patterns. Then if Etot >Egoal, the learning process will continue by expanding the network by adding a new layer to the tree. The left link will be expanded by introducing a child E2. So, the new network output will be:

$$Y_{new} = E1(u_2 + E2(u_1)) + E3(u_1).$$

The new error will be:

$$E_{res-new} = d - (w\,(u_2 + E2(u_1))^v + E3(u_1))$$
$$= E_{res} + w(u_2)^V - (w\,(u_2 + E2(u_1))^v$$

Let $E_{tot-new}$ be the sum of the square $E_{res-new}$ of all the training patterns. So, if there exists any $E2(u_1)$ such that $E_{diff} \equiv E_{tot-new} - E_{tot} < 0$, then this link is useful as it will reduce the overall error, and it will be added to the network. Else, this link will not be added. We call this process 'Link admission process.' To avoid the uncontrolled expansion of the tree, we used the following modified admission rule. If there exists any $E2(u1)$; where $E_{diff} < \varepsilon < 0$, then this link will be added to the network. Else, this link will not be added. 'ε' is a small negative number called 'admission threshold' that is introduced to guarantee that the added link is valuable enough.

The above process continues until achieving the target performance or reaching the maximum permitted network depth. If the resulted network is just a single layer network, then the network represents a single level symbolic function; else, if the resulted network is a multilevel network, then it represents a multilevel symbolic function. The model is growing in a tree hierarchy; the terminal Bands are linear networks and these networks are connected together using activation functions to build the big nonlinear network. To organize the network construction process, some definitions have to be introduced:

- **Band:** assuming the pool of candidate features consists of N pure input. Therefore, the number of candidate nonlinear transformations is: '3N' (N features times 3, the number of possible basic functions, i.e. E1, E2, and E3). Each Band consists of such candidate links plus the dummy link.
- **Link Group:** each Band consists of three Link Groups: E1, E2, and E3 Link groups. Where each group consists of N links.
- **Band Group:** all Bands under the same parent Band belong to a Band group. There are 3N Bands in each Band group. In addition, the number of Band groups in each layer ℓ is $(3N)^{\ell-2}$, $\ell \geq 2$.
- **Cluster:** the Band group is split to N clusters. The cluster contains all Bands in the Band group that its parent links affect the same pure input. Therefore, the dummy links in these Bands transfer the same pure input to the parent link.

- **Segment:** the Band group is split to three segments: E1, E2, and E3 segments. The segment contains all Bands in the Band group that its parent links have the same function. For the Band, segments called link groups. See Figure 2 for illustration.

This figure represents the full links network. In practice, the constructed network is a sparse network, which means not all available links are added to the network, but only the links that reduces the value of the error by a specific threshold are added. The resulted network will vary according to the application. The proposed training algorithm tries to find the smallest number of links that represents the function to be modeled with the minimum value of error.

In addition, each band is split to N clusters. The cluster contains all links that affect the same pure input. Figure 3 represents an example of a sparse network that constructed by the training algorithm. The constructed network contains 3 layers, 7 nonlinear links, and 3 linear dummy links.

This network represents a nonlinear Symbolic function Y where

$$Y = E1(u_2 + E1(u_1) + E3(u_2)) + E1(u_2) + E3(u_2 + E2(u_1 + E3(u_2))).$$

Figure 3. Example of a constructed symbolic network

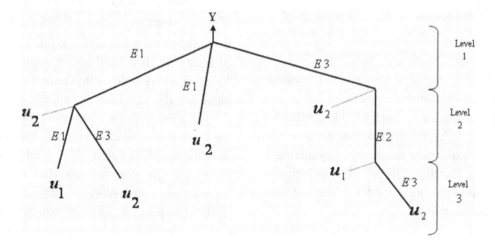

3.2. Model Notations and Forward Computations

The forward computations are derived to calculate the matrix of node outputs. Here the computations are done assuming a single input model then it will be generalized to a multi input model.

3.2.1. Single-Input Network

Referring to Figure 2, each layer ℓ consists of H_ℓ Bands where:

$$H_{\ell=} \quad 3^{(\ell-1)} \tag{3}$$

Each Band can be indexed by (ℓ, h) where h is the index of the Band's head node; $h \in [1, H_\ell]$. Each Band is a linear network of the three basic nonlinear transformations: $E1$, $E2$, and $E3$.

Define a matrix $W \{ W_{(L*H_L)} \}$, where

$$H_{L=} \quad 3^{(L-1)} \text{ (See Box 1).}$$

Also, define

$$V_{(L*H_L)}, Q_{(L*H_L)}, \alpha_{(L*H_L)},$$
$$P_{(L*H_L)}, WU_{(L*H_L)} \quad :$$

the weight matrices that have the same structure as W, V, Q, α, P are the nonlinear links' weights that could be tuned through the learning process. WU is the dummy link that is kept fixed during learning.

For each (ℓ, h) where

$$\ell \in [1:L]; \, h \in [1, H\ell]$$

$$E1_{\ell h} = w_{\ell h} (in^2 + 1)^{v_{\ell h}} \tag{5}$$

$$E2_{\ell h} = q_{\ell h} e^{\alpha_{\ell h} in} \tag{6}$$

$$E3_{\ell h} = p_{\ell h} \log(in^2 + 1) \tag{7}$$

Where in is the output of the child node, i.e. the input to the link. Each level ℓ; where $\ell \in [1, L]$ contains 'K' nodes where

$$K(\ell) = 3 * h(\ell) = 3^\ell \tag{8}$$

Any node 'k' in the tree could be (Selected/ Unselected), (Open/ Closed).

Define a matrix 'KS' that represents the nodes' (Selected/ Unselected) status

$$KS = \begin{pmatrix} ks_{11} & 0 & \cdots & \cdots & \cdots & \cdots & \cdots & \cdots & 0 \\ ks_{21} & ks_{22} & ks_{23} & 0 & \cdots & \cdots & \cdots & \cdots & 0 \\ \vdots & \vdots & \vdots & \vdots & \cdots & \cdots & \cdots & \cdots & \vdots \\ ks_{\ell 1} & ks_{\ell 2} & ks_{\ell 3} & \cdots & ks_{\ell k} & \cdots & ks_{\ell K_\ell} & \cdots & 0 \\ \vdots & \vdots & \vdots & \vdots & \cdots & \cdots & \vdots & \cdots & \vdots \\ ks_{L1} & ks_{L2} & ks_{L3} & \cdots & \cdots & \cdots & \cdots & \cdots & ks_{LK_L} \end{pmatrix} \tag{9}$$

$KS_{(L*K_L)}$; where $K_L = 3^{(L)}$. $ks_{\ell k} = 1$ If the link terminated at this node is selected during the learning process. Initially, $KS = (0)$.

Define 'KO' that represents the (Open/ Closed) status of $KO_{(L*K_L)}$, and have the same structure as KS. $ko_{\ell k} = 1$ If the node (ℓ, k) is selected, i.e. $ks_{\ell k} = 1$, and it is a terminal node (not closed by a child), and so it is sensing the pure (not transformed) input, else $ko_{\ell k} = 0$. Initially $KO = (0)$.

Let the output of a Band indexed by (ℓ, h) is $Z_{\ell h}$. That could be computed using the following recursive function:

Figure 2. Multi-layer symbolic function neural network: N=3, L=3

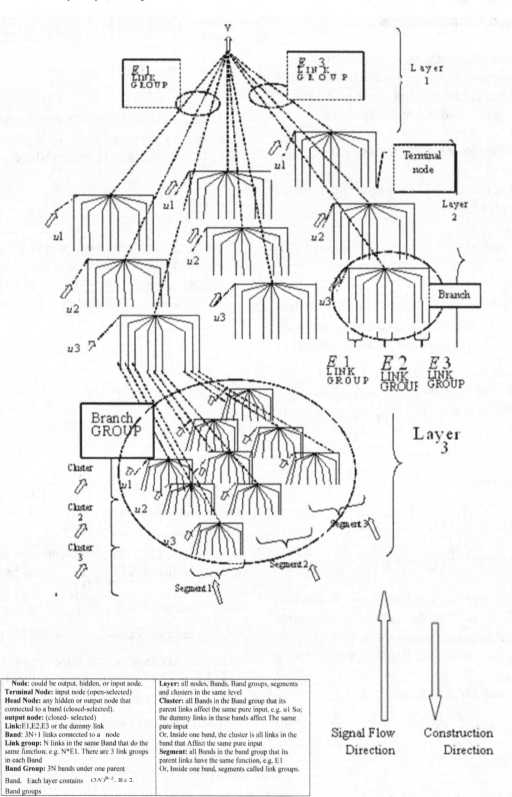

Node: could be output, hidden, or input node.
Terminal Node: input node (open-selected)
Head Node: any hidden or output node that connected to a band (closed-selected).
output node: (closed- selected)
Link:E1,E2,E3 or the dummy link
Band: 3N+1 links connected to a node
Link group: N links in the same Band that do the same function; e.g. N*E1. There are 3 link groups in each Band
Band Group: 3N bands under one parent Band. Each layer contains $(3N)^{B-2}$, $B \geq 2$. Band groups

Layer: all nodes, Bands, Band groups, segments and clusters in the same level
Cluster: all Bands in the Band group that its parent links affect the same pure input, e.g. u1 So; the dummy links in these bands affect The same pure input
Or, Inside one band, the cluster is all links in the band that Affect the same pure input
Segment: all Bands in the band group that its parent links have the same function, e.g. E1
Or, Inside one band, segments called link groups.

Signal Flow Direction

Construction Direction

Box 1.

$$
W = \begin{pmatrix}
w_{11} & 0 & \cdots & \cdots & \cdots & \cdots & \cdots & \cdots & 0 \\
w_{21} & w_{22} & w_{23} & 0 & \cdots & \cdots & \cdots & \cdots & 0 \\
\vdots & \vdots & \vdots & \vdots & \cdots & \cdots & \cdots & \cdots & \vdots \\
w_{\ell 1} & w_{\ell 2} & w_{\ell 3} & \cdots & w_{\ell h} & \cdots & w_{\ell H_\ell} & \cdots & 0 \\
\vdots & \vdots & \vdots & \vdots & \cdots & \cdots & \vdots & \cdots & \vdots \\
w_{L1} & w_{L2} & w_{L3} & \cdots & \cdots & \cdots & \cdots & \cdots & w_{LH_L}
\end{pmatrix} \quad (4)
$$

$$
\begin{aligned}
Z_{\ell h} &= bu + E1(w_{\ell h}, v_{\ell h}, z_{\ell+1, c1(h)}) \\
&+ E2(q_{\ell h}, \alpha_{\ell h}, z_{\ell+1, c2(h)}) + E3(p_{\ell h}, z_{\ell+1, c3(h)}) \\
&= bu + E1_{\ell h}(z_{\ell+1, c1(h)}) \\
&+ E2_{\ell h}(z_{\ell+1, c2(h)}) + E3_{\ell h}(z_{\ell+1, c3(h)})
\end{aligned} \quad (10)
$$

Where: $b = 1$ if $\ell > 1$, b=0 if $\ell = 1$.

$z_{\ell+1, cx(h)}$; $x \in [1, 2, 3]$ Is the output of the x_{st} child band.

The child index is $cx(h)$ where $cx(h) = 3 * (h - 1) + x$ (11)

$$
E1_{\ell h} = w_{\ell h}(z_{\ell+1c1(h)}^2 + 1)^{v_{\ell h}} \quad (12)
$$

$$
E2_{\ell h} = q_{\ell h} e^{\alpha_{\ell h} z_{\ell+1c2(h)}} \quad (13)
$$

$$
E3_{\ell h} = P_{\ell h} \log(z_{\ell+1c3(h)}^2 + 1) \quad (14)
$$

Each Band is a linear network

$$
\begin{aligned}
Z_{\ell h} &= bu + E1_{\ell h}(z_{\ell+1c1(h)}) \\
&+ E2_{\ell h}(z_{\ell+1c2(h)}) + E3_{\ell h}(z_{\ell+1c3(h)})
\end{aligned} \quad (15)
$$

The network output Y is the output of the first layer Band

Where

$$
\begin{aligned}
Y &= Z_{11} = E1_{11}(z_{21}) \\
&+ E2_{11}(z_{22}) + E3_{11}(z_{23})
\end{aligned} \quad (16)
$$

3.2.2. Multi-Input Network

Let the input vector U, Where

$$
U^T = (u_1 \ u_2 \ \ldots\ldots u_N),
$$

N is the number of pure inputs. For each triple (i, ℓ, h)

where $\ell \in [1 : L]$; $i \in [1, N]$; $h \in [1, H_\ell]$

$$
E1_{i\ell h} = w_{i\ell h}(u_i^2 + 1)^{v_{i\ell h}} \quad (17)
$$

$$
E2_{i\ell h} = q_{i\ell h} e^{\alpha_{i\ell h} u_i} \quad (18)
$$

Box 2.

$$W_i = \begin{pmatrix} w_{i11} & 0 & \cdots & \cdots & \cdots & \cdots & \cdots & \cdots & 0 \\ w_{i21} & w_{i22} & w_{i23} & 0 & \cdots & \cdots & \cdots & \cdots & 0 \\ \vdots & \vdots & \vdots & \vdots & \cdots & \cdots & \cdots & \cdots & \vdots \\ w_{i\ell 1} & w_{i\ell 2} & w_{i\ell 3} & \cdots & w_{i\ell h} & \cdots & w_{i\ell H_\ell} & \cdots & 0 \\ \vdots & \vdots & \vdots & \vdots & \cdots & \cdots & \vdots & \cdots & \vdots \\ w_{iL1} & w_{iL2} & w_{iL3} & \cdots & \cdots & \cdots & \cdots & \cdots & w_{iLH_L} \end{pmatrix} \quad (20)$$

$$E3_{i\ell h} = P_{i\ell h} \log(u_i^2 + 1) \quad (19)$$

All the matrices of the single dimension model are scaled here and represents as three dimensional matrices.

$$W_{(N*L*H_L)} = \begin{pmatrix} W_1 & W_2 & \cdots & W_i & \cdots & W_N \end{pmatrix},$$

Where (See Box 2).
Also,

$$V_{(N*L*H_L)}, Q_{(N*L*H_L)}$$
$$, \alpha_{(N*L*H_L)}, P_{(N*L*H_L)}$$

are the weight matrices that have the same structure as $W_{(N*L*H_L)}$, and

$$KS_{(N*L*K_L)}, KO_{(N*L*K_L)}.$$

While the dummy weight matrix $WU_{(L*H_L)}$

has different structure as each Band has only one dummy weight.

Each layer ℓ consists of H_ℓ Bands where

$$H_{\ell=} N*3^{(\ell-1)}.$$ Each Band can be identified by (ℓ, h) where h is the index of the Band's head

node, $h \in [1, H_\ell]$. Each Band output is a linear network of the Band links where Band consists of $3*N + 1$ links, that are the basic elementary functions $E1, E2, E3$ for each pure input and one dummy link.

The network output the output of the first layer band and given by:

$$Y = Z_{111}$$
$$= \sum_{n=1}^{N} \frac{E1_{n11}(z_{n21}) + E2_{n11}(z_{n22})}{+ E3_{n11}(z_{n23})}$$

$$(21)$$

4. SFN OPTIMIZATION

SFN networks are optimized through two simultaneous processes: weights optimization and structure optimization. In weight optimization process, all free weights and parameters of the network are updated in order minimize a specific cost function. As some nodes are hidden, the effect of parameters associated with such nodes on the cost function cannot be inferred directly. To overcome this, a back propagation of error signals can be derived to compute the impact of changing of individual parameters on the cost function. Once such gradient values are computed, they could be used to update the network parameters by applying steepest descent methodology. The proposed gradient- steepest descent based optimization method is inspired by the Backpropagation approach used in optimizing Multilayer Perceptron (MLP) (Haykin, 1999). While various optimization techniques can be applied to do the task.

The network structure can be optimized by adding new items to the network, or through removing some of the already admitted terms. Whenever such structure update occurs, all network parameters are re-optimized.

In this section, the aforementioned design steps are illustrated. First, the gradient computations are derived and followed by illustrating how steepest descent approach could be applied to update network parameters using the computed gradients. Second, the overall network optimization process is discussed by illustrating suggested network structure evolving approaches and the corresponding parameters update processes.

4.1. Computation of the Gradient

The proposed training algorithm is based on steepest descent concept. We, therefore, need to compute the gradient of the error w.r.t. the network weights. The backward computations are derived to compute the matrix of gradients in a recursive manner.

For illustration, consider Figure 4. Consider a particular path along the tree: Y- Z1- Z2- Z3- ---- where the functions encountered along the path are: $E_{i_1} - E_{i_2} - E_{i_3} -----$

Then, $z_{j-1} = E_{i_j}(z_j) + E_{oth}(z_{oth})$

(22)

Where $E_{oth}(z_{oth})$ is the sum of other transformations that are affecting z_{oth} which are the brothers of z_j.

Let the error function be

Figure 4. Particular path along the tree

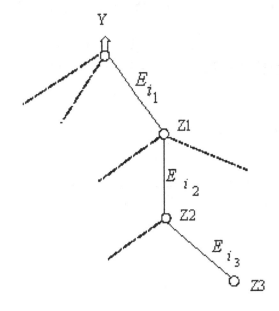

$$J = \sum_{m=1}^{M} (y(m) - d(m))^2 = \sum_{m=1}^{M} e(m)^2$$

(23)

Where $y(m)$ and $d(m)$ are the actual network output and the target output for training example (m) respectively, and M is the size of the training set.

The instantaneous gradient w.r.t some weight ω is

$$\frac{\delta J}{\delta \omega}(m) = 2\,e(m)\,\frac{\delta y(m)}{\delta \omega}$$

(24)

However the total gradient for the whole training set is

$$\frac{\delta J}{\delta \omega} = 2\sum_{m=1}^{M} e(m)\,\frac{\delta y(m)}{\delta \omega}$$

(25)

To obtain $\frac{\delta y}{\delta \omega}$ (we skipped the index m for ease notations), a key quantity has to be evaluated namely $\frac{\delta y}{\delta z_j}$. It is obtained using the chain rule by starting up the tree with $j=1$, and tracing the tree going downward as follows:

$$\frac{\delta y}{\delta z_j} = \frac{\delta y}{\delta z_{j-1}} \frac{\delta z_{j-1}}{\delta z_j} \qquad (26)$$

The above equation is used to compute the partial derivative of the network output w.r.t any hidden node in a recursive manner.

Using Equation (22) and Equation (26) we get:

$$\frac{\delta y}{\delta z_j} = \frac{\delta y}{\delta z_{j-1}} E'_{i_j}(z_j) \qquad (27)$$

Where $E'_{i_j}(z_j)$ is obtained by differentiating the basic functional forms

(Equation 1) w.r.t its argument u and evaluated at $u=z_j$

Once $\frac{\delta y}{\delta z_j}$'s are evaluated for all the tree, the gradient can be obtained.

Let ω be the weight associated with node, i.e.

$$z_j = E_{i_{j+1}}(z_{j+1},\omega) + E_{oth}(z_{oth}) \qquad (28)$$

$$\frac{\delta y}{\delta \omega} = \frac{\delta y}{\delta z_j} \frac{\delta E_{i_{j+1}}}{\delta \omega} \qquad (29)$$

$\frac{\delta E_{i_{j+1}}}{\delta \omega}$ Can be evaluated by differentiating the basic functional forms Equation (1) w.r.t the weights w,v,q,α,p whatever ω represents.

The above equations are the general gradient equations. We will write them in terms of the model notations mentioned in the above section.

Rewriting Equation (26):

$$\frac{\delta y}{\delta z_j} = \frac{\delta y}{\delta z_{j-1}} \frac{\delta z_{j-1}}{\delta z_j}$$

For $\ell>1$;

$$\frac{\delta y}{\delta z_{\ell,h}} = \frac{\delta y}{\delta z_{\ell-1,hp}} * \frac{\delta z_{\ell-1,hp}}{\delta z_{\ell,h}} \qquad (30)$$

For $\ell=1$; $\frac{\delta y}{\delta z_{1h}} = 1$

Rewriting Equation (27):

$$\frac{\delta y}{\delta z_j} = \frac{\delta y}{\delta z_{j-1}} E'_{i_j}(z_j)$$

If $\mod(h,3) =1$, i.e. $i=1$

$$E'_{1_h}(z_h)$$
$$=2*w_{\ell hp}*v_{\ell hp}*z_{\ell h}*(z_{\ell h}^2+1)^{(v_{\ell hp}-1)} \qquad (31)$$

If $\mod(h,3) =2$, i.e. $i=2$

$$E'_{2_h}(z_h) = q_{\ell hp}*\alpha_{\ell hp}*\exp(\alpha_{\ell hp}*z_{\ell h}) \qquad (32)$$

If $\mod(h,3) =0$, i.e. $i=3$

$$E'_{3_h}(z_h) = 2*p_{\ell hp}*z_{\ell h}/(z_{\ell h}^2+1) \qquad (33)$$

Rewriting Equation (29):

$$\frac{\delta y}{\delta \omega} = \frac{\delta y}{\delta z_j} \frac{\delta E_{i_{j+1}}}{\delta \omega}$$

$$\frac{\partial y}{\partial \omega_{\ell h}} = \frac{\partial y}{\partial z_{\ell h}} * \frac{\partial z_{\ell h}}{\partial \omega_{\ell h}} = \frac{\partial y}{\partial z_{\ell h}} * \frac{\delta E_{1_{\ell,h+1}}}{\delta \omega} \tag{34}$$

For $\omega = w$;

$$\frac{\delta E_{1_{\ell,h+1}}}{\delta w} = (z_{\ell-1,h_{c1(h)}}{}^2 + 1)^{v_{\ell h}} \tag{35}$$

For $\omega = v$;

$$\frac{\delta E_{1_{\ell,h+1}}}{\delta v} = w_{\ell h} * \log(z_{\ell-1,h_{c1(h)}}{}^2 + 1)$$

$$* (z_{\ell-1,h_{c1(h)}}{}^2 + 1)^{v_{\ell h}} \tag{36}$$

Where $c1(h) = 3*(h-1)+1$
For $\omega = q$;

$$\frac{\delta E_{2_{\ell,h+1}}}{\delta q} = \exp(\alpha_{\ell h} * z_{\ell-1,h_{c2(h)}}) \tag{37}$$

For $\omega = \alpha$;

$$\frac{\delta E_{2_{\ell,h+1}}}{\delta \alpha} = q_{\ell h} * z_{\ell-1,h_{c2(h)}}$$

$$* \exp(\alpha_{\ell h} * z_{\ell-1,h_{c2(h)}}) \tag{38}$$

Where $c2(h) = 3*(h-1)+2$

For $\omega = p$;

$$\frac{\delta E_{3_{\ell,h+1}}}{\delta p} = \log(z_{\ell-1,h_{c3(h)}}{}^2 + 1) \tag{39}$$

Where $c3(h) = 3*(h-1)+3$

4.2. Steepest Descent Computations

The steepest descent algorithm may run in two modes: pattern mode or batch mode. For pattern mode Equation (24) is used to compute the instantaneous gradient matrix, and all weights matrices are being updated according to the following equations:

For each pattern $m \in [1,M]$

$$\Delta \omega(m) = -\eta * \frac{\delta J}{\delta \omega}(m)$$

$$\Delta \omega_{\ell h}(m) = -\eta * \frac{\delta J}{\delta \omega_{\ell h}}(m) \tag{40}$$

$$\Delta w_{\ell h}(m) = -2\eta e(m)$$

$$* (z_{\ell-1,h_{c1(h)}}(m)^2 + 1)^{v_{\ell h}(m)} * \frac{\partial y(m)}{\partial z_{\ell h}(m)} \tag{41}$$

$$\Delta v_{\ell h}(m) = -2\eta e(m)^* w_{\ell h}(m)$$

$$^*\log(z_{\ell-1,h_{c1(h)}}(m)^2+1)$$

$$^*(z_{\ell-1,h_{c1(h)}}(m)^2+1)^{v_{\ell h}(m)} * \frac{\partial y(m)}{\partial z_{\ell h}(m)}$$

$$(42)$$

$$\Delta q_{\ell h}(m) = -2\eta e(m)^*\exp(\alpha_{\ell h}(m)$$

$$^* \; z_{\ell-1,h_{c2(h)}}(m)) * \frac{\partial y(m)}{\partial z_{\ell h}(m)}$$

$$(43)$$

$$\Delta \alpha_{\ell h}(m) = -2\eta e(m)^* q_{\ell h}(m)^* z_{\ell-1,h_{c2(h)}}(m)$$

$$^*\exp(\alpha_{\ell h}(m)^* z_{\ell-1,h_{c2(h)}}(m)) * \frac{\partial y(m)}{\partial z_{\ell h}(m)}$$

$$(44)$$

$$\Delta p_{\ell h}(m) = -2\eta e(m)$$

$$^*\log(z_{\ell-1,h_{c3(h)}}(m)^2+1) * \frac{\partial y(m)}{\partial z_{\ell h}(m)}$$

$$(45)$$

However, for the batch mode, the gradient matrix is computed by accumulating the instantaneous gradients according to Equation (25). All of the weight matrices are updated just one time after each epoch according to the following rule:

$$\Delta\omega = -\eta * \frac{\delta J}{\delta\omega} \qquad (46)$$

4.3. Network Optimization

As a result of being an evolving neural network model, the process of optimizing the network should include two major processes; finding the best network structure that represents the problem at hand, and finding the best values of the network weights. These steps could be done simultaneously until achieving the optimal design. Actually, there is unlimited number of various techniques that could be developed and applied to optimize the tree network. We developed some constructive algorithms to build the network and to find the optimal weights. It is open for future work to try and develop other methods.

4.3.1. Structure Optimization

In this section, we explain the proposed algorithm and its variants in details. Mainly, we have designed three model variants: forward (F-SFN), backward (B-SFN), and forward-backward (FB-SFN) model. Structure optimization deals with the issue of constructing the tree; that is determining the strategy and sequence of node additions. We have proposed several algorithms for structure optimization. These algorithms are described as follows:

4.3.1.1. Forward Algorithm (F-SFN)

In the forward algorithm, the network components are added to the network in an incremental way. The network component can be a single link (FLK-SFN) or a complete layer (FLY-SFN). The algorithm builds the network incrementally from top to down. It starts with an empty network then adds the network elements one by one. After adding each element and training the network, it measures the network performance and decides based on that to keep this added item or to restore the previous network configurations. The following are the steps of the proposed algorithm:

Algorithm Steps:

1. Start from a blank network. Initialize all weights to zero.
2. Test the effect of adding a link (a layer) on the network performance, as follows:

2a. Store the current network configuration.

2b. Add a link (a layer) to the network by selecting the link (layer) terminating node(s). Then initialize its associated weights to small random values (the weights for the nodes already existing in the network are initialized by their original values, i.e. the values they currently have.)

2c. Run the optimization algorithm on the updated network scheme (by updating all network weights) and find the resulting network performance.

2d. Decide to keep the new added link (layer) or to restore the network to the old scheme based on comparing the performance improvement to a threshold set by the designer.

3. Repeat step 2 until trying all possible elementary functions/input variables or achieving the performance goal.

Forward Model with Reduced Random Set Capability (FRS-SFN)

When the number of features (N) is too large, then each layer in the network would grow by too much as we go down the tree. The number of links of the complete Band (CB) in a Layer (L) to be searched is given by: $CB(L) = (3*N)^L$.

To limit the resulting computational burden, we have proposed the following variant. Instead of going through all the features one by one, at each step we randomly select distinct links from the available complete set. We introduced a parameter called a reduction factor 'RF' that controls the number of links to be selected at each layer. The Reduced Band set (RB) is given by: $RB(L) = ceil(CB(L)* (RF^L) = ceil(3*N*RF)^L$.

4.3.1.2. Backward Algorithm (B-SFN)

For some applications that involve high nonlinearities it is often not practical to train the network in a forward greedy approach by adding a single link each time. The other option is to apply the forward algorithm by adding a complete layer each time. This scenario has an advantage that the network is being constructed and approximates the target in a short time, but it has a disadvantage that the constructed network is not a sparse one and probably contains many superfluous links. For this reason we have designed the backward model. It jumps to a good approximating but not sparse network in a short time- using the forward model by adding a layer each time- but then it applies a pruning algorithm in order to remove the redundant weights from the network. Here are the details of the algorithm:

Algorithm Steps:

1. Start from a blank network. Initialize all weights to zero.

2. Test the effect of adding a complete layer on the network performance, as follows:

2a. Store the current network configuration.

2b. Add a layer to the network by selecting the layer terminating nodes, then initializing its associated weights to random values.

2c. Run the optimization algorithm on the updated network scheme and find the associated network performance.

2d. Decide to keep the new added layer, or to restore the network to the old scheme based on comparing the performance improvement to a threshold set by the designer.

3. Repeat step 2 until reaching the maximum depth or achieving the performance goal.

4. Run the pruning algorithm, as follows:

4a. Start from the full weights network designed in steps 1, 2, and 3 and apply pruning in a bottom-up direction starting from the last layer.

4b.   Test the effect of removing a terminal link on the network performance, as follows:

4b.1. Store the current network configuration.

4b.2. Remove this terminal link from the network.

4b.3. Run the optimization algorithm on the updated network scheme and find the associated network performance.

4b.4. Decide to keep this link removed or to restore the network to the old configuration based on comparing the performance degradation to a threshold set by the designer.

4c.   Repeat step 4-b until testing all terminal nodes.

Note: When applying a pruning step and one node is removed, its parent node could become a terminal node. So next time pruning is applied, it could be removed as well. This is the way pruning can possibly ultimately access all nodes, not just the terminal nodes.

4.3.1.3. Forward Backward Algorithm (FB-SFN)

By applying the forward algorithm on some regression applications, we noticed that often while the training error is getting better by adding more links, the generalization performance is getting worse. This is due to the well-known "overfitting" effect. Therefore, we have designed a model variant that is based on running a pruning algorithm in parallel with the constructive algorithm. We found that this scenario enhances the generalization performance and solves the problem of "training error- generalization error" trade off. In addition, by applying pruning in parallel there is a chance to re-evaluate the already admitted links.

Algorithm Steps:

1.   Start with a blank network. Initialize all weights to zero.

2.   Test the effect of adding a link on the network performance, as follows:

2a.   Store the current network configurations.

2b.   Add a link to the network by selecting the link terminating node, and then initializing its associated weights to small random values.

2c.   Run the optimization algorithm on the updated network scheme and find the associated network performance.

2d.   Decide to keep the new added link, or to restore the network to the old scheme based on comparing the performance improvement to a threshold set by the designer.

3.   If the number of consecutively added links reaches K (K is a parameter set by the designer), then run the following pruning algorithm:

3a.   Store the current network configurations.

3b.   Remove a link selected from the set of terminal links.

3c.   Run the optimization algorithm on the updated network scheme and find the resulting network performance.

3d.   Restore the network configuration stored in 3-b.

3e.   Repeat steps 3-b-d for all of the candidate links.

3g.   Compare the network performances computed in 3-c, and identify the worst link and remove this link.

4.   Repeat steps 2 and 3 until trying all possible links or achieving the performance goal.

4.3.2. Weights Optimization

The gradient equations introduced in sections 4.1 and 4.2 could be used by any optimization algorithm in order to find the optimal weight matrices that reduce the performance measure. We used the steepest descent method to optimize the network weights. In this case, we have to set the learning rate(s) to a suitable specific value(s). We used a different learning rate for each weight. These rates could be set as fixed with time or changed during the course of the training process based on the training performance. In most applications, we kept the rates fixed. We designed the training algorithm to run in pattern mode, i.e. whenever a new pattern applied to the network, the training process updates all weights in the network. We found that updating all links (old and newly added links) is better than just updating the added one. Surely, for this method the training time complexity is higher.

We used the holdout validation technique in the training algorithm. The data is split into two main groups: learning data and testing data. The learning data group is split into two groups as well: training data and validation data. After training the network for a specific number of data epochs using the training data, the algorithm validates the network using the validation data and decides to continue or stop training the current network structure depending of the slope of the training performance. We add some threshold on the slope value to guarantee that the training algorithm will stop training using the current structure and test another structure if the training performance curve is not getting better by a valuable amount.

After completing the training of the current network, whatever the applied optimization method is, the training algorithm decides to admit the new added link (remember the added unit could be a band or a complete layer instead of a single link) based on the performance of the network using the validation data set. In addition, we add a threshold on the admission criteria that is to guarantee that the added unit increases the network performance by a minimum percentage, e.g. 5%. This helps to build the sparsest network. Finally, after completing the network determination and

weight optimization processes, the constructed network performance is tested using the test data set that is unseen during the learning phase.

5. ILLUSTRATIVE EXAMPLES

In this section, some illustrative examples are reported to show the SFN modeling ability. All versions of the proposed method: 1) Forward Layer by Layer (FLY-SFN), 2) Forward Link by Link (FLK-SFN), 3) Backward (B-SFN), 4) Forward Backward (FB-SFN), and 5) Forward with Reduced Random Set (FRS-SFN) have been tested. The data points are partitioned into 75% training set and 25% validation set. In addition, there is a test set for the final test of the performance of the models. The training set is used for the weight optimization process and the validation set is used to evaluate the network structure in the link admission process. The error measure used to assess the networks performance is Mean Square Error (MSE); where

$$MSE = \frac{\sum\limits_{m=1}^{M} (y(m) - d(m))^2}{M}$$

and $; y(m), d(m)$ are the network output, and the desired output at any sample m respectively; and, M is the length of the investigated data set. Besides the error measures, the number of resulted networks' weights are reported to compare their complexity. To obtain a comparative idea about the performance of the proposed model, we have implemented on these same problems a Multilayer Perceptron neural network (MLP) (a single hidden layer network). We have considered the following methods for training the MLP: 1) The Basic Backpropagation (B-BP): It uses the standard gradient descent with the momentum term, and 2) Bayesian Regularization Backpropagation (BR-BP). In this approach, the cost function is the error function plus a regularization term that penalizes network complexity. This penalty term is based on a Bayesian formulation.

In the simulation results, we used the abbreviations of the learning methods followed by the number of hidden nodes for the trained MLP network, and by maximum network depth for the SFN networks.

5.1. Single Input Function Approximation

The problem is to approximate the Function: $f(X) = \sin(2\pi X)$. We generated two data sets, each set represents two complete cycles of the sin wave; the first is the training set and consists of 41 samples, $X \in [-1:0.05:1]$. The second set is used for the network testing and also consists of 40 samples, $X \in [-0.975:0.05:0.975]$. The test

data points are therefore shifted from the training points by a constant shift that equals 0.025. It is well known that for MLP, the most critical parameter is the number of hidden nodes. We used the validation set to determine this parameter. We trained networks with numbers of hidden nodes being 3, 6, 9, 12, 15, and 20, and selected the one that gives best validation set performance.

For both SFN and MLP networks, all of the network structures' performances are evaluated using a validation data set. However, only the winning structure is tested using the test data set and reported. Table 1 shows the test performance for SFN and its variants as well as the competing methods. One can see that for SFN good performance is achieved when setting the maximum network depth to a suitable value. The performance is getting better with going to deeper

Table 1. Training and testing error (in MSE) for example 1 for the proposed model variants: FLY-SFN, FLK-SFN, B-SFN, FB-SFN, and FRS-SFN, each applied on different maximum depth networks, and for some competing methods B-BP, ES-BP, and BR-BP. Also shown are the average number of weights for all resulted networks.

| Algorithm | Training | | | Testing | | | Average # Weights |
	Best MSE	Worst MSE	Average MSE	Best MSE	Worst MSE	Average MSE	
B-BP (6)	0.0025	0.0027	0.00258	0.0031	0.0037	0.00336	19
ES- BP (6)	0.0026	0.0055	0.00328	0.0033	0.0056	0.00398	19
BR –BP (12)	2.36E-14	2.94E-11	6.14E-12	1.28E-09	7.43E-09	5.49E-09	37
FLY-SFN (2)		0.0088			0.0098		20
FLY-SFN (3)		1.49 E-4			1.66 E-4		65
FLK-SFN (2)		0.0053			0.0069		10
FLK-SFN (3)		0.0045			0.0056		13
B-SFN (2)		0.0085			0.0096		17
B-SFN (3)		1.16 E-4			1.42 E-4		50
FB-SFN (2) (K=5)		9.22 E-4			0.0012		16
FB-SFN (3) (K=5)		7.38 E-5			7.31 E-5		25
FRS-SFN(2) (RF=0.5))	4.68E-04	0.0022	0.0016	4.50E-04	0.003	0.0021	12
FRS-SFN(3) (RF=0.5))	4.38E-04	8.30E-04	6.29E-04	3.38E-04	0.0013	8.06E-04	17

Figure 5. SFN output of the function approximation problem

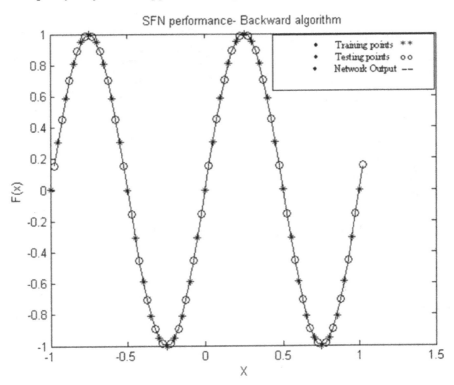

layers. One can observe that the FB-SFN and FRS-SFN methods give a good compromise of sparseness (as measured by the number of weights) and performance. Figure 5 illustrates the fitting performance for the B-SFN (3) (i.e. a three layer backward-algorithm SFN).

Figure 6 illustrates a constructed SFN network. The network is evolved using FRS-SFN (2) (i.e.

a two layer forward reduced random set-algorithm SFN). It consists of seven elementary functions and twelve parameters. The performance fitness of the constructed function of the testing set measured in MSE is: 4.50 e-004.

The network output is given by:

Figure 6. SFN network for the function approximation problem

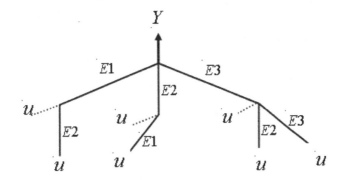

$Y = E1(u + E2(u)) + E2(u + E1(u)) + E3(u$
$+E2(u) + E3(u)).$

$Y = 0.3304 (1 + [u - 0.0009 \, e^{4.5983u}]^2)^{4.6275}$

$+ \ 10.0713 \, e^{(-4.4452[u + 0.3396(u^2 + 1)^{1.3831}])}$

$-3.7065 \log(1 + [u - 1.0049 \, e^{-3.3430u}$

$+1.1832 \log(u^2 + 1)]^2)$

5.2. Multiple Input Function Approximation

We considered the example and we compare the SFN performance with a related neural tree model (FNT). For this example, the problem is to design a network to approximate a nonlinear static function. The system is described by the equation:

$$y = (1 + x1^{-2} + x2^{-1.5})^2. \quad 1 \le x1, x2 \le 5.$$

50 training and 200 test samples are randomly generated in the interval [1, 5]; Table 2 shows the comparison results. For such problem where there is no random noise added, all runs typically lead to the same network (and same performance). In such a case, only one run's result is reported. One can observe that the performance of B-SFN (2) (i.e. a single layer backward-algorithm SFN) is the best and outperform that of the FNT model.

Figure 7 illustrates a constructed SFN network that evolved using the FLK-SFN (2) algorithm. (I.e. a two layer Forward link by link-algorithm SFN). The constructed network contains 18 nonlinear transformations, and involves 31 tuned parameters; however, The FNT network contains 12 hidden nodes, these nodes involve 24 tuned parameters; and, 30 tuned linear weights. Therefore, the network consists of 54 parameters.

The resultant network weight matrices are:

Table 2. Testing error (in MSE) for the proposed model variants FLY-SFN, FLK-SFN, B-SFN, FB-SFN, and FRS-SFN, and for the FNT method

Algorithm	Testing MSE
FNT	8.60 E-4
FLY-SFN (2)	4.45E-04
FLK-SFN (2)	0.001
B-SFN (2)	4.00 E-4
FB-SFN (2)	0.0079
FRS-SFN(2)(RF=0.5)	0.0021

$$WU = \begin{pmatrix} 0 & 0 & 0 & 0 & 0 & 0 \\ 1 & 0 & 0 & 1 & 0 & 1 \end{pmatrix}$$

$$W_1 = \begin{pmatrix} 11.2586 & 0 & 0 & 0 & 0 & 0 \\ -1.9812 & 0 & 0 & -0.2343 & 0 & 0.0937 \end{pmatrix}$$

$$W_2 = \begin{pmatrix} 10.4547 & 0 & 0 & 0 & 0 & 0 \\ 1.2834 & 0 & 0 & 0.0269 & 0 & 0.0988 \end{pmatrix}$$

$$\alpha_1 = \begin{pmatrix} 0 & 0 & 0 & 0 & 0 & 0 \\ 0 & 0 & 0 & 0.2298 & 0 & 0.0966 \end{pmatrix}$$

$$\alpha_2 = \begin{pmatrix} -0.2867 & 0 & 0 & 0 & 0 & 0 \\ 0 & 0 & 0 & 0.0997 & 0 & 0.1000 \end{pmatrix}$$

$$P_1 = \begin{pmatrix} 0 & 0 & 0 & 0 & 0 & 0 \\ 0.8502 & 0 & 0 & 0.0858 & 0 & 0.0889 \end{pmatrix}$$

$$P_2 = \begin{pmatrix} 0.1932 & 0 & 0 & 0 & 0 & 0 \\ 0.1115 & 0 & 0 & 0 & 0 & 0 \end{pmatrix}$$

Figure 7. Evolved SFN for approximating a static nonlinear function

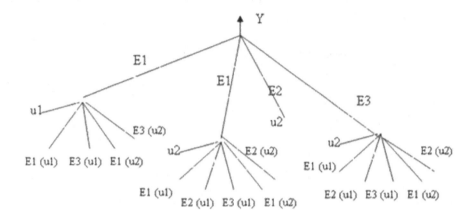

$$V_1 = \begin{pmatrix} -1.0776 & 0 & 0 & 0 & 0 & 0 \\ -0.2864 & 0 & 0 & -0.0945 & 0 & 0.0977 \end{pmatrix}$$

$$V_2 = \begin{pmatrix} -2.0828 & 0 & 0 & 0 & 0 & 0 \\ 0.0240 & 0 & 0 & 0.0948 & 0 & 0.0999 \end{pmatrix}$$

$$Q_1 = \begin{pmatrix} 0 & 0 & 0 & 0 & 0 & 0 \\ 0 & 0 & 0 & -0.0597 & 0 & 0.0936 \end{pmatrix}$$

$$Q_2 = \begin{pmatrix} 1.8631 & 0 & 0 & 0 & 0 & 0 \\ 0 & 0 & 0 & 0.0733 & 0 & 0.0993 \end{pmatrix}$$

5.3. Regression of Single Input Noisy Function

In this example, there are two major tasks have to be accomplished: capturing the model of the underlying systems and filtering the noise out. The designed model has to be the optimal representation that fits the pure model curve without approximating the noise component with it. More complex model representation may result in overfitting; however, too simple model representation may result in underfitting.

Here we examine the model ability in linear regression problems using a single dimensional function: $f(X) = 2X - 2 + \varepsilon$; $X \in [-1,1]$, where ε is a normally distributed random noise with mean $\mu = 0$, and standard deviation σ. We generated two data sets; the first is the training set and consists of 41 samples. The second set is used for the network testing and also consists of 40 samples. The test data points are, therefore, shifted from the training points by a constant shift that equals 0.0125.

For all algorithms trials, different noise levels are tried. In addition, since it is a random process, all tests are repeated 10 times and the average values are used to indicate the network performance.

Table 3 shows the test performance for SFN and its variants as well as the competing methods. Different levels of noise are used to train the SFN. Tables 3a and 3b shows the results when $\sigma = 0.1$ and 0.5, respectively. One can observe that the FB-SFN and B-SFN methods give a good compromise of sparseness (as measured by the number of weights) and performance. Figure 8 illustrates the fitting performance for the B-SFN (1) (i.e. a single layer backward-algorithm SFN) in case of the system noise is of standard deviation $\sigma = 0.5$.

Table 3. Training and testing error (in MSE) for example 5.3 for the proposed model variants FLY-SFN, FLK-SFN, B-SFN, and FB-SFN, and for some competing methods B-BP, and BR-BP. Also shown are the average number of weights for all resulted networks

Standard deviation of the noise signal $\sigma = 0.1$							
	Training			Testing			Average # Weights
Algorithm	Best MSE	Worst MSE	Average MSE	Best MSE	Worst MSE	Average MSE	
B-BP (5)	0.0023	0.0091	0.0046	0.00252	0.00503	0.00388	16
BR –BP (5)	0.0026	0.0064	0.0047	0.00018	0.00057	0.00035	16
FLY-SFN (2)	0.0092	0.0698	0.0217	0.00046	0.00152	0.00106	20
FLK-SFN (1)	0.008	0.0136	0.0108	0.00037	0.00173	0.00101	5
FLK-SFN (2)	0.009	0.0149	0.0113	0.00034	0.00205	0.00086	6
B-SFN (2)	0.0076	0.0097	0.0084	0.0003	0.00073	0.00052	17
FB-SFN (2)(K=4)	0.0071	0.0147	0.0113	0.00019	0.00188	0.00063	5
Standard deviation of the noise signal $\sigma = 0.5$							
	Training			Testing			Average # Weights
Algorithm	Best MSE	Worst MSE	Average MSE	Best MSE	Worst MSE	Average MSE	
B-BP (5)	0.0594	0.1443	0.1031	0.0161	0.0629	0.043	16
BR –BP (5)	0.0406	0.1294	0.0924	0.0165	0.0635	0.0413	16
FLY-SFN (2)	0.1663	0.2516	0.2267	0.0072	0.0438	0.0205	20
FLK-SFN (1)	0.2014	0.4212	0.2674	0.0046	0.0563	0.0296	4
FLK-SFN (2)	0.1673	0.358	0.2325	0.0033	0.0256	0.0181	6
B-SFN (1)	0.1408	0.2503	0.2038	0.0035	0.0157	0.0074	4
FB-SFN (2)(K=4)	0.148	0.2647	0.2094	0.0032	0.0235	0.0136	5

5.4. Two-Dimension Nonlinear Regression

We considered here a regression problem, namely approximating a noisy two-dimensional function. We considered the function: $f(X) = X1^2 * X2^2 + \varepsilon$; . where ε is a normally distributed random noise with mean $\mu = 0$, and standard deviation $\sigma = 0.05$. The training set consists of 100 samples generated in the grid [-1:0.2:0.8]x[-1:0.2:0.8], and the test set consists of 100 samples generated using the grid [-0.975:0.2:0.825]x[-0.975:0.2:0.825] (i.e. the

testing points are shifted from the learning points by a constant shift equals 0.025 in both dimensions). Table 4 shows the test comparison results. Figure 9a shows the noisy data used in training the network, and Figure 9b shows the SFN network's fitting performance for the B-SFN (2) (i.e. a two layer backward-algorithm SFN). The results show that B-SFN produces the best performance (beating the MLP methods as well as the other SFN methods). However, FB-SFN and FRS-SFN produce very sparse networks, yet the performance is reasonable.

Figure 8. SFN network output for the linear regression problem

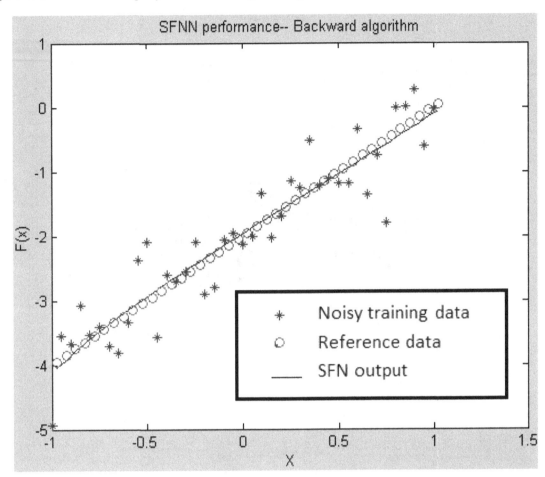

Table 4. Training and testing error (in MSE) for example 5.4 for the proposed model variants FLY-SFN, FLK-SFN, B-SFN, FB-SFN, and FRS-SFN, and for some competing methods B-BP, ES-BP, and BR-BP. Also shown are the average number of weights for all resulted networks

Algorithm	Training			Testing			Average # Weights
	Best MSE	Worst MSE	Average MSE	Best MSE	Worst MSE	Average MSE	
B-BP (12)	0.0038	0.0067	0.0055	0.0023	0.0069	0.0047	49
ES- BP (20)	0.0044	0.016	0.0074	0.0052	0.0087	0.006	81
BR –BP (15)	0.0012	0.0025	0.0019	6.24 E-4	0.0016	0.001	61
FLY-SFN (2)	0.0018	0.0028	0.0023	6.23 E-4	0.0018	0.0012	70
FLK-SFN (2)	0.0091	0.015	0.0012	0.0055	0.009	0.0079	13
B-SFN (2)	0.0017	0.0036	0.0025	6.69 E-4	0.0013	9.41E-04	62
FB-SFN (2)(K=5)	0.0128	0.0149	0.0013	0.0086	0.0091	0.0088	8
FRS-SFN(2)(RF=0.5)	0.0063	0.0171	0.012	0.0045	0.0097	0.0076	12

Figure 9. a) Noisy data for the linear regression problem, b) SFN network output for the regression problem

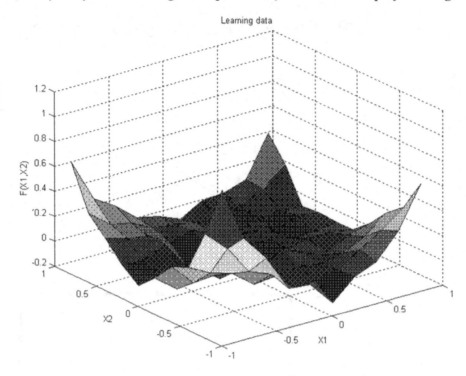

a)

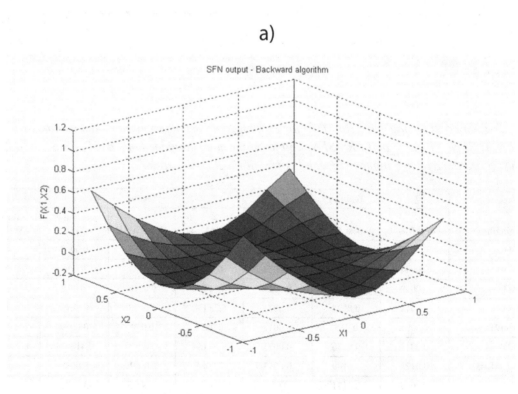

b)

5.5. System Identification Problem

Here we considered the dynamical system

$$y(k+1) = 0.4y(k) + 0.4y(k)y(k-1) + 0.6u(k)^3 + 0.1$$

The problem is to design a network that identifies the given system using input-output data. We generated a two sequences of 200 points each by considering the input signal as an independent random noise (uniform in $[0, 0.5]$). The first sequence is used for learning and the second sequence is used for testing the network performance. Table 5 shows the comparison results. Figure 10 shows the SFN network testing performance for the B-SFN (1) (i.e. a single layer backward-algorithm SFN). The results show that FB-SFN and FRS-SFN methods result in the sparsest network however, with just 4 parameters each and in spite of that the performance is still very reasonable. On the other hand, B-SFN's performance is the best, and is still quite sparse, with the network having just 10 weights.

5.6. Time Series Forecasting

In this example, we test the SFN model power in time series forecasting problems. As a real world case study, we used SFN to predict the river flow based on historical measures. We used the readings of the average daily flow of the river Nile in Egypt. The flow is measured as a volume in millions of cubic meters during the ten years period from 1985 to 1995. Two modes of prediction are tested: "single-step-ahead prediction" where only one step forward is predicted based on current available data and "multi-step ahead prediction" where longer horizon is predicted. We created the time series from the original data by computing the ten-day flow average. The time series is scaled before used in the forecasting process and then the output of the forecasting model is being rescaled to get the predicted flow volume. The original time series consists of 3600 points, this is the daily average flow time series in the period of 1985-1994, taking the ten days average results in a 360 points time series. We divided this new time series into two data sets, the first is a testing set and consists of 180 points represents the period of 1985-1989, and is used for training

Table 5. Training and testing error (in MSE) for example 5.5 for the proposed model variants FLY-SFN, FLK-SFN, B-SFN, FB-SFN, and FRS-SFN, and for some competing methods B-BP, ES-BP, and BR-BP. Also shown are the average number of weights for all resulted networks.

Algorithm	Training			Testing			Average # Weights
	Best MSE	Worst MSE	Average MSE	Best MSE	Worst MSE	Average MSE	
B-BP (9)	7.65E-05	3.01E-04	1.53E-04	9.63E-05	2.67E-04	1.87E-04	46
ES- BP (9)	9.29E-05	2.13E-04	1.42E-04	1.76E-04	6.90E-04	3.21E-04	46
BR –BP (3)	1.64E-07	3.92E-05	8.80E-06	6.42E-05	2.51E-04	1.39E-04	16
FLY-SFN (1)	5.39E-05	1.42E-04	8.75E-05	5.13E-05	1.33E-04	8.03E-05	15
FLK-SFN (1)	2.95E-04	4.54E-04	3.77E-04	2.14E-04	4.70E-04	3.42E-04	6
B-SFN (1)	7.65E-05	1.09E-04	9.29E-05	5.88E-05	6.42E-05	5.89E-05	10
FB-SFN (1)(K=3)	3.28E-04	4.87E-04	4.04E-04	2.67E-04	4.28 E-04	3.26E-04	4
FRS-SFN(1)(RF=0.5)	3.28E-04	4.60E-04	3.84E-04	2.37E-04	3.83E-04	3.17E-04	4

Figure 10. SFN network output for the system identifiacation problem

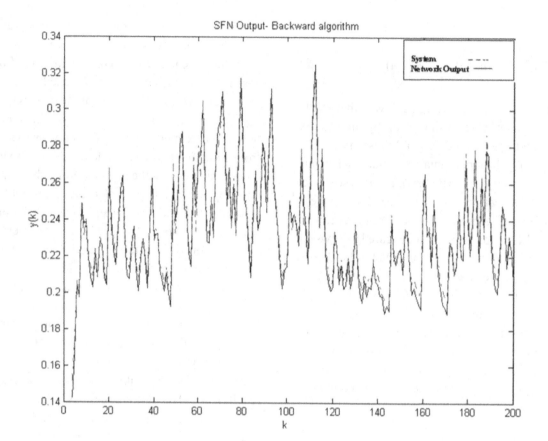

the SFN network. The second set is the testing set, which consists of the remaining 180 points representing the period 1990:1994, and is used to test the constructed network.

5.6.1. Single Step Ahead Prediction

In this experiment, we tried to train the SFN using various algorithms and compared the results with the performance of a single layer MLP. Table 6 shows the comparison results. Figure 11 shows the SFN network testing performance for the B-SFN (1) (i.e. a single layer backward-algorithm SFN). The results show that: FRS-SFN method results in the sparsest network with the best performance that outperforms all of the other methods.

As shown in the results, that the prediction is accurate and all SFN variants outperform the MLP performance, and also with more sparse constructed networks.

5.6.2. Multi Step Ahead Prediction

In addition of predicting just the next step of the time series, we considered here the problem of predicting several steps away, in other words, we are to design a network that gets the available values of the time series as inputs: $x(1)$, $x(2)$,...$x(t)$, and predicts the time series value $x(t+k)$; where $k>1$. Surely, the larger k is, the more difficult problem is. We tried to design a SFN networks for $k = 2$ and 3.

Table 6. Single step ahead prediction (ten-days ahead) of river flow

Algorithm	Training			Testing			Average # Weights
	Best MSE	Worst MSE	Average MSE	Best MSE	Worst MSE	Average MSE	
B-BP (9)	0.0456	0.0837	0.0685	0.113	0.272	0.158	46
ES- BP (15)	0.0806	0.113	0.088	0.116	0.115	0.128	76
BR –BP (3)	0.102	0.105	0.103	0.0858	0.147	0.113	16
FLY-SFN (1)		0.115			0.107		15
FLK-SFN (1)		0.129			0.0937		9
B-SFN (1)		0.122			0.0975		9
FB-SFN (1) (K=5)		0.133			0.0987		7
FRS-SFN(1) (RF=0.5)	0.127	0.147	0.137	0.0837	0.094	0.0884	5

Figure 11. SFN network output for the single step ahead prediction (ten-days ahead) of river flow

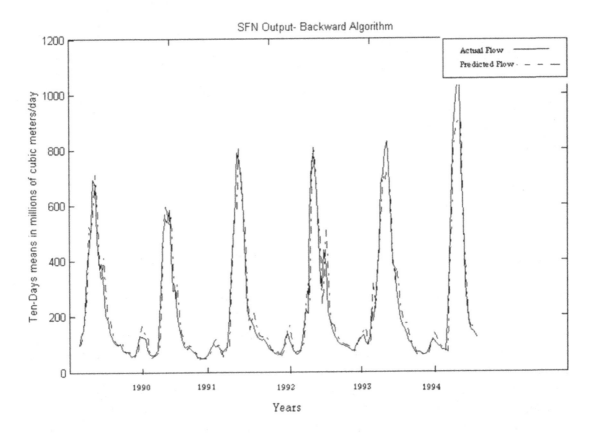

Table 7. Two step ahead prediction (double ten-days ahead) of river flow

Algorithm	Training			Testing			Average # Weights
	Best MSE	Worst MSE	Average MSE	Best MSE	Worst MSE	Average MSE	
B-BP (6)	0.191	0.216	0.201	0.21	0.308	0.271	31
ES- BP (15)	0.203	0.302	0.231	0.207	0.262	0.231	76
BR –BP (9)	0.051	0.606	0.167	0.496	1.419	0.803	46
FLY-SFN (1)		0.357			0.253		15
FLK-SFN (1)		0.373			0.248		12
B-SFN (1)		0.359			0.247		6
FB-SFN (1)(K=5)		0.272			0.213		9
FRS-SFN(1)(RF=0.5)	0.37	0.4	0.392	0.245	0.258	0.253	6

Table 8. Three step ahead prediction (triple ten-days ahead) of river flow

Algorithm	Training			Testing			Average # Weights
	Best MSE	Worst MSE	Average MSE	Best MSE	Worst MSE	Average MSE	
B-BP (3)	0.312	0.542	0.429	0.386	0.513	0.447	16
ES- BP (12)	0.298	0.375	0.335	0.344	0.388	0.361	61
BR –BP (3)	0.296	0.316	0.306	0.425	0.45	0.44	16
FLY-SFN (1)		0.582			0.439		15
FLK-SFN (1)		0.542			0.446		8
B-SFN (1)		0.581			0.436		7
FB-SFN (1) (K=5)		0.484			0.389		12
FRS-SFN(1) (RF=0.5)	0.617	0.618	0.618	0.439	0.444	0.441	6

Tables 7 and 8 and Figures 12 and 13 show the results for k = 2 (two step ahead), k = 3 (three step ahead), respectively.

As shown in the results, SFN gives the best prediction accuracy, and the constructed networks are sparser than the resulted MLP networks. For example, while the results of B-BP algorithm in MSE was 0.158, 0.271, and 0.447 for a single, double, and triple Steps ahead respectively; the results of the B-SFN algorithm in MSE was 0.0975, 0.247, and 0.436.

6. CONCLUSION

Symbolic modeling concept has been recently introduced to the machine learning community. The promising results of such models in many fields such as; time series forecasting and system modeling encouraged us to introduce this concept to the neural networks area by developing a novel neural network like model that can extract the most relevant features and discover the sparse symbolic representation of the modeled system. Developing such symbolic representations of systems has

Figure 12. Two step ahead prediction "double ten-days ahead"

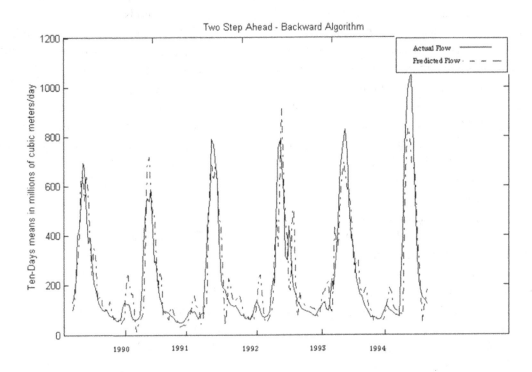

Figure 13. Three step ahead prediction "triple ten-days ahead"

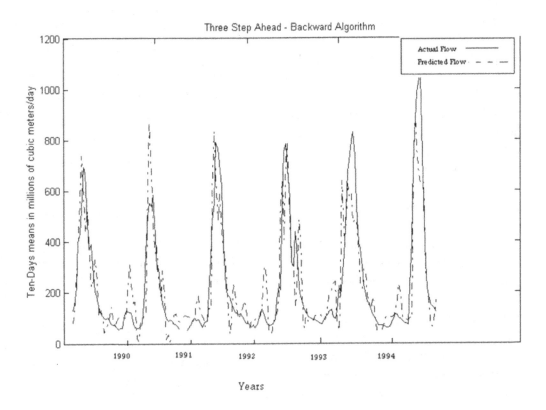

been achieved recently by applying evolutionary algorithms such as Genetic programming. In addition, much work has been done to design sparse neural networks that contain just the most effective synapses and features with all redundant and irrelevant connections being removed. Structure based neural networks, such as tree-based structure, are found to be more suitable for designing such sparse networks than the fully connected networks, such as MLP. Due to all of the above, the suggested implementation of the sparse basis neural network model was a tree structure-based neural network that can be evolving using a reliable evolutionary algorithm. Moreover, the new model is motivated by the current needs of developing more enhanced predictors. The accuracy and the recall speed of solutions of some critical applications such as the telecommunications network time series forecasting are still not enough to support the developing of reliable quality control strategies. Therefore, new neural networks models with higher approximation ability will help improving such applications.

SFN proved to have high ability in function approximation, regression, and time series forecasting problems compared with some of the traditional neural networks models, such as feed forward multilayer perceptron and recurrent networks, and with some advanced related models, such as the Flexible Tree Network (FNT) (Eskander & Atiya, 2009; Eskander, Atiya, Chong, Kim, & Yoo, 2007; Eskander & Atiya, 2007).

This work opened the door for many interesting research points that need further investigation:

- Extend the application of The SFN model to be applied to the classification problems.
- Develop new evolutionary learning algorithms and using them to optimize the SFN network structure and weights in order to get sparser, and more fitting symbolic functions through a much faster training process. The evolutionary algorithms can be designed based on one or a combination of population based and evolutionary methods like: Genetic Algorithms (GA), Genetic Programming (GP), Particle Swarm Optimization (PSO), and Evolutionary Programming (EP).
- Improve the symbolic expressions represented by the SFN network by getting sparser symbolic representation through applying symbolic reduction procedures.
- Improve the SFN model by trying other basic nonlinear transformations.

REFERENCES

Angeline, P. J., Sunders, G. M., & Pollack, J. B. (1994). An evolutionary algorithm that constructs recurrent artificial neural networks. *IEEE Transactions on Neural Networks*, 5, 54–65. doi:10.1109/72.265960

Atiya, A. F., Aly, M. A. A., & Parlos, G. (2005). Sparse basis selection: New results and application to adaptive prediction of video source traffic. *IEEE Transactions on Neural Networks*, 16(5), 1136–1146. doi:10.1109/TNN.2005.853426

Behnke, S., & Karayiannis, N. B. (1998). CNeT: Competitive neural trees for pattern classifications. *IEEE Transactions on Neural Networks*, 9(6), 1352–1369. doi:10.1109/72.728387

Chen, S. S., Donoho, D. L., & Saunders, M. A. (1998). Atomic decomposition by basis pursuit. *SIAM Journal on Scientific Computing*, 20(1), 33–61. doi:10.1137/S1064827596304010

Chen, Y., & Abraham, A. (2005). Feature selection and intrusion detection using hybrid flexible neural trees. *Lecture Notes in Computer Science*, 3498, 439–444. doi:10.1007/11427469_71

Chen, Y., Yang, B., & Abraham, A. (2006). *Flexible neural trees ensemble for stock index modeling*. London, UK: Elsevier Science. doi:10.1016/j. neucom.2006.10.005

Chen, Y., Yang, B., & Dong, J. (2004a). Nonlinear system modeling via optimal design of neural trees. *International Journal of Neural Systems, 4*(2), 125–137. doi:10.1142/S0129065704001905

Chen, Y., Yang, B., & Dong, J. (2004b). Evolving flexible neural networks using ant programming and PSO algorithm. *Lecture Notes in Computer Science, 3173,* 211–216. doi:10.1007/978-3-540-28647-9_36

Chen, Y., Yang, B., Dong, J., & Abraham, A. (2004). Time series forecasting using flexible neural tree model. *Information Science, 174,* 219–235. doi:10.1016/j.ins.2004.10.005

Chen, Y., Yang, J., Zhang, Y., & Dong, J. (2005). Evolving additive tree models for system identification. *International Journal of Computational Cognition, 3*(2).

Chen, Y., Zhang, Y., Dong, J., & Yang, J. (2004). System identification by evolved flexible neural tree. In *Proceedings of the 5th Congress of Intelligent Control and Automation.* IEEE.

Coinfman, R. R., & Wickerhauser, M. V. (1992). Entropy–based algorithms for best basis selection. *IEEE Transactions on Information Theory, 38,* 713–718. doi:10.1109/18.119732

Cotter, S., Delgado, K. K., & Rao, B. (2001). Backward elimination for sparse vector subset selection. *Signal Processing, 81,* 1849–1864. doi:10.1016/S0165-1684(01)00064-0

Eskander, G., & Atiya, A. (2009). Symbolic function network. *Neural Networks, 22*(4), 395–404. doi:10.1016/j.neunet.2009.02.003

Eskander, G. S., Atiya, A., Chong, K. T., Kim, H., & Yoo, S. G. (2007). Round trip time prediction using the symbolic function network approach. In *Proceedings of the 2007 International Symposium on Information Technology Convergence (ISITC 2007).* Jeonju, South Korea: IEEE Press.

Eskander, G. S., & Atiya, A. F. (2007). A novel symbolic type neural network model- Application to river flow forecasting. In *Proceedings International Computer Engineering Conference (ICENCO 2007).* Cairo, Egypt: ECENCO.

Fahlman, S. E., & Lebiere, C. (1990). The cascade- correlation learning architecture. *Advances in Neural Information Processing Systems, 2,* 524–532.

Gori, M., Kuchler, A., & Sperduti, A. (1999). On implementation of frontier- to – root automata in recursive neural networks. *IEEE Transactions on Neural Networks, 10*(6). doi:10.1109/72.809076

Haykin, S. (1999). *Neural networks- A comprehensive foundation* (2nd ed.). Upper Saddle River, NJ: Prentice Hall.

John, G. H., Kohavi, R., & Pfleger, K. (1994). Irrelevant features and the subset selection problem. In *Proceedings of the 11th International Conference on Machine Learning,* (pp. 121-129). IEEE.

Koza, J. R. (1991). A genetic approach to econometric modeling. In *Proceedings of the 2nd International Conference on Economics.* IEEE.

Narendra, P. M., & Fuknaga, K. (1997). A branch and bound algorithm for feature subset selection. *IEEE Transactions on Computers, 26*(9), 917–922. doi:10.1109/TC.1977.1674939

Natarjan, B. K. (1995). Sparse approximate solutions to linear system. *SIAM Journal on Computing, 24*(2), 227–234. doi:10.1137/S0097539792240406

Poggio, T., & Girosi, F. (1998). A sparse representation for function approximation. *Neural Computation, 10*(6), 1445–1454. doi:10.1162/089976698300017250

Reeves, J. (1999). An efficient implementation of backward greedy algorithm for sparse signal reconstruction. *IEEE Signal Processing Letters, 6*(10), 266–268. doi:10.1109/97.789606

Sanger, T. D. (1991). A tree- structured adaptive network for function approximation in high-dimensional space. *IEEE Transactions on Neural Networks, 2*(2). doi:10.1109/72.80339

Sankar, A., & Mammone, R. J. (1991a). Optimal pruning of neural tree networks for improved generalization. In *Proceedings of the International Joint Conference on Neural Networks*, (pp. 219-224). Seattle, WA: IEEE.

Sankar, A., & Mammone, R. J. (1991b). Speaker independent vowel recognition using neural tree networks. In *Proceedings of the International Joint Conference on Neural Networks*, (pp. 809-814). Seattle, WA: IEEE.

Sankar, A., & Mammone, R. J. (1993). Growing and pruning neural tree networks. *IEEE Transactions on Computers, 42*, 291–299. doi:10.1109/12.210172

Sethi, I. K. (1990). Entropy nets: From decision trees to neural networks. *Proceedings of the IEEE, 78*(10), 1605–1613. doi:10.1109/5.58346

Sethi, I. K., & Jan, A. K. (1991). Decision tree performance enhancement using an artificial neural networks implementation. In *Artificial Neural Networks and Statistical Pattern Recognition* (pp. 71–88). Amsterdam, The Netherlands: Elsevier.

Suykens, J. A. K., Lukas, L., & Vandewalle, J. (2000). Sparse approximation using least squares support vector machines. In *Proceedings of IEEE International Symposium on Circuits and Systems (ISCAS 2000)*, (pp. 11757-11760). IEEE Press. Adas, A. N. (1998). Using adaptive linear prediction to support real–time VBR video under RCBR network service model. *IEEE Transactions on Networking, 6*(5).

Yao, X. (1997). A new evolutionary system for evolving artificial neural networks. *IEEE Transactions on Neural Networks, 8*, 694–713. doi:10.1109/72.572107

Yao, X. (1999). Evolving artificial neural networks. *Proceedings of the IEEE, 87*(9), 1423–1447. doi:10.1109/5.784219

Yao, X., Lin, Y., & Lin, G. (1999). Evolutionary programming made faster. *IEEE Transactions on Evolutionary Computation, 3*, 82–122. doi:10.1109/4235.771163

Yoo, S.-J. (2002). Efficient traffic prediction scheme for real time VBR MPEG video transmission over high speed networks. *IEEE Transactions on Broadcasting, 48*(1).

Zhang, B. T. (1997). Evolutionary induction of sparse neural tree. *Evolutionary Computation, 5*(2), 213–236. doi:10.1162/evco.1997.5.2.213

Zhang, B. T. (2002). A Bayesian evolutionary approach to the design and learning of heterogeneous neural trees. *Integrated Computer-Aided Engineering, 9*(1), 73–86.

Zhang, B. T., & Muhlenbein, H. (1994). Synthesis of sigma-pi neural networks by breeder genetic programming. In *Proceedings of the IEEE Conference on Evolutionary Computations*. IEEE Press.

Zhang, G. P. (2003). Time series forecasting using a hybrid ARIMA and neural network model. *Neurocomputing, 50*, 159–175. doi:10.1016/S0925-2312(01)00702-0

Chapter 15
City Manager Compensation and Performance:
An Artificial Intelligence Approach

Jean X. Zhang
Virginia Commonwealth University, USA

ABSTRACT

This chapter proposes a nonlinear artificial Higher Order Neural Network (HONN) model to study the relation between manager compensation and performance in the governmental sector. Using a HONN simulator, this study analyzes city manager compensation as a function of local government perfor-mance, and compares the results with those from a linear regression model. This chapter shows that the nonlinear model generated from HONN has a smaller Root Mean Squared Error (Root MSE) of 0.0020 as compared to 0.06598 from a linear regression model. This study shows that artificial HONN is an effective tool in modeling city manager compensation.

1. INTRODUCTION

Executive compensation has been rigorously stud-ied in the corporate sector (e.g. Sloan, 1993; Baber, et al., 1996; Core, et al., 2003, 2008); however, few examine compensation and performance in the nonprofit and governmental sectors (Werner & Gemeinhardt, 1995; Frumkin & Keating, 2001; Baber, et al., 2002; Gore, 2009; Gore, et al., 2011; Zhang, 2012). For example, Gore (2009) finds that municipalities with agency problems spend more on manager salaries and bonuses. In addition,

Gore et al. (2011) investigate the determinants of severance offered to municipal managers. They find that managers with excessive salaries, or exposed to greater political risk, receive more severance pay. Moreover, Zhang (2012) examines the relation between compensation and financial performance measures for city managers by us-ing a linear model. However, no prior study in the accounting literature focuses on modeling a nonlinear relation between city manager compen-sation and financial performance measures using artificial neural networks.

This chapter employs artificial HONN as a tool to develop a nonlinear model for the rela-

DOI: 10.4018/978-1-4666-2175-6.ch015

tion between city manager compensation and performance and compares the performance of both linear and nonlinear models. This study uses HONN models rather than the standard Artificial Neural Network (ANN) models since the standard ANN models employed by the current studies are unable to provide explanations for their behavior. In contrast, HONN models (Redding, Kowalczyk, & Downs, 1993; Zhang, Zhang, & Fulcher, 2000) are regarded as "open box" rather than "black box" since they provide some rationale for the simulations they produce. In addition, HONNs are capable of simulating higher frequency and higher order nonlinear data, hence, providing superior results as compared to those from standard ANN models. Results show that HONN models are able to simulate the nonlinear relation between city manager compensation and financial performance measures with less Root MSE.

This study offers several contributions to the extant literature. First, this research is the first to model city manager compensation using artificial intelligence. This is an important step in studying the stewardship role of the municipality. Second, this study extends research in executive compensation. While Zhang (2012) studies the association between compensation and performance using a linear model, this chapter models compensation by employing a nonlinear model.

The remainder of this chapter is organized as follows. Section 2 presents the background for this study. Section 3 describes the data and sample selection procedure. Section 4 discusses the results and Section 5 concludes this chapter.

2. BACKGROUND: NEURAL NETWORK IN ACCOUNTING RESEARCH

Artificial neural network is widely used in accounting literature. Previous researchers use neural networks to predict takeover targets (Cheh, et

al., 1999), earnings (Charitou & Charalambous, 1996), and pricing of initial public offerings (Jain & Nag, 1995). More recently, using 178 mergers from 1996-2001, Shawver (2005) developed and tested neural network models for predicting bank merger premiums. The evidence shows that a neural network methodology provides more explanation between bank merger premiums and financial variables in the model than a traditional regression model. The author attributes the results to the ability of a neural network model to recognize patterns in complicated financial relationships.

Ragothaman and Lavin (2008) employ the neural networks methodology for modeling revenue restatements. The authors use six financial and governance variables to train the neural network, and the model is validated using a holdout sample of 51 firms. Compared to the multiple discriminant analysis and Logit models, the results suggest that the neural network model has greater predictive power for revenue restatement modeling. While examining misclassification costs, the authors find that the neural network model outperforms the other models by having the lowest relative misclassification costs.

Using a sample of 50 fraud and 50 non-fraud companies from 1995 to 2002, McKee (2009) uses artificial intelligence models to predict all categories of financial statement fraud. The author uses fifteen financial fraud predictors to create a variety of neural network, logistic regression, and classification tree models. This methodology increases classification accuracy from 71 percent to 83 percent, decreases the estimated overall error rate from 0.0057 to 0.0035, and the relative misclassification costs from 2.79 to 0.58.

2.1. Background: Polynomial Higher Order Neural Networks

Linear models are used in many of the studies that examine compensation; however, many researchers also use nonlinear models in their analysis (Kaplan & Welam, 1974; Brock & Sayers, 1988; Lee & Wu, 1988). For example, Schipper (1991) finds that the usual regression approach in evaluating the earnings-share price relation may not be descriptive since it implies a linear loss function. Due to the limitations of the traditional statistical approaches, alternative approaches, i.e. ANNs, have been considered in modeling and predicting financial data (Azoff, 1994). In overcoming the limitations of the standard ANNs, researchers have developed HONN models (Karayiannis & Venetsanopoulos, 1993; Redding, et al., 1993; Zhang, et al., 2000). Since polynomial functions are often used in modeling financial data, this chapter employs Polynomial HONN (PHONN) to model the nonlinear relation between city manager compensation and local government performance.

Polynomial curve fitting is an example of non-linear mapping from input space to output space. By minimizing an error function, polynomial curve fitting aims to fit a polynomial to a set of n data points (Zhang, et al., 2000). The function f(x, y) is determined by the values of the parameters a_{k1k2}, which is equivalent to ANN weights w0, w1, w2 . . . etc. The Polynomial HONN (PHONN) model utilizes a combination of linear, power and multiplicative neurons. In addition, the training of this ANN uses the standard back propagation. The PHONN model is able to extract coefficients a_{k1k2} of the general nth-order polynomial form as follows:

$$z = \sum_{k1,k2=0}^{n} a_{k1k2} x^{k1} y^{k2} \qquad (1)$$

3. DATA AND SAMPLE SELECTION

The sample begins with 11,489 municipal-year observations available in the International City/County Management Association (ICMA), Census, and Government Finance Officers Association (GFOA) databases. This study excludes 5,330 observations without manager characteristics and 4,034 with missing financial performance measures. The final sample consists of 658 observations, after removing additional observations for cities experiencing manager turnover and cities with missing salary change information.

Zhang (2012) finds that city manager compensation is associated with financial performance measures. Following Zhang (2012), the dependent variable is the percent change in the chief administrative officers' base salary *(%∆BASE SALARY)*. The independent variables are measures of local government performance that includes efficiency and surplus. Following Gore (2009), the administration expense ratio (*Admin*) is used to measure municipal inefficiency. This measure is defined as the ratio of total administrative expenses less manager salary to total operating expenses, where administrative expenses include central staff services, financial administration, and unallocable expenses. Assuming the goal of municipalities is to spend more toward programs and services for citizens rather than on administrative expenses, then a higher *Admin* ratio is associated with lower efficiency. *Surplus* is defined as the per capita total revenues less total expenditures (see Table 1).

4. RESULTS AND ANALYSIS

Zhang (2012) uses multiple linear regressions to explore the relation between city manager compensation and performance. Her results indicate that changes in city manager's salary are related to fiscal responsibility, which is consistent with statements in GASB (2006) that state the role of government includes providing services in a "sustainable" manner. In addition, the significantly positive coefficient for *Admin* suggests agency problems since city managers receive greater pay increases at inefficient cities. The Root MSE is

Table 1. Sample selection

	Salary (1999-2003)
Total cities and towns in ICMA compensation database	11,489
Less governments with missing manager characteristics	(5,330)
	6,159
Less governments with missing financial information	(4,034)
	2,125
Less governments with manager turnover	(199)
	1,926
Less governments with Missing salary change data	(1,278)
Final Sample	648

0.06598 for the multiple linear regression. This study extends Zhang (2012) by examining the use of HONN for predicting city manager salary changes. This is the first study that examines the use of artificial intelligence expert systems in predicting compensation.

The HONN model employed in this study has one output (dependent) and two input (independent) variables. Figure 1 shows an illustration of the structure of the neural network. To ensure better simulation results for the HONN model, all input and output values are converted to a number ranges from 0 to 1. Table 2 shows the input and output values for the HONN model. Input 1 and Input 2 show the scaled values for *Admin* and *Surplus*, while Act0/P-0 and Des0/P-0 shows the actual and desired output values. The following coefficients are generated by HONN to model city manager compensation for the converted data.

$\%\Delta BASE\ SALARY = 0.817 + 0.004*Admin + 0.497*Admin^2$

$+ 0.042*Surplus + 0.295*Surplus*Admin + 0.142*Surplus*Admin^2$

$-0.012*Surplus^2 + 0.075*Surplus^2*Admin + 1.000*Surplus^2*Admin^2$

The results show that the Root MSE from the nonlinear HONN model is 0.0020 which is smaller than that from the linear model of 0.06598. This suggests that the nonlinear model generated by HONN is more superior compared to the linear model from SAS. This study is also the first step toward studying the usefulness of neural networks in predicting compensation.

5. CONCLUSION

This chapter extends the current studies in manager compensation by examining whether there is a nonlinear relation between city manager compensation and performance using artificial neural network. The multiple linear regression model generated from Zhang (2012) shows a positive association between city manager compensation and local government surplus, which is consistent with the stewardship role of the municipality since city managers are compensated for generating a surplus for the municipality. In addition, her study also finds that city manager pay is directly related to inefficiency, which suggests agency problems in the local government. This multiple linear regression model has a Root MSE of 0.06598.

Figure 1. Weights of PHONN to predict city manager salary

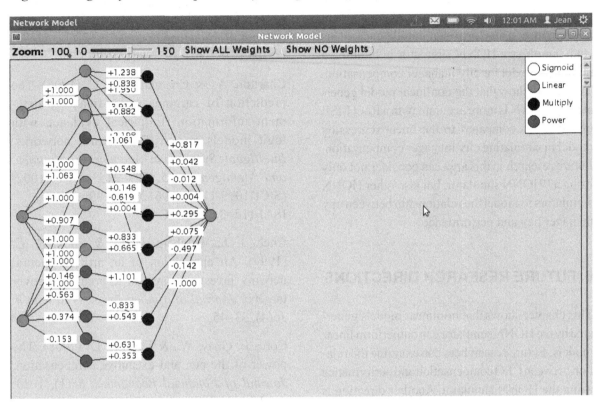

Table 2. HONN input and output

Input-0	Input-1	ActO/P-0	DesO/P-0	Error	%Error
0.429439	0.63738	0.875246	0.866772	0.008474	0.59
0.476696	0.673077	0.875997	0.821252	0.054746	3.84
0.582959	0.682156	0.876184	0.887912	-0.01173	0.82
0.818462	0.643623	0.873207	0.84857	0.024637	1.73
0.351063	0.668943	0.875421	0.857848	0.017573	1.23
0.346414	0.668934	0.87539	0.880987	-0.0056	0.39
0.318061	0.729909	0.875658	0.87218	0.003478	0.24
0.320849	0.705442	0.875538	0.857668	0.01787	1.25
1	0.645257	0.870256	0.844003	0.026252	1.84
0.459816	0.67331	0.875966	0.858659	0.017307	1.22
0.694019	0.620384	0.873767	0.848577	0.02519	1.77
0.362936	0.653286	0.875282	0.851603	0.023679	1.66
0.367944	0.67441	0.875594	0.848879	0.026715	1.88
0.361176	0.658806	0.875349	0.856532	0.018817	1.32
0.305054	0.169735	0.858291	0.860827	-0.00254	0.18
0.298731	0.774086	0.875515	0.848557	0.026958	1.89
0.265135	0	0.847552	0.839458	0.008094	0.57

This chapter is the first to study the relation between city manager pay and local government performance using artificial intelligence. This study employs a HONN simulator in building a nonlinear model for city manager compensation. The results show that the nonlinear model generated by HONN is more accurate with a Root MSE of 0.0020 as compared to the linear regression model in simulating city manager compensation. Future research in this area can consider not only using a PHONN simulator, but also other HONN simulators to model the relationship between city manager pay and performance.

6. FUTURE RESEARCH DIRECTIONS

This chapter shows that nonlinear models generated by the HONN simulator can outperform linear models. Future researchers can examine the relation between CEO compensation and performance using the HONN simulator. Another direction is to examine other top management pay using the method above. References of this new direction are included in the 'Additional Reading' section.

REFERENCES

Azoff, E. (1994). *Neural network time series forecasting of financial markets*. Chichester, UK: Wiley.

Baber, W., Daniel, P., & Roberts, A. (2002). Compensation to managers of charitable organizations: An empirical study of the role of accounting measures of program activities. *Accounting Review, 77*(3), 679–693. doi:10.2308/accr.2002.77.3.679

Baber, W., Janakiraman, S., & Kang, S. (1996). Investment opportunities and the structure of performance-based executive compensation. *Journal of Accounting and Economics, 21*(3), 297–318. doi:10.1016/0165-4101(96)00421-1

Brock, W., & Sayers, C. (1988). Is the business cycle characterized by deterministic chaos? *Journal of Monetary Economics, 22*(1), 71–91. doi:10.1016/0304-3932(88)90170-5

Charitou, A., & Charalambous, C. (1996). The prediction of earnings using financial statement information: Empirical evidence with logit models and artifical neural networks. *Intelligent Systems in Accounting, Finance, and Management, 5*, 199–215. doi:10.1002/(SICI)1099-1174(199612)5:4<199::AID-ISAF114>3.0.CO;2-C

Cheh, J. J., Weinberg, R. S., & Yook, K. C. (1999). An application of an artificial neural network investment system to predict takeover targets. *Journal of Applied Business Research, 15*(4), 33–45.

Core, J., Guay, W., & Larcker, D. (2008). The power of the pen and executive compensation. *Journal of Financial Economics, 88*(1), 1–25. doi:10.1016/j.jfineco.2007.05.001

Core, J., Guay, W., & Verrecchia, R. (2003). Price versus non-price performance measures in optimal CEO compensation contracts. *Accounting Review, 78*(4), 957–981. doi:10.2308/accr.2003.78.4.957

Freeman, R., & Tse, S. (1992). A non-linear model of security price responses to unexpected earnings. *Journal of Accounting Research, 30*(2), 85–109. doi:10.2307/2491123

Frumkin, P., & Keating, E. K. (2001). *The price of doing good: executive compensation in nonprofit organizations*. Working paper. Boston, MA: Harvard University.

GASB. (2006). *GASB white paper: Why governmental accounting and financial reporting is – and should be – different*. Retrieved November 15, 2009, from http://www.gasb.org/white_paper_mar_2006.html

Gore, A. (2009). Why do cities hoard cash? Determinants and implications of municipal cash holdings. *Accounting Review, 84*(1), 183–207. doi:10.2308/accr.2009.84.1.183

Gore, A., Kulp, S., & Li, Y. (2011). *Golden handcuffs for bureaucrats? Ex ante severance contracts in the municipal sector*. Working paper. Washington, DC: The George Washington University.

Jain, B. A., & Nag, B. N. (1995). Artificial neural network models for pricing initial public offerings. *Decision Sciences, 26*(3), 283–302. doi:10.1111/j.1540-5915.1995.tb01430.x

Kaplan, R., & Welam, U. (1974). Overhead allocation with imperfect markets and nonlinear technology. *Accounting Review, 49*(3), 477–484.

Karayiannis, N., & Venetsanopoulos, A. (1993). *Artificial neural networks: Learning algorithms, performance evaluation and applications*. Boston, MA: Kluwer Academic.

McKee, T. E. (2009). A meta-learning approach to predicting financial statement fraud. *Journal of Emerging Technologies in Accounting, 6*(1), 5–26. doi:10.2308/jeta.2009.6.1.5

Ragothaman, S., & Lavin, A. (2008). Restatements due to improper revenue recognition: A neural networks perspective. *Journal of Emerging Technologies in Accounting, 5*(1), 129–142. doi:10.2308/jeta.2008.5.1.129

Redding, N., Kowalczyk, A., & Downs, T. (1993). Constructive high-order network algorithm that is polynomial time. *Neural Networks, 6*, 997–1010. doi:10.1016/S0893-6080(09)80009-9

Shawver, T. (2005). Merger premium predictions using neural network approach. *Journal of Emerging Technologies in Accounting, 1*, 61–72. doi:10.2308/jeta.2005.2.1.61

Sloan, R. (1993). Accounting earnings and top executive compensation. *Journal of Accounting and Economics, 16*, 55–100. doi:10.1016/0165-4101(93)90005-Z

Werner, S., & Gemeinhardt, G. (1995). Nonprofit organizations: What factors determine pay levels? *Compensation and Benefits Review, 27*(5), 53–60. doi:10.1177/088636879502700511

Zhang, J. (2012). *Compensation and financial performance measures: The case of municipal managers*. (Unpublished Doctoral Dissertation). The George Washington University. Washington, DC.

Zhang, M., Zhang, J. C., & Fulcher, J. (2000). Higher order neural network group models for data approximation. *International Journal of Neural Systems, 10*(2), 123–142. doi:10.1016/S0129-0657(00)00011-9

ADDITIONAL READING

Baber, W., Kang, S., & Kumar, K. (1998). Accounting earnings and executive compensation: The role of earnings persistence. *Journal of Accounting and Economics, 25*(2), 169–193. doi:10.1016/S0165-4101(98)00021-4

Baber, W., Kang, S., & Kumar, K. (1999). The explanatory power of earnings levels and earnings changes in the context of executive compensation. *Accounting Review, 74*(4), 459–472. doi:10.2308/accr.1999.74.4.459

Banker, R. D., & Datar, S. M. (1989). Sensitivity, precision, and linear aggregation of signals for performance evaluation. *Journal of Accounting Research, 27*(1), 21–39. doi:10.2307/2491205

Bebchuk, L. A., & Fried, J. M. (2003). Executive compensation as an agency problem. *The Journal of Economic Perspectives*, *17*(3), 71–92. doi:10.1257/089533003769204362

Bushman, R. M., Indjejikian, R. J., & Smith, A. (1995). Aggregate performance measures in business unit manager compensation: The role of intrafirm interdependencies. *Journal of Accounting Research*, *33*, 101–128. doi:10.2307/2491377

Fama, E. (1980). Agency problems and the theory of the firm. *The Journal of Political Economy*, *88*(2), 288–307. doi:10.1086/260866

Fisher, J., & Govindarajan, V. (1992). Profit center manager compensation: An examination of market, political and human capital factors. *Strategic Management Journal*, *13*(3), 205–217. doi:10.1002/smj.4250130304

Gore, A., Matsunaga, S. R., & Yeung, E. (2010). The role of technical expertise in firm governance structure: Evidence from chief financial officer contractual incentives. *Strategic Management Journal*, *32*(7), 771–786. doi:10.1002/smj.907

Holzer, M. (2002). Performance measurement and improvement in state agencies . In *The Book of the States* (*Vol. 35*, pp. 361–369). Lexington, KY: The Council of State Governments.

Hwang, B., & Kim, S. (2009). It pays to have friends. *Journal of Financial Economics*, *93*, 138–158. doi:10.1016/j.jfineco.2008.07.005

Jensen, M., & Meckling, W. (1976). Theory of the firm: managerial behavior, agency costs and ownership structure. *Journal of Financial Economics*, *3*(4), 305–360. doi:10.1016/0304-405X(76)90026-X

Jensen, M., & Murphy, K. J. (1990). Performance pay and top management incentives. *The Journal of Political Economy*, *98*(2), 225–264. doi:10.1086/261677

Keating, A. (1997). Determinants of divisional performance evaluation practices. *Journal of Accounting and Economics*, *24*(3), 243–273. doi:10.1016/S0165-4101(98)00008-1

Kim, O., & Suh, Y. (1993). Incentive efficiency of compensation based on accounting and market performance. *Journal of Accounting and Economics*, *16*, 25–53. doi:10.1016/0165-4101(93)90004-Y

Lambert, R., & Larcker, D. (1987). An analysis of the use of accounting and market measures of performance in executive compensation contracts. *Journal of Accounting Research*, *25*, 85–125. doi:10.2307/2491081

Murphy, K. (1985). Corporate performance and managerial remuneration. *Journal of Accounting and Economics*, *7*, 11–42. doi:10.1016/0165-4101(85)90026-6

Streib, G., & Poister, T. H. (1989). Established and emerging management tools: A 12-year perspective. In *The Municipal Yearbook 1989* (pp. 45–54). Washington, DC: International City Management Association.

Tiebout, C. M. (1956). A pure theory of local expenditures. *The Journal of Political Economy*, *64*(5), 416–424. doi:10.1086/257839

KEY TERMS AND DEFINITIONS

Admin: Ratio of total administrative expenses less manager salary to total operating expenses, where administrative expenses include central staff services, financial administration, and unallocable expenses.

ANN: Artificial Neural Network.

Compensation: The percent change in the chief administrative officers' base salary.

HONN: Higher Order Neural Network.

PHONN: Polynomial Higher Order Neural Network.

Surplus: Per capita total revenues less total expenditures.

Chapter 16
On Some Dynamical Properties of Randomly Connected Higher Order Neural Networks

Hiromi Miyajima
Kagoshima University, Japan

Noritaka Shigei
Kagoshima University, Japan

Shuji Yatsuki
Kyoto Software Research, Inc., Japan

ABSTRACT

This chapter presents macroscopic properties of higher order neural networks. Randomly connected Neural Networks (RNNs) are known as a convenient model to investigate the macroscopic properties of neural networks. They are investigated by using the statistical method of neuro-dynamics. By applying the approach to higher order neural networks, macroscopic properties of them are made clear. The approach establishes: (a) there are differences between stability of RNNs and Randomly connected Higher Order Neural Networks (RHONNs) in the cases of the digital state $\{-1,1\}$-model and the analog state $[-1,1]$ model; (b) there is no difference between stability of RNNs and RHONNs in the cases of the digital state $\{0,1\}$-model and the analog state $[0,1]$-model; (c) with neural networks with oscillation, there are large differences between RNNs and RHONNs in the cases of the digital state $\{-1,1\}$-model and the analog state $[-1,1]$-model, that is, there exists complex dynamics in each model for $k = 2$; (d) behavior of groups composed of RHONNs are represented as a combination of the behavior of each RHONN.

INTRODUCTION

It is well known that the brain has a stable structure in the sense that damage of a part of neurons does not always destroy its function and may use dynamic attractors to hold memory rather than static states as in most (artificial) neural networks (Amari & Maginu, 1988; Hopfield, 1982; Kohonen, 1988; McEliece, et al., 1987; Palm, 1980; Rumelhart & McClelland, 1986; Wang & Ross, 1991). For this reason, studying dynamics of interconnected neural networks from the macroscopic viewpoint gives a method of approach to understand the information processing

DOI: 10.4018/978-1-4666-2175-6.ch016

method of the brain and a suggestion to construct artificial neural networks. Many studies have been done with macroscopic behavior of neural networks (Amari, 1971, 1972, 1974; Annios, et al., 1970; Venzl, 1976). Amari (1971, 1972, 1974) has investigated macroscopic behavior by using the statistical method of neuro-dynamics. As a result, it is shown that there exist only monostable, bistable, and oscillatory networks in this case (Amari, 1974). Macroscopic dynamics of the traditional model whose potential is represented as the linear sum of weights and input vector is simple and it gives the limit of this model. Therefore, in the traditional model, complex behavior is performed by combining simple neural networks, using nonmonotone output function and changing signals from the outside (Hjelmfelt & Ross, 1994; Hopfield, 1982; Moreira & Auto, 1993; Morita, et al., 1990; Morita, 1993; Yao, et al., 1991). On the other hand, Higher Order Neural Networks (HONNs), whose potential is computed by using the second- and third-order product, have been proposed as a generalized model of the traditional one (Rumelhart & McClelland, 1986). It is known that HONNs are superior in associative memory and combinatorial optimization problems to the traditional neural networks (Cheng & Lee, 1993; Cooper, 1995; Gile & Maxwell, 1988; Miyajima, et al., 1996, 1995; Perantonis & Lisboa, 1992; Psaltis, et al., 1988; Simpson, 1990; Villalobos & Merat, 1995; Yatsuki & Miyajima, 1997). In particular, in associative memory complex dynamics of HONNs leads to development of a powerful algorithm (Psaltis, et al., 1988; Simpson, 1990; Yatsuki & Miyajima, 1997). Then, can HONNs perform complex dynamics in the macroscopic or microscopic sense really? It is necessary to investigate not only superiority for application of networks but also qualitative difference of characteristics between HONNs and the traditional neural networks. Such studies of HONNs from the macroscopic viewpoint are little made. Randomly connected neural networks are

proposed as a convenient model for investigating the macroscopic properties of neural networks and can easily extend to the case of HONNs (Amari, 1971, 1972, 1974; Cooper, 1995).

In this chapter, we introduce Randomly connected Higher Order Neural Networks (RHONNs), and we describe macroscopic dynamics, transformations and stability of the activities for various models of RHONNs such as the digital state $\{0, 1\}$- and $\{-1, 1\}$-models, the analog state models, and systems composed of RHONNs by using the statistical method of neuro-dynamics. Specifically, the following problems for RHONNs are investigated:

- How is the behavior of networks affected by changing of the parameters such as weights and thresholds?
- How is the number of equilibrium points in RHONNs?
- What sort of dynamics is performed in RHONNs?
- Does there exist the difference of qualitative ability between the analog and digital models?

Next section, higher order neural networks and RHONNs are defined. In the third section, the activities for states of networks are defined first, global transformation formulas of activities for various models are derived and dynamics for them are made clear. In the fourth, with systems connected RHONNs with different statistical properties to each other, the transformation formulas are shown and the results for them are obtained.

RANDOMLY CONNECTED HIGHER ORDER NEURAL NETWORKS

First, we consider a circuit (network) consisting of n elements as shown in Figure 1. Each element has m inputs and one output, and each of the

Figure 1. A higher order neural network: $L = L_1 \cdots L_k$ $L_t \in Z_m$, $t \in Z_k$, and $w_{i,L}$ is a weight of products of k pieces of input variables

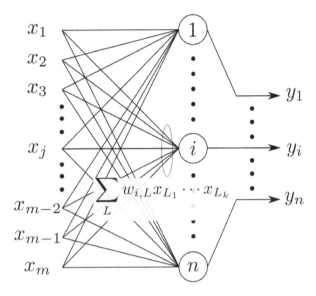

input and the output takes a value $y \in Q$, where Q is called the state set. When $Q = \{0,1\}$ ($\{-1,1\}$) we call it the digital state $\{0,1\}$- ($\{-1,1\}$–) model. When Q is the set of all real numbers from 0 to 1 (-1 to 1), it is called the analog state $[0,1]$- ($\{-1,1\}$-) model. The output of an element, which is also called the state of an element, is represented as a function of potential u. Let $Z_m = \{1, 2, \cdots, m\}$ and $Z_m^k = Z_m \times \cdots \times Z_m$ be defined as k tuples of Z_m. The potential u increases in proportion to the weighted sum

$$\sum_{L \in Z_m^k} w_{i,L} \prod_{j=1}^{k} x_{L_j}$$ of all combinations of products of

k pieces chosen from m input variables $x_i (i \in Z_m)$ and a threshold s_i, where $L = L_1 \cdots L_k$, $L_t \in Z_m$, $t \in Z_k$ and $w_{i,L}$ is called a weight of products of k pieces of input variables. Then, each output of the elements, $y_i (i \in Z_n)$, is determined as follows.

$$y_i = f_i \left(\sum_{L \in Z_m^k} w_{i,L} \prod_{j=1}^{k} x_{L_j} + s_i \right) \qquad (1)$$

where f_i is an output function. If $k = 1$, the linear model is formed (Rumelhart & McClelland, 1986). Corresponding to y_i of Equation 1, we define a (global) mapping $G : Q^m \to Q^n$ as follows: Let $X = (x_1, x_2, \cdots, x_m) \in Q^m$

and

$$y_i = f_i \left(\sum_{L \in Z_m^k} w_{i,L} \prod_{j=1}^{k} x_{L_j} + s_i \right),$$

for $i \in Z_n$. Then $Y = (y_1, \cdots, y_n) \in Q^n$ and we define $G(X) = Y$. The vectors X and Y are called the states of the network.

In the case of the digital state model, when each of f_i's is any Boolean function, a global mapping composed of $f_i (i \in Z_n)$ is called a parallel mapping. It is clear that any Boolean function is represented by a higher order neural network, so any parallel mapping is also represented by a higher order neural network. The set of higher order neural networks also includes the set of cellular networks (Miyajima & Yatsuki, 1994).

Then, how is the macroscopic dynamics of higher order neural networks? In order to show it, we introduce the following statistical assumptions on the networks.

1. Any weight $w_{i[L]}$ is a random variable and is selected mutually independent from a probabilistic distribution.
2. Each threshold s_i is also a random variable and has a normal distribution with an average $\bar{s}$ and a variance σ_s.
3. The numbers m and n are sufficiently large.

Since $n \cdot (m^k + 1)$ parameters of the weights and the thresholds are random variables, the potentials are also random variables depending on them. We call the networks Randomly connected Higher Order Neural Networks (RHONNs).

TRANSFORMATION AND STABILITY OF THE NETWORKS

In this section, we define the activity of a state of a network as a macroscopic value and we statistically characterize the dynamics of the activity.

First, the activities $\bar{X}$ and $\bar{Y}$ of input X and output Y are defined as follows:

$$\bar{X} = \frac{1}{m} \sum_{i=1}^{m} x_i, \quad \bar{Y} = \frac{1}{n} \sum_{i=1}^{n} y_i, \qquad (2)$$

where $\min Q \le \bar{X}, \bar{Y} \le \max Q$.

In the following, we omit the overbar of $\bar{X}$ and $\bar{Y}$ for simplicity, and we use the expected value $\bar{w}$ and the variance σ_w^2 of weight $w_{i,L}$ rather than the value of weight $w_{i,L}$ in order to characterize the relation $Y = F(X)$ between input activity X and output activity Y. The parameters $\bar{w}$ and σ_w are defined as follows:

$$\bar{w} = m^k E[w_{i,L}], \quad \sigma_w^2 = m^k V[w_{i,L}], \qquad (3)$$

where $E[x]$ and $V[x]$ are the expected value and the variance of x, respectively. In the following subsections, we show the transformation and the stability of networks for the digital and analog models.

The Digital State $\{0,1\}$-Model

When $f_i = \text{sgn}$ and $Q = \{0,1\}$, Equation 1 is rewritten as follows:

$$y_i = \text{sgn}\left(\sum_{L \in Z_m^k} w_{i,L} \prod_{j=1}^{k} x_{L_j} + s_i \right), \qquad (4)$$

where $\text{sgn}(u) = 1$ for $u \ge 0$ and 0 for $u < 0$.

First, let us show the relation $Y = F(X)$ between input activity X and output activity Y. The following equation of the expected value $E[Y]$ over all networks holds from Equation A-1 in Appendix.

$$E[Y] = \frac{1}{n} E[\sum y_i] = E[y_i]$$

$$= 1 \times \Pr\{u_i \ge 0\} + 0 \times (1 - \Pr\{u_i \ge 0\})$$
$$= \Pr\{u_i \ge 0\},$$
$$(5)$$

where $u_i = \sum_{L \in Z_m^k} w_{i,L} \prod_{j=1}^{k} x_{L_j} + s_i$ and $\Pr\{u_i \ge 0\}$ means the probability that $u_i \ge 0$. The following equality holds.

$$V[Y] = \frac{1}{n^2} V[\sum y_i] = \frac{1}{n} V[y_i]$$

$$= \frac{1}{n}\left\{ E[y_i^2] - (E[y_i])^2 \right\} \qquad (6)$$

$$= \frac{1}{n}\left\{ E[Y](1 - E[Y]) \right\}$$

Since the variance of Y is in proportion to $1/n$, $Y = E[Y]$ holds for the sufficiently large n. Therefore, we must compute $E[Y]$, i.e. $\Pr\{u_i \geq 0\}$, in order to show the relation of $Y = F(X)$. Let us compute $\Pr\{u_i \geq 0\}$. Since m is sufficiently large, the Central Limit Theorem holds in this case (See Equation A-2 in Appendix). Therefore, the distribution of $\sum_{L \in Z_m^k} w_{i,L} \prod_{j=1}^{k} x_{L_j}$ is normal. From the assumption that s_i has the normal distribution, u_i has also normal one. Then the expected value and the variance of $u_i - s_i$ are computed by Equation 3 as follows:

$$E\left[\sum_{L \in Z_m^k} w_{i,L} \prod_{j=1}^{k} x_{L_j}\right] = \sum_{L \in Z_m^k} \left(\prod_{j=1}^{k} x_{L_j}\right) E[w_{i,L}]$$
$$= m^k X^k E[w_{i,L}] = \overline{w} X^k \quad (7)$$

$$V\left[\sum_{L \in Z_m^k} w_{i,L} \prod_{j=1}^{k} x_{L_j}\right] = \sum_{L \in Z_m^k} \left(\prod_{j=1}^{k} x_{L_j}\right)^2 V[w_{i,L}]$$
$$= \sigma_w^2 X^k \quad (8)$$

Therefore, the following equations for the expected value $\overline{u}$ and the variance σ^2 of u_i hold:

$$\overline{u} = \overline{w} X^k + \overline{s}, \; \sigma^2 = \sigma_w^2 X^k + \sigma_s^2 \quad (9)$$

As the distribution of u_i is normal, the probability $\Pr\{u_i \geq 0\}$ in Equation 5 is represented as follows.

$$\Pr\{u_i \geq 0\} = \Phi\left(\frac{\overline{u}}{\sigma}\right) \quad (10)$$

where

$$\Phi(u) = \frac{1}{\sqrt{2\pi}} \int_{-\infty}^{u} \exp\left[-\frac{z^2}{2}\right] dz. \quad (11)$$

From Equations 4, 9 and 10, the global transformation of activity, $F(X)$, is represented as follows (Miyajima et al., 1996):

$$Y = F(x) = \Phi\left(\frac{\overline{u}}{\sigma}\right) = \Phi\left(\frac{\overline{w} X^k + \overline{s}}{\sqrt{\sigma_x^2 X^k + \sigma_s^2}}\right) \quad (12)$$

Note that the activity X is included in both denominator and numerator for Equation 12.

Example 1

If $k = 1$, the following relation holds.

$$F(X) = \Phi\left(\frac{\overline{w} X + \overline{s}}{\sqrt{\sigma_w^2 X + \sigma_s^2}}\right)$$

If $k = 2$ and 3, the following relations hold.

$$F(X) = \Phi\left(\frac{\overline{w} X^2 + \overline{s}}{\sqrt{\sigma_w^2 X^2 + \sigma_s^2}}\right) \text{ for } k = 2,$$

$$F(X) = \Phi\left(\frac{\overline{w} X^3 + \overline{s}}{\sqrt{\sigma_w^2 X^3 + \sigma_s^2}}\right) \text{ for } k = 3.$$

Figure 2 shows graphs of the function $F(X)$ with $\overline{w} = 1$, $\overline{s} = 0$ and $\sigma_w^2 = \sigma_s^2 = 0.5$. As k increases, the graph changes rapidly. However, there is little difference of dynamics between the case of $k = 1$ and others in the digital state $\{0, 1\}$-model.

Next, let us consider the dynamics of the networks for the digital state $\{0, 1\}$-model by using Equation 12. Although the function $F(X)$ of Equation 12 has four parameters, $\overline{w}$, $\overline{s}$, σ_w, σ_s, the number of independent parameters is three. The reason is shown in the following. Let Z be defined as follows.

Figure 2. Transformations of activities of the networks for $k = 1, 2$ and 3 with $\overline{w} = 1$, $\overline{s} = 0$ and $\sigma_w^2 = \sigma_s^2 = 0.5$

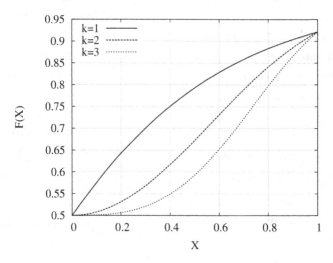

$$Z = \frac{\overline{w}X^2 + \overline{s}}{\sqrt{\sigma_w^2 X^2 + \sigma_s^2}}$$

$$= \frac{(\overline{w}X^k + \overline{s}) / \sigma_w}{\sqrt{X^k + (\sigma_s / \sigma_w)^2}}$$

From the above relation, Z depends on $\overline{w} / \sigma_w$, $\overline{s} / \sigma_w$, σ_s / σ_w as parameters. So, for any Z with $\overline{w}$, $\overline{s}$, σ_w, σ_s, we can select $\overline{w} / \sigma_w$, $\overline{s} / \sigma_w$, σ_s / σ_w as three parameters which realize the same value Z. This is the reason why the number of independent parameters is three. Therefore let us consider $\overline{w}$, $\overline{s}$ and the ratio σ_s^2 / σ_w^2 of σ_w^2 and σ_s^2 such that $\sigma_w^2 + \sigma_s^2 = 1$. Now let us consider two extreme cases, $(1)\sigma_w^2 \gg \sigma_s^2$ and $(2)\sigma_w^2 \ll \sigma_s^2$ such that $\sigma_w^2 = 0.99, \sigma_s^2 = 0.01$ and $\sigma_w^2 = 0.01, \sigma_s^2 = 0.99$ for $k = 1, 2, 3$. As a result, there exists little difference between the above cases (1) and (2). Therefore, we will consider only the case where $\sigma_w^2 + \sigma_s^2 = 1$, $0 \le \sigma_w^2 \le 1$ and $0 \le \sigma_s^2 \le 1$.

In the following, we show the stability of the networks by using the transformation F with the parameters $\overline{w}$, and $\overline{s}$ for fixed σ_w and σ_s. There-

fore, the transition of the network is represented by using the parameters $\overline{w}$, and $\overline{s}$ as follows:

$$X_{t+1} = F(X_t, \overline{w}, \overline{s}), [1]$$

where X_t means the state X at step t.

A network is called monostable when it has only one stable equilibrium state (of activity) to which any state (of activity) X converges. A network is called bistable when it has exactly two stable equilibrium states to either of which any state converges. Likewise, tristable with three stable equilibrium states is defined. A network is called non-equilibrium when there exists an initial state from which the network does not converge to any stable equilibrium state. Oscillatory network is a kind of non-equilibrium networks. In addition, there exist networks which are monostable (bistable or tristable) and non-equilibrium.

As is well known, equilibrium states are defined as the states satisfying the equation $F(X_0, \overline{w}, \overline{s}) = X_0$, that is, they are obtained as the intersections of two graphs $Y = F(X, \overline{w}, \overline{s})$ and $Y = X$. It is also known that an equilibrium state X_0 is stable when $|F'(X_0, \overline{w}, \overline{s})| < 1$ and unstable when $|F'(X_0, \overline{w}, \overline{s})| \ge 1$, where

$$\left|F'(X_0, \bar{w}, \bar{s})\right| = \frac{dF(X, \bar{w}, \bar{s})}{dX}\Bigg|_{X=X_0} .$$

Amari (1971, 1972, 1974) investigated the dynamics of RHONNs for $k = 1$, i.e. RNNs, in detail. For $k = 1$, it is shown that, there exist networks which are monostable, bistable and oscillatory with period 2.

Let us consider the case of $\sigma_w^2 = \sigma_s^2 = 0.5$. For $k = 2$, the following equation is obtained.

$$F(X_0, \bar{w}, \bar{s}) = \frac{1}{\sqrt{2\pi}} \int_{-\infty}^{\frac{\bar{w}X^2 + \bar{s}}{\sqrt{0.5X^2 + 0.5}}} \exp\left(-\frac{z^2}{2}\right) dz \tag{13}$$

$$F(X_0, \bar{w}, \bar{s}) = X_0 \tag{14}$$

In the case of Equations 13 and 14, it is impossible to solve it analytically. Therefore, the dynamics are calculated by numerical simulation based on Equation 13. Figure 3 shows the dynamics of the networks for $k = 1$ and $k = 2$. The case of $k = 3$ is almost the same result as the case of $k = 2$. For every cases, there exist only monostable, bistable, and oscillatory networks and the qualitative characteristics of the networks depend on parameters $\bar{w}$ and $\bar{s}$ only. The values of σ_w and σ_s determine only the coordinate of $\bar{w}$ which changes from being monostable to being bistable. There is little difference of dynamics between the case of $k = 1$ and the other cases. It suggests that the number of equilibrium states in HONNs does not increase so much with k.

The Digital State $\{-1, 1\}$-Model

When $f_i = \text{sign}$ and $Q = \{-1, 1\}$, Equation 1 is rewritten as follows:

$$y_i = \text{sign}\left(\sum_{L \in Z_m^k} w_{i,L} \prod_{j=1}^{k} x_{L_j} + s_i\right), \tag{15}$$

Figure 3. Stability of RHONNs in the digital state $\{0, 1\}$-model

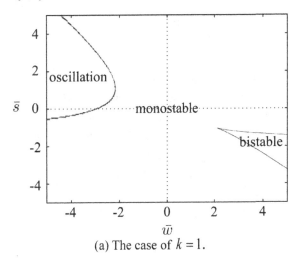

(a) The case of $k = 1$.

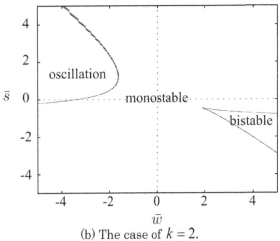

(b) The case of $k = 2$.

where $\text{sign}(u) = 1$ for $u \geq 0$ and -1 for $u < 0$.

Let us show the relation $Y = F(X)$ between input activity X and output activity Y. The following equation of the expected value $E[Y]$ over all networks holds as the same as Equation 5.

$$\begin{aligned}
E[Y] &= \frac{1}{n} E\left[\sum y_i\right] \\
&= 2 \times \Pr\{u_i \geq 0\} - 1
\end{aligned} \tag{16}$$

where $u_i = \sum_{L \in Z_m^k} w_{i,L} \prod_{j=1}^{k} x_{L_j} + s_i$. The following equality also holds.

$$V[Y] = \frac{1}{n^2} V\left[\sum y_i\right]$$

$$= \frac{1}{n} E[Y](1 - E[Y]) \tag{17}$$

Since the variance of Y is in proportion to $1/n$, $Y = E[Y]$ also holds for the sufficiently large n. Therefore, we must compute $E[Y]$, i.e. $\Pr\{u_i \geq 0\}$, in order to show the relation of $Y = F(X)$. Let us compute $\Pr\{u_i \geq 0\}$. Since m is sufficiently large, the Central Limit Theorem holds in this case (See the Equation A-2 in Appendix). Therefore, the distribution of $\sum_{L \in Z_m^k} w_{i,L} \prod_{j=1}^k x_{L_j}$ is normal. Then the expected value and the variance of $u_i - s_i$ are computed by Equation 3 as follows:

$$E\left[\sum_{L \in Z_m^k} w_{i,L} \prod_{j=1}^k x_{L_j}\right] = m^k X^k E\left[w_{i,L}\right] = \bar{w} X^k \tag{18}$$

$$V\left[\sum_{L \in Z_m^k} w_{i,L} \prod_{j=1}^k x_{L_j}\right] = m^k V\left[w_{i,L}\right] = \sigma_w^2, \tag{19}$$

where $x^2 = 1$ for any input x. Therefore, the following equations for the expected value $\bar{u}$ and the variance σ^2 of u_i hold:

$$\bar{u} = \bar{w} X^k + \bar{s}, \quad \sigma^2 = \sigma_w^2 + \sigma_s^2 \tag{20}$$

From the above relation, the probability $\Pr\{u_i \geq 0\}$ in Equation 16 is represented as follows:

$$\Pr\{u_i \geq 0\} = \Phi\left(\frac{\bar{u}}{\sigma}\right), \tag{21}$$

From Equations 16, 20, and 21, the global transformation of activity, $F(X)$, is represented as follows (Miyajima, et al., 1995):

$$F(X) = 2\Phi\left(\frac{\bar{u}}{\sigma}\right) - 1$$

$$= 2\Phi\left(\frac{\bar{w} X + \bar{s}}{\sqrt{\sigma_w^2 + \sigma_s^2}}\right) - 1 \tag{22}$$

Example 2

If $k = 1$, the following relation holds (Amari, 1972).

$$F(X) = 2\Phi\left(\frac{\bar{w} X + \bar{s}}{\sqrt{\sigma_w^2 + \sigma_s^2}}\right) - 1$$

If $k = 2$ and 3, the following relation holds, respectively.

$$F(X) = 2\Phi\left(\frac{\bar{w} X^2 + \bar{s}}{\sqrt{\sigma_w^2 + \sigma_s^2}}\right) - 1 \text{ for } k = 2$$

$$F(X) = 2\Phi\left(\frac{\bar{w} X^3 + \bar{s}}{\sqrt{\sigma_w^2 + \sigma_s^2}}\right) - 1 \text{ for } k = 3$$

As is shown later, if k is odd, then $F(X)$ is similar to the case of $k = 1$, and if k is even, then $F(X)$ is similar to parabola. From this viewpoint, one may say that, depending on whether k is even or not, the qualitative properties of them are different.

Next, let us consider the dynamics of networks. First, let us normalize $\bar{w}$ and $\bar{s}$ as follows:

$$W = \frac{\bar{w}}{\sqrt{\sigma_w^2 + \sigma_s^2}}, \quad S = \frac{\bar{s}}{\sqrt{\sigma_w^2 + \sigma_s^2}}$$

From this, we can substitute two parameters for four parameters. Now, W and S are new macroscopic parameters. Then, Equation 22 is transformed into Equation 23.

$$F(X_t, W, S) = 2\Phi(WX_t^k + S) - 1 \qquad (23)$$

Let $\Psi(X) = 2\Phi(X) - 1$. Then, Equation 24 holds.

$$X_{t+1} = \Psi\left(WX_t^k + S\right) \qquad (24)$$

In the following, we show the stability of the networks by using the transformation F with the parameters W and S. As discussed in the case of $\{0,1\}$-model, the stability of the graph $F(X, W, S)$ is obtained by investigating $\max |F'(X, W, S)| = 1$.

Figure 4 shows the area of monostable networks obtained by solving the equation.

Next, let us consider the case of $\max |F'(X, W, S)| \geq 1$. In order to investigate the dynamics for this case, the relation between W and S satisfying the following equations must be shown:

$$F(X_0, W, S) = \sqrt{\frac{2}{\pi}} \int_0^{WX_0^2 + S} \exp\left(-\frac{z^2}{2}\right) dz \qquad (25)$$

$$F(X_0, W, S) = X_0 \qquad (26)$$

It is, however, impossible to solve it analytically. Instead, Figure 5 shows the dynamics for W and S obtained by numerical simulation. The dynamics is explained in Figure 5(b). For $S = 2$, let W be changed as follows. When W is small, for example $W = 0, -1$ or -2, the number of intersections of two graphs $Y = F(X, W, S)$ and $Y = X$ is one, where $|F'(X_0, W, S)| < 1$ for $W = 0$ and -1, that is the network are monos-

Figure 4. The area of monostable networks: the graph is obtained by solving $\max |F'(X, W, S)| = 1$.

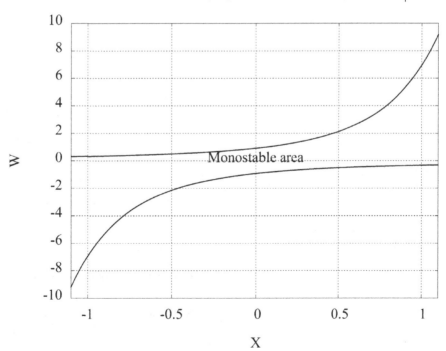

Figure 5. Stability of RHONNs for $k = 1, 2, 3$ in the digital state $\{-1, 1\}$-models: by numerical calculation, the number of intersections between $Y = F(X)$ and $Y = X$ is determined and classified based on whether they are stable or not

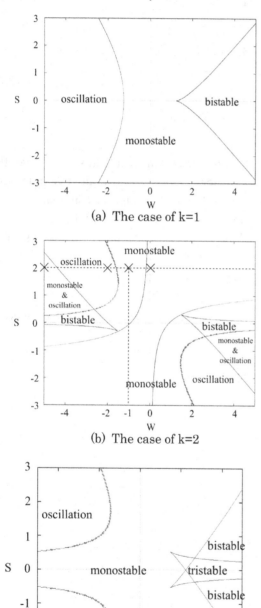

(a) The case of k=1

(b) The case of k=2

(c) The case of k=3

table, and $|F'(X_0, W, S)| < -1$ for $W = -2$, that is the network is non equilibrium. When W is large, for example $W = -5$, the number of intersections of the graphs are three which are a stable point and two unstable points (see Figure 6). Note that $F(X, W, S)$ changes rapidly as W increases. As well, the dynamics for $k = 3$ is obtained by numerical simulation.

The qualitative properties for $k = 3$ are similar to the ones for $k = 1$, though there exist tristable networks. Note that the number of equilibrium states for $k = 3$ is larger than the one for $k = 1$. In the Case of $k = 2$ there exist networks, which are monostable and oscillatory, and neither equilibrium state nor oscillatory. The qualitative properties for $k = 2$ are different from the ones for $k = 1$. We will deal with these networks in the section of Behavior of Non-Equilibrium RHONNs.

At the end of this Section, we describe the relation between the activity X and the threshold S. As the equilibrium state X_0 determined by Equation 22 depends on W and S, the relation between X_0, W and S is represented as follows:

$$X_0 = g(S, W) \tag{27}$$

In the case of $k = 2$ with a fixed W, the relation between X_0 and S is shown in Figure 7. In the figure, X_0 is three-valued function when the absolute of W is large (at least $|W| > 2$), and one-valued function when the absolute of W is small ($|W| < 1$). The case of $k = 3$ is shown in the Figure 8. In the figure, X_0 is one-valued function for $W \leq 0$, and one-, three- or five-valued function for $0 < W < 3$, and five-valued function for $W \geq 3$.

The Analog State Models

First, let us consider the case where Q is the set of all real numbers from 0 to 1 and an output

Figure 6. A figure to explain the Figure 5: as W increases, the number of intersections of graphs $Y = F(X,W,S)$ *and* $Y = X$ *increases*

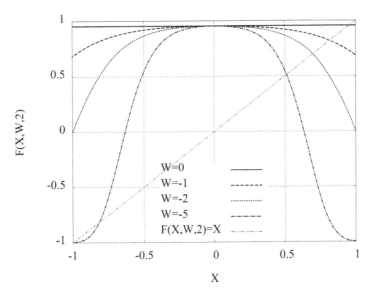

Figure 7. A figure to explain the relation $X_0 = g(S,W)$ *for* $k = 2$

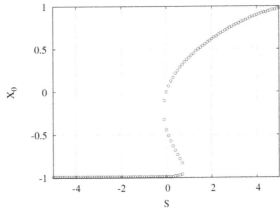

(a). Three-valued function for a large absolute value of W

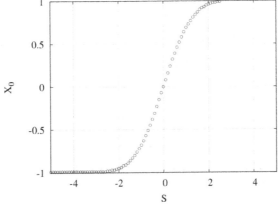

(b) One-valued function for a small absolute value of W

Figure 8. A figure to explain the relation $X_0 = g(S, W)$ *for* $k = 3$

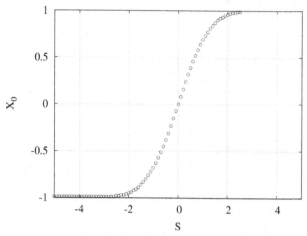

(a) One-valued function for $W = 0$

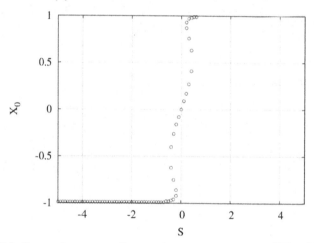

(b) One-, three-, or five-valued function for $W = 2.0$

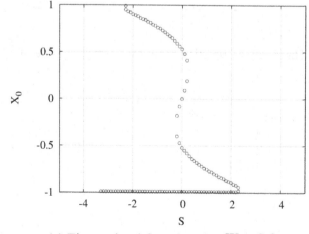

(c) Five-valued function for $W = 5.0$

function f_i is $0 \le f_i(u) \le 1$ and monotone increasing. Then, the following relation holds for the expected value $\bar{u}$ and the variance σ^2 of u_i.

$$\bar{u} = E[u_i] = \bar{w}X^k + \bar{s},$$

$$\sigma^2 = V\left[\sum_{L \in Z_m^k} w_{i,L} \prod_{j=1}^k x_{L_j}\right] + \sigma_s^2$$

$$= \sum_{L \in Z_m^k} \left(\prod_{j=1}^k x_{L_j}\right)^2 V[W_{i,L}] + \sigma_s^2$$

$$= \sigma_w^2 \frac{1}{m^k} \sum_{L \in Z_m^k} \left(\prod_{j=1}^k x_{L_j}\right)^2 + \sigma_s^2 \qquad (28)$$

$$= \sigma_w^2 \left(\frac{1}{m}\sum_{j=1}^m x_j^2\right)^2 + \sigma_s^2$$

$$= \sigma_w^2 \tilde{X}^k + \sigma_s^2,$$

where $\tilde{X} = \dfrac{1}{m}\displaystyle\sum_{j=1}^m x_j^2$

From Equation 28, the distribution of u_i depends on not only activity of input but also the expected value of squares of input, $\tilde{X}$ In order to reduce the number of variables, let us consider to represent $\tilde{X}$ by using X. $\tilde{X}$ is, however, not represented directly by using X. Therefore we introduce X_v which is the variance of x_j.

$$X_v = \frac{1}{m}\sum_{j=1}^m (x_j - X)^2 = \tilde{X} - X^2 \qquad (29)$$

Then σ^2 is rewritten as follows:

$$\sigma^2 = \sigma_w^2(X_v + X^2)^k + \sigma_s^2$$

As $0 \le X_V \le X(1-X)$, the following equation holds.

$$\sigma_w^2 X^{2k} + \sigma_s^2 \le \sigma^2 \le \sigma_w^2 X^k + \sigma_s^2 \qquad (30)$$

Therefore, from Equation 30, we will approximate the variance σ^2 as two values of $\sigma_2^2 = \sigma_w^2 X^{2k} + \sigma_s^2$ and $\sigma_1^2 = \sigma_w^2 X^k + \sigma_s^2$. Now let us assume that an output function $f(u)$ is represented as follows:

$$f(u) = \begin{cases} 0 & (u \le 0) \\ u/a & (0 < u < a) \\ 1 & (a \le a) \end{cases} \qquad (31)$$

Then the average of y_i for the analog state $[0,1]$-model is as follows:

$$E[y_i] = E[f(u)] = \int f(u)p(u)du, \qquad (32)$$

where $p(u)$ is the normal distribution function represented as follows.

$$p(u) = \frac{1}{\sqrt{2\pi}\sigma}\exp\left(-\frac{(u-\bar{u})^2}{2\sigma^2}\right) \qquad (33)$$

When n is sufficiently large, the following holds from the Central Limit Theorem by using the same way as Equation 6.

$$Y = E(f(u)) \qquad (34)$$

Equation 34 is computed as follows:

$$Y = F(X) = \int_{-\infty}^0 0 \times p(u)du$$

$$+ \int_0^a \frac{u}{a}p(u)du + \int_a^\infty 1 \times p(u)du \qquad (35)$$

$$\int_0^a \frac{u}{a} p(u) du =$$

Hence, Equation 36 is obtained (Miyajima, et al., 1996).

$$\frac{\sigma}{\sqrt{2\pi a}} \left[\exp\left(-\frac{\bar{u}^2}{2\sigma^2}\right) - \exp\left(-\frac{(a-\bar{u})^2}{2\sigma^2}\right) \right]$$

$$Y = F(X) = \frac{\sigma}{\sqrt{2\pi a}} [E_2 - E_1]$$

$$+ \left[\Phi\left(\frac{a-\bar{u}}{\sigma}\right) - \Phi\left(\frac{-\bar{u}}{\sigma}\right) \right]$$

$$+ \left(\frac{\bar{u}}{a} - 1\right)\Phi_1 - \frac{\bar{u}}{a}\Phi_2 + 1,$$

(36)

$$\int_a^\infty 1 \times p(u) du = \Pr\{a < u\} = 1 - \Phi\left(\frac{a-\bar{u}}{\sigma}\right)$$

Figure 9. Transformations of activities of two extreme networks with (1) $\sigma_1^2 = \sigma_w^2 X^k + \sigma_w^2$ *and (2)* $\sigma_2^2 = \sigma_w^2 X^{2k} + \sigma_s^2$ *for* $\sigma_w^2 = 1$, $\sigma_s^2 = 1$, $a = 2$, $\bar{w} = 6$, $\bar{s} = -2.5$, *as* σ^2

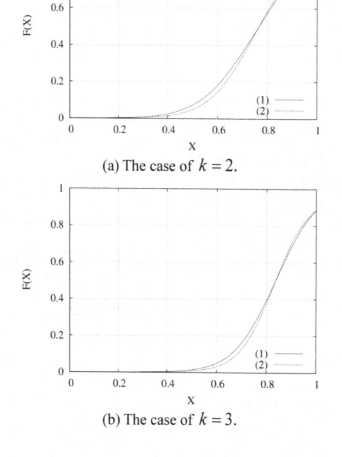

(a) The case of $k = 2$.

(b) The case of $k = 3$.

Figure 10. Stability of RHONNs in the analog state $[0,1]$-*model*

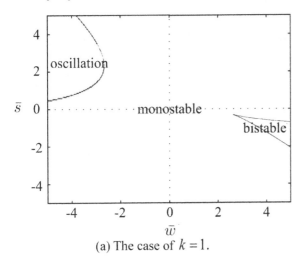

(a) The case of $k = 1$.

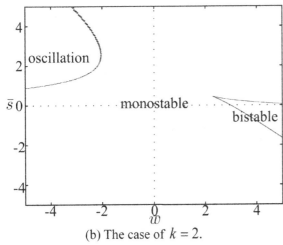

(b) The case of $k = 2$.

where $\Phi_1 = \Phi\left(\dfrac{a - \overline{u}}{\sigma}\right)$, $\Phi_2 = \Phi\left(\dfrac{-\overline{u}}{\sigma}\right)$,

$E_2 = \exp\left(-\dfrac{\overline{u}^2}{2\sigma^2}\right)$, $E_1 = \exp\left(-\dfrac{(a - \overline{u})^2}{2\sigma^2}\right)$.

Figure 9 shows two graphs, (1) and (2), for $k = 2$ and 3 with σ_1^2 and σ_2^2 as σ^2, respectively. Since there is little difference between the graphs (1) and (2), we use σ_1^2 as σ^2 Therefore, by using the same method as the case of digital state $\{0, 1\}$-model, dynamics is shown as Figure 10. It is shown that the obtained results are the same ones as the case of the digital state $\{0, 1\}$-model, that

is, dynamics of the networks of this case is monostable, bistable and oscillatory with period 2.

Next, let us consider the case where Q is the set of all real numbers from -1 to 1 and a output function f_i is $-1 \leq f_i(u) \leq 1$ and monotone increasing. Then, the following relation holds in the same way as the case of the analog state $[0, 1]$-model.

$$\overline{u} = \overline{w}X^k + \overline{s}$$

$$\sigma^2 = \sigma_w^2(X_V + X^2)^k + \sigma_s^2 \tag{37}$$

However, as $X_V \leq X(1 - X)$ does not hold in this case, we will approximate σ by the following two cases.

$$\sigma_0^2 = \sigma_w^2 + \sigma_s^2, \quad \sigma_2^2 = \sigma_w^2 X^{2k} + \sigma_s^2, \tag{38}$$

because $\sigma_w^2 X^{2k} + \sigma_s^2 \leq \sigma^2 \leq \sigma_w^2 + \sigma_s^2$.

Assume that the output function $f(u)$ is as follows:

$$f(u) = \begin{cases} -1 & (u \leq -a) \\ u / a & (-a < u < a) \\ 1 & (a \leq u) \end{cases} \tag{39}$$

Then we can get the following result by using the same method as the case of the analog state $[0, 1]$-model.

$$Y = F(X) = \int_{-\infty}^{-a} (-1) \times p(u)du$$
$$\tag{40}$$
$$+ \int_{-a}^{a} \frac{u}{a} p(u)du + \int_{a}^{\infty} 1 \times p(u)du$$

$$\int_{-\infty}^{a} (-1) \times p(u)du = -\Phi\left(\dfrac{-a - \overline{u}}{\sigma}\right),$$

$$\int_{-a}^{a} \frac{u}{a} p(u) du =$$

$$\frac{\sigma}{\sqrt{2\pi}a}\left[\exp\left(-\frac{(-a-\bar{u})^2}{2\sigma^2}\right) - \exp\left(-\frac{(a-\bar{u})^2}{2\sigma^2}\right)\right]$$

$$+\frac{\bar{u}}{a}\left[\Phi\left(\frac{a-\bar{u}}{\sigma}\right) - \Phi\left(\frac{-a-\bar{u}}{\sigma}\right)\right],$$

$$\int_{a}^{\infty} 1 * p(u) du = 1 - \Phi\left(\frac{a-\bar{u}}{\sigma}\right).$$

Therefore, the following relation holds (Miyajima, et al., 1996).

$$Y = F(X) = \frac{\sigma}{\sqrt{2\pi}a}[E_3 - E_1]$$

$$+\left(\frac{\bar{u}}{a} - 1\right)\Phi_1 - \left(\frac{\bar{u}}{a} + 1\right)\Phi_3 + 1,$$

(41)

where

$$\Phi_3 = \Phi\left(\frac{-a-\bar{u}}{\sigma}\right)$$

Figure 11. Transformations of activities of two extreme networks with (1) $\sigma_0^2 = \sigma_w^2 + \sigma_s^2$ and (2) $\sigma_2^2 = \sigma_w^2 X^{2k} + \sigma_s^2$ for $\sigma_w^2 = 0.5$, $\sigma_s^2 = 1$, $a = 1$, $\bar{w} = 6$, and $\bar{s} = 0.2$

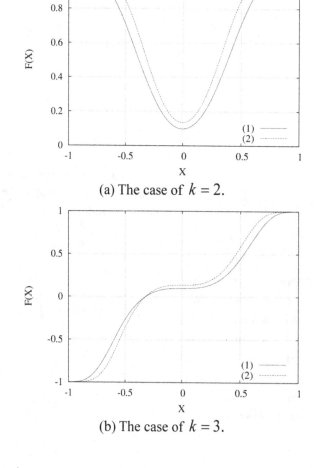

(a) The case of $k = 2$.

(b) The case of $k = 3$.

Figure 12. Stability of RHONNs in the analog state $[-1,1]$-*model*

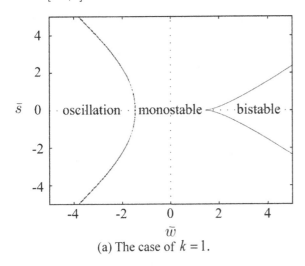

(a) The case of $k = 1$.

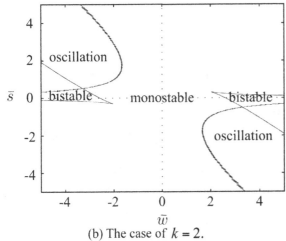

(b) The case of $k = 2$.

and $E_3 = \exp\left(-\dfrac{(-a - \bar{u})^2}{2\sigma^2}\right)$.

In this case, there exist monostable, bistable, tristable and non-equilibrium networks as the same as the case of the digital state $\{-1,1\}$-model. The graphs, (1) and (2), for $k = 2$ and 3 with σ_0 and σ_2 as σ are shown in Figure 11. Although there is a little difference between two cases with the graphs, (1) and (2), we will neglect the difference in order to get the qualitative properties of networks. So, dynamics of the networks of the cases for $k = 1, 2$ with σ_2 as σ are shown in the Figure 12. The case of $k = 3$ is almost the same result as Figure 5(c). As a result, it is shown

that dynamics of the analog $[-1,1]$-model is very similar to one of the digital $\{-1,1\}$-model. Therefore, it is shown that there is little difference of dynamics between analog and digital models.

Behavior of Non-Equilibrium RHONNs

Let us consider the dynamics of non-equilibrium RHONNs. Let J be an interval and let $H : J \to J$ be a mapping. For $x \in J$, $H^0(x) = x$, and $H^{n+1}(x) = H(H^n(x))$ for $n = 0, 1, 2, \cdots$. A point p is called periodic or a periodic point with period n if $p \in J$ and $p = H^n(p)$ and $p \neq H^k(p)$ for $1 \leq k < n$.[2] A point p is called periodic or a periodic point if p is periodic for some $n \geq 1$. A point q is (eventually) periodic if for some positive integer m, $p = H^m(q)$ is a periodic point.

In the case of $k = 1$, it is known that any state of any oscillated RNN is periodic with period 2 (Amari, 1972).

Then, how is the case of $k > 1$? Let us explain that the case of $k = 2$ is different one of $k = 1$.

First, let us consider Figure 13 of the transformation F with $W = -4$, $S = 2.5$ in the digital state $\{-1,1\}$-model with $k = 2$. Then the point -0.826 is periodic with period 3 as shown in Figure 13. Is this the special case? In fact, many cases have the period more than or equal to 3 in non-equilibrium RHONNs with $k = 2$.

By the numerical simulation with starting point -0.5 until $n = 1000$ step, the sequence $\{F^n(-0.5) \mid n \in I\}$ are classified into three cases, (1) period 2^n for some $n \geq 1$, (2) $m > 1$ is not the power of 2, and (3) not periodic.

Remark that the period of the sequence $\{F^n(-0.5) \mid n \in I\}$ is at most 2^m in the case of the digital state $\{-1,1\}$-model, as the number of neurons is m. However, there does not exist such restriction in the case of the analog state $[-1,1]$-model. The three cases for the sequence $\{F^n(-0.5) \mid 0 \leq n \leq 500\}$ in the analog state $[-1,1]$-model with $k = 2$, $a = 1$, $\sigma_w^2 = 0.5$, and $\sigma_s^2 = 1.0$ are shown in Figure 14. Figure 14(c)

Figure 13. An example of a point with period 3: the point $a = -0.826$ is periodic with period 3 and the point -0.5 is eventually periodic under the transformation F with $W = -4$ and $S = 2.5$

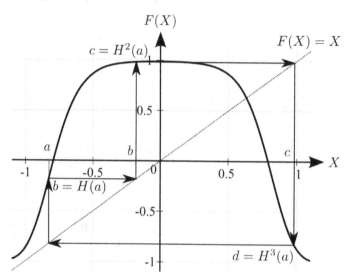

and a part of Figure 14(b) may exist a chaotic network. For the case of $k = 3$, it seems that there is no such area. This is because, in order to exist complex dynamics such as chaotic one, symmetric curves such as parabola are needed. However the graph of the case of $k = 3$ is similar to the case of $k = 1$ rather than the case of $k = 2$.

We conjecture that (1) there exist chaotic networks in the case where k is even, and (2) non-equilibrium networks are oscillatory with period 1 or 2 in the case where k is odd.

At the end of the section, let us consider whether Chaos Assumption holds or not.

Let us consider the states:

$$X(0) = (x_1, x_2, \cdots, x_n)$$

and

$$Y_i = (y_1^i, y_2^i, \cdots, y_n^i) \in Q$$

such that $Y_i = G^i(X(0))$ for $i = 1, 2, \cdots$, where G is a global mapping defined by Equation 1. Let the activities of the state $X(0)$ and Y_i be defined by $\bar{X} = \dfrac{1}{n}\sum_{j=1}^{n} x_j$ and $\bar{Y}_i = \dfrac{1}{n}\sum_{j=1}^{n} y_j^i$, respec-

tively. Let F be a global transformation of the activities. Then Chaos Assumption holds if $F^i(\bar{X}) \approx \bar{Y}_i$ for $i = 2, 3, \cdots,$. That is the activities of the states after transitions by G nearly equals to the activities after transitions by F^i. As it is difficult to prove theoretically the relation for $i = 2, 3, \cdots,$ some numerical simulations has been performed. Figure 15 shows the results of $\bar{Y}_1$, $\bar{Y}_4$ and $\bar{Y}_7$ for input $X(0)$'s for $k = 1$. The results show $F^1(\bar{X}) \approx \bar{Y}_1$, $F^4(\bar{X}) \approx \bar{Y}_4$ and $F^7(\bar{X}) \approx \bar{Y}_7$. Figures 16 and 17 show that the relation holds for $k = 2$ and 3, respectively. As a result, it seems that Chaos Assumption holds for $k = 1, 2, 3$ from numerical simulations.

DYNAMICS OF GROUPS OF RHONNS

In this section, we describe the dynamics of groups composed of RHONNs. We consider systems composed of a plural RHONNs connected mutually and multi-layered systems composed of a plural kinds of RHONNs.

Figure 14. Classification for oscillated RHONNs for the analog state $[-1,1]$-model with $k = 2$, $a = 1$, $\sigma_w^2 = 0.5$, and $\sigma_s^2 = 1.0$

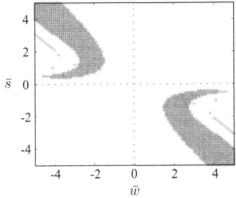

(a) The case with period 2^n for some $n \geq 2$.

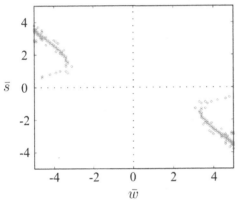

(b) The case with $m > 1$, where m is not the power of 2.

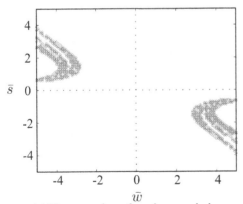

(c) The case where there is no period.

Dynamics of Interconnected Groups

In this section, we consider systems composed of a plural RHONNs connected mutually. Figure 18 shows a system composed of m pieces of subnetworks. Each network N_α is a kind of RHONNs and its dynamics has already been shown.

First let us consider the case of the digital state $\{-1,1\}$-model. Let s_i^α and n_α be the threshold and the number of elements for subnetwork N_α, respectively. Then let the potential of the i-th element for n_α be denoted by u_i^α as follows.

$$u_i^\alpha = \sum_{\beta=1}^{m} \sum_{L_\beta \in Z^{k_\beta}} w_{i,L_\beta}^{\alpha\beta} \prod_{j=1}^{k_\beta} x_{l_j}^\beta + s_i^\alpha, \qquad (42)$$

where $L_\beta = l_1 \cdots l_{k_\beta}$, $l_j \in Z_m$ $(j \in Z_{k_\beta})$, and $x_{l_j}^\beta$ is a state of the l_j-th element for N_β. Note that the product $x_{l_1}^\beta \cdots x_{l_{k_\beta}}^\beta$ with the weight $w_{i,L_\beta}^{\alpha\beta}$ as a coefficient is input to the i-th element for N_α. From the assumption of networks, any weight $w_{i,L_\beta}^{\alpha\beta}$ and any threshold s_i^α are selected mutually independent from a probabilistic distribution. Further, assume that the probabilistic distribution of $w_{i,L_\beta}^{\alpha\beta}$ depends on α and β, but not on i and L_β. Now let us approximate u_i^α by a normal distribution. Assume that a distribution of s_i^α is the normal one with the expected value $\bar{s}_\alpha$ and the variance $\sigma_{s\alpha}^2$ as follows.

$$\bar{s}_\alpha = \mathrm{E}\left[s_i^\alpha\right], \quad \sigma_{s\alpha}^2 = \mathrm{V}\left[s_i^\alpha\right] \qquad (43)$$

In the same method as Equationd 18 and 19, we use the expected value and the variance of weights rather than each value of weights. So, we define Equations 44 and 45. Let $w_i^{\alpha\beta}$ be defined as follows.

Figure 15. Comparison between $F(X,W,S)$ *and simulation results for* $k=1$, $W=3.16$, *and* $S=0$

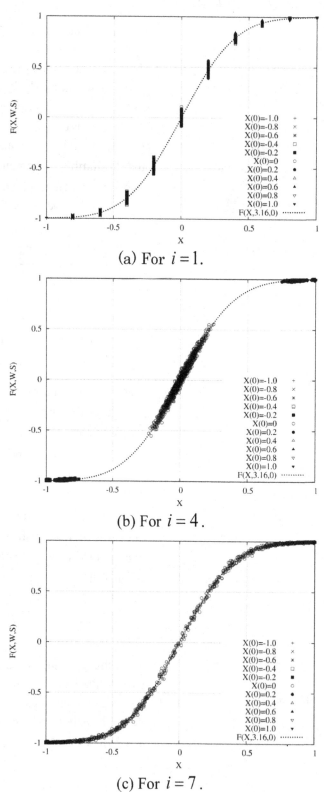

(a) For $i=1$.

(b) For $i=4$.

(c) For $i=7$.

Figure 16. Comparison between $F(X,W,S)$ and simulation results for $k = 2$, $W = 8.0$ and $S = 0$

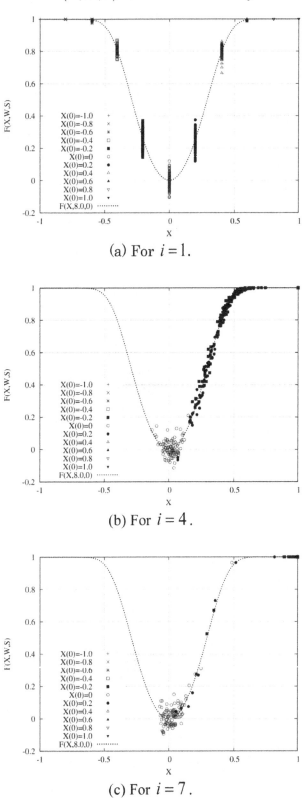

(a) For $i = 1$.

(b) For $i = 4$.

(c) For $i = 7$.

Figure 17. Comparison between $F(X, W, S)$ *and simulation results for* $k = 3$, $W = 10.0$ *and* $S = 0$

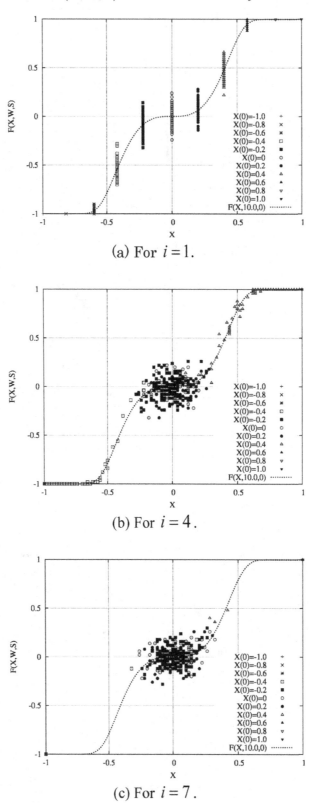

(a) For $i = 1$.

(b) For $i = 4$.

(c) For $i = 7$.

Figure 18. A system composed of m pieces of subnetworks

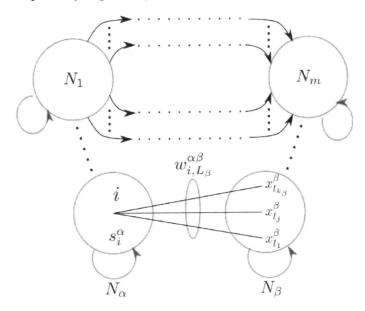

$$w_i^{\alpha\beta} = \sum_{L_\beta} w_{i,L_\beta}^{\alpha\beta} \tag{44}$$

Then, the expected value and covariance for $w_i^{\alpha\beta}$ are defined as follows.

$$E[w_i^{\alpha\beta}] = \bar{w}_{\alpha\beta}, \quad V[w_i^{\alpha\beta}] = \sigma_{\alpha\beta}^2 \tag{45}$$

Further, the activity for the subnet N_α is represented as follows.

$$X_\alpha = \frac{1}{n_\alpha} \sum_{i=1}^{n_\alpha} x_i^\alpha \tag{46}$$

As a result, corresponding to Equation 20, the following equation is obtained by using the same method as the case of digital state $\{-1, 1\}$-model.

$$\bar{u}^\alpha = E[u_i^\alpha] = \sum_{\beta=1}^{m} \bar{w}_{\alpha\beta} X_\beta^{k_\beta} + \bar{s}_\alpha$$

$$\sigma_\alpha^2 = V[u_i^\alpha] = \sum_{\beta=1}^{m} \sigma_{\alpha\beta}^2 + \sigma_{s\alpha}^2 \tag{47}$$

Therefore, the following equation is obtained by using Ψ of Equation 24.

$$F(X_\alpha) = \Psi \left(\frac{\sum_{\beta=1}^{m} \bar{w}_{\alpha\beta} X_\beta^{k_\beta} + \bar{s}_\alpha}{\sigma_\alpha} \right) \tag{48}$$

It follows from Equation 48 that the transition of the activity X_α for N_α depends on the activity X_β for subnet N_β which connects to N_α. Let $w_{\alpha\beta} = \dfrac{\bar{w}_{\alpha\beta}}{\sigma_\alpha}$ and $s_\alpha = \dfrac{\bar{s}_\alpha}{\sigma_\alpha}$. Then Equation 48 is rewritten as follows:

Figure 19. with $w_{11} = w_{12} = 1$, $s_1 = 0$

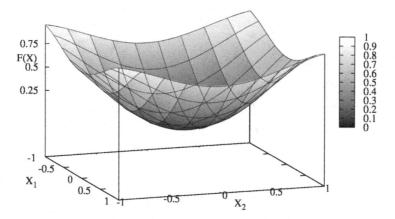

Figure 19. with $w_{11} = w_{12} = 1$, $s_1 = 0$

$$F(X_a) = \Psi\left(\sum_{\beta=1}^{m} w_{\alpha\beta} X_{\beta}^{k_\beta} + s_\alpha\right)$$

(49)

$$= \Psi\left(w_{\alpha\alpha} X_{\beta}^{k_\alpha} + \sum_{\beta=1,\beta\neq\alpha}^{m} w_{\alpha\beta} X_{\beta}^{k_\beta} + s_\alpha\right)$$

It follows from Equation 49 that the transition of activity X_α for N_α depends on the activity X_α and the activity X_β for another subnet N_β. We will take an example to explain Equation 49.

Example 3

Let $m = 3$, $k_1 = k_2 = 2$.

$$F(X_1) = \Psi(w_{11}X_1^2 + w_{12}X_2^2 + s_1)$$ (50)

$$F(X_2) = \Psi(w_{22}X_2^2 + w_{21}X_1^2 + s_2)$$ (51)

Figure 19 shows an example of $F(X_1)$ with $w_{11} = w_{12} = 1$ and $s_1 = 0$.

From Equation 50, $F(X_1)$ depends on the sum of the states X_1^2 with the weight w_{11} and $s_1^* = w_{12}X_2^2 + s_1$. So we will consider s_1^* as a threshold of Equation 50. For Equation 51, we also consider $s_2^* = w_{21}X_1^2 + s_2$ as a threshold of

Figure 20. Two intersecting curves of g_1 and g_2, where the number of intersections is 25

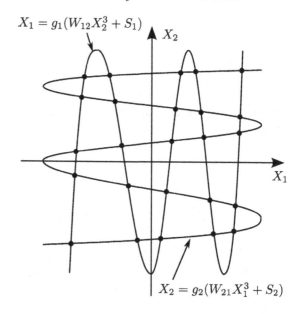

the Equation 51. Let us investigate equilibrium states of the network for Equations 50 and 51. As is shown in Equation 27 of digital state $\{-1, 1\}$-model, equilibrium states X_1^* and X_2^* for the networks N_1 and N_2 depend on s_1^*, w_{11} and s_2^*, w_{22}, respectively. The relation is represented as follows:

$$X_1^* = g\left(s_1^*, w_{11}\right) = g_1(s_1^*)$$
$$X_2^* = g\left(s_2^*, w_{22}\right) = g_2(s_2^*)$$

$$(52)$$

When we consider X_1^* and X_2^* as function of X_2^* and X_1^*, respectively, each graph is one that expands and contracts the graph $g(X, w_{\alpha\alpha})$ to $1 / w_{\alpha\beta}$ times in the horizontal direction and shifts it by $s_\alpha / w_{\alpha\beta}$. We can draw the graph g_1 by taking X_1 as the vertical axis and X_2 as the horizontal axis, and graph g_2 by taking X_2 as the vertical axis and X_1 as the horizontal axis. Intersections between two graphs g_1 and g_2, are equilibrium states. Corresponding to various kinds of graphs as shown in Figure 7, the number of intersections is ranging from 1 to 9. As well, in the case of $m = 2$, $k_1 = k_2 = 3$ by using Figure 8, the number of intersections is ranging from 1 to 25 (See Figure 20). It means that the number of equilibrium states is determined by each of RHONNs.

In the case of the digital state $\{0,1\}$-model, the following equation holds corresponding to

Equation 49 by using the same method as digital state $\{0,1\}$-model.

$$F(X_a) = \Phi\left(\frac{\displaystyle\sum_{\beta=1}^m \bar{w}_{\alpha\beta} X_\beta^{k_\beta} + \bar{s}_\alpha}{\sigma_\alpha}\right)$$

$$(53)$$

where $\sigma_\alpha^2 = V[u_i^\alpha] = \displaystyle\sum_{\beta=1}^m \sigma_{\alpha\beta}^2 X_\beta^{k_\beta} + \sigma_{s\alpha}^2$.

In the case of the analog state models, the following variance is substituted for Equations 36 and 41.

$$\sigma_\alpha^2 = \sum_{\beta=1}^m \sigma_{\alpha\beta}^2 \tilde{X}_\beta^{k_\beta} + \sigma_{s\alpha}^2$$

$$(54)$$

Dynamics of Multi-Layered Groups

Then, is a network with complex dynamics such as chaotic networks constructed by combining simple RHONNs with $k = 1$? In this section we

Figure 21. A three-layered system composed of input, hidden and output layers, where each of hidden and output layers is another kind of RHONN

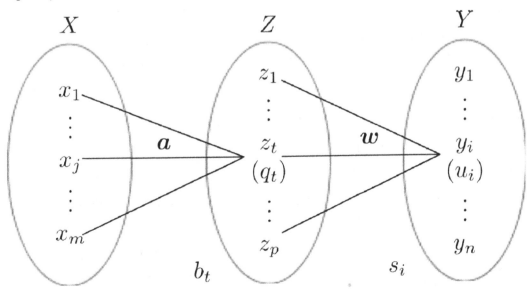

consider three-layered systems as an example of multi-layered groups. First let us consider Figure 21 as a three-layered system, in the digital state $[-1,1]$-model Let $X = (x_1, \cdots, x_m)$, $Z = (z_1, \cdots, z_p)$, and $Y = (y_1, \cdots, y_n)$ be states of input, hidden, and output layers, respectively. Let q_t, b_t, u_i, and s_i be the potential and threshold of $z_t (t \in Z_p)$ and $y_i (i \in Z_n)$, respectively. Let a_{tj} and w_{it} be the weights to the t-th element of Z from the j-th element of X and the i-th element of Y from the t-th element of Z, respectively. Then y_i and z_t are represented as follows:

$$y_i = \text{sgn}(u_i)$$

$$= \text{sgn}\left(\sum_{L_z \in Z_p^{k_1}} w_{i,L_z} \prod_{j=1}^{k_1} z_{l_j} + s_i \right) \tag{55}$$

$$z_{ti} = \text{sgn}(q_t)$$

$$= \text{sgn}\left(\sum_{L_x \in Z_m^{k_2}} w_{i,L_z} \prod_{j=1}^{k_2} x_{l_j} + b_t \right) \tag{56}$$

where $L_z = l_1 \cdots l_{k_1}, l_j \in Z_p$, $L_x = l_1 \cdots l_{k_2}$, $l_t \in Z_m$, and $w_{i,L_z}(a_t, L_x)$ is a weight of products of $k_1 (k_2)$ pieces of variables. And let the expected value and covariance for w_{it} and a_{tj} be defined as follows.

$$\bar{w} = p^{k_1} E[w_{1,L_z}], \quad \bar{a} = m^{k_2} E[a_{t,L_x}],$$
$$\bar{s} = E[s_i], \qquad\qquad b = E[b_t], \tag{57}$$

$$\sigma_w^2 = p^{k_1} V[w_{i,L_z}], \quad \sigma_a^2 = m^{k_2} V[a_{t,L_x}],$$
$$\sigma_s^2 = V[s_i], \qquad\qquad \sigma_b^2 = V[b_t], \tag{58}$$

Figure 22. Classification for oscillated RHONNs for the analog state $[-1,1]$-model with $k = 2$, $a = 1$, $\sigma_w^2 = 0.5$, and $\sigma_s^2 = 1.0$.

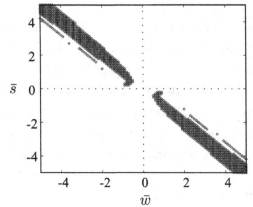

(a) The case with period 2^n for some $n \geq 2$.

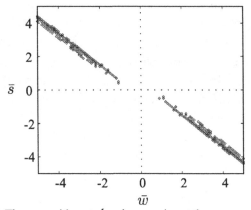

(b) The case with $m > 1$, where m is not the power of 2.

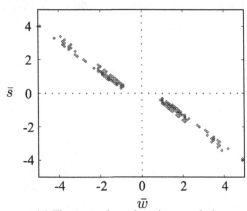

(c) The case where there is no period.

Then the following result for the expected value and variance of u_i is obtained by using the same method as the case of digital state $\{-1, 1\}$ -model.

$$E[u_i] = \overline{w}(E[z_t])^{k_2} + \overline{s} \tag{59}$$

$$\sigma_u^2 = \sigma_w^2 + \sigma_s^2 \tag{60}$$

Further the following result holds for the expected value and variance of z_t.

$$E[z_t] = 2\Phi\left(\frac{\overline{q}}{\sigma}\right) - 1 = 2\Phi\left(\frac{\overline{a}X^{k_2} + \overline{b}}{\sigma_q}\right) - 1$$

$$= \Psi(AX^{k_2} + B), \tag{61}$$

$$\overline{q} = E[q_t] = \overline{a}X^{k_2} + \overline{b},$$
$$\sigma_q^2 = V[q_t] = \sigma_a^2 + \sigma_b^2,$$

where $A = \overline{a} / \sigma_q$, $B = \overline{b} / \sigma_q$.

As a result, the following equation holds.

$$F(X) = \Psi\left(W\left(\Psi\left(AX^{k_2} + B\right)\right)^{k_1} + S\right), \tag{62}$$

where $W = \overline{w} / \sigma_u$, $S = \overline{s} / \sigma_u$.

Let us consider an example of dynamics of networks which have feedback from outputs to inputs as $m = n$. Figure 22 shows an example of three-layered systems with $k_1 = 2$, $k_2 = 1$, $A = 4$, $B = 0$. It is classified by the same method as Figure 14. Each point of the area shown in (a), (b), (c) of Figure 22 shows non-equilibrium points. Note that there does not exist any system with bifurcation diagram like this in simple RHONNs.

In the case of the digital state $\{0, 1\}$ -model, the following equation holds by using the same method as digital state $\{0, 1\}$ -model.

$$F(X) = \Phi\left(\frac{\overline{w}\left(\Phi\left(\dfrac{\overline{a}X^{k_2} + \overline{b}}{\sigma_q}\right)\right)^{k_1} + \overline{S}}{\sigma_u}\right), \tag{63}$$

where $\sigma_u^2 = \sigma_w^2 X^{k_1} + \sigma_s^2$ and $\sigma_q^2 = \sigma_a^2 X^{k_2} + \sigma_b^2$.

In the case of the analog state models, the following variance is used to get the result.

$$\sigma_u^2 = \sigma_w^2 \tilde{X}^{k_1} + \sigma_s^2, \ \sigma_q^2 = \sigma_a^2 \tilde{X}^{k_2} + \sigma_b^2 \tag{64}$$

In this section, transformation formulas for interconnected systems composed of RHONNs are obtained. In this case, it is clarified that each RHONN behaves as a neuron and characteristic of the system is determined by them. Although it is interesting problem to investigate whether complex dynamics is performed by interconnected systems composed of RHONNs, it is difficult to find the result. This is because we cannot select appropriate parameters from many ones.

CONCLUSION

This chapter describes the macroscopic dynamics of Randomly connected Higher Order Neural Networks (RHONNs). The dynamics was obtained by using the statistical method of neuro-dynamics. First, 1) it is shown that there are some differences between dynamics of RNNs and RHONNs in the cases of the digital state $\{-1, 1\}$ -model and the analog state $[-1, 1]$ -model. This indicates that the dynamics of RHONNs is more complex than the one of RNNs. Specifically, it seems that there exist chaotic networks in the cases of $k = 2$. Their complex dynamics may be able to be utilized to improving the storage capacity and the basin of attractor in associative memory. Morita (1993) has proposed a model of associative memory by using monotone increasing neurons and has shown that the dynamics in failure of recalling process becomes a chaotic behavior and does not converge to any sable state (Morita, et al., 1990; Morita, 1993). HONNs may be able to perform the same behavior without using monotone increasing neurons. On the other hand, it may be possible to avoid converging to shallow local minima for combinatorial optimization problems by using HONNs with complex behavior. Further, 2) it is shown that there is little difference of the dynamics between RNNs and RHONNs in the cases of the digital state $\{0,1\}$-model and the analog state $[0,1]$-model. The number of equilibrium states does not increase so much in HONNs. This means that, for the $\{0,1\}$-model and the analog state $[0,1]$-model, the dynamics of RHONNs are not complex. However, with a combinatorial optimization problem, Cooper (1995) has shown high ability of HONNs by effective use of the property. Furthermore, 3) it is shown that the behavior of a group of RHONNs is the combination of behaviors of individual RHONNs, and the transformation formulas for three-layered systems are also shown. However, we do not perform high period by using special combination of RHONNs as shown in Amari (1974). Further, it is interesting to show whether there exists any complex (chaotic) network in three-layered networks composed of RHONNs with $k = 1$. With cellular automata, Wolfram (1984) has shown that there exist networks with chaotic behavior. It is interesting to investigate the relation between HONNs and cellular automata.

The authors investigate applying complex dynamics to static and time-learning sequence patterns in associative memory. Further, the detailed dynamics of groups of RHONNs will be considered as the future work.

ACKNOWLEDGMENT

This work is supported by Grant-in-Aid for Scientific Research (C) (No.22500207) of Ministry of Education, Culture, Sports, Science, and Technology of Japan.

REFERENCES

Amari, S. (1971). Characteristics of randomly connected threshold element networks and network systems. *Proceedings of the IEEE*, *59*, 35–47. doi:10.1109/PROC.1971.8087

Amari, S. (1972). Characteristics of random nets of analog neuron-like elements. *IEEE Transactions on Systems, Man, and Cybernetics*, *2*(5), 643–657. doi:10.1109/TSMC.1972.4309193

Amari, S. (1974). A method of statistical neurodynamics. *Kybernetik*, *14*, 201–215.

Amari, S., & Maginu, K. (1988). Statistical neurodynamics of associative memories. *Neural Networks*, *1*, 63–73. doi:10.1016/0893-6080(88)90022-6

Annios, P. A., Csermely, B., & Harth, E. M. (1970). Dynamics of neural structures. *Journal of Theoretical Biology*, *26*, 121–148. doi:10.1016/S0022-5193(70)80036-4

Cheng, K. W., & Lee, T. (1993). On the convergence of neural network for higher order programing. In *Proceedings of IJCNN 1993*, (vol 2), (pp. 1507-1511). Nagoya, Japan: IJCNN.

Cooper, B. S. (1995). Higher order neural networks for combinatorial optimization improving the scaling properties of the hopfield network. In *Proceedings of the IEEE ICNN 1995*, (vol 4), (pp. 1855-1890). IEEE Press.

Giles, C. L., & Maxwell, T. (1988). Learning, invariance and generalization high-order neural networks. *Applied Optics*, *26*, 4972–4978. doi:10.1364/AO.26.004972

Hjelmfelt, A., & Ross, J. (1994). Pattern recognition, chaos, and multiplicity in neural networks and excitable systems. *Proceedings of the National Academy of Sciences of the United States of America*, *91*, 63–67. doi:10.1073/pnas.91.1.63

Hopfield, J. J. (1982). Neural networks and physical systems with emergent collective computational abilities. *Proceedings of the National Academy of Sciences of the United States of America*, *79*, 2554–2558. doi:10.1073/pnas.79.8.2554

Kohonen, T. (1988). *Self organization and associative memory* (2nd ed.). New York, NY: Springer-Verlag. doi:10.1007/978-3-662-00784-6

Li, T. Y., & Yorke, J. A. (1975). Periodic three implies chaos. *The American Mathematical Monthly*, *82*, 985–992. doi:10.2307/2318254

McEliece, R. J., Posner, E. C., Rodemich, E. R., & Venkatesh, S. S. (1987). The capacity of the Hopfield associative memory. *IEEE Transactions on Information Theory*, *33*, 461–482. doi:10.1109/TIT.1987.1057328

Miyajima, H., Ma, L., & Suwa, H. (1996). Dynamical properties of higher order random neural networks. in *Proceedings of the IEEE ICTAI 1996*, (vol 1), (pp. 430-431). IEEE Press.

Miyajima, H., & Yatsuki, S. (1994). On some dynamical properties of threshold and homogeneous networks. *IEICE Transactions on Fundamentals*, *77*(11), 1823–1830.

Miyajima, H., Yatsuki, S., & Maeda, M. (1996). Some characteristics of higher order neural networks with decreasing energy functions. *IEICE Transactions on Fundamentals*, *99*(10), 1624–1629.

Miyajima, H., Yatsuku, S., & Kubota, J. (1995). Dynamical properties of neural networks with product connections. In *Proceedings of the IEEE ICNN 1995*, (vol 6), (pp. 3198-3203). IEEE Press.

Moreira, J. M., & Auto, D. M. (1993). Intermittency in a neural network with variable threshold. *Europhysics Letters*, *21*(6), 639. doi:10.1209/0295-5075/21/6/001

Morita, M. (1993). Associative memory with non-monotone dynamics. *Neural Networks*, *6*, 115–126. doi:10.1016/S0893-6080(05)80076-0

Morita, M., Yoshizawa, S., & Nakano, K. (1990). Analysis and improvement of the dynamics of autocorrelation associative memory. *Transactions on Institutional Electronics, Information . Communication Engineers Japan*, *73*(2), 232–242.

Palm, G. (1980). On associative memory. *Biological Cybernetics*, *36*, 19–31. doi:10.1007/BF00337019

Perantonis, S. J., & Lisboa, P. J. G. (1992). Translation, rotation and scale invariant pattern recognition by high-order neural networks and moment classifiers. *IEEE Transactions on Neural Networks*, *3*, 241–251. doi:10.1109/72.125865

Psaltis, D., Park, C. H., & Hong, J. (1988). High order associative memories and their optical implementations. *Neural Networks*, *1*, 149–163. doi:10.1016/0893-6080(88)90017-2

Ross, S. M. (1970). *Applied probability models with optimization applications*. New York, NY: Dover Publications.

Rumelhart, D. E., & McClelland, J. L. (1986). *Parallel distributed processing*. Cambridge, MA: The MIT Press.

Schuster, H. G. (1989). *Deterministic chaos- An introduction* (2nd ed.). Weinheim, Germany: VCH Verlagsgeshellschaft.

Simpson, P. K. (1990). Higher-ordered and interconnected bidirectional associative memories. *IEEE Transactions on Systems, Man, and Cybernetics*, *20*, 637–653. doi:10.1109/21.57276

KEY TERMS AND DEFINITIONS

Higher Order Neural Networks: The conventional neural network is composed of numerous neurons whose potential is given by the linear combination $\sum w_i x_i$ of inputs x_i with the weights w_i. A higher order neural network is composed of higher order neurons whose potential is computed by the linear combination $\sum w_{ij} x_i x_j$ or $\sum w_{ijk} x_i x_j x_k$ of the second- or third-order product of inputs with the weights w_{ij} or w_{ijk}.

Oscillated Neural Networks: Dynamics of neural network is called non-equilibrium when there exists an initial state for which the network does not converge to any stable equilibrium state. Oscillated network is a kind of non-equilibrium networks.

Randomly Connected Neural Networks: The weights and the thresholds in neural networks are random variables and selected mutually independent from a probabilistic distribution. The neural networks are called randomly connected neural networks. With respect to randomly connected neural networks, the statistical properties with ensembles of networks are discussed rather than the property of each neural network.

The Analog state Model: Any neural network is composed of numerous neurons. Each neuron has a large number of inputs and one output, and each of the input and the output takes a value $y \in Q$, where Q is called the state set. When Q is the set of all real numbers from 0 to 1 (-1 to 1), it is called the analog state $[0,1]$- ($[-1,1]$-) model.

The Digital State Model: When $Q = \{0,1\}$ ($\{-1,1\}$), we call it the digital state $\{0,1\}$- ($\{-1,1\}$-) model.

ENDNOTES

1   Correctly speaking, the relation holds only for $t = 0$. However, assuming Chaos Assumption, it holds for any t. We will argue with Chaos Assumption in the section "Behavior of Non-Equilibrium RHONNs."

2   When $n = 1$, we call it an equilibrium state (point) in Section of digital state $\{0, 1\}$-model and when $n > 1$, it is called an oscillatory point.

APPENDIX

In this appendix, a few basic theorems in probability theory (Ross, 1970) are introduced. These theorems are often used in this chapter.

$$E\left(\sum_{i=1}^{n} X_i\right) = \sum_{i=1}^{n} E(X_i), \text{(A-1)}$$

When random variables $X_1, X_2, \cdots, X_n$ are independent and n is sufficient large, the mean of these random variables is approximately normally distributed. This phenomenon is well known as the following theorem.

Central Limit Theorem

If $X_1, X_2, \cdots$ are independent and identically distributed with mean μ and variance σ^2 then

$$\lim_{n \to \infty} \Pr\left\{ \frac{X_1 + \cdots + X_n - n\mu}{\sigma\sqrt{n}} \le a \right\} \text{(A-2)}$$
$$= \int_{-\infty}^{a} \frac{1}{\sqrt{2\pi}} e^{\frac{-x^2}{2}} \, dx.$$

Chapter 17
A Hybrid Higher Order Neural Structure for Pattern Recognition

Mehdi Fallahnezhad
Norwegian University of Science and Technology (NTNU), Norway

Salman Zaferanlouei
Amirkabir University of Technology (Tehran Polytechnic), Iran

ABSTRACT

Considering high order correlations of selected features next to the raw features of input can facilitate target pattern recognition. In artificial intelligence, this is being addressed by Higher Order Neural Networks (HONNs). In general, HONN structures provide superior specifications (e.g. resolving the dilemma of choosing the number of neurons and layers of networks, better fitting specs, quicker, and open-box specificity) to traditional neural networks. This chapter introduces a hybrid structure of higher order neural networks, which can be generally applied in various branches of pattern recognition. Structure, learning algorithm, and network configuration are introduced, and structure is applied either as classifier (where is called HHONC) to different benchmark statistical data sets or as functional behavior approximation (where is called HHONN) to a heat and mass transfer dilemma. In each structure, results are compared with previous studies, which show its superior performance next to other mentioned advantages.

INTRODUCTION

Among many different structures of Artificial Neural Networks (ANNs), backpropagation networks (BPNs; Rumlhart, et al., 1986) are most widely used in many different areas. Al-

though these networks are recognized for their excellent performance in mathematical function approximation, nonlinear classification, pattern matching, and pattern recognition, they have several limitations. They do not excel in discontinuous or non-smooth (small changes in inputs cause large changes in outputs) data mining and knowledge learning (Fulcher, et al., 2006; Zhang,

DOI: 10.4018/978-1-4666-2175-6.ch017

et al., 2002). In addition, they cannot deal well on incomplete or noisy data (Dong, 2007; Peng & Zhu, 2007; Wang, 2003). A traditional ANN with single connections having no hidden layer only can map neuron inputs linearly to neuron outputs. Single hidden layer Feedforward Neural Networks (FNNs) are known for their ability of function approximation and learning pattern recognition but cannot realize every nonlinear mapping. FNNs incorporating more hidden layers are well known for their long time convergence and usually stuck in local minima rather than a global.

In order to improve various limitations of traditional neural network, Higher Order Neural Networks (HONNs) can be considered. By combining inputs, nonlinearly, HONNs make a higher order correlation among inputs (Zurada, 1992). Leaving necessity of hidden layers, HONN structures turn out simpler than FNN structures and initialization of learning parameters (weights) will become less challenging. Especially method presented in this chapter, there is no need for hidden layers (and consequently hidden neurons) which, in turn, eases the process of finding appropriate network structure. In addition, unlike BPN, HONN successfully can provide an efficient open-box model of nonlinear input-output mapping, which provides easier understanding of data mining. Moreover, HONNs most often run faster than FNNs. Examples in implementation of two-input and three-input XOR functions by using Second Order Neural Network (SONN) proved that SONN is several times faster than FNN (Gupta, et al., 2009; Zhang, 2009).

In following sections, we introduce a hybrid higher order structure, which is firstly proposed as a classifier form in Fallahnezhad et al. (2011) and were developed afterwards to more general form. We discuss its pros and cons either as a classifier (where is called HHONC) in the classification of the Iris data set, the breast cancer data set, the Wine recognition data set, the Glass identification data set, the Balance scale data set, and the Pima diabetes data set, or as functional behavior approximation (where it is called HHONN) to a heat and mass transfer dilemma.

HIGHER ORDER NEURAL NETWORK STRUCTURES AND MODELS

In recent years, many different structures of high order neural networks have been developed. The simplest structure is a network with productive terms as additional inputs next to the original inputs (Lee, et al., 1986). However, "high-order" concept is widely used in neuron type (linear, power, multiplicative, sigmoid, etc.), neuron activation function type (polynomial, sigmoid, cosine, sine, SINC, etc.) (Fulcher, et al., 2006; Zhang, 2009), and as higher order neural networks with adaptive functions (Xu, 2008), etc. In summary, HONN uses a higher correlation of input neurons for better fitting properties, which often leads to a higher number of learning parameters (weights). The greater the order is used the higher the number of parameters will be. Many efforts for decreasing the number of parameters in different areas have been done. In summary, two major forms of HONN have been considered, sigma-pi network known as Higher-order Processing Unit (HPU) and Pi-Sigma Network (PSN). The former uses all of the combination of inputs up to the specified order. As a result, HPU models need more number of learning parameters to be updated which causes a longer run time. However, it provides an investigation of all correlations among different inputs. In contrast, the latter is developed to comprise a high order correlation between inputs by using lower number of weights which causes faster learning while avoids the high loss of performance. Shin and Ghosh (1991) have introduced an efficient higher-order neural network as a PSN model and they have studied several pattern classification and function approximation problems. They claimed that a generalization of PSN can approximate any measurable function. Homma and Gupta (2002) developed a sigma-pi Artificial Second Order Neural Unit (ASONU) without losing the higher performance. Recurrent PSN (RPSN) and converging challenges is proposed and used in predicting the foreign currency exchange rates and results are compared with feed-forward and other recurrent structures (Hussain & Liatsis, 2008). Since, PSN is not a universal approximator, a generalization of PSN is the Ridge Polynomial Higher Order Neural Network (RPHONN) proposed by Shin and Ghosh (1995). Dynamic RPHONN is used in prediction of the exchange rate time series (Ghazali, et al., 2007). More general sigma-pi models are proposed in three structures named 1b, 1, and 0 models (Zhang, 2009). Equations (1), (2), and (3) show the presented models for a network including two features, x1 and x2, in every sample.

HONN Model 1b:

$$Z = \sum_{i,j=0}^{N} a_{ij}^{0} \cdot \left\{ a_{ij}^{kx_1} \cdot f_i^{x_1} \left(a_i^{x_1} \cdot x_1 \right) \right\} \tag{1}$$
$$\cdot \left\{ a_{ij}^{hx_2} \cdot f_j^{x_2} \left(a_j^{x_2} \cdot x_2 \right) \right\}$$

HONN Model 1:

$$Z = \sum_{i,j=0}^{N} a_{ij}^{0} \cdot \left\{ f_i^{x_1} \left(a_i^{x_1} \cdot x_1 \right) \right\} \cdot \left\{ f_j^{x_2} \left(a_j^{x_2} \cdot x_2 \right) \right\}$$

$$\tag{2}$$

HONN Model 0:

$$Z = \sum_{i,j=0}^{N} a_{ij}^{0} \cdot \left\{ f_i^{x_1} \left(x_1 \right) \right\} \cdot \left\{ f_j^{x_2} \left(x_2 \right) \right\} \tag{3}$$

The Kernel function (f) can be a variety of functions. It has been proposed as six different types: Polynomial Higher Order Neural Network (PHONN), Trigonometric Higher Order Neural Networks (THONN), SINC Higher Order Neural Network (SINCHONN), Sigmoid Polynomial Higher Order Neural Network (SPHONN), Ultra High Frequency Cosine and Sine Higher Order Neural Network (UCSHONN), SINC and Sine Polynomial Higher Order Neural Network (SXSPHONN).

Each of these six kernels can be used in one of the structures 1b, 1, and 0. By changing one of these six models to another, neuron activation function inside the sigma symbol changes. It has been proved mathematically that presented HONN models always converge and have better accuracy than Statistical Analysis System Nonlinear (SAS NLIN) models.

In these models (1 to 3) model 0 is the simplest. Although it may not perform excellent in dealing with more complex patterns, it has less number of learning parameters and usually run much faster. It is shown that different structures of model 0 get smaller residual mean squared error than SAS NLIN for the US population growth data and for the Quadratic with Plateau data. Using this model (model 0) implemented by different kernels including PHONN, THONN, UCSHONN (Ultra High Frequency Cosine and Sine Higher Order Neural Networks), SXSPHONN (SINC and Sine Polynomial Higher Order Neural Networks), SINCHONN, MSE, and run time of the best models for the exchange rate Yen vs. US dollar year 2004 have been reported. The Best model 0 is reported to be a UCSHONN model of order 5.

Figure 1 presents a graphical theme of model 0. This is a general implementation of model 0 which we use it as basic kernel of our hybrid structure.

STRUCTURE AND LEARNING ALGORITHM OF HYBRID HIGHER ORDER NEURAL NETWORK

General Scheme, Structure and Learning Algorithm

As Equations (1) and (2) demonstrate, in spite of better fitting properties, the number of learning parameters in HONN model 1b and 1 is more than

Figure 1. General structure of model 0 as a basic kernel of each higher order unit in hybrid HONN

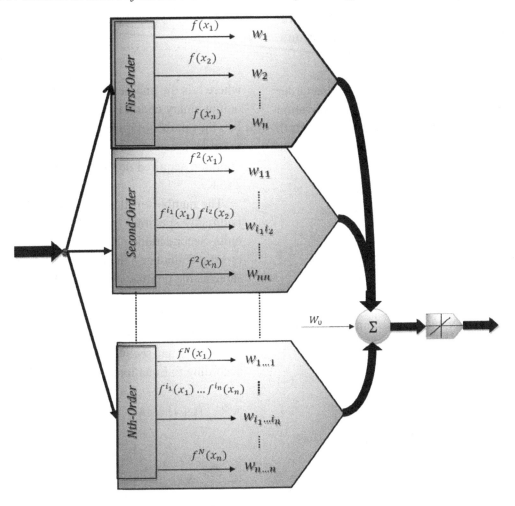

HONN model 0 and as the order of model gets higher, updating the parameters will become more difficult. We propose a two-hidden-layered higher order neural network, which forms as a selective and linear combination of model 0 HONNs. In first layer it incorporates some or all of high-order units including PHONN, SPHONN (involving both LOGSIG and TANSIG), SINCHONN and THONN models implemented as model 0. In second layer, a linear combination of selected units is chosen.

Different high-order units in the first layer are organized as follows (Zhang, 2009):

1. PHONN Model: Polynomial Higher Order Neural Networks (PHONNs) are developed by choosing the activation function as a polynomial function. The learning formula of PHONN and other five models are presented by Zhang (2009). Accordingly, in this model neuron activation function, f(x), in model presented in Figure 1, is linear.

2. THONN Model: In Trigonometric Higher Order Neural Networks (THONN) the activation functions are trigonometric (sine and cosine) functions. We use cosine and sine alternately over the features e.g. for data set including two features: f(x1) = cos(x1), f(x2) = sin(x2)

3. SINCHONN: In SINC Higher Order Neural Networks (SINCHONN) all of the activation functions are SINC functions;

$$f(x) = \frac{\sin(x)}{x}$$

SPHONN: In Sigmoid Polynomial Higher Order Neural Networks (SPHONN) the activation functions are SIGMOID functions. Both LOGSIG and TANSIG functions can be used.

Tansig : $f(x) = \dfrac{1 - e^{-x}}{1 + e^{-x}}$

Logsig : $f(x) = \dfrac{1}{1 + e^{-x}}$

Equations (4) and (5) mathematically demonstrate HHONN outputs as a function of input features.

$$y_j(\overline{x}) = \qquad (4)$$

$$w_{j0}^{(1)} + \sum_{i_1=1}^{P} w_{ji_1}^{(1)} f_1(x_{i_1}) + \sum_{i_1=1}^{P}\sum_{i_2=i_1}^{P} w_{ji_1i_2}^{(1)} f_1(x_{i_1}) f_1(x_{i_2})$$

$$+ .. + \sum_{i_1=1}^{P} .. \sum_{i_{N_1}=i_{N_1-1}}^{P} w_{ji_1 \dots i_{N_1}}^{(1)} f_1(x_{i_1}) .. f_1(x_{i_{N_1}})$$

$$+ \quad w_{j0}^{(2)} + \sum_{i_1=1}^{P} w_{ji_1}^{(2)} f_2(x_{i_1}) + \sum_{i_1=1}^{P}\sum_{i_2=i_1}^{P} w_{ji_1i_2}^{(2)} f_2(x_{i_1}) f_2(x_{i_2})$$

$$+ .. + \sum_{i_1=1}^{P} .. \sum_{i_{N_2}=i_{N_2-1}}^{P} w_{ji_1 \dots i_{N_2}}^{(2)} f_2(x_{i_1}) .. f_2(x_{i_{N_2}})$$

$$+ \dots$$

$$+ \quad w_{j0}^{(K)} + \sum_{i_1=1}^{P} w_{ji_1}^{(K)} f_K(x_{i_1}) + \sum_{i_1=1}^{P}\sum_{i_2=i_1}^{P} w_{ji_1i_2}^{(K)} f_K(x_{i_1}) f_K(x_{i_2})$$

$$+ .. + \sum_{i_1=1}^{P} .. \sum_{i_{N_K}=i_{N_K-1}}^{P} w_{ji_1 \dots i_{N_K}}^{(K)} f_K(x_{i_1}) .. f_K(x_{i_{N_K}})$$

$$z_1 = Y \times V = v_{j0} + \sum_{j=1}^{K} v_{jl} y_j(\overline{x}),$$

$$Z = [z_1, \dots, z_1, \dots, z_L] \qquad (5)$$

where L is the number of outputs (bit number of output binary code), P is the number of features, K is the number of higher order units which have the order greater than 0 and N_1, N_2, ..., N_K are optimum acquired order of higher order units 1, 2 to K.

The number of hidden neurons in first layer is directly specified by the order of high-order units. Second hidden layer of HHONN is a linear order and number of neurons in this layer will be same as the number of outputs. For example, as a classifier output, when we have 2, 3, or 7 class, the number of hidden neurons in second layer will be 1, 2, and 3, respectively.

The first and second layer weights are updated according to Equations (6) and (7), respectively.

$$w_{ji_1 \dots i_{N_k}}^{(k)}(t+1) = w_{ji_1 \dots i_{N_k}}^{(k)}(t) - \; \cdot .\left(\partial E \big/ \partial w_{ji_1 \dots i_{N_k}}^{(k)}\right)$$

$$\frac{\partial E}{\partial w_{ji_1 \dots i_{N_k}}^{(k)}} = \frac{\partial E}{\partial y_j} \cdot \frac{\partial y_j}{\partial w_{ji_1 \dots i_{N_k}}^{(k)}}$$

$$= \frac{\partial E}{\partial y_j} \cdot f_K(x_{i_1}) \dots f_K(x_{i_{N_K}})$$

$$\frac{\partial E}{\partial y_j} = \frac{\partial}{\partial y_j}\left[\frac{1}{2}\sum_{l=1}^{L}(d_l - z_l)^2\right]$$

$$= \sum_{l=1}^{L}(d_l - z_l)\frac{\partial}{\partial y_j}(Y \times V) = \sum_{l=1}^{L}(d_l - z_l)v_{jl} \qquad (6)$$

$$v_{jl}(t+1) = v_{jl}(t) - \; \cdot .\left(\partial E \big/ \partial v_{jl}\right)$$

$$\frac{\partial E}{\partial v_{jl}} = \frac{\partial E}{\partial z_l} \cdot \frac{\partial z_l}{\partial v_{jl}} = \frac{\partial E}{\partial z_l} \cdot y_j = y_j \cdot \sum_{l=1}^{L}(d_l - z_l) \qquad (7)$$

where t is training state, · is learning coefficient, E is error, W is weight matrix of first hidden layer, and V is weight matrix of second hidden layer, L is the number of outputs, P is the number of input samples, K is the number of higher order units which have a non-zero order, and N_1, N_2, ..., N_K are optimum acquired orders of higher order units 1, 2, to K.

Since each HONN unit (PHONN, THONN, SPHONN, and SINCHONN) converges solely, each linear combination of these units will converge as well. In addition, by adding a hidden layer including linear neurons, convergence of network will not change, so proposed network always converges.

In summary, formation and updating algorithm of HHONN is organized as follows:

- Initialize N_1, N_2, N_3, N_4, N_5 by 0; set order of model according to N.

- Increase one to previous order of model (N) (e.g. when order is [0 0 0 0 1], the next orders will be [0 0 0 1 0], [0 0 0 1 1], [0 0 1 0 0], [0 0 1 0 1], ...).
- Set weights to current model and initialize them.
- Update weights by using Equations (7) and (8); calculate the accuracy and mean squared error for training samples and more especially for validation samples.
- If the accuracy (or MSE) of validation samples reached to desired value, stop. Otherwise, go to step 2.

HHONN: A GENERAL STRUCTURE FOR PATTERN RECOGNITION

Proposed structure can be used in various areas such as pattern classification, pattern behavior approximation, process optimization, etc. A general scheme of this structure is given in Figure 2.

Figure 2. Block diagram of the HHONN

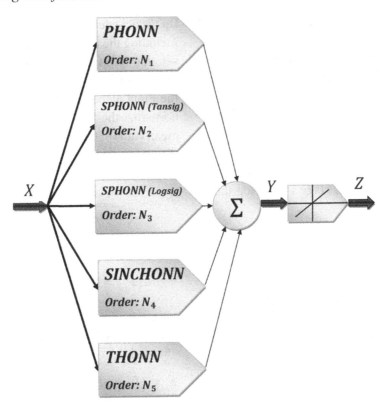

Network input assumes to be a numerical matrix type M×N input where M is the number of inputs and N is the number of features. Appropriate normalization of input matrix for having a meaningful scale of features is usually needed. If under-study data is not numerical or if it is not in appropriate shape, a conversion stage prior to input stage will be necessary. In output stage, according to the target problem a conversion stage might be needed. For example, in next session we will show how a stage will be added to output to provide a classifier concept to the network. The order of each high-order unit dynamically changes during training process (decrease and increase) to obtain a desired accuracy for validation samples (or MSE). We apply proposed HHONN structure to a well-known pattern recognition problem in the heat and mass transfer area. In regard to the data structure and maximum specified order for each high-order unit, the best fitted model of HHONN will be considered. Additionally, we use a multilayered back propagation feed-forward neural network (BPN/FNN) and find the best-fitted model to the problem. Finally, we compare results achieved by FNN model with HHONN one.

HHONC: A Classifier Structure for Classification Problems

Structure, weights updating, network algorithm and mathematical formulation of this network (HHONC) is similar to HHONN. The only difference is that in HHONC there is a shifted-step stage (Figure 3) in output stage to provide the

Figure 3. Output stage of HHONC during testing process

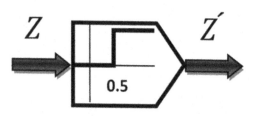

network outputs in a binary format. One should note that, this unit is just used in testing process and it is because of our binary bit coding (0, 1) of output for identifying different classes. As shown in Figure 3, this stage is a shifted hard limit function. Since the output values of HHONN are values between 0 and 1, this stage divides each feature of output to two codes: 0 if value of output feature falls between 0 and 0.5 and 1 if value of output feature falls between 0.5 and 1.

As an example, in Figure 4, we have shown outputs of different stages including before (Z) and after (Z´) the shifted hard-limit unit of the one HHONC implemented for breast cancer dataset. This dataset includes 699 samples and 9 features. The output class numbers are 2: Malignant (241 instances) and Benign (458 instances). This dataset contains 16 samples with missing features that are not considered in our process.

HHONC: EXPERIMENTAL RESULTS

We use six different kinds of UCI datasets (ftp://ftp.ics.uci.edu/pub/machine-learning-databases/) including the Iris data set, the Breast cancer data set, the Wine recognition data set, the Glass identification data set, the Balance scale data and the Pima diabetes data set. For each dataset, we normalize the data over each feature value to have mean value of 0 and variance value of 1. Equation (8) covers this concept:

$$\hat{f}_i = \frac{f_i - mean(F_j)}{\sqrt{var(F_j)}}$$

$$mean\left(F_j\right) = \frac{\sum_{i=1}^{n} f_i}{n}$$

$$var\left(F_j\right) = \frac{\sum_{i=1}^{n} (f_i - mean(F_j))^2}{n},$$
$$F_j = \left[f_1, \ldots, f_i, \ldots, f_n\right] \tag{8}$$

Figure 4. Output of different stages of HHONC for breast cancer dataset

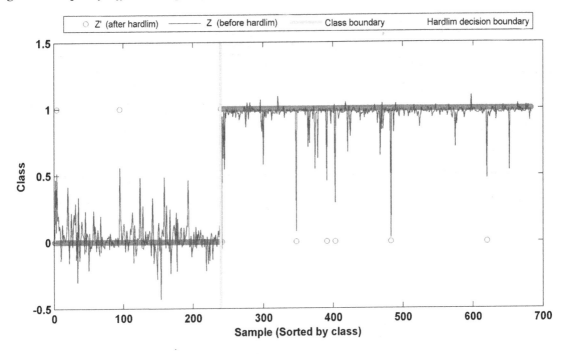

Where, f_i is the normalized value of feature *j*th of sample *i*th, f_i is the original value of feature *j*th of sample *i*th, F_j is the values of feature *j*th of all samples.

Meant for providing excellent comparison with other classifiers, two kinds of experiments are carried out on different datasets. At the first one, we use the original datasets including all of features, and at the second experiment, we apply our proposed HHONC to a selected subset of features. In both experiments we compare the proposed method with other classifiers.

Experiments on Original Datasets

In this experiment, we use original datasets and try to find a HHONC model for each one. For each dataset, we use 65% of data as training instances, 10% as validation instances, and 25% as testing instances, which are randomly selected over dataset. In fact, for providing a good comparison with previous works we use 25% of dataset as test samples; however, in spite the other compared classifiers, we need to choose validation samples over the dataset for our training stop epoch. For probing the robustness of the method over the various testing instances, we repeat the method 200 times on each data set by differing train, validation, and test instances.

Table 1 presents the resultant orders of different high-order units for each HHONC.

Figure 5 presents the comparison of presented method with the Naive Bayes method (John & Langley, 1995), the C4.5 method (Quinlan, 1993), the Sequential Minimal Optimization (SMO) (Platt, 1999), and fuzzy gain measure (Shie & Chen, 2006; Chen & Shie, 2008). The reported values are organized as: Mean value ± Standard deviation, which are computed from 200 independent trials.

From Figure 5 we can see that while the number of features of a data set is low enough (about four features), the proposed method gets higher average classification accuracy rates than the others. Meanwhile, the accuracy of data sets with more features is acceptable.

Table 1. HHONC configuration: order of different high-order units for original datasets

Data sets	Orders of different units of HHONC				
	PHONN	SPHONN TANSIG	SPHONN LOGSIG	SINCHONN	THONN
Iris data set	0	0	2	0	1
Breast cancer data set	0	1	0	1	1
Wine recognition data set	1	0	1	0	0
Glass identification data set	1	1	0	1	0
Balance scale data set	1	1	3	0	0

Figure 5. Comparison of the average classification accuracy rates of proposed method by prior presented classifiers: for original datasets

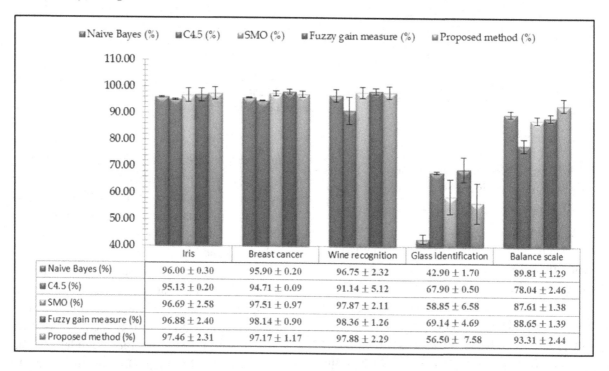

	Iris	Breast cancer	Wine recognition	Glass identification	Balance scale
Naive Bayes (%)	96.00 ± 0.30	95.90 ± 0.20	96.75 ± 2.32	42.90 ± 1.70	89.81 ± 1.29
C4.5 (%)	95.13 ± 0.20	94.71 ± 0.09	91.14 ± 5.12	67.90 ± 0.50	78.04 ± 2.46
SMO (%)	96.69 ± 2.58	97.51 ± 0.97	97.87 ± 2.11	58.85 ± 6.58	87.61 ± 1.38
Fuzzy gain measure (%)	96.88 ± 2.40	98.14 ± 0.90	98.36 ± 1.26	69.14 ± 4.69	88.65 ± 1.39
Proposed method (%)	97.46 ± 2.31	97.17 ± 1.17	97.88 ± 2.29	56.50 ± 7.58	93.31 ± 2.44

Experiments on Feature Subset Selected Datasets

In this section, we use a method based on fuzzy entropy measures proposed by Shie and Chen (2008) for feature subset selection. Then we apply again the proposed HHONC to the new datasets with selected features. In this experiment, we use the 10 times 10 fold cross validation method for acquiring the average accuracy of different clas-

sifiers. Table 2 indicates the order of different high-order units for each dataset. Figure 6 draws a comparison between acquired accuracy of using HHONC with the other classifiers reported in Shie and Chen (2008) including LMT (Landwehr, et al., 2003), Naive Bayes (John & Langley, 1995), C4.5 (Quinlan, 1993), and SMO (Pal, et al., 2000). All of the classifiers use the same subset of data features selected by fuzzy entropy measures.

Table 2. HHONC configuration: order of each high-order units for feature subset selected datasets

Data sets	Orders of different units of HHONC				
	PHONN	SPHONN TANSIG	SPHONN LOGSIG	SINCHONN	THONN
Iris data set	2	1	0	0	0
Breast cancer data set	0	1	0	1	0
Pima diabetes data set	3	3	0	1	0

Figure 6. Comparison of average classification accuracy rates of proposed method by prior presented 7 classifiers: for feature subset selected datasets

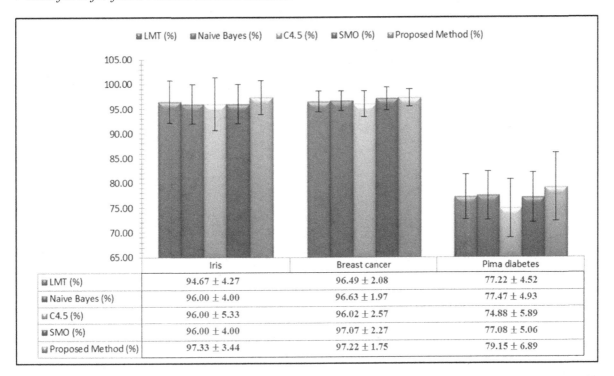

	Iris	Breast cancer	Pima diabetes
LMT (%)	94.67 ± 4.27	96.49 ± 2.08	77.22 ± 4.52
Naive Bayes (%)	96.00 ± 4.00	96.63 ± 1.97	77.47 ± 4.93
C4.5 (%)	96.00 ± 5.33	96.02 ± 2.57	74.88 ± 5.89
SMO (%)	96.00 ± 4.00	97.07 ± 2.27	77.08 ± 5.06
Proposed Method (%)	97.33 ± 3.44	97.22 ± 1.75	79.15 ± 6.89

As the detailed results given in Figure 6 demonstrate, the lower the number of features of dataset is, the higher the accuracy of HHONC will be.

For ensuring the accurate operation of proposed classifier, we have recorded all 10 tests, train and validation degrees of accuracy of 623 examined models in the case of Breast cancer data set. Figure 7a and 7b show the test, validation, and train accuracy of each model sorted by highest test accuracy for Wisconsin breast cancer data set and for Pima diabetes data set, respectively. From these figures, it can be achieved that accuracy of validation samples vary similar to that of test samples while this trend is different for those of training instances. As a result of the nature of validation and test instances, this similarity of accuracy value trends is expected which certifies our procedure for finding the best model. Figure 8a and Figure 8b, respectively, show the accuracy and complexity of each model and Figure 8c shows the accuracy of each model respect to the

Figure 7. Accuracy of train, validation, and test samples: a) 623 models for Wisconsin breast cancer data set, b) 1023 models for Pima diabetes data set

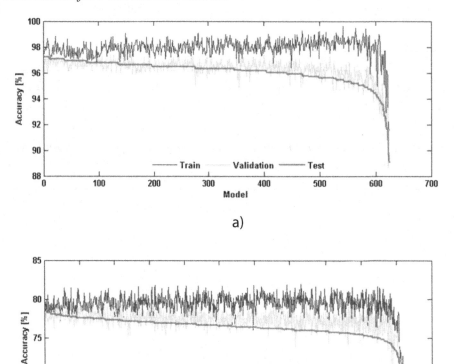

a)

b)

model complexity for the Pima diabetes data set. We have assumed the Model Complexity (MC) of each HHONC to be the number of additive terms in open-box model. It is the summation of high-order unit's terms ($MC = MC_1 + MC_2 + MC_3 + MC_4 + MC_5$ where MC_i is the model complexity of ith high-order unit).

As mentioned above, one of the advantages of proposed classifier, compared with other neural classifiers and most of commonly used classifiers, is its open-box property. For example, as shown in Table 2, the open-box model achieved for the Iris data set with selected features is given by Equation (9). The coefficients of each output are given in Table 3 (since the Iris data set includes

3 classes, it's coded by 2 bit output). This capability can be more notable whenever data set includes 2 classes (i.e. breast cancer data set and Pima diabetes data set).

$$Z = [Z_1, Z_2]$$
$$Z_i = a_{i0} + a_{i1}x_1 + a_{i2}x_2 + a_{i3}x_1^2 + a_{i4}x_1x_2 + a_{i5}x_2^2$$
$$+ a_{i6}T(x_1) + a_{i7}T(x_2), \ i = 1, 2$$
$$T(x) = \frac{1 - e^{-x}}{1 + e^{-x}}.$$

(9)

where x_1 and x_2 are 3rd and 4th feature of the Iris data set, respectively.

Figure 8. Accuracy and model complexity of 623 tested models for Wisconsin breast cancer data set. Green dashed-line identifies the accuracy value given in Figure 6 for this dataset: a) sorted highest-to-lowest accuracy values of models, b) model complexity of each model according to sorting in (a), c) accuracy of different 623 models versus model complexity.

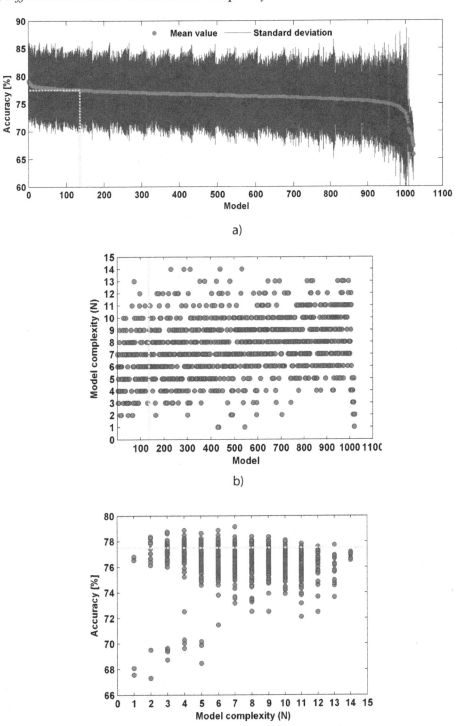

Table 3. HHONC model coefficients of Iris data set

	a_{i0}	a_{i1}	a_{i2}	a_{i3}	a_{i4}	a_{i5}	a_{i6}	a_{i7}
$i=1$	0.1220	1.3861	0.7877	-0.8811	0.5141	-0.5153	-0.2855	-0.4799
$i=2$	1.3314	-1.3341	-2.3523	3.5471	-3.9824	2.7494	-0.0502	3.1171

HHONN: EXPERIMENTAL RESULTS

Here, we want to investigate the pros and cons of HHONN in comparison with FNN in prediction of CHF, which is a well-known problem in heat and mass transfer process optimization. Therefore, in the following sections, firstly, our pattern recognition problem, the FNN structure and its best selected model are briefly described and then both FNN and HHONN algorithms are applied on the current problem. Finally, the final results compared with each other. A general dataset, which has been obtained from experimental tests, has been selected for training and testing of HHONN and FNN.

Introduction to Heat and Mass Transfer Dilemma

In heat flux-controlled systems, such as nuclear reactors, the Critical Heat Flux (CHF) condition causes an intense reduction of heat transfer coefficient which subsequently results in a sudden rise in the wall temperature and a fault to the heated surface. Thus, accurate prediction of the CHF is important for safe and economic design of nuclear reactors.

There are basically two classes of CHF situations: Departure from Nucleate Boiling (DNB) and departure from convective boiling in vapor-continuous flow or Dry-Out (DO). DNB is often related to subcooled boiling and can be associated with phenomena like micro layer evaporation under a bubble, bubble crowding, or vapor blanketing at the wall. The essential features of DO are a liquid film flowing on the channel wall and a vapor core containing entrained droplets. These droplets are continually tearing off the liquid film, mainly due to large disturbance waves on the liquid film, and are redeposited onto the film again. While the DNB usually occurs at bubbly or churn flow and low qualities, DO is connected to annular flow and higher qualities (Hoyer, 1998). DNB and DO are complex phenomena, which are affected by many parameters, thus various models are created to predict them. A great volume of experimental and theoretical studies on the CHF has been carried out by many researchers, which have resulted to several reliable prediction models and correlations. Low-pressure correlations and models (Hoyer, 1998; Jayanti & Valette, 2004) which are suited at pressures below the reduced pressure P/P_{cr}, were insufficient to predict DO at much higher pressures and the other factors such as nucleation-induced entrainment and vapor-inhibited redeposition became important. Thus, the present study was motivated by the inadequacy of extension of low-pressure correlations and models to predict CHF at high pressure. Three main methods for calculation and prediction of CHF are:

- Experimental data (look-up tables).
- Empirical correlations.
- Analytical models (Kandlikar, 2001).

Predicting CHF with Artificial Neural Network (ANN), as an empirical prediction method, has been the subject of many researches since 1990s. Thibault and Grandjean (1991) showed that ANN could be used to model heat transfer data. Yapo et al. (1992) predicted CHF by using hybrid kohen back propagation ANN. Moon and Chang (1994) and Moon et al. (1996), Mazzola (1997), Su et al. (2002, 2003), Vaziri et al. (2007) also applied this method to CHF prediction. Furthermore, Zaferanlouei et al. (2010) predicted CHF by using Adaptive Neuro-Fuzzy Inference System (ANFIS) in fixed inlet, outlet, and local conditions.

Identifying a black-box model, which includes sophisticated input-output correlations, has been a challenging problem in function approximation and pattern recognition field. Therefore, we use an input-output dataset which includes continues range of data to compare and discuss HHONN and FNN results.

CHF Dataset

The dataset of considered problem which includes 111 experimental data was selected from the experimental results of Vijayarangan et al. (2006). The range of the parameters of dataset is listed in Table 4. To train a neural network model, the most common approach is to divide the data samples collected from experiments into two groups, the training and validation datasets. The training group is used to train the neural network model by adjusting the weight matrices of the network model. The validation group is used to ensure that the neural network has properly learned the relationship between inputs and outputs and has been able to generalize the results. The validation dataset should include samples, which are not included in the training dataset. Based on this method, for both FNN and HHONN models, we divide 111 data samples into 88 training samples and 23 validation samples. In our algorithm, Root-Mean Square (RMS) error of validation samples is a criterion to prevent overfitting of training sample. An overfitted network acts as a look-up table. Thereby prediction is meaningless for an overfitted network.

Based on the chosen dataset, DO prediction model at near critical pressure can be expressed as in the following:

$$Q_{DO} = f(P, G, X)$$

Thus the three variables were selected as the input parameters and DO is selected as the output of the HHONN and FNN.

There was significant variation in the magnitude of the values of the input variables. These different magnitudes of the inputs led to ill-conditioning of the problem. To avoid this problem, the input data were normalized using the Equation (8).

Table 4. Experimental range of the DO data

Parameters	Unit	Range/type
Working fluid	------	R-134a
Pressure (P)	kPa	10-39.7
Mass flow (G)	Kg/m²s	200-2000
Inlet subcooling (ΔT_{sub})	°C	3
Heat flux (q)	(kW/m²)	2.8-80
The heated length to tube diameter ratio (L/D)	------	236.21
Number of data	------	111

Table 5. HHONN configuration: order of different high-order units for original datasets

Data set	Orders of different units of HHONN				
	PHONN	SPHONN TANSIG	SPHONN LOGSIG	SINCHONN	THONN
data set	0	2	3	0	3

Network Configuration

In this experiment, we use all of the features of the dataset and try to find a HHONN model over the dataset. For probing the robustness of the method over the various testing instances, we repeat the method 200 times on data set by differing train, validation, and test instances. Table 5 represents the resulting orders of different high-order units for each HHONN model.

Results of FNN and HHONN Nonlinear Models

Structure and Learning Algorithm of FNN

A FNN consists of at least three layers, input, output and hidden layer. The schematic diagram of a neuron is shown in Figure 9. Each neuron in a layer receives weighted inputs from a previous layer and transmits its output to neurons in the next layer. The summation of weighted input

signals are calculated by Equation (10), and it is transferred by a nonlinear activation function given in Equation (11). The results of network are compared with the actual observation results and the network error is calculated using Equation (12). The training process continues until this error reduces to an acceptable value.

$$Y_{net} = \sum_{i=1}^{N} X_i W_i + W_0 \qquad (10)$$

$$Y = f(Y_{net}) = \frac{1}{1 + e^{-Y_{net}}} \qquad (11)$$

$$J_r = \frac{1}{2} \sum_{i=1}^{k} (Y_i - O_i)^2 \qquad (12)$$

Where Y_i is the response of neuron i, $f(Y_{net})$ is the nonlinear activation function, Y_{net} is the summation of weighted inputs, X_i is the neuron input, W_i is weight coefficient of each neuron input, W_0 is bias, J_r is the error between observed

Figure 9. A neuron that constructs FNN's structure

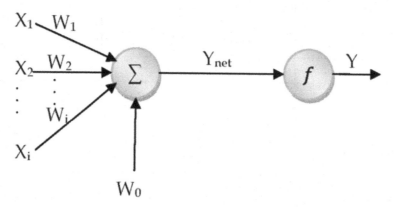

value and network response, O_i is the observed value of neuron i. N is the number of input variables and M is the number of the hidden neurons in hidden layer. In this study, the back propagation learning algorithm, the supervised learning and sigmoid activation functions are used in training and testing the models. Further details of these methods can be found in Yapo et al. (1992). Back propagation algorithm is one of the most popular algorithms for training a network due to its success from both simplicity and applicability viewpoints. The simplest algorithm of back propagation updates the network weights and biases in the direction in which the performance function decreases most rapidly, i.e. the negative of the gradient. The training of the network is based on the delta training rule method (Artyomov & Yadid-Pecht, 2005; Foresti & Dolso, 2004). The sigmoid activation function is most commonly used in the structure of feed forward neural networks (Artyomov & Yadid-Pecht, 2005; Foresti & Dolso, 2004). Supervised learning is the most commonly used method for training the feed forward neural network. In supervised learning, the purpose of a neural network is to change its weights according to the input and output samples. After a network has established its input output mapping with a defined minimum error value, the training task has been completed (Foresti & Dolso, 2004). The procedure of the BPN is that the error at the output layer propagates backward to the input layer through the hidden layer in the network to obtain the final desired outputs.

The gradient descent method is utilized to calculate the weight of the network and adjust the weight of interconnections to minimize the output error (Foresti & Dolso, 2004).

FNN Models for Prediction of DO at Near Critical Pressures

There exist no analytical methods to determine the optimum number of hidden layers and optimum number of hidden neurons in each layer required for a specific problem. For FNN, several rules of thumb to select the number of hidden neurons have been proposed by various researchers (Rovithakis, et al., 2004; Wang & Lin, 1995). It should be mentioned that the number of hidden neurons generally depends on many factors, especially the distribution of training data and the number of data samples and exactly defining of that is yet controversial. However, in this work, each FNN was trained with a different number of hidden layers (from 1 to 3) and different number of neurons in each hidden layer. The error value is high when the number of layers and neurons is low. Although increasing the number of hidden layers and hidden neurons decreases the final error value and makes the network move toward the global minimum, it usually leads to an overfitting over the training data. In this case, the number of network parameters that are adjusted through the learning algorithm is more than the required ones. For each FNN, a combination of sigmoid activation function and linear transfer function are used in the hidden and output layers, respectively. This combination has been shown to be sufficient to learn any types of mapping. We tried to find the best model including the number of hidden layers, neuron numbers in each hidden layer and activation function. Our investigations demonstrate that Tangent Sigmoid (TANSIG) function has better result than Logarithm Sigmoid (LOGSIG) function. So by differing the number of hidden layers (1 to 3) and neuron numbers (1 to 20) in every hidden layer, we achieved the final FNN model which is best fitted to input-output mapping.

Numerical Discussions

In this study, two types of ANNs (FNN and HHONN) are trained with the experimental CHF data. Table 6 makes a comparison of these two models in prediction of DO. It also shows the number of data, which are in the range of ±10% either in the training set or in the testing set.

Table 6. Accuracy and RMS error of the HHONN and FNN

Model	Training data		Test data		
	No. of experimental data	Data no. inside band of ±10%	No. of experimental data	Data no. inside band of ±10%	RMS error (%)
HHONN	88	84	23	2	3.24
FNN	88	81	23	3	4.7

Thus, the accuracies of the HHONN and FNN are considered at the range of ±10%.

In this section, according to the results of previous sections for finding the best nonlinear model of FNN and HHONN, we compare the efficiency of models based on characteristics including output linear regression (R^2) and root-mean square (RMS) of error.

In statistics, R2 with one independent variable is performed using Equation (13):

$$R^2 = 1 - \frac{\sum_{i=1}^{n}(y_i - \hat{y}_i)^2}{\sum_{i=1}^{n}(y_i - \overline{y})^2}$$

$$\overline{y} = \frac{1}{n}\sum_{i=1}^{n} y_i \qquad (13)$$

where $\overline{y}$ is the mean value of output, y_i is the ith output of network and $\hat{y}_i$ is the desired value. In addition, to evaluate the precision of estimations, we calculated the RMS defined by Equations presented in (14):

Mean Square Error: $MSE = \frac{1}{n}\sum_{i=1}^{n}(\hat{y}_i - y_i)^2$

$$RMS = \sqrt{MSE} = \sqrt{\frac{1}{n}\sum_{i=1}^{n}(\hat{y}_i - y_i)^2} \qquad (14)$$

Figure 10 shows the linear regression of DO prediction by FNN and HHONN and draws a

Figure 10. The prediction results with HHONN and FNN: a) prediction of DO with HHONN, b) prediction of DO with FNN

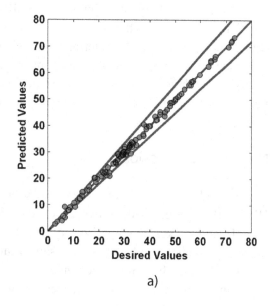

a)

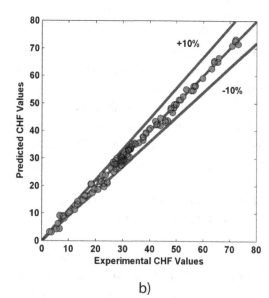

b)

comparison with the desired values. As it can be seen in Figures 10a and 10b, all points are located nearby the diagonal line and this shows that the results obtained from FNN and HHONN agree with the desired values. However, the value of regression for the HHONN is better than FNN. Figures 10a and 10b illustrate all 111 data samples including training and validation samples. In validation data R^2 value of HHONN is 0.96104 while this value for FNN is 0.93813 which shows the great strength of nonlinear function approximation of HHONN model for predicting DO at near critical pressures. HHONN and FNN predict DO with RMS error of 3.24%, 4.7%, respectively.

Figure 11 draws a comparison between the look-up table method of Groeneveld (1986), the generalized DO correlation of Katto and Ohno (1984) with HHONN and FFN models. As shown in Figure 11, it is clear that prediction of HHONN and FNN are superior to other methods, especially at high reduced pressure.

Structural Discussion

However, the FNN mapping can be presented in an Equation. It needs more discussion to be clarified. There is a substantial difference between the FNN and HONN structures. As it can be seen in Equation (3), the HONN model is non-linear combination of inputs in each term, and summation of these terms directly construct the model, as Figure 2 represents the concept. In contrast, the general FNN model is constructed by Equation (15):

$$Y^1_{net} = \sum_{i=1}^{N} X_i W^1_i + W^1_0$$

$$Y^1 = f(Y^1_{net}) = \frac{1}{1 + e^{-Y^1_{net}}}$$

$$Y^2_{net} = \sum_{i=1}^{N} Y^1_i W^2_i + W^2_0$$

$$Y^2 = f(Y^2_{net}) = \frac{1}{1 + e^{-Y^2_{net}}} \quad (15)$$

$$Y^n_{net} = \sum_{i=1}^{N} Y^{n-1}_i W^n_i + W^n_0$$

$$Y^n = f(Y^n_{net}) = \frac{1}{1 + e^{-Y^n_{net}}}$$

Equation (15) represents the connections between layers. The final output is combination of last layer neurons. The obtained formula from FNN will be more intricate than HONN. Furthermore, HONN inputs directly construct the output, it means that in FNN models the, input passes from several different functions to build output. It should be noted that the one layer FNN can be accounted for an open-box model. Only in this case, the input transmits from one function.

A traditional ANN with single connections having no hidden layer just can map neuron inputs linearly to neuron outputs. Single hidden layer FNNs are known for their ability of function approximation and learning pattern recognition. In spite of these, they cannot realize every nonlinear mapping. FNNs incorporating more hidden layers are known to have long convergence time and usually stuck in local minima rather than global minima. They have more complex structure than others, so that initializing the weights will be difficult and also investigating of the input-output mapping might be a disaster. Furthermore, most often the purpose of using an intelligent unit is to have an open-box model of input-output mapping. BPNs are acting like black-box models and as the number of hidden layers increases, this black-box becomes harder to understand.

Figure 11. The comparison of methods of prediction: a) prediction of DO with Katto and Ohno (1984) correlation, b) prediction of DO with Groeneveld (1986) method, c) prediction of DO with Vijayarangan et al. (2006) correlation, d) prediction of DO with FNN method, e) prediction of DO with HHONN method

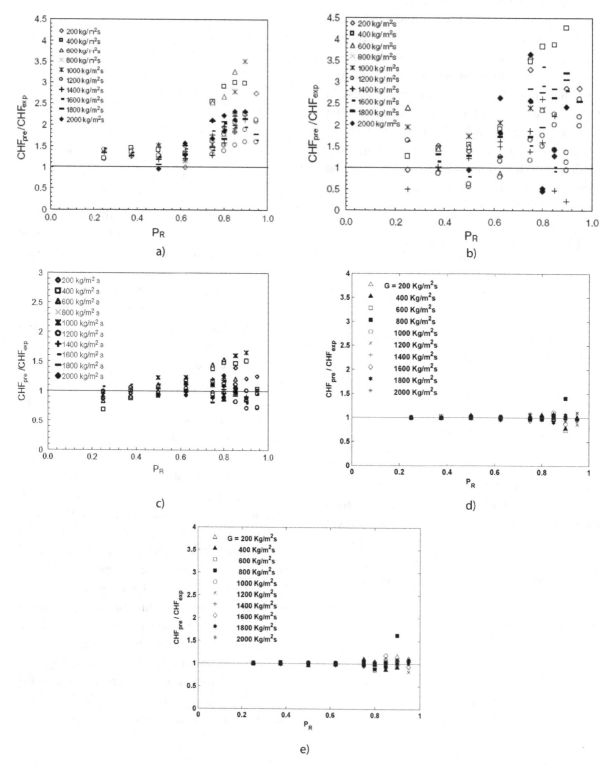

Table 7. Nomenclature and abbreviations

Nomenclature	Abbreviations	
D diameter of tube (m)	ANN	artificial neural network
G mass flow rate (kgm^{-2} s^{-1})	ASONU	artificial second order neural unit
L heated length (m)	BPN	backpropagation network
L/D the heated length to tube	CHF	critical heat flux
diameter ratio	DNB	departure from nucleate boiling
P pressure (kPa)	DO	dryout
P$_R$ reduced pressure	FNN	feed-forward neural network
q heat flux	HONN	high order neural network
X dry-out quality R^2 linear regression	HHONN HHONC	hybrid HONN hybrid higher order neural classifier
a$_i$ weight coefficient of each each neuron input	HPU	higher-order processing unit
	MC	Model Complexity
a$_{ij}$ weight between the neurons i and j	MSE	mean square error
	PHONN	polynomial HONN
x Feature of input vector W_0 bias	PSN RMS	pi-sigma network root-mean square
Y$_i$ Response of neuron i	RPSN	recursive PSN
J_r error between observed value and network response	RPHONN	ridge polynomial HONN
	SAS NLIN	system nonlinear
O_i observed val$^{\text{ue of neuron}}$ i	SINCHONN	SINC HONN
Y_{net} summation of weighted inputs	SONN	second order neural network
Z output of HONN model	SPHONN	sigmoid polynomial HONN
normalized value of feature *j*th of sample *i*th	SXSPHONN	SINC and sine polynomial HONN
original value of feature *j*th of sample *i*th	THONN	trigonometric HONN
values of feature *j*th	UCSHONN	ultra high frequency cosine and sine HONN

CONCLUSION

In this chapter, a hybrid higher order neural structure has been introduced and applied in two different areas, pattern classification, and functional behavior approximation of a heat and mass transfer dilemma. As a classifier, the results demonstrated the strength of designed classifier more specifically when dealing with datasets containing few features (less than 8). This network was used as a general structure for functional behavior approximation of a well-known problem.

The selected problem is a process identification and optimization in heat and mass transfer area. Comparisons between results of the developed structure and previous works show that structure can be useful in a general scheme and can be applied to a variety of pattern behavior approximation and recognition (see Table 7).

REFERENCES

Abdelbar, A. (1998). Achieving superior generalization with a high order neural network. *Neural Computing & Applications, Volume, 7*(Issue: 2), 141–146. doi:10.1007/BF01414166

Artyomov, E., O. Y.-P. (2005). Modified high-order neural network for invariant pattern recognition. *Pattern Recognition Letters, 26*(6), 843–851. doi:10.1016/j.patrec.2004.09.029

Banerji, R. B. (1964). A language for the description of concepts. *General Systems, 9*(1), 135–141.

Boser, B. E. (1992). A training algorithm for optimal margin classifiers. *In Proceedings of the fifth annual workshop on computational learning theory, Pittsburgh, Pennsylvania*, pp. 144–152.

Chen, S. M. (2002). Automatically constructing membership functions and generating fuzzy rules using genetic algorithms. *Cybernetics and Systems, 33*(8), 841–862. doi:10.1080/01969720290040867

Chen, S. M. (2002). Generating fuzzy rules from training data containing noise for handling classification problems. *Cybernetics and Systems, 33*(7), 723–748.

Chen, S. M. (2005). A new method to construct membership functions and generate weighted fuzzy rules from training instances. *Cybernetics and Systems, 36*(4), 397–414. doi:10.1080/01969720490929562

Chen, S. M. (2008). Fuzzy classification systems based on fuzzy information gain measures,. *International journal of Expert Systems with Applications.*, in press.

Cover, T. M. (1967). Nearest neighbor pattern classification. *IEEE Transactions on Information Theory, IT-13*(1), 21–27. doi:10.1109/TIT.1967.1053964

Dong, G. P. (2007). *Sequence Data Mining.* Springer.

Fisher, R. A. (1936). The use of multiple measurements in taxonomic problems. *Annals of Eugenics, 7*(2), 179–188.

Foresti, G.L, T. D. (2004). An adaptive high-order neural tree for pattern recognition. *IEEE Transactions on Systems, Man, and Cybernetics. Part B, Cybernetics, 34*(2), 988–996. doi:10.1109/TSMCB.2003.818538

Fulcher, J. Z. (2006). Application of higher-order neural networks to financial time series prediction. In J. B. Kamruzzaman, *Artificial neural networks in finance and manufacturing* (pp. (pp. 80-108)). New York: Idea Group Inc (IGI).

Ghazali, R. H.-j. (2007). Dynamic Ridge Polynomial Neural Networks in Exchange Rates Time Series Forecasting. In B. Beliczynski, A. Dzielinski, M. Iwanowski, & B. Ribeiro, *Adaptive and Natural Computing Algorithms.* (pp. 123-132). Berlin: Springer Berlin / Heidelberg.

Gomez, J. G. (2005). A fuzzy rule coevolutionary approach for multiclass classification problems. *In Proceedings of the 2005 IEEE congress on evolutionary computation, Edinburgh, UK*, pp. 1637–1644.

Gupta, M. M. (2009). Fundamental theory of artificial higher order neural networks. In M. Zhang, *Artificial higher order neural networks for economics and business.* (pp. pp. 368-388). Idea Group Inc (IGI).

Hagan, M. T. (1996). *Neural network design*. PWS Publishing Company.

Homma, N. (2002). A general second order neural unit. *Bull. Coll. Med. Sci. Tohoku Univ.*, *11*(1), 1–6.

Hsing Chih Tsai (in press). (2008). Hybrid high order neural networks. *International Journal of Applied Soft Computing* .

Hussain, A. L. P. (2008). A Novel Recurrent Polynomial Neural Network for Financial Time Series Prediction. In Z. M., *Higher Order Neural Networks for Economics and Business.* (pp. 190-211). Idea Group Inc (IGI)

Jakubowski, J. K. (2002). Higher Order Statistics and Neural Network for Tremor Recognition. *IEEE TRANSACTIONS ON BIOMEDICAL ENGINEERING, VOL.*, *49*(2), 152–159. doi:10.1109/10.979354

Jin-Yan Li Chow, T. Y.-L. (1995). The estimation theory and optimization algorithm for the number of hidden units in the higher-order feedforward neural network. *Neural Networks. Proceedings., IEEE International Conference on*, Volume: 3, On page(s): 1229-1233 vol.3.

John, G. H. (1995). Estimating continuous distributions in Bayesian. *In Proceedings of the 11th conference on uncertainty in artificial intelligence, Montreal, Canada*, pp. 338–345.

John, G. H. (1995). Estimating continuous distributions in Bayesian. *In Proceedings of the 11th conference on uncertainty in artificial intelligence, Montreal, Canada,* pp. 338–345.

John, G. H. (1995). Estimating continuous distributions in baysian classifiers. *In Proceedings of the 11th conference on uncertainty in artificial intelligence, Montreal, Canada*, pp. 338–345.

Lee, Y. D. (1986). Machine learning using a higher order correlation network. *Physica D. Nonlinear Phenomena*, *22*, 276–306.

Lippmann, R. (1989). Pattern classification using neural networks. *Communications Magazine, IEEE*, Volume: 27, Issue: 11.

Peng, H. Z. (2007). Handling of incomplete data sets using ICA and SOM in data mining. *Neural Computing & Applications*, 167–172. doi:10.1007/s00521-006-0058-6

Platt, J. C. (1999). Using analytic QP and sparseness to speed training of support vector machines. *In Proceedings of the 13th annual conference on neural information processing systems, Denver, Colorado*, pp. 557–563.

Quinlan, J. R. (1986). Induction of decision trees. *Machine Learning*, *1*(1), 81–106. doi:10.1007/BF00116251

Quinlan, J. R. (1986). Induction of decision trees. *Machine Learning*, *1*(1), 81–106. doi:10.1007/BF00116251

Quinlan, J. R. (1993). *C.45 Programs for machine learning Kaufmann.*

Ramanathan, K. G. (2007). Multiorder neurons for evolutionary higher-order clustering and growth. *Neural Computation, Volume*, *19*(Issue: 12), 3369–3391. doi:10.1162/neco.2007.19.12.3369

Reid, M. S. (1989). Rapid training of higher-order neural networks for invariant pattern recognition. *Neural Networks. IJCNN., International Joint Conference on*, 689-692 vol.1.

Reynolds, D. R. (1995). Robust text-independent speaker identification using Gaussian mixture speaker models. *IEEE Transactions on Speech and Audio Processing*, 72–83. doi:10.1109/89.365379

Rovithakis, G., Maniadakis, M., & Zervakis, M. (2000). Artificial neural networks for feature extraction and classification of vascular tissue fluorescence spectrums. *Acoustics, Speech, and Signal Processing, 2000. ICASSP apos;00. Proceedings. 2000 IEEE International Conference on*, Page(s):3454 - 3457 vol.6.

Rovithakis, G. I. (2004). High-order neural network structure selection for function approximation applications using genetic algorithms. *IEEE Transactions on Systems, Man, and Cybernetics. Part B, Cybernetics, 34*(1), 150–158. doi:10.1109/TSMCB.2003.811767

Rovithakis, G. M. (2000). Artificial neural networks for feature extraction and classification of vascular tissue fluorescence spectrums. *Acoustics, Speech, and Signal Processing. ICASSP '00. Proceedings.IEEE International Conference on*, 3454 - 3457 vol.6.

Shin, Y. a. (1991). The Pi-Sigma Networks: An Efficient Higher-order Neural Network for Pattern Classification and Function Approximation. *Proceedings of International Joint Conference on Neural Networks*, Vol.1, pp.13-18.

Shin, Y. a. (1995). Ridge Polynomial Networks. *IEEE Transactions on Neural Networks, 6*(3), 610–622. doi:10.1109/72.377967

Shin, Y. G. (1995). Ridge polynomial networks. *Neural Networks, IEEE Transactions on*, Volume: 6, Issue: 3, On page(s): 610-622.

Shu, M. M. (2007). Genetic Algorithms Designed for Solving Support Vector Classifier. *Data, Privacy, and E-Commerce, 2007. ISDPE 2007. The First International Symposium on*, 167 - 169.

Shuxiang Xu, L. C. (2008). Application of New Adaptive Higher Order Neural Networks in Data Mining. *Computer Science and Software Engineering, 2008 International Conference on*, Volume: 1, On page(s): 115-118.

Spirkovska, L. R. (1990). Connectivity strategies for higher-order neural networks applied to pattern recognition. *Neural Networks, 1990., 1990 IJCNN International Joint Conference on*, 21-26 vol.1.

Takeshi Kaita, S. T. (2002). On a higher-order neural network for distortion invariant pattern recognition. *Pattern Recognition Letters, 23*(Issue 8), 977–984. doi:10.1016/S0167-8655(02)00028-4

Wang, J. H. J. L. (1995). Qualitative analysis of the BP composed of product units and summing units. *IEEE International Conference on Systems, Man and Cybernetics 1*, 35–39.

Wang, S. H. (2003). Application of self-organising maps for data mining with incomplete data sets. *Neural Computing & Applications*, 42–48. doi:10.1007/s00521-003-0372-1

Wei Chu Keerthi, S. C. (2002). A new Bayesian design method for support vector classification. *Neural Information Processing. ICONIP '02. Proceedings of the 9th International Conference on*, 888 - 892 vol.2.

Winkler, S. M. (2006). Advances in applying genetic programming to machine learning, focusing on classification problems. *In Proceedings of the 20th international symposium on parallel and distributed processing, Rhodes Island, Greece*, pp. 2295–2302.

Xu, S. (2008). Adaptive Higher Order Neural Network Models and Their Applications in Business. In M. Zhang, *Artificial Higher Order Neural Networks for Economics and Business* (pp. 314-329). IGI Global.

Zhang, M. (2008). *Artificial Higher Order Neural Networks for Economics and Business*. Hershey: IGI Global. doi:10.4018/978-1-59904-897-0

Zhang, M. X. (2002). Neuron-adaptive higher order neural-network models for automated financial data modeling. *Neural Networks, IEEE Transactions on*, Volume 13, Issue 1, Page(s):188 - 204.

ZHENGQUAN HE. M. Y. (1999). Improvement on higher-order neural networks for invariant object recognition. *Springer, Neural processing letters ISSN 1370-4621*, vol. 10, no1, pp. 49-55 (11 ref.).

Zurada, J. M. (1992). *Introduction to Artificial Neural Systems*. St. Paul: West Publishing Company.

KEY TERMS AND DEFINITIONS

Backpropagation: A supervised method of updating learning parameters used for neural networks where error of each layer is backward propagation of errors of other forward layers.

Backpropagation Network (BPN): A network which learning parameters are updated using back propagation method.

Classification: Expressing outputs in a set of classes and mapping each input data to one of those classes.

Critical Heat Flux (CHF): Describes the thermal limit of a phenomenon where a phase change occurs during heating (such as bubbles forming on a metal surface used to heat water), which suddenly decreases the efficiency of heat transfer, thus causing localized overheating of the heating surface.

Departure from Nucleate Boiling (DNB): If the heat flux of a boiling system is higher than the Critical Heat Flux (CHF) of the system, the bulk fluid may boil. Thus large bubbles form, sometimes blocking the passage of the fluid. This results in a departure from nucleate boiling.

Dry-Out (DO): Condition represents the termination of continuous liquid contact with the wall. It follows the gradual depletion of liquid due to evaporation and entrainment of the liquid film. The vapor, from the continuous vapor phase in the bulk flow, covers the heated surface, and the discrete liquid droplets flowing in the vapor core may make occasional contact with the heated surface.

Feedforward Neural Network (FNN): A simplest type of artificial neural network which direction is forward from inputs to hidden layer(s) and to outputs.

Hybrid Higher Order Neural Network (HHONN): A hybrid structure incorporating linear combination of high-order terms.

Pattern Recognition: Data mapping of outputs to specific inputs according to a behavior.

Compilation of References

Abdelbar, A. (1998). Achieving superior generalization with a high order neural network. *Neural Computing & Applications, Volume,* 7(Issue: 2), 141–146. doi:10.1007/BF01414166

Abdelbar, A. M. (1998). Achieving superior generalisation with a high order neural network. *Neural Computing & Applications,* 7(2), 141–146. doi:10.1007/BF01414166

Abolhassani, N., Patel, R., & Moallem, M. (2007). Needle insertion into soft tissue: A survey. *International Journal of Medicine and Engineering Physics,* 29, 413–431. doi:10.1016/j.medengphy.2006.07.003

Adas, A. N. (1998). Using adaptive linear prediction to support real – time VBR video under RCBR network service model. *IEEE Transactions on Networking,* 6(5).

Alanis, A. Y., Sanchez, E. N., & Loukianov, A. G. (2006). Discrete-time recurrent neural induction motor control using Kalman learning. In *Proceedings of International Joint Conference on Neural Networks,* (pp. 1993–2000). IEEE.

Alanis, A. Y., Leon, B. S., Sanchez, E. N., & Ruiz-Velazquez, E. (2011). Blood glucose level neural model for type 1 diabetes mellitus patients. *International Journal of Neural Systems,* 21(6), 491–504. doi:10.1142/S0129065711003000

Alanis, A. Y., Sanchez, E. N., & Loukianov, A. G. (2010). Real-time discrete neural block control using sliding modes for electric induction motors. *IEEE Transactions on Control Systems Technology,* 18, 11–21. doi:10.1109/TCST.2008.2009466

Alanis, A. Y., Sanchez, E. N., Loukianov, A. G., & Perez-Cisneros, M. A. (2010). Real-time discrete neural block control using sliding modes for electric induction motors. *IEEE Transactions on Control Systems Technology,* 18(1), 11–21. doi:10.1109/TCST.2008.2009466

Alanis, A. Y., Sanchez, E. N., Loukianov, A. G., & Perez-Cisneros, M. A. (2011). Real-time neural-state estimation. *IEEE Transactions on Neural Networks,* 22(3), 497–505. doi:10.1109/TNN.2010.2103322

Alcaraz-Gonzalez, V., & Gonzalez-Alvarez, V. (2007). Robust nonlinear observers for bioprocesses: Application to wastewater treatment. In *Selected Topics in Dynamics and Control of Chemical and Biological Processes* (pp. 119–164). Berlin, Germany: Springer-Verlag. doi:10.1007/978-3-540-73188-7_5

Al-Rawi, M. S., & Al-Rawi, K. R. (2010). On the equivalence between ordinary neural networks and higher order neural networks. In Zhang, M. (Ed.), *Artificial Higher Order Neural Networks for Computer Science and Engineering – Trends for Emerging Application* (pp. 138–158). Hershey, PA: IGI Global.

Alterovitz, R., Goldberg, K., & Okamura, A. (2005). Planning for steerable bevel-tip needle insertion through 2D soft tissue with obstacles. In *Proceedings of ICRA,* (pp. 1652-1657). Barcelona, Spain: ICRA.

Amari, S. (1971). Characteristics of randomly connected threshold element networks and network systems. *Proceedings of the IEEE,* 59, 35–47. doi:10.1109/PROC.1971.8087

Amari, S. (1972). Characteristics of random nets of analog neuron-like elements. *IEEE Transactions on Systems, Man, and Cybernetics,* 2(5), 643–657. doi:10.1109/TSMC.1972.4309193

Amari, S. (1974). A method of statistical neurodynamics. *Kybernetik,* 14, 201–215.

Amari, S., & Maginu, K. (1988). Statistical neurodynamics of associative memories. *Neural Networks,* 1, 63–73. doi:10.1016/0893-6080(88)90022-6

Amartur, S. C., Piraino, D., & Takefuji, Y. (1992). Optimization neural networks for the segmentation of magnetic resonance images. *IEEE Transactions on Medical Imaging, 11*(2), 215–220. doi:10.1109/42.141645

An, Z. G., Mniszewski, S. M., Lee, Y. C., Papcun, G., & Doolen, G. D. (1988). HIERtalker: A default hierarchy of high order neural networks that learns to read English aloud. In *Proceedings of the Fourth Conference on Artificial Intelligence Applications,* (p. 388). IEEE.

Angeline, P. J., Sunders, G. M., & Pollack, J. B. (1994). An evolutionary algorithm that constructs recurrent artificial neural networks. *IEEE Transactions on Neural Networks, 5,* 54–65. doi:10.1109/72.265960

Annios, P. A., Csermely, B., & Harth, E. M. (1970). Dynamics of neural structures. *Journal of Theoretical Biology, 26,* 121–148. doi:10.1016/S0022-5193(70)80036-4

Aquino, R. R. B., Lira, M. M. S., Oliveira, J. B., Carvalho, M. A., Jr., & Neto, O. N. (2009). Application of wavelet and neural network models for wind speed forecasting and power generation in a Brazilian experimental wind park. In *Proceedings of the IEEE International Joint Conference on Neural Networks,* (pp. 172-178). Atlanta, GA: IEEE Press.

Arai, M., Kohon, R., & Imai, H. (1991). Adaptive control of a neural network with a variable function of a unit and its application. *Transactions on Institutional Electronic Information Communication Engineering, 74*(A), 551-559.

Artyomov, E., O. Y.-P. (2005). Modified high-order neural network for invariant pattern recognition. *Pattern Recognition Letters, 26*(6), 843–851. doi:10.1016/j.patrec.2004.09.029

Aseltine, J. A., Mancini, A. R., & Sartune, C. W. (1958). A survey of adaptive control systems. *I.R.E. Transactions on Automatic Control, 3*(6), 102–108. doi:10.1109/TAC.1958.1105168

Asuncion, A., & Newman, D. J. (2007). *UCI machine learning repository*. Irvine, CA: University of California. Retrieved from http://www.ics.uci.edu/~mlearn/MLRepository.html

Atiya, A. F. (2001). Bankruptcy prediction for credit risk using neural networks: A survey and new results. *IEEE Transactions on Neural Networks, 12*(4), 929–935. doi:10.1109/72.935101

Atiya, A. F., Aly, M. A. A., & Parlos, G. (2005). Sparse basis selection: New results and application to adaptive prediction of video source traffic. *IEEE Transactions on Neural Networks, 16*(5), 1136–1146. doi:10.1109/TNN.2005.853426

Atiya, A. F., Yoo, S. G., Chong, K. T., & Kim, H. (2007). Packet loss rate prediction using the sparse basis prediction model. *IEEE Transactions on Neural Networks, 18*(3), 950–954. doi:10.1109/TNN.2007.891681

Azema-Barac, M., & Refenes, A. (1997). Neural networks for financial applications. In Fiesler, E., & Beale, R. (Eds.), *Handbook of Neural Computation*. Oxford University Press. doi:10.1887/0750303123/b365c125

Azoff, E. (1994). *Neural network time series forecasting of financial markets*. Chichester, UK: Wiley.

Baber, W., Daniel, P., & Roberts, A. (2002). Compensation to managers of charitable organizations: An empirical study of the role of accounting measures of program activities. *Accounting Review, 77*(3), 679–693. doi:10.2308/accr.2002.77.3.679

Baber, W., Janakiraman, S., & Kang, S. (1996). Investment opportunities and the structure of performance-based executive compensation. *Journal of Accounting and Economics, 21*(3), 297–318. doi:10.1016/0165-4101(96)00421-1

Babu, B. V., & Sheth, P. N. (2006). Modeling and simulation of reduction zone of downdraft biomass gasifier: Effect of char reactivity factor. *Energy Conversion and Management, 47*(15–16), 2602–2611. doi:10.1016/j.enconman.2005.10.032

Baesens, B., Setiono, R., Mues, C., & Vanthienen, J. (2003). Using neural network rule extraction and decision tables for credit-risk evaluation. *Management Science, 49*(3). doi:10.1287/mnsc.49.3.312.12739

Baldi, P., & Venkatesh, S. S. (1993). Random interactions in higher order neural networks. *IEEE Transactions on Information Theory, 39*(1), 274–283. doi:10.1109/18.179374

Banerji, R. B. (1964). A language for the description of concepts. *General Systems, 9*(1), 135–141.

Barbe, L., & Bayle, B., De Mathelin, et al. (2007). Needle insertions modeling: Identifiability and limitations. *International Journal of Biomedical Signal Processing and Control, 2,* 191–198. doi:10.1016/j.bspc.2007.06.003

Barbounis, T. G., Theocaris, J. B., Alexiadis, M. C., & Dokoupoulos, P. S. (2006). Long-Term wind speed and power forecasting using local recurrent neural network models. *IEEE Transactions on Energy Conversion, 21*(1), 273–284. doi:10.1109/TEC.2005.847954

Barron, R., Gilstrap, L., & Shrier, S. (1987). Polynomial and neural networks: Analogies and engineering applications. In *Proceedings of International Conference of Neural Networks*, (Vol. 2), (pp. 431-439). New York, NY: IEEE.

Barron, A. R. (1994). Approximation and estimation bounds for artificial neural networks. *Machine Learning, 14*, 115–133. doi:10.1007/BF00993164

Baruch, I. S., Galvan-Guerra, R., & Nenkova, B. (2008). Centralized indirect control of an anaerobic digestion bioprocess using recurrent neural identifier. *Lecture Notes in Computer Science*, 297–310. doi:10.1007/978-3-540-85776-1_25

Bastin, G., & Dochain, D. (1990). *On-line estimation and adaptive control of bioreactors*. Amsterdam, The Netherlands: Elsevier Science Publications. doi:10.1016/S0003-2670(00)82585-4

Basu, P., & Kaushal, P. (2009). Modeling of pyrolysis and gasification of biomass in fluidized beds: A review. *Chemical Product and Process Modeling, 4*(1).

Behnke, S., & Karayiannis, N. B. (1998). CNeT: Competitive neural trees for pattern classifications. *IEEE Transactions on Neural Networks, 9*(6), 1352–1369. doi:10.1109/72.728387

Belmonte-Izquierdo, R., Carlos-Hernandez, S., & Sanchez, E. N. (2009). Hybrid intelligent control scheme for an anaerobic wastewater treatment process. In *Proceedings of the Second International Workshop on Advanced Computational Intelligence (IWACI 2009)*. Mexico City, Mexico: IWACI.

Belmonte-Izquierdo, R., Carlos-Hernandez, S., & Sanchez, E. N. (2010). A new neural observer for an anaerobic bioreactor. *International Journal of Neural Systems, 20*(1), 75–86. doi:10.1142/S0129065710002267

Bernstein, D. S. (2005). *Matrix mathematics*. Princeton, NJ: Princeton University Press.

Beteau, J. F. (1992). *An industrial wastewater treatment bioprocess modelling and control*. (Unpublished Doctoral Dissertation). INPG. France.

Bhattacharya, A., Parlos, A. G., & Atyia, A. F. (2003). Prediction of MPEG-coded source traffic using recurrent neural networks. *IEEE Transactions on Signal Processing, 51*(8). doi:10.1109/TSP.2003.814470

Bigus, J. P. (1996). *Data mining with neural networks*. New York, NY: McGraw-Hill.

Bishoff, J. T. RCM-PAKY. (1998). Clinical application of a new robotic system for precise needle placement. *Journal of Endourology*. Retrieved from http://www.ncbi.nlm.nih.gov/pmc/articles/PMC3099458/

Blum, E., & Li, K. (1991). Approximation theory and feed-forward networks. *Neural Networks, 4*, 511–515. doi:10.1016/0893-6080(91)90047-9

Boser, B. E. (1992). A training algorithm for optimal margin classifiers. *In Proceedings of the fifth annual workshop on computational learning theory, Pittsburgh, Pennsylvania*, pp. 144–152.

Boutalis, Y. S., Christodoulou, M. A., & Theodoridis, D. C. (2010). Identification of nonlinear systems using a new neuro-fuzzy dynamical system definition based on high order neural network function approximators. In Zhang, M. (Ed.), *Artificial Higher Order Neural Networks for Computer Science and Engineering – Trends for Emerging Application* (pp. 423–449). Hershey, PA: IGI Global.

Boutalis, Y. S., Theodoridis, D. C., & Christodoulou, M. A. (2009). A new neuro FDS definition for indirect adaptive control of unknown nonlinear systems using a method of parameter hopping. *IEEE Transactions on Neural Networks, 20*(4), 609–625. doi:10.1109/TNN.2008.2010772

Brachman, R. J., Khabaza, T., Kloesgen, W., Piatetsky-Shapiro, E., & Simoudis, E. (1996). Mining business databases. *Communications of the ACM, 39*(11), 42–48. doi:10.1145/240455.240468

Bridgwater, A. V. (2003). Renewable fuels and chemicals by thermal processing of biomass. *Chemical Engineering Journal, 91*, 87–102. doi:10.1016/S1385-8947(02)00142-0

Brock, W., & Sayers, C. (1988). Is the business cycle characterized by deterministic chaos? *Journal of Monetary Economics*, *22*(1), 71–91. doi:10.1016/0304-3932(88)90170-5

Brown, D., Fuchino, T., & Marechal, F. (2006). Solid fuel decomposition modelling for the design of biomass gasification systems. In W. Marquardt & C. Pantelides (Eds.), *Proceedings of the 16th European Symposium on Computer Aided Process Engineering and 9th International Symposium on Process Systems Engineering,* (pp. 1661–1666). Garmisch-Partenkirchen, Germany: IEEE.

Browne, A., Hudson, B. D., Whitley, D. C., Ford, M. G., & Picton, P. (2004). Biological data mining with neural networks: Implementation and application of a flexible decision tree extraction algorithm to genomic problem domains. *Neurocomputing*, *57*, 275–293. doi:10.1016/j.neucom.2003.10.007

Brucoli, M., Carnimeo, L., & Grassi, G. (1997). Associative memory design using discrete-time second-order neural networks with local interconnections. *IEEE Transactions on Circuits and Systems. I, Fundamental Theory and Applications*, *44*(2), 153–158. doi:10.1109/81.554334

Bukovsky, I., & Simeunovic, G. (2006). Dynamic-order-extended time-delay dynamic neural units. In *Proceedings of the 8th Seminar on Neural Network Applications in Electrical Engineering NEUREL-2006*. IEEE Press.

Bukovsky, I., Bila, J., & Gupta, M. M. (2006). Stable neural architecture of dynamic neural units with adaptive time delays. In *Proceedings of the 7th International FLINS Conference on Applied Artificial Intelligence,* (pp. 215-222). FLINS.

Bukovsky, I., Homma, N., Smetana, L., Rodriguez, R., Mironovova, M., & Vrana, S. (2010). Quadratic neural unit is a good compromise between linear models and neural networks for industrial applications. In *Proceedings of the ICCI 2010: the 9th IEEE International Conference on Cognitive Informatics*. Beijing, China: IEEE Press.

Bukovsky, I., Bila, J., & Gupta, M. M. (2005). Linear dynamic neural units with time delay for identification and control. *Automatizace*, *48*(10), 628–635.

Bukovsky, I., Bila, J., Gupta, M. M., Hou, Z.-G., & Homma, N. (2010). Foundation and classification of nonconventional neural units and paradigm of nonsynaptic neural interaction. In Wang, Y. (Ed.), *Discoveries and Breakthroughs in Cognitive Informatics and Natural Intelligence* (pp. 508–523). Hershey, PA: IGI Global. doi:10.4018/978-1-60566-902-1.ch027

Burns, T. (1986). The interpretation and use of economic predictions. *Proceedings of the Royal Society A*, 103-125.

Burshtein, D. (1998). Long-term attraction in higher order neural networks. *IEEE Transactions on Neural Networks*, *9*(1), 42–50. doi:10.1109/72.655028

Butt, N. R., & Shafiq, M. (2006). Higher-order neural network based root-solving controller for adaptive tracking of stable nonlinear plants. In *Proceedings of IEEE International Conference on Engineering of Intelligent Systems,* (pp. 1 – 6). IEEE Press.

Campolucci, P., Capparelli, F., Guarnieri, S., Piazza, F., & Uncini, A. (1996). Neural networks with adaptive spline activation function. [Bari, Italy: IEEE Press.]. *Proceedings of IEEE MELECON*, *1996*, 1442–1445.

Campos, J., Loukianov, A. G., & Sanchez, E. N. (2003). Synchronous motor VSS control using recurrent high order neural networks. In *Proceedings of 42nd IEEE Conference on Decision and Control,* (vol. 4), (pp. 3894 – 3899). IEEE Press.

Cao, J., Lin, Z., & Huang, G. B. (2010). Composite function wavelet neural networks with extreme learning machine. *Neurocomputing*, *73*(7–9), 1405–1416. doi:10.1016/j.neucom.2009.12.007

Cao, J., Ren, F., & Liang, J. (2009). Dynamics in artificial higher order neural networks with delays. In Zhang, M. (Ed.), *Artificial Higher Order Neural Networks for Economics and Business* (pp. 389–429). Hershey, PA: IGI Global. doi:10.4018/978-1-59904-897-0.ch018

Carlos-Hernandez, S., Oudaak, N., Beteau, J. F., & Sanchez, E. N. (2004). Fuzzy observer for the anaerobic digestion process. In *Proceedings of IFAC Symposium on Structures Systems and Control*. Oaxaca, Mexico: IFAC.

Carlos-Hernandez, S., Sanchez, E. N., & Bueno, J. A. (2010). *Neurofuzzy control strategy for an abattoir wastewater treatment process*. Paper presented at the 11th IFAC Symposium on Computer Applications in Biotechnology. Leuven, Belgica.

Carlos-Hernandez, S., Sanchez, E. N., & Beteau, J.-F. (2009). Fuzzy observers for anaerobic wwtp: Synthesis and implementation. *Control Engineering Practice, 17*(6), 690–702. doi:10.1016/j.conengprac.2008.11.008

Charitou, A., & Charalambous, C. (1996). The prediction of earnings using financial statement information: Empirical evidence with logit models and artifical neural networks. *Intelligent Systems in Accounting, Finance, and Management, 5*, 199–215. doi:10.1002/(SICI)1099-1174(199612)5:4<199::AID-ISAF114>3.0.CO;2-C

Cheh, J. J., Weinberg, R. S., & Yook, K. C. (1999). An application of an artificial neural network investment system to predict takeover targets. *Journal of Applied Business Research, 15*(4), 33–45.

Chen, G., & Lewis, F. L. (2011). Distributed adaptive tracking control for synchronization of unknown networked Lagrangian systems. *IEEE Transactions on Systems, Man, and Cybernetics, Part B, 41*(3).

Chen, J. S. (1987). *Kinetic engineering modelling of co-current moving bed gasification reactors for carbonaceous material*. (Unpublished Doctoral Dissertation). Ithaca, NY: Cornell University.

Chen, L., & Narendra, K. S. (2002). Nonlinear adaptive control using neural networks and multiple models. In *Proceedings of the 2000 American Control Conference*, (pp. 4199-4203). Chicago, IL: IEEE.

Chen, S. M. (2008). Fuzzy classification systems based on fuzzy information gain measures,. *International journal of Expert Systems with Applications.*, in press.

Chen, Y., Chen, F., & Wu, Q. (2007). An artificial neural networks based dynamic decision model for time-series forecasting. In *Proceedings of the IEEE International Joint Conference on Neural Networks*, (pp. 696-699). Orlando, FL: IEEE Press.

Chen, Y., Zhang, Y., Dong, J., & Yang, J. (2004). System identification by evolved flexible neural tree. In *Proceedings of the 5th Congress of Intelligent Control and Automation*. IEEE.

Chen, C. T., & Chang, W. D. (1996). A feedforward neural network with function shape autotuning. *Neural Networks, 9*(4), 627–641. doi:10.1016/0893-6080(96)00006-8

Chen, F. C., & Khalil, H. K. (1992). Adaptive control of nonlinear systems using neural networks. *International Journal of Control, 55*(6), 1299–1317. doi:10.1080/00207179208934286

Cheng, K. W., & Lee, T. (1993). On the convergence of neural network for higher order programing. In *Proceedings of IJCNN 1993*, (vol 2), (pp. 1507-1511). Nagoya, Japan: IJCNN.

Chen, H. H., Lee, Y. C., Maxwell, T., Sun, G. Z., Lee, H. Y., & Giles, C. L. (1986). High order correlation model for associative memory. *AIP Conference Proceedings, 151*, 86. doi:10.1063/1.36224

Chen, S. M. (2002). Automatically constructing membership functions and generating fuzzy rules using genetic algorithms. *Cybernetics and Systems, 33*(8), 841–862. doi:10.1080/01969720290040867

Chen, S. M. (2002). Generating fuzzy rules from training data containing noise for handling classification problems. *Cybernetics and Systems, 33*(7), 723–748.

Chen, S. M. (2005). A new method to construct membership functions and generate weighted fuzzy rules from training instances. *Cybernetics and Systems, 36*(4), 397–414. doi:10.1080/01969720490929562

Chen, S. S., Donoho, D. L., & Saunders, M. A. (1998). Atomic decomposition by basis pursuit. *SIAM Journal on Scientific Computing, 20*(1), 33–61. doi:10.1137/S1064827596304010

Chen, Y., & Abraham, A. (2005). Feature selection and intrusion detection using hybrid flexible neural trees. *Lecture Notes in Computer Science, 3498*, 439–444. doi:10.1007/11427469_71

Chen, Y., Cheng, J. J., & Creamer, K. S. (2007). Inhibition of anaerobic digestion process: A review. *Bioresource Technology, 99*(10), 4044–4064. doi:10.1016/j.biortech.2007.01.057

Chen, Y., Wu, P., & Wu, Q. (2009). Foreign exchange rate forecasting using higher order flexible neural tree. In Zhang, M. (Ed.), *Artificial Higher Order Neural Networks for Economics and Business* (pp. 94–112). Hershey, PA: IGI Global. doi:10.4018/978-1-59904-897-0.ch005

Chen, Y., Wu, P., & Wu, Q. (2009). Higher order neural networks for stock index modeling. In Zhang, M. (Ed.), *Artificial Higher Order Neural Networks for Economics and Business* (pp. 113–132). Hershey, PA: IGI Global. doi:10.4018/978-1-59904-897-0.ch006

Chen, Y., Yang, B., & Abraham, A. (2006). *Flexible neural trees ensemble for stock index modeling.* London, UK: Elsevier Science. doi:10.1016/j.neucom.2006.10.005

Chen, Y., Yang, B., & Dong, J. (2004). Nonlinear system modeling via optimal design of neural trees. *International Journal of Neural Systems, 4*(2), 125–137. doi:10.1142/S0129065704001905

Chen, Y., Yang, B., & Dong, J. (2004). Evolving flexible neural networks using ant programming and PSO algorithm. *Lecture Notes in Computer Science, 3173*, 211–216. doi:10.1007/978-3-540-28647-9_36

Chen, Y., Yang, B., Dong, J., & Abraham, A. (2004). Time series forecasting using flexible neural tree model. *Information Science, 174*, 219–235. doi:10.1016/j.ins.2004.10.005

Chen, Y., Yang, J., Zhang, Y., & Dong, J. (2005). Evolving additive tree models for system identification. *International Journal of Computational Cognition, 3*(2).

Cheung, K.-W., & Lee, T. (1993). On the convergence of neural network for higher order programming. In *Proceedings of IJCNN*, (vol 2), (pp. 1507—1511). IJCNN.

Cho, K. B., & Wang, B. H. (1996). Radial basis function based adaptive fuzzy systems and their applications to system identification and prediction. *Fuzzy Sets and Systems, 83*, 325–339. doi:10.1016/0165-0114(95)00322-3

Chopra, N., & Spong, M. W. (2006). Passivity-based control of multi-agent systems. In *Advances in Robot Control* (pp. 107–134). Berlin, Germany: Springer. doi:10.1007/978-3-540-37347-6_6

Chopra, N., & Spong, M. W. (2009). On exponential synchronization of Kuramoto oscillators. *IEEE Transactions on Automatic Control, 54*(2), 353–357. doi:10.1109/TAC.2008.2007884

Christodoulou, M. A., & Iliopoulos, T. N. (2006). Neural network models for prediction of steady-state and dynamic behavior of MAPK cascade. In *Proceedings of 14th Mediterranean Conference on Control and Automation,* (pp. 1 – 9). IEEE.

Chung, S., & Slotine, J. J. E. (2009). Cooperative robot control and concurrent synchronization of Lagrangian systems. *IEEE Transactions on Robotics, 25*(3), 686–700. doi:10.1109/TRO.2009.2014125

Cichochi, A., & Unbehauen, R. (1993). *Neural networks for optimization and signal processing.* Chichester, UK: Wiley.

Cios, K. J., Pedrycz, W., Swiniarski, R. W., & Kurgan, L. A. (2007). *Data mining: A knowledge discovery approach.* Berlin, Germany: Springer.

Coello, C. A., Lamont, G. B., & Veldhuizen, D. A. V. (2007). *Evolutionary algorithms for solving multi-objective problems* (2nd ed.). Berlin, Germany: Springer.

Coinfman, R. R., & Wickerhauser, M. V. (1992). Entropy–based algorithms for best basis selection. *IEEE Transactions on Information Theory, 38*, 713–718. doi:10.1109/18.119732

Cooper, B. S. (1995). Higher order neural networks for combinatorial optimization improving the scaling properties of the hopfield network. In *Proceedings of the IEEE ICNN 1995*, (vol 4), (pp. 1855-1890). IEEE Press.

Core, J., Guay, W., & Larcker, D. (2008). The power of the pen and executive compensation. *Journal of Financial Economics, 88*(1), 1–25. doi:10.1016/j.jfineco.2007.05.001

Core, J., Guay, W., & Verrecchia, R. (2003). Price versus non-price performance measures in optimal CEO compensation contracts. *Accounting Review, 78*(4), 957–981. doi:10.2308/accr.2003.78.4.957

Cotter, N. (1990). The stone-weierstrass theorem and its application to neural networks. *IEEE Transactions on Neural Networks, 1*(4), 290–295. doi:10.1109/72.80265

Cotter, S., Delgado, K. K., & Rao, B. (2001). Backward elimination for sparse vector subset selection. *Signal Processing, 81*, 1849–1864. doi:10.1016/S0165-1684(01)00064-0

Cover, T. M. (1967). Nearest neighbor pattern classification. *IEEE Transactions on Information Theory, IT-13*(1), 21–27. doi:10.1109/TIT.1967.1053964

Crane, J., & Zhang, M. (2005). Data simulation using SINCHONN model. In *Proceedings of IASTED International Conference on Computational Intelligence*, (pp. 50-55). Calgary, Canada: IASTED.

Crouch, J. R., Pizer, S. M., & Chaney, E. L. (2007). Automated finite-element analysis for deformable registration of prostate images. *IEEE Transactions on Medical Imaging, 26*, 1379–1390. doi:10.1109/TMI.2007.898810

Cuoci, A., Faravelli, T., Frassoldati, A., Grana, R., Pierucci, S., Ranzi, E., & Sommariva, S. (2009). Mathematical modelling of gasification and combustion of solid fuels and wastes. *Chemical Engineering Transactions, 18*, 989–994.

Dantigny, P., Ninow, J. L., & Lakrori, M. (1989). A new control strategy for yeast production based on the L/A* approach. *Applied Microbiology and Biotechnology, 36*(3), 352–357.

Das, A., Lewis, F. L., & Subbarao, K. (2010). Backstepping control of quadrotor: A dynamically tuned higher order like neural network approach. In Zhang, M. (Ed.), *Artificial Higher Order Neural Networks for Computer Science and Engineering – Trends for Emerging Application* (pp. 484–513). Hershey, PA: IGI Global.

Das, T., & Kar, I. N. (2006). Design and implementation of an adaptive fuzzy logic-based controller for wheeled mobile robots. *IEEE Transactions on Control Systems Technology, 14*, 501–510. doi:10.1109/TCST.2006.872536

Dayhoff, J. E. (1990). *Neural network architectures: An introduction*. New York, NY: Van Nostrand Reinhold.

De Souza, M. B., Jr., Barreto, A. G., Jr., Nemer, L. C., Soares, P. O., & Quitete, C. P. B. (2010). A study on modeling and operational optimization of biomass gasification processes using neural networks. In *Proceedings of 2010 Annual Meeting of AIChE*. Salt Lake City, UT: AIChE.

Dehuri, S., & Chao, S. (2010). A theoretical and empirical study of functional link neural networks (FLANNs) for classification. In Zhang, M. (Ed.), *Artificial Higher Order Neural Networks for Computer Science and Engineering – Trends for Emerging Application* (pp. 545–573). Hershey, PA: IGI Global.

Detournay, M., Hemati, M., & Andreux, R. (2011). Biomass steam gasification in fluidized bed of inert or catalytic particles: Comparison between experimental results and thermodynamic equilibrium predictions. *Powder Technology, 208*, 558–567. doi:10.1016/j.powtec.2010.08.059

Diao, Y., & Passino, K. M. (2002). Adaptive neural/fuzzy control for interpolated nonlinear systems. *IEEE Transactions on Fuzzy Systems, 10*(5), 583–595. doi:10.1109/TFUZZ.2002.803493

DiMaio, S. P., & Salcudean, S. E. (2003). Needle insertion modeling and simulation. *IEEE Transactions on Robotics and Automation, 19*, 864–875. doi:10.1109/TRA.2003.817044

Ding, Y. (2010). A high order neural network to solve n-queens problem. In *Proceedings of IJCNN*, (pp. 1-6). IJCNN.

Dochain, D., & Perrier, M. (1997). Dynamical modelling, analysis, monitoring and control design for nonlinear bioprocesses. *Advances in Biochemical Engineering/Biotechnology, 56*, 147–197. doi:10.1007/BFb0103032

Do, K. D., Jiang, Z. P., & Pan, J. (2004). Simultaneous tracking and stabilization of mobile robots: An adaptive approach. *IEEE Transactions on Automatic Control, 49*, 1147–1152. doi:10.1109/TAC.2004.831139

Dong, G. P. (2007). *Sequence Data Mining*. Springer.

Doulamis, A. D., Doulamis, N. D., & Kollias, S. D. (2000). Recursive nonlinear models for online traffic prediction of VBR MPEG coded video sources. In *Proceeding of IEEE-INNS-ENNS International Joint Conference on Neural Networks IJCNN*, (pp. 114-119). IEEE Press.

Doulamis, A. D., Doulamis, N. D., & Kollias, S. D. (2000). Nonlinear traffic modeling of VBR MPEG-2 video sources. In *Proceedings IEEE International Conference on Multi Media, ICME*, (pp. 1318-1321). IEEE Press.

Doulamis, A. D., Doulamis, N. D., & Kollias, S. D. (2003). An adaptable neural network model for recursive nonlinear traffic prediction and modeling of MPEG video sources. *IEEE Transactions on Neural Networks, 14*(1), 150–166. doi:10.1109/TNN.2002.806645

Draye, J. S., Pavisic, D. A., Cheron, G. A., & Libert, G. A. (1996). Dynamic recurrent neural networks: A dynamic analysis. *IEEE Transactions SMC- Part B, 26*(5), 692-706.

Dunis, C. L., Laws, J., & Evans, B. (2006). Modelling and trading the soybean-oil crush spread with recurrent and higher order networks: A comparative analysis. *Neural Network World, 3*(6), 193–213.

Dunis, C. L., Laws, J., & Evans, B. (2009). Modeling and trading the soybean-oil crush spread with recurrent and higher order networks: A comparative analysis. In Zhang, M. (Ed.), *Artificial Higher Order Neural Networks for Economics and Business* (pp. 348–367). Hershey, PA: IGI Global.

Dupont, D., Nocquet, T., Da Costa, J. A. Jr, & Verne-Tournon, C. (2011). Kinetic modelling of steam gasification of various woody biomass chars: Influence of inorganic elements. *Bioresource Technology*, *102*, 9743–9748. doi:10.1016/j.biortech.2011.07.016

Durbin, R., & Rumelhart, D. E. (1989). Product units: A computationally powerful and biologically plausible extension to backpropagation networks. *Neural Computation*, *1*(1), 133–142. doi:10.1162/neco.1989.1.1.133

El-Fouly Tarek, H. M., El-Saadany Ehab, F., & Salama Magdy, M. A. (2008). One day ahead prediction of wind speed and direction. *IEEE Transactions on Energy Conversion*, *23*(1), 191–201. doi:10.1109/TEC.2007.905069

Epitropakis, M. G., Plagianakos, V. P., & Vrahatis, M. N. (2010). Evolutionary algorithm training of higher order neural networks. In Zhang, M. (Ed.), *Artificial Higher Order Neural Networks for Computer Science and Engineering – Trends for Emerging Application* (pp. 57–85). Hershey, PA: IGI Global. doi:10.1016/j.asoc.2009.08.010

Eskander, G. S., & Atiya, A. F. (2007). A novel symbolic type neural network model- Application to river flow forecasting. In *Proceedings International Computer Engineering Conference (ICENCO 2007)*. Cairo, Egypt: ECENCO.

Eskander, G. S., Atiya, A., Chong, K. T., Kim, H., & Yoo, S. G. (2007). Round trip time prediction using the symbolic function network approach. In *Proceedings of the 2007 International Symposium on Information Technology Convergence (ISITC 2007)*. Jeonju, South Korea: IEEE Press.

Eskander, G., & Atiya, A. (2009). Symbolic function network. *Neural Networks*, *22*(4), 395–404. doi:10.1016/j.neunet.2009.02.003

Fahlman, S. E., & Lebiere, C. (1990). The cascade- correlation learning architecture. *Advances in Neural Information Processing Systems*, *2*, 524–532.

Fallahnezhad, M., Moradi, M. H., & Zaferanlouei, S. (2011). A hybrid higher order neural classifier for handling classification problems. *Expert Systems with Applications*, *38*, 386–393. doi:10.1016/j.eswa.2010.06.077

Fax, J. A., & Murray, R. M. (2004). Information flow and cooperative control of vehicle formations. *IEEE Transactions on Automatic Control*, *49*(9), 1465–1476. doi:10.1109/TAC.2004.834433

Feldkamp, L. A., Prokhorov, D. V., & Feldkamp, T. M. (2003). Simple and conditioned adaptive behavior from Kalman filter trained recurrent networks. *Neural Networks*, *16*, 683–689. doi:10.1016/S0893-6080(03)00127-8

Feng, G., Huang, G.-B., Lin, Q., & Gay, R. (2009). Error minimized extreme learning machine with growth of hidden nodes and incremental learning. *IEEE Transactions on Neural Networks*, *20*(8), 1352–1357. doi:10.1109/TNN.2009.2024147

Fiori, S. (2003). Closed-form expressions of some stochastic adapting equations for nonlinear adaptive activation function neurons. *Neural Computation*, *15*(12), 2909–2929. doi:10.1162/089976603322518795

Fisher, R. A. (1936). The use of multiple measurements in taxonomic problems. *Annals of Eugenics*, *7*(2), 179–188.

Fitzek, F., & Reisslein, M. (1998). *MPEG-4 and h.236 video traces for network performance evaluation*. Berlin, Germany: Technical University of Berlin.

Foka, A. (1999). *Time series prediction using evolving polynomial neural networks*. (MSc Thesis). University of Manchester Institute of Science & Technology. Manchester, UK.

Foo, Y. P. S., & Szu, H. (1989). Solving large-scale optimization problems by divide-and-conquer neural networks. In *Proceedings of IJCNN*, (vol 1), (pp. 507—511). IJCNN.

Foresti, G.L, T. D. (2004). An adaptive high-order neural tree for pattern recognition. *IEEE Transactions on Systems, Man, and Cybernetics. Part B, Cybernetics*, *34*(2), 988–996. doi:10.1109/TSMCB.2003.818538

Fox, B., Flynn, D., Bryans, L., Jenkis, N., Milborrow, D., & O'Malley, M. … Anaya-Lara, O. (2007). *Wind power integration: Connection and system operational aspects*. London, UK: The Institution of Engineering and Technology.

Fradkov, A. L., & Pogromsky, A. Y. (1998). *Introduction to control of oscillations and chaos*. Singapore: World Scientific Publishing Co.doi:10.1142/9789812798619

Freeman, R., & Tse, S. (1992). A non-linear model of security price responses to unexpected earnings. *Journal of Accounting Research*, 30(2), 85–109. doi:10.2307/2491123

Frost, V. S., & Melamed, B. (1994, March). Traffic modeling for telecommunications networks. *IEEE Communications Magazine*, 70–81. doi:10.1109/35.267444

Frumkin, P., & Keating, E. K. (2001). *The price of doing good: executive compensation in nonprofit organizations*. Working paper. Boston, MA: Harvard University.

Fulcher, J. Z. (2006). Application of higher-order neural networks to financial time series prediction. In J. B. Kamruzzaman, *Artificial neural networks in finance and manufacturing* (pp. (pp. 80-108)). New York: Idea Group Inc (IGI).

Fulcher, G. E., & Brown, D. E. (1994). A polynomial neural network for predicting temperature distributions. *IEEE Transactions on Neural Networks*, 5(3), 372–379. doi:10.1109/72.286909

Fulcher, J., Zhang, M., & Xu, S. (2006). Application of higher-order neural networks to financial time-series prediction. In Kamruzzaman, J., Begg, R., & Sarker, R. (Eds.), *Artificial Neural Networks in Finance and Manufacturing*. Hershey, PA: IGI Global. doi:10.4018/978-1-59140-670-9.ch005

Galán-Marín, G. (2007). A study into the improvement of binary hopfield networks for map coloring. *Lecture Notes in Computer Science*, 4432, 98–106. doi:10.1007/978-3-540-71629-7_12

Gallant, A. R., & White, H. (1988). There exists a neural network that does not make avoidable mistakes. In *Proceedings of the IEEE Second International Conference on Neural Networks*, (pp. 657-665). San Diego, CA: SOS Printing.

Gao, M. (2008). Robust exponential stability of Markovian jumping neural networks with time-varying delay. *International Journal of Neural Systems*, 18(3), 207–218. doi:10.1142/S0129065708001531

Garcia, C., Molina, F., Roca, E., & Lema, J. M. (2007). Fuzzy-based control of an anaerobic reactor treating wastewaters containing ethanol and carbohydrates. *Industrial & Engineering Chemistry Research*, 46(21), 6707–6715. doi:10.1021/ie0617001

GASB. (2006). *GASB white paper: Why governmental accounting and financial reporting is – and should be – different*. Retrieved November 15, 2009, from http://www.gasb.org/white_paper_mar_2006.html

Gasser, T. C., Gudmundson, P., & Dohr, G. (2009). Failure mechanisms of ventricular tissue due to deep penetration. *Journal of Biomechanics*, 42, 626–633. doi:10.1016/j.jbiomech.2008.12.016

Gellings, C. W. (2009). *The smart grid: Enabling energy efficiency and demand response*. Boca Raton, FL: CRC Press.

Ge, S. S., & Wang, C. (2004). Adaptive neural control of uncertain MIMO nonlinear systems. *IEEE Transactions on Neural Networks*, 15(3), 674–692. doi:10.1109/TNN.2004.826130

Ge, S. S., Zhang, J., & Lee, T. H. (2004). Adaptive neural network control for a class of MIMO nonlinear systems with disturbances in discrete-time. *IEEE Transactions on Systems, Man, and Cybernetics*, 34, 1–4.

Ghazali, R. (2005). *Higher order neural network for financial time series prediction*. Retrieved from http://www.cms.livjm.ac.uk/research/doc/ConfReport2005.doc

Ghazali, R. H.-j. (2007). Dynamic Ridge Polynomial Neural Networks in Exchange Rates Time Series Forecasting. In B. Beliczynski, A. Dzielinski, M. Iwanowski, & B. Ribeiro, *Adaptive and Natural Computing Algorithms*. (pp. 123-132). Berlin: Springer Berlin / Heidelberg.

Ghazali, R., & Al-Jumeily, D. (2009). Application of pi-sigma neural networks and ridge polynomial neural networks to financial time series prediction. In Zhang, M. (Ed.), *Artificial Higher Order Neural Networks for Economics and Business* (pp. 271–294). Hershey, PA: IGI Global. doi:10.4018/978-1-59904-897-0.ch012

Ghazali, R., Hussain, A. J., & Nawi, N. M. (2010). Dynamic ridge polynomial higher order neural network. In Zhang, M. (Ed.), *Artificial Higher Order Neural Networks for Computer Science and Engineering – Trends for Emerging Application* (pp. 255–268). Hershey, PA: IGI Global.

Ghosh, J., & Shin, Y. (1992). Efficient higher-order neural networks for function approximation and classification. *International Journal of Neural Systems, 3*(4), 323–350. doi:10.1142/S0129065792000255

Giles, C. L., & Maxwell, T. (1987). Learning, invariance, and generalization in higher order neural networks. *Applied Optics, 26*(23), 4972–4978. doi:10.1364/AO.26.004972

Giles, L., & Maxwell, T. (1987). Learning, invariance and generalization in high-order neural networks. *Applied Optics, 26*(23), 4972–4978. doi:10.1364/AO.26.004972

Giltrap, D. L., McKibbin, R., & Barnes, G. R. G. (2003). A steady state model of gas–char reactions in a downdraft gasifier. *Solar Energy, 74*, 85–91. doi:10.1016/S0038-092X(03)00091-4

Gøbel, B., Henriksen, U., Jensen, T. K., Qvale, B., & Houbak, N. (2007). The development of a computer model for a fixed bed gasifier and its use for optimization and control. *Bioresource Technology, 98*, 2043–2052. doi:10.1016/j.biortech.2006.08.019

Goldberg. (1998). *Genetic algorithms in search, optimization, and machine learning.* Reading, MA: Addison-Wesley.

Gomez, J. G. (2005). A fuzzy rule coevolutionary approach for multiclass classification problems. *In Proceedings of the 2005 IEEE congress on evolutionary computation, Edinburgh, UK*, pp. 1637–1644.

Goodwin, G. C., & Mayne, D. Q. (1987). A parameter estimation perspective of continuous time model reference adaptive control. *Automatica, 23*(1), 57–70. doi:10.1016/0005-1098(87)90118-X

Gopalsamy, K. (2007). Learning dynamics in second order networks. *Nonlinear Analysis Real World Applications, 8*(9), 688–698. doi:10.1016/j.nonrwa.2006.02.007

Gordillo, E. D., & Belghit, A. (2011). A two phase model of high temperature steam-only gasification of biomass char in bubbling fluidized bed reactors using nuclear heat. *International Journal of Hydrogen Energy, 36*, 374–381. doi:10.1016/j.ijhydene.2010.09.088

Gore, A., Kulp, S., & Li, Y. (2011). *Golden handcuffs for bureaucrats? Ex ante severance contracts in the municipal sector.* Working paper. Washington, DC: The George Washington University.

Gore, A. (2009). Why do cities hoard cash? Determinants and implications of municipal cash holdings. *Accounting Review, 84*(1), 183–207. doi:10.2308/accr.2009.84.1.183

Gori, M., Kuchler, A., & Sperduti, A. (1999). On implementation of frontier- to − root automata in recursive neural networks. *IEEE Transactions on Neural Networks, 10*(6). doi:10.1109/72.809076

Gouze, J. L., Rapaport, A., & Hadj-Sadok, Z. (2000). Interval observers for uncertain biological systems. *Ecological Modelling, 133*(1–2), 45–56. doi:10.1016/S0304-3800(00)00279-9

Grossberg, S. (1986). Some nonlinear networks capable of learning a spatial pattern of arbitrary complexity. *Proceedings of the National Academy of Sciences of the United States of America, 59*, 368–372. doi:10.1073/pnas.59.2.368

Grover, R., & Hwang, P. Y. C. (1992). *Introduction to random signals and applied Kalman filtering* (2nd ed.). New York, NY: John Wiley and Sons.

Güler, M. (1999). Neural classifiers for learning higher-order correlations. *Transactions Journal of Physics, 23*, 39–46.

Guo, B., Li, D., Cheng, C., Lu, Z. A., & Shen, Y. (2001). Simulation of biomass gasification with a hybrid neural network model. *Bioresource Technology, 76*, 77–83. doi:10.1016/S0960-8524(00)00106-1

Gupta, M. M. (2009). Fundamental theory of artificial higher order neural networks. In M. Zhang, *Artificial higher order neural networks for economics and business.* (pp. pp. 368-388). Idea Group Inc (IGI).

Gupta, M. M., Homma, N., Hou, Z., Solo, A. M. G., & Bukovsky, I. (2010). Higher order neural networks: Fundamental theory and applications. In Zhang, M. (Ed.), *Artificial Higher Order Neural Networks for Computer Science and Engineering – Trends for Emerging Application* (pp. 397–422). Hershey, PA: IGI Global.

Gupta, M. M., Homma, N., Hou, Z., Solo, A. M. G., & Goto, T. (2009). Fundamental theory of artificial higher order neural networks. In Zhang, M. (Ed.), *Artificial Higher Order Neural Networks for Economics and Business* (pp. 368–388). Hershey, PA: IGI Global. doi:10.4018/978-1-59904-897-0.ch017

Gupta, M. M., Jin, L., & Homma, N. (2003). *Static and dynamic neural networks: From fundamentals to advanced theory*. Hoboken, NJ: IEEE & Wiley. doi:10.1002/0471427950

Haemmerich, D., Lee, F. T., & Schutt, D. J. (2005). Large-volume radiofrequency ablation of ex-vivo bovine liver with multiple cooled cluster electrodes. *Journal de Radiologie, 234*, 563–568.

Hagan, M. T. (1996). *Neural network design*. PWS Publishing Company.

Hagan, M. T., Demuth, H. B., & Beale, M. (1996). *Neural network design*. Boston, MA: PWS Publishing Company.

Haidar, A. M. A. (2009). An intelligent load shedding scheme using neural networks and neuro-fuzzy. *International Journal of Neural Systems, 19*(6), 473–479. doi:10.1142/S0129065709002178

Hammadi, N. C., & Ito, H. (1998). On the activation function and fault tolerance in feedforward neural networks. *IEICE Transactions on Information & Systems. E (Norwalk, Conn.), 81D*(1), 66–72.

Han, J., & Kamber, M. (2006). *Data mining: Concepts and techniques*. Amsterdam, The Netherlands: Elsevier.

Han, J., Li, M., & Guo, L. (2006). Soft control on collective behavior of a group of autonomous agents by a shill agent. *Journal of Systems Science and Complexity, 19*, 54–62. doi:10.1007/s11424-006-0054-z

Hansen, J. V., & Nelson, R. D. (1997). Neural networks and traditional time series methods: A synergistic combination in state economic forecasts. *IEEE Transactions on Neural Networks, 8*(4), 863–873. doi:10.1109/72.595884

Hansen, J. V., & Nelson, R. D. (2002). Data mining of time series using stacked generalizers. *Neurocomputing, 43*, 173–184. doi:10.1016/S0925-2312(00)00364-7

Harston, C. T. (1990). The neurological basis for neural computation. In Maren, A. J., Harston, C. T., & Pap, R. M. (Eds.), *Handbook of Neural Computing Applications* (Vol. 1, pp. 29–44). New York, NY: Academic.

Haykin, S. (1999). *Neural networks- A comprehensive foundation* (2nd ed.). Upper Saddle River, NJ: Prentice Hall.

Haykin, S. (1999). *Neural networks: A comprehensive foundation*. Upper Saddle River, NJ: Prentice Hall.

Haykin, S. (Ed.). (2001). *Kalman filtering and neural networks*. New York, NY: John Wiley & Sons, Inc. doi:10.1002/0471221546

Haykin, S. S. (1994). *Neural networks: A comprehensive foundation*. New York, NY: Macmillan.

He, X., & Asada, H. (1993). A new method for identifying orders of input-output models for nonlinear dynamic systems. In *Proceedings of the IEEE American Control Conference,* (pp. 2520-2523). San Francisco, CA: IEEE Press.

Hensen, R. H. A., Angelis, G. Z., van de Molengraft, M. J. G., de Jager, A. G., & Kok, J. J. (2000). Grey-box modeling of friction: An experimental case-study. *European Journal of Control, 6*(3), 258–267.

Hinton, G. E. (1989). Connectionist learning procedure. *Artificial Intelligence, 40*, 251–257. doi:10.1016/0004-3702(89)90049-0

Hjelmfelt, A., & Ross, J. (1994). Pattern recognition, chaos, and multiplicity in neural networks and excitable systems. *Proceedings of the National Academy of Sciences of the United States of America, 91*, 63–67. doi:10.1073/pnas.91.1.63

Ho, D. W. C., Liang, J. L., & Lam, J. (2006). Global exponential stability of impulsive high-order BAM neural networks with time-varying delays. *Neural Networks, 19*(10), 1581–1590. doi:10.1016/j.neunet.2006.02.006

Holden, S. B., & Rayer, P. J. W. (1995). Generalisation and PAC learning: Some new results for the class of generalised single-layer networks. *IEEE Transactions on Neural Networks, 6*(2), 368–380. doi:10.1109/72.363472

Holubar, P., Zani, L., Hager, M., Froschl, W., Radak, Z., & Braun, R. (2002). Advanced controlling of anaerobic digestion by means of hierarchical neural networks. *Water Research, 36*, 2582–2588. doi:10.1016/S0043-1354(01)00487-0

Homma, N. (2002). A general second order neural unit. *Bull. Coll. Med. Sci. Tohoku Univ., 11*(1), 1–6.

Homma, N., & Gupta, M. M. (2002). A general second order neural unit. *Bulletin of Collected Medical Science, 11*(1), 1–6.

Hong, Y., Chen, G. R., & Bushnell, L. (2008). Distributed observers design for leader following control of multi-agent networks. *Automatica, 44*(3), 846–850. doi:10.1016/j.automatica.2007.07.004

Hopfield, J. J. (1982). Neural networks and physical systems with emergent collective computational abilities. *Proceedings of the National Academy of Sciences of the United States of America, 79*(8), 2554–2558. doi:10.1073/pnas.79.8.2554

Hopfield, J. J., & Tank, D. W. (1985). Neural computation of decisions in optimization problems. *Biological Cybernetics, 52*(1), 141–152.

Horan, P., Uecker, D., & Arimoto, A. (1990). Optical implementation of a second-order neural network discriminator model. *Japanese Journal of Applied Physics, 29*, 361–365. doi:10.1143/JJAP.29.L1328

Hornik, K. (1991). Approximation capabilities of multilayer feedforward networks. *Neural Networks, 4*, 251–257. doi:10.1016/0893-6080(91)90009-T

Hornik, K., Stinchcombe, M., & White, H. (1989). Multilayer feed forward networks are universal approximators. *International Journal of Neural Networks, 2*, 359–366. doi:10.1016/0893-6080(89)90020-8

Horn, R. A., & Johnson, C. R. (1987). *Matrix analysis*. Cambridge, UK: Cambridge University Press.

Hou, Z. G., Cheng, L., & Tan, M. (2009). Decentralized robust adaptive control for the multiagent system consensus problem using neural networks. *IEEE Transactions on Systems, Man, and Cybernetics. Part B, 39*(3), 636–647.

Hsing Chih Tsai (in press). (2008). Hybrid high order neural networks. *International Journal of Applied Soft Computing*.

Huang, G. B., & Siew, C.-K. (2004). Extreme learning machine: RBF network case. In *Proceedings of the Eighth International Conference on Control, Automation, Robotics and Vision (ICARCV 2004)*, (vol. 2), (pp. 1029-1036). Kunming, China: ICARCV.

Huang, G. B., Zhu, Q.-Y., & Siew, C.-K. (2004). Extreme learning machine: A new learning scheme of feedforward neural networks. In *Proceedings of International Joint Conference on Neural Networks (IJCNN2004)*, (vol. 2), (pp. 985-990). Budapest, Hungary: IJCNN.

Huang, C. L., & Wang, C. J. (2006). A GA-based feature selection and parameters optimization for support vector machines. *International Journal of Experimental Systems Applications, 31*, 231–240. doi:10.1016/j.eswa.2005.09.024

Huang, G. B., & Chen, L. (2007). Convex incremental extreme learning machine. *Neurocomputing, 70*, 3056–3062. doi:10.1016/j.neucom.2007.02.009

Huang, G. B., Chen, L., & Siew, C.-K. (2006). Universal approximation using incremental constructive feedforward networks with random hidden nodes. *IEEE Transactions on Neural Networks, 17*(4), 879–892. doi:10.1109/TNN.2006.875977

Huang, G. B., Li, M. B., Chen, L., & Siew, C. K. (2008). Incremental extreme learning machine with fully complex hidden nodes. *Neurocomputing, 71*, 576–583. doi:10.1016/j.neucom.2007.07.025

Huang, G. B., & Siew, C. K. (2005). Extreme learning machine with randomly assigned RBF kernels. *International Journal of Information Technology, 11*(1), 16–24.

Huang, G. B., Zhu, Q. Y., & Siew, C. K. (2006). Extreme learning machine: Theory and applications. *Neurocomputing, 70*, 489–501. doi:10.1016/j.neucom.2005.12.126

Huang, G.-B., & Chen, L. (2008). Enhanced random search based incremental extreme learning machine. *Neurocomputing, 71*, 3460–3468. doi:10.1016/j.neucom.2007.10.008

Huang, G.-B., Ding, X., & Zhou, H. (2010). Optimization method based extreme learning machine for classification. *Neurocomputing, 74*, 155–163. doi:10.1016/j.neucom.2010.02.019

Huang, H. J., & Ramaswamy, S. (2009). Modeling biomass gasification using thermodynamic equilibrium approach. *Applied Biochemistry and Biotechnology, 154*, 193–204. doi:10.1007/s12010-008-8483-x

Hui, Q., & Haddad, W. M. (2008). Distributed nonlinear control algorithms for network consensus. *Automatica, 44*, 2375–2381. doi:10.1016/j.automatica.2008.01.011

Hu, S., & Yan, P. (1992). Level-by-level learning for artificial neural groups. *ACTA Electronica SINICA, 20*(10), 39–43.

Hussain, A. L. P. (2008). A Novel Recurrent Polynomial Neural Network for Financial Time Series Prediction. In Z. M., *Higher Order Neural Networks for Economics and Business.* (pp. 190- 211). Idea Group Inc (IGI)

Hussain, A., Knowles, A., Lisboa, P., El-Deredy, W., & Al-Jumeily, D. (2006). Polynomial pipelined neural network and its application to financial time series prediction. *Lecture Notes in Artificial Intelligence, 4304*, 597–606.

Hussain, A., & Liatsis, P. (2009). A novel recurrent polynomial neural network for financial time series prediction. In Zhang, M. (Ed.), *Artificial Higher Order Neural Networks for Economics and Business* (pp. 190–211). Hershey, PA: IGI Global. doi:10.4018/978-1-59904-897-0.ch009

Hu, Z., & Shao, H. (1992). The study of neural network adaptive control systems. *Control and Decision, 7*, 361–366.

Igelnik, B., & Pao, Y. H. (1995). Stochastic choice of basis functions in adaptive function approximation and the functional-link net. *IEEE Transactions on Neural Networks, 6*, 1320–1329. doi:10.1109/72.471375

Inui, T., Tanabe, Y., & Onodera, Y. (1978). *Group theory and its application in physics*. Heidelberg, Germany: Springer-Verlag. doi:10.1007/978-3-642-80021-4

Ioannou, P., & Fidan, B. (2006). *Adaptive control tutorial*. SIAM. doi:10.1137/1.9780898718652

Ioannou, P., & Sun, J. (1996). *Robust adaptive control*. Upper Saddle River, NJ: Prentice Hall.

Jadbabaie, A., Lin, J., & Morse, A. S. (2003). Coordination of groups of mobile autonomous agents using nearest neighbor rules. *IEEE Transactions on Automatic Control, 48*(6), 988–1001. doi:10.1109/TAC.2003.812781

Jain, B. A., & Nag, B. N. (1995). Artificial neural network models for pricing initial public offerings. *Decision Sciences, 26*(3), 283–302. doi:10.1111/j.1540-5915.1995.tb01430.x

Jakubowski, J. K. (2002). Higher Order Statistics and Neural Network for Tremor Recognition. *IEEE TRANSACTIONS ON BIOMEDICAL ENGINEERING, VOL., 49*(2), 152–159. doi:10.1109/10.979354

Jarungthammachote, S., & Dutta, A. (2007). Thermodynamic equilibrium model and second law analysis of a downdraft waste gasifier. *Energy, 32*, 1660–1669. doi:10.1016/j.energy.2007.01.010

Jayah, T. H., Aye, L., Fuller, R. J., & Stewart, D. F. (2003). Computer simulation of a downdraft wood gasifier for tea drying. *Biomass and Bioenergy, 25*, 459–469. doi:10.1016/S0961-9534(03)00037-0

Jeffries, C. (1989). Dense memory with high order neural networks. In *Proceedings of Twenty-First Southeastern Symposium on System Theory,* (pp. 436 – 439). Washington, DC: IEEE.

Jiang, M., Gielen, G., & Wang, L. (2010). Analysis of quantization effects on higher order function and multilayer feedforward neural networks. In Zhang, M. (Ed.), *Artificial Higher Order Neural Networks for Computer Science and Engineering – Trends for Emerging Application* (pp. 187–222). Hershey, PA: IGI Global.

Jiang, T., & Baras, J. S. (2009). *Graph algebraic interpretation of trust establishment in autonomic networks. Preprint Wiley Journal of Networks*. New York, NY: Wiley.

Jin-Yan Li Chow, T. Y.-L. (1995). The estimation theory and optimization algorithm for the number of hidden units in the higher-order feedforward neural network. *Neural Networks. Proceedings., IEEE International Conference on*, Volume: 3, On page(s): 1229-1233 vol.3.

John, G. H. (1995). Estimating continuous distributions in Bayesian. *In Proceedings of the 11th conference on uncertainty in artificial intelligence, Montreal, Canada,* pp. 338–345.

John, G. H., Kohavi, R., & Pfleger, K. (1994). Irrelevant features and the subset selection problem. In *Proceedings of the 11th International Conference on Machine Learning,* (pp. 121-129). IEEE.

Juang, C. F., & Lin, C. T. (1998). An on-line self-constructing neural fuzzy inference network and its applications. *IEEE Transactions on Fuzzy Systems, 6*(1), 12–32. doi:10.1109/91.660805

Kaplan, R., & Welam, U. (1974). Overhead allocation with imperfect markets and nonlinear technology. *Accounting Review, 49*(3), 477–484.

Karayiannis, N. B., & Venetsanopoulos, A. N. (1993). *Artificial neural networks: Learning algorithms, performance evaluation, and applications.* Berlin, Germany: Springer.

Karayiannis, N., & Venetsanopoulos, A. (1993). *Artificial neural networks: Learning algorithms, performance evaluation and applications.* Boston, MA: Kluwer Academic.

Kariniotakis, G. N., Stavrakakis, G. S., & Nogaret, E. F. (1996). Wind power forecasting using advanced neural networks models. *IEEE Transactions on Energy Conversion, 11*(4), 762–767. doi:10.1109/60.556376

Karnavas, Y. L. (2010). Electrical machines excitation control via higher order neural networks. In Zhang, M. (Ed.), *Artificial Higher Order Neural Networks for Computer Science and Engineering – Trends for Emerging Application* (pp. 366–396). Hershey, PA: IGI Global.

Karppanen, E. (2000). *Advanced control of an industrial circulating fluidized bed boiler using fuzzy logic.* (Doctoral Dissertation). University of Oulu. Oulu, Finland.

Kaushal, P., Abedi, J., & Mahinpey, N. (2010). A comprehensive mathematical model for biomass gasification in a bubbling fluidized bed reactor. *Fuel, 89,* 3650–3661. doi:10.1016/j.fuel.2010.07.036

Kawato, M., Uno, Y., Isobe, M., & Suzuki, R. (1987). A hierarchical model for voluntary movement and its application to robotics. In *Proceedings of the IEEE International Conference Network,* (vol 4), (pp. 573-582). IEEE Press.

Kay, A. (2006). Artificial neural networks. *Computerworld.* Retrieved on 27 November 2006 from http://www.computerworld.com/softwaretopics/ software/appdev/story/0,10801,57545,00.html

Kendi, T. A., & Doyle, F. J. (1996). Nonlinear control of a fluidized bed reactor using approximate feedback linearization. *Industrial & Engineering Chemistry Research, 35,* 746–757. doi:10.1021/ie950334a

Kesavadas, T., Srimathveeravalli, G., & Arulesan, V. (2005). Parametric modeling and simulation of Trocar insertion. *Journal of Studies in Health Technologies and Informatics, 119,* 252–254.

Khalil, H. (1996). *Nonlinear systems* (3rd ed.). Upper Saddle River, NJ: Pearson Education.

Khalil, H. K. (2002). *Nonlinear systems* (3rd ed.). Upper Saddle River, N.J: Prentice Hall.

Khalil, H. K. (2002). *Nonlinear systems.* Upper Saddle River, NJ: Prentice-Hall.

Khoo, S., Xie, L., & Man, Z. (2009). Robust finite-time consensus tracking algorithm for multirobot systems. *IEEE Transaction on Mechatronics, 14*(2), 219–228. doi:10.1109/TMECH.2009.2014057

Kim, S. H., & Noh, H. J. (1997). Predictability of interest rates using data mining tools: a comparative analysis of Korea and the US. *Expert Systems with Applications, 13*(2), 85–95. doi:10.1016/S0957-4174(97)00010-9

Klass, D. L. (1998). Biomass for renovable energy. In *Fuels and Chemicals* (pp. 225–256). Longon, UK: Elsevier.

Klassen, M., Pao, Y., & Chen, V. (1988). Characteristics of the functional link net: A higher order delta rule net. In *Proceedings of IEEE 2nd Annual International Conference on Neural Networks.* IEEE Press.

Knowles, A., Hussain, A., Deredy, W. E., Lisboa, P. G. J., & Dunis, C. (2005). *Higher-order neural network with bayesian confidence measure for prediction of EUR/USD exchange rate.* Paper presented at the Forecasting Financial Markets Conference. Marseilles, France.

Knowles, A., Hussain, A., Deredy, W. E., Lisboa, P., & Dunis, C. L. (2009). Higher order neural networks with bayesian confidence measure for the prediction of the EUR/USD exchange rate. In Zhang, M. (Ed.), *Artificial Higher Order Neural Networks for Economics and Business* (pp. 48–59). Hershey, PA: IGI Global. doi:10.4018/978-1-59904-897-0.ch002

Kobayashi, S. (2006). *Sensation world made by the brain – Animals do not have sensors.* Tokyo, Japan: Corona.

Kobayashi, Y., Onishi, A., & Watanabe, H. (2010). Development of an integrated needle insertion system with image guidance and deformation simulation. *Computerized Medical Imaging and Graphics, 34,* 9–18. doi:10.1016/j.compmedimag.2009.08.008

Kohonen, T. (1988). *Self organization and associative memory* (2nd ed.). New York, NY: Springer-Verlag. doi:10.1007/978-3-662-00784-6

Kohonen, T., Kaski, S., Lagus, K., Salojarvi, J., Honkela, J., Paatero, V., & Saarela, A. (2000). Self organization of a massive document collection. *IEEE Transactions on Neural Networks, 11,* 574–585. doi:10.1109/72.846729

Kosmatopoulos, E. B., Ioannou, P. A., & Christodoulou, M. A. (1992). Identification of nonlinear systems using new dynamic neural network structures. In *Proceedings of the 31st IEEE Conference on Decision and Control,* (vol. 1), (pp. 20 – 25). IEEE Press.

Kosmatopoulos, E. B., Polycarpou, M. M., Christodoulou, M. A., & Ioannou, P. A. (1995). High-order neural network structures for identification of dynamical systems. *IEEE Transactions on Neural Networks, 6*(2), 422–431. doi:10.1109/72.363477

Koza, J. R. (1991). A genetic approach to econometric modeling. In *Proceedings of the 2nd International Conference on Economics.* IEEE.

Kros, J. F., Lin, M., & Brown, M. L. (2006). Effects of neural networks s-sigmoid function on KDD in the presence of imprecise data. *Computers & Operations Research, 33,* 3136–3149. doi:10.1016/j.cor.2005.01.024

Kumar, N., Panwar, V., Sukavanam, N., Sharma, S. P., & Borm, J. H. (2011). Neural network-based nonlinear tracking control of kinematically redundant robot manipulators. *Mathematical and Computer Modelling, 53*(9), 1889–1901. doi:10.1016/j.mcm.2011.01.014

Kuramoto, Y. (1975). Self-entrainment of a population of coupled non-linear oscillators. *Lecture Notes in Physics, 39,* 420–422. doi:10.1007/BFb0013365

Kurbel, K., Singh, K., & Teuteberg, F. (1998). Search and classification of "interesting" business applications in the world wide web using a neural network approach. In *Proceedings of the 1998 IACIS Conference.* Cancun, Mexico: IACIS.

Kuroe, Y. (2004). Learning and identifying finite state automata with recurrent high-order neural networks. In *Proceedings of SICE 2004 Annual Conference,* (vol. 3), (pp. 2241 – 2246). SICE.

Kuroe, Y., Ikeda, H., & Mori, T. (1997). Identification of nonlinear dynamical systems by recurrent high-order neural networks. In *Proceedings of IEEE International Conference on Systems, Man, and Cybernetics,* (Vol. 1), (pp. 70 – 75). IEEE Press.

Lagerburg Marinus, V., Moerland, A., & Vulpen, M. V. (2006). A new robotic needle insertion method to minimize attendant prostate motion, prostate brachytherapy. *Radiotherapy and Oncology, 80,* 73–77. doi:10.1016/j.radonc.2006.06.013

Lakrori, M. (1989). Control of a continuous bioprocess by simple algorithms of P and L/A types. In *Proceedings of International IFAC Symposium on Nonlinear Control System Design.* Capri, Italy: IFAC.

Lan, Y., Soh, Y. C., & Huang, G.-B. (2008). Extreme learning machine based bacterial protein subcellular localization prediction. In *Proceedings of the IEEE International Joint Conference on Neural Networks 2008,* (pp. 1859–1863). IEEE Press.

Lange, M. (2003). *Analysis of the uncertainty of wind power predictions.* (Unpublished Doctoral Dissertation). Carl von Ossietzky Universität Oldenburg. Oldenburg, Germany.

Laurendeau, M. (1978). Kinetics of coal char gasification and combustion. *Journal of Energy Combustion, 4,* 221–270. doi:10.1016/0360-1285(78)90008-4

Lee, M., Lee, S. Y., & Park, C. H. (1992). Neural controller of nonlinear dynamic systems using higher order neural networks. *Electronics Letters, 28*(3), 276–277. doi:10.1049/el:19920170

Lee, Y. C., Doolen, G., Chen, H., Sun, G., Maxwell, T., Lee, H., & Giles, C. L. (1986). Machine learning using a higher order correlation network. *Physica D. Nonlinear Phenomena, 22,* 276–306.

Lee, Y. D. (1986). Machine learning using a higher order correlation network. *Physica D. Nonlinear Phenomena, 22,* 276–306.

Leon, B. S., Alanis, A. Y., Sanchez, E. N., Ornelas, F., & Ruiz-Velazquez, E. (2011). Inverse optimal trajectory tracking for discrete time nonlinear positive systems. In *Proceedings of 50th IEEE Conference on Decision and Control and European Control Conference (IEEE CDC-ECC)*. Orlando, FL: IEEE Press.

Leshno, M., Lin, V., Ya, P. A., & Schocken, S. (1993). Multilayer feedforward networks with a nonpolynomial activation function can approximate any function. *Neural Networks, 6,* 861–867. doi:10.1016/S0893-6080(05)80131-5

Leunga, C., & Chan, L. (2003). Dual extended Kalman filtering in recurrent neural networks. *Neural Networks, 16,* 223–239. doi:10.1016/S0893-6080(02)00230-7

Lewis, F. L., Jagannathan, S., & Yesildirek, A. (1998). *Neural network control of robot manipulators and nonlinear systems*. New York, NY: Taylor & Francis.

Lewis, F. L., Yesildirek, A., & Liu, K. (1996). Multilayer neural-net robot controller with guaranteed tracking performance. *IEEE Transactions on Neural Networks, 7*(2), 388–399. doi:10.1109/72.485674

Lewis, F., Jagannathan, S., & Yesildirek, A. (1999). *Neural network control of robot manipulators and nonlinear systems*. London, UK: Taylor and Francis.

Liatsis, P., Hussain, A., & Milonidis, E. (2009). Artificial higher order pipeline recurrent neural networks for financial time series prediction. In Zhang, M. (Ed.), *Artificial Higher Order Neural Networks for Economics and Business* (pp. 164–189). Hershey, PA: IGI Global. doi:10.4018/978-1-59904-897-0.ch008

Li, M. B., Huang, G.-B., Saratchandran, P., & Sundararajan, N. (2005). Fully complex extreme learning machine. *Neurocomputing, 68,* 306–314. doi:10.1016/j.neucom.2005.03.002

Lin, Y. H., & Cunningham, G. A. (1995). A new approach to fuzzy-neural system modelling. *IEEE Transactions on Fuzzy Systems, 3*(2), 190–198. doi:10.1109/91.388173

Lippman, R. P. (1989). Pattern classification using neural networks. *IEEE Communications Magazine, 27,* 47–64. doi:10.1109/35.41401

Li, R. P., & Mukaidono, M. (1995). A new approach to rule learning based on fusion of fuzzy logic and neural networks. *IEICE Transactions on Information and Systems, 78*(11), 1509–1514.

Lisboa, P., & Perantonis, S. (1991). Invariant pattern recognition using third-order networks and zernlike moments. In *Proceedings of the IEEE International Joint Conference on Neural Networks,* (Vol. 2), (pp. 1421-1425). Singapore: IEEE Press.

Li, T. Y., & Yorke, J. A. (1975). Periodic three implies chaos. *The American Mathematical Monthly, 82,* 985–992. doi:10.2307/2318254

Little, R. J., & Rubin, D. B. (1987). *Statistical analysis with missing data*. New York, NY: John Wiley and Sons.

Li, X. T., Grace, J. R., Lim, C. J., Watkinson, A. P., Chen, H. P., & Kim, J. R. (2004). Biomass gasification in a circulating fluidized bed. *Biomass and Bioenergy, 26,* 171–193. doi:10.1016/S0961-9534(03)00084-9

Li, X., Chen, Z. Q., & Yuan, Z. Z. (2002). Simple recurrent neural network-based adaptive predictive control for nonlinear systems. *Asian Journal of Control, 4*(2), 231–239. doi:10.1111/j.1934-6093.2002.tb00350.x

Li, X., Wang, X., & Chen, G. (2004). Pinning a complex dynamical network to its equilibrium. *IEEE Transactions on Circuits and Systems, 51*(10), 2074–2087. doi:10.1109/TCSI.2004.835655

Li, Y. M. (2008). An improvement to ant colony optimization heuristic. *Lecture Notes in Computer Science, 5263*, 816–825. doi:10.1007/978-3-540-87732-5_90

Li, Z., Duan, Z., & Chen, G. (2009). Consensus of multi-agent systems and synchronization of complex networks: A unified viewpoint. *IEEE Transactions on Circuits and Systems, 57*(1), 213–224.

Lo, J. T.-H. (1992). A new approach to global optimization and its applications to neural networks. *Neural Networks, 2*(5), 367–373.

Lu, B., Qi, H., Zhang, M., & Scofield, R. A. (2000). Using PT-HONN models for multi-polynomial function simulation. In *Proceedings of IASTED International Conference on Neural Networks,* (pp. 1-5). Pittsburgh, PA: IASTED.

Lu, J., & Chen, G. (2005). A time-varying complex dynamical network model and its controlled synchronization criteria. *IEEE Transactions on Automatic Control, 50*(6), 841–846. doi:10.1109/TAC.2005.849233

Lumer, E. D. (1992). Selective attention to perceptual groups: The phase tracking mechanism. *International Journal of Neural Systems, 3*(1), 1–17. doi:10.1142/S0129065792000024

Lu, Y., Guo, L., Zhang, X., & Yan, Q. (2007). Thermo-dynamic modeling and analysis of biomass gasification for hydrogen production in supercritical water. *Chemical Engineering Journal, 131*, 233–244. doi:10.1016/j.cej.2006.11.016

Lu, Z., Shieh, L., & Chen, G. (2009). A new topology for artificial higher order neural networks - Polynomial kernel networks. In Zhang, M. (Ed.), *Artificial Higher Order Neural Networks for Economics and Business* (pp. 430–441). Hershey, PA: IGI Global.

Lu, Z., Song, G., & Shieh, L. (2010). Improving sparsity in kernel principal component analysis by polynomial kernel higher order neural networks. In Zhang, M. (Ed.), *Artificial Higher Order Neural Networks for Computer Science and Engineering – Trends for Emerging Application* (pp. 223–238). Hershey, PA: IGI Global.

Lyapunov, A. M. (1992). *The general problem of the stability of motion* (Fuller, A. T., Trans.). New York, NY: Taylor and Francis.

Machado, R. J. (1989). Handling knowledge in high order neural networks: The combinatorial neural model. In *Proceedings of the International Joint Conference on Neural Networks,* (vol. 2), (pp. 582). IEEE.

Machine Learning Repository, U. C. I. (2007). *Website.* Retrieved from ftp://ftp.ics.uci.edu/pub/ machine-learning-databases/auto-mpg/auto-mpg.data

Mafidziuk, J. (1995). Solving the n-queens problem with a binary Hopfield-type network. *Biological Cybernetics, 72*(1), 439–445. doi:10.1007/BF00201419

Mahvash, M., & Dupont, P. E. (2009). Fast needle insertion to minimize tissue deformation and damage. In *Proceedings of the IEEE International Conference on Robotics and Automation,* (pp. 3097-3102). IEEE Press.

Mahvash, M., & Dupont, P. E. (2010). Mechanics of dynamic needle insertion into a biological material. *IEEE Transactions on Bio-Medical Engineering, 57*, 934–943. doi:10.1109/TBME.2009.2036856

Mailleret, L., Bernard, O., & Steyer, J. P. (2004). Nonlinear adaptive control for bioreactors with unknown kinetics. *Automatica, 40*, 1379–1385. doi:10.1016/j.automatica.2004.01.030

Malone, J., McGarry, K., Wermter, S., & Bowerman, C. (2006). Data mining using rule extraction from Kohonen self-organising maps. *Neural Computing & Applications, 15*(1), 9–17. doi:10.1007/s00521-005-0002-1

Mao, Z. Q., Selviah, D. R., Tao, S., & Midwinter, J. E. (1991). Holographic high order associative memory system. In *Proceedings of the Third IEE International Conference on Holographic Systems, Components and Applications,* (vol 342), (pp. 132-136). Edinburgh, UK: IEE.

Masamune, K., Kobayashi, E., & Masutani, Y. (1995). Development of an MRI-compatible needle insertion manipulator for stereotactic neurosurgery. *Computer Aided Surgery, 1*(4), 242–248. doi:10.3109/10929089509106330

Matsuba, I. (2000). *Nonlinear time series analysis.* Tokyo, Japan: Asakura-syoten.

Matsuoka, T., Hamada, H., & Nakatsu, R. (1989). Syllable recognition using integrated neural networks. In *Proceedings of the International Joint Conference on Neural Networks,* (pp. 251-258). Washington, DC: IEEE.

Maurel, W. (1999). *3D modeling of the human upper limb including the biomechanics of joints, muscles and soft tissues*. (PhD Thesis). Laboratoire d'Infographie-Ecole Polytechnique Federale de Lausanne. Lausanne, Switzerland.

McCue, C. (2007). *Data mining and predictive analysis: Intelligence gathering and crime analysis*. London, UK: Butterworth-Heinemann.

McCulloch, W. S., & Pitts, W. H. (1943). A logical calculus of the ideas imminent in nervous activity. *The Bulletin of Mathematical Biophysics*, *5*, 115–133. doi:10.1007/BF02478259

McEliece, R. J., Posner, E. C., Rodemich, E. R., & Venkatesh, S. S. (1987). The capacity of the Hopfield associative memory. *IEEE Transactions on Information Theory*, *33*, 461–482. doi:10.1109/TIT.1987.1057328

McKee, T. E. (2009). A meta-learning approach to predicting financial statement fraud. *Journal of Emerging Technologies in Accounting*, *6*(1), 5–26. doi:10.2308/jeta.2009.6.1.5

Meiqin, M., Ming, D., Jianhui, S., Chang, L., Min, S., & Guorong, Z. (2008). *Testbed* for microgrid with multi-energy generators. In *Proceedings of the Canadian Conference on Electrical and Computer Engineering CCECE*, (pp. 637-640). CCECE.

Melgar, A., Pérez, J. F., Laget, H., & Horillo, A. (2007). Thermochemical equilibrium modelling of a gasifying process. *Energy Conversion and Management*, *48*, 59–67. doi:10.1016/j.enconman.2006.05.004

Mendel, J. M. (1991). Tutorial on higher-order statistics (spectr) in signal processing and system theory: Theoretical results and some applications. *Proceedings of the IEEE*, *79*(3), 278–305. doi:10.1109/5.75086

Mendez-Acosta, H. O., Campos-Delgado, D. U., & Femat, R. (2003). Intelligent control of an anaerobic digester: Fuzzy-based gain scheduling for a geometrical approach. In *Proceeding of IEEE International Symposium on Intelligent Control*, (pp. 298–303). Houston, TX: IEEE Press.

Miche, Y., Sorjamaa, A., Bas, P., Simula, O., Jutten, C., & Lendasse, A. (2010). OP-ELM: Optimally pruned extreme learning machine. *IEEE Transactions on Neural Networks*, *21*(1).

Mishra, S. (2006). Neural-network-based adaptive UPFC for improving transient stability performance of power system. *IEEE Transactions on Neural Networks*, *17*(2), 461–470. doi:10.1109/TNN.2006.871706

Misra, S., Macura, K., & Ramesh, K. (2009). The importance of organ geometry and boundary constraints for planning of medical interventions. *Medical Engineering & Physics*, *31*(2), 195–206. doi:10.1016/j.medengphy.2008.08.002

Mitra, S., & Hayashi, Y. (2000). Neuro-fuzzy rule generation: Survey in soft computing framework. *IEEE Transactions on Neural Networks*, *11*(3), 748–768. doi:10.1109/72.846746

Miyajima, H., Ma, L., & Suwa, H. (1996). Dynamical properties of higher order random neural networks. in *Proceedings of the IEEE ICTAI 1996*, (vol 1), (pp. 430-431). IEEE Press.

Miyajima, H., Yatsuku, S., & Kubota, J. (1995). Dynamical properties of neural networks with product connections. In *Proceedings of the IEEE ICNN 1995*, (vol 6), (pp. 3198-3203). IEEE Press.

Miyajima, H., & Yatsuki, S. (1994). On some dynamical properties of threshold and homogeneous networks. *IEICE Transactions on Fundamentals*, *77*(11), 1823–1830.

Miyajima, H., Yatsuki, S., & Maeda, M. (1996). Some characteristics of higher order neural networks with decreasing energy functions. *IEICE Transactions on Fundamentals*, *99*(10), 1624–1629.

Monnet, F. (2003). *An introduction to anaerobic digestion of organic wastes. Technical Report*. Edinburgh, UK: Remade Scotland.

Moreira, J. M., & Auto, D. M. (1993). Intermittency in a neural network with variable threshold. *Europhysics Letters*, *21*(6), 639. doi:10.1209/0295-5075/21/6/001

Morita, M. (1993). Associative memory with nonmonotone dynamics. *Neural Networks*, *6*, 115–126. doi:10.1016/S0893-6080(05)80076-0

Morita, M., Yoshizawa, S., & Nakano, K. (1990). Analysis and improvement of the dynamics of autocorrelation associative memory. *Transactions on Institutional Electronics, Information. Communication Engineers Japan*, *73*(2), 232–242.

Mountouris, A., Voutsas, E., & Tassios, D. (2006). Plasma gasification of sewage sludge: Process development and energy optimization. *Energy Conversion and Management, 47*, 1723–1737. doi:10.1016/j.enconman.2005.10.015

Munehisa, T., Kobayashi, M., & Yamazaki, H. (2001). Cooperative updating in the Hopfield model. *IEEE Transactions on Neural Networks, 12*(5), 1243–1251. doi:10.1109/72.950153

Murata, J. (2010). Analysis and improvement of function approximation capabilities of pi-sigma higher order neural networks. In Zhang, M. (Ed.), *Artificial Higher Order Neural Networks for Computer Science and Engineering – Trends for Emerging Application* (pp. 239–254). Hershey, PA: IGI Global.

Naimark, M. A., & Stern, A. I. (1982). *Theory of group representations*. Berlin, Germany: Springer-Verlag. doi:10.1007/978-1-4613-8142-6

Najarian, S., Hosseini, S. M., & Fallahnezhad, M. (2010). Artificial tactile sensing and robotic surgery using higher order neural networks. In Zhang, M. (Ed.), *Artificial Higher Order Neural Networks for Computer Science and Engineering – Trends for Emerging Application* (pp. 514–544). Hershey, PA: IGI Global.

Narendra, K. S., & Parthasarathy, K. (1990). Identification and control of dynamical systems using neural networks. *IEEE Transactions on Neural Networks, 1*, 4–27. doi:10.1109/72.80202

Narendra, P. M., & Fuknaga, K. (1997). A branch and bound algorithm for feature subset selection. *IEEE Transactions on Computers, 26*(9), 917–922. doi:10.1109/TC.1977.1674939

Narendra, S., & Parthasarathy, K. (1990). Identification and control of dynamical systems using neural networks. *IEEE Transactions on Neural Networks, 1*(1), 4–27. doi:10.1109/72.80202

Natarjan, B. K. (1995). Sparse approximate solutions to linear system. *SIAM Journal on Computing, 24*(2), 227–234. doi:10.1137/S0097539792240406

Nath, S. (2000). Dosimetric effects of needle divergence in prostate seed implant using 125I and 103Pd radioactive seeds. *Medical Physics, 27*, 1058–1066. doi:10.1118/1.598971

Neto, J. P. (2010). Higher order neural networks for symbolic, sub-symbolic and chaotic computations. In Zhang, M. (Ed.), *Artificial Higher Order Neural Networks for Computer Science and Engineering – Trends for Emerging Application* (pp. 37–56). Hershey, PA: IGI Global.

Noguchi, W., & Pham, C.-K. (2006). A proposal to solve n-queens problems using maximum neuron model with a modified hill-climbing term. In *Proceedings of IJCNN*, (pp. 2679—2683). IJCNN.

Norgaard, M., Ravn, O., Poulsen, N. K., & Hansen, L. K. (2000). *Neural networks for modelling and control of dynamic systems: A practitioner's handbook*. London, UK: Springer-Verlag. doi:10.1007/978-1-4471-0453-7

Okamura, M., Simone, C., & O'Leary, M. D. (2004). Force modeling for needle insertion into soft tissue. *IEEE Transactions on Bio-Medical Engineering, 51*, 1707–1716. doi:10.1109/TBME.2004.831542

Olfati-Saber, R., Fax, A. J., & Murray, R. M. (2007). Consensus and cooperation in networked multi-agent systems. *Proceedings of the IEEE, 95*(1), 215–233. doi:10.1109/JPROC.2006.887293

Olfati-Saber, R., & Murray, R. M. (2004). Consensus problems in networks of agents with switching topology and time-delays. *IEEE Transactions on Automatic Control, 49*(9), 1520–1533. doi:10.1109/TAC.2004.834113

Onwubolu, G. C. (2009). Artificial higher order neural networks in time series prediction. In Zhang, M. (Ed.), *Artificial Higher Order Neural Networks for Economics and Business* (pp. 250–270). Hershey, PA: IGI Global. doi:10.4018/978-1-59904-897-0.ch011

Ornelas, F., Sanchez, E. N., & Loukianov, A. G. (2010). Discrete-time inverse optimal control for nonlinear systems trajectory tracking. In *Proceedings of the 49th IEEE Conference on Decision and Control*. Atlanta, GA: IEEE Press.

Ou, C. (2008). Anti-periodic solutions for high-order Hopfield neural networks. *Computers & Mathematics with Applications (Oxford, England)*, *56*(3), 1838–1844. doi:10.1016/j.camwa.2008.04.029

Paes, T. (2005). *Modeling for control of a biomass gasifier*. (Unpublished Doctoral Dissertation). Technische Universiteit Eindhoven. Eindhoven, The Netherlands.

Palm, G. (1980). On associative memory. *Biological Cybernetics*, *36*, 19–31. doi:10.1007/BF00337019

Pao, Y. H. (1989). *Adaptive pattern recognition and neural networks*. Reading, MA: Addison-Wesley.

Park, B. S., Yoo, S. J., Park, J. B., & Choi, Y. H. (2010). A simple adaptive control approach for trajectory tracking of electrically driven nonholonomic mobile robots. *IEEE Transactions on Control Systems Technology*, *18*, 1199–1206. doi:10.1109/TCST.2009.2034639

Park, J., & Sandberg, I. W. (1993). Approximation and radial-basis-function networks. *Neural Computation*, *5*, 305–316. doi:10.1162/neco.1993.5.2.305

Parlos, A. G. (2002). *Identification of the internet end to end delay dynamics using multi - step neuro - predictors*. New York, NY: IEEE Press. doi:10.1109/IJCNN.2002.1007528

Passino, K. M., & Yurkovich, S. (1998). *Fuzzy control*. Menlo Park, CA: Addison Wesley Longman.

Pearlmutter, B. A. (1995). Gradient calculation of recurrent neural networks: A survey. *IEEE Transactions on Neural Networks*, *6*(5), 1212–1228. doi:10.1109/72.410363

Pedro, J., & Dahunsi, O. (2011). Neural network based feedback linearization control of a servo-hydraulic vehicle suspension system. *International Journal of Applied Mathematics and Computer Science*, *21*(1), 137–147. doi:10.2478/v10006-011-0010-5

Peng, H. Z. (2007). Handling of incomplete data sets using ICA and SOM in data mining. *Neural Computing & Applications*, 167–172. doi:10.1007/s00521-006-0058-6

Peng, H., & Zhu, S. (2007). Handling of incomplete data sets using ICA and SOM in data mining. *Neural Computing & Applications*, *16*(2), 167–172. doi:10.1007/s00521-006-0058-6

Pentland, A., & Turk, M. (1989). Face processing: Models for recognition. In *Proceedings of SPIE - Intelligent Robots and Computer Vision VIII: Algorithms and Technology*, (pp. 20-35). SPIE.

Perantonis, S. J., & Lisboa, P. J. G. (1992). Translation, rotation and scale invariant pattern recognition by high-order neural networks and moment classifiers. *IEEE Transactions on Neural Networks*, *3*, 241–251. doi:10.1109/72.125865

Petre, E., Selisteanu, D., & Sendrescu, D. (2008). Adaptive control strategies for a class of anaerobic depollution bioprocesses. In *Proceedings of the IEEE Automation, Quality and Testing, Robotics*, (vol 2), (pp. 159–164). Cluj-Napoca, Romania: IEEE Press.

Picton, P. (2000). *Neural networks*. Basingstoke, UK: Palgrave.

Platt, J. C. (1999). Using analytic QP and sparseness to speed training of support vector machines. *In Proceedings of the 13th annual conference on neural information processing systems, Denver, Colorado*, pp. 557–563.

Plett, G. L. (2003). Adaptive inverse control of linear and nonlinear systems using dynamic neural networks. *IEEE Transactions on Neural Networks*, *14*(2), 360–376. doi:10.1109/TNN.2003.809412

Poggio, T., & Girosi, F. (1998). A sparse representation for function approximation. *Neural Computation*, *10*(6), 1445–1454. doi:10.1162/089976698300017250

Polycarpou, M. M. (1996). Stable adaptive neural control scheme for nonlinear systems. *IEEE Transactions on Automatic Control*, *41*(3), 447–451. doi:10.1109/9.486648

Polycarpou, M. M., & Ioannou, P. A. (1996). A robust adaptive nonlinear control design. *Automatica*, *32*(3), 423–427. doi:10.1016/0005-1098(95)00147-6

Poznyak, A. S., Sanchez, E. N., & Yu, W. (2001). *Differential neural networks for robust nonlinear control*. Singapore, Singapore: World Scientific.

Poznyak, A. S., Yu, W., Sanchez, E. N., & Perez, J. P. (1999). Nonlinear adaptive trajectory tracking using dynamic neural networks. *IEEE Transactions on Neural Networks*, *10*(6), 1402–1411. doi:10.1109/72.809085

Psaltis, D., Park, C. H., & Hong, J. (1988). High order associative memories and their optical implementations. *Neural Networks, 1,* 149–163. doi:10.1016/0893-6080(88)90017-2

Puig-Arnavat, M., Carles Bruno, J., & Coronas, A. (2010). Review and analysis of biomass gasification models. *Renewable & Sustainable Energy Reviews, 14,* 2481–2851. doi:10.1016/j.rser.2010.07.030

Qi, H., Zhang, M., & Scofield, R. (2001). Rainfall estimation using M-PHONN model. In *Proceedings of the International Joint Conference on Neural Networks 2001,* (pp. 1620-1624). Washington, DC: IJCNN.

Quinlan, J. R. (1993). *C.45 Programs for machine learning Kaufmann.*

Quinlan, J. R. (1986). Induction of decision trees. *Machine Learning, 1*(1), 81–106. doi:10.1007/BF00116251

Qu, Z. (2009). *Cooperative control of dynamical systems: Applications to autonomous vehicles.* New York, NY: Springer-Verlag. doi:10.1109/TAC.2008.920232

Qu, Z., Wang, J., & Hull, R. A. (2008). Cooperative control of dynamical systems with application to autonomous vehicles. *IEEE Transactions on Automatic Control, 53*(4), 894–911. doi:10.1109/TAC.2008.920232

Ragothaman, S., & Lavin, A. (2008). Restatements due to improper revenue recognition: A neural networks perspective. *Journal of Emerging Technologies in Accounting, 5*(1), 129–142. doi:10.2308/jeta.2008.5.1.129

Ra, J. B., Kwon, S. M., & Kim, J. K. (2002). Spine needle biopsy simulator using visual and force feedback. *Computer Aided Surgery, 7,* 353–363. doi:10.3109/10929080209146524

Ramanathan, K., & Guan, S. U. (2007). Multiorder neurons for evolutionary higher-order clustering and growth. *Neural Computation, 19*(12), 3369–3391. doi:10.1162/neco.2007.19.12.3369

Rashid, T., Huang, B. Q., & Kechadi, T. (2007). Auto regressive recurrent neural network approach for electricity load forecasting. *International Journal of Computational Intelligence, 3*(1), 66–71.

Redding, N. J., Kowalczyk, A., & Downs, T. (1993). Constructive higher-order network algorithm that is polynomial time. *Neural Networks, 6*(7), 997–1010. doi:10.1016/S0893-6080(09)80009-9

Reed, T. B. (1981). *Biomass gasification principle and technology.* Upper Saddle River, NJ: Noyes Data Corporation.

Reed, T. B., Levie, B., & Graboski, M. S. (1988). *Fundamentals, development and scaleup of the air-oxygen stratified downdraft gasifier.* Columbus, OH: Battelle.

Reeves, J. (1999). An efficient implementation of backward greedy algorithm for sparse signal reconstruction. *IEEE Signal Processing Letters, 6*(10), 266–268. doi:10.1109/97.789606

Reid, M. S. (1989). Rapid training of higher-order neural networks for invariantpattern recognition. *Neural Networks. IJCNN., International Joint Conference on,* 689-692 vol.1.

Reid, M. B., Spirkovska, L., & Ochoa, E. (1989). Simultaneous position, scale, rotation invariant pattern classification using third-order neural networks. *International Journal of Neural Networks, 1,* 154–159.

Ren, F., & Cao, J. (2006). LMI-based criteria for stability of high-order neural networks with time-varying delay. *Nonlinear Analysis Series B: Real World Applications, 7*(5), 967–979. doi:10.1016/j.nonrwa.2005.09.001

Ren, W. (2009). Distributed leaderless consensus algorithms for networked Euler–Lagrange systems. *International Journal of Control, 82*(11), 2137–2149. doi:10.1080/00207170902948027

Ren, W., & Beard, R. W. (2005). Consensus seeking in multiagent systems under dynamically changing interaction topologies. *IEEE Transactions on Automatic Control, 50*(5), 655–661. doi:10.1109/TAC.2005.846556

Ren, W., & Beard, R. W. (2008). *Distributed consensus in multi-vehicle cooperative control.* New York, NY: Springer-Verlag.

Ren, W., Beard, R. W., & Atkins, E. M. (2007). Information consensus in multivehicle cooperative control. *IEEE Control Systems Magazine, 27*(2), 71–82. doi:10.1109/MCS.2007.338264

Reynolds, D. R. (1995). Robust text-independent speaker identification using Gaussianmixture speaker models. *IEEE Transactions on Speech and Audio Processing,* 72–83. doi:10.1109/89.365379

Ricalde Castellanos, L. J. (2005). *Inverse optimal adaptive recurrent neural control with constrained inputs.* (Unpublished Doctoral Dissertation). Centro de Investigación y de Estudios Avanzados (CINVESTAV) del Instituto Politécnico Nacional (IPN). Guadalajara, México.

Ricalde, L., Sanchez, E., & Alanis, A. Y. (2010). Recurrent higher order neural network control for output trajectory tracking with neural observers and constrained inputs. In Zhang, M. (Ed.), *Artificial Higher Order Neural Networks for Computer Science and Engineering – Trends for Emerging Application* (pp. 286–311). Hershey, PA: IGI Global.

Rizun, P. R. (2004). Robot-assisted neurosurgery. *Semin Laporasc Surgery, 11,* 99–106.

Rodriguez-Angeles, A., & Nijmeijer, H. (2004). Mutual synchronization of robots via estimated state feedback: A cooperative approach. *IEEE Transactions on Control Systems Technology, 12*(4), 542–554. doi:10.1109/TCST.2004.825065

Rong, H. J., Huang, G.-B., Sundararajan, N., & Saratchandran, P. (2009). Online sequential fuzzy extreme learning machine for function approximation and classification problems. *IEEE Transactions on Systems, Man, and Cybernetics. Part B, Cybernetics, 39*(4), 1067–1072. doi:10.1109/TSMCB.2008.2010506

Roos, K. F. (1991). *Profitable alternatives for regulatory impacts on livestock waste management.* Paper presented at the National Livestock, Poultry and Aquacultural Waste Management National Workshop. Kansas City, MO.

Ross, S. M. (1970). *Applied probability models with optimization applications.* New York, NY: Dover Publications.

Rovithakis, G. A. (2000). Paper. In *Proceedings of the IEEE International Symposium on Intelligent Control,* (pp. 7-12). Patras, Greece: IEEE Press.

Rovithakis, G. A., Kosmatopoulos, E. B., & Christodoulou, M. A. (1993). Robust adaptive control of unknown plants using recurrent high order neural networks-application to mechanical systems. In *Proceedings of International Conference on Systems, Man and Cybernetics,* (vol. 4), (pp. 57 – 62). IEEE.

Rovithakis, G. M. (2000). Artificial neural networks for feature extraction and classification of vascular tissue fluorescence spectrums. *Acoustics, Speech, and Signal Processing. ICASSP '00. Proceedings. IEEE International Conference on,* 3454 - 3457 vol.6.

Rovithakis, G., Gaganis, V., Perrakis, S., & Christodoulou, M. (1996). A recurrent neural network model to describe manufacturing cell dynamics. In *Proceedings of the 35th IEEE Conference on Decision and Control,* (vol. 2), (pp. 1728 – 1733). IEEE Press.

Rovithakis, G., Maniadakis, M., & Zervakis, M. (2000). Artificial neural networks for feature extraction and classification of vascular tissue fluorescence spectrums. *Acoustics, Speech, and Signal Processing, 2000. ICASSP apos; 00. Proceedings. 2000 IEEE International Conference on,* Page(s):3454 - 3457 vol.6.

Rovithakis, G. A., Chalkiadakis, I., & Zervakis, M. E. (2004). High-order neural network structure selection for function approximation applications using genetic algorithms. *IEEE Transactions on Systems, Man and Cybernetics. Part B, 34*(1), 150–158.

Rovithakis, G. A., & Christodoulou, M. A. (2000). Adaptive control with recurrent high order neural networks. In Grible, M. A., & Johnson, M. A. (Eds.), *Advances in Industrial Control.* London, UK: Springer Verlag. doi:10.1007/978-1-4471-0785-9

Rovithakis, G. I. (2004). High-order neural network structure selection for function approximation applications using genetic algorithms. *IEEE Transactions on Systems, Man, and Cybernetics. Part B, Cybernetics, 34*(1), 150–158. doi:10.1109/TSMCB.2003.811767

Rumelhart, D., Hinton, G., & McClelland, J. (1986). Learning internal representations by error propagation. In D. Rumelhart & J. McClelland (Eds.), *Parallel Distributed Processing: Explorations in the Microstructure of Cognition, Volume 1: Foundations.* Cambridge, MA: MIT Press.

Rumelhart, D. E., Hinton, G. E., & Williams, R. (1986). Learning representation by back-propagation errors. *Nature, 323,* 533–536. doi:10.1038/323533a0

Rumelhart, D. E., & McClelland, J. L. (1986). *Parallel distributed computing: Exploration in the microstructure of cognition.* Cambridge, MA: MIT Press.

Saad, E. W., Prokhorov, D. V., & Wunsch, D. C. II. (1998). Comparative study of stock trend prediction using time delay recurrent and probabilistic neural networks. *IEEE Transactions on Neural Networks*, *9*(6), 1456–1470. doi:10.1109/72.728395

Sagüés, C., García-Bacaicoa, P., & Serrano, S. (2007). Automatic control of biomass gasifiers using fuzzy inference systems. *Bioresource Technology*, *98*, 845–855. doi:10.1016/j.biortech.2006.03.004

Salcedo-Sanz, S., & Yao, X. (2004). A hybrid Hopfield network-genetic algorithm approach for the terminal assignment problem. *IEEE Transactions on Systems, Man, and Cybernetics*, *34*(6), 2343–2353. doi:10.1109/TSMCB.2004.836471

Sanchez Camperos, E. N., & Alanis Garcia, A. Y. (2006). *Redes neuronales: Conceptos fundamentales y aplicaciones a control automatico*. Madrid, Spain: Pearson-Prentice Hall.

Sanchez, E. N., & Ricalde, L. J. (2003). Trajectory tracking via adaptive recurrent neural control with input saturation. In *Proceedings of International Joint Conference on Neural Networks 2003*. Portland, OR: IJCNN.

Sanchez, E. N., Alanis, A. Y., & Rico, J. (2004). Electric load demand prediction using neural networks trained by Kalman filtering. In *Proceedings of the IEEE International Joint Conference on Neural Networks*, (pp. 2771-2775). Budapest, Hungary: IEEE Press.

Sanchez, E. N., Alanis, A. Y., & Chen, G. R. (2006). Recurrent neural networks trained with the Kalman filtering for discrete chaos reconstruction. *Continuous Discrete Impulsive Systems B*, *13*, 1–18.

Sanchez, E. N., Alanis, A. Y., & Loukianov, A. G. (2007). Discrete-time recurrent high order neural observer for induction motors. In Melin, P. (Eds.), *Foundations of Fuzzy Logic and Soft Computing*. Berlin, Germany: Springer-Verlag. doi:10.1007/978-3-540-72950-1_70

Sanchez, E. N., Alanis, A. Y., & Loukianov, A. G. (2008). *Discrete time high order neural control trained with Kalman filtering*. Berlin, Germany: Springer-Verlag. doi:10.1007/978-3-540-78289-6

Sanchez, E. N., Alanis, A. Y., & Rico, J. (2009). Electric load demand and electricity prices forecasting using higher order neural networks trained by kalman filtering. In Zhang, M. (Ed.), *Artificial Higher Order Neural Networks for Economics and Business* (pp. 295–313). Hershey, PA: IGI Global.

Sanchez, E., Urrego, D. A., Alanis, A. Y., & Carlos-Hernandez, S. (2010). Recurrent higher order neural observers for anaerobic processes. In Zhang, M. (Ed.), *Artificial Higher Order Neural Networks for Computer Science and Engineering – Trends for Emerging Application* (pp. 333–365). Hershey, PA: IGI Global.

Sanger, T. D. (1991). A tree- structured adaptive network for function approximation in high-dimensional space. *IEEE Transactions on Neural Networks*, *2*(2). doi:10.1109/72.80339

Sankar, A., & Mammone, R. J. (1991). Optimal pruning of neural tree networks for improved generalization. In *Proceedings of the International Joint Conference on Neural Networks*, (pp. 219-224). Seattle, WA: IEEE.

Sankar, A., & Mammone, R. J. (1991). Speaker independent vowel recognition using neural tree networks. In *Proceedings of the International Joint Conference on Neural Networks*, (pp. 809-814). Seattle, WA: IEEE.

Sankar, A., & Mammone, R. J. (1993). Growing and pruning neural tree networks. *IEEE Transactions on Computers*, *42*, 291–299. doi:10.1109/12.210172

Schmidt, W., & Davis, J. (1993). Pattern recognition properties of various feature spaces for higher order neural networks. *IEEE Transactions on Pattern Analysis and Machine Intelligence*, *15*, 795–801. doi:10.1109/34.236250

Schuster, G., Löffler, G., Weigl, K., & Hofbauer, H. (2001). Biomass steam gasification--An extensive parametric modeling study. *Bioresource Technology*, *77*, 71–79. doi:10.1016/S0960-8524(00)00115-2

Schuster, H. G. (1989). *Deterministic chaos- An introduction* (2nd ed.). Weinheim, Germany: VCH Verlagsgeshellschaft.

Schwartz, J. M., Denninger, M., & Rancourt, D. (2005). Modeling liver tissue properties using a non-linear viscoelastic model for surgery simulation. *Medical Image Analysis*, *9*, 103–112. doi:10.1016/j.media.2004.11.002

Seiffertt, J., & Wunsch, D. C. II. (2009). Higher order neural network architectures for agent-based computational economics and finance. In Zhang, M. (Ed.), *Artificial Higher Order Neural Networks for Economics and Business* (pp. 79–93). Hershey, PA: IGI Global.

Sekhar Barman, N., Ghosh, S., & De, S. (2012). Gasification of biomass in a fixed bed downdraft gasifier – A realistic model including tar. *Bioresource Technology, 107*, 505–511. doi:10.1016/j.biortech.2011.12.124

Selviah, D. (2009). High speed optical higher order neural network for discovering data trends and patterns in very large databases. In Zhang, M. (Ed.), *Artificial Higher Order Neural Networks for Economics and Business* (pp. 442–465). Hershey, PA: IGI Global.

Selviah, D. R., & Shawash, J. (2009). Generalized correlation higher order neural networks for financial time series prediction. In Zhang, M. (Ed.), *Artificial Higher Order Neural Networks for Economics and Business* (pp. 212–249). Hershey, PA: IGI Global. doi:10.4018/978-1-59904-897-0.ch010

Selviah, D., & Shawash, J. (2010). Fifty years of electronic hardware implementations of first and higher order neural networks. In Zhang, M. (Ed.), *Artificial Higher Order Neural Networks for Computer Science and Engineering – Trends for Emerging Application* (pp. 269–285). Hershey, PA: IGI Global.

Senjyu, T., Yona, A., Urasaki, N., & Funabashi, T. (2006). Application of recurrent neural network to long-term-ahead generating power forecasting for wind speed generator. In *Proceedings of the Power Systems Conference and Exposition PSCE*, (pp. 1260-1265). PSCE.

Sethi, I. K. (1990). Entropy nets: From decision trees to neural networks. *Proceedings of the IEEE, 78*(10), 1605–1613. doi:10.1109/5.58346

Sethi, I. K., & Jan, A. K. (1991). Decision tree performance enhancement using an artificial neural networks implementation. In *Artificial Neural Networks and Statistical Pattern Recognition* (pp. 71–88). Amsterdam, The Netherlands: Elsevier.

Shawash, J., & Selviah, D. (2010). Artificial higher order neural network training on limited precision processors. In Zhang, M. (Ed.), *Artificial Higher Order Neural Networks for Computer Science and Engineering – Trends for Emerging Application* (pp. 312–332). Hershey, PA: IGI Global.

Shawver, T. (2005). Merger premium predictions using neural network approach. *Journal of Emerging Technologies in Accounting, 1*, 61–72. doi:10.2308/jeta.2005.2.1.61

Shi, J., Lee, W. J., Liu, Y., Yang, Y., & Wang, P. (2011). Short term wind power forecasting using Hilbert-Huang transform and artificial neural network. In *Proceedings of the Fourth International Conference on Electric Utility Deregulation and Restructuring and Power Technologies*, (pp. 162-167). Weihai, China: IEEE.

Shi, D., Tan, S., & Ge, S. S. (2009). Automatically identifying predictor variables for stock return prediction. In Zhang, M. (Ed.), *Artificial Higher Order Neural Networks for Economics and Business* (pp. 60–78). Hershey, PA: IGI Global. doi:10.4018/978-1-59904-897-0.ch003

Shin, Y. G. (1995). Ridge polynomial networks. *Neural Networks, IEEE Transactions on*, Volume: 6, Issue: 3, On page(s): 610-622.

Shin, Y., & Ghosh, J. (1991). The pi-sigma network: An efficient higher-order neural network for pattern classification and function approximation. In *Proceedings of the International Joint Conference on Neural Networks*, (pp. 13-18). IEEE.

Shin, Y. a. (1995). Ridge Polynomial Networks. *IEEE Transactions on Neural Networks, 6*(3), 610–622. doi:10.1109/72.377967

Shin, Y., & Ghosh, J. (1995). Ridge polynomial networks. *IEEE Transactions on Neural Networks, 6*, 610–622. doi:10.1109/72.377967

Shu, M. M. (2007). Genetic Algorithms Designed for Solving Support Vector Classifier. *Data, Privacy, and E-Commerce, 2007. ISDPE 2007. The First International Symposium on*, 167 - 169.

Shuxiang Xu, L. C. (2008). Application of New Adaptive Higher Order Neural Networks in Data Mining. *Computer Science and Software Engineering, 2008 International Conference on*, Volume: 1, On page(s): 115-118.

Siddiqi, A. A. (2005). Genetically evolving higher order neural networks by direct encoding method. In *Proceedings of Sixth International Conference on Computational Intelligence and Multimedia Applications*, (pp. 62 – 67). IEEE.

Simeonov, I., & Queinnec, I. (2006). Linearizing control of the anaerobic digestion with addition of acetate (control of the anaerobic digestion). *Control Engineering Practice*, *14*, 799–810. doi:10.1016/j.conengprac.2005.04.011

Simpson, P. K. (1990). Higher-ordered and interconnected bidirectional associative memories. *IEEE Transactions on Systems, Man, and Cybernetics*, *20*, 637–653. doi:10.1109/21.57276

Singhal, S., & Wu, L. (1989). In Touretzky, D. S. (Ed.), *Training multilayer perceptrons with the extended Kalman algorithm* (*Vol. 1*, pp. 133–140). Advances in Neural Information Processing Systems San Mateo, CA: Morgan Kaufmann.

Sinha, N., Gupta, M. M., & Zadeh, L. (1999). *Soft computing and intelligent control systems: Theory and applications*. New York, NY: Academic.

Sloan, R. (1993). Accounting earnings and top executive compensation. *Journal of Accounting and Economics*, *16*, 55–100. doi:10.1016/0165-4101(93)90005-Z

Softky, R. W., & Kammen, D. M. (1991). Correlations in high dimensional or asymmetrical data sets: Hebbian neuronal processing. *Neural Networks*, *4*, 337–347. doi:10.1016/0893-6080(91)90070-L

Solo, A. M. G. (2010). Multidimensional Matrix Algebra and Multidimensional Matrix Calculus: Part 1 of 5. *Proceedings of the 2010 International Conference on Scientific Computing* (CSC'10), 353-359. CSREA Press.

Solo, A. M. G. (2010). Multidimensional Matrix Algebra and Multidimensional Matrix Calculus: Part 2 of 5. *Proceedings of the 2010 International Conference on Scientific Computing* (CSC'10), 360-366. CSREA Press.

Solo, A. M. G. (2010). Multidimensional Matrix Algebra and Multidimensional Matrix Calculus: Part 3 of 5. *Proceedings of the 2010 International Conference on Scientific Computing* (CSC'10), 367-372. CSREA Press.

Solo, A. M. G. (2010). Multidimensional Matrix Algebra and Multidimensional Matrix Calculus: Part 4 of 5. Proceedings of the 2010 International Conference on Scientific Computing (CSC'10), 373-378. CSREA Press.

Solo, A. M. G. (2010). Multidimensional Matrix Algebra and Multidimensional Matrix Calculus: Part 5 of 5. Proceedings of the 2010 International Conference on Scientific Computing (CSC'10), 379-381. CSREA Press.

Song, Y., & Grizzle, J. W. (1995). The extended Kalman filter as a local asymptotic observer for discrete-time nonlinear systems. *Journal of Mathematical Systems. Estimation and Control*, *5*(1), 59–78.

Spanos, D. P., Olfati-Saber, R., & Murray, R. M. (2005). *Dynamic consensus on mobile networks*. Paper presented at the 2005 IFAC World Congress. Prague, Czech Republic.

Spirkovska, L. R. (1990). Connectivity strategies for higher-order neural networks applied to pattern recognition. *Neural Networks, 1990., 1990 IJCNN International Joint Conference on*, 21-26 vol.1.

Stone, M. H. (1948). The generalized weierstrass approximation theorem. *Mathematics Magazine*, *21*(4-5), 167–184, 237–254. doi:10.2307/3029750

Strogatz, S. (2000). From Kuramoto to Crawford: Exploring the onset of synchronization in populations of coupled oscillators. *Physica D. Nonlinear Phenomena*, *143*, 1–20. doi:10.1016/S0167-2789(00)00094-4

Sun, D., Shao, X., & Feng, G. (2007). A model-free cross-coupled control for position synchronization of multi-axis motions: Theory and experiments. *IEEE Transactions on Control Systems Technology*, *15*(2), 306–314. doi:10.1109/TCST.2006.883201

Suykens, J. A. K., Lukas, L., & Vandewalle, J. (2000). Sparse approximation using least squares support vector machines. In *Proceedings of IEEE International Symposium on Circuits and Systems (ISCAS 2000)*, (pp. 11757-11760). IEEE Press. Adas, A. N. (1998). Using adaptive linear prediction to support real – time VBR video under RCBR network service model. *IEEE Transactions on Networking, 6*(5).

Takeshi Kaita, S. T. (2002). On a higher-order neural network for distortion invariant pattern recognition. *Pattern Recognition Letters, 23*(Issue 8), 977–984. doi:10.1016/S0167-8655(02)00028-4

Talebi, H., Abdollahi, F., Patel, R., & Khorasani, K. (2010). *Neural network-based state estimation of nonlinear systems* (3rd ed.). New York, NY: Springer. doi:10.1007/978-1-4419-1438-5

Tawfik, H., & Liatsis, P. (1997). Prediction of nonlinear time-series using higher-order neural networks. In *Proceeding IWSSIP 1997 Conference*. Poznan, Poland: IWSSIP.

Taylor, J. G., & Commbes, S. (1993). Learning higher order correlations. *Neural Networks, 6*, 423–428. doi:10.1016/0893-6080(93)90009-L

Taylor, R. H., & Kazanzides, P. (2007). Medical robotics and computer-integrated interventional medicine. *International Journal of Advance in Computers, 73*, 219–260.

Tenti, P. (1996). Forecasting foreign exchange rates using recurrent neural networks. *Applied Artificial Intelligence, 10*, 567–581. doi:10.1080/088395196118434

Thammano, A., & Ruxpakawong, P. (2010). Nonlinear dynamic system identification using recurrent neural network with multi-segment piecewise-linear connection weight. *Memetic Computing, 2*(4), 273–282. doi:10.1007/s12293-010-0042-7

Thangavel, P., & Gladis, D. (2007). Hopfield hysteretic Hopfield network with dynamic tunneling for crossbar switch and N-queens problem. *Neurocomputing, 70*, 2544–2551. doi:10.1016/j.neucom.2006.06.006

Theilliol, D., Ponsart, J. C., Harmand, J., Join, C., & Gras, P. (2003). On-line estimation of unmeasured inputs for an aerobic wastewater treatment processes. *Control Engineering Practice, 11*(9), 1007–1019. doi:10.1016/S0967-0661(02)00230-7

Theodoridis, D. C., Boutalis, Y. S., & Christodoulou, M. A. (2009). A new neuro-fuzzy dynamical system definition based on high order neural network function approximators. In *Proceedings* of the *European Control Conference ECC 2009*, (pp. 3305-3310). Budapest, Hungary: ECC.

Theodoridis, D. C., Boutalis, Y. S., & Christodoulou, M. A. (2010). A new adaptive neuro-fuzzy controller for trajectory tracking of robot manipulators. *International Journal of Robotics and Automation, 26*(1), 1–12.

Theodoridis, D. C., Christodoulou, M. A., & Boutalis, Y. S. (2010). Neuro – fuzzy control schemes based on high order neural network function aproximators. In Zhang, M. (Ed.), *Artificial Higher Order Neural Networks for Computer Science and Engineering: Trends for Emerging Applications* (pp. 450–483). Hershey, PA: IGI Global.

Thimm, G., & Fiesler, E. (1997). High-order and multilayer perceptron initialization. *IEEE Transactions on Neural Networks, 8*(2), 349–359. doi:10.1109/72.557673

Tou□cAzar, & Hayward, V. (2008). Estimation of the fracture toughness of soft tissue from needle insertion. *Lecture Notes in Computer Science, 5104*, 166-175.

Tsao, T.-R. (1989). A group theory approach to neural network computing of 3D rigid motion. In *Proceedings of the International Joint Conference on Neural Networks*, (vol 2), (pp. 275-280). IJCNN.

Tseng, Y.-H., & Wu, J.-L. (1994). Constant-time neural decoders for some BCH codes. In *Proceedings of IEEE International Symposium on Information Theory*, (p. 343). IEEE Press.

Tsitsiklis, J. N. (1984). *Problems in decentralized decision making and computation*. (Ph.D. Dissertation). Massachusetts Institute of Technology. Cambridge, MA.

Tsoi, A. C., & Back, A. D. (1994). Locally recurrent feed forward networks: A critical review of architectures. *IEEE Transactions on Neural Networks, 5*(2), 229–239. doi:10.1109/72.279187

Van Impe, J. F., & Bastin, G. (1995). Optimal adaptive control of fed-batch fermentation processes. *Control Engineering Practice, 3*(7), 939–954. doi:10.1016/0967-0661(95)00077-8

Vecci, L., Piazza, F., & Uncini, A. (1998). Learning and approximation capabilities of adaptive spline activation function neural networks. *Neural Networks, 11*, 259–270. doi:10.1016/S0893-6080(97)00118-4

Vicsek, T., Czirok, A., Jacob, E. B., Cohen, I., & Schochet, O. (1995). Novel type of phase transitions in a system of self-driven particles. *Physical Review Letters*, *75*, 1226–1229. doi:10.1103/PhysRevLett.75.1226

Villalobos, L., & Merat, F. (1995). Learning capability assessment and feature space optimization for higher-order neural networks. *IEEE Transactions on Neural Networks*, *6*, 267–272. doi:10.1109/72.363427

Viuela, P. I., & Galvn, I. M. (2004). *Redes de neuronas artificiales un enfoque práctico* (3rd ed.). Madrid, Spain: Pearson, Prentice Hall.

Waerden, B. L. (1970). *Algebra*. New York, NY: Frederick Ungar Publishing Co.

Wang, J. H. J. L. (1995). Qualitative analysis of the BP composed of product units and summing units. *IEEE International Conference on Systems, Man and Cybernetics 1*, 35–39.

Wang, J. (2007). A memetic algorithm with genetic particle swarm optimization and neural network for maximum cut problems. *Lecture Notes in Computer Science*, *4688*, 297–306. doi:10.1007/978-3-540-74769-7_33

Wang, J., & Tang, Z. (2004). An improved optimal competitive Hopfield network for bipartite subgraph problems. *Neurocomputing*, *61*(5), 413–419. doi:10.1016/j.neucom.2004.03.012

Wang, L. (1994). *Adaptive fuzzy systems and control*. Englewood Cliffs, NJ: Prentice Hall.

Wang, L. P., Li, S., Tian, F. Y., & Fu, X. J. (2004). A noisy chaotic neural network for solving combinatorial optimization problems: Stochastic chaotic simulated annealing. *IEEE Transactions on Systems, Man, and Cybernetics. Part B, Cybernetics*, *34*(5), 2119–2125. doi:10.1109/TSMCB.2004.829778

Wang, S. H. (2003). Application of self-organising maps for data mining with incomplete data sets. *Neural Computing & Applications*, *12*(1), 42–48. doi:10.1007/s00521-003-0372-1

Wang, X. F., & Chen, G. (2002). Pinning control of scale-free dynamical networks. *Physica A*, *310*(3), 521–531. doi:10.1016/S0378-4371(02)00772-0

Wang, Y., & Kinoshita, C. M. (1993). Kinetic model of biomass gasification. *Solar Energy*, *51*(1), 19–25. doi:10.1016/0038-092X(93)90037-O

Wang, Z., Liu, Y., & Liu, X. (2009). On complex artificial higher order neural networks: Dealing with stochasticity, jumps and delays. In Zhang, M. (Ed.), *Artificial Higher Order Neural Networks for Economics and Business* (pp. 466–483). Hershey, PA: IGI Global.

Wei Chu Keerthi, S. C. (2002). A new Bayesian design method for support vector classification. *Neural Information Processing. ICONIP '02. Proceedings of the 9th International Conference on*, 888 - 892 vol.2.

Wei, Z., Wan, G., & Gardi, L. (2004). Robot-assisted 3D-TRUS guided prostate brachytherapy: System integration and validation. *Medical Physics*, *31*, 539–548. doi:10.1118/1.1645680

Welch, R. L., Ruffing, S. M., & Venayagamoorthy, G. K. (2009). Comparison of feedforward and feedback neural network architectures for short term wind speed prediction. In *Proceedings of the IEEE International Joint Conference on Neural Networks*, (pp. 3335-3340). Atlanta, GA: IEEE Press.

Werbos, P. J. (2009). Putting more brain-like intelligence into the electric power grid: What we need and how to do it. In *Proceedings of the IEEE International Joint Conference on Neural Networks*, (pp. 3356-3359). Atlanta, GA: IEEE Press.

Werbos, P. J. (1990). Backpropagation through time: What it is and how to do it. *Proceedings of the IEEE*, *78*(10), 1550–1560. doi:10.1109/5.58337

Werner, S., & Gemeinhardt, G. (1995). Nonprofit organizations: What factors determine pay levels? *Compensation and Benefits Review*, *27*(5), 53–60. doi:10.1177/088636879502700511

Willcox, C. R. (1991). Understanding hierarchical neural network behavior: A renormalization group approach. *Journal of Physics. A. Mathematical Nuclear and General*, *24*, 2655–2644. doi:10.1088/0305-4470/24/11/030

Williams, R. J., & Zipser, D. (1989). A learning algorithm for continually running fully recurrent neural networks. *Neural Computation*, *1*, 270–280. doi:10.1162/neco.1989.1.2.270

Winkler, S. M. (2006). Advances in applying genetic programming to machine learning, focusing on classification problems. *In Proceedings of the 20th international symposium on parallel and distributed processing, Rhodes Island, Greece*, pp. 2295–2302.

Wood, J., & Shawe-Taylor, J. (1996). A unifying framework for invariant pattern recognition. *Pattern Recognition Letters, 17*, 1415–1422. doi:10.1016/S0167-8655(96)00103-1

Wu, C. W. (2007). *Synchronization in complex networks of nonlinear dynamical systems*. Singapore: World Scientific. doi:10.1142/6570

Wu, J., Chen, S., Zeng, J., & Gao, L. (2009). Control technologies in distributed generation systems based on renewable energy. *Asian Power Electronics Journal, 3*(1), 39–52.

Xia, G., Tang, Z., Li, Y., & Wang, J. (2005). A binary Hopfield neural network with hysteresis for large crossbar packet-switches. *Neurocomputing, 67*, 417–425. doi:10.1016/j.neucom.2004.09.004

Xiao, G., Ni, M. J., Chi, Y., Jin, B. S., Xiao, R., Zhong, Z. P., & Huang, Y. J. (2008). Gasification characteristics of MSW and an ANN prediction model. *Waste Management (New York, N.Y.), 29*(1), 240–244. doi:10.1016/j.wasman.2008.02.022

Xu, S. (2008). Adaptive Higher Order Neural Network Models and Their Applications in Business. In M. Zhang, *Artificial Higher Order Neural Networks for Economics and Business* (pp. 314-329). IGI Global.

Xu, S. (2009). A novel higher order artificial neural networks. In *Proceedings of the Second International Symposium on Computational Mechanics (ISCM II)*, (pp. 1507-1511). Hong Kong, China: ISCM.

Xu, S., & Chen, L. (2009). Adaptive higher order neural networks for effective data mining. In *Proceedings of the Sixth International Symposium on Neural Networks (ISNN 2009)*, (pp. 165-173). Wuhan, China: ISNN.

Xu, S., & Zhang, M. (1999). Approximation to continuous functions and operators using adaptive higher order neural networks. In *Proceedings of International Joint Conference on Neural Networks 1999*. Washington, DC: IEEE.

Xu, S., & Zhang, M. (2002). An adaptive higher-order neural networks (AHONN) and its approximation capabilities. In *Proceedings of the 9th International Conference on Neural Information Processing*, (Vol. 2), (pp. 848 – 852). IEEE.

Xu, B., Liu, X., & Liao, X. (2005). Global asymptotic stability of high-order Hopfield type neural networks with time delays. *Computers & Mathematics with Applications (Oxford, England), 45*(10-11), 1729–1737. doi:10.1016/S0898-1221(03)00151-2

Xu, B., Liu, X., & Teoc, K. L. (2009). Global exponential stability of impulsive high-order Hopfield type neural networks with delays. *Computers & Mathematics with Applications (Oxford, England), 57*(3), 1959–1967. doi:10.1016/j.camwa.2008.10.001

Xu, L., Oja, E., & Suen, C. Y. (1992). Modified Hebbian learning for curve and surface fitting. *Neural Networks, 5*, 441–457. doi:10.1016/0893-6080(92)90006-5

Xu, S. (2009). Adaptive higher order neural network models and their applications in business. In Zhang, M. (Ed.), *Artificial Higher Order Neural Networks for Economics and Business* (pp. 314–329). Hershey, PA: IGI Global. doi:10.4018/978-1-59904-897-0.ch014

Xu, S. (2010). Adaptive higher order neural network models for data mining. In Zhang, M. (Ed.), *Artificial Higher Order Neural Networks for Computer Science and Engineering – Trends for Emerging Application* (pp. 86–98). Hershey, PA: IGI Global.

Xu, S. (2010). Data mining using higher order neural network models with adaptive neuron activation functions. *International Journal of Advancements in Computing Technology, 2*(4), 168–177. doi:10.4156/ijact.vol2.issue4.18

Yamada, T., & Yabuta, T. (1992). Remarks on a neural network controller which uses an auto-tuning method for nonlinear functions. In *Proceedings of IJCNN*, (vol 2), (pp. 775-780). IJCNN.

Yang, X. (1990). Detection and classification of neural signals and identification of neural networks (synaptic connectivity). *Dissertation Abstracts International - B, 50*(12), 5761.

Yao, X. (1997). A new evolutionary system for evolving artificial neural networks. *IEEE Transactions on Neural Networks*, 8, 694–713. doi:10.1109/72.572107

Yao, X. (1999). Evolving artificial neural networks. *Proceedings of the IEEE*, 87(9), 1423–1447. doi:10.1109/5.784219

Yao, X., Lin, Y., & Lin, G. (1999). Evolutionary programming made faster. *IEEE Transactions on Evolutionary Computation*, 3, 82–122. doi:10.1109/4235.771163

Yatsuki, S., & Miyajima, H. (2000). Statistical dynamics of associative memory for higher order neural networks. In *Proceedings of The 2000 IEEE International Symposium on Circuits and Systems,* (Vol. 3), (pp. 670 – 673). Geneva, Switzerland: IEEE Press.

Yeap, T. H., & Ahmed, N. U. (1994). Feedback control of chaotic systems. *Dynamics and Control*, 4(1), 97–114. doi:10.1007/BF02115741

Yih, G. L., Wei, Y. W., & Tsu, T. L. (2005). Observer-based direct adaptive fuzzy-neural control for nonaffine nonlinear systems. *IEEE Transactions on Neural Networks*, 16(4), 853–861. doi:10.1109/TNN.2005.849824

Yi, X., Shao, J., & Yu, Y. (2008). Global exponential stability of impulsive high-order Hopfield type neural networks with delays. *Journal of Computational and Applied Mathematics*, 219(3), 216–222. doi:10.1016/j.cam.2007.07.011

Yoo, S.-J. (2002). Efficient traffic prediction scheme for real time VBR MPEG video transmission over high speed networks. *IEEE Transactions on Broadcasting*, 48(1).

Young, S., & Downs, T. (1993). Generalisation in higher order neural networks. *Electronics Letters*, 29(16), 1491–1493. doi:10.1049/el:19930996

Yousefi, H., Ramezanpour, H., & Rostami, M. (2010). Applications of needle insertion with rotating capability in manipulator. In *Proceedings of the ICBME 17th Iranian Conference on Biomedical Engineering,* (pp. 1-4). ICBME.

Yu, W. (2010). Robust adaptive control using higher order neural networks and projection. In Zhang, M. (Ed.), *Artificial Higher Order Neural Networks for Computer Science and Engineering – Trends for Emerging Application* (pp. 99–137). Hershey, PA: IGI Global.

Zhang, B. T., & Muhlenbein, H. (1994). Synthesis of sigma-pi neural networks by breeder genetic programming. In *Proceedings of the IEEE Conference on Evolutionary Computations*. IEEE Press.

Zhang, H. T., Xu, F. Y., & Zhou, L. (2010). Artificial neural network for load forecasting in smart grid. In *Proceedings of the Ninth Conference on Machine Learning and Cybernetics,* (pp. 3200-3205). Qingdao, China: IEEE.

Zhang, J. (2005). *Polynomial full naïve estimated misclassification cost models for financial distress prediction using higher order neural network*. Paper presented at the 14th Annual Research Work Shop on Artificial Intelligence and Emerging Technologies in Accounting, Auditing, and Ta. San Francisco, CA.

Zhang, J. (2012). *Compensation and financial performance measures: The case of municipal managers*. (Unpublished Doctoral Dissertation). The George Washington University. Washington, DC.

Zhang, J. C., Zhang, M., & Fulcher, J. (1997). Financial simulation system using a higher order trigonometric polynomial neural network group model. In *Proceedings of the IEEE/IAFE 1997 Computational Intelligence for Financial Engineering (CIFEr),* (pp. 189 – 194). Houston, TX: IEEE Press.

Zhang, M. (2001). Financial data simulation using A-PHONN model. In *Proceedings of the International Joint Conference on Neural Networks 2001,* (pp. 1823 – 1827). Washington, DC: IJCNN.

Zhang, M. (2003). Financial data simulation using PL-HONN model. In *Proceedings IASTED International Conference on Modelling and Simulation,* (pp. 229-233). Marina del Rey, CA: IASTED.

Zhang, M. (2005). A data simulation system using sinx/x and sinx polynomial higher order neural networks. In *Proceedings of IASTED International Conference on Computational Intelligence,* (pp. 56 – 61). Calgary, Canada: IASTED.

Zhang, M. (2006). A data simulation system using CSINC polynomial higher order neural networks. In *Proceedings of the 2006 International Conference on Artificial Intelligence,* (Vol. 1), (pp. 91-97). Las Vegas, NV: IEEE.

Zhang, M. X. (2002). Neuron-adaptive higher order neural-network models for automated financial data modeling. *Neural Networks, IEEE Transactions on*, Volume 13, Issue 1, Page(s):188 - 204.

Zhang, M., & Lu, B. (2001). Financial data simulation using M-PHONN model. In *Proceedings of the International Joint Conference on Neural Networks 2001*, (pp. 1828-1832). Washington, DC: IJCNN.

Zhang, M., & Scofield, R. A. (2001). Rainfall estimation using A-PHONN model. In *Proceedings of International Joint Conference on Neural Networks*, (Vol. 3), (pp. 1583 – 1587). Washington, DC: IJCNN.

Zhang, M., Fulcher, J., & Scofield, R. A. (1996). Neural network group models for estimating rainfall from satellite images. In *Proceedings of World Congress on Neural Networks*, (pp. 897-900). San Diego, CA: IEEE.

Zhang, M., Murugesan, S., & Sadeghi, M. (1995). Polynomial higher order neural network for economic data simulation. In *Proceedings of International Conference on Neural Information Processing*, (pp. 493-496). Beijing, China: IEEE.

Zhang, M., Xu, S., & Lu, B. (1999). Neuron-adaptive higher order neural network group models. In *Proceedings of International Joint Conference on Neural Networks*, (Vol. 1), (pp. 333 - 336). IJCNN.

Zhang, M., Zhang, J. C., & Fulcher, J. (1997). Financial prediction system using higher order trigonometric polynomial neural network group model. In *Proceedings of the IEEE International Conference on Neural Networks*, (pp. 2231-2234). Houston, TX: IEEE Press.

Zhang, M., Zhang, J. C., & Keen, S. (1999). Using THONN system for higher frequency non-linear data simulation & prediction. In *Proceedings of IASTED International Conference on Artificial Intelligence and Soft Computing*, (pp. 320-323). Honolulu, HI: IASTED.

Zhang, B. (2007). Delay-dependent robust exponential stability for uncertain recurrent neural networks with time-varying delays. *International Journal of Neural Systems*, *17*(3), 207–218. doi:10.1142/S012906570700107X

Zhang, B. T. (1997). Evolutionary induction of sparse neural tree. *Evolutionary Computation*, *5*(2), 213–236. doi:10.1162/evco.1997.5.2.213

Zhang, B. T. (2002). A Bayesian evolutionary approach to the design and learning of heterogeneous neural trees. *Integrated Computer-Aided Engineering*, *9*(1), 73–86.

Zhang, G. P. (2003). Time series forecasting using a hybrid ARIMA and neural network model. *Neurocomputing*, *50*, 159–175. doi:10.1016/S0925-2312(01)00702-0

Zhang, J. (2006). *Linear and nonlinear models for the power of chief elected officials and debt*. Pittsburgh, PA: Mid-Atlantic Region American Accounting Association.

Zhang, L., Simoff, S. J., & Zhang, J. C. (2009). Trigonometric polynomial higher order neural network group models and weighted kernel models for financial data simulation and prediction. In Zhang, M. (Ed.), *Artificial Higher Order Neural Networks for Economics and Business* (pp. 484–503). Hershey, PA: IGI Global. doi:10.4018/978-1-59904-897-0.ch022

Zhang, M. (2008). *Artificial higher order neural networks for economics and business*. Hershey, PA: IGI Global. doi:10.4018/978-1-59904-897-0

Zhang, M. (2009). Artificial higher order neural network nonlinear model - SAS NLIN or HONNs. In Zhang, M. (Ed.), *Artificial Higher Order Neural Networks for Economics and Business* (pp. 1–47). Hershey, PA: IGI Global.

Zhang, M. (2009). Ultra high frequency trigonometric higher order neural networks for time series data analysis. In Zhang, M. (Ed.), *Artificial Higher Order Neural Networks for Economics and Business* (pp. 133–163). Hershey, PA: IGI Global. doi:10.4018/978-1-59904-897-0.ch007

Zhang, M. (2010). Higher order neural network group-based adaptive trees. In Zhang, M. (Ed.), *Artificial Higher Order Neural Networks for Computer Science and Engineering – Trends for Emerging Application* (pp. 1–36). Hershey, PA: IGI Global. doi:10.4018/978-1-61520-711-4.ch001

Zhang, M. (2010). Rainfall estimation using neuron-adaptive artificial higher order neural networks. In Zhang, M. (Ed.), *Artificial Higher Order Neural Networks for Computer Science and Engineering – Trends for Emerging Application* (pp. 159–186). Hershey, PA: IGI Global. doi:10.4018/978-1-61520-711-4.ch007

Zhang, M., & Fulcher, J. (2004). Higher order neural networks for satellite weather prediction. In Fulcher, J., & Jain, L. C. (Eds.), *Applied Intelligent Systems* (*Vol. 153*, pp. 17–57). Berlin, Germany: Springer.

Zhang, M., Xu, S. X., & Fulcher, J. (2002). Neuron-adaptive higher order neural-network models for automated financial data modeling. *IEEE Transactions on Neural Networks, 13*(1), 188–204. doi:10.1109/72.977302

Zhang, M., Xu, S. X., & Fulcher, J. (2007). ANSER: An adaptive-neuron artificial neural network system for estimating rainfall using satellite data. *International Journal of Computers and Applications, 29*(3), 215–222. doi:10.2316/Journal.202.2007.3.202-1585

Zhang, M., Xu, S., & Fulcher, J. (2002). Neuron-adaptive higher order neural-network models for automated financial data modeling. *IEEE Transactions on Neural Networks, 13*(1), 188–204. doi:10.1109/72.977302

Zhang, M., Zhang, J. C., & Fulcher, J. (2000). Higher order neural network group models for data approximation. *International Journal of Neural Systems, 10*(2), 123–142. doi:10.1016/S0129-0657(00)00011-9

Zhang, R., Huang, G.-B., & Sundararajan, N. P. (2007). Multi-category classification using an extreme learning machine for microarray gene expression cancer diagnosis. *IEEE/ACM Transactions on Computational Biology and Bioinformatics, 4*(3), 485–495. doi:10.1109/tcbb.2007.1012

Zhang, T., Ge, S. S., & Hang, C. C. (1999). Design and performance analysis of a direct adaptive controller for nonlinear systems. *Automatica, 35*(11), 1809–1817. doi:10.1016/S0005-1098(99)00098-9

Zhan, R., & Wan, J. (2006). Neural network-aided adaptive unscented Kalman filter for nonlinear state estimation. *IEEE Signal Processing Letters, 13*(7), 445–448. doi:10.1109/LSP.2006.871854

ZHENGQUAN HE. M. Y. (1999). Improvement on higher-order neural networks for invariant object recognition. *Springer, Neural processing letters ISSN 1370-4621*, vol. 10, no1, pp. 49-55 (11 ref.).

Zhu, Q. Y., Qin, P. N., & Huang, G.-B. (2005). Evolutionary extreme learning machine. *Pattern Recognition, 38*, 1759–1763. doi:10.1016/j.patcog.2005.03.028

Zivanovic, A., & Davies, B. L. (2000). A robotic system for blood sampling. *IEEE Transactions in Information Technology Biomedical Engineering, 4*, 8–14. doi:10.1109/4233.826854

Zurada, J. M. (1992). *Introduction to Artificial Neural Systems*. St. Paul: West Publishing Company.

About the Contributors

Ming Zhang received the M.S. degree in Information Processing and Ph.D. degree in the research area of Computer Vision from East China Normal University, Shanghai, China, in 1982 and 1989, respectively. He held Postdoctoral Fellowships in Artificial Neural Networks with the Chinese Academy of the Sciences in 1989 and the USA National Research Council in 1991. He was a face recognition airport security system project manager and Ph.D. co-supervisor at the University of Wollongong, Australia, in 1992. Since 1994, he was a Lecturer at the Monash University, Australia. From 1995 to 1999, he was a Senior Lecturer and Ph.D. Supervisor at the University of Western Sydney, Australia. He also held Senior Research Associate Fellowship in Artificial Neural Networks with the USA National Research Council in 1999. He is currently a full Professor and Graduate Student Supervisor in Computer Science at the Christopher Newport University, VA, USA.

* * *

Alma Y. Alanis was born in Durango, Durango, Mexico, in 1980. She received the B.Sc degree from Instituto Tecnologico de Durango (ITD), Durango Campus, Durango, Durango, in 2002, the M.Sc. and the Ph.D. degrees in Electrical Engineering from the Advanced Studies and Research Center of the National Polytechnic Institute (CINVESTAV-IPN), Guadalajara Campus, Mexico, in 2004 and 2007, respectively. Since 2008, she has been with University of Guadalajara, where she is currently a Professor in the Department of Computer Science. She is also member of the Mexican National Research System (SNI-1). She has published papers in international journals and conferences, as well as two international books. Her research interest centers on neural control, backstepping control, block control, chaos reproduction, and their applications to electrical machines, power systems, and robotics.

N. Arana-Daniel received the M.S. and Ph.D. degrees in Computer Science, both from the Center of Research and Advanced Studies, CINVESTAV Unidad Guadalajara, Jalisco, México. She is currently a Research Fellow with the Department of Computer Science, University of Guadalajara, Guadalajara, Jalisco, where she is working, in the Intelligent Systems Research Group. Her current research interests include applications of geometric algebra, machine learning, optimization, computer vision, pattern recognition, and visually guided robotics.

Amir Atiya received his B.S. degree from Cairo University, Egypt, and the M.S. and Ph.D. degrees from Caltech, Pasadena, CA, all in Electrical Engineering. He held positions in academia, as well as several positions in financial firms. From 1997 to 2001, he was a Visiting Associate at Caltech. He held research positions in the firms Simplex Risk Management, Hong Kong, Countrywide Corporation in Los Angeles, Dunn Capital Management, Florida, and Veros Systems, Texas. He received the Egyptian State Prize for Best Research in Science and Engineering in 1994. He also received the Young Investigator Award from the International Neural Network Society in 1996. In addition, he received the prestigious Kuwait Prize by the Kuwait Foundation for the Advancement of Sciences. Currently, he is an Associate Editor for *IEEE Transactions on Neural Networks*. His research interests include statistical learning, neural networks, computational finance, trading system design, optimization, pattern recognition, and time series forecasting.

Yiannis Boutalis (M'86) received the diploma of Electrical Engineer in 1983 from Democritus University of Thrace (DUTH), Greece, and the PhD degree in Electrical and Computer Engineering (topic Image Processing) in 1988 from the Computer Science Division of National Technical University of Athens, Greece. Since 1996, he serves as a faculty member at the Department of Electrical and Computer Engineering, DUTH, Greece, where he is currently an Associate Professor and director of the Automatic Control Systems lab. Currently, he is also a Visiting Professor for research cooperation at Erlangen-Nuremberg University of Germany, Chair of Automatic Control. His current research interests are focused in the development of computational intelligence techniques with applications in control, pattern recognition, signal, and image processing problems.

J. Andrés Bueno was born in Guanajuato, México. He received the Engineering degree from the Universidad de Guanajuato in 2007. He studies a Master in the Centro de Investigacióny de Estudios Avanzados (Cinvestav), Unidad Guadalajara, México. His research interest is automatic control applications with neural networks.

Ivo Bukovsky graduated from Czech Technical University (CTU) in Prague, where he received his Ph.D. in the field of Control and System Engineering in 2007. His Ph.D. thesis on nonconventional neural units and adaptive approach to evaluation of complicated systems was recognized by the Verner von Siemens Excellence Award 2007. His research interests include higher-order neural networks, adaptive evaluation of time series and dynamical systems, multiscale-analysis approaches, control, and biomedical applications. In 2004, Ivo became a head of the Division of Automatic Control and Engineering Informatics at the Department of Instrumentation and Control Engineering, Faculty of Mechanical Engineering, CTU, in Prague, in 2010. He was a Visiting Researcher at the Intelligent Systems Research Laboratory at the University of Saskatchewan (2003), at the Cyberscience Center at the Tohoku University in Japan (2009), and at the University of Manitoba in Canada (2010), and recently he was a Visiting Professor at the Tohoku University in 2011.

Salvador Carlos-Hernández was born in Jilotepec, México. He received the Engineering degree from the Instituto Tecnológico de Toluca in 1999 and the Master degree in 2001 from the Centro de Investigación y de Estudios Avanzados (Cinvestav), Unidad Guadalajara, México. He obtained the Ph.D. degree in Automatic Control from the Institut National Polytechnique de Grenoble, France, in 2005. Since 2006, he is with the Grupo de Recursos Naturales y Energéticos, a research team in Cinvestav, Unidad Saltillo, México. His research interests are: a) automatic control applications and b) organic wastes valorisation for energy production by biological and thermochemical processes.

Rocío Carrasco-Navarro was born in Briseñas, Michoacán, México. She received the B.Sc. degree in Communication and Electronics Engineering from the University of Guadalajara, Guadalajara, México, in 2006, and the M.Sc. degree in Electrical Engineering from the Research and Advanced Studies Center of the National Polytechnic Institute (CINVESTAV-IPN), Guadalajara, México, in 2009. Her research interests include neural networks to estimate and control nonlinear systems and their applications to biological processes.

Glendy A. Catzin was born in 1986, in Uman, Yucatan, Mexico. She received the BEng Major in Mechatronics from Facultad de Ingenieria of the Universidad Autonoma de Yucatan (UADY), Merida, Mexico, in 2011. During her formation in that career, she participated in research projects funded by the CONACYT and the Government of Yucatan, all of them related to the renewable energy area. Among the awards granted to her, it highlights her distinction as an Academic Council Member of the Facultad de Ingenieria of the UADY. She has published one journal paper and two conferences papers. Her research interests include artificial intelligence, signal processing, renewable energy sources, wavelet neural networks, and forecasting in smart grids, among other subjects.

Gang Chen was born in Chongqing, China. He received the Ph.D. degree in Control Engineering from Zhejiang University, Hangzhou, China, in 2006. Since 2006, he has been with the College of Automation, Chongqing University, Chongqing. From 2009 to 2010, he was a Visiting Scholar at the Automation and Robotics Research Institute, The University of Texas at Arlington. His current research interests include distributed control, cooperative control, intelligent control, nonlinear control, and control applications.

Manolis Christodoulou (S'78–M'82–SM'89) was born in Kifissia, Greece, in 1955. He received the diploma degree (EE'78) from the National Technical University of Athens, Greece, the M.S. degree (EE'79) from the University of Maryland, College Park, the Engineer Degree (EE'82) from the University of Southern California, Los Angeles, and the Ph.D. degree (EE'84) from the Democritus University, Thrace, Greece. He joined the Technical University of Crete, Greece, in 1988, where he is currently a Professor of Control. He has been a Visiting Professor at Georgia Tech, Syracuse University, the University of Southern California, Tufts University, Victoria University, and the Massachusetts Institute of Technology. He has authored and co-authored more than 200 journal articles, book chapters, books, and conference publications in the areas of control theory and applications, robotics, factory automation, computer integrated manufacturing in engineering, neural networks for dynamic system identification, and control in the use of robots for minimally invasive surgeries and recently in systems biology.

Abhijit Das was born in Kharagpur, India. He received his B.E. degree from Bengal Engineering College (Deemed University), Shibpur, in 2003, M.S. degree from Indian Institute of Technology, Kharagpur, in 2006, and Ph.D. degree from the University of Texas at Arlington, in 2010, all in Electrical Engineering. From 2003 to 2006, he was involved with several projects with Defense Research and Development Organization (DRDO), India. In 2007, he joined Automation and Robotics Research Institute as a Research Assistant. His Ph.D. dissertation won Dean Dissertation Fellowship award in 2010. He worked as a Fuel Systems Controls Engineer at Technical Center, Caterpillar Inc., from Aug'10 to Feb'12. Currently, he is an Advanced Systems Engineer at Sauer-Danfoss Inc. He is the author of 1 book, 3 book chapters, and several journal and conference articles. He is life member of Systems Society of India. His profile has also appeared in Marquis Who's Who in America.

Yuxin Ding received his Ph.D. degree in Computer Software from the Institute of Software, Chinese Academy of Sciences. He is currently an Associate Professor in the Department of Computer Science at the Harbin Institute of Technology Shenzhen Graduate School. His current research interests are primarily in machine learning and pattern recognition and their applications in computer security.

George Eskander received his B.S. degree from Ain Shams University, Egypt, in Systems and Control Engineering, and M.S. degree from Cairo University, Egypt, in Computer Engineering. Since May 2009, he has been working towards his PhD degree in ETS, Quebec University, Canada, in Automatic Production Engineering. He is conducting research in biometric-cryptography, part of a larger research project in document security funded by Natural Sciences and Engineering Research Council (NSERC) and Banctec Canada. He recently received the Postgraduate Scholarship (PGS) award from NSERC and the Doctoral Scholarship from Québec Funds for Research in Nature and Technologies. His research interests include machine learning, pattern recognition, neural networks, biometrics, bio-cryptography, handwritten recognition, and mathematical modeling.

Mehdi Fallahnezhad was born in Karaj, Iran, in December 1982. He received his B.Sc. degree in Electrical Engineering from Sharif University of Technology, Tehran, and his M.Sc. degree in Biomedical Engineering at Bioelectronics Department of Amirkabir University of Technology (Tehran Polytechnic), Tehran, Iran. He has published several technical/review articles in international journals and conference proceedings on artificial intelligence, pattern recognition, robotic and neuroscience scopes. He is currently working toward a Ph.D. in Neuroscience, at Kavli Institute for Systems Neuroscience/CBM, NTNU, Norway.

Madan M. Gupta is a Professor (emeritus) and Distinguished Research Chair in the College of Engineering and the Director of the Intelligent Systems Research Laboratory at the University of Saskatchewan. Dr. Gupta has authored or co-authored over 900 published research papers. He co-authored *Static and Dynamic Neural Networks: From Fundamentals to Advanced Theory*, *Introduction to Fuzzy Arithmetic: Theory and Applications*, and *Fuzzy Mathematical Models in Engineering and Management Science*. In addition, Dr. Gupta has edited or co-edited 20 other books as well as many conference proceedings and journals in the fields of his research interests, such as adaptive control systems, fuzzy computing, neuro-computing, neuro-vision systems, and neuro-control systems. Dr. Gupta was elected fellow of the Institute of Electrical and Electronics Engineers (IEEE) for his contributions to the theory of fuzzy sets and adaptive control systems and for the advancement on the diagnosis of cardiovascular disease. He was elected fellow of the International Society for Optical Engineering (SPIE) for his contributions to the field of neuro-control and neuro-fuzzy systems. He was also elected fellow of the International Fuzzy Systems Association (IFSA) for his contributions to fuzzy-neural computing systems. In 1998, Dr. Gupta was honored by the III-Kaufmann Prize and Gold Medal for his research in the field of fuzzy logic. This gold medal was presented by the foundation FEGI (Fundació per a l'Estudi de la Gestió en la Incertesa: Fuzzy Management Research Foundation) and SIGEF (Sociedad Internacional de Gestión Economia: Fuzzy International Association for Fuzzy Set Management and Economy) in Reus, Spain. In 1991, Dr. Gupta was the co-recipient of the Institute of Electrical Engineering Kelvin Premium. He was elected as a Visiting Professor and a Special Advisor in the area of high technology to the European Centre for Peace and Development (ECPD), University for Peace, which was established by the United Nations.

Kelly Joel Gurubel-Tun was born at Mérida, in Yucatán, México, on July 02, 1980. He studied in Instituto Tecnológico de Mérida, where he received the Chemical Engineer degree in 2006, and in 2007 he entered the Centro de Investigación y de Estudios Avanzados (Cinvestav), Unidad Guadalajara, in Jalisco, México, where he received Master degree in Electrical Engineering. Nowadays, he is Ph. D. student in Automatic Control Engineering from Cinvestav, Unidad Guadalajara, where he researches Control for Methane Production in an Anaerobic Process. His research interests are renewable energy sources, chemical reactors, artificial neural networks, and optimal control.

Noriyasu Homma received a BA, MA, and PhD in Electrical and Communication Engineering from Tohoku University, Japan, in 1990, 1992, and 1995, respectively. From 1995 to 1998, he was a Lecturer at the Tohoku University, Japan. He is currently an Associate Professor of the Cyberscience Center at the Tohoku University. From 2000 to 2001, he was a Visiting Professor at the Intelligent Systems Research Laboratory, University of Saskatchewan, Canada. His current research interests include neural networks, complex and chaotic systems, soft computing, cognitive sciences, intelligent medical systems, and brain sciences. He has published over 100 papers, and co-authored 1 book and 10 chapters in 10 research books in these fields.

Zeng-Guang Hou received the B.E. and M.E. degrees in Electrical Engineering from Yanshan University, China, in 1991 and 1993, respectively, and the Ph.D. degree in Electrical Engineering from Beijing Institute of Technology, China, in 1997. From May 1997 to June 1999, he was a Postdoctoral Research Fellow with the Institute of Systems Science, Chinese Academy of Sciences, Beijing, China. From July 1999 to May 2004, he was an Associate Professor with the Key Laboratory of Complex Systems and Intelligence Science, Institute of Automation, Chinese Academy of Sciences, where he has been a Full Professor since June 2004. From September 2003 to October 2004, he was a Visiting Professor with the Intelligent Systems Research Laboratory, College of Engineering, University of Saskatchewan, Saskatoon, Canada. His current research interests include neural networks, optimization algorithms, robotics, and intelligent control systems.

F. L. Lewis, Fellow IEEE, Fellow IFAC, Fellow UK Institute of Measurement and Control, PE Texas, UK Chartered Engineer, is Distinguished Scholar Professor and Moncrief-O'Donnell Chair at University of Texas at Arlington's Automation and Robotics Research Institute. He obtained the Bachelor's Degree in Physics/EE and the MSEE at Rice University, the MS in Aeronautical Engineering from University of West Florida, and the Ph.D. at Georgia Tech. He works in feedback control, intelligent systems, distributed control systems, and sensor networks. He is the author of 6 US patents, 216 journal papers, 330 conference papers, 14 books, 44 chapters, and 11 journal special issues. He received the Fulbright Research Award, NSF Research Initiation Grant, ASEE Terman Award, International Neural Network Society Gabor Award 2009, UK Institute of Measurement and Control Honeywell Field Engineering Medal 2009. Received Outstanding Service Award from Dallas IEEE Section, selected as Engineer of the Year by Fort Worth IEEE Section. Listed in Fort Worth Business Press Top 200 Leaders in Manufacturing. Received the 2010 IEEE Region 5 Outstanding Engineering Educator Award and the 2010 UTA Graduate Dean's Excellence in Doctoral Mentoring Award. He served on the NAE Committee on Space Station in 1995. He is an elected Guest Consulting Professor at South China University of Technology and Shanghai Jiao Tong University. Founding Member of the Board of Governors of the Mediterranean

Control Association. Helped win the IEEE Control Systems Society Best Chapter Award (as Founding Chairman of DFW Chapter), the National Sigma Xi Award for Outstanding Chapter (as President of UTA Chapter), and the US SBA Tibbets Award in 1996 (as Director of ARRI's SBIR Program).

Carlos Lopez-Franco gained his Ph.D. in Computer Science in 2007 from the Center of Research and Advanced Studies, CINVESTAV Unidad Guadalajara, Jalisco, México. At the present, he is a Full Professor at the University of Guadalajara, México, Department of Computer Science. He is currently working with the Intelligent Systems Group. His current research interests include geometric algebra, computer vision, robotics, and pattern recognition.

Michel Lopez-Franco was born in Guadalajara, Mexico, in 1986. His first interest for science was in computer engineering, and he received the Bachelor's degree in Computer Engineering from the University of Guadalajara, Guadalajara, Mexico, in 2008. However, contacts with his teachers awakened his interest for neural networks; then, he turned away from computer studies. He received the M. S. degree in Computer and Electrical Engineering from the University of Guadalajara, Guadalajara, Mexico, in 2011. He currently studies for his Ph. D. in Electrical Engineering from the Center for Research and Advanced Studies of the National Polytechnic Institute, Guadalajara, Mexico. His current research interests include inverse optimal control, decentralized control, and adaptive and neural networks controllers for dynamic systems.

Xuejun Meng is a Master Student in the Department of Computer Science at the Harbin Institute of Technology Shenzhen Graduate School. Her research interests are machine learning and computer security.

Hiromi Miyajima received the B.E. degree in Electrical Engineering from Yamanashi University, Japan, in 1974, and the M.E. and D.E. degrees in Electrical and Communication Engineering from Tohoku University, in 1976 and 1979, respectively. He is currently a Professor in Graduate School of Science and Engineering at Kagoshima University. His current research interests include fuzzy modeling, neural networks, quantum computing, and parallel computing.

Luis J. Ricalde was born in 1975, in Merida, Yucatan, Mexico. He received the Mechanical Engineer Degree, from Instituto Tecnologico de Merida, Yucatan, Mexico, in 1999, the MSEE major in Automatic Control and the PhD in Automatic Control from CINVESTAV-IPN (Advanced Studies and Research Center of the National Polytechnic Institute), Guadalajara, Mexico, in 2001 and 2005. He was a Professor of the Graduate Program in Electronics and Mechatronics Engineering of the Universidad Autonoma de Guadalajara (UAG), Jalisco, Mexico, from 2005 to 2006. Since 2007, he has been with Universidad Autonoma de Yucatan (UADY), Merida, Mexico, as Professor of Mechatronics Engineering Graduate Program. His research interests center in neural network control, adaptive nonlinear control, constrained inputs nonlinear control, and wind energy generation systems. He was granted the Arturo Rosenblueth's Award in 2005 and is a member of the Mexican National Research System (SNI-C). He has published several technical papers, and served as reviewer for different international journals and conferences.

Edgar N. Sanchez was born in 1949, in Sardinata, Colombia, South America. He obtained the BSEE, major in Power Systems, from Universidad Industrial de Santander (UIS), Bucaramanga, Colombia, in 1971, the MSEE from CINVESTAV-IPN (Advanced Studies and Research Center of the National

Polytechnic Institute), major in Automatic Control, Mexico City, Mexico, in 1974, and the Docteur Ingenieur degree in Automatic Control from Institut Nationale Polytechnique de Grenoble, France, in 1980. In 1971, 1972, 1975, and 1976, he worked for different Electrical Engineering consulting companies in Bogota, Colombia. In 1974, he was Professor of Electrical Engineering Department of UIS, Colombia. From January 1981 to November 1990, he worked as a Researcher at the Electrical Research Institute, Cuernavaca, Mexico. He was a Professor of the Graduate Program in Electrical Engineering of the Universidad Autonoma de Nuevo Leon (UANL), Monterrey, Mexico, from December 1990 to December 1996. Since January 1997, he has been with CINVESTAV-IPN, Guadalajara Campus, Mexico, as a Professor of Electrical Engineering graduate programs. His research interest centers on neural networks and fuzzy logic as applied to automatic control systems. He has been the advisor on 10 Ph.D. theses and 40 M.Sc theses. He was granted a USA National Research Council Award as a Research Associate at NASA Langley Research Center, Hampton, Virginia, USA (January 1985 to March 1987). He is also member of the Mexican National Research System (promoted to highest rank, III, in 2005), the Mexican Academy of Science, and the Mexican Academy of Engineering. He has published more than 150 technical papers in international journals and conferences, and has served as reviewer for different international journals and conferences. He has also been member of many international conference IPCs, both IEEE and IFAC.

Noritaka Shigei received the B.E., M.E., D.E. degrees from Kagoshima University, Japan, in 1992, 1994, and 1997, respectively. He is currently an Associate Professor in Graduate School of Science and Engineering at Kagoshima University. His current research interests include neural network, wireless sensor network, digital communication system, digital circuit design, and parallel computing systems.

Ashu M. G. Solo is an interdisciplinary researcher, electrical engineer, computer engineer, intelligent systems engineer, political and public policy engineer, mathematician, progressive political writer, entrepreneur, and former infantry platoon commander understudy. Solo is the creator of multidimensional matrix mathematics and its subsets, multidimensional matrix algebra and multidimensional matrix calculus. Solo originated and defined the new interdisciplinary fields of public policy engineering, computational public policy, political engineering, and computational politics. Solo has over 400 engineering and math research and political commentary publications. He is the principal of Maverick Technologies America Inc. and Trailblazer Intelligent Systems, Inc. Solo has served on 169 international program committees for research conferences. He is a city committee representative on the Saskatoon Cultural Diversity and Race Relations Committee. Solo is a fellow of the British Computer Society. He won two Outstanding Achievement Awards, two Distinguished Service Awards, and two Achievement Awards from research conferences. Solo served honorably as an infantry officer and platoon commander understudy in the Cdn. Army Reserve.

Dimitrios C. Theodoridis was born in Solingen (Germany) in 1974. He received a diploma in Physics and a M.Sc. degree in Electrical Physics (Radioelectrology) from the Aristotle University of Thessaloniki (AUTH) in 1997 and 1999, respectively. He received the Ph.D. degree in Electrical and Computer Engineering in 2011 from the Democritus University of Thrace (DUTH). Since 2005, he serves as a Teacher in Secondary Grade education. In addition, he is a scientific co-operator in the Department of Electrical and Computer Engineering in the Democritus University of Thrace. His main research interests lie in the field of neuro-fuzzy networks, neural networks, adaptive control, intelligent control, nonlinear control systems, robot manipulators, and applications to electric drive systems. He has served as a reviewer for scientific journals in the area of neural networks, translational medicine, adaptive control, signal processing, robotics, and automation, as well as member of scientific conference committees.

Xiao Xiao is a Master Student in the Department of Computer Science at the Harbin Institute of Technology Shenzhen Graduate School.

Shuxiang Xu has been a Lecturer of Computing (since 1999) in the School of Computing and Information Systems at the University of Tasmania, Tasmania, Australia. He holds a Bachelor of Applied Mathematics from the University of Electronic Science and Technology of China (1986), Chengdu, China, a Master of Applied Mathematics from Sichuan Normal University (1989), Chengdu, China, and a PhD in Computing from the University of Western Sydney (2000), Sydney, Australia. He received an Overseas Postgraduate Research Award from the Australian government in 1996. His current interests include the theory and applications of artificial neural networks, and data mining.

Shuji Yatsuki received the B.E., M.E., Ph.D. degrees in System Information Engineering from Kagoshima University, Japan, in 1993, 1995, and 1998, respectively. He is currently working at Kyoto Software Research, Inc. His research interests are neural networks, artificial intelligence, and file systems for embedded systems.

Qingzhen You is a Master Student in the Department of Computer Science at the Harbin Institute of Technology Shenzhen Graduate School.

Hashem Yousefi was born in Alamoot, Qazvin, Iran, in April 1986. He received his B.Sc. degree from School of Mechanical Engineering, University College of Engineering, University of Tehran, Tehran, Iran in 2004 and the M.Sc. degree in Biomechanics from the Biomedical Engineering Department at Amirkabir University of Technology (Tehran Polytechnic), Tehran, Iran, in 2011. He is currently a member of Motion Analysis Laboratory, in the Department of Biomedical Engineering, Amirkabir University of Technology. His current research interests include robot-aided surgeries, image guided surgeries, rehabilitation robots, and soft tissue biomechanics. He has also worked on several projects in soft tissue finite element modeling, MEMS, dynamic systems, and control.

Salman Zaferanlouei was born in Mashhad, Iran, in August 1982. He received his B.Sc. in Mechanical Engineering from Azad University of Takestan, Iran, and his M.Sc. in Nuclear Engineering from Amirkabir University of Technology, in 2009. He has worked on adaptive wavelet neural network controllers, two-phase flow natural circulation, and heat transfer. His current research interests include control systems, neural computing, and pattern recognition.

Jean X. Zhang is an Assistant Professor of Accounting at Virginia Commonwealth University. She earned a B.B.A. in Accounting from the College of William and Mary in 2004 and a M.S. in Accounting from the University of Virginia in 2005. She received her Ph.D. from The George Washington University in 2012. Her research focuses on compensation, performance measures, governance, corruption, and artificial intelligence. Her coauthored paper on the consequences of financial restatements in the market for municipal debt received the Outstanding Research Paper Award for the American Accounting Association Government and Nonprofit section in 2007. Her dissertation on city manager compensation and performance measures received the AAA Government and Nonprofit Section Competitive Dissertation Grant in 2011.

Index

A

Absolute Relative Error (ARE) 258
Adaptive Fuzzy Systems (AFS) 142, 158
Adaptive Neuro-Fuzzy Inference System (ANFIS) 377
additive generalized 84, 91
Additive Tree model (EAT) 295
administration expense ratio 327
Artificial Intelligent (AI) 2
Artificial Neural Network (ANN) 2, 5, 81, 326, 376
Artificial Second Order Neural Unit (ASONU) 63, 366

B

Bayesian Network (BN) 81
Boolean function 335
Bose Chaudhuri Hocquenghem (BCH) 5

C

Center Membership Value (CMV) 140
Center Process Units (CPUs) 2
Central Limit Theorem 337, 340, 345, 363
Chaos Assumption 350, 362
Char Reduction (CR) 181
Chemical Oxygen Demand (COD) 163
Competitive Neural Tree model (CNeT) 295
complete Band (CB) 307
Completely Stirred Tank Reactor (CSTR) 172
complex ELM algorithm (C-ELM) 280
cooperative tracking control 215
Correlation HONN (CHONN) 5
Critical Heat Flux (CHF) 376, 387
crossbar switch 44-45, 52-57

D

degree of accuracy 2, 78, 85, 88, 93, 282
Dry-Out (DO) 376, 387
Dynamic Ridge Polynomial Higher Order Neural Network (DRPHONN) 80

E

Electric Load Demand (ELD) 254, 258
Elman Recurrent Neural Network (ERNN) 258
Equilibrium Real Exchange Rates (ERER) 79
Evolutionary Programming (EP) 251, 322
Extended Kalman Filter Derivative Free (EKFDF) 256
Extended Kalman Filter (EKF) 30-31, 35, 162, 175, 256
Extreme Learning Machine (ELM) 276, 279, 287

F

Flaming Pyrolysis (FP) 180
Flexible Neural Tree model (FNT) 295
Forward Error Correction (FEC) 239, 248
Frobenius norm 201, 206
Functional Link Neural Networks (FLNNs) 5
fuzzy entropy 372

G

Genetic Algorithms (GA) 251, 322
Genetic Programming (GP) 251, 322
Government Finance Officers Association (GFOA) 327
Group of pictures (GOPs) 243

H

Higher-order Processing Unit (HPU) 278, 281, 365
High-order Discrete Hopfield Neural Networks (HDHNN) 45
    Discrete Hopfield Neural Network (DHNN) 45
high-order Hopfield Neural Networks (HHNNs) 44
    Continuous Hopfield Neural Network (CHNN) 45
    Hopfield Neural Network (HNN) 45
High-order Processing Unit (HPU) 63

I

Incremental Extreme Learning Machine (I-ELM) 280
inorganic carbon (IC) 174
International City 327, 332

K

Kalman Filter (KF) 168, 260

L

Lagrange systems 214-217, 221-222, 229, 231-232, 234, 236
Levenberg-Marquardt algorithm 64, 69, 125, 128
Lipschitz quotients 254, 258, 262, 266-267, 274
local neighborhood synchronization error 198, 206
Logarithm Sigmoid (LOGSIG) 379
Lyapunov function 171, 195, 201, 203, 206, 222, 225-226, 229
Lyapunov-like function 134, 144-147
Lyapunov stability theory 215-216

M

Mean Absolute Percentage Error (MAPE) 257
Mean Square Error (MSE) 256, 309
mean square prediction error (MSE) 242
Model Complexity (MC) 374
multi-agent systems 194, 211-212, 214-217, 235-236
Multi-Layer Feed-forward Neural Networks (MLFNN) 83
Multi-Layer Perceptron (MLP) 3, 284-286
Multi-Objective Evolutionary Algorithm (MOEA) 61
Multi-Objective Genetic Algorithm (MOGA) 61
Multi-Objective Problems (MOPs) 61

Multiple-Input/Single-Output (MISO) 104
    Axon 104-105
    Dendrites 104
    Soma 104-105
    Synapse 104-105
multiple linear regressions 327
Multi-Polynomial Higher Order Neural Network Group (MPHONNG) 2
Multi-Polynomial Higher Order Neural Network (MPHONN) 1

N

National Renewable Energy Laboratory (NREL) 258
National Wind Technology Center (NWTC) 258
Neural Network Output Error (NNOE) 264
Neural Tree Network model (NTN) 295
Neuro-Fuzzy Dynamical Systems (NFDS) 158
Neuron-adaptive Activation Function (NAF) 82
Neuron-Adaptive Higher Order Neural Network (NAHONN) 3
nonholonomic mobile robot 30-31, 35-37, 41
nonlinear surface fitting 119
Numerical Weather Prediction (NWP) 256
NxN neuron matrix 50

O

Optimally Pruned Extreme Learning Machine (OP-ELM) 281
Oscillatory network 338

P

Packet Loss Ratio (PLR) 238-239, 252
Particle Swarm Optimization (PSO) 251, 257, 295, 322
Permanent Magnet Synchronous Generator (PMSG) 263
pi-sigma network 25, 101, 122, 129, 217, 236, 365
Polynomial Higher Order Neural Network (PHONN) 6, 22, 76, 78-79, 85, 94, 366
Polynomial Neural Network (PNN) 82
Probabilistic Incremental Program Evolution (PIPE) 295
product generalized 84, 91
Pseudo Higher Order Neural Net (PHONN) 197
Pseudo Random Binary Sequences (PRBS) 38

Q

Quality-of-Service (QoS) 238, 243

R

Radial Basis Function Neural Network (RBFNN) 5
Radial Basis Function (RBF) 127, 279, 287
Random Vector Functional Link (RVFL) 197
Recurrent Higher Order Neural Networks (RHONN) 31, 33, 135, 167, 256
Recurrent High Order Neural Observer (RHONO) 174, 186
Recurrent Multilayer Perceptron (RMLP) 256
Recurrent Neural Networks (RNN) 31-32, 135
Recursive Least Square with Covariance Resetting (RLS-CR) 60
Renegotiated Constant Bit Rate (RCBR) 238
renewable energy 192, 254-255, 258, 272, 274
ridge function 122
ridge polynomial 5, 27, 63, 74, 80, 82, 95, 122, 366, 384, 386
Ridge Polynomial Neural Network (RPNN) 5, 122
Root Mean Square (RMS) 5
Round-Trip-Time (RTT) 238

S

Second Order Neural Network (SONN) 365
Second Order Neural Units (SONUs) 108
Second Order Polynomial Neural Networks (SOPNN) 68
Self-Organising Map (SOM) 278
Semi-Globally Uniformly Ultimately Bounded (SGUUB) 35
sigma-pi network 121-123, 365
Sigmoid polynomial Higher Order Neural Network (SPHONN) 6, 22, 93-94, 366
Simultaneous Recurrent Neural Network (SRNN) 258
SINC Higher Order Neural Network (SINCHONN) 366

Single hidden Layer Feedforward Networks (SLFNs) 281
Somatic Operation 105, 107, 113
Statistical Analysis System Nonlinear (SAS NLIN) 366
subnetwork 351
surplus 327-328, 332
Symbolic Function Network (SFN) 237-239, 293
Synaptic Operation 105, 113

T

Tactile Tumor Detector (TTD) 4
tapped delay feedbacks of neural output (TptDNN) 113
Third Order Polynomial Network 64-65, 69
Trigonometric Polynomial Higher Order Neural Network Group (THONNG) 78, 92
Trigonometric polynomial Higher Order Neural Network (THONN) 6, 78, 92

U

Uniformly Ultimately Bounded (UUB) 148, 202, 222

V

Variable Bit Rate (VBR) 238
Visual Object Plane (VOP) 244

W

Wavelet Neural Network (WNN) 281
Weierstrass approximation theorem 205, 212
Weighted Indicator Function (WINF) 140
Wind Energy Generation (WEG) 254, 258
Wind Speed (WS) 254, 258

Z

ZWICK 62